Racial Politics in
American Cities

Racial Politics in American Cities

Third Edition

Edited by

RUFUS P. BROWNING
San Francisco State University

DALE ROGERS MARSHALL
Wheaton College

DAVID H. TABB
San Francisco State University

New York   San Francisco   Boston
London   Toronto   Sydney   Tokyo   Singapore   Madrid
Mexico City   Munich   Paris   Cape Town   Hong Kong   Montreal

Vice President and Publisher: *Priscilla McGeehon*
Executive Editor: *Eric Stano*
Senior Marketing Manager: *Megan Galvin-Fak*
Project Coordination, Text Design, and Electronic Page Makeup: *Sunflower Publishing
    Services*
Cover Design Manager: *Wendy Ann Fredericks*
Cover Designer: *Kay Petronio*
Cover Photo: © *Mark Richards/Photoedit*
Manufacturing Buyer: *Roy Pickering*
Printer and Binder: *The Maple-Vail Book Manufacturing Group*
Cover Printer: *Lehigh Press, Inc.*

Library of Congress Cataloging-in-Publication Data

Racial politics in American cities/edited by Rufus Browning, Dale Rogers Marshall, David H.
Tabb.—3rd ed.
    p. cm.
Includes bibliographical references and index.
    ISBN 0-321-10035-2
    1. African Americans—Politics and government. 2. Hispanic Americans—Politics and
government. 3. United States—Race relations. 4. Municipal government—United States—
History—20th century. I. Browning, Rufus P. II. Marshall, Dale Rogers. III. Tabb, David H.
    E185.615.R214 2002
    324.'089'9607301732—dc21
                        2002010341

Please visit our website at http://www.ablongman.com

ISBN 0-321-10035-2

1 2 3 4 5 6 7 8 9 10—MA—05040302

Contents

Preface

Earlier editions of this book, published in 1990 and 1997, were well received and widely used in colleges and universities. Since that time, dramatic demographic shifts and qualitative changes in racial politics have become increasingly apparent.

This third edition is a major revision. All of the chapters have been substantially revised to take account of recent events and interpret emerging patterns. The chapter authors are among the most highly regarded political scientists writing about urban politics. Several of our chapter authors—Richard DeLeon, Rodney Hero, Marion Orr, and Raphael Sonenshein—as well as the editors have won national book awards for their work on urban and ethnic politics. Two new authors, Michael Rich and Michael Owens, bring their own high competence and fresh perspective to the analysis of Atlanta, replacing Clarence Stone, whose excellent work on that city appeared in the previous editions. Also new in this edition, Susan Clarke joins Rodney Hero on the Denver chapter, and Dario Moreno joins Christopher Warren on the Miami chapter.

We wish to express our thanks to all the authors who shared their expertise, to the University of California Press and the American Political Science Association for permission to draw heavily on earlier work, and to the good people at Longman and at Sunflower Publishing Services who worked with skill and commitment on the book. We benefited from the counsel of Robert P. Haro, Ph.D., professor emeritus of La Raza Studies and director emeritus of research, Cesar Chavez Institute, and Helen Hyun, Ph.D., senior researcher at the Public Research Institute, both at San Francisco State University; and we acknowledge with gratitude the assistance of David Lee, executive director of the Chinese American Voters Education Committee, and Kevin Rafter, Ph.D. candidate at the City University of New York.

We dedicate this book to our children and their children. We hope that their generations will continue to give priority to the cause of racial justice.

Marla, Ross, Charles, and Mark Browning
Jessica, Cynthia, and Clayton Marshall
Kevin, Lisa, and Jonah Tabb

RUFUS P. BROWNING
DALE ROGERS MARSHALL
DAVID H. TABB

About the Authors

Rufus P. Browning, Dale Rogers Marshall, and David H. Tabb are the authors of *Protest Is Not Enough: The Struggle of Blacks and Hispanics in Urban Politics* (University of California Press, 1984). The book received the 1985 Ralph J. Bunche Award for best book in political science on ethnic and cultural pluralism and the 1985 Gladys Kammerer Award for best book on national policy, both from the American Political Science Association.

Rufus P. Browning is professor of political science and senior faculty researcher at the Public Research Institute, San Francisco State University. He is currently working on a study of the use of ethnic news media.

Susan Clarke is professor of political science at University of Colorado at Boulder. Professor Clarke's research and teaching interests center on public policy and urban political economy, particularly issues of globalization and local democracy. Recent books reflecting these interests include *The New Localism* (coedited with Edward Goetz, Sage Publications, 1993) and *The Work of Cities* (coauthored with Gary L. Gaile, University of Minnesota Press, 1998).

Richard E. DeLeon is professor of political science at San Francisco State University, where he has taught since 1970. He is the author of *Left Coast City: Progressive Politics in San Francisco, 1975–1991* (University Press of Kansas, 1992), which received the 1993 award for best book on urban politics from the Urban Politics Section of the American Political Science Association. He is currently writing a follow-up to *Left Coast City*, focusing on land use policy, electoral reform, social movements, and identity politics during Mayor Willie Brown's administration.

Rodney E. Hero is Packey J. Dee Professor of American Democracy in the Department of Political Science, University of Notre Dame. His book *Latinos and the U.S. Political System: Two-Tiered Pluralism* (Temple University Press, 1992) received the American Political Science Association's 1993 Ralph J. Bunche Award. He also authored *Faces of Inequality: Social Diversity in American Politics* (Oxford University Press, 1998), which was awarded the 1999 Woodrow Wilson Foundation Award of the American Political Science Association.

Richard Keiser is associate professor of political science and associate director of the program in American Studies at Carleton College. He has written on minority politics in Philadelphia, Chicago, Atlanta, Gary, and New York, and is the author of *Subordination or Empowerment? African American Leadership and the Struggle for Urban Political Power* (Oxford University

Press, 1997). His most recent book is *Minority Politics at the Millennium* (Garland, 2000), coedited with Katherine Underwood.

Dale Rogers Marshall is president and professor of political science at Wheaton College in Massachusetts. Previously she was academic dean at Wellesley College and professor of political science and associate dean of the College of Letters and Sciences at the University of California at Davis. Educated at Cornell University and the University of California, Los Angeles, she has published widely in urban politics and has been active in the Western Political Science Association and the American Political Science Association.

Dario Moreno is associate professor of political science at Florida International University. His areas of specialization are Cuban-American politics and U.S.-Latin American relations. The author of two books on U.S. policy in Central America, he has also written numerous articles and book chapters on Cuban-American politics in Miami, and has served as an expert witness on three voting rights cases in Florida. He is currently working on a book on Cuban-American politics in Miami.

John Mollenkopf is Director of the Center for Urban Research and professor of political science and sociology at the City University of New York Graduate Center. Educated at Carleton College and Harvard University, he has published ten books on urban policy and politics, most recently *Place Matters: A Metropolitics for the 21st Century* (University Press of Kansas, 2001) with Peter Dreier and Todd Swanstrom; *E Pluribus Unum? The Political Incorporation of Immigrants in America* (Russell Sage Foundation, 2001), coedited with Gary Gerstle; and *Rethinking the Urban Agenda* (Century Foundation Press, 2001), coedited with Ken Emerson. He is working on a study of the immigrant second generation in metropolitan New York. Other publications have included *A Phoenix in the Ashes: The Rise and Fall of the Koch Coalition in New York City Politics* (Princeton University Press, 1992) and *The Contested City* (Princeton University Press, 1983). He consulted to the 1991 New York City Redistricting Commission and the 1989–1990 Charter Commissions that reformed New York City government.

Marion Orr is an associate professor of political science and urban studies at Brown University. His book *Black Social Capital: The Politics of School Reform in Baltimore, 1986–1998* (Princeton University Press, 1999) won the Policy Studies Organization's 2000 Aaron Wildavsky Award for the best policy studies book published in 1999. He is coauthor of *The Color of School Reform: Race, Politics, and the Challenge of Urban Education* (Princeton University Press, 1999), which was deemed the best book on urban politics in 1999 by the Urban Politics Section of the American Political Science Association. He is currently engaged in a study of the organizing experiences of the Industrial Areas Foundation (IAF) in various regions of the United States.

Michael Leo Owens is visiting assistant professor of political science and visiting fellow at the Office for University-Community Partnerships at Emory University. He earned his Ph.D. from the State University of New York at Albany and is the recipient of the 2000 Sage Publications/Urban Affairs Association Young Scholar Award. His research interests are urban politics, religion and politics, and community development policy. He is completing a book on the changing politics of urban black churches.

Dianne Pinderhughes is professor of political science and Afro-American studies and director of the Afro-American Studies and Research Program at the University of Illinois Urbana-Champaign. She is the author of *Race and Ethnicity in Chicago Politics: A Reexamination of Pluralist Theory* (University of Illinois Press, 1987) and numerous other publications on race, public policy, and electoral politics. Active in many professional associations, she was vice-president of the American Political Science Association in 1995–1996 and president of the National Conference of Black Political Scientists from 1988–1989.

Huey L. Perry is professor of political science and coordinator of the Office of Research and Services at Southern University, Baton Rouge. Perry's principal area of research focuses on the impact of the increased black political participation that has occurred in the South since the national civil rights legislation of the mid-1960s. His research examines the political, social, and economic impact of black political participation in the South. He has edited two books, *Blacks and the American Political System* (coedited with Wayne Parent, University Press of Florida, 1995) and *Race, Politics, and Governance in the United States* (University Press of Florida, 1996), and has written several articles and book chapters.

Michael J. Rich is associate professor of political science and director of the Office of University-Community Partnerships at Emory University. He is the author of *Federal Policymaking and the Poor* (Princeton University Press, 1993) as well as several publications on federalism and a variety of urban policy topics. His current research focuses on community building, neighborhood revitalization strategies, and welfare reform.

Raphael J. Sonenshein, professor of political science at California State University, Fullerton, received his Ph.D. in political science from Yale University. He is the author of *Politics in Black and White: Race and Power in Los Angeles* (Princeton University Press, 1993), the winner of the 1994 Ralph J. Bunche Award from the American Political Science Association for the best book in political science on ethnic and cultural pluralism. In 2001, Dr. Sonenshein was selected as the 2001–2002 Fellow of the John Randolph Haynes and Dora Haynes Foundation to assist in the Foundation's Initiative on Governing Los Angeles.

David H. Tabb, professor of political science at San Francisco State University, has written or coauthored more than 20 articles and three books on the politics of race and political incorporation.

Christopher Warren is associate professor of political science at Florida International University where he teaches urban and American politics. His research and publications have focused on the politics of ethnicity and class in urban political environments, Miami politics, and the reform of local governmental structures. He is presently working on a book on Cuban-American politics in Miami.

Part I

Problems and Possibilities

Can People of Color Achieve Equality in City Government? The Setting and the Issues

Rufus P. Browning,
Dale Rogers Marshall, and
David H. Tabb

The long and terrible history of racial domination in the United States has twice led to great national movements, prolonged conflict, and death and destruction. The movement to abolish slavery finally achieved the Fourteenth Amendment but failed to secure for the former slaves the rights of citizens. Nearly a century later, the civil rights movement endeavored to span the chasm between the ideals of democracy and political equality and the American practice of extreme inequality, violent suppression, and denial of the most fundamental rights and liberties for people of African descent—the right to vote, the right to equal treatment before the law, the rights of free speech and assembly.

THE CIVIL RIGHTS MOVEMENT AND BLACK PROTEST

Waves of political mobilization, demand, and protest—sometimes peaceful, but often violent—swept across the United States from the late 1950s to the mid-1970s. African Americans and their allies mounted assaults on the institutionalized structures of racial exclusion and domination nationwide and in all cities with significant black populations. Latinos, who have a long history of engagement with civil rights issues, accelerated their mobilization too.

First came the civil rights movement, challenging the exclusion of African Americans from politics, government, and education, etching scenes that will forever mark the American consciousness: National Guardsmen escorting black children into school through mobs of enraged whites, lunch counter sit-ins, Governor George Wallace—"segregation today, segregation tomorrow, segregation forever"—blocking the doorway of the University of Alabama to federal officials, Martin Luther King, Jr.'s, impassioned plea for equality from the steps of the Lincoln Memorial, marches in Selma and Birmingham in

3

Alabama and the attacks on them, the murder of civil rights workers, burnings of black churches.

Mass violence erupted in the mid-1960s. Riots in Los Angeles, Detroit, Newark, and dozens of other cities both expressed and aroused fear, anger, and hatred. Leaders struggled to control events and prevent cities from burning. The riots were followed by recriminations, investigations, and heightened demands.

The federal government initiated programs aimed at poverty, racial inequality, and discrimination—and at defusing protest. President Lyndon Johnson pushed aggressively for passage of the Civil Rights Act of 1964, the Voting Rights Act of 1965, and the "war on poverty" created by the Economic Opportunity Act of 1964. These were followed by Model Cities and a tidal wave of other programs in employment, housing, education, and health, many of which changed the activities and resources of city governments but also the prospects and resources of blacks, Latinos, the unemployed, low-income workers, and inner-city residents. During the first Nixon administration (1969–1973), the federal system of grants to cities was reorganized but continued to expand with the institution of general revenue sharing and block grants.

Since the 1970s, the great passion and commitment of the civil rights movement has been defused by its achievements, both real and symbolic. The support of whites for fundamental civil rights, evoked with the deeply moral and religious voice of Martin Luther King, Jr., could not be sustained and transformed into support for the economic agenda that beckoned after federal power had been applied to voting registration and the integration of schools and universities. The movements for civil rights and black power were also suppressed by assassination of their strongest and most charismatic leaders—King and Malcolm X—and eclipsed by other issues, in particular the war in Vietnam. They suffered the attrition of exhaustion, fear, and generational change.

With a series of Republican and moderate Democratic presidencies beginning in 1969, the organizations that carry the mantle of the black civil rights movement, such as the National Association for the Advancement of Colored People, the Southern Christian Leadership Conference, and the Urban League, lost visibility and access to the federal government and became less active. Electoral organization and officeholding at all levels, by African Americans especially but also by Latinos and Asians, have grown nationwide, while the dramatic protests that so gripped public attention in the 1960s and 1970s virtually ceased, though with notable exceptions: violent civil unrest in Los Angeles in 1992 and Louis Farrakhan's Million Black Men march in 1995.

In many cities, biracial or multiethnic coalitions formed, and African Americans and Latinos rose from exclusion to positions of authority as mayors, council members, and top managers and administrators. Where this happened, the politics of mobilization and mass action were replaced by the politics of administration, implementation, planning, and economic development—and sometimes by crises of competence and corruption, as in governments generally. Open conflict both within and between minority groups now represented in city governments has sometimes replaced the unity that was once attained when city government and its white powerholders were the common enemy.

THE STRUGGLE FOR DEMOCRACY IN CITY POLITICS

Much of the denial of civil rights and of rights to equality in employment, education, housing, and government services occurred at the local level, where people lived, worked, voted, and were subject to the imposition of police power and other local regulation. Accordingly, much of the civil rights movement and of local mobilization by African Americans, Latinos, and other groups aimed to force city governments to end their massive, blatant, common, and virtually complete discrimination and exclusion, and to engage the power of city governments on the side of reducing discrimination in private employment and housing. These historic efforts became tests not only of the ability of groups to sustain a high level of political activity and achieve their goals, but tests as well of the American polity itself, a running experiment on the proposition that excluded groups in a racially obsessed society could realize the democratic promise of the American political ideal.

The continuing efforts of African Americans and Latinos—and of Asians, in some cities—to achieve access to government and responsive policies from cities, and the response to their efforts, are the subjects of this book. As we shall see, these struggles have achieved changes that are striking in their scope and significance. Standing in 1960 and looking forward from the near-total exclusion of African, Latino, and Asian-American people from government in the United States at that time, it would have seemed incredible that an African American could become a general in the U.S. Army, Chairman of the Joint Chiefs of Staff, and Secretary of State or the powerful Speaker of the California Assembly; or that blacks would be mayors of New York, Los Angeles, Chicago, Philadelphia, Washington, DC, Seattle, San Francisco, and many other cities.

Such achievements stemmed from rapid social and economic gains, including the breakdown of barriers to higher education and the professions, a change in attitudes and practices that had kept minority people out of many trades and jobs, and the extraordinarily rapid growth of an African-American middle class from the 1940s on (Thernstrom and Thernstrom 1997). On the other hand, while "the American condition is overall dramatically improved" in racial matters, it remains "in important respects, continually depressing," and "tenacious ills remain," including intractable gaps in education, employment, and income; continued segregation and racial isolation; and "the vastly disproportionate involvement of black males in the criminal justice system" (Foreman 1999, 5). Even the astonishing long boom of the 1990s, though it reduced unemployment and poverty among many groups, fell considerably short of prosperity for all (Cherry and Rodgers 2000).

In city politics, the value of the benefits gained through mobilization and participation is questioned by some. The momentum of the movement has slowed, its successes have been uneven over time and from city to city, and its gains have been subject to attack and reversal. A long tide of reaction to racial and other social changes of the 1960s strengthened forces at all levels of government that dismantled programs intended to undo or counterbalance discrimination and cut funding that many people of color (and many whites) as well as their organizations and leaders believe is necessary for continued progress toward equality and regard as rightful compensation for the barriers and deprivations of a racialized society. In the courts, decisions were entered against affirmative action in government contracting and in both admissions and financial aid in higher education.

In California, four successful ballot initiatives that had their greatest impact on people of color were sponsored by conservative interests and the California Republican Party.[1] The cleverly misnamed "California Civil Rights Initiative" (Proposition 209, 1996) prohibited by constitutional amendment a wide range of state affirmative action programs that provided selective educational and employment support to people of color. Its success led to similar efforts in other states—some successful, some not. And in the largest cities in the country—Los Angeles, New York, Chicago, Philadelphia—African-American mayors were replaced by significantly more conservative whites. It was not unreasonable to fear that the great expansion of officeholding by African Americans was only temporary or would fail to sustain long-term equality in law and policy and be followed by re-establishment of white rule at the local level and reversal of legislative gains at all levels.

Even with the expansion of officeholding by blacks, Latinos, and Asians in some cities, many with substantial black, Latino, or Asian populations still have no, or very little, minority representation in city council and mayoral offices. Even where they hold office, how much power do they have? Can black, Latino, and Asian officeholders really make city governments responsive to the interests of their groups?

Clearly, in some cities, people of color can control local policies on some issues and at least some departments of city government. Control of police departments in particular remains especially difficult and onerous in many settings, as in Los Angeles. Even where people of color hold office, can they make any headway against unemployment and poverty, which remain painful and intractable problems in a racialized society, especially for people of color? If they try to reallocate resources to their people, can they still attract the investors and financial institutions on which cities depend for investment and economic growth? Will economic and demographic forces—recession, globalization, high rates of immigration, and reaction to immigration—hinder or support political equality? These questions ask us to look beyond the achievement of local office to the problematic nature of local office in a racialized society, in which by far the greater power remains in the hands of the dominant group in the economy and at the higher levels of government.

In short, even with the growing number of black, Latino, and Asian officials, it may be that the limited powers of cities in a federal system and in a racialized, cap-

---

[1] "Three Strikes and You're Out" (Proposition 184, 1994) provided for mandatory and long prison terms for repeat offenders that produced 5,000 life sentences by 1999, half involving non-violent offenders. It shifted state funding from education to prisons. The "Save Our State" initiative (Proposition 187, 1994), attempted to deny education and medical care to undocumented immigrant children and their families but was almost entirely overturned by the Federal District Court in Los Angeles in 1995 and again in 1998. The "California Civil Rights Initiative" (Proposition 209, 1996) overturned affirmative action in California. The "English for the Children" initiative (Proposition 227, 1998) forced widespread abandonment of bilingual education programs. See Gibbs and Bankhead (2001).

italist society render that gain more symbolic than real. When forces succeed in reversing policies of the 1960s and 1970s, as with the dismantling of race-targeted affirmative action in California, the future of progress for African Americans and Latinos especially is thrown into doubt (Gibbs and Bankhead 2001). (Whether the end of race-targeted affirmative action will actually improve the status of those groups in the long run is, of course, a point of contention.)

African Americans and Latinos are the two largest minority groups in the United States. Together, they comprised 21 percent of the population in 1990 and 25 percent in 2000, about equally split between the two groups, and much larger proportions in many states and cities. Include Asians, and we have 29 percent. The quality of their mobilization and their capacity to sustain political power in cities are crucial to their ability to gain continuing access at the national level of government as well as a voice in the governance of the cities where most of them live. And because many contenders for state and national office first hold local office and learn from their formative experience in city politics, it is important to understand local officeholding and the diverse lessons that experience teaches.

Most important, this book offers a current report on the efforts of racially subordinated, excluded groups to gain equality by election—continuing experiments in democracy. Their efforts often arise out of frustration over persistent, racially determined inequality. We know from experience in Los Angeles and elsewhere—for example, the videotaped police beating of Rodney King in 1991 and the racially charged violence of April 1992—that racialized official violence and explosions of rage among inner-city black and Latino populations can still occur. We know that racially motivated crimes continue to be a problem. We know that racial profiling and differential treatment of suspects based on race remain intensely hated practices of state and local police in many parts of the country. We know that educational opportunities are typically much worse for low-income groups, especially people of color, than for middle- and upper-income groups. Whether governments are really able to respond effectively to demands for equal treatment and social justice remains an open question to be decided in the ebb and flow of social and political contention.

THE CITIES

This book addresses these questions by bringing together 13 chapters on the political mobilization and political power of African, Latino, and Asian Americans in twenty cities. Table I.1 shows the fundamental demographics of these cities. In the top half of the table, the 10 U.S. cities that are the focus of Chapters 2 through 12 are presented; in the bottom half, the 10 cities in Northern California that are discussed in Chapter 1. In each half, cities are shown in order of increasing percentage of white, non-Hispanic residents.

These 20 cities include the four largest cities in the country—New York, Los Angeles, Chicago, and Philadelphia—and other major cities in diverse regions. Black mayors hold office in six of the cities (30%) as of early 2002—Philadelphia,

TABLE I.1   Populations of the 20 cities studied in this book

City	Total Population in 2000 (1,000s)	White	Black	Latino	Asian
Ten U.S. Cities					
Miami	363	11.8	19.9	65.8	0.6
Birmingham	243	23.5	73.2	1.6	0.8
New Orleans	485	26.6	66.7	3.1	2.3
Los Angeles	3,695	29.7	10.9	46.5	9.9
Baltimore	651	31.0	64.0	1.7	1.5
Chicago	2,896	31.3	36.4	26.0	4.3
Atlanta	417	31.3	61.0	4.5	1.9
New York City	8,008	35.0	24.5	27.0	9.7
Philadelphia	1,518	42.5	42.6	8.5	4.4
Denver	555	51.9	10.8	31.7	2.7
Mean	1,883	31.5	41.0	21.6	3.8
Ten Northern California Cities					
Daly City	104	17.7	4.3	22.3	50.3
Richmond	99	21.2	35.6	26.5	12.2
Oakland	400	23.5	35.1	21.9	15.1
Hayward	140	29.2	10.6	34.2	18.7
Vallejo	117	30.4	23.3	15.9	23.8
Stockton	244	32.2	10.8	32.5	19.3
San Jose	895	36.0	3.3	30.2	26.6
Sacramento	407	40.5	15.0	21.6	16.4
San Francisco	777	43.6	7.6	14.1	30.7
Berkeley	103	55.2	13.3	9.7	16.3
Mean	328	33.0	15.9	22.9	22.9

Percentage[a]

[a]"White," "Black," and "Asian" are non-Hispanic in this table; "Latino" means Latino or Hispanic of any race.

Source: U.S. Census Bureau, *Census 2000 Redistricting Data (Public Law 94-171) Summary File Matrices PL1, PL2, PL3, and PL4.*

Atlanta, San Francisco, Birmingham, New Orleans, and Denver—a net gain of one since 1995. Oakland and Baltimore lost black mayors; Philadelphia, San Francisco, and Denver added them. Latinos hold the mayoral office in Miami and San Jose (10% of the cities), with no net change since 1995: San Jose added, Denver lost. One city has an Asian (Filipino) mayor: Daly City, CA, where the Asian population, mainly Filipino, spurted to slightly more than 50 percent by the 2000 Census.

The 10 U.S. cities studied are larger and blacker on average than the 10 California cities. The California cities have much larger Asian populations, in percentage terms, than the 10 U.S. cities.

To locate these 20 cities in the universe of U.S. cities, Figure I.1 places them in a scatterplot with the other 230 U.S. cities with populations of 100,000 or more in 2000. The vertical axis is the relative size of the white, non-Hispanic population; the

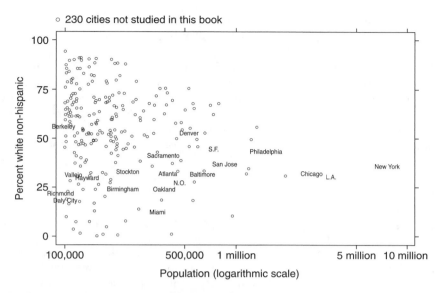

FIGURE I.1   Percent white non-Hispanic by city population for 20 cities studied in this book and 230 other cities with 100,000 or more population in 2000

horizontal axis is total population. As you can see, most cities with at least 100,000 people are relatively small and mostly white compared to the cities studied in this book. The cities of this book include the largest cities and other cities of various sizes, and 18 of them are in the range of 20 to 55 percent white, non-Hispanic population. In this middle range, the non-white and Hispanic population is large enough to win or influence elections if they can be united and mobilized but, typically, not so large that the role of whites is negligible. (Even where whites comprise only 20 percent of the total population, they may be a majority of the voting population for many reasons, including more adults, fewer noncitizens, and higher levels of education among whites.) In short, this is a range in which the political opportunities for ethnoracial minorities are good, but coalitions will typically be necessary if control over city government is the goal.

Race and Ethnicity

Measurement is social and political. The measurement method of Table I.1 maximizes the reported sizes of Latino populations by including in them all persons who identify themselves as Hispanic or Latino, regardless of their racial self-identification on U.S. Census forms. Why is this a problem? As Orlando Patterson has pointed out, "Although all reports routinely note that 'Hispanics can be of any race,' they almost always go on to neglect this critical fact, treating Hispanics as if they were, in fact, a sociological race comparable to 'whites' and 'blacks'." In fact, however, "48 percent of so-called Hispanics classified themselves as solely white" in the 2000 Census (Patterson 2001).

As Patterson argues, repeatedly naming and classifying a group under a single category, in the context of an explicitly racial classification, is part of the process by which a group is racialized in a racially obsessed society (Haslanger 2000).

We do not wish to aid the process of racialization. On the other hand, we do want to use indicators of group presence that approximate the size of the group *if it were politically mobilized as a group.* Because bad things *do* happen to people who can be identified as Hispanic/Latino and *do* lead to political mobilization, a measure of the maximum size of that group is relevant. The real racial and ethnic diversity of Latinos is also politically relevant in some settings, as the studies in this book point out. This point applies also to Asians, who are wholly a socially constructed category and even more diverse in terms of ethnicity and language than Latinos.

WHAT IS POLITICAL POWER IN CITIES?

All the chapters in this book use a framework that we developed studying cities in northern California (Browning, Marshall, and Tabb 1984). Here we identify its main outlines in order to frame the fundamental political problem faced by excluded minorities.

Look at the question—What is political power?—from the perspective of people who have long been excluded from holding office or from any significant influence over city government. Suppose they decide to contest their exclusion from city politics, and suppose power over city government is the target of their efforts. They know they have achieved power when they wrest concessions from an unwilling city hall, when they win office against determined opposition, when they succeed in forming a coalition that defeats an incumbent group, when their coalition is able to change the policies and personnel of city government, and when they are able, over a period of years, to institutionalize the changes they sought.

Examples of demands that African Americans and other groups have won in this way include representation in elective offices, access to employment in city government, appointments to head city agencies, application of the enforcement powers of city government to reduce or punish discrimination, and equitable allocation of funds for city services. These are fundamental and legitimate interests clearly within the authority of city governments.

The goal of representation has been at the center of the struggle for political equality. Considering their virtual exclusion from city governments in the late 1950s, it is an astonishing achievement that many people of color now hold office as mayors, council members, and other officials. As important as representation is, however, it is not enough. The presence of people of color in office is essential, but it does not ensure that they will pursue and realize the substantive demands.

To change the direction of city government in the face of opposition requires control of local legislation, programs, spending, governmental structure, and governmental personnel over a period of years. This means that blacks, Latinos, and Asians, if they are to achieve their political goals in any city, must secure control of city council and the mayor's office and hold it for years in the face of opposition. A group must either constitute a majority on its own or participate in a *governing coalition* that can dominate city council on issues of greatest concern to it and secure re-election. Such a coalition does not have to consist entirely of people of color, but it does need a strong commitment to their interests if they are to obtain the changes in city government that they want.

The key is not just representation but a coalition that controls city government. Even substantial minority-group representation—30 to 40 percent of a city council—will have no effect on policy if they are opposed at every turn by an entrenched and intransigent governing coalition. Where minority groups fall short of 50 percent of the voting-age population, as they usually do, biracial or multiracial coalitions between groups and with liberal whites are necessary to replace a resistant governing coalition if these groups are to gain control of city government.

Political Incorporation

We use the term *political incorporation* to refer to the extent to which group interests are effectively represented in policy making. We *measure* the political incorporation of a group by the extent to which it is represented in a coalition that dominates city policy making on issues of greatest concern to that group. This measure involves a supposition—that coalition control of city government really does, at least on key issues, "effectively represent" a group in policy making. This is not an assumption; it is a hypothesis to be tested against the results of such control.

Political incorporation, as a measure, thus refers to a range of possibilities for group presence in city government. At the lowest level, a group is not represented at all—there are no officials from the group, and the group does not participate in a coalition that controls city government on the issues of greatest concern to it. At the next level, there is some representation, but on a council dominated by a coalition that is resistant to minority interests. Finally—the strongest form of incorporation—a group has an equal or leading role in a dominant coalition that is strongly committed to minority interests. The highest levels of political incorporation may afford substantial influence over policy.

What Did Blacks, Then Latinos and Asians, Want of City Governments?

First, they wanted to end their exclusion from government and the political process. In the twentieth century before the 1960s, *they were almost universally and totally excluded*. And exclusion remains an issue in some cities. Weak mobilization and lack of political incorporation is common, especially in smaller cities.

They wanted respect from government, access to it, and real influence over policies and programs of special interest to them. They wanted to have their concerns taken seriously, to hold office, and to shape city policies and spending priorities. Real influence is very much an issue, or is nonexistent, in many cities.

They wanted a share of the benefits of government and an end to discrimination. Starting from nearly zero in many cities, they wanted—and often still want—increased minority employment in city government. They want to see minority administrators in top city jobs. They want minority businesses to get some of the city's contracts and purchases. If economic development funds are considered, they want minority business districts to get a share. They want police to stop shooting and beating minority suspects and to end racial profiling, which imposes real risk and unending humiliation. They want low-income housing, parks and recreation programs, police protection, libraries, and health and other services in minority neighborhoods.

They wanted, in short, government that includes them, that is fair, and that is responsive to a broad range of deeply felt demands. However, because in 1960 racism was pervasive, not rare; because whites controlled all the functions of city governments and discrimination was accepted practice; and because people in power do not willingly give it up, a prolonged struggle was necessary if minority demands were to be met, even in part.

What Forms Did the Struggle Take?

Groups pursue political objectives in several ways. Aside from terrorism, groups may petition or pressure government from outside—the interest-group and protest strategy—or they may achieve representation and a position of influence inside— the electoral strategy. These are not mutually exclusive approaches, and large groups typically pursue both. The strategy that is dominant in a given setting and the intensity of protest will shape the political struggle that ensues.

In 1960, African Americans, Latinos, and Asians had almost no representation in city governments and not even a serious audience for their concerns. In the 1950s, African Americans commonly met steadfast resistance to even the most basic requests for an end to discrimination. The great force of the national civil rights and black power movements pushed these encounters from request to demand to protest. Mobilization of Latinos came later, and of Asians later still. Latinos and Asians also face real civil rights issues and significant barriers to political mobilization and incorporation, but their mobilization in cities has been less intense than the urban mobilization of African Americans was in the 1960s and 1970s—less enraged, less violent, less disruptive, and more consistently oriented toward electoral mobilization.

We can portray a successful protest strategy for a newly mobilizing group as follows:

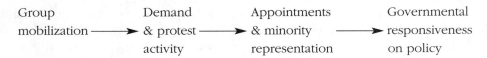

The group mobilizes and applies pressure to city government with demands backed by protest—marches, pickets, displays of anger and determination, disruptions of public meetings, and the like. A co-optative or a responsive governing coalition in city government may respond by appointing one or more minority representatives to vacancies as they occur on city council or to managerial positions in city government; in any case, the coalition responds positively to some of the group's demands. The short-term success of the strategy depends on the responsiveness of the governing coalition—a quality in short supply during the 1950s and 1960s.

Where a group is sufficiently large or can find allies for a coalition, an electoral strategy might be feasible. A successful electoral strategy looks like this:

Group mobilization———▶	Candidates run for elective offices	Representation ———▶ & incorporation into government	Governmental ———▶ responsiveness on policy

In this scenario, the focus is on electoral mobilization. If successful, it leads to representation and some level of group incorporation into city government; in turn, the extent of incorporation determines the extent to which city government is responsive to group interests. Protests may be carried out, but their primary function is to arouse minority populations and their potential supporters, to raise the level of anger and create the possibility and the determination to act. The position of power in city government achieved by minority-group officeholders, rather than solely group pressure on city government from the outside, leads to changes in city government that make it more responsive.

There is nothing inevitable to these scenarios: a coalition in power may be utterly unresponsive to minority demands, or electoral effort may lead to no victories and no representation. Still, they constitute possible ways of influencing city governments. Both strategies were and are employed by mobilizing groups.

URBAN POLITICS AND ECONOMIC POWER

The interest-group and electoral strategies are commonplace for all of us, because they are the stuff of public discourse about politics and political power. The formation of coalitions, the importance of political leaders in framing issues and building coalitions, mobilization for protest and for elections, public disputes about policy and public funds—these elements of news and talk about politics are both familiar and real, but it is important to understand that the emphasis on them—the assumption that they are important—is a matter of perspective. In political science, this perspective is called the *pluralist* perspective. It is a view of politics as contention among many groups for control of political institutions, with the presumption that those institutions are significantly autonomous, possess real authority, and control important resources.[2]

A *class* or *structural* perspective, in contrast, sees politics from a different vantage point, looking not at the decisions of a given city government but at the relationship between government and the economic structure of society. Through the

---

[2] Here and in subsequent paragraphs we are drawing on Mollenkopf (1992, ch. 2), and on Alford and Friedland (1985).

structural lens, we observe that government is not autonomous, that it is fundamentally constrained by the structure of business interests:

> Private property, market competition, wealth and income inequality, the corporate system, and the stage of capitalist development pervasively shape the terrain on which political competition occurs (Mollenkopf 1992, 27).

In the structural view, city politics reveal deep and lasting inequalities that government can do little about, and the forces that produce and maintain inequality are likely to be more important than the limited autonomy of local government and the limited benefits that governmental action might secure. The structure and dynamic of capitalism, the institutional power of local corporations, and the cumulative inequalities embedded in capitalist institutions exert profound effects on urban politics and government.

Consider how the transformative dynamic of capitalism can undermine the prosperity of a group. African Americans migrate from the South to escape the oppression of sharecropping and seek employment in the great industries of Detroit, Chicago, and Cleveland. Decades of struggle to overcome the racism of both employers and white workers eventually yield great gains in employment and income. Then, beginning in the 1970s, these gains are steadily undermined as global competition drains market share and employment from steel, automobiles, machinery, and other manufacturing industries. Unemployment and poverty among African Americans increase again, and a portion of the African-American population is mired without hope or opportunity in big-city ghettoes. The wealth those industries created is no longer available to finance local governments and local needs; it disappears or moves elsewhere, leaving behind the people who depended on it. Even if people of color have gained control of city governments in such a setting, they will be under constant pressure to compete with other cities for outside investment—to reduce taxes and channel resources toward infrastructure that is attractive to investors, thus reducing resources for new programs.

In addition to the overarching structure and transformative dynamic of the global capitalist system, organized and powerful local economic elites may dominate city government. To express the likelihood that strong economic institutions mold city government to their interests, we must refer to a broader governing coalition—a network of political and economic leaders that these institutions seek to form and control according to their economic objectives and that, in turn, is able to control city government. To differentiate this broader coalition from a governing coalition located entirely within the political/governmental sphere, it is called a *regime* (Stone 1989, 2). While electoral coalitions are typically public because they depend on public support, regimes are partly hidden—they thrive on secrecy about the extent of their power and their ability to produce governmental actions that enhance their power and profits.

Seen from the structural perspective, elections and voting are of limited interest, because they cannot explain why city governments behave as they do. Instead, the extent of structural inequality and the power and objectives of local economic elites in a city constitute the fundamental explanation: "the unequal distribution of economic, organizational, and cultural resources has a substantial bearing on the character of actual governing coalitions" in cities (Stone 1989, 9).

Though often presented as being opposed, the pluralist and structural perspectives are, we believe, complementary. They are both necessary. They offer different truths and allow us to see different possibilities, but neither has a viable claim to be *the* truth. Their different central claims are both at least sometimes true, and we must employ both to understand urban politics fully.

Between them, the two theoretical perspectives identify five fundamental elements of urban political systems. This list does not exhaust the institutions with power over city governments—for example, it does not include state and federal governments—but it does identify the key actors in the immediate vicinity of local institutions:

1. Political *entrepreneurs*, leaders who are typically coalition builders and who seek to lead city government.
2. Public sector *producer interests* within government—administrators, employees, unions.
3. *Popular or constituency interests,* who may express their demands through elections and interest-group activity.
4. *Private market interests,* especially corporations with discretion over local capital investment.
5. A *dominant political coalition*—"a working alliance among different interests that can win elections for executive office and secure the cooperation it needs from other public and private power centers in order to govern" (Mollenkopf 1992, 38). This *governing coalition* is the product of the efforts of political entrepreneurs who build support from the other key actors.

This *governing-coalition approach* borrows from the pluralist view the proposition that a key interaction takes place between popular interests (3) and political entrepreneurs (1) as the latter seek to develop viable coalitions (5). From the structural approach, the governing-coalition perspective borrows the proposition that an exercise of power occurs in the broader sphere between the political coalition that is able to dominate city government (5) and private market interests (4), with market interests almost always influential but with a wide range of possibilities for dominance, collaboration, or stalemate. It is also possible that public employees (2) play significant roles in the allocation of public money and privilege.

While we accord private market interests a prominent place in any account of the capabilities and inclinations of city government, we also look for the possibility that political entrepreneurs and the alliances they may build may create some autonomy for the political sphere and obtain the co-operation, support, or forebearance of market interests.

Thus, the achievement of political power by a hitherto excluded group in or over city government must overcome two potential obstacles—the presence of a dominant political coalition that will not give up power without a struggle, and the presence of market interests that may organize to dominate and shape any political coalition.

HOW THIS BOOK WORKS

The authors of the chapters in this book apply these frameworks to the cities they know best, testing the adequacy of the frameworks against new evidence and extending them as they encounter patterns of power and frustration not readily encompassed by them. By the end of the book, you should understand not only how the movement for political power unfolded in some of the largest and most important American cities, but also the possibilities (and limitations) of the present and future—the adequacy of political incorporation of the previously excluded groups, the extent to which they pursue the broader goals of the movement, what they might now do in pursuit of those goals, and the obstacles they encounter.

REFERENCES

Alford, Robert R. and Roger Friedland. 1985. *Powers of Theory: Capitalism, the State, and Democracy*. Cambridge, UK: Cambridge University Press.

Browning, Rufus P., Dale Rogers Marshall, and David H. Tabb. 1984. *Protest Is Not Enough: The Struggle of Blacks and Hispanics for Equality in Urban Politics*. Berkeley: University of California Press, pp. 3–5.

Cherry, Robert, and William M. Rodgers III, eds. 2000. *Prosperity for All? The Economic Boom and African Americans*. New York: Russell Sage Foundation.

Foreman, Christopher H., Jr. 1999. The Rough Road to Racial Uplift. In Foreman, ed. *The African–American Predicament*. Washington, DC: Brookings Institution.

Gibbs, Jewelle Taylor, and Teiahsha Bankhead. 2001. *Preserving Privilege: California Politics, Propositions and People of Color*. Westport, CT: Praeger.

Haslanger, Sally. 2000. Gender and Race: (What) Are They? (What) Do We Want Them To Be? *Noûs* 34(1): 31–55.

Mollenkopf, John H. 1992. *A Phoenix in the Ashes: The Rise and Fall of the Koch Coalition in New York City Politics*. Princeton, NJ: Princeton University Press.

Patterson, Orlando. 2001. Race by the Numbers. *New York Times,* May 8, A31.

Stone, Clarence N. 1989. *Regime Politics: Governing Atlanta 1946–1988*. Lawrence: University Press of Kansas.

Thernstrom, Stephan, and Abigail Thernstrom. 1997. *America in Black and White: One Nation, Indivisible*. New York: Simon and Schuster.

Chapter 1

Mobilization, Incorporation, and Policy in 10 California Cities

Rufus P. Browning, Dale Rogers Marshall, and David H. Tabb

In the 1960s and 1970s, a tremendous wave of political mobilization swept through minority communities in the United States. First and foremost, their political energy and anger released by the civil rights movement, this was a movement of black people. Their mobilization was more active and more pervasive in many ways—and more intensely suffused with the rage that stemmed from their history of racial oppression. Latinos also mobilized in some cities, and Asians began a process of mobilization that has continued and grown.

Why did these groups mobilize strongly in some cities but not in others? Why did mobilization lead to significant minority incorporation in some city governments but not in others? Where incorporation was achieved, did it lead to power and responsive policies? Overall, was the movement successful? Is it still? How has it changed?

This chapter describes the racial politics of 10 northern California cities during the intense political mobilization of the 1960s and 1970s. The cities were revisited three times between 1989 and 2002 to reassess the political mobilization and incorporation and the policy influence of people of African, Latino, and Asian origin; to re-examine the conditions for biracial and multiracial coalitions; and to review developments and differences in racial politics.

We elaborate on the framework presented in the Introduction to understand why minority mobilization unfolded in diverse ways—and with notably different results—in various cities.[1] Study of these cities enables us to assess the successes and failures of minority mobilization in local settings and the conditions that led to success or failure. This assessment, valid for cities in northern California, forms a set of hypotheses about the achievements and evolution of minority political mobilization in other regions and in cities with

---

[1] Portions of this chapter are drawn from the authors' previous work on this subject (1984, 1990, 1995, 1997, and 2000).

very different characteristics and histories.[2] To understand the emergence and evolution of the national movement in the cities is to understand why it evolved in different ways depending on social, economic, historical, and political factors that varied—and still vary—from city to city.

Understanding variation is essential for political action as well. Political action occurs in the context of each city's distinctive history. Political activists and leaders as well as the public would profit from reviewing how their city differs from others to apply effectively the lessons learned elsewhere. Thus, to make our understanding relevant to action, we must understand variation—both what is different about particular cities and the patterns of difference across all cities.

Looking at many cities at once inevitably brings out aspects of city politics that differ from those in an examination of one city. Studies of one city take the population makeup of the city as a given and search in the ebb and flow of political competition, leadership, and policy for explanations and evaluations of change. The population differences between cities, however, are likely of great interest in comparative studies of many cities. So it is here. In the comparative view of 10 cities presented in this chapter, we bring out the structure of population characteristics that shape the political dynamics and possibilities of cities. When you read Chapters 2 through 12 on particular cities, keep this structure in mind to assess how it shapes the politics of each.

TEN CITIES IN THE 1960s

We studied the largest cities in northern California—San Francisco, San Jose, Oakland, and Sacramento—and a group of smaller cities with substantial black or Latino populations—Berkeley, Stockton, Richmond, Hayward, Daly City, and Vallejo. In 2000, their total populations ranged from 99,000 to 895,000; combined black, Latino, and Asian populations ranged from 39.3 percent to 74.3 percent. Black populations have decreased in percentage terms in many of these cities since 1970; Latino and Asian populations have greatly increased, mainly because of immigration. Even in 1970, however, total group populations and populations eligible to vote were large enough in all these cities to have substantial influence in city politics—if they could mobilize and unite or form an alliance with liberal whites and each other. (See Table 1.1 for city-specific data on population and other variables.)

Constitutionally, all these cities are in the progressive reform tradition, with nonpartisan elections, city managers, and professional civil service systems. All had at-large elections for city council in the early 1960s, but the larger cities later

---

[2] Without intending to diminish in any way the social conditions and political efforts of other groups, we use the terms *minority* or *people of color* to refer, for ease of expression, to people of African, Asian, and Latino origin. We do not mean to imply that these groups are generally united or have identical goals and interests.

TABLE 1.1 **Minority population and representation in 10 northern California cities**[a]

City	Total (1,000s)	Population, 2000 Black	Percentage Latino	Asian	City council electoral system[b] (year of adoption)	Size[c]	City council, 2002 Black	Latino	Asian
San Jose	894↑	3.3↓	30.2↑	26.6↑	D (1980)	11	1—	4↑	1—
Daly City	104↑	4.3↓	22.3—	50.3↑	A-L	5	0—	1—	1—
San Francisco	777↑	7.6↓	14.1—	30.7—	D (1996)[d]	12	2↑	2↑	1—
Hayward	140↑	10.6—	34.2↑	18.7↑	A-L	7	2↑	2↑	0—
Stockton	244↑	10.8↑	32.5↑	19.3↑	D/A-L (1986)[e]	7	1—	0↓	1—
Berkeley	103—	13.3↓	9.7↓	16.3↑	D (1986)	9	2—	0—	0—
Sacramento	407↑	15.0—	21.6↑	16.4—	D (1971)	9	2↑	0↓	1—
Vallejo	117↑	23.3—	15.9↑	23.8—	A-L	7	1↑	0—	1—
Oakland	399↑	35.1↓	21.9↑	15.1↑	D (1981)[f]	9	2↓	1—	2↑
Richmond	99↑	35.6↓	26.5↑	12.2—	A-L	9	6↑	1—	0—
Average	328↑	15.9↓	22.9↑	22.9↑	Total	85	18↑	11↑	8↑
Standard deviation	293	11.7	8.1	11.1	No. in late 1970s, 1994		11,13	5,9	1,7
Coefficient of variation[g]		.74	.35	.49	Average % of council		21	13	10

No. of cities group size . . . since 1990:				No. of cities group representation . . . since 1994:			
Increased	1	7	6	Increased	5	3	1
Stayed the same	3	2	4	Stayed the same	4	5	9
Decreased	6	1	0	Decreased	1	2	0

[a] ↑ = increased, ↓ = decreased, — = group percentage of 2000 population stayed within ±10 percent of 1990 percentage or number of city council members did not change from 1994. For example, if a group was 16 percent of a city's population in 1990, it would be coded "same" if its 2000 percentage fell within the interval 16 ± 1.6, or 14.4 to 17.6 percent.

[b] A-L = at large, D = district elections.

[c] Includes mayors of all cities, even though the mayors of San Francisco and Oakland do not sit on San Francisco's Board of Supervisors or on Oakland's city council. The actual size of the San Francisco Board of Supervisors is 11, and of the Oakland City Council, 8.

[e] Stockton approved district elections in 1971 when the city's elite woke up too late to the fact that district elections were intended by their supporters to guarantee black representation on the city council. In 1986, the city charter was amended to create a mixed system in which candidates for council living in and chosen in a primary election in a district would face each other in an at-large election, in which considerations of money and the views of all the city's voters would loom large. The change was successful in removing from the council two black members who were regarded by Stockton's governing regime as, among other things, excessively racialized in their approach to city government.

[d] San Francisco voters chose district elections in 1977 but reverted to at-large elections in 1980, then adopted district elections again in 1996. See Chapter 6 of this volume.

[f] Oakland elects seven council members from districts and one at-large.

[g] Standard deviation divided by the mean; a measure of dispersion in a batch of data, standardized by the mean of the batch.

Source: U.S. Census Bureau, *Census 2000 Redistricting Data (Public Law 94-171) Summary File, Matrices PL1, PL2, PL3, and PL4*; city clerks.

adopted district elections, typically as part of efforts to secure the representation of minorities. Despite the presence of city managers (or a county administrator in San Francisco), the authority and prominence of the mayor's office is much greater in the larger cities than the reform tradition implies.

As noted in the Introduction, groups pursue political objectives in two ways: They petition government from outside (the interest-group strategy), or they achieve representation and a position of influence inside (the electoral strategy). By the late 1950s, African Americans in several of these California cities already had considerable experience both with electoral mobilization and with moderate forms of protest. Blacks in Berkeley during the 1930s focused on picketing and on increasing black voter turnout to demonstrate opposition to discrimination in public accommodations and employment; black candidates ran organized campaigns for city council, not with the expectation of winning but as a way of registering protest (Nathan and Scott 1978, 10).[3] With the rapid influx of blacks to work in defense plants during World War II and continuing migration afterward, their electoral prospects improved. Blacks became active in the state Democratic party and were instrumental in selecting black delegates to the 1948 Democratic convention. In that year, the Black Caucus was formed in Berkeley, and W. Byron Rumford became the first black elected to the California State Assembly, from a district of predominantly black neighborhoods in north Oakland and south Berkeley. The Caucus screened and selected black candidates so that multiple candidates would not split the black vote (Nathan and Scott 1978, 133). As the civil rights movement gathered force during the late 1950s and early 1960s, the electoral strategy in particular was already at least well practiced—if not well established—where leadership and conditions were optimal in parts of the San Francisco Bay Area.

As the civil rights movement spread through northern California in the early 1960s, it was testing with nonviolent protest the boundaries of the rights of assembly and petition in many cities and towns nationwide. Those gatherings—large-scale marches and rallies, boycotts, and sit-ins—were peaceful, usually intensely unwanted or forbidden by local authorities, and sometimes disruptive or costly to their targets. Nonviolent protest became civil disobedience, and organized nonviolent activity was increasingly overshadowed by spontaneous violent protest. A range of strategies acted out in cities across the country in the late 1950s erupted in widespread violence in the mid-1960s.

In northern California as elsewhere, African Americans and Latinos wanted the most basic civil rights—to hold public office, to be treated equally under the law,

---

[3] We retain in this discussion of the 1960s and 1970s the term *black*. People of African descent in the United States were called *Negro* well into the 1960s. In the late 1960s and 1970s, the term *black* became increasingly common and preferred, a usage that fit the real and dramatic polarization of black and white in the civil rights and, especially, the black power movement. In the 1980s, *African American* or *Afro-American* were increasingly adopted, a contemporary usage that signals a sort of terminological equivalence between Americans of African origin and Americans of Irish, Asian, or any other national or world-region origin.

and to end discrimination. They wanted access to education, to government, and to government employment and business. They wanted to enjoy the same benefits of local government that white citizens took for granted. They certainly wanted police to stop shooting, beating, and harassing people of color.

What path would blacks and Latinos in northern California take as they pursued these goals? Would it be a peaceful path, focused on voter registration and turnout and the recruitment of minority candidates? Would it follow the direction of traditional interest-group effort, concentrating on articulation of interests and demands rather than on elections? Would it take the more threatening stance of sometimes violent protest?

The answer was not one but many paths in different cities as the movement unfolded. The dominant effort in a given city was shaped by characteristics of the minority community, of the white population and historical race relationships, and of the local political system and its response to minority mobilization.

The Structure of the Situation—Resources of Population and Political Commitment

For activists, a fundamental political resource is the size of minority populations. Black and Latino populations, the most active in these cities during the 1960s and 1970s, varied greatly in 1970, from a mere 2 percent to 36 percent and from tiny communities of less than 2,000 to groups of more than 100,000. We should expect the politics of mobilization and competition to play out very differently in cities where group populations are relatively large than in cities where they are small.

Both the magnitude of protest and the importance of group voting are contingent on how many people can be mobilized, but the incentive to pursue protest or voting in a given city depends on different aspects of group size. The ability to mount large-scale protest depends on the absolute *number* of people who can be mobilized for protest. In contrast, the ability to mount a powerful electoral challenge depends not on numbers but on the *percentage* of the electorate that those numbers constitute. In these cities, numbers and percentages of group populations are not closely related. For instance, San Francisco's large black population in 1970—about 96,000—constituted only 13 percent of the city's population and somewhat less of the voting-age population, but Richmond's 29,000 blacks were a potent 36 percent of its population. Groups in these cities varied not only in their basic population resources but also in the extent to which those resources equipped them for protest, for electoral mobilization, for neither, or for both.

As black and Latino populations increased after World War II, the partisan balance in these cities also shifted. Democratic voter registration grew rapidly. By 1962, it ranged from 53 percent to 73 percent of registered voters, but Republicans still constituted majorities on half of these city councils. At the same time the civil rights movement was gaining momentum, Democrats in these cities were moving to capitalize on Democratic majorities among voters. For Democrats, the task was to mobilize voters to replace Republicans; blacks and

Latinos were likely sources of such support. For blacks and Latinos, the task was to mobilize people of color and form alliances with liberal whites to replace all-white, conservative coalitions that had no intention of responding positively to minority demands, and racially liberal whites were likely to come from the ranks of liberal Democrats.

The civil rights movement and the replacement of Republican, conservative coalitions were related but not identical. Many Democrats were not sufficiently tolerant or liberal on the racial, social, and economic issues important to blacks and Latinos to support a minority-oriented coalition. Many whites of both parties did not want to concede anything to blacks and Latinos, and even those who were willing to grant some minority demands often preferred not to share leadership with minorities. The extent to which white Democrats were eager or willing to work closely and co-operatively with blacks and Latinos varied considerably from one city to the next.

As black mobilization intensified, local activists thus faced quite different structures of political opportunities and problems. Both the ideological commitments of liberal activists and the structure of the situations in which they sought control of city government powerfully shaped their incentives to actively seek minority support—and to make significant concessions to get it.

PATTERNS OF MINORITY MOBILIZATION

We can summarize the evolution of the movement in these 10 cities by describing minority initiatives as well as white responses and their consequences, ranging from continued exclusion of minorities from city government to some form of inclusion in a governing coalition, often in a subordinate role but, occasionally, in an equal or dominant role.

Demand-Protest

The pattern of group mobilization in a given city was very strongly shaped by group size. In every city where black or Latino populations were large in an absolute sense, intense, sustained demand and protest activity developed.

Mobilization was shaped also by the extent of political support from white liberals. Where white populations were more willing to support black and Latino candidates and their positions on issues, demand and protest tended to occur at higher levels and with greater frequency.

During the 1960s and 1970s, San Francisco and Oakland experienced intense, racially related rioting and other violence in addition to organized and persistent pressure on city government, including rallies, marches, sit-ins, picketing, and numerous dramatic and successful efforts to focus media attention on issues. In several smaller cities, local minority groups generated some demand activity, such as meetings with city officials to request consideration of problems. The relationship between absolute size of the black population and the level of black demand-protest was very close (r^2 =.94; Browning, Marshall, and Tabb 1984, 88). Size of the black population was not the only factor involved in the production of intense demand-protest, however. Cities with large black populations were also large cities, and organizers intent on growing the movement gravitated to them with big-city media attention in mind. A very large, vociferous rally in San Francisco—with clever arrangements to involve the mayor as the target of demands—would almost certainly hit the San Francisco media, be distributed throughout the greater Bay Area, and stand a chance of making the national media. Events in the larger cities were intrinsically more interesting to the media and, therefore, more valuable to organizers.

White hostility to black political interests typically diminished demand-protest in a city; liberal support encouraged it—no doubt by raising expectations that demand-protest would be effective. More recently, while the level of demand-protest is certainly lower than in the 1960s, it is still evoked by the same types of events that gave rise to it then, such as deaths of African-American suspects during police chases or in police custody. The largest cities—Oakland, San Francisco and San Jose—remain the major sites of protest activity, but not on the scale and intensity of the 1960s.

Electoral Mobilization

The electoral mobilization of black populations was shaped by a different calculus of resources and opportunities. Numbers can generate massive protest, but percentages win elections. Black and Latino populations in all 10 cities fell well short of electoral majorities in 1960 and 1970, so electoral victory depended on the support of liberal whites. The most successful electoral efforts always involved the creation of cohesive electoral coalitions of blacks and whites, and sometimes with Latinos as well. These coalitions formed slates of candidates, carefully recruited and controlled the number of minority and white candidates so as not to split the minority vote, developed common platforms, shared funds, and organized common publicity and canvassing; sometimes they established continuing citywide, party-like organizations.

In the often tense atmosphere of minority protest during the 1960s and 1970s, conditions did not always permit the formation of coalitions. Nevertheless, the extent of coalition formation efforts by blacks was strongly shaped by the combination of black population and racially liberal support by whites, Latinos, and other groups. Figure 1.1 shows the exceptionally close relationship between black electoral organization and coalition formation and a measure of total support for black candidates and interests. In cities where black populations and supportive nonblacks, mostly whites, were found in adequate numbers, blacks mobilized for electoral politics and formed coalitions with their nonblack supporters. Where the numbers were insufficient, electoral mobilization was less intense, and coalitions did not emerge.

Black population and nonblack liberal support are represented by their product rather than their sum on the horizontal axis of Figure 1.1, because their effects

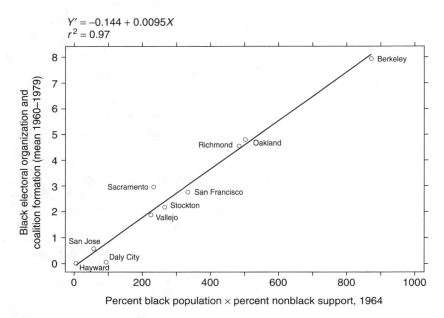

FIGURE 1.1   Black electoral organization and coalition formation, 1960–1979, as a function of black population and liberal support in 1964

Key to electoral mobilization/coalition formation scale: 8—Black leaders conduct centralized recruitment of black candidates on bi/multiracial coalition slates; 6—Coalition formation negotiations between black and white organizations over black candidates on coalition slates; 4—Recruitment and endorsement of black candidates by black organizations; no bi/multiracial coalition; 2—Endorsements of black candidates by black organizations; 0—Occasional black candidates run without significant endorsements

Source: Adapted from Browning, Marshall, and Tabb 1984, 119.

on coalition formation are interdependent.[4] Consider a black population that makes up 25 percent of a city's electorate. If there is no support for black candidates by racially liberal nonblacks, that 25 percent cannot elect sufficient council members to control city government. In this situation, blacks have little incentive to expend a great deal of energy in a futile effort to contest elections. If liberals other than blacks also constitute 25 percent of the electorate, however, both groups stand an excellent chance of winning control of city council if they can unite around a common slate of candidates. In that situation, the incentive to organize a cohesive biracial slate and to establish party-like control over minority candidacies is very strong. That political incentive depends on the presence of

---

[4] Support among nonblacks for black candidates and interests was estimated from votes on a 1964 statewide proposition widely understood to be antiblack; see Browning, Marshall, and Tabb (1984, 282).

both groups in sufficient numbers in a city's electorate. Thus, the impact on electoral mobilization of black population and of support from nonblack liberals is contingent on the level of the other factor. Neither group can go it alone; together, they can win.

In cities where blacks and liberals together accounted for nearly half or more of the electorate—Berkeley, Oakland, and Richmond—blacks did indeed consistently take the long step from recruitment and endorsement of black candidates to formation of biracial coalitions with racially liberal whites and others.

The strategies of electoral organization and coalition formation that were used successfully between 1960 and 1979 began to change in the 1980s, however, for two main reasons. First, citywide coalitions of blacks and other racially liberal voters had been necessary to win citywide elections for the mayor's office and at-large elections for city council in the 1960s, but between 1970 and 1996, six of the 10 cities adopted district elections (Table 1.1, middle column). Motivation for district elections varied from city to city, but a common desire was to create a politics based on grass roots activism, requiring less money and name recognition than in citywide elections, by removing influence over elections from the hands of developers and downtown business interests and placing it in the neighborhoods. Minority groups often favored district elections—but not always, depending on the size of the group. A group with a large plurality of a city's voters, such as African Americans in Richmond, benefits from at-large elections: in 2002, six of nine council members in Richmond are black (Table 1.1, right columns). A relatively small minority population, such as African Americans in San Francisco, protects its ability to elect an African American to the Board of Supervisors with district elections, even though the group comprises only 7.6 percent of the city's population.

District elections completely changed the incentive for coalition formation. With at-large elections, only a biracial or a multiracial citywide coalition could hope to be successful against a well-financed conservative coalition accustomed to power. With district elections, it is not necessary to form a citywide coalition to elect people from minority communities; what is necessary is to develop constituency relationships in a district. The shift to district elections affects everyone's calculations and greatly reduces the need for citywide electoral organization.

Under district elections, black candidates would still win in districts with substantial back populations, but white, Latino, and Asian activists would come to the fore in districts with few black residents. In Berkeley, black representation on city council is down from 44 percent to 55 percent at its peak to 22 percent as of this writing.

The success of the movement is the second reason why intense electoral organization by biracial coalitions gradually loosened its hold. The necessity of the 1960s and 1970s was to overcome first the conservatives who controlled city council and then an entrenched bureaucracy that was staffed by whites and thoroughly accustomed to the policies and routines of white business interests that controlled city government and to the assumption that people of color could be indefinitely excluded from city government employment and other city-controlled goods. Overcoming the bureaucracies took 10 years or more, but once a newly dominant biracial coalition held itself in place through many elections, the goals of the move-ment were largely achieved—and the urgency of mobilization seeped away. We describe the strongest coalitions and their successes below under "Patterns of Coalition and Political Incorporation."

The Population Revolution

Biracial coalitions have also given way to a new multiracial, multiethnic reality. The growth of Latino and Asian populations and the decline of black populations has been dramatic (Table 1.1). Black populations have *decreased* in percentage terms in six of the cities since 1990, while Latino and Asian populations have *increased* in seven and six of the cities, respectively. Across all 10 cities, both Latino and Asian populations now stand at substantially higher levels than African-American popula-tions (Table 1.1, average percentage of population). Latinos comprise more than 20 percent of the population in four cities and more than 30 percent in three others. Asians comprise more than 15 percent in six cities and more than 25 percent in three others. African Americans in 2000 made up more than 20 percent of the pop-ulation in only three cities.

More immigrants come to the United States—and to California—from Mexico and China than from any other country. The growth of Latino and Asian popula-tions, mainly Mexican and Chinese, continues the effects of a great wave of immi-gration triggered by their quest for economic opportunity and education and, for Asians, by the Immigration and Nationality Act of 1965, which eliminated the national-origins quota system and greatly increased the number of immigrants who could be admitted each year from Asian countries.

Other Asian groups are also increasingly well organized and politically mobilized, but Chinese immigrants are by far the largest Asian group in northern California. Population figures for Asians and references to Asian mobilization in this chapter refer primarily to people of Chinese origin.

Rates of political participation by Asians and Latinos have also grown, but they lag far behind their total populations for many reasons:

- All these groups—black, Latino, and Asian—are somewhat younger on average than the rest of the population, so group populations of voting age are between 7 percent and 11 percent less than group percentages of the total population.
- Large numbers of Latinos and Asians are not citizens and, therefore, cannot vote. In many of these cities, more than one-third of the Latino and Asian populations are noncitizens. Thus, their population figures greatly overstate their ability to get voters to the polls.
- Latinos and Asians, more recent arrivals in these cities, are, on average, bet-ter off than African Americans; despite the long history of San Francisco's Chinatown, most Asians are also more recent arrivals than Latinos and, on average, better off than both Latinos and blacks. These factors work against mobilization.

- Many Latinos consider themselves to be culturally—but not racially—different from whites and are therefore less inclined to insist on a racialized and separate group political role. There is some evidence that both Latinos and Asians, while acknowledging the existence of discrimination in the United States, are determined to avoid self-identification as a racialized group akin to African Americans.
- In some cities, Latinos and Asians are culturally and politically fragmented into different nationality groups, in contrast to the group cohesion that African Americans could count on. Latinos are from Central and South America as well as from Mexico; Asians are from the Philippines, Vietnam, and Korea as well as from China. Diversity of origin and ethnicity works against mobilization.

The broad categories of Latino and Asian mask great diversity. *Latino* is a fairly recent creation, identifying and creating communication among people of diverse origins and races who have a common language and partly shared experiences both abroad and in the United States (Rodriguez 1999). Like all identities, Latino identity is partly situational and goal-oriented. People of Hispanic origin from many different countries identify with other Latinos to ease their social and political relationships and to maximize group size for political purposes. Alongside that expression of political purpose and pan-ethnic alliance, a community of immigrants from Mexico may still profess a strongly Mexican identity in community cultural practices.

Like Latinos, Asians vary in their country of origin, but their cultural and language diversity is greater. *Asian* lumps together peoples from an enormous region who speak more than 50 very different languages and have very different societies, histories, religions, and relationships to each other. While *Asian* and *Asian American* are commonly known terms with real resonance especially among scholars, commentators, activists, and the politically aware, many Asians identify with their Chinese, Filipino, Korean, or East Indian origins but see themselves as Asian or Asian American only as a classification—not as an identity (Espiritu 1992). On the other hand, the process of racialization in the United States can produce a degree of pan-ethnic identity and bloc voting across Asian groups in some situations (Lien 2001, 195–96), and legislative threats to immigrants in California in the 1990s (Introduction, footnote 1) did produce upsurges in citizenship applications and voter registration among both Latinos and Asians. All in all, Latinos at this time seem to have adopted their pan-ethnic identity more readily than Asians have adopted theirs.

Latinos and Asians are also more evenly distributed than blacks in these 10 cities, partly because they experience less intense housing discrimination than African Americans do. Note from the much larger coefficient of variation in Table 1.1 that African Americans are more concentrated in a few cities. Until very recently, in no city did Latinos or Asians come close to the 43 percent to 44 percent peak of black population reached in Richmond and Oakland in the 1990 U.S. Census. In no city, therefore, could Latinos or Asians be a clearly dominant political force even if they wished to be. Now, however, both Asians and Latinos constitute larger fractions of total population than blacks in five of the 10 cities, including San Francisco and San Jose. They are likely to comprise larger fractions of voting-eligible populations within a few years as well.

Latino and Asian Mobilization

Latinos and Asians also mobilized in many cities beginning in the 1960s and continuing through the last decades of the twentieth century—but typically less vigorously than blacks. For many reasons, Latino and Asian mobilization not only occurred later but also usually was not so unified, so well organized, so intensely pursued, or so racialized.

Latino mobilization, because it came later and the black power movement was already underway, was activated by black mobilization to some extent. In a given city, black demand-protest tended to stimulate Latino demand-protest. And just as black coalition formation depended on the presence of liberals (including Latinos), the ability of Latinos to participate in electoral coalitions was contingent on the presence of sizable black populations. In Sacramento, smallish communities of blacks, Latinos, and liberal whites achieved a genuinely multi-ethnic coalition.

Latinos in several cities have mobilized strongly at the community level. In the Fruitvale district of Oakland, for example, Latino organizations banded together to operate a community clinic and other services, and they persuaded city hall to build a new library as part of an effort to develop the community and generate employment. The Unity Council, in conjunction with council member Ignacio de la Fuente, spearheaded the Fruitvale Bay Area Rapid Transit Village—a $100 million, federally sponsored project. This initiative is a plan to build a cluster of housing, shops, and neighborhood-oriented services surrounding a pedestrian plaza at the Fruitvale station of the BART system. The Unity Council (formerly the Spanish Speaking Unity Council), one of Fruitvale's oldest community-based institutions, spearheaded this plan with the participation of a broad spectrum of neighborhood residents, merchants, and other community organizations. These activities grew out of a history of development of community-based organizations with real reach, capabilities, and resources.

Like blacks and Latinos, Chinese-American activists were mobilized by the civil rights movement and by federal funding for antipoverty programs. These programs bypassed established local government authority and, in the hands of the young, bilingual activists who organized the required grass roots participation, challenged—and then replaced—the traditional leadership of the Chinese community in San Francisco's Chinatown. Since the 1960s, dense networks of community organizations have been built in San Francisco as well as in Oakland and other Bay Area cities focusing on health, education, job training, employment, housing, civil rights, and self-sufficiency issues. Some of the most vigorous and successful Chinese-American political leaders, often women and including members of the San Francisco Board of Education and Board of Supervisors as well as candidates for higher office, are graduates of leadership and management experience in community nonprofit organizations and neighborhood associations.[5] In Oakland, Asians are represented on the city council, school board, and county board of supervisors, and an Asian woman, Wilma Chan, represents Oakland in the state assembly, where she has become the majority floor whip.

Where African Americans were natural coalition partners for white liberals in the 1960s on the basis of size and cohesion and in the context of the civil rights movement, the rapid growth of Latino and Asian (especially Chinese) populations relative to African Americans suggest that prospects for the future mobilization of Latinos and Asians are improving steadily. Citizenship and participation have been stimulated by political threats to immigrants in the 1990s, by the continuing efforts of organizations such as the Southwest Voter Registration Education Project and the Chinese American Voters Education Project, and by the awareness and focus of ethnic media such as Univision and *Sing Tao Daily*.

COALITIONS, POLITICAL INCORPORATION, AND RESPONSIVENESS

This section combines the two critical stages of political incorporation and governmental responsiveness to show first how the civil rights and black power movement played out during the period of its greatest force and then the transformation in racial and ethnic politics that has occurred since 1980.

Between 1960 and 1979, African Americans overcame their exclusion from the political and governmental systems of these 10 cities. They achieved very high levels of political incorporation in two—Berkeley and Oakland—where they became equal or dominant partners in liberal or progressive biracial coalitions that controlled city governments continuously for many years.

In other important cities of the region—San Francisco, Sacramento, San Jose, and the smaller city of Richmond—African Americans became major political forces and major partners in coalitions led by whites that also took strongly liberal positions on racial issues and produced rapid gains in government employment, government contracting, and group representation on boards and commissions. Political incorporation resulted directly from—and was very closely related to—electoral organization and biracial coalition formation: The higher the level of electoral organization, the greater the resulting political incorporation.

The results of the strongest forms of political incorporation—leadership of or partnership in sustained, dominant coalitions—were striking. African Americans in

---

[5] We are indebted to David Lee, executive director of the Chinese American Voters Education Committee (CAVEC) in San Francisco for his knowledge and insights into the mobilization of Chinese Americans in the Bay Area.

these cities went within a decade from virtually complete exclusion to positions of substantial equality both in the kinds of office and authority they held and in the assumptions about policy that guided those city governments. African Americans became mayors, council members, and department heads. They were active partners and leaders of strong coalitions, and their concerns were taken seriously.

In a group of smaller cities with more conservative white populations or smaller, poorer, and less well-organized black populations—Hayward, Vallejo, Daly City, and Stockton—mobilization was weaker. In these cities, African Americans achieved little political incorporation.

Latinos gained less incorporation from 1960 to 1979 but made a significant start. Where they did gain access to government as coalition partners, such as in Sacramento, blacks and supportive whites were both present in significant numbers and needed Latino support to challenge conservative coalitions that controlled city governments. In San Francisco, Latinos mobilized and gained control of major Model Cities programs in the Mission district. Where Latinos were fewer in number, not well organized, or not needed, they were not brought into the biracial coalitions that formed in many cities to take control of city government from the conservative, business-oriented coalitions then in power.

Asians were scarcely visible on the broader political radar screen in northern California, and their populations were much smaller than they are now. While Asians were numerous enough to make a difference if mobilized—for example, they comprised 15.6 percent of the population of San Francisco in 1970—they had not yet done so vigorously.[6]

The sequence of mobilization, formation of biracial coalitions (in one city, multiethnic), successful electoral challenge, officeholding and exercise of governmental powers, and implementation of responsiveness was a path tightly structured first by the passionate determination of the civil rights and black power movements and then the political realities of these diverse cities:

1. *Electoral mobilization and coalition formation.* In the context of the civil rights and black power movements, the most vigorous mobilization and coalition formation occurred if—and only if—African Americans and racially liberal supporters and coalition partners were present in sufficient numbers to approach an electoral majority.

---

[6] However, two of the first minority council members were Japanese American. Frank Ogawa returned from World War II internment to become an advocate for minority rights in Oakland; he was appointed to the at-large position on the Oakland City Council in 1966 and held it until his death in 1994. Norman Mineta was a council member in San Jose from 1967 to 1971, and then mayor from 1971 to 1974, the first Japanese-American mayor of a large American city. Mineta was elected to Congress in 1974 and later served in the cabinets of presidents Bill Clinton and George W. Bush. While indicative of changing times, the beginnings of these noteworthy political careers were not the product of the concerted biracial and multiracial mobilizations that characterized the black power movement.

2. *Political incorporation.* The strongest forms of political incorporation of blacks and Latinos appeared where—and only where—numbers, commitment, and timing could be brought together successfully to replace conservative governing coalitions for years at a time.
3. *Responsiveness.* The most vigorous and complete institutional change and policy response to the demands of African Americans and Latinos was achieved where the strongest forms of incorporation were instituted.

The relationships between these three main stages of governmental change are very strong (Browning, Marshall, and Tabb 1984, 1997). Rank orders of these cities on measures of support, electoral mobilization and biracial coalition formation, political incorporation, and governmental responsiveness from 1960 to 1979 are virtually identical.

Did Minority Incorporation Make Governments More Responsive?

Some commentators have answered this question in the negative, arguing that the protest of the 1960s and a few black and Latino officeholders in the 1960s and 1970s did not really make much difference in what city governments did. Cities are, after all, severely constrained by economic pressures and by the limits and mandates of federal and state governments (Peterson 1981). The politics of city governments are also strongly influenced by a formidable array of local forces, including the rules and operating procedures established by bureaucrats (Levy, Meltsner, and Wildousky 1974; Lineberry 1977). Under such limitations, how can we expect demonstrations, the efforts of a few minority officeholders, or even a change of allegedly dominant coalitions to have much impact?

The answer is that minority incorporation *did* make city governments more responsive, and Figure 1.2 provides a simple demonstration. Here, we take as a measure of responsiveness the averages of city government responses to common minority demands in four key areas: establishment of civilian police review boards, appointment of minority members to city boards and commissions, provisions for minority shares of city contracts, and minority employment in city government. Figure 1.2 shows a close relationship between these average responsiveness values and black political incorporation. City governments in which blacks achieved strong incorporation were more responsive on this measure, and for the most part, only such governments were responsive.

At its strongest, the governmental response to minority interests extended across the programs and agencies of city government and permeated routine decision making and service delivery. At its weakest, the response was sporadic, half-hearted, undertaken only under duress, and limited to verbal assurances and occasional, isolated action.

Across a wide range of issues and routine actions that never became issues, the responsive governments were pervasively different. Economic development funds were channeled to minority business districts. Several of the cities where the political incorporation of African Americans was strongest—Berkeley, Richmond and

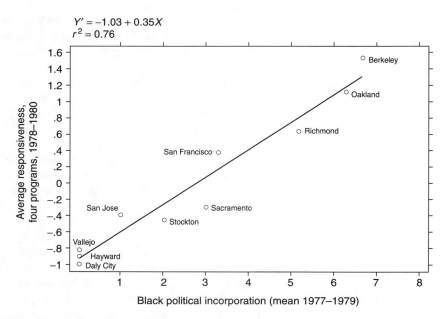

FIGURE 1.2   Average responsiveness as a function of black incorporation

The measure of responsiveness is the mean of the standard scores of measures of city government responsiveness in four policy areas: minority employment in city government, establishment of police review boards, minority representation on commissions, and city contracting with minority businesses. Its mean is 0, and its units are standard deviations. Scale of political incorporation: 0 = No minority representation on city council; 1–2 = Minority representation on city council but not in the dominant coalition; 3–4 = 1–2 minority council members in the dominant coalition; 5–6 = Several minority council members in the dominant coalition; 7–8 = Minority control of mayor's office; mayor leads dominant coalition in which other minority council members participate.

Source: Browning, Marshall, and Tabb 1984, 166.

Oakland—established elaborate housing rehabilitation programs as a way of maintaining housing affordability. Senior centers were deliberately located in minority neighborhoods, which were also beneficiaries of programs for street tree planting, sidewalk repairs, and undergrounding of utility lines and poles. City-supported and minority-oriented health services, such as sickle cell anemia and blood pressure control programs, were located in minority neighborhoods. Funding for homeless services, including emergency shelters, transitional houses, independent living, and related services, increased markedly. Police departments were retrained and their command structures replaced, with African-American and Latino officers moving up the hierarchy. Though the federal government decreased funding for employment programs, Berkeley and Oakland in particular continued to fund and refine a series of employment and social services programs focused on reducing poverty in the city, particularly in minority areas. Major parks were developed or improved in minority districts. Support was given to dozens of community-based organizations that offered employment, health, educational, social, and cultural services to residents. Even city libraries developed responsive programs, such as the tool-lending office behind the South Berkeley Branch, where residents were able to borrow tools for nothing or at modest cost. Major city projects, such as public housing and redevelopment, were planned with minority participation in the more responsive cities.

Although the picture was uneven from city to city, demand-protest clearly produced some responsiveness. Very strong incorporation, as in Berkeley and later in Oakland, clearly could produce across-the-board change at the highest levels of city government and significant changes in the allocation of neighborhood improvements, prevention of unwanted change in minority neighborhoods, provision of new social services, redistribution and reorientation of traditional city services (including police), and minority employment.

The presence of people of color on councils changed decision making to include them as a matter of course and sensitized whites to their concerns. Blacks and Latinos talked about how different it was to be "on the inside," to attend council meetings and see minority representatives, and to be able to call them on the telephone. Council members talked about a new atmosphere—and new pressure—on the council once minorities were members. As one city official said, "When minorities talk to the city council now, council members nod their heads in agreement rather than yawn."

Measured by the standards of the dream of integration and an end to poverty, these gains still fall short. They were nevertheless of enormous importance to people of color and dramatically different from what had gone before. Decades of political effort had produced a great breakthrough in political equality and reduction of governmental discrimination.

Still, this breakthrough was unevenly achieved, and many problems were not alleviated by it. Widespread unemployment, poverty, and health problems associated or intensified with poverty remained. Inner-city populations continued to face inadequate education with constrained funding induced by the tax-revolt victories of Proposition 13 in 1978 and its successor tax- and spending-limitation initiatives and by cutbacks at the federal level. Even strong and determined biracial coalitions that controlled city governments felt compelled to compete for private investment with the usual tools available to cities, though they were also sometimes able to make arrangements with developers that produced low- and moderate-income housing and other essentials and amenities that otherwise would not have been realized.

The goals of eliminating poverty and achieving integration were not realized. However, the goals of ending racial exclusion, gaining elective office, bringing people of color into government at all levels, changing the perspectives and practices of city agencies, and reallocating the resources of city government were achieved in many cities.

As noted earlier, the very successes of the movement removed much of the incentive to maintain the structures that produced them. When employment of a minority group in city government approaches or exceeds the group's relative size in the city and occurs at all levels, the proposition that continued intense mobilization and coalition unity are necessary to achieve equity in city government employment is not persuasive. And when women, gays, Latinos, Asians, and environmentalists entered local politics in increasing numbers, there were new faces to respond to, new demands for representation, and new issues to contest. The successes of the movement and the entry of other claimants and issues have made race less prominent in the politics of many of these cities and transformed the terms of political engagement in other ways as well.

From the Struggle to Overcome Exclusion to the Politics of Issue-Based Coalitions

If the 1960s and 1970s were times in which racial issues suffused urban politics and racial exclusion was overcome by political struggle in most of the 10 cities, subsequent decades have witnessed a gradual transition to a different form of politics. The interests of ethnoracial groups continue to play a significant role, but the ideology of the black power movement is not as commonly evoked, and sustained, intense polarization on racial lines is also less common. Nevertheless, exclusion is still not unknown, and racially charged issues arise periodically.[7]

In contrast to the 1960s, more groups participate and have access to government, and other issues shape shifting coalitions among them. At its best in these cities, the hitherto excluded groups occupy a place of respect by right and by organization and persistence.

The transition was marked by change in five main areas: enforcement by other governmental authorities, acceptance of minority participation in government, spread of minority representation, issue succession, and the rise of competing coalitions.

Enforcement by Other Governmental Authorities   Governmental authorities at state and federal levels pushed the adoption of racially fair policies in cities where African Americans were not strongly incorporated—in effect compensating for political weakness in those cities. For example, in the 1970s, the California Fair Employment Practices Commission (FEPC) investigated and surveyed city employment practices in Vallejo, Daly City, and Stockton, which resulted in stronger affirmative action plans and increased minority hiring. Court orders and FEPC actions even in cities with strong black incorporation led to hiring changes in police and fire departments. People of color increasingly were incorporated at all levels of government, and this helped local groups to achieve their objectives.

---

[7] As we write these words, the Bayview-Hunters Point community of San Francisco is seething over an incident in which police, acting on a tip about guns that probably referred to another vehicle beat an onlooker after they surrounded and aggressively searched a group of African-American teens listening to music in a parked car at midnight (Sward 2002, A21; Costa 2002, 1).

Acceptance of Minority Participation in Government   More political activists and officeholders in more cities now accept people of color as rightful participants in government. In the cities where black incorporation is strongest, their political resources tend to be protected. For example, when Berkeley drew new lines for city council districts in response to the 2000 U.S. Census, the lines of every district were manipulated by opposing coalitions in search of partisan advantage—except the boundaries of the two with African-American incumbents. This is the sort of unspoken protection of interests one associated in the past only with business interests. There is still racism, but it is less common—and certain to be immediately and strongly condemned when it does emerge.

Spread of Minority Representation   Representation of African Americans, Latinos, and Asians in city governments continues to increase. The right columns of Table 1.1 show the numbers of each group on city councils plus mayors in each city as well as instances of increase or decrease since 1994; at the bottom of the right side are the average percentages of each group on city councils in 2002, the number of group council members in the late 1970s and 1994, and the number of cities in which the group representation increased or decreased since 1994. Taking the 1970s-1994-2002 sequence, we find that African-American representation increased from 11 to 13 to 18 in 2002; as a percent of councils, it now exceeds African-American population in seven of the 10 cities. Latino representation rose from 5 to 9 to 11, and Asian from 1 to 7 to 8.

With continued growth in population and citizenship, Latino and Asian representation is likely to continue to grow as well. Absent a grievous turn of events for these groups, we do not see the signs of a broad-based, racialized mobilization but, rather, of a somewhat uneven growth in candidacies, organization, and representation with the growth of the population. Because of the superior organization of African Americans and their more acute focus on defense of the race through political mobilization, their representation is not likely to decrease overall even with their gradually declining populations in many cities. In several cities, they are both more plentifully represented and more influential than their numbers would suggest. Overall, their council-plus-mayor representation is substantially higher than their share of population, and they are well organized and outspoken in many cities.

Issue Succession   Other issues arose that could not be readily identified or labeled as black, Latino or Asian issues, and still other issues were reconstituted in universalistic form. Rent control, development and land use, environmental quality, public transportation and control of autos, affordable housing, child care, homelessness, and living wage issues have occupied much of the attention of these city governments in recent years. Although blacks and Latinos, with larger low-income populations, were more likely to support affordable housing and living wage initiatives than other groups, members of all groups could be found on both sides of most issues. Issues such as rent control could not be racial issues, because they divided homeowners and tenants regardless of color.

The discourse of policy shifted. As it became much more difficult for cities to pursue many kinds of affirmative action in the wake of Proposition 209 in 1996, which overturned affirmative action in California, initiatives arose for universalistic policies that might, for example, benefit all low-wage employees in a city (living wage) or give an advantage in city contracting to all small businesses. African Americans, Latinos, and in some cities, Asians are numerous among the low-income population and among small business owners, but race and racial justice are not the explicit focus of this issue.

On one issue, racial polarization remains strong and racial groups call in their political debts and demand committed action—police harassment and injury or death inflicted by police on people of color, primarily African Americans and Latinos. Occasions for protest on issues of police violence occur less often than in the past but are still distressingly frequent.

Rise of Competing Coalitions   New ideologically based coalitions emerged around the new and reframed issues. These coalitions oppose unrestricted corporate development and the replacement of neighborhood businesses with cookie-cutter copies of corporate chain outlets. They may oppose housing development, except for affordable public housing. They have most recently worked—with mixed success— to pass local living wage and universal health care legislation in several cities.

These coalitions and their supporters are increasingly labeled "progressive" to distinguish them on the left from conventional liberals who are willing to permit development with fewer restraints and who resist redistributive policies. There is no single progressive ideology or group, but restrictions on development, environmental issues, grass roots activism, anticorporate positions, and mildly redistributive policies are typical.

How do the new "progressive" coalitions interact with race? Because members of every racial group are found in both progressive and moderate coalitions, the ideological divisions of these coalitions cross-cut racial allegiances, and vice versa. In Berkeley, the two African-American council members belong to the progressive coalition; however, on affordable housing issues, they vote with the moderate coalition, enabling privately financed, affordable housing to be built as part of larger developments that include market-rate housing. This introduces a fluidity to council politics, a practice of switching sides depending on the issue that could not exist unless both coalitions accepted the autonomy and standing of these members. One coalition doesn't just face off against another—there are multiple coalitions depending on the issue. It's not random, but it's not a fully polarized politics on racial or ideological grounds.

In other cities with less clearly ideological politics and less clearly defined coalitions, council politics are still more fluid and individualistic. Members may swing back and forth between coalitions as allegiances are tested by issues and constituency demands, as leaders attempt to mobilize support, and as elections and officeholder succession change the political environment.

The Bottom Line on Political Incorporation

Overall, the political incorporation and policy influence of African Americans seems about the same in these 10 cities today as in the late 1970s. The *scale* of incorporation (Figure 1.2) captured essential aspects of minority political strength from 1960 to 1980, but it does not encompass the *qualitative* shift in the political standing of these groups that has occurred since then. Partnership in a new, biracial, dominant coalition was necessary then; our measure of incorporation is based on equal participation in such a coalition, on the number of council seats held, and on control of the mayor's office. These elements were necessary to dominate a city's political system for years and to turn its practices of exclusion and discrimination around. They are not necessary when that task has been completed, the group is on the inside, and its presence and importance are acknowledged. The scale of incorporation measured well the officeholding that ensured representation of a group's interests during the period of struggle to overcome exclusion, but it does not capture so well different structures that strongly represent group interests after exclusion has been overcome.

Is there any readily observable aspect of a city's politics that we can use to measure political incorporation when inclusion is a fact of a group's political life in a city? Various configurations of coalitions and groups might qualify as strong political incorporation once exclusion has been overcome. One pattern that puts a smallish group in a strong position is the present configuration in Berkeley, where two African-American council members hold the balance of power between competing liberal and progressive coalitions. The structure of the situation means that both of the coalitions must respect the African-American members and heed the interests they represent. During the time of turning city government around, full partnership in a dominant, biracial coalition and representation more than double the size of the African-American population were necessary. Now, much smaller representation sustains the interests of the group in a setting where they hold the balance of power between competing coalitions. A place of power in the coalitional system is still the key, but the system is different. Then, a biracial coalition drove a conservative, whites-only coalition into extinction. Now, competing coalitions both require the inclusion of African Americans.

The example in not reassuring. A position holding the balance of power between competing coalitions may be uncommon—minority groups in many cities will not find themselves in such a favorable position—and it may not endure, especially if group populations continue to shrink, as African-American populations have shrunk in most of these cities in recent years (see Table 1.1).

Inclusion is not a passive condition. It is a dynamic of vigilance, assertiveness, effective use of ideology and interest to forge coalitional support and attention to strategy and to the recruitment and election of candidates The disproportionate representation that symbolized and strengthened the movement to overcome exclusion in some cities, including control of the mayor's office for many years in cities with relatively small black populations such as Berkeley and Los Angeles, may no longer be necessary, but representation remains essential. A group that has lost council representation altogether may still experience fairness in hiring in city government, but it is less likely to exert strong influence over major new policy decisions. Representation still counts.

Latinos and Asians, now more numerous in most of these cities, are considerably more active politically, more strongly incorporated, and more influential than they once were, but they are not so cohesive, well organized, or strongly focused on political incorporation as African Americans are.

We can summarize patterns of mobilization, coalition, and incorporation of these groups by comparing our classification of cities in the period 1960 to 1977 with our classification for 2002 (Table 1.2). The classification of cities in the earlier period stemmed almost entirely from the activity and success of African Americans—they were by far the most strongly mobilized and incorporated group. Now it refers to the combined activity and incorporation of all three groups.

The most important difference from the 1970s is that exclusion is a thing of the past. Minorities are no longer completely excluded from governance in any city. Not only does every city council have some minority representation, all these councils have at least two minority council members (Table 1.1). In six of the 10 cities, including all the largest ones, these groups overall are well established, politically important, and strongly incorporated. A second difference is that protest, common during the 1960s, is not a defining aspect of politics in these cities now; it is nevertheless employed from time to time in several cities with determination, insistence, and some success—even if with less defiance.

Within groups, greater diversity of interests is now expressed on issues such as rent control, taxation, economic development, and regulation of the urban environment. Blacks, Latinos, Asians, and whites are all typically represented both in progressive and in moderate (traditional liberal) coalitions in cities such as San Francisco, Oakland, and Berkeley, where progressive coalitions are active and, at times, significant political forces. Coalitions between groups are now more likely to be organized around particular, diverse, and fluid issues rather than around fixed electoral slates centered on fundamental fairness in housing, employment, contracting, and services that formerly defined racial liberalism in the struggle against exclusion. Above all, the political incorporation of people of color is now not a struggle—in most places in this region, it is an accomplished and accepted fact.

TABLE 1.2   Incorporation and mobilization, 1960s to 2002 (alphabetical within categories)

Incorporation and Mobilization	1960s to 1977 (Black Incorporation)	2002 (Blacks, Latinos, and Asians combined)
Established to very strong	Berkeley Richmond Sacramento San Francisco	Berkeley Oakland Richmond Sacramento San Francisco San Jose
Weak mobilization and incorporation	—	Daly City Hayward Stockton Vallejo
Protest and exclusion	Oakland San Jose Stockton	—
Weak mobilization and exclusion	Daly City Hayward Vallejo	—

City Government Employment

Employment discrimination in general, and city government employment of people of color in particular, was at the center of group demands in the 1960s and of governmental responsiveness in the 1970s. The rate of gain in black employment especially was closely related to the political incorporation of African Americans (Browning, Marshall, and Tabb 1984, ch. 5). How do these groups fare now in this respect?

The easiest way to grasp the relevant relationships is to look at each group's city government employment in relation to its percentage of adult population in 2000, which we can take as a more appropriate measure than percentage of total population, more appropriate because adult population is more closely related both to the share of votes a group can bring to the polls and to the group's share of the workforce in a city.[8] Figure 1.3 shows the relationship for African Americans and their share of city government employment.

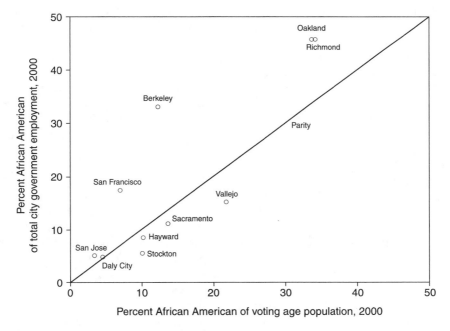

FIGURE 1.3   **Percent African American of city government employment by percent of voting age population**

---

[8]   Remember, however, that the Latino and Asian shares of the actual voting-eligible populations are substantially lower than these voting-age population shares, because so many are not citizens. Most of the voting-age population in these groups have green cards or other work permits and are eligible for employment even if not for voting

First, note in Figure 1.3 the wide variation in African-American populations among these cities, ranging from 3.3 percent of voting-age population in San Jose to more than 35 percent in Oakland and Richmond. Remember that black populations have recently declined in percentage terms in most of the 10 cities. As housing prices have risen, sizable numbers have moved to more affordable suburban and Central Valley areas as well as out of state.

Second, note the line of parity—the line of equal percentage employment and percentage of the voting-age population. Parity is a commonly accepted target for minority-group employment. In *all* 10 cities, total black employment in city government is close to parity. Berkeley and San Francisco, which are well above parity, had already made black employment a high priority by the mid-1960s; no city is disastrously below parity, even those where blacks are not strongly incorporated. African Americans are strongly incorporated in Berkeley and San Francisco, given their share of the populations of those cities, and their record speaks to the importance of political incorporation. However, the achievement of parity, even in cities without strong incorporation, speaks clearly to the diffusion of nondiscrimination in government employment. Nowhere do we see the sort of exclusion—near-zero employment—that was still common in the 1960s. This does not mean that racist harassment in work settings of city governments is unheard of (Ratcliff 2002); it does mean that official fair employment practices have been broadly instituted.

Latino employment displays a pattern somewhat similar to that of blacks, but without the markedly higher-than-parity rates found for blacks in Berkeley and San Francisco (Figure 1.4). City government employment is closely related to the size of the Latino population, and six cities are at or only slightly below parity. That is the main message: Employment close to parity with size of adult population has been achieved whether or not the Latino population is large or its political incorporation is particularly strong.

The pattern of Asian employment (Figure 1.5) looks different, partly because people of Asian origin are rather evenly distributed among most of these cities and, therefore, are clustered in a range between 12 percent and 28 percent Asian. The exceptions are San Francisco, with a large Chinese population of long standing combined with a large new-immigrant Chinese population, and Daly City, with a rapidly increasing Filipino population. Compared to blacks and Latinos, employment of Asians lies farther below parity in more cities.

In San Francisco, the greater-than-parity Asian share of city government employment reflects a long-established population, high levels of education, and political strength. In most of the 10 cities, Asian employment in city government has increased rapidly in recent years, and the lag of employment behind population probably reflects the fact that the growth of Asian populations is so rapid and so recent. It takes time for employment—a process largely of attrition and replacement—to catch up with population. In no city is Asian employment so low as to suggest exclusion.

How do the groups compare? African Americans have resided in these cities in substantial numbers for a longer period of time, they pushed for affirmative action in government employment earlier and more vigorously than Latinos and Asians, they have a strong orientation toward public-sector employment, and they have probably been subject to greater discrimination in private employment.

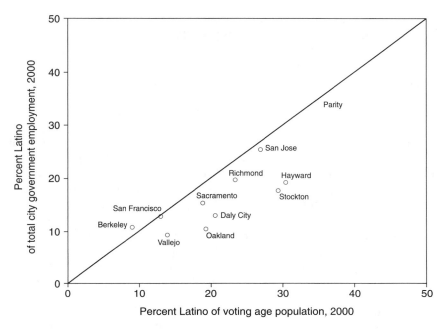

FIGURE 1.4   Percent Latino of city government employment by percent Latino of voting age population

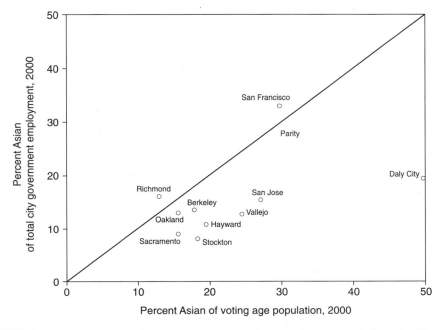

FIGURE 1.5   Percent Asian of city government employment by percent Asian of voting age population

Consequently, African Americans display higher levels of city government employ-ment than Latinos relative to voting-age/working-age population—in Figure 1.3, the cities are generally farther above or closer to the line of parity than in Figure 1.4—and the data for Latinos shows higher levels than for Asians.

For all three groups, the message of the graphs is that exclusion from city gov-ernment employment is a thing of the past.

Higher-level employment in city government presents a partly different, partly similar picture. Graphs for group shares of employment as officials and administrators in city government suggest that these groups are excluded nowhere, their employ-ment is well above parity in a few cities, is positively related to population shares, but is typically at somewhat lower levels than total city government employment. African and Asian Americans generally have gained shares of official/administrator employ-ment at substantially higher rates than Latinos have. Differences in group political incorporation make a greater difference for group shares of employment as officials and administrators than for group shares of total employment. For example, in cities where Latinos are not strongly incorporated and hiring fairness is not a high priority, their share of employment as officials and administrators falls far short of parity.

We can still see the effects of high levels of political incorporation: Biracial and multiracial coalitions that controlled city governments significantly elevated city government employment of nonwhite groups, especially African Americans, and incorporation still has a substantial impact, especially for employment of officials and administrators. In addition, however, we see a widespread reduction of dis-crimination in city government employment even in cities where these groups do not have strong political incorporation. For example, Vallejo has had neither a black nor a Latino city council member for almost all of its history, yet total government employment of blacks and Latinos in Vallejo is not far from parity. Early, strong political incorporation did make a difference—city government employment of blacks approached or exceeded parity in the middle and late 1970s in Berkeley, San Francisco, Sacramento, and San Jose, much earlier than in other cities (Browning, Marshall, and Tabb 1984, 173), and it remains considerably higher than parity in Berkeley and San Francisco despite their smallish and shrinking black populations. Fairness in hiring also has continued to spread even to cities where minority polit-ical incorporation has not changed much.

The reduction of employment discrimination, rise of a black middle class, and upward mobility of people of color in general is a significant success story, and gov-ernment employment has played a significant role. It is also true that the success is still somewhat uneven, and too many have not benefitted.

Civilian Police Review Boards

Civilian police review boards are an instrument that African Americans in particular have used to attempt to exert control over police departments and to reduce the level of police violence against them. Police review boards are an imperfect tool given the centrality, cohesiveness, and control over the means of violence that police depart-ments commonly possess. Other tools in this urgent and ongoing effort include the appointment of black police chiefs in cities where black political incorporation is strongest; hiring and promotion of black police officers, sometimes using the courts to force the departments to do so; training and retraining of police; and protest.

The establishment of police review boards was clearly related to black political incorporation, but only Berkeley and Oakland had created them by 1979. By 2002, five of the 10 cities, including the three largest, had them, and their establishment was closely related to black political incorporation (Table 1.3).

POLITICAL ECONOMY

The Introduction noted that the overarching structure of capitalism exerts profound effects on cities. As a consequence, powerful economic elites may dominate the local political process and its governing coalition. Those forces can shape or nullify the acts of political leadership, coalition formation, and elections.

The political economy of a region affects:

- *The power of government relative to investors.* Cities that are attractive to investors can extract concessions from them; cities that are not must grant concessions to them to attract investment.
- *The power of government relative to particular employers.* A single large employer determined to preserve its advantages can be very powerful, because the city's prosperity depends on it. Many smaller employers in a diversified economy are less able to dominate city government.
- *The nature of the population.* A highly educated work force is likely to be significantly more tolerant on racial issues and sensitive to environmental concerns.

These 10 cities have had significant political-economic advantages. The San Francisco Bay Area has experienced rapid growth—consider the electronics industry in Silicon Valley and its impact on the region—and has been enormously attractive for investors, thus potentially increasing the power of city governments somewhat in relation to investors. Other than the electronics industry, however, it is not blue-collar manufacturing firms but public agencies, universities, hospitals, and the military that are the largest employers. Public investment in services and administration on this scale diversifies local economies, attracts highly educated

TABLE 1.3   Black incorporation and civilian police review boards

	Black Incorporation, 2002		
Police Review Board	**Weak**	**Moderate**	**Strong**
Yes	—	San Francisco San Jose	Berkeley Oakland Richmond
No	Daly City Hayward Stockton Vallejo	Sacramento	—

people and private investment in services and research, and buffers city governments somewhat from the demands of private investors and employers.

Not all the political-economic determinants have been favorable. Heavy manufacturing and other blue-collar employment was concentrated during World War II in
San Francisco, Oakland, Vallejo, and Richmond, which produced rapid growth of
black populations attracted by job opportunities in those cities. As industry shrank in
the post–World War II period, San Francisco was able to stay prosperous on the shoul-
ders of a growing tourism industry and service sector, including education, health,
banking, and legal services. Oakland and Richmond in general, and their black and
Latino populations in particular, experienced persistently higher unemployment. The
economic boom of the late 1990s helped to reduce rates of unemployment, but reces-
sions still produce the typical disproportionate increases in unemployment and
poverty among black and Latino residents, particularly in Oakland and Richmond.

The presence of many highly educated and highly skilled people had direct
political implications in many of these cities. As noted earlier, support by nonblacks
for black candidates and interests was crucial to the formation of racially liberal
coalitions that could take control of city governments in the 1960s and 1970s. Figure
1.6 shows that the level of such support varied widely among cities and was closely
related to their levels of white-collar employment, which we take as a rough indicator for the size of a well-educated professional class. The higher the level of
white-collar employment, the greater the support for black candidates and interests
among nonblacks—mainly whites—in the 1960s.

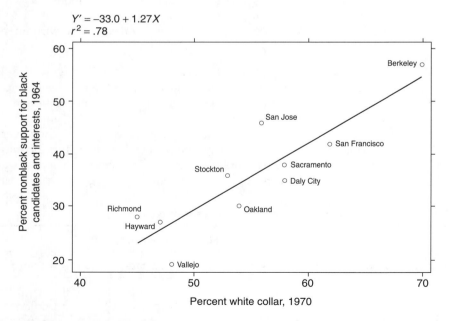

FIGURE 1.6   Nonblack support for black candidates and interests by percent white collar

Source: Percent white collar; 1970 census. Nonblack Support: see fn. 4 and Figure 1.1.

Historically, these cities have experienced distinctive patterns of economic development. Such distinctive economic development led to distinctive clustering both of ethnoracial groups and of educated whites. The resulting characteristics of the economy and the population made it likely that some of these cities would be relatively responsive to the civil rights movement and the movement to gain access to city government and relatively autonomous in relation to investors and local economic elites.

The historical, social, and political history of San Francisco also predisposed people of the major cities of this region to respond more favorably than most regions to the civil rights politics of the 1960s and the gay politics of the 1970s to the present. The city is famous both for its tolerance of alternative lifestyles and for the left-liberal cast of its politics, and it has been so since the mid-nineteenth century. These conditions continue to attract like-minded people to the region.

PRESENT PROBLEMS AND EMERGING THREATS

To shift our vision from the restricted sphere of local government to the problems of these groups is to focus on a different set of concerns. At the core of poverty, unemployment, and crime—and of some drug abuse leading to poverty—must be lack of skills, the loss of hope and community, and rage. In turn, these might be addressed in part through education, but education is not in the sphere of general local government in California. Some of these cities invest in youth and drug programs, affordable housing, and health programs directed toward particular neighborhoods and groups, but the core interest of education still cannot be addressed through these city governments in which so much political effort has been invested.

Citizens' groups in many of these cities have vigorously pursued their interests at the neighborhood and school-district levels. No overarching coalitions exist, however, that make education a foundation of their programs and that work in a unified way in both the education and city-government arenas. Mayor Jerry Brown's recent partly successful effort to gain control of the Oakland School Board and to establish a military academy may be an interesting exception to this rule.

In California as a whole, the success of antitax, antiexpenditure forces beginning in 1978 means that schools and local governments generally are restricted in their funding options. The tax and spending limits now part of the state constitution by initiative drag down the level and scope of public spending for state government—and for all local governments and school boards. The structure of tax and spending limits, however, does not totally eliminate variation among localities in what they can do. The cities in this region in which African Americans, Latinos, and Asians are most strongly incorporated are also the cities that do best in the struggle to bend or circumvent the tax and spending limits and to maintain relatively high levels of spending for public education. Educational spending has fluctuated with the state's shifting economy. During the late 1990s, efforts were made to reduce inequality in per-student expenditure for schools with a variety of state and local propositions. The recession of 2001 ended the state government budget surplus and has led to cutbacks in state contributions to local education budgets. In some cities, like Berkeley, schools are experiencing large, unexpected budget deficits; little state help is anticipated. Education remains a serious problem and contentious issue in many cities.

CONCLUSION

When the energy unleashed by the civil rights movement flowed across the country in the 1960s, some of these northern California cities were ready for a new political coalition—a coalition between diverse liberals, who were unusually numerous in these cities but faced conservative coalitions in power, and African Americans seeking to end their exclusion from city government and its benefits. The civil rights and black power movements made the mobilization of black people possible and necessary, and created the opportunity and incentive for blacks and white, Asian, and Latino liberals to build alliances that took over city governments and changed them. Where there weren't enough black people given the size of the racially liberal electorate, that didn't happen; where there weren't enough liberals given the size of the black population, it didn't happen.

The struggle to overcome exclusion achieved its goal in most of these cities. Some city governments were remade to end discrimination and transform city policies toward minority populations. Even in the cities at the other end of the spectrum, where political incorporation of African Americans and other people of color made little progress, governments became less discriminatory in hiring and other areas as state and federal agencies and courts pressured them to change.

Mobilization of Latinos and Asians was also stimulated by the civil rights movement and has continued to develop, supported by rapid population growth and boosted by anti-immigrant initiatives in the 1990s. All three groups have substantially increased their representation in city council and mayoral positions since the late 1970s; every city council has at least two members of color in mid-2002; and all three groups hold a majority of council seats in three cities. With further growth in Asian and Latino populations and increasing naturalization, citizenship, and voter registration, we can expect their representation to continue to increase. The allegiance of an ethnic group is a potential political resource that will usually be exploited by someone. Even where groups do not feel a strongly racialized sense of grievance, the threats posed by anti-immigrant legislation, by scapegoating (e.g., the Wen Ho Lee case), and by other evidence of prejudice is enough to convince reasonable people that they should become citizens and voters. Representation does not lead inevitably to participation in strong coalitions, but it creates a basis for coalition formation on issues important to the group.

Although the number of African-American council members and mayors grew from 13 to 18 in these cities between 1994 and 2002 (an increase of 39 percent), that level of representation and other gains such as city government employment are likely to come under pressure if black populations continue to decline in these cities. In cities where biracial coalitions took over city governments, African

Americans hold much larger shares of city employment at all levels than other groups, in proportion to population. Control of top positions and of city employment overall has become turf that African-American officeholders strive to preserve against the demands of Latinos and Asians for greater shares—not a stance that enhances prospects for coalition (Tilove 1996). Overall, African-American leaders and organizations appear to us more vigilant, better organized, and more assertive about group interests, and they are likely to continue to need those political resources.

The civil rights and black power movement was a force that produced many of the same kinds of political effort in many cities at once. With the achievement of some of its objectives, the movement is less of a unifying force; greater variation in conditions and strategies has unfolded. Although issues such as police violence continue to arise and evoke a struggle for racial justice, highly racialized issues are much less common now than they were in the 1960s and 1970s, and they occupy a much smaller part of the agenda of city governments.

In place of issues that evoked race as their central theme, activists have brought new issues to the fore such as affordable housing, living wage, child care, homelessness, rent control, and environmental cleanup and protection. Six of these ten cities have adopted living wage ordinances, and living wage is coming up on the agenda of others. Such issues create opportunities for groups to come together in shifting coalitions depending on the issue. On living wage, there is no unified biracial coalition in place that can dominate city policy making; rather, issue-centered coalitions of diverse progressives and people of color are created, with labor unions and faith-based and other community organizations playing significant roles. The significance of race is not forgotten, but race is not the unifying, public principle at work pulling diverse interests and organizations together.

REFERENCES

Browning, Rufus P., Dale Rogers Marshall, and David H. Tabb. 1984. *Protest Is Not Enough.* Berkeley: University of California Press.

Browning, Rufus P., Dale Rogers Marshall, and David H. Tabb, eds., 1990. *Racial Politics in American Cities.* White Plains, N.Y.: Longman.

Browning, Rufus P., Dale Rogers Marshall, and David H. Tabb, eds., 1995. Mobilization, Incorporation, and Policy: Ten California Cities Revisited. Paper prepared for the 1995 Annual Meeting of the American Political Science Association, Aug. 31–Sept. 3, Chicago.

Browning, Rufus P., Dale Rogers Marshall, and David H. Tabb, eds., 1997. *Racial Politics in American Cities,* 2nd ed. White Plains, N.Y.: Longman.

Browning, Rufus P., Dale Rogers Marshall, and David H. Tabb, eds., 2000. Taken In or Just Taken? Political Incorporation of African Americans in Cities. In Richard C. Keiser and Katherine Underwood, eds., *Minority Politics at the Millenium.* New York: Garland, pp. 131–156.

Costa, Francisco da. 2002. Hunters Point Crowd Denounces Police Terrorism. *San Francisco Bay View,* February 20, 1.

Espiritu, Yen Le. 1992. *Asian American Panethnicity: Bridging Institutions and Identities.* Philadelphia: Temple University Press.

Levy, Frank, Arnold Meltsner, and Aaron Wildavsky. 1974. *Urban Outcomes*. Berkeley: University of California Press.

Lien, Pei-te. 2001. *The Making of Asian American Through Political Participation*. Philadelphia: Temple University Press.

Lineberry, Robert L. 1977. *Equality and Urban Policy: The Distribution of Municipal Public Services*. Beverly Hills: Sage.

Nathan, Harriet, and Stanley Scott, eds. 1978. *Experiment and Change in Berkeley*. Berkeley: Institute of Governmental Studies, University of California.

Peterson, Paul E. 1981. *City Limits*. Chicago: University of Chicago Press.

Ratcliff, Willie. 2002. Despite Noose, HRC Rules No Racism at SFO. *San Francisco Bay View*. February 20, 1.

Rodriguez, América. 1999. *Making Latino News: Race, Language, Class*. Thousand Oaks, Calif.: Sage.

Sward, Susan. 2002. Parents Outraged at S.F. Cops, Female Students Groped, Teen Beaten, They Say. *San Francisco Chronicle*, March 3, A21.

Tilove, Jonathan. 1996. Minorities Fighting Each Other for Power: Many Ready to Abandon Idea of Rainbow Coalitions. Newhouse News Service. In *The Times-Picayune*, December 8, A20.

Part II

Biracial Coalitions

Chapter 2

Post-Incorporation Politics in Los Angeles

Raphael J. Sonenshein

EDITORS' NOTE

In the study of minority incorporation, Los Angeles stands as the leading big city example of the political success of minority incorporation through biracial electoral coalition. Despite a black population that has never exceeded 17 percent of the city (now reduced to 11 percent), blacks won a major share of power at city hall under the five-term leadership of African-American mayor Tom Bradley.

In this chapter, Raphael J. Sonenshein traces the circumstances and leadership techniques that made this extraordinary coalition successful in the face of widespread beliefs that interracial politics were dead. He highlights the roles of shared ideology, common political interests, and creative leadership in the development of cross-racial coalitions.

Yet even in Los Angeles, the general decline of such alliances has been severely felt. In 1993, Republican Richard Riordan defeated Bradley's ideological heir, and the black community found itself out of power. Coalition lines fell into disrepair, and Latinos and Asian Americans chafed at the notion of a solely black–white politics. Sonenshein discusses the decline of the coalition and the dramatic rise of a Republican mayor in the Democratic city. When Riordan was succeeded by a black-supported Democrat, James K. Hahn, in 2001, it was not simply a re-creation of the black-centered Bradley coalition, but rather the mix-and-match coalition politics of the post–Bradley era. The driving forces of the city's politics were increasingly Latinos and suburban whites.

In the post–Bradley era in Los Angeles politics, racial and ethnic minority groups are pursuing their interests and beliefs in different ways than before. In the face of a strong suburban secession movement and the rise of Latinos, coalition patterns have become deeply unsettled. The earlier politics of ideology and race has now expanded to include ethnicity and "place" in the evolving political geography of Los Angeles.

Sonenshein argues that while there is still a basis for interracial coalition politics in Los Angeles, shared liberal ideology and common political interests no longer provide the sole guideposts for minority politics.

I n their 1984 book *Protest Is Not Enough,* Browning, Marshall, and Tabb contended that biracial coalitions are powerful vehicles for achieving minority incorporation in the political life of cities. Their relatively optimistic view of biracial and multiracial coalitions contrasted strikingly with the more common pessimism about cross-racial politics. Racial polarization in such major cities as New York and Chicago (as well as in a number of medium- and smaller-size cities) fed the belief that the black protests and white backlash of the 1960s doomed biracial politics.

In that light, the success of biracial coalition politics in Los Angeles was extremely significant. In Los Angeles, the urban center of traditionally conservative Southern California, a small black community won a major share of political power through membership in a biracial coalition with white liberals. Under the leadership of African-American mayor Tom Bradley, this liberal coalition dominated city politics for two decades (1973–1993). Latinos, who significantly outnumbered blacks in the city, were junior partners in the coalition and were less successful than blacks in winning political incorporation. Asian Americans, allies of Bradley since his first election to the city council, were also important, if secondary, members of the Bradley mayoral coalition (Sonenshein 1993).

By the mid-1990s, however, the Los Angeles coalition was on its last legs, torn asunder by racial and class conflicts. After the videotaped beating of Rodney King in 1991 and the massive civil unrest of April 1992, the city seemed to be careening out of control. Bradley chose not to run for a sixth term in 1993. He was replaced by a white Republican businessman, Richard Riordan; the question for the future was not the relationship between blacks and whites that had so animated city politics for decades but the stresses and strains among the city's many diverse groups. In 2001, city voters nearly elected a liberal Latino to the mayoralty, and he was only defeated by a fellow Democrat who built an unlikely coalition of African Americans and conservative and moderate whites.

What do these changes mean for the theory of political incorporation set forth by Browning, Marshall, and Tabb? More specifically,

1. What demographic and economic factors underlay the development of a winning biracial coalition and then its demise?
2. What benefits were gained for minorities through the strong political incorporation achieved by the biracial coalition, and what has been the fate of those changes since the passing of the liberal ruling coalition?
3. What is the future of minority politics in the puzzling new world of Los Angeles? What are the prospects for the development of multiracial coalitions?

BACKGROUND

Los Angeles is the prototype of the newer western city. Its expansion began in the 1880s and continued well beyond World War II, as its population rank among cities rose from 135 (in 1880) to 2 (in 1982). Los Angeles added nearly a half-million more people in the 1980s, and several hundred thousand more in the 1990s. During its period of greatest growth, the city was dominated and shaped by white Protestant migrants from the Midwest who hoped to create an urban model of the heartland lifestyle (Fogelson 1967). Their explicit intention was to avoid the political character of the big eastern and midwestern cities, which were dominated by Catholic immigrants, labor unions, and minority groups.

Midwestern values helped to create and sustain the nonpartisanship of California cities. In both formal structure and actual practice, Los Angeles has been a strongly nonpartisan city (Adrian 1959). As a result, party organizations have been virtually non-existent. Despite a clear majority in party registration, Democrats failed for many years to take over city hall (Mayo 1964; Carney 1964) until the rise of the liberal coalition in the early 1970s.

Unlike many big cities in the East and Midwest, but more like the Sunbelt of which it was a part, Los Angeles was dominated by its business leaders for the first half of the twentieth century. It was very much an "entrepreneurial political economy," as defined by Elkin (1987, 61):

> All entreprenurial cities have in common a relatively unimpeded alliance at work composed of public officials and local businessmen, an alliance that is able to shape the workings of city political institutions so as to foster economic growth. In each, moreover, electoral politics is organized so that businessmen play an important role, and urban bureaucracies are adept at organizing their domains so that they are neither dominated by elected officials nor in the service of local businessmen.

The homogeneous community ideal of the midwesterners' new city implicitly excluded such minority groups as blacks, Jews, Mexicans, and Japanese. The steady migration of minorities into Los Angeles before and after World War II, however, slowly eroded the predominance of conservative whites. The city's economy also dramatically changed, as Greater Los Angeles became the most important aircraft production center in the nation. Los Angeles rapidly industrialized, and thousands of black workers migrated from the South for highly desirable industrial jobs (Smith 1978).

It took several decades for these wartime economic changes to generate political effects, but by the 1950s and early 1960s, the growing black community was actively organizing for political power. The much less economically grounded Latino community was also growing in numbers, but it developed politically at a much slower pace. Asian Americans were even farther from the center of political action.

During these same decades, the Jewish community also grew by leaps and bounds (Vorspan and Gartner 1970). Economically adaptable, Jews moved steadily from the downtown area through the mid-city and out to West Los Angeles, and then a large group moved over the mountains to the San Fernando Valley.

Jews responded to their exclusion from the business and civic world of white Protestants by building their own economic power centers away from downtown (Davis 1991). The social provincialism of the city's Protestant economic leaders therefore helped to generate competition that divided and weakened their own dominance of city life. Indeed, the election of maverick Sam Yorty as mayor in 1961, despite the near-total opposition of the business corrimunity, suggested that the downtown alliance of corporate leaders and the *Los Angeles Times* was not an unbeatable monolith (Carney 1964).

Jews (included in the white category by the U.S. Bureau of the Census) have been an important and distinctive group in the city, representing about 7 percent of the population in 1970 and 6 percent in 2000. Highly mobilized, Jews comprised an estimated 15 percent of the local electorate in 1973. Twenty years later, Jews cast an astonishing 19 percent of the votes in the mayoral runoff, and in the 2001 mayoral election, Jews cast 18 percent of all votes. Los Angeles Jews have remained Democratic in very large numbers. Private polling in the mid-1990s indicated that more than three-quarters were Democrats (Fairbank, Maslin, Maullin, and Associates, various dates). According to the *Los Angeles Times* exit poll in 1993, more than 80 percent of Los Angeles Jews were Democrats (Gold, 2001).

THE RISE OF A BIRACIAL COALITION

The political and cultural exclusion of Jews from the homogeneous community during the first half of the twentieth century suggests that despite their economic success, they experienced the feeling of being an "out-group" (Vorspan and Gartner 1970, ch. 5). This sense of being left out combined with their liberalism and activism to establish the basis for a political coalition with blacks. Blacks and Jews were drawn together by liberal ideology as well as by shared political interests. In the early 1960s, Jewish liberals and blacks formed a powerful coalition that was able to challenge both the rigidities of the downtown establishment and the conservative reactionaries led by Mayor Sam Yorty. In 1973, this coalition elected a black mayor, Tom Bradley, and dominated city politics for the next two decades.

With Bradley's election, racial minorities attained strong incorporation. Before 1973, minority incorporation had been minimal in Los Angeles and followed a pattern similar to that found by Browning, Marshall, and Tabb in 10 northern Califomia cities. For the first half of the twentieth century, blacks and Latinos were largely invisible in city politics, and to a much greater degree than in the East and Midwest, where party organizations sometimes provided partial incorporation. The first minority council member, Edward Roybal, a Latino, was elected in 1949, and until 1962, there were no black city council members.

In 1962 and 1963, blacks organized with remarkable effectiveness to elect three members to the 15-seat council—a 20 percent proportion they have held into the twenty-first century (Sonenshein 1993, ch. 3; Patterson 1969). In the process, Latinos lost their one seat to blacks and would not attain another of their own until 1985. The black gains on the council were diluted, however, by the extreme hostility of the incumbent mayor, Sam Yorty. Elected in 1961 with strong minority support, Yorty became a relentless foe of minorities and progressives, backing the hated Police Chief William Parker and using racist appeals to defeat Bradley's strong challenge in 1969. At best, minorities had some representation before 1973, but very little incorporation.

The biracial coalition gained its first great success with the election of Bradley to the city council in 1963. In a district only one-third black, Bradley's black and Jewish allies built a powerful biracial alliance that overwhelmed the conservative white appointee to a vacant council seat. As the central focus of these interracial efforts, Bradley became well known citywide, and he soon made plans to challenge Yorty for the mayoralty.

In 1969, Bradley made a stunning showing in the nonpartisan primary, far out-distancing Yorty with 42 percent (to 26 percent) of the vote. Yorty's blatantly racist appeals dominated the runoff campaign, however, and the mayor succeeded in por-traying the moderate Bradley as a tool of black militants and white leftists. To the profound dismay of his followers, Bradley lost. He had, however, set a record for black mayoral candidates in major American cities, winning more than one-third of the white vote (Hahn, Klingman, and Pachon 1976).

In 1973, Bradley again challenged Yorty and utilized a highly effective cam-paign organization that had matured significantly since the 1969 crusade. Dominating the media with powerful television commercials and keeping Yorty on the defensive, the Bradley forces reversed the outcome of 1969 and solidly defeated the three-term mayor. Bradley's allies were also dominant in the city council, pro-viding a strong base for a moderately progressive mayoralty.

With Bradley's election as mayor in 1973, minorities—especially blacks and their liberal Jewish allies—gained strong incorporation. Three council seats were held by blacks, and the biracial coalition controlled a majority of the council. The mayor appointed allies to city commissions and boards, and the coalition's electoral fortunes were assured with the solid support of highly mobilized blacks and Jewish liberals.

The biracial coalition was built on a foundation of shared liberal ideology, com-mon political interest, and strong, trusting leadership. Contrary to the point of view presented in Carmichael and Hamilton's *Black Power* (1967), self-interest was not the only guiding force of the coalition. Liberal ideology among whites, particularly Jews, was essential to Bradley's majority coalition. This role for ideology confirms the analysis by Browning, Marshall, and Tabb, but neither view explains the human dimensions of coalition success, which ultimately depended on leadership.

Bradley's coalition was immeasurably strengthened by the close political and personal ties among the black and white liberal activists who had worked together since the early 1960s. Trust among leaders is an underrated element of coalition development (Hinckley 1981). Trust in the Bradley coalition showed its value in 1979, when controversy over the forced resignation of United Nations Ambassador Andrew Young led to black–Jewish conflicts in numerous cities. Only in Los Angeles was the pre-existing leadership able to defuse the potentially deadly con-troversy (Sonenshein 1993, ch. 8).

The role of Latinos was less clear. Courted by Yorty, Latinos came over to the Bradley coalition in his 1973 election (Hahn, Klingman, and Pachon 1976). Over the years, Latino voters strongly backed Bradley's re-election, and they were well rewarded with commission posts. It was 12 years into Bradley's mayoralty, however, before Latinos regained council representation with Richard Alatorre's election in the eastside Fourteenth District. The next year, Gloria Molina was elected in the neighboring First District—a district created only after a lawsuit against the city by Latino activists. In 1993, Richard Alarcon was elected in the Seventh District of the San Fernando Valley. By the time Bradley left office in 1993, the council was 40 percent black and Latino, with half from each group.

Asian Americans gained greater political representation through the Bradley coalition, especially in appointments to city commissions. The first Asian-American city council member, Michael Woo, was elected in 1985 and became a Bradley ally. When the city council tried to redistrict Woo out of his new district in 1986, Bradley saved Woo's seat by his veto of the ordinance.

DID MINORITIES BENEFIT FROM THE BIRACIAL COALITION?

Minorities gained important benefits from the political incorporation they enjoyed during the heyday of the biracial coalition. The main benefits came in four areas: representation, city hiring, federal aid, and police accountability (Sonenshein 1993, ch. 9).

Representation

Bradley brought an entirely new body of people into Los Angeles city government. Whereas Yorty's appointees had tended to be older white businessmen, apolitical minorities, and wives of prominent politicians, Bradley appointed a diverse array of politically active men and women from both minority and white communities. Tables 2.1 and 2.2 show the Bradley style in appointments to city commissions compared with Mayor Yorty's appointees. On such key commissions as public works and civil service, the Bradley appointees aggressively pursued an agenda that was favorable to minority interests.

Affirmative Action in City Hiring

With the help of his appointed civil service commissioners, Bradley aggressively increased minority hiring at city hall, both in overall percentage and in the higher ranks of job categories. Significant gains in city hiring were obtained by blacks,

TABLE 2.1   Minority representation among Yorty commissioners, 1973

	%	N
Black	6	11
Latino	9	12
Asian American	1	5
Jewish	11	15
Women	17	23
Total N		133

Source: Los Angeles Times, 8 August 1973.

TABLE 2.2   Minority representation among Bradley commissioners, 1973, 1984, and 1991

	1973		1984		1991	
	N	*%*	*N*	*%*	*N*	*%*
Black	21	15	23	19	42	20
Latino	13	9	19	16	34	16
Asian American	10	7	11	9	28	13
Women	43	32	40	33	99	47
Total appointments	140		120		213	

Sources: 1973—*Los Angeles Times*, 8 August 1973; 1984—*Los Angeles Times*, 2 August, 3 August 1984; 1991—Office of the Mayor.

Latinos, Asian Americans, and women (Tables 2.3 to 2.6). All four groups also registered solid gains in the two most desirable categories: officials/administrators and professionals.

Even though African Americans were declining as a share of the city's population, they were holding their position in city hiring. Despite a lower degree of political incorporation, Latinos and Asian Americans were markedly improving their positions. In a quiet way, the regime did a respectable job of developing a secure and upwardly mobile occupational base for some elements of minority communities.

Federal Aid

Again in stark contrast to Yorty, Bradley sought to improve city services through the search for federal and state assistance. He became an outstanding mayoral grantsperson, bringing tens of millions of dollars into the city for physical improvements and social services (Saltzstein, Sonenshein, and Ostrow 1986).

The pressure to make redistributive choices was anticipated and eased by an emphasis on increasing overall resources. In this sense, the federal funding boom of the 1970s was a godsend. Using federal money, the city undertook a wide range of new social service programs while hardly tapping the city treasury. Many, though

TABLE 2.3   Composition of city government workforce, 1973 and 1991

	1973		1991	
	N	*%*	*N*	*%*
White	26,681	64.1	21,088	46.0
Black	9,135	21.9	10,286	22.4
Latino	3,879	9.3	9,112	19.9
Asian American	1,659	4.0	3,452	7.5
Women	6,660	16.0	11,705	25.5

Source: Analysis of data drawn from City of Los Angeles, *Numerical Progress, 1973–1991.*

TABLE 2.4   Job classifications of Latino, Asian-American, and women city employees, 1973 and 1991 (percentage of group)

	Latinos		Asian Americans		Women	
	1973	1991	1973	1991	1973	1991
Officials	0.2	0.5	0.2	1.5	0.1	0.8
Professionals	6.8	10.1	27.8	37.3	10.3	21.2
Technical	8.2	8.3	17.5	13.9	7.0	4.9
Protective services	15.4	24.2	2.0	7.6	3.0	13.0
Paraprofessionals	0.8	1.2	0.4	1.4	1.0	2.0
Service	23.2	18.4	6.6	3.4	2.2	4.0
Skilled	23.3	18.8	14.3	14.3	0.1	1.0
Clerical	22.1	18.5	31.2	20.7	76.3	52.8

Source: Analysis of data drawn from City of Los Angeles, *Numerical Progress, 1973–1991.*

TABLE 2.5   Minority representation in top-level city jobs, 1973 and 1991 (percentage of jobs)

	Officials and Administrators		Professionals	
	1973	1991	1973	1991
White	94.7	70.9	81.4	54.9
Black	1.3	10.5	5.0	12.0
Latino	2.6	7.5	4.6	11.1
Asian American	1.3	8.0	8.0	15.4
Women	3.0	14.9	11.9	29.9

Source: Analysis of data drawn from City of Los Angeles, *Numerical Progress, 1973–1991.*

TABLE 2.6   African Americans in low-level city jobs, 1973 and 1991 (percentages)

	1973	1991
Share of service and maintenance jobs held by blacks	57.6	42.6
Share of jobs held by blacks that were service and maintenance jobs	40.0	23.5

Source: Analysis of data drawn from City of Los Angeles, *Numerical Progress, 1973–1991.*

not all, of these programs were in poor and minority communities. A study of grants in the Bradley era indicated that overall, they had the effect of redistributing resources downward (Ross 1980).

Using federal and private dollars, the Bradley administration pursued a major economic redevelopment program. Bradley's Los Angeles received a greatly increased share of federal economic development funds, and millions of dollars were invested in the redevelopment of downtown.

Police Accountability

Progress was exceedingly slow in reforming the highly entrenched Los Angeles Police Department. Although Bradley's police commissioners were often perceived by police officials as antagonists, reformers frequently felt that the Bradley group was too cautious. Even so, the Bradley forces won several important battles, including some limits on police shootings and a tighter rein on the police budget and pension fund. It was the videotaped beating of black motorist Rodney King in March 1991, however, that set off the climactic battle between the biracial coalition and the department.

From March 1991 until the summer of 1992, liberal and conservative forces were locked in mortal combat. Bradley's allies on the police commission tried to remove Police Chief Daryl Gates but were overruled by the city council. Bradley's appointed Christopher Commission had more success. The Commission's report was exhaustive and dramatic, and the city council placed most of the report's recommendations for police reform on the June 1992 ballot as Proposition F. The most important recommendation was that the police chief no longer have civil service protection.

Perhaps the greatest victory achieved by the Bradley coalition was the voters' approval of Proposition F in 1992—even in the wake of the civil disorder several months before. The biracial coalition shone through one more time as black voters joined with white liberals and Latinos to carry Proposition F to an easy victory (Table 2.7).

Although the Bradley forces had won a great victory, the political damage to Bradley himself was fatal. His support among white voters fell so dramatically that his biracial base could no longer deliver for him, and he decided not to seek a sixth term.

Economic Policy

Minorities obtained only mixed benefits from the biracial alliance in terms of neighborhood economic development. In the area of economic policy, the Bradley coalition was unquestionably committed to a downtown development strategy. With the close ties between the mayor and the Community Redevelopment Agency, the

TABLE 2.7 Proposition F vote and margin in four key council districts, 1992

District	Main Voter Group	Yes (%)[a]	No (%)[a]	Margin (N)
5th	White liberal/Jewish	71.1	28.9	+22,645
8th	Black	92.0	8.0	+24,024
12th	White conservative	46.3	53.7	−3,420
14th	Latino/moderate white	65.4	34.6	+6,408

[a] Percentage of all votes cast on Proposition F.

Source: Analysis of data from County of Los Angeles Registrar-Recorder.

Bradley administration embarked in 1975 on one of the grandest downtown building programs of any American city. Within the next decade, the Los Angeles skyline
grew dramatically, and downtown was filled with gleaming skyscrapers. Tax-incre-
ment financing made the massive project self-sustaining, because the increased
property values generated tax revenue that was plowed back into development.

The downtown building boom helped to cement the economic alliance between
the Bradley regime and downtown business and labor (Regalado 1991)—in uneasy
coexistence with the minority–liberal coalition that sustained its electoral success. It
also increased the alienation of poor, minority neighborhoods, which continued to
deteriorate as Los Angeles became a global city with a world reputation.

While Bradley ceaselessly pursued programs to draw business into the inner
city, it was only near the end of his mayoralty that he invested substantial political
capital in programs that would ease bank lending practices in poor and minority
neighborhoods. During those later years, he developed a creative program to use
redevelopment funds to provide after-school care in the city schools and supported
council efforts to push banks to increase their lending in the inner city.

One Bradley critic set forth the paradox of Bradley's economic policy:

> Critics who accuse the Bradley administration of "killing Southcentral L.A."
> usually ignore its achievements in integrating the public workforce. . . . It
> may be equally true that Black political leadership in Los Angeles County has
> sponsored significant economic advance and contributed to the community's
> benign neglect at the same time. (Davis 1991, 304)

Thus, the Bradley regime generated substantial political and social benefits for
minority communities, and at great political cost, some police accountability was
achieved. Even in South Central Los Angeles, many families owed their livelihoods
to affirmative action programs in city hiring and to federally funded projects pursued aggressively by Bradley. The economic development of the inner city, however, languished alongside the shining towers of downtown. As thousands of young
men roamed the streets without work, the potential for civil violence became a reality in 1992 (Morrison and Lowry 1994).

THE DECLINE AND FALL OF THE BIRACIAL COALITION

The steady obliteration of the city's industrial base and the rise of a global service
economy, sustained by massive immigration, ultimately changed the foundations of
the city's life. As with the previous industrial economy, the political effects of this
new economy were not immediately felt. It helped to seal the doom of the biracial
coalition, however, and sent the political system into a post-incorporation world
marked by confusion and conflict. Ironically, Tom Bradley's dream to create a world-
class city was coming true, but with consequences he would never have imagined.

For all the dramatic demographic changes that Los Angeles had experienced,
the city's political system seemed poised to continue resembling what it had been

for decades: politics in black and white. In the 1993 mayoral runoff, 84 percent of all votes were cast by blacks and whites. Blacks and Jews, the core groups of the biracial alliance, alone cast nearly one-third of all the runoff votes.

The gap between Latino population and Latino participation in 1993, meanwhile, was truly astonishing: four times as many people as their share of the vote. Table 2.8, which compares the highest- and lowest-participation districts among the 15 council districts, reveals the components of this participation gap. The First is a low-income, largely Latino district on the east side. The Fifth is the principal westside liberal district, nearly 40 percent Jewish and heavily Democratic.

Table 2.8 clearly shows the hole in the electorate. Age opens up one important gap—the Latino community is much younger. However, the huge drop is citizenship, the lack of which reduced the potential voting bloc in the First District to only one-third of the Fifth. Then, registration and voting brought the First down to only one-fifth of the Fifth District's votes per population. Standard turnout figures obscure this difference. Whereas about one-third of the registered voters turned out in each district for the April primary, there were more than five times as many actual voters in the Fifth.

It was not the changing economy alone that spelled the end of the biracial coalition; there were many political factors as well. For example, increasing conflict between blacks and Jews had a chilling effect on the elite ties that had been essential to the coalition's success. When Louis Farrakhan came to town in 1985, the leaders of the Bradley coalition were unable to surmount the intergroup divisions that resulted. The increasing fear of crime among middle-class whites made it extremely difficult for progressive candidates to build majority coalitions crossing lines of race and class.

Economic changes, however, made a big difference. The downtown growth boom sustained by the Bradley coalition alienated disparate groups. Inner-city blacks and Latinos felt that their neighborhoods had been shortchanged in the midst of an economic restructuring. At the same time, whites in West Los Angeles and in the San Fernando Valley felt there had been too much growth in their areas—too much traffic, too many stores, too big a jump in home costs. While few in either area felt that the quality of their lives had been improved by Los Angeles's growth machine, the divergent complaints and conflicts of interest provided little ground for coalition building.

The immigration issue also significantly weakened coalition politics. In the diverse global city, there were increasingly cross-cutting conflicts at the street level,

TABLE 2.8   Mobilization gap between two council districts, 1992–1993

District	Population[a]	18 Yrs of Age and Older[a]	Citizens 18 Yrs of Age[a]	Registered Voters[a]	Votes Cast in 1993
1	228,695	160,576	58,547	36,804	10,118
5	236,423	203,451	174,199	151,020	53,018

[a] In 1992.

Source: Pactech Consultants, *Report to the Los Angeles City Council;* 1993 votes cast from city clerk election division.

particularly in South Central Los Angeles. Citywide issues of black and white were replaced by localized conflicts between blacks and immigrant Latinos for construction jobs and between blacks and Korean-American storeowners (Oliver and Johnson 1984; Johnson and Oliver 1989; Sonenshein 1996).

Less visibly, but crucially, the immigration issue was leading to a wide concern among whites—and many blacks—that the city was changing in an unpredictable and uncomfortable direction. In 1994, white conservatives and half of blacks voted on the same side for Proposition 187 (to prevent undocumented residents from receiving public services), while Latinos and white liberals voted against it. Immigration was one of the few issues that seemed capable of fracturing the basic structure of Los Angeles politics and establishing new—and jarring—coalition patterns.

The new global economy was not creating the sorts of jobs that had sustained the political activism of an up-and-coming black community after World War II. Although immigrant Latinos in South Central Los Angeles were employed at high levels, they were not earning high wages (Pastor 1995). Many were not citizens and were struggling to make ends meet. Unlike the workers in World War II Los Angeles, those now doing the hard work of the city were not in a position to build a foundation for future civic involvement. Indeed, they were virtually invisible in the city's politics, unenfranchised, formally represented by black elected officials, and often ignored by Latino elected officials with their own districts to represent.

The city's population was changing rapidly (Table 2.9). Until the 1980 Census, whites had been a majority of the city's population. By 1990, whites represented less than 40 percent of the city's nearly 3.5 million people. The single largest group were Latinos, who had increased in number significantly from 1980. By 2000, Latinos represented more than 45 percent of the population and African Americans only 10 percent.

The city's political system, however, was becoming a much narrower version of the "lived" city. Table 2.10 contrasts the actual population of the city with the politically eligible and active population.

Indeed, despite the enormous demographic changes in Los Angeles, the political community in the mid-1990s looked remarkably similar to what it was when Bradley fought Yorty in 1969 and 1973: a white majority; a stable, one-sixth black base; and a significant, but surprisingly small, Latino bloc.

TABLE 2.9 Population of Los Angeles by race/ethnicity, 1990

	Percent[a]	N
White[a]	37.3	1,299,604
Black[a]	13.0	454,289
Latino	39.9	1,391,411
Asian or Pacific Islanders[a]	9.2	320,668
Other	0.6	19,426
Total		3,485,398

[a]Non-Hispanic.

Source: U.S. Census, 1990, Table P010, Hispanic origin by race.

TABLE 2.10   **Population versus registration, Los Angeles (in percentages)**

			Votes for Mayor	
	1990 Population	**Registration**	*1993 primary*	*1993 runoff*
White[a]	37.3	65	68	72
Jewish	6.0 (est.)	15	16	19
Black	13.0	15	18	12
Latino[b]	39.9	11	8	10
Asian or Pacific Islander	9.2	4	4	4

Sources: Population, U.S. Census 1990, Table P010. *Hispanic Orgin by Race.* Registration, summary of various estimates; vote in 1993 from *Los Angeles Times* exit polls.

[a] Non-Hispanic white population, including Jews.

[b] Latinos of any race.

In this context, the 1992 civil disturbance and the 1993 election of Richard Riordan as mayor represented two sides of a coin: the appearance or reappearance of characters in the drama of Los Angeles politics. The violence came from the poor and unaffiliated to a far greater degree than the more political Watts riot of 1965 (Sears 1994). Alienated poor people had not been much of a presence in the upwardly mobile, middle-class biracial coalition, and they were out in inchoate force, even burning down such landmarks of the minority movement as the Watts Labor Community Action Center. Latinos on the more established eastside displayed little inclination to participate, but Latinos in South Central and Koreatown represented a core component of the violence.

A year later, white conservatives, long marginalized under the Bradley regime, burst back into the politics they had dominated during the era of Sam Yorty. They voted in a large bloc, with a very high turnout, for a Republican candidate who promised a tough and business-like approach.

With both the minority poor and white conservatives out in force, Los Angeles politics was certain to become more diverse, more polarized, and more unpredictable than it had been under the long and stable rule of the Bradley coalition. In that context, how did the rollback of minority incorporation occur, and what have been its consequences?

THE RISE OF A CONSERVATIVE COALITION

In the 1993 Los Angeles municipal elections, the long era of strong minority incorporation ended. City councilman Michael Woo, a Chinese American associated with the progressive ideal of multiracial politics, was soundly defeated by Republican businessman Richard Riordan. In a city where two-thirds of registered voters were Democrats and whites represented less than 40 percent of the population, how did this occur? How did a Woo aide's confident prediction that "Los Angeles will never elect an old, rich, white Republican" turn out to be 1993's epitaph for Los Angeles liberalism?

The first explanation has already been presented: Voter registration in 1993 Los Angeles was quite different from the population. Whites represented two-thirds of the voters, and in that sense, nothing much had changed. This, however, is only the first part of the answer, because a liberal coalition had triumphed five consecutive times behind Tom Bradley by drawing off large blocs of Latinos and both liberal and moderate whites, especially Jews.

As an Asian American drawing on a multicultural constituency, Woo came to symbolize the uncertain future of a city that was becoming more diverse but also more confusing and even threatening. The declining popularity of the Bradley coalition, combined with the gloomy outlook held by the great majority of the city's voters, made the road for a liberal candidate rocky indeed. Los Angeles is a moderately liberal city, with a strong Democratic majority. Winning progressive alliances join the left and the center, but Woo found himself largely on the left and with little appeal to the center.

There had arisen a vast new level of *interest* conflicts among the various groups likely to form a progressive multiracial coalition. Some were neighborhood based, such as the interminority battles in an increasingly diverse South Central Los Angeles. Others concerned the distribution of resources and power between the inner city and the more affluent parts of the community. And there was a serious decline in the leadership capabilities of the liberal forces compared with those of the Bradley coalition in its heyday.

Woo's runoff opponent, Republican businessman Richard Riordan, seemed an easy target in a city of Democrats. But he had a personal fortune from which he spent freely, and a simple and compelling pledge—"Tough enough to turn L.A. around." Riordan quickly staked out the highest ground on the two key issues: public safety and the economy. He promised to hire 3,000 more police officers and to remove barriers to private investment in Los Angeles. Woo's private polling showed that on most indicators of leadership, the voters preferred Riordan by a wide margin (Fairbank, Maslin, Maullin, and Associates, various dates). Even those who eventually voted for Woo were only "mild about Mike." In areas where Woo had his greatest strength, the turnout was significantly lower than in his weakest areas (Sonenshein and Valentino 1995).

Riordan held a near-monopoly of elite support across party lines. To many of the city's leaders, Riordan was a *mensch*, a real grown-up with weight. To city council president John Ferraro, his colleague Woo was "a snot-nosed kid." Woo was not widely liked on the council, and leaders flocked to Riordan's campaign. Even President Clinton, in his tepid endorsement of fellow Democrat Woo, praised Riordan. Riordan was certainly no Yorty-style populist, but neither did he draw his support only from the business elites. He gained endorsements from Latino council member Richard Alatorre and from J. Stanley Sanders, who had been the leading black candidate in the mayoral primary.

In the election, the traditional patterns of the city's coalitions held firm. Woo, the liberal candidate, had the great share (86 percent) of the black vote due to his prominent role in opposing Chief Gates. He won handily among white liberals, and he won bare majorities among Jews and Latinos. He also won the great majority of

Asian American votes. In a city that only a year before had witnessed assaults on Asian American stores by black and Latino rioters, Woo managed to craft a strong "rainbow" coalition.

Woo was crushingly defeated among white non-Jews, however, and his support among Jews and Latinos was well below Tom Bradley levels. Most remarkably, Riordan won a solid majority of the Fifth Council District—the most liberal, most Jewish, and most participatory of all 15 districts. While some of the change may have been due to a 1992 redistricting that increased the San Fernando Valley portion of the Fifth District, something was different. The Fifth had been a pillar of the Bradley coalition. Clearly, the liberal side of Los Angeles politics, although still competitive, was less unified, less enthusiastic, and less able to hold the center than in its glory days.

MINORITY INCORPORATION IN THE RIORDAN ERA

Under Richard Riordan, minority influence significantly declined at city hall. After enjoying 20 years at the head table in the mayor's office, black voters saw the top executive job go to a person who was backed by fewer than 15 percent of African-American voters and by a minority of Latinos and Asian Americans.

The Riordan era in Los Angeles politics was one of partial, inconsistent incorporation by minority groups—certainly a far cry from the full incorporation of the Bradley era (1973–1993), although more positive than the earlier Yorty era of minority exclusion (1961–1973). African Americans, on the outs during the Riordan years, took the brunt of the decline in minority incorporation. Riordan had closer ties to Latinos, including the head of the newly energized County Federation of Labor, Miguel Contreras.

With a white conservative Republican businessman as mayor, minorities (especially African Americans) lost the full incorporation they had enjoyed under Tom Bradley. Elected with the Sam Yorty coalition of Valley conservatives and a minority of Latinos and Jews in the face of near-unanimous opposition by blacks, Riordan could be expected to roll back many of the gains made by minorities under the previous regime. The Riordan record, however, was mixed. His politics and policies were in some ways conservative and reactionary to Bradley's. In other ways, however, he was more like a moderate, centrist Democrat of the Bill Clinton variety.

Riordan had been a Bradley commissioner and an active campaign donor to such Democrats as Bradley. He was a principal financial supporter of Bradley's run for Governor in 1982. Many of his closest associates were Democrats, and his campaign operatives were mostly retreads from the 1992 Clinton campaign in California. State Republicans derisively referred to Riordan as R.I.N.O. (Republican In Name Only). Riordan's record of support for Democratic candidates came back to haunt him during his failed bid for the 2002 Republican gubernatorial nomination, as conservative Republican voters turned against him.

During his first months in office, Riordan allied himself with Democratic president Bill Clinton. He flew to Washington to lobby Congress for Clinton's crime bill, and in 1994, he went against his party to back Democratic Senator Dianne Feinstein for re-election.

Riordan was acceptable to local Democrats and provided relatively nonpartisan leadership. His image was "tough," but only "tough enough"—an important distinction for white moderates and even white liberals. On social issues important to white liberals, such as gay rights and abortion, Riordan was unthreatening. In fact, shortly after he took office, Riordan marched in the Gay Rights Parade and was photographed hugging a participant.

Riordan worked aggressively to keep existing companies in the city. Applying for federal empowerment zone funds, Riordan seemed to be pledging more economic development for the inner city than the Bradley administration had. This would certainly have never been a program of a Sam Yorty.

In fact, Riordan's ability to meet his campaign pledges was almost entirely dependent on the success of the Clinton administration's policies regarding crime and economic development. Riordan counted on the Clinton crime bill to help him meet his promise to add 3,000 police officers to the city's force. His strategy of investment in the city became heavily tied to the Clinton administration's empowerment zone program.

Riordan's initial appointments to city commissions were eclectic and surprising. Although they did not follow the coalition pattern of the Bradley years, these appointments placed a number of progressive Democrats in very important positions. Police and fire commissioners included several who were very willing to confront the departments on minority hiring and promotion. In fact, Riordan's fire commission took on the department's popular chief on this very question—and far more publicly than Bradley's people had (Rainey 1995).

Riordan's appointments to city commissions were substantially less oriented toward minorities, however, and were skewed more to the Valley, to Republicans, and to mobile economic elites than were those of Bradley (Rainey 1993; Connell 1993). More striking was Riordan's selection of commissioners with less visible stakes in city politics. Half the members of Riordan's transition team did not live in Los Angeles (Rohrlich 1993).

Schockman (1996, 68–69) found that a surprising number of Riordan's inner circle lived far beyond the city's borders, and that they disproportionately represented affluent white areas. Despite a significant degree of racial and economic diversity in commission appointments, Schockman concluded that Riordan had assembled a "neo-rainbow coalition, based on class, not on race."

Riordan survived—and thrived—by holding his white conservative and moderate base and expanding it to include more than 60 percent of both Latinos and Jews in his 1997 re-election, thereby occupying the center of Los Angeles politics. His political high point came in 1999, before the Rampart police scandal hit, when his endorsement carried the new City Charter and several school board and city council candidates to victory.

Despite his elite ties, Riordan increasingly turned against the inside system of government. Coming to city hall as an experienced behind-the-scenes string-puller, Riordan built alliances outside the city government with business leaders, county labor officials, elected charter reform commissioners, anybody except those who worked for the city as elected officials or as city employees who did not report directly to him. He could draw on his own private fortune and a well-tuned political group. His main opponents were white liberals, city and school district employees and their unions, and African Americans.

Riordan's hostility to city employees and their unions was a defining feature of his mayoralty—and extremely disturbing to African Americans. Bradley's success in opening the lines of city employment to African Americans was a signal achievement. Riordan's treatment of the city government as a hostile entity that should be fought at every turn alarmed African Americans. African American leaders strongly defended African-American general managers of city departments under rhetorical assault from Riordan.

Not surprisingly, Riordan's attempt to reform the City Charter to increase his authority over general managers was fiercely resisted by African-American city council members. Although the Charter adopted by the voters in 1999 only moderately increased the mayor's authority, it lost heavily in the African-American voting districts. African Americans and city employee unions later combined to elect James K. Hahn, Riordan's nemesis as city attorney, to the mayor's office with a sweet taste of revenge.

Where Riordan ultimately diverged most directly from the progressive positions of the Bradley regime was on police reform. As a private citizen, he had supported Proposition F for police reform in 1992, but his mayoral campaign received critical help from the Police Protective League, then a largely white union profoundly hostile to police reform. His campaign promise to hire 3,000 new police officers without raising taxes placed him on a collision course with the equally costly and popular policy of community-based policing championed by African-American Police Chief Willie Williams, a holdover from the Bradley administration.

Some of Riordan's appointed civilian police commissioners were highly committed to reform, but the mayor himself seemed to define reform as manpower expansion. Not surprisingly, Riordan's early support for Williams soon evaporated, and the two men entered a long period of conflict that ended with Williams' inability to win a second term in 1997.

Following the departure of Williams, Riordan's police commission appointed Bernard C. Parks to be police chief. An African-American veteran officer, Parks had strong support from African Americans and within the city council. In office, Parks turned out to be a vociferous opponent of civilian oversight of the Department and, with Riordan's support, undercut and virtually controlled the civilian police commission. Parks continued to be strongly popular among black leaders, however, even though his positions on civilian oversight were diametrically opposed to the reform positions championed by Tom Bradley. Parks's popularity among African Americans, based in part on the perception that he had greatly improved the behavior of police officers in minority communities, drove a wedge into the police reform coalition, isolating white liberals as the main advocates of civilian oversight.

With the reform coalition thus weakened and divided, Riordan reversed some of the hard-won gains of the Bradley coalition. He allowed Parks to eliminate the popular Senior Lead Officer program, which had been a bastion of community involvement. Riordan battled the city council, undermined his own civilian police commission, and backed Parks against civilian oversight. Then, in 1999, a major scandal erupted with the revelation that officers within the Rampart division had shot, beaten, and framed civilians. The Rampart scandal, which will end up costing the city millions of dollars in legal judgments, was politically contained by the alliance of Riordan and Parks.

Parks became seriously unpopular with the police union because of his strict discipline and hierarchical control. With the mayor tightly allied with a chief unpopular among the troops, police morale plummeted. In turn, the police ranks steadily declined, crime started going back up, and critics charged that the rapid hiring effort made training and oversight dangerously thin. The police union that had backed Riordan in 1993 supported Riordan's long-time adversary James K. Hahn in 2001. The historically conservative union joined with other city employees and the group that Riordan could never reach—African Americans—to elect the next mayor.

The confusing lines of Los Angeles coalitions in the post-Bradley era are shown in the battle over Chief Parks. Once, police reform represented the principal fault line of Los Angeles politics. Police reformers were blacks and white liberals; opponents of reform were white conservatives. Parks, however, was an African American deeply rooted in his community, yet a bitter foe of civilian oversight. Riordan, unpopular among blacks, strongly backed Parks. The chief's greatest support came from blacks, however—the group least likely to back Riordan. The white-led police union loathed the chief, and even flirted with police reform. Something was changing in the structure of race and ideology in Los Angeles politics.

Despite their defeat in 1993, African Americans remained important players at city hall. While he threatened some of the employment gains of the Bradley years, Riordan was not the hostile force that Yorty had been. It is testimony to the long-run impact of minority incorporation that a new victor at city hall did not simply dismantle all of its successes.

As Table 2.11 indicates, minority gains in city hiring persisted and expanded even during the years that minority incorporation declined at city hall. The data reveal that whites continued to decline as a share of the city workforce, and in the top positions. Despite the decline in African-American population share, their piece of the city employment pie continued to grow. Hispanics also made major strides.

One of the most resistant departments to minority hiring had been the Fire Department. The city was placed under a federal consent decree in 1974 to improve its record of minority employment in the Fire Department. On April 8, 2002, a federal judge withdrew the consent decree, ruling that the city had met its mandate (Rosenzweig 2002, B1, B9).

SECESSION, LATINOS, AND THE 2001 ELECTIONS

Between the two riots of 1965 and 1992, racial division was the fundamental wedge that shaped issues in Los Angeles politics. By the turn of the twenty-first century, racial division remained, but it was sharing the stage with the rise of discontent in the historically white San Fernando Valley and the drive for representation by Latinos.

TABLE 2.11   **Share of city employment by group, 1993, 1997, 2001**

| | (a) Total city employment (percentages) | | |
	1993	*1997*	*2001*
Black	22.0	21.0	20.8
Hispanic	20.4	23.4	25.9
Asian	8.0	8.4	8.9
White	45.2	42.4	38.9

| | (b) Officials/administrators (percentages) | | |
	1993	*1997*	*2001*
Black	11.0	11.9	12.1
Hispanic	7.9	10.0	10.4
Asian	8.7	9.7	12.7
White	69.5	65.1	60.9

| | (c) Professionals (percentages) | | |
	1993	*1997*	*2001*
Black	12.2	13.1	14.1
Hispanic	11.7	13.2	14.9
Asian	16.5	17.0	18.1
White	52.8	48.6	43.1

Source: Analysis of data in *Work Force Analysis Reports,* City of Los Angeles, Personnel Department.

The Valley, which was annexed to the city in 1915, had long fostered movements for detachment from Los Angeles. Separated from the rest of Los Angeles by the Santa Monica Mountains, the Valley had been the bastion of middle-class homeownership. It had also been the base of Los Angeles conservatism, backing Yorty for Mayor, Proposition 13 to reduce property taxes, and anti-busing movement. Having helped to elect Riordan in 1993, Valley voters increasingly turned toward a secession movement. Secessionists showed enough strength to win changes in state law that made secession easier to accomplish, and they gathered sufficient signatures to make a ballot measure possible in 2002.

Secession sentiment became a strong enough force to compel the attention of city policy makers. It provided the political impetus for a major reform of the City Charter between 1997 and 1999 that strengthened the office of the mayor and established the city's first system of neighborhood councils. A citizen commission established by the new charter to propose district lines for city council seats began with the assumption that the Valley would receive additional representation. The impact of secession on minority power and on policies relating to minorities was likely to become an important part of the secession debate.

As secession moved to the center of the city's agenda, Latinos began their rapid and dramatic political rise. In fact, the movements overlapped because of a large increase of the Latino population in the eastern portion of the San Fernando Valley. By 2000, non-Hispanic whites represented less than half of all Valley residents.

The 2001 municipal elections reflected the sudden accession of Latinos to a competitive position in city politics (Sonenshein and Pinkus 2002). In 2001, the Riordan mayoralty ended in a runoff battle between two labor Democrats, former Assembly Speaker Antonio Villaraigosa and City Attorney James K. Hahn. The 2001 election revealed that Los Angeles had evolved from the politics of black and white into a multileveled, multiracial politics. Evidence that the Riordan era had passed could be found in the defeat of his endorsed primary candidate, Steven Soboroff, a Republican businessman who pledged to continue Riordan's policies.

The context for the runoff election was the dramatic increase in Latino participation and the possibility that a Latino could win the mayoralty with a Bradley-style coalition of an insurgent minority group and liberals, particularly Jews. There had been a major surge of Latino participation after the passage of Proposition 187 in 1994. Proposition 187 would have deprived undocumented residents of public services, and it was widely seen among Latinos as a measure hostile to their community. The surge of Latino participation after Proposition 187 in 1994 helped to generate growth of the Latino share of the vote between 1993 and 2001 (Table 2.12) and began to close the gap between voting and population (Table 2.13)

While many observers had believed that Latinos were at least one mayoral election away from having a chance to win that office, events moved much more swiftly than expected. Under the surface, the mobilization of Latino voters that started with the reaction to Proposition 187 in 1994 had continued. From 8 percent of the voters who went to the polls in 1993, Latinos were expected to represent as much as 20% in 2001. Whites were declining as a share of the electorate, but Jews were holding their position. There were also fewer Republicans in the electorate than in 1993.

Organized labor had accomplished a major increase in its strength by recruiting and representing low-wage Latino workers. While the County Federation of Labor banked heavily on Latino political participation, city employee unions continued to have strong representation of African Americans.

TABLE 2.12   Group share of the vote, 1993–2001 (in percentages)

| | 1993 | | 1997 | 2001 | |
	Primary	*General*	*Primary*	*Primary*	*General*
Black	18	12	13	14	17
White*a*	68	72	65	52	52
Jewish	16	19	15	16	18
Latino	8	10	15	20	22
Asian American	4	4	4	4	6

*a*Includes Jews.

Source: Los Angeles Times exit polls.

TABLE 2.13 **Population of Los Angeles by race and ethnicity, 2000 (in percentages)**

Black	10.9
White	29.7
Latino	46.5
Asian American	9.9
Total Population	3,694,820

Source: U.S. Census.

The prospects for a Latino mayoralty were complicated by the presence of two competing Latino candidates—former Speaker of the Assembly Antonio Villaraigosa and Congressman Xavier Baccerra. There were strong white candidates who seemed likely to fill the two spots in the nonpartisan runoff reserved for the top two finishers. City attorney James K. Hahn, heir to the one of the few political dynasties in Los Angeles, was the clear favorite. Ironically, despite the presumption that African-American politics was in decline in Los Angeles, Hahn's base in the black community made him the front-runner overall.

The chemistry of the race was dramatically changed by Villaraigosa's ability to create a new coalition model that bore a strong resemblance to the Tom Bradley coalition. With strong endorsements from state Democrats, including Governor Gray Davis, as well as from the County Federation of Labor, Villaraigosa went directly after the support of the Jewish voters he had been cultivating for years. He was clearly the most liberal candidate in the race—and the most oriented toward multiracial coalition building. His goal was to build a labor, liberal, Latino coalition. Hahn, however, had the strong and underestimated support of an array of city employee unions.

In a major surprise, Villaraigosa finished first in the April primary, with 30 percent of the vote to Hahn's 25 percent. The *Los Angeles Times* exit poll reported that Villaraigosa had made a better showing than Hahn among whites and among Jews (Gold 2001). The two Jewish moderate candidates—Steven Soboroff, a Republican, and Joel Wachs, an independent—also did better than Hahn with these groups. Hahn made it into the runoff because of his overwhelming support from African Americans. If Villaraigosa could retain and expand his support among whites, particularly Jews, he would win the election with a Latino-led, Bradley-style coalition in opposition to African Americans.

Villaraigosa's hopes rested largely with Jewish voters. Although the Jewish population was only 6 percent of the city, Jews cast 18 percent of all votes in the primary and general elections of 2001. In 1993, they had cast 19 percent. White non-Jews were leaving the city, but Jews were staying. In 1993, Jews cast one-fourth of all white votes; in 2001, they cast one-third. As Latinos replaced non-Jewish whites in the electorate, Jews were holding their steady role. And the political differences between Jews and non-Jewish whites persisted (Sonenshein and Valentino 2000).

Villaraigosa developed strong support among liberal Jews. In fact, columnist Marlene Adler Marks wrote in the *Jewish Journal*: "A good case could be made, and many in the Jewish community are making it, that Villaraigosa is the 'Jewish candidate" (Marks 2001, 7). Villaraigosa himself campaigned heavily with Jews and won the support of liberal rabbis and other community leaders. County Supervisor Zev Yaroslavsky, the most popular Jewish politician in Los Angeles, endorsed Villaraigosa. The unknown factor was the preference of those Jews who had supported Soboroff or Wachs, who were more likely to be moderate voters.

After an awkward post-primary delay, Riordan endorsed Villaraigosa, but the Riordan endorsement was less important than Hahn's support from the energetic police union. Hahn hurt Villaraigosa badly with his law-and-order campaign, charging that the liberal former Assembly Speaker was soft on crime. Hahn used a tough ad about Villaraigosa's letter to President Clinton on behalf of a convicted drug dealer. Like Yorty in 1969, Hahn was able to play on white fears of the new group coming up and to challenge the liberal leanings of Jewish voters with their instinct for security and self-preservation. The oddity was that Hahn's principal base of support was African Americans—the victims of Yorty's attacks in 1969. The minority movement had bifurcated into African Americans seeking to hold onto their gains from before and Latinos playing the role of insurgents shaking up the system.

In the mayoral race, the black-supported candidate won. When the final votes were counted, Hahn had defeated Villaraigosa by 54 to 46 percent. According to the *Los Angeles Times* exit poll, white voters went heavily for Hahn to join more than three-quarters of black voters (Gold and Daunt 2001). Hahn won a large majority of conservative white voters and Republicans. Jewish voters were split—52 percent for Hahn, and 48 percent for Villaraigosa. Jews were divided along geographical lines. Among Jewish voters, Villaraigosa did much better on the urban westside than in the suburban Valley. Hahn defeated Villaraigosa by 57 to 43 percent among Valley Jews. Villaraigosa won by 54 to 46 percent among westside Jews, but the westside only comprised 18 percent of the city electorate compared to the Valley's 42 percent.

Jews as a whole were more likely to vote for Villaraigosa than were non-Jewish whites, but a majority were not ready to take the step of electing a liberal Latino to the mayoralty—especially when there was a reliable, moderate, tough-on-crime Democrat available. In this case, liberal ideology was not strong or intense enough to overcome threats to self-interest or community interest.

The Villaraigosa campaign showed both the potential for a renewed multiracial liberal alliance and the obstacles that stand before it. Jews were obviously more attuned than non-Jewish whites to the idea that the time had come for a Latino mayor, and they were more willing than non-Jewish whites to vote for a liberal Latino for that job. Had Villaraigosa been better-known locally, with fewer vulnerabilities on the crime issue, he might well have won enough Jewish votes to defeat Hahn. Tom Bradley, after all, was a well-known city councilman and former police officer who found a way to blunt the crime issue and won huge Jewish support.

Even though Los Angeles was becoming more Democratic—Republicans cast only 18 percent of the vote in 2001, compared to more than 30 percent in 1993—and more labor-oriented, it was not becoming more liberal. Citywide candidates who are seen as liberal on the issue of crime and public safety still suffer at the polls.

Los Angeles politics are being transformed by the aspirations of Latinos to become incorporated into city politics. Swing voters like Jews, who are crucial to biracial coalitions, are in flux. Latinos and Jews could look to the Bradley coalition model, in which shared liberal and Democratic values join with ethnic identification to create a liberal biethnic alliance. In other cases, however, Jews and Latinos could be opposed, as in the city attorney race between Latino Rocky Delgadillo and Jewish councilman Mike Feuer. In that citywide race, the moderate Latino candidate defeated the liberal Jewish candidate by drawing massive Latino support, a majority of African Americans, and of non-Jewish and non-liberal whites.

The more dramatic and disorienting change is the new role for African Americans as defenders of the political status quo, threatened by both the resurgence of Valley whites and the rise of Latinos. These changes have greatly altered the context for minority politics in Los Angeles. Jews feeling the pressure of social change might end up in a status quo coalition, at times, with African Americans. In other elections, African-Americans may become free agents, forming new alliances based on perceived self-interest.

The new role of African-Americans was highlighted in early 2002, when Mayor Hahn announced his preference that Chief Parks not be retained by the Police Commission for a second five-year term. A furious reaction ensued from African-American political and religious leaders that seemed likely to permanently damage Hahn's ties to his strongest base of political support. Some in the African-American community even talked of allying with Valley secessionists in order to create a new Los Angeles in which their proportion of the vote would be higher than in the existing city.

WHITHER MINORITY POLITICS IN LOS ANGELES?

Where did minority groups end up in 2001 after the Bradley and Riordan years and heading into the Hahn era? The key issues driving city politics were secession, Latino incorporation, and police reform. No clear, consistent minority position has emerged on these issues. There is now a two-headed minority movement in Los Angeles, with African Americans and Latinos eyeing each other warily. There are grounds for alliance, and there are reasons for conflict.

Issues that concern minorities have become seriously fragmented. At one time, the city's warring factions were divided clearly into two main groups: those who sided with minorities against those who were unfriendly to minorities. That is no longer the case. The issues that defined minority progress then were well known: affirmative action in city hiring, obtaining federal funds, and police accountability. No such clarity exists in today's Los Angeles, where the old biracial alliance shares space with angry white conservatives and assertive Latinos.

Los Angeles politics still retains important vestiges of the racialized politics of the Bradley era, but superimposed above that has been a new level of political activity centered around the incorporation of Latinos and the alienation of suburban voters. As a result, minority politics in the twenty-first century is likely to be played simultaneously in several dimensions, with cross-cutting and shifting alliances.

Issues of class and ethnicity are likely to re-emerge centered around the social and economic incorporation of immigrant communities. Conflicts over growth, housing, transportation, and education are likely to be reforged along class and ethnic lines rather than along the old black–white divide.

As city leaders devised new council district boundaries following the 2000 Census, these issues came into focus. The need to placate the Valley called for an increase in that area's seats. At the same time, a political imperative existed to hold the three seats of the African-American community, and to keep or increase Latino representation. The answer to meeting all three of these demands was found in the removal of one seat on the white liberal Westside. Thus the politics of race, ethnicity, and place emerged as key factors in the new Los Angeles.

African-Americans are still important players in city government, even though their position is largely defensive. They have not lost the full measure of the gains they made during the period of incorporation, and their influence is institutionalized in city politics and government.

Measuring minority incorporation in Los Angeles, however, cannot be done by adding African Americans and Latinos together. The thin line between conflict and coalition that marks the relationship between these two groups calls for caution in treating their power as mutually reinforcing.

The story of the Riordan mayoralty is that conservative coalitions are viable but unlikely to dominate Los Angeles permanently. Liberal forces are a long way from resolving the issues that caused them to lose the support of an electoral and governing majority. The political future is up for grabs. As a result, the minority agenda is also being reshaped.

Los Angeles coalition politics in the post-incorporation period has developed a mix-and-match quality. Rather than the stable structure of race and ideology that defined the Bradley years, temporary voting alliances have formed—and have then been reshaped. The racial divide remains influential, but it is overlaid by other divides. Blacks are now both insurgents and status quo defenders. Latinos are Democrats, often liberal, but ethnically assertive. Jews are Democrats, often liberal, but often worried about crime and other issues.

The old lines of interest and ideology remain, but new divisions based on a two-headed minority search for power and the weaker attachments between groups have created an atmosphere of shifting alliances and coalitions. With liberal ideology fragmented, it is harder than before to identify and pursue a progressive agenda (and just as hard for conservatives to pursue a coherent agenda of their own). If secession occurs, the division of the city will create an entirely new set of governmental structures and incentives on which minority interests can be pursued and alliances built. Even if the city stays together, the path to coalition and incorporation will likely depend on flexible and movable coalitions.

The new Los Angeles confirms the power of minority incorporation through the continuing role played by African Americans in city politics and policy and by persistent ideological differences among whites. The impact of white suburban alienation and the rise of Latino political assertion, however, suggest that the framework of ideology, interest, and leadership that animated the movement for minority incorporation will be profoundly altered in the years to come.

REFERENCES

Adrian, Charles R. 1959. A Typology for Nonpartisan Elections. *Western Political Quarterly* 12: 449–458.

Browning, Rufus P., Dale Rogers Marshall, and David H. Tabb. 1984. *Protest Is Not Enough: The Struggle of Blacks and Hispanics for Equality in Urban Politics.* Berkeley: University of California Press.

Carmichael, Stokely, and Charles V. Hamilton. 1967. *Black Power: The Politics of Liberation in America.* New York: Random House.

Carney, Francis M. 1964. The Decentralized Politics of Los Angeles. *The Annals of the American Academy of Political and Social Science* 353: 107–121.

Connell, Richard. 1993. City Hall Power Shifts to Eclectic, Pragmatic Team Government: Emphasis for Riordan Commissioners Is on the Bottom Line. *Los Angeles Times,* November 29.

Davis, Mike. 1991. *City of Quartz: Excavating the Future in Los Angeles.* London: Haymarket Press.

Elkin, Stephen L. 1987. *City and Regime in the American Republic.* Chicago: University of Chicago Press.

Fairbank, Maslin, Maullin, and Associates. Various dates. Public opinion poll reports (unpublished). Santa Monica, Calif.

Fogelson, Robert M. 1967. *The Fragmented Metropolis: Los Angeles, 1850–1930.* Cambridge, Mass.: Harvard University Press.

Gold, Matea. 2001. New Coalitions Forged in an Upbeat L.A. *Los Angeles Times,* April 11.

Gold, Matea, and Tina Daunt. 2001. L.A. Takes a Turn to the Left with a Democrat in Charge. *Los Angeles Times,* June 6.

Hahn, Harlan, David Klingman, and Harry Pachon. 1976. Cleavages, Coalitions, and the Black Candidate: The Los Angeles Mayoralty Elections of 1969 and 1973. *Western Political Quarterly* 29: 521–530.

Hinckley, Barbara. 1981. *Coalitions and Politics.* New York: Harcourt Brace Jovanovich.

Johnson, James, Jr., and Melvin Oliver. 1989. Interethnic Minority Conflict in Urban America: The Effects of Economic and Social Dislocations. *Urban Geography* 10: 449–463.

Marks, Marlene Adler. 2001. Mayors R Us. *Jewish Journal,* March 16, 7.

Mayo, Charles G. 1964. The 1961 Mayoralty Election in Los Angeles: The Political Party in a Nonpartisan Election. *Western Political Quarterly* 17: 325–337.

Morrison, Peter A., and Ira S. Lowry. 1994. A Riot of Color: The Demographic Setting. In Mark Baldassare, ed., *The Los Angeles Riots: Lessons for the Urban Future,* 19–46. Boulder, Colo.: Westview Press.

Oliver, Melvin L., and James H. Johnson, Jr. 1984. Inter-ethnic Conflict in an Urban Ghetto: The Case of Blacks and Latinos in Los Angeles. *Research in Social Movements, Conflict, and Change* 6: 57–94.

Pactech Consultants. 1992. Report to the Los Angeles City Council for the Redistricting Process.

Pastor, Manuel, Jr. 1995. Economic Inequality, Latino Poverty, and the Civil Unrest in Los Angeles. *Economic Development Quarterly* 9 (August): 238–258.

Patterson, Beeman. 1969. Political Action of Negroes in Los Angeles: A Case Study in the Attainment of Councilmanic Representation. *Phylon* 30: 170–183.

Rainey, James. 1995. Fire Department's Shining Image Clouded by Audit Bias. *Los Angeles Times,* January 3.

Rainey, James. 1993. Inner City Still Mostly on Outside at City Hall. *Los Angeles Times,* September 9.

Regalado, James. 1991. Organized Labor and Los Angeles City Politics: An Assessment in the Bradley Years, 1973–1989. *Urban Affairs Quarterly* 27 (September): 87–108.

Rohrlich, Ted. 1993. More Than Half on Transition Team Don't Live in L.A. *Los Angeles Times,* June 16.

Rosenzweig, David. 2002. Firefighter Hiring Quotas Ended. *Los Angeles Times,* April 9.

Ross, Ruth. 1980. *The Impact of Federal Grants on the City of Los Angeles.* Federal Aid Case Studies Series, paper no. 8. Washington, DC: Brookings Institution.

Saltzstein, Alan, Raphael Sonenshein, and Irving Ostrow. 1986. Federal Aid to the City of Los Angeles: Implementing a More Centralized Local Political System. In Terry Clark, ed., *Research in Urban Policy,* vol. 2, 55–76. Greenwich, Conn.: JAI Press.

Schockman, H. Eric. 1996. Is Los Angeles Governable? Revising the City Charter. In Michael Dear, H. Eric Schockman, and Greg Hise, eds., *Rethinking Los Angeles,* 57–72. Thousand Oaks, Calif.: Sage.

Sears, David O. 1994. Urban Rioting in Los Angeles: A Comparison of 1965 with 1992. In Mark Baldassare, ed., *The Los Angeles Riots: Lessons for the Urban Future,* 237–254. Boulder, Colo.: Westview Press.

Smith, Alonzo Nelson. 1978. Black Employment in the Los Angeles Area, 1938–1948. PhD dissertation, University of California, Los Angeles.

Sonenshein, Raphael J. 1993. *Politics in Black and White: Race and Power in Los Angeles.* Princeton, NJ: Princeton University Press.

Sonenshein, Raphael J. 1996. The Battle over Liquor Stores in South Central Los Angeles: The Management of an Interminority Conflict. *Urban Affairs Review* 31: 710–737.

Sonenshein, Raphael J., and Nicholas Valentino. 1995. A New Alignment in City Politics? Evidence from the 1993 Los Angeles Mayoral Election. Paper presented at the annual meeting of the Western Political Science Association, San Francisco.

Sonenshein, Raphael J. and Nicholas Valentino. 2000. The Distinctiveness of Jewish Voting: A Thing of the Past? *Urban Affairs Review,* 95 (January): 358–389.

Sonenshein, Raphael J. and Susan Pinkus. 2002. The Dynamics of Latino Political Incorporation: The 2001 Los Angeles Mayoral Election As Seen in *Los Angeles Times* Exit Polls. *PS,* 35 (March): 67–74.

Vorspan, Max, and Lloyd P. Gartner. 1970. *History of the Jews of Los Angeles.* San Marino, Calif.: The Huntington Library.

Chapter 3

Philadelphia's Evolving Biracial Coalition

Richard A. Keiser

EDITORS' NOTE

Like Los Angeles, Philadelphia is a case of black political success. Like Chicago, Philadelphia is a large, old, eastern city with partisan elections and a history of machine politics. Yet Philadelphia presents many contrasts to both. Blacks constituted more than twice the proportion of the population in Philadelphia than in Los Angeles, but the election of a black mayor came a full decade later—Wilson Goode in 1983.

Why such a long delay? Richard A. Keiser shows how a liberal reform movement that had displaced a long-lived Republican machine began the job of black political incorporation, but a rejuvenated Democratic party halted this progress. During periods when the alliance of white liberals and blacks temporarily overcame the machine, black incorporation progressed. Even when the organization politicians governed the city, the biracial reform alliance dampened the efforts of the machine to roll back black political gains. Eventually, a moderate biracial reform coalition elected a black city council president and a black mayor. Keiser's account of the origins and evolution of this coalition is worth studying for the light it sheds on the displacement of conservative coalitions, the linkages between electoral competitiveness and the emergence of political leadership, the nurturing of trust, and the avoidance of the extreme racial polarization that we observe in Chicago.

After the first black mayor lost control of that office in Philadelphia, maintaining the unity of the dominant coalition became a problem. In Philadelphia, divisions between powerful black leaders that had been papered over in the effort to elect the first black mayor now emerged and contributed to the election of a white mayor, Ed Rendell. However, Rendell headed a biracial coalition that was neither liberal nor reformist, and his election did not represent a backlash against black interests.

After Rendell, John Street, an African American, was elected mayor with the support of African Americans, the traditional (machine) Democratic Party organization, and conservative labor unions. Racially based voting—that is, white Democrats who voted for a white Republican rather for than a black Democrat—was a primary factor in a close election in a city with a 7-2 ratio of registered Democrats to registered Republicans. Philadelphia demonstrates that a machine government with blacks as full-fledged partners—leaders—in the governing coalition may also create significant gains for blacks and, so far, appears to represent a viable machine path to political incorporation. African Americans in Philadelphia are strongly incorporated both in the current machine coalition and in a reform coalition that may again attempt to gain control of city government.

INTRODUCTION

In Philadelphia, black leaders had been participating in biracial coalitions that had delivered incremental political incorporation since the 1950s. In 1983, W. Wilson Goode was elected as the first black mayor of Philadelphia. Goode was one among a cadre of prominent liberal black politicians in Philadelphia who gained legitimacy and could garner the votes of both blacks and whites. Goode served the limit of two consecutive terms and was followed by Ed Rendell, a moderate white Democrat who also served two terms. In 1999, City Council President John Street, an African-American Democrat, was elected. Though Goode and Street were both Democrats and black—and were elected by multiracial coalitions of blacks, a small share of whites, and a majority of Latinos—their politics diverge. Street is a master of machine-style politics, something that made Goode quite uncomfortable.[1] This chapter presents a history and analysis of the biracial coalitions in Philadelphia that were the forerunners of the coalitions that elected Wilson Goode and John Street. The intermittent successes of these coalitions in gaining the political incorporation of blacks are reviewed. The opposition that a biracial coalition dedicated to an incrementalist strategy faces from within the black community and from whites is also examined. The accomplishments of these two administrations, focusing particularly on the extent to which they enhanced the status and furthered the political incorporation of blacks and Hispanics, is highlighted as well—as is the significance of the Rendell years, in which a biracial coalition headed by a white Democrat governed the city.

The last 20 years or so of politics in Philadelphia presents interesting data regarding some of the most crucial questions for students of urban politics. Are machine and

---

[1] Following Wolfinger (1977, 79), I define machine politics as "the manipulation of certain incentives to partisan political participation: favoritism based on political criteria in personnel decisions, contracting, and administration of the laws." Wolfinger drew the important and oft-forgotten distinction between political machines—the complex and sometimes centralized organizations—and the machine politics—which may be practiced by centralized party organizations, party factions, or personalistic organizations.

reform politics still useful designations that advance analytical understanding of con-temporary politics? Are traditional party organizations ever anything more than retro-grade vehicles that protect the hegemony of white ethnic political interests? Do labor unions play any meaningful role in urban electoral politics? Has there been a rollback in black political power in Philadelphia, as allegedly took place in New York and Chicago after white mayors defeated incumbent black mayors? Are black mayoral can-didates winning the votes of whites and Latinos? If so, are these votes for black can-didates coming predominantly from better-educated voters who are typically more liberal?

Before addressing these questions in the context of the current administration, a discussion of the political environment of Philadelphia is necessary. At the same time that John Street was elected, Frank Rizzo, Jr., and Wilson Goode, Jr.—both sons of former mayors—were elected to the city council. It is impossible to explain Street's election margin of less than 8,000 votes (out of about 420,000) without first understanding the circumstances that brought to office these mayoral predecessors, whose legacies impacted contemporary Philadelphia politics in far more important ways than the presence of their sons.

INCREMENTAL CONSTRUCTION OF A BIRACIAL REFORM COALITION

In the late 1940s, Philadelphia government was rocked by scandals that disgraced the formerly dominant Republican party, a party that had governed Philadelphia since 1881 and had rebuffed all efforts by blacks to gain political power. Joseph Clark, a reformer who promised "good government" in the wake of this corruption, led a coalition that ushered in a period of Democratic party domination of the city's politics after he was elected mayor in 1951. This new coalition included the Greater Philadelphia Movement (GPM), an umbrella business organization that mobi-lized the city's business leadership against their former GOP allies; the Americans for Democratic Action (ADA), home of the city's liberal activists; and significant aspects of the black community. Since then, politics in Philadelphia has been characterized by competition between (1) an amalgam of white liberal activists and "good-govern-ment" reformers, including many of the city's civic, religious, and business leaders, and (2) the regular organization ethnic politicians of the Democratic party, many of whom defected (with their neighborhood ties intact) from the discredited Republican organization. The reformers and the organization politicians have battled largely within the confines of the Democratic party (e.g., in primary elections); however, when either the reformers or the ethnic pols have been defeated in such battles, they have not hesitated to shift their support to Republicans and to use this otherwise mori-bund party as an alternative front for the ongoing battle. One of the major battle lines in this competition has been for the votes of the expanding black electorate. These conditions of electoral competitiveness made black voters a potentially decisive force in electoral outcomes and gave black political leaders leverage with which they could bargain for group political incorporation or more particularistic benefits (Keiser 1997).

Seeking to put machine-style politics out of business, the reformers instituted a new city charter that included a rigid civil service system for awarding city jobs. Because of private sector discrimination, an especially well-educated pool of blacks was available to take the examinations and win city employment (Lowe 1967; Weiler 1974). The crucial contribution that black voters, defecting from the GOP, made to the reform coalition was rewarded in a number of ways. Mayor Clark and his reform-minded successor, Richardson Dilworth, began the incorporation of blacks into city government by backing black community leaders (especially clergymen) for elected and appointed offices that heretofore had not been held by blacks. Mayor Dilworth, seeking to remedy police brutality against blacks, created the first civilian police review board in the nation (Rogers 1971). Aside from this latter benefit—the value of which should not be gainsaid—poorer blacks received little other than the vicarious satisfaction of seeing better-educated members of the race employed in city government (Reichley 1959). This intangible reward would not prove sufficient to maintain the loyalty of poor blacks to the reform wing of the Democratic party.

THE SHORT LADDER OF BLACK PATRONAGE

When Democrat George Leader was elected governor in 1955, the weak Philadelphia Democratic organization finally obtained the means to compete effectively with the reformers for control of the party and the city government. Leader strengthened the organization by placing nearly 3,000 patronage jobs at its disposal. The organization cultivated a mass base of support among low-income blacks by distributing patronage jobs, albeit those with the lowest salaries (Reichley 1959; Strange 1966). In 1958, the organization co-opted a prominent black councilman, who until then had been allied with the reformers, by promising him the next available judgeship. That same year, the organization further increased its black support by slating the first black Philadelphian elected to the U.S. Congress, Robert N. C. Nix. Even after an organization ward leader and councilman, James Tate, was elevated to the mayor's office in 1962 (because of Mayor Dilworth's resignation to run unsuccessfully for governor) and elected in 1963, the organization wing and the reform wing of the Democratic party remained highly competitive. Hence, the regular organization (not just white liberal reformers) deserved some credit for early advances of black incorporation; the electoral competition between machine and reform factions is the variable that explains these parallel paths of black incorporation (Keiser 1997).

That politics in Philadelphia remained highly competitive is significant, because it meant that Tate and the regular Democratic organization were forced to court black voters at the same time that they were trying to keep the blue-collar white ethnic vote from defecting to the GOP, as happened in the 1968 presidential election of Richard Nixon. In classic machine fashion, Tate developed a political organization in black neighborhoods by creating new leaders to administer the federally funded antipoverty program and placing patronage jobs at their disposal so they could mobilize others in their neighborhoods (Peterson 1967). In both mayoral elections, Tate's victory came on the strength of the black vote, largely from poorer black wards (*Philadelphia Bulletin* 1965; Ekstrom 1973). Tate had earned this support by delivering about 39 percent of the city's jobs (more than 11,000) to blacks. Although these were entry-level jobs or menial labor, for most of the recipients the alternative was poverty (Ershkowitz and Zikmund 1973, 58).

It is important to recognize that while Tate used particularistic rewards to ensure that blacks remained the nucleus of the Democratic organization's *electoral coalition,* blacks were not part of the *governing coalition* (nor had they been with the liberal reformers). Blacks who aspired to leadership positions within the organizational structure of the party were rebuffed (Strange 1969). Moreover, blacks were no longer slated for visible public offices from which they could influence the formation of policy. Consequently, policies emanating from city hall on such issues as school discrimination, police brutality, enforcement of housing codes, and prohibition of discrimination in municipal contracting were less responsive to their needs (Keiser 1997).

The growing unresponsiveness to demands of the black middle class on the part of Tate and the Democratic organization was part of their attempt to halt massive electoral defections by the white ethnic working class (Ekstrom 1973; Edsall and Edsall 1991). White voters who viewed black advancement as threatening had been defecting to Republican candidates like District Attorney Arlen Specter, who promised to "get tough on crime." To increase the party's lagging support among these voters, Tate promoted a charismatic policeman, Frank Rizzo, to the post of chief of police. Additionally, Tate moved to shore up white ethnic support by eliminating the city's civilian police review board. Tate was betting that black levels of electoral support for Democratic party candidates could be maintained even as the party adopted a less sympathetic view toward the policy concerns of blacks (*Philadelphia Bulletin* 1974).

PROTEST STIMULUS AND REFORM RESPONSE

In response to city hall's inattention to their substantive policy concerns, a black protest movement emerged under the leadership of Cecil Moore, the president of the National Association for the Advancement of Colored People (NAACP). Moore and the protest movement that he led did win some battles—and provoked a few brutal responses by the police—yet city hall remained largely unresponsive to black policy demands.

Moore's separatist approach and antibiracial coalition rhetoric was contradicted by the successes that moderate blacks continued to achieve through biracial co-operation even though white liberal reformers no longer occupied city hall. After a group of 400 black ministers led a series of well-co-ordinated boycotts against selected Philadelphia businesses that failed to respond to requests that they hire more blacks, Philadelphia's business community seemed to require no further prodding to begin major efforts to create employment and employment training programs specifically for the black community (Strange 1973). Philadelphia's premier business leadership organ, the GPM, echoed the pragmatism for which

Atlanta's business leadership has become known by candidly admitting that their motivation was to preclude an escalation from peaceful boycotts to violent riots:

> Most of greater Philadelphia's business and industrial leaders realized that unless the plight of the Black Americans became the central concern for all Americans, there will be no racial peace in this nation for possibly generations to come. (*New York Times* 1968, 34)

The most notable example of co-operation between the black leadership and the business community was the Opportunities Industrialization Center, which was created in 1964 by Reverend Leon Sullivan and his Zion Baptist Church to provide job training and business skills for blacks. After a year of success, local business leaders and the Ford Foundation began contributing money, training machinery, and program guidance. This is one example of the significant organizational vehicles by which the biracial reform alliance begun under Mayor Clark was continued in the period of rollback that this alliance faced in the Tate/Rizzo years; this alliance was further strengthened by the tenure of Mayor Frank Rizzo (discussed below).

By the close of the 1960s, then, three distinct political segments existed among Philadelphia's black community; a group linked to Mayor Tate and the Democratic organization through patronage; a group that followed Moore on a radical, protest path that condemned any biracial alliances; and a group led by black ministers and business people that sought electoral and civic alliances with white liberal reformers.

RIZZO UNIFIES THE OPPOSITION: THE REFORM-BLACK ALLIANCE OF THE 1970s

Because Mayor Tate was prevented by the city charter from running for a third consecutive term, the 1971 Democratic primary became a pivotal contest. With the endorsement of Tate and the Democratic organization, Frank Rizzo captured 48 percent of the vote and defeated three liberal candidates.

In the general election, Rizzo faced Thacher Longstreth, executive vice-president of the Philadelphia Chamber of Commerce. Rizzo confined his appearances to working-class white neighborhoods. He promised the residents of these neighborhoods no unwanted public housing projects, opposition to busing children to schools for purposes of racial balance, no tax hikes, and a get-tough attitude toward crime that he boasted "would make Atilla the Hun look like a faggot."

Longstreth had the support of the Republican organization, much of Philadelphia's business and civic leadership (including the GPM), former mayors Clark and Dilworth, and the endorsement of the *Bulletin*. However, this was not enough. With a record turnout of 77 percent of the city's registered voters, Rizzo defeated Longstreth by just under 50,000 votes.

Frank Rizzo's 1971 mayoral campaign catalyzed a previously unseen degree of mobilization in the black community. In the primary, black voters demonstrated a greater willingness to support a white liberal who could win rather than a black who was relatively unknown to white voters. Bill Green won 51 percent of the vote in predominantly black wards, while State Senator Hardy Williams captured only 37 percent (Keiser 1989). In retrospect, Williams' candidacy has been viewed as a milestone in independent black politics, both because it represented a first black mayoral candidacy and because a young housing activist named W. Wilson Goode was the campaign manager. Williams, however, was the wrong black for the job of mobilizing a united black vote to take advantage of the split in the white vote, and quite significantly, the majority of black voters recognized this.

In the general election, white liberals and blacks chose neither to stay at home nor to passively accept defeat and vote for their party's candidate. Instead, they unified behind Longstreth and came close to defeating Rizzo. This was most noteworthy for black voters, because it represented their first massive defection from the Democratic party to join in alliance with white liberal reformers. In the 10 wards in which more than 90 percent of the registered voters were black, Rizzo won only 23 percent of the vote. Sixty-four percent of the city's registered black voters cast ballots, and Rizzo was rejected by an amazing 77 percent of the voters in predominantly black wards. That Tate had captured approximately 70 percent of the vote in these black wards four years earlier indicates that the black vote represented a "sophisticated" defection from the candidate of the Democratic party. If contrasted to Chicago, where Mayor Richard J. Daley consistently won more black votes than any candidate he faced, including white liberal and black challengers, this demonstration of black independence from the Democratic party seems particularly significant.

As mayor, Rizzo continued to foster black unity. In addition to condoning a policy of police brutality against blacks that ultimately led to a federal investigation of the police force, Mayor Rizzo systematically waged war on the city's black leadership (Keiser 1990). Even so, in 1975, Rizzo defeated Republican Thomas Foglietta and Charles Bowser, a black who ran as an independent candidate in the mayoral election. With two candidates dividing the anti-Rizzo vote, the election was really a contest for second place. Rizzo won with 57 percent of the vote. Bowser garnered 25 percent, and Foglietta received 18 percent. Yet, it is most significant that voters in the city's white reform wards demonstrated their willingness to support a qualified, non-divisive black candidate by giving Bowser 41 percent of their vote. Even in the face of certain defeat, black and white leaders who favored a moderate biracial coalition continued to work together to preserve the trust and norms of mutual support created under Clark and Dilworth and reaffirmed in the Longstreth campaign.

ELECTORAL MOBILIZATION AND FORMATION OF A DOMINANT BIRACIAL COALITION

By the middle of his second term, Mayor Rizzo had begun a campaign to amend the city charter to eliminate the prohibition against more than two consecutive mayoral terms. "Good government" business leaders (including the GPM), liberal activists from the ADA and similar groups, and black reformers organized, financed, and provided the leadership for a coalition to protect the charter.

When Mayor Rizzo followed a strategy of attempting to divide the city along racial lines by calling on white citizens to "Vote White," the city's civic leadership joined with the black community in unequivocally condemning and repudiating such tactics. After this blatant attempt to foster racial polarization, Rizzo was constantly on the defensive (*Philadelphia Inquirer* 1978). The election results suggest—and interviews conducted by the author confirm—that the wide spectrum of leaders that condemned Rizzo's polarizing strategy produced an anti-Rizzo coalition broader than any he had ever—or would subsequently—face. Sixty-seven percent of the voters rejected changing the charter. The winning coalition was composed of blacks, reformers, liberals, and Jews (Featherman and Rosenberg 1979). Displaying unprecedented unanimity, voters in predominantly black wards cast 96 percent of their ballots against Mayor Rizzo's proposal to change the charter.

Perhaps even more significant than black unanimity was the degree of mobilization in the black community. The voter registration drives in the black community were hugely successful and raised the black proportion of total registered voters by seven points to 38 percent. The rate of turnout in predominantly black wards was 63 percent. Only three years before, when Charles Bowser ran as an independent mayoral candidate, blacks comprised 31 percent of the city's registered voters, and the rate of turnout in the black wards was 54 percent. Bowser's mayoral candidacy had not succeeded in getting unregistered black voters to register, nor in getting enough registered black voters to vote for him. Rizzo's blatantly racial appeal, however, did succeed in catalyzing massive black voter registration and turnout against Rizzo. Commenting on the decade-long effort to fight Frank Rizzo through the ballot box, Wilson Goode said, "Biracial coalitions and reformers were dominant forces in city politics. No longer regarded as an anomaly, black and liberal white voters were now taken seriously and had often become pivotal in deciding the outcome of close elections" (Goode 1992, 148).

In the race to fill the vacuum left by the removal of Frank Rizzo from the 1979 mayoral race, Congressman Bill Green, Jr., jumped out to an early lead. Green, who narrowly lost to Rizzo in the 1971 Democratic primary, aimed his appeal at the biracial coalition of white reformers and blacks. Within the black community, however, there were leaders who argued that after the massive registration and turnout of blacks precipitated by the charter referendum, a black mayor could be elected even with minimal white support. They convinced Charles Bowser to be their candidate. Seeking to remobilize the additional 100,000 blacks who had registered to vote against the charter change, Bowser shifted from the moderate tenor of his 1975 campaign and relentlessly attacked Bill Green, who he tried to equate with the Rizzo gang. Green, however, refused to be provoked into confrontation and spoke only of healing the wounds left from Rizzo's tenure.

Green captured 53 percent of the vote and defeated Bowser (44 percent) in the Democratic primary. Bowser won every black ward and two predominantly white wards, but he was not able to mobilize the degree of support in the black wards that was necessary for victory. Turnout in the 13 predominantly black wards was only 54 percent, which although high for a primary election in Philadelphia was lower than the 63 percent black turnout for the charter referendum.

Green faced Republican David Marston in November. Marston immediately began to try to build support in the black community. He publicly pledged that, if elected, he would name a black as the city's managing director (city manager), the second most powerful post in the city government. Marston also initiated a dialogue with Bowser and attempted to win his endorsement.

Arguing that a third party black candidate would have a better chance in the general election against the two white candidates, Marston and Green, than Bowser had had in the primary head-to-head with Green, Councilman Lucien Blackwell entered the mayoral race. Green recognized that Bowser's attacks had diminished the support that Green could expect from blacks, especially against Blackwell and Marston. Such considerations led Green to strike a deal—in exchange for the endorsements of Bowser and black senior statesman Samuel Evans, Green matched Marston's promise (in a written agreement) to appoint a black as managing director. Again, competition for the pivotal black vote produced a major step forward in the incorporation of blacks into the dominant political coalition.

Green emerged victorious, with 53 percent of the vote to Marston's 29 percent and Blackwell's 17 percent. Green waged an especially vigorous campaign in the black community, and an analysis of the 13 wards in which at least 90 percent of the registered voters were black showed that Green and Blackwell evenly split the black vote (Keiser 1989). The rate of turnout in predominantly black wards was 55 percent.

Bowser's endorsement was a watershed event that gains significance when compared with other cases in the literature on urban minority politics. Many of the city's black leaders followed Bowser and endorsed Green over Blackwell, thereby pre-empting the possibility of a polarizing campaign based on dividing the white vote and mobilizing a black bloc. Because of the history of mutually advantageous coalition between middle-class white liberals and blacks, lining up behind Green was not perceived by blacks to be "selling out." Rather, it yielded a black managing director and brought blacks one step closer to the mayor's office—the man Mayor Green named as managing director was Wilson Goode. Bowser, Evans, and the other black leaders who endorsed Green after he agreed to name a black managing director were sharply criticized by the Blackwell camp, yet charges of "Uncle Tom-ism" were not perceived as credible and did not stick. The iterative process of biracial co-operation that had historically yielded incremental black empowerment provided legitimacy for this historic step.

Within Green's first two months, he delivered on what was undoubtedly the most pressing issue for the black citizenry, their fear of harassment and brutality from Frank Rizzo's police department. A black aide to Congressman William H. Gray, III, said, "I used to warn my own son, 'If a cop stops you, smile, do everything he tells you, and pray he doesn't kill you.' It was very real" (Paolantonio 1993). The Green administration issued new rules for the use of firearms by police officers, mandating that use of a gun should come only after all other methods of suspect apprehension were exhausted. The police rank-and-file were livid about this new policy that made them subject to a panel of Monday-morning quarterbacks. After only two years of this policy, the incidence of police shooting civilians was halved (Paolantonio 1993).

The unions and the black city council members were not satisfied with the procedural, good-government initiatives of Mayor Green. Ultimately, these groups pressed their particularistic agendas over the objections of the mayor. The unions prompted the city council to ignore the wishes of Green and city business leaders and to enact the first city-level plant closing legislation in the nation in 1982. The law required firms employing 50 or more to give 60 days of notice before closing (Portz 1990). Green clashed with black city council members over an affirmative action hiring program for black police officers. Although in 1980 only 17 percent of Philadelphia's police force but 39 percent of its population was black, Mayor Green opposed legislation to redress this balance, because earlier in his administration he had laid-off policemen and did not want to now hire new officers. Yet Councilman Blackwell and others argued that blacks deserved preferential treatment from Green, not only to remedy an unjust system built on past discrimination initiated by then Police Commissioner Rizzo but also because, as crucial members of the mayor's electoral coalition, they had earned such rewards. Blacks and white liberals on the city council also clashed with Mayor Green over set-aside legislation to aid minority-owned firms in winning city contracts on a range of services from construction to consulting. The legislation called for minority-owned businesses to get 15 percent of the city's contracts. Green vetoed this bill, but the city council overrode the mayor's veto. In both these instances, black elected officials were in a position to advance the progress of black empowerment through their domination of city council, a development that resulted not only from black electoral mobilization but also from scandals produced by a federal sting operation that forced three conservative "Rizzocrats" to resign and gave blacks and white liberals a dominant coalition in the city council. Students of the relationship between the local state and capital should note that the successes on plant closing and set-aside legislation came over the opposition of the city's business community.

Before the emerging split between Green and his black supporters could splinter the biracial coalition, Green shocked everyone in Philadelphia by announcing that he would not be a candidate for mayor in 1983. Attention immediately focused on two men—Green's predecessor, Frank Rizzo, who had long been hinting that he would run again; and Green's right-hand man and natural successor, Wilson Goode.

Wilson Goode is part of the moderate, reformist black political leadership group that has captured biracial legitimacy. This legitimacy has long existed in cities like Philadelphia and Atlanta, and it distinguishes them from a city like Chicago, which has not fostered a moderate black political cadre (Keiser 1993). Like many in this group, Goode has strong ties to the black clergy, having long been a deacon in his church. He also worked closely with the business community and many black neighborhood activists as the president of a nonprofit agency that built low-income housing. Goode was a familiar face to the city's liberal activists as well, having long been a member of the ADA. He was an early member of the Black Political Forum, a group of reformers dedicated to black political empowerment. In 1978, Governor Milton Shapp appointed Goode to the Public Utilities Commission. There, Goode gained attention for his skillful handling of the Three Mile Island nuclear facility disaster. Later, he went to the most powerful post in Philadelphia government aside from the mayor, the office of managing director, where he earned a sterling reputation for effective, non-political service delivery in the black community and beyond (*Philadelphia Daily News* 1982).

ELECTING THE FIRST BLACK MAYOR

To the surprise of almost every observer, the campaign between Rizzo and Goode was almost totally free of overt racial divisiveness (*New York Times* 1983). What had changed since 1978, when Rizzo had mobilized his base of support with a call for them to "Vote White"? Rizzo's campaign had an amicable, non-divisive tenor, because that was the most expedient strategy for being elected mayor in the Philadelphia of the 1980s. Given an electorate in which blacks comprised 39 percent of the registered voters, a Rizzo victory hinged on three factors: (1) a large turnout of white ethnic, blue-collar voters; (2) winning some black votes; and (3) minimizing his losses among white middle- and upper-class reformers. Blacks and white liberal reformers previously had turned out and voted against Rizzo in heavy numbers because of his racially divisive tactics. Therefore, to Rizzo and his campaign strategists, the way to diminish the turnout and anti-Rizzo voting of blacks and liberal whites was to avoid the race issue. In short, although a "Vote White" strategy would be successful nationally for George Bush when he used Willie Horton to defeat Michael Dukakis in 1988, it would not work in a city with a 40 percent black population.

Goode understood the political environment in much the same way that Rizzo did. The failure of blacks and of white liberals to unify in the 1971 Democratic primary produced a Rizzo victory that lasted eight years. Conversely, in 1978, Rizzo was stopped by a coalition of registered, mobilized black voters in alliance with the business community and liberal white voters. Goode reached the same conclusion as Rizzo: The road to victory was not to be found in an overtly racial appeal to blacks, which might polarize the electorate, but in an inclusive, reformist appeal to white liberals and the business community. Neither the black vote nor the white ethnic, blue-collar vote was big enough to win alone.

Goode was very successful in galvanizing the business community to make a strong effort on his behalf (*Philadelphia Inquirer* 1983a). Among Goode's backers in the business community, which included the Greater Philadelphia Partnership (the new name for the former GPM), two themes were consistently evident. First, the business and banking leadership believed that electing Goode would improve the city's position in the economic competition for new and relocating capital. Second, Goode would "unify the city" and be fair to all neighborhoods as well as to the downtown interests (*Philadelphia Inquirer* 1983b).

Goode also had strong ties to community groups and liberal organizations. As managing director, he had demonstrated a genuine desire to improve the conditions of the city's neighborhoods. He had approached representatives of more than 30 neighborhood groups seeking to familiarize them with ways that they could influence city hall to improve program and service delivery in their neighborhoods. Because of Goode's historic ties to liberal activism and his pervasive presence as a problem-solver while he was managing director, he received substantial support from white liberals.

Goode won the primary, capturing 53 percent of the vote, while Rizzo received 43 percent. Goode's general election victory would turn out to be a virtual replay of the primary vote. In the primary, black turnout was 69 percent, while about 70 percent of registered whites voted. In predominantly black wards, Goode won 91 percent of the vote in the primary and 97 percent in the general election. Goode won about 18 percent of the white vote in the primary and 23 percent in the general election against Republican John Egan, a successful businessman, and against independent candidate Thomas Leonard, formerly a Democrat and the city's controller. Rizzo's non-divisive campaign failed to win over liberal, upper-class voters in Chestnut Hill and Center City. In those wards (which Bowser had failed to win in the 1979 primary against Green), Goode captured 70 percent of the vote. In addition, Rizzo won only 44 percent of the vote in West Philadelphia/Overbrook and in the Logan Circle area, both of which were largely white (65 percent of the registered voters), middle-class areas with growing black populations.

WHO GOT WHAT? EVALUATING GOODE'S RECORD

Evaluating the performance of Goode and his administration is a contentious issue. Goode and his supporters argued that he compiled a record of accomplishments that, if compared to those of his predecessors or of mayors in other cities, would inspire praise. Yet Goode's record has been eclipsed by the MOVE disaster, in which the mayor gave the order to drop a bomb on a neighborhood that ultimately killed 11 people—including five children—and destroyed 61 homes in the resulting fire. MOVE is a radical, back-to-nature group that has existed in Philadelphia since the 1970s. In Mayor Rizzo's second term, an armed confrontation between the police and MOVE led to the death of an officer. MOVE had received virtually no sympathy or support from Philadelphians of any stripe, and in the areas where MOVE settled, they quickly alienated their neighbors. In May 1985, after members of the group refused to evacuate a heavily fortified house they were occupying, a Philadelphia police helicopter dropped a bomb on the house. The bomb started the fire that killed 11 MOVE members and burned two city blocks of the surrounding black neighborhood.

This outcome shocked and outraged even the most passionate enemies of MOVE, and the mayor drew sharp criticism from a blue-ribbon investigative commission. Much ink has been spilled regarding the MOVE disaster, and space limitations preclude examination here of any of the issues. One thing is certain, however—the basis for Goode's political appeal beyond his black base, Goode's reputation as an effective administrator and manager, was damaged beyond repair in the episode.

Aside from the MOVE debacle, the mayor's supporters claimed that his performance was measured, especially by the media, against the lofty and, given the constraints on mayoral leadership, unrealistic expectations people had of him. One example was the decline in the quality of city services, for which the Goode administration was unfairly blamed (*Christian Science Monitor* 1986; *Philadelphia*

Inquirer 1987a). These declines had more to do with the dramatic cuts in federal funding that the city suffered than with who sat in the mayor's office. During Frank Rizzo's second term, the mayor used Comprehensive Employment and Training Act (CETA) funds to pay the salaries of 4,442 city workers. During Mayor Goode's two terms in office, the Reagan administration's attack on urban America fully eliminated CETA funds. Overall, federal aid to the city fell during the decade Goode was managing director and mayor from more than $250 million to only $54 million (*Philadelphia Inquirer* 1987b; Adams 1991).

A second example of the unfair treatment Mayor Goode received was the way that he was blamed for failing to solve problems when the blame should have been shared with the city council. This was most notable in the city's inability to solve its expensive garbage disposal crisis, a problem that had stymied the Green administration as well. The city was paying enormous sums to bury its garbage in landfills outside the city limits. Both mayors and the business community agreed that the best policy was to build an incinerator in the city that would burn trash and use the steam produced in the process for energy needs. The city council basically took a "not-in-my-backyard" approach to the location of an incinerator that some feared was an environmental hazard and potential producer of carcinogens. No location for a trash-to-steam facility could be agreed on by the city council, and the bill for landfill dumping continued to drain the city budget. During the Green years, the city council deservedly received the blame for this stalemate. During the Goode years, however, the argument was that the mayor lacked the political skills to forge a compromise, which although accurate, constitutes only half of the explanation, because the City Council remained an obstructionist body.

The fiscal crisis that engulfed the city in Goode's second term was a third failure unjustly put on Goode's balance sheet. Certainly, as chief executive of the city during the crisis, Wilson Goode must share in the responsibility and blame. Yet as with most fiscal crises, the seeds of the problem were sown long before. One of the most significant aspects of Frank Rizzo's re-election strategy in 1975 was his granting of a 12.8 percent pay increase to municipal unions, a raise that was three times the 4.2 percent increases the unions had enjoyed in each of the prior two years. Rizzo was running without the party endorsement, and this whopping increase (along with the sweetening of their benefits package) no doubt contributed to Rizzo's ability to defeat the organization's candidate in a party primary. That Frank Rizzo was President Richard Nixon's favorite mayor ultimately contributed to the city's fiscal crisis as well. Federal revenue sharing funneled money into Philadelphia at a time when other cities were beginning the belt-tightening process. According to Paolantonio, "The city got double per capita more than Chicago, reaping $65 million, or about 10 percent of the city's operating budget, in the first 18 months of the program. It enabled the city to balance the budget. In Philadelphia, an inevitable fiscal crisis had been forestalled" (Paolantonio 1993, 154). During Goode's administration he was unable to gain the co-operation of Democratic state legislators in his efforts to address the city's mounting debt and its inability to borrow in municipal bond markets because of its junk bond status. To a significant extent, the failure of the Democratically controlled state legislature to rescue the state's largest

Democratic stronghold was because the speaker of the house wanted to be elected governor and recognized that it might be unwise to appear to be the orchestrator of a bailout of a city that many non-urbanites saw as a repository for acquired immunodeficiency syndrome (AIDS) victims, welfare recipients, and the homeless. Meanwhile, the two most powerful black city councilmen—without whom no budget legislation could be passed—refused to offer co-operation or alternative leadership. Lucien Blackwell did not want to support any tax increases, because he was planning to run for mayor in 1991 when Goode stepped aside. Appropriations Committee chair John Street wanted first to become city council president (he was the heir apparent but would not be elected until after the 1991 election cycle) and then take as much credit as possible for solving the city's fiscal crisis.

Finally, though Goode took credit for resolving a long-standing impasse that blocked the legislation necessary for establishing cable TV franchises in the city, the politics behind the resolution of this issue indicate some of the constraints that a technocratic reformer like Goode faces (and black mayors increasingly have technocratic backgrounds). Mayor Green believed that the licenses and contracts for cable TV service should go to the one company that made the best offers on the basis of cost per customer and extent of service. Members of the city council wanted multiple cable vendors to serve different parts of the city. Goode was expected to come in as a strong mayor and force the city council to be a vehicle for "good government." Instead, he balked at confronting the city council. Goode chose to cede to the council control of awarding four separate contracts (with four different opportunities for council oversight and potentially corrupting relationships) and thereby satisfy the demands of the citizenry for cable TV service.

Two other issues that Goode promised to resolve—the future plan for trash disposal in the city, and construction of a major convention center—languished in the city council, however, because the mayor, in his own words, refused to "do the kind of political trading that goes with that. . . . We simply can't afford to satisfy the insatiable appetite of members of Council if you're going to base votes on political trading" (*Philadelphia Inquirer* 1987c). The mayor offered a number of sound proposals to resolve these issues, yet he could not proceed without the approval of the city council. Goode's administration faltered in much the same way as Green's. Neither mayor was enough of a politician (and Goode was too much the technocrat) to "go along to get along" with the city council's dominant coalition of bipartisan, patronage-minded, neighborhood representatives. The reformist faction (mostly blacks aligned with Congressman William Gray, III) were too few to pass legislation in the city council. Both mayors were also good-government advocates who could not bring themselves to threaten using their power to punish the constituents of their opponents as a tactic for expanding their coalitions. Goode's discussion of this factional split within the black community is worth quoting at length (Goode 1992, 279–280):

> Over the years Black politicians had gained significant power. Bill Gray was now majority whip in Congress. . . . Our reform movement had broken down the racial barriers, but it was threatening to create others as these new

"bosses" sought to solidify and hold on to their power, not through merit, but by political control.

Essentially, they were saying they didn't like the way the first wave of reformers had played the political game. It was too altruistic, they didn't like this "community good" stuff—working primarily for the best interests of the community rather than themselves. Basically, they wanted now to play politics the same way the "old boy" establishment had played. Their goal was not to reform politics, but to change the complexion of who was in charge.

Realizing this, I knew the only way I could get some things passed by the council in my final administration would be to work on behalf of their interests. I was out of the equation. So I started strategizing, doing things like getting Blackwell to see that by supporting some of my reforms he wasn't helping me, but painting a favorable portrait of himself as future mayor in the eyes of the people and the business establishment. I made similar suggestions to Street as he pursued his desire to become council president.

When the Philadelphia Eagles professional football team threatened to leave the city for financial reasons, Mayor Goode personally negotiated with the team's ownership and carved out an agreement. Goode received heavy criticism, because he agreed to have the city pay the costs—and receive partial rental rights—for deluxe corporate sky boxes to be built atop the stadium. By September 1987, however, when the Eagles wanted to buy back the skyboxes because of their popularity, Goode appeared to have scored a coup that promised financial gains for the city. This is but one example of the successes the mayor has had in convincing mobile capital to remain in Philadelphia and in attracting new companies to the city because of his personal involvement. The dramatically changed appearance of Center City Philadelphia, with numerous office towers framing the statue of William Penn atop City Hall, is testimony to the service Goode performed on behalf of the growth coalition (Summers and Luce 1987). Goode deserves more credit than he has received for facilitating Philadelphia's belated movement into the corporate era, yet Goode has been criticized for being too subservient to capital (Jennings 1992)—another criticism his defenders consider to be unfair. A mayoral aide said, "Scholars are always talking or writing about the tragic consequences of suburban competition with cities. Yet when our mayor takes steps to compete with suburbs and attract good jobs, he is criticized as a lackey for the business elite" (Personal Interview, July 1986).

It would be inaccurate to view the Goode administration simply as a corporate-centered regime. Goode believed that job creation was the number one issue in the black community (*Philadelphia Magazine* 1984). The vast majority of the city's blacks continued to support Wilson Goode in his successful re-election bid of 1987—not only because he was the city's first black mayor and he brought blacks into many positions of real power and responsibility (discussed below), but also because Goode delivered on his promise by creating 37,000 new jobs (*Philadelphia Inquirer* 1987a).

In the area of executive appointments, where the mayor of Philadelphia is given near-total discretion by the city's charter, Wilson Goode was the only black appointed to Mayor Green's four-man cabinet. In Goode's six-person cabinet, there were three blacks (one female), and three whites (two female), marking a doubling of the proportion of blacks in the cabinet. In 1980, the U.S. Census reported that 39 percent of the city's population was black. Goode's appointments went beyond parity: Sixty percent of the commissioners heading city agencies in the Goode administration were black, while in the Green administration, the comparable figure had been 30 percent. In 1987, after a number of top-level reorganizations, 43 percent of these executive appointments were black. In 1988, Goode appointed the city's first black police commissioner, Willie Williams, capping a restructuring of the police force that was begun by Mayor Green and District Attorney Ed Rendell and continued by Goode.

The Green administration had not enthusiastically attacked the problem of racial and gender discrimination in the awarding of contracts with the city. After the city council overrode a mayoral veto of set-aside legislation, the Green administration awarded only a total of $2.4 million to minority- and female-owned firms. In contrast, the Goode administration in 1984 awarded $43 million worth of contracts to such firms (32 percent to female-owned firms), while in 1985, $63 million worth of contracts went to minority-owned firms and $27 million to female-owned firms. This still represented only 26 percent of the city's aggregate contract expenditures. When the U.S. Supreme Court struck down set-asides in the Croson case of 1989 (Richmond v. Croson, 1095, Ct. 706), Goode refused to modify the city's plan. When a U.S. district judge struck down the city's minority set-aside plan in April 1990, Goode signed an executive order mandating a new set-aside plan.

Critics point to some blemishes in Goode's record regarding black employment, although defenders are quick to point out that Goode's actions were designed to protect the tenuous economic position of the city rather than to advance any narrow interests (e.g., those of growth barons). For instance, Goode was criticized for opposing a measure that called for affirmative action hiring preferences for city residents, minorities, and women in construction jobs funded even partially by the city. Goode was not alone in his opposition to this bill, however; the city council's two most prominent black leaders also opposed it. Beauregard (1989) concluded that Goode's argument against the legislation—that it would produce similar retaliatory legislation by surrounding suburbs that would hurt Philadelphia construction workers who, in the aggregate, were successful in finding employment outside the city— was sound.

Goode's efforts to restore fiscal discipline to the city led him to refuse the demands of the public employees union and withstand a 20-day strike by predominantly black sanitation workers. Goode eventually endorsed plans for reduction of the size of trash collection crews from three or four to two. This decision seemed reasonable considering the design of modern trash trucks; nevertheless, it promised to eliminate the jobs of about 1,500 workers (Paolantonio 1993).

With respect to affirmative action in the municipal workforce, the record of the Goode administration also is noteworthy. According to Equal Employment Opportunity (EEO) reports filed by the city with the federal government, during the last year of Mayor Green's administration (1982–1983), blacks represented 28 percent of the municipal workforce, Hispanics 1 percent, and whites 70 percent. By the end of Goode's second term, Blacks held about 45 percent of the jobs in the city government. The Goode administration was not satisfied with simply raising the aggregate numbers of minorities in city jobs. It increased the proportion of blacks in the top three EEO job classifications from 24 percent under Mayor Green to 28 percent by 1987 and 31 percent by 1991.

In the neighborhoods, the Goode administration used the meager trickle of federal Urban Development Action Grants to supplement private capital and bring to fruition efforts to revitalize neighborhood shopping areas. This created construction jobs as well as permanent service industry jobs, in addition to upgrading the quality of life in the neighborhoods. Though these projects developed throughout the city, the Goode administration, unlike its predecessors, did not ignore the low-income black and Hispanic sections of North Philadelphia, where private capital was least willing to invest. Goode spent one-half of the city's $60 million block grant on low-income housing rehabilitation in predominantly black North Philadelphia, yet these efforts were considered disappointing because of the high expectations engendered by Goode's previous involvement with housing issues. Importantly, the Goode administration was responding to pressure from an activist neighborhood organization headed by City Councilman John Street and his flamboyant brother, Milton. Protest is not enough, but without it, resources probably would have been less forthcoming.

The Goode administration also did not ignore the city's poor. The single largest shift in spending in the budget ($2 million during the first year of the program) was toward programs that provided shelter and provisions for the homeless of the city—a program that earned national recognition (U.S. Conference of Mayors 1987). Unfortunately, in the midst of the national recession of 1990 to 1992 and impending municipal bankruptcy, spending on the homeless and on AIDS treatment was dramatically cut (*New York Times* 1989). With the city's bonds rated at junk bond status and the city council refusing to enact adequate tax increases, services were cut across the board. Wages of municipal employees were also targeted.

Does this suggest that Goode failed to deliver to the poorer segment of the black community, or that the mayor and the black city councilmembers who passed his budget were puppets of a growth coalition (Jennings 1992)? This is a conclusion that can be reached only by divorcing theory from empirical realities and exigencies. Clearly, the Goode administration did not limit political and economic advancement to the middle-class beneficiaries of affirmative action and minority business set-aside programs. Less educated, less skilled blacks also won a greater share of low-skill city jobs, the likes of which are disappearing in the private sector. As well, the mayor's efforts improved employment prospects in the private sector. Goode improved the quality of life in poor neighborhoods that were largely ignored in the past, and his administration temporarily took steps that represented a comprehensive, humanitarian response to the problems of homelessness and AIDS. Although much more certainly needs to be done for the city's disproportionately black poor, the problems go far beyond what even a united mayor and city council can do. Federal aid to the cities has declined dramatically, as already noted. The national epidemic of family breakup that has been correlated with poverty exacerbates the problems of Philadelphia's poor as well; by 1988, "about 45% of the city's Black families and 13% of its White families were headed by single women" (Adams 1991, 31). As the economy of Philadelphia and the greater metropolitan area changes in step with domestic and international rearrangements, the demand for a better-educated workforce grows while wages for low-skilled service jobs decline. By the 1980s, according to Adams (1991, 31), "three quarters of the Black men who had not finished high school were out of the workforce." Educational initiatives should be at the top of the agenda for all big city mayors, as should strategies for linking employable blacks to jobs in the suburbs.

LATINOS IN PHILADELPHIA

In contrast to several other chapters in this volume, discussion of the Latino population of Philadelphia has been conspicuously absent. This is because Latinos have, until recently, played a very minor role in the city's politics. According to U.S. Census Bureau data, in 1970 only about 2 percent of the city's population was Latino; by the 1990 Census, this figure was almost 6 percent, with nearly three-quarters of these being Puerto Rican. Even with the small numbers they represent, however, the competitiveness of the city's politics has forced politicians seeking citywide offices to give attention to the political demands of Latino voters.

Wilson Goode did this assiduously, and under his administration, black empowerment initiated Latino incorporation. In his initial mayoral campaign, Goode listed liberal lawyer Angel Ortiz on his sample ballot for an at-large seat on the City Council. While Ortiz was not elected, he came very close to winning. As mayor, Goode appointed him to the post of commissioner of records, the first Latino to head a city department. Due to the death of a councilman, Ortiz ran in a special election and won, with Goode's support, becoming the first Latino to serve on the city council.

Wilson Goode received strong electoral support from the Latino community. He received approximately 66 percent of the vote in predominantly Latino precincts in the 1983 Democratic primary against Frank Rizzo and 77 percent of their votes in the general election. In the 1987 general election, Ortiz, who was again elected to an at-large seat on the City Council, campaigned vigorously for Goode against Republican candidate Frank Rizzo by warning that a Rizzo victory would mean a "return to slavery . . . and racism." Goode won about 75 percent of the Latino vote in his narrow victory over Rizzo. Because he was elected at-large, however, Ortiz has not been able to devote himself solely to Latino community concerns. For instance, Ortiz was a leader in the fight for domestic partnership benefits for gay and lesbian city employees.

The most pressing issue for the Latino community seems to be police brutality. Hispanics have been vociferous in their demands for a strong, independent civilian police review board that would punish and deter brutality. Mayor Rendell (discussed below) had originally sought to create a weak, advisory police review board, but a high degree of pressure from black city council members and Latino activists forced the mayor to accede completely to community demands (*Philadelphia Inquirer* 1993, 1994a; *Philadelphia Inquirer Magazine* 1994a).

GOODE'S 1987 RE-ELECTION

In the Democratic mayoral primary, Goode won 57 percent of the vote and defeated Ed Rendell, the very popular former district attorney. Rendell had previously enjoyed the backing of the biracial reform coalition and been an ally of Goode. In 1987, however, Rendell was vigorously opposed by the city's black clergy who claimed that he had broken a promise not to challenge Goode in exchange for black support of his unsuccessful 1986 gubernatorial bid. Rendell received the support of many of the white liberals and business executives who had supported Goode in 1983 as well as both of the city's newspapers, which had endorsed Goode in 1983. In personal interviews, these reform-minded former supporters of Mayor Goode indicated that while they were backing away from a mayor whom they perceived to be incompetent, they had not lost faith in the ethos of biracial reform coalitions. Some already were looking toward 1991 and the opportunity to vigorously support another black reformer.

In the general election, Goode faced Frank Rizzo, who had switched to the Republican party. About 50,000 voters followed Rizzo and changed their registration to Republican. However, the Democratic party organization, under the unifying leadership of ward leader and former union leader Robert Brady, turned out voters on behalf of Goode and black city council candidates (*Philadelphia Inquirer Magazine* 1994b). There had been rumors anticipating defections of white Democratic politicians to Rizzo and the Republicans, but none materialized. Only one of the city's 28-member Democratic delegation to the state House and Senate defected to the Rizzo team. Credit for Goode's 1987 mayoral victory goes foremost to blacks, who turned out at a rate of about 70 percent and gave Goode 97 percent of their votes. Among whites, Goode received 18 percent of the vote. The mayor received diminished but significant support from those living in the city's upper-income reform areas, who gave Goode 54 percent of their votes. Goode could not have eked out his 18,000 vote victory without the support of Democratic party ward leaders, however, who persuaded their friends, families, and city jobholders to vote for Goode. Even though most of these ward leaders and voters had been lifelong supporters of Rizzo, a significant minority remained loyal to the party's candidate. Party loyalty and precinct-level organization were crucial ingredients in Goode's re-election, suggesting that while his electoral coalition was biracial, it was no longer unequivocally liberal or reformist.

Brady and the Democratic ward leaders of course had pragmatic reasons for re-electing Goode. Goode had appointed Brady to head the party in 1986 and knew what he was getting. He gave control over patronage jobs in the court system and Parking Authority to Brady (Balchunis 1992). In addition, Brady amassed patronage jobs by becoming a board member of the Pennsylvania Turnpike Authority, the city Redevelopment Authority, and the Delaware River Port Authority. A Republican administration would have been a major setback to the resurgent Democratic organization—regardless of the race of the mayor. More significantly, these white leaders of the Democratic organization believed that in 1991 they might elect a black Democrat who was not a reformer and was amenable to their machine style of politics, a position Goode was already moving toward. They accomplished this goal not in 1991, when Ed Rendell won election, but in 1999, when John Street was elected mayor.

FAULT LINES AFTER THE FIRST BLACK MAYOR

In the post-Rizzo era, the city council shifted from an arena in which Rizzocrats fought the white reform/black coalition over the issue of political incorporation to one in which a biracial coalition of politicians who favor a machine style of politics are in conflict with a biracial coalition of procedural reformers interested in good government. The business community of the city has been severely decimated by national corporate restructuring, and many positions that were formerly held by CEOs are now filled by local managers of firms headquartered elsewhere. Black leaders such as former Councilman and Congressman Lucien Blackwell, State Rep. Dwight Evans, and former City Council President (and current Mayor) John Street are now powerful figures within the Democratic organization that once tried to subordinate them. Issues of patronage, dispensation of city contracts, selection of candidates for political offices, and spoils of large-scale economic development are all areas in which they can align with union officials and party politicians (including Republicans). Other black leaders, however, many of whom are political disciples of former Congressman William Gray, III, and former Councilman John F. White, remain committed to the good-government tenets they share with the city's dwindling white liberal and business communities.

In short, two biracial coalitions now exist in Philadelphia. Mayor Goode walked the line between both, and depending on the issue, he was a champion or a disappointment to either group. In October 1986, even before Goode's re-election campaign had begun, the leaders of these black factions unanimously endorsed Goode for a second term. They stated that they did not want the city "to go the way of Cleveland"—a city where an incumbent black mayor lost to a white challenger. But in 1991, the black vote divided between Blackwell and an Ivy League–educated black reformer, Councilman George Burrell. Maintaining unity in the election of a second black mayor represents a major crisis point in black political development, as other cases in this book also illustrate.

Like New York's Rudolph Giuliani and Chicago's Richard M. Daley, Ed Rendell's election in 1991 replaced a black mayor with a white mayor. That these three mayors shared certain policy strategies—for instance, privatization of some city services—and that all three followed African-American mayors has led some observers to posit that a new "type" of mayor emerged in the 1990s as part of some hostile backlash against identity politics, affirmative action, and other assertions of African-American political empowerment (Sleeper 1993; for a contrary argument, see Keiser 2000). The evidence presented in the rest of this chapter suggests that Rendell's election did not represent a backlash against black political interests and a reassertion of white political power.

Councilman Lucien Blackwell was the leading mayoral contender in the black community, and although he had high negative ratings among white voters, he would have won the Democratic party primary, in which blacks were a majority of the registered voters, *if he had been the only black candidate.* He would have received strong support from the black clergy, including good-government clergy, because of their opposition to his leading opponent, Ed Rendell. He probably would have also won the general election, because the Democratic party organization would have had little trouble turning out a sizable minority of white voters willing to support this patronage-oriented, former union leader (as they did for Goode in 1987). The business community would have financially supported Blackwell, because he had engineered the consent of the fractious city council on a number of major development projects (a task for which they could not count on Mayor Goode). Why, then, did Blackwell lose?

For reasons that have more to do with the kinds of natural divisions within the black community that are sublimated until a first black mayor is elected but emerge after this event, Blackwell lost. Congressman William Gray, III, and City Councilman Blackwell had long been ideological (and personal) opponents. Even if blacks would be at the helm of the city, Gray and his reformist allies could not support a candidate who would turn the city's coffers into a spoils trough. Perhaps more important, Gray and his black clergy allies feared that Blackwell's abrasive style and attitude—and the overlain racial and class resentments he shared with his working class and poor constituents regarding white privilege—would foment racial polarization in the citizenry. The efforts that Gray's predecessors and contemporaries had made to demonstrate to whites they could work harmoniously with blacks, particularly middle-class blacks, for mutual development and advancement would be jeopardized by a Blackwell mayoralty. Gray persuaded one of his city council protégés, George Burrell, to enter the race early and to declare that under no circumstances would he withdraw. Gray twisted the arms of other black ministers to either support Burrell or remain uncommitted. Either Burrell would be the one black candidate, in which case he would cruise to victory, or the black vote would be divided. A term or two with the mayor's office occupied by Ed Rendell or Republican Frank Rizzo (or the other leading GOP candidate) would not do damage comparable to a Blackwell victory. Rendell would likely hand the mayoral baton to a moderate black (as Bill Green had done), whereas Rizzo would unify and rejuvenate the black-white liberal alliance as he had always done. Even after revelations about Burrell's finances and ethics devastated his candidacy, he refused to withdraw. The black vote divided and Rendell easily won the Democratic primary. Rizzo captured the GOP nomination, but he died soon after, and his replacement was unable to mount a serious campaign.

Does Rendell represent a repudiation of biracial coalitions and governance? No substantial evidence would support this claim. He earned support in the black community in part because of his aggressive actions as district attorney against police brutality, and this support was not dramatically eroded by the virulent opposition he faced from black clergy who believed he had promised to not run against Goode in 1987. Rendell became the most esteemed mayor in the nation during the 1990s, because in his first year, he produced a small budgetary surplus in a city that had a junk bond rating and a $250 million dollar cumulative deficit. Not only was he a friend of Bill Clinton, he also was a poster boy for the *Wall Street Journal*, *The Economist*, and the conservative Manhattan Institute, because he rolled back union benefits and froze wages to save $78 million annually. He has also persuaded the state legislature to underwrite some of the city's continuing economic development efforts. The entire budgetary process during his mayoral tenure smoothly sailed through the city council—because Council President John Street received at least half the credit for everything. Rendell headed a biracial coalition, and Street was his closest advisor aside from the mayor's chief of staff. Rendell was a charismatic cheerleader for the city and capitalized on the fiscal crisis environment to divide the city's municipal unions against other unionized workers (whose high taxes pay for the salary and benefit packages that Rendell slashed), but he ultimately took only a few meager steps toward privatization. Only about 10 percent of the city's total budget in the Rendell years was subjected to the competitive bidding process (i.e., privatization). Total savings were about $70 million in one year, split between contracting out jobs previously done by municipal employees (e.g., tree trimming, golf course management) and trimming costs in city bureaucracies and unionized work force.

Although his coalition was biracial, Rendell did not govern as a reformer who sought to root out patronage, corruption, or abuse of power. On the contrary, he supported a number of changes to the city charter (which failed) that would have increased either the power of the mayor or the president of city council at the expense of independent boards and commissions. When the local Democratic Party was implicated in a plot to tamper with and falsify absentee ballots in a crucial state legislative race, the mayor refused to treat the episode as anything deserving of concern—let alone a cause for a thorough housecleaning of the party that he now headed. Hence, although Rendell headed a biracial coalition that continued to advance black incorporation, it was neither liberal nor reformist.

When Rendell took office, the city had about a quarter-billion dollar deficit. By the end of 1999, the city treasury had a surplus of almost a quarter-billion dollars ($206 million). It accomplished this while cutting wage and business taxes, hiring more police officers, and signing new union contracts. Credit for this accomplishment goes to disciplined budgeting, no doubt. Even more credit, however, should go to the booming economy of the Clinton years, which enabled the city to collect about $66 million dollars more in wage, business and real estate taxes in 1999 than had been projected.

MAYORAL PRIMARIES OF 1999

In 1999, the Republican party nominated Sam Katz, who was unopposed. Katz, a Jewish liberal and long-time Democrat, had previously run for mayor and governor and was a very successful municipal financial strategist. Katz raised lots of money and attracted a talented team of advisers.

The Democratic primary was a bit more complicated. The eventual winner, John Street, faced four serious opponents in the Democratic mayoral campaign; two other African Americans, and two white challengers. These circumstances produced numerous calls by leaders among the black clergy and the outspoken leader of the Philadelphia NAACP for at least one of the black candidates to withdraw. At one point, there was even considerable discussion in the black community about holding an "all-black" primary before the official Democratic primary to reduce the field from three black candidates to one. None of these calls were heeded, however, and the candidates universally condemned them as an unnecessary injection of race into the campaign.

John Street grew up poor, living in a house in the outskirts of the city that did not have electricity or indoor plumbing until he was 11 years old. He first became visible in Philadelphia politics during the mid-1970s in the shadow of his radical older brother, Milton. Milton Street was a hot-dog vendor who thought that existing zoning ordinances gave all the best vending spots in the city to white food truck and pushcart operators. He decided to park his hot-dog cart wherever he felt and argued that the rules were racist. He relied on his younger brother, John, a lawyer, to get him out of legal trouble. The two brothers later turned from vendors' rights to protesting the discriminatory housing policies of the Rizzo administration. Then they entered electoral politics, with John winning a seat on the city council that was vacated after the death of the incumbent and Milton winning a seat in the state legislature.

John Street represented the Fifth District, which includes a bit of Center City, the Temple University area, and some of the city's poorest black neighborhoods. After entering the city council, he became a serious student of politics; he shocked members of the council when he admitted that he had read a considerable amount of the testimony of the council from the previous 10 years. In the 1980s, John Street slugged and wrestled to the floor another city councilman and publicly harassed the council president. This was done in the midst of Abscam, however, the FBI sting of the Philadelphia City Council, and Street's activity was part of a call for council members who were implicated in the bribery investigation to resign. Due to hard work and intelligence, Street became a budget whiz (even as he failed to pay his own utility bill and twice declared bankruptcy, facts that opponents are quick to underscore) in an era of urban fiscal crisis. He learned all the tricks of shifting funds from one bureaucracy to another and of creative accounting based on anticipated intergovernmental funding. When Wilson Goode sought to continue using these widely practiced tactics of budgetary finagling, Street, as chairman of the budget committee, refused to go along. His actions precipitated a budgetary crisis in Philadelphia for which Goode was blamed. Street wanted to take the credit for fixing Philadelphia's financial problems, and he knew that he had an excellent chance of becoming president of the city council (due to retirement of the incumbent) in the next election. He let the Goode administration flounder financially and then, after Rendell's election, played a most important role in getting the city's finances in order.

Once Street became city council president, he started practicing pinstripe patronage. In contrast to blue-collar patronage, these lucrative opportunities go to lawyers, financial analysts, business owners, and other highly educated individuals or firms who will, in turn, replenish the campaign coffers of the mayor and the party. Street helped to enrich many African Americans who later became the bankrollers of his mayoral campaign. For example, when the Goode administration negotiated a waste-hauling and incineration contract, the council president signaled he was dissatisfied with it. Contractors submitted new proposals, and their lawyers surmised that hiring local attorneys who were friends of Street could only help them. On this deal alone, two friends of the council president, both of whom emerged as part of his innermost circle during the mayoral election, earned nearly $100,000 apiece. As well, with the consent of Mayor Rendell, the city's bond counsel work—perhaps the most lucrative source of money flowing from city coffers—was shared between the mayor and the council president. Huge fees were earned by small firms with African-American lawyers, firms that had never been players in this game.[2]

One of the most important assets that Street had in his mayoral bid was the very strong endorsement of Mayor Rendell. Street had built a very impressive record of public service, but so had a number of his competitors in the Democratic primary. Voters were very concerned that the economic revitalization that Rendell had guided would be threatened by a change in leadership; within the region, many continue to see the economic rebound as quite tenuous. Rendell never faltered in his sharing of credit with Street. The outgoing mayor donated $100,000 to the Street campaign and taped TV commercials endorsing Street.

The two other black candidates were John White and Dwight Evans. White had a long and distinguished resume that included being the director of both the state welfare agency and the city's housing authority. He won endorsements from the teachers union, the city employees union, gay rights organizations, and the local chapter of the National Organization for Women. State Senator Dwight Evans, who had served 18 years in the state legislature and was formerly a gubernatorial candidate, could match any of the candidates in terms of policy knowledge and innovative ideas. He tried to focus his campaign around the issue of gun control and lawsuits against gun makers.

The two white candidates in the primary were Happy Fernandez and Marty Weinberg. Fernandez was an incumbent member of city council who had been a university professor. Although she was the first serious female candidate for mayor in the city's history, her campaign never drew the interest of the public. Weinberg was city solicitor in the Rizzo administration and had been one of Mayor Rizzo's most important advisors—making him a villain in the eyes of many black voters. For many Rizzo supporters, he represented an opportunity to return to bet-

---

[2] Although a 1994 U.S. Securities and Exchange Commission ruling bans municipal bond dealers, who sell the bonds, from giving more than $250 a year to candidates who could send business to them, companies circumvent the ruling by having banking arms, which are permitted to contribute.

ter days. He also was a successful lawyer who had leveraged his political connections to advance the financial interests of his firm and his white ethnic political allies.

White and Weinberg were the targets of $750,000 in TV and radio ads launched by Republican candidate Sam Katz. Katz did not want to run against another white candidate, Weinberg, in a city dominated by Democrats. He also did not want to have to compete against a black candidate like White, who could woo liberal, good-government voters who might otherwise cross over to him. Katz, who was white, reform-oriented, and portrayed as a policy wonk, wanted to face Street, who was black, machine-oriented, and portrayed as arrogant. At the same time, White lost some support in the black community because of fears that a divided black vote could deliver a victory for Weinberg. Evans's campaign stumbled early and was constantly beset by calls for his withdrawal. The Democratic primary ultimately came down to a battle between the two largest fund-raisers, Street and Weinberg.

Citywide, about 50 percent of registered voters were white and 45 percent were black, which was slightly more than their proportion of the population. Within the Democratic party, blacks had an edge of about 6 percent in registration over whites. Turnout for the May 18th primary was basically even between blacks and whites (Latinos will be discussed below) at about 40 percent according to official data. Street won with 35 percent of the vote. Weinberg received 31 percent, White captured 22 percent, Fernandez received 6 percent, Evans received 5 percent, and a fringe candidate received 1 percent.

The interpretation? The pessimistic view would argue that Street had everything going for him and still eked out only a narrow victory. He had nearly universal name recognition, a huge bankroll, the strong support of a wildly popular mayor, and a polished resume. He conducted himself with dignity and poise throughout the election, he received the endorsements of both major newspapers, and he faced Marty Weinberg—a candidate with no electoral experience, who had not been in public service for about 25 years, and who had very high negatives. Yet Street received only about 12 percent of the white vote. Furthermore, Republican Sam Katz was seen as a having an excellent chance at winning the general election in a city that had not elected a Republican mayor in 52 years, simply because many thought it unlikely that white voters would support Street.

A more optimistic—and I believe realistic—analysis of the election results would focus on how many white voters did not vote for Weinberg, who was seen as the only real chance to pre-empt a black victory. Analysis of the vote at the ward level shows that the three black candidates received between 20 and 40 percent of the vote in many of the white ethnic wards—wards in which the black candidates who lost to Ed Rendell in 1991 did poorly (about 10 percent or less). Thus, in many of the ethnic wards that, as late as 1990, were Rizzo strongholds, Rendell's endorsement of Street and the resumes and demeanor of all three black candidates deprived Weinberg of votes that would have come to him if race were the only factor of electoral calculus. A ward-level analysis of white voting shows that John White sometimes did better than Street in white wards, and that Fernandez sometimes did better than White and Street, finishing second to Weinberg. Yet the fact that so many white voters were willing to vote for one of the black candidates, or for a white candidate who clearly had no chance of winning, suggests that electoral polarization by race has declined among whites. Blacks in Philadelphia have long been willing to support qualified white candidates, as evidenced in earlier discussions of black voting for Longstreth, Green, and Rendell. In this election, more than 20 percent of white voters were willing to support a black candidate.

THE GENERAL ELECTION OF 1999

In the general election of 1999, Democrat John Street defeated Republican Sam Katz by about 8,000 votes—the narrowest margin in the city's history. Official turnout for the mayoral election, on a day when it rained in sheets and was extremely windy, was 43 percent of registered voters. Black turnout was estimated at about 5 percent lower than white turnout, which was better than average for all Philadelphia elections except the 1983 mayoral election of Wilson Goode, in which black turnout topped white turnout (Zausner 1999). Knowledgeable observers agreed, however, that a more accurate assessment of turnout was in the range of 60 to 65 percent of registered voters. (Turnout in the 1991 mayoral race was 61 percent of registered voters.) The discrepancy between the official statistic and the informed estimate is due to what might be called *registration inflation*, the increase in the rolls of registered voters due to new laws that prohibit the purging of names of inactive voters (those who have not voted for years) from the voter rolls. Since 1991, the adult population of Philadelphia has dropped by more than 115,000, yet the number of registered voters has increased by almost 200,000. New in-migration and the Motor Voter Law are adding new names to the registration rolls at the same time that removal of names has been halted.

Why was the election so close in a city with a 7-2 ratio of registered Democrats to Republicans? Answers to this question fall into three broad categories. Deserving of first mention is race—and not merely that blacks voted for Street and whites voted for Katz, but that many white Democrats could not bring themselves to vote for the black Democratic nominee and crossed party lines to vote for a white candidate. Was Katz really such an attractive candidate? No; aside from differences on a few issues, his platform was similar to Street's. Furthermore, Street hewed more to the Rendell record, a record that had proven itself to be wildly popular with voters. If Rendell had been running against Katz, the outcome would have been as lopsided as the voter registration figures.

A second factor would be character, something that is often hard to separate from race. This entails those (largely white) voters who distrusted John Street because of behavior early in his governmental service career, such as his fighting on the floor of the city council with a colleague, his shoving of a reporter, or his declaration of bankruptcy. Certainly, this argument cannot be dismissed, but one does have to question whether voters pay as much heed to the early career mistakes of white candidates for office.

Finally, there are ideological and policy reasons that could explain defection from Street and voting for Katz.[3] These would include Street's historic opposition to the agenda of gay and lesbian rights advocates, Katz's call for a much sharper reduction in wage and business taxes than Street (or Rendell) advocated, and Street's unabashed willingness to practice the politics of patronage and the steering of financial opportunities to associates.

Excluded from this list of explanations are all arguments about urban realignments of formerly liberal voters, such as Jews, Latinos, and African Americans, either to the GOP or away from black, identity-oriented candidates. The data for elections to the city council, in which Democrats won 14 of the 17 seats (10 district and seven at-large, two of which are reserved for the minority party), and the fact that the only two non-incumbents to win at-large seats were African Americans, offer only refutation for mayor-centric, realignment arguments. However, ideological and issue-based explanations for crossing party lines to vote for a particular candidate like Katz cannot be gainsaid. The question students must ask is whether the total number of voters who are dissuaded by positions on issues like gay rights and lower business taxes approaches the size of the white defection from the Democratic candidate. To the extent that it does not, we must turn back to the earlier explanations.

The view offered here is that racially based voting is the primary factor for the narrowness of Street's victory. Yes, character and ideology do play a role in electoral preference, and their impact in the election of Mayor John Street will be elaborated momentarily. However, race remains the trump card. This is an unfortunate state of affairs for our society, but it comes as no surprise to any but the most naïve of observers. Black candidates for public office have a great deal of difficulty in winning white votes even when party identification and issue orientation is shared. Scholars are so inured to this reality that we focus more of our attention on the exception to this rule—that is, when white voters do vote for black candidates. The Browning, Marshall, and Tabb argument (see Chapter 1) has called attention to the electoral support of white liberals (and Latinos) for black candidates. The election of John Street confirms an argument proffered in the second edition of this book—that an electorally significant minority of non-liberal white ethnics who give allegiance to the Democratic party organization (not merely to the party label) and to blue-collar unions are willing to support a similarly oriented African-American candidate. We will discuss this important finding after a brief description and analysis of the role of character and ideology in the election, but our focus on this segment of white voters who supported Street should not obscure the fact that the majority of white Democrats who cast ballots supported the white Republican.

---

[3] Here it is worth noting that in 1991, the issue most prominent in the minds of voters in Philadelphia and across the nation was crime, an issue that cuts against African-American politicians. In 1999, in contrast, the most salient issue in Philadelphia was maintenance of the economic health linked to the Rendell administrations. This concern no doubt aided Street.

The most significant events that took place after the primary election were symbolized by the distribution of endorsements by key players and organizations. Among the losers in the Democratic primary, Marty Weinberg and Dwight Evans endorsed John Street, but John White and Happy Fernandez endorsed Sam Katz. For Fernandez, the issue was character. She did not like the way John Street ran the city council when he presided over that body. She felt that he ran roughshod over the council's sovereignty vis-à-vis the mayor and that he manipulated and mistreated individual members. She feared that if elected mayor, Street would become even more imperious and that his prickly personality would limit the city's forward movement. John White took a very dramatic step in endorsing Katz. He could have offered a lukewarm endorsement and remained a team player. White's team wasn't merely the Democratic party, however. It was the liberal, good-government strain that, as discussed earlier, has run so strongly in Philadelphia. White had worked closely with Katz back in 1976 when Katz, then a Democrat, had managed Bill Gray's first congressional campaign. This same ideological argument explains why it was an open secret that Jerry Mondesire—president of the Philadelphia NAACP and the loudest voice in the African-American community calling for one of the black mayoral candidates to drop out (on the theory that three black mayoral candidates and two whites would produce an easy victory for a white candidate in the primary)—was supporting Katz. Mondesire cut his teeth in politics by being Congressman Gray's henchman, and there is no doubt that John White could have emerged as the power broker to the African-American community if Katz won but that a Street victory offered White nothing. Still, White's decision was probably based on ideology, not on prospects of personal gain. Simply put, these good-government African Americans opposed the machine politics, honest graft style of John Street. Recall the insight offered by Wilson Goode (Goode, 1992, 279–280):

> Our reform movement had broken down the racial barriers, but it was threatening to create others as these new "bosses" sought to solidify and hold on to their power, not through merit, but by political control.
>
> Essentially, they were saying they didn't like the way the first wave of reformers had played the political game. It was too altruistic, they didn't like this "community good" stuff—working primarily for the best interests of the community rather than themselves. Basically, they wanted now to play politics the same way the "old boy" establishment had played. Their goal was not to reform politics, but to change the complexion of who was in charge.

The other surprising twist in the endorsement sweepstakes was the decision by the two major newspapers, both of which had endorsed Street in the Democratic primary, to endorse Katz in the general election. This was a factor that helped to rouse the Street campaign from a complacency that had set in after the primary election. Newspapers in this overwhelmingly Democratic city endorsed the Republican candidate Sam Katz. Katz had no real political experience, but he was a policy wonk and consistently called for a sizable decrease in the city's tax rate on businesses. Street meanwhile pledged to continue to lower business taxes in the incremental and minimalist way that Mayor Rendell had done. Business leaders and their newspaper editorial page spokesmen argued that the way to clean up the blight of the city—one of Street's most pronounced goals—was to reduce business taxes enough to entice businesses to locate in the city and conduct the cleanup themselves. New businesses would also create jobs and thereby address another major problem of the city, the loss of population, which did not abate during the Rendell years. As a candidate and as a mayor, Street's view has been that the businesses and taxpayers who would leave because of tax sensitivity had already left. To attract new investment, Street argued that the city must first remove blight (e.g., abandoned cars and trash-filled lots), and then business would see the city as a place of opportunity. Street also believes that fighting blight helps to improve the quality of life for Philadelphians. In the mayoral election, Street constantly juxtaposed Katz's emphasis on tax reduction with his own emphasis on improving quality of life. The mayor continues to govern with the philosophy that blight removal and the towing of abandoned cars is more tangible to citizens than a few dollars more in their wallets due to tax reductions (Burton 2000). The newspapers, as voices of the growth coalition, have continued to focus on the city's high taxes on business as a criticism of the Street administration. Their endorsement of Katz flowed from their obeisance to business interests.

Unsurprising, but very significant, were the endorsements of the labor unions. The unions had been divided among the Democratic candidates during the primary but united behind John Street for the general election. This was not merely a proforma set of endorsements for the Democratic candidate, however. The unions, in a joint effort with the Democratic party ward organization, launched a massive and expensive field operation to mobilize supporters of Street. The unions declared election day a union holiday, giving members time to vote and work on behalf of the candidate. The Street campaign contributed considerable money to the Democratic organization to build an election day operation, including $250,000 that was spent on paying field operatives $75 apiece to get people to the polls. This effort was successful in delivering white ethnic blue-collar voters, many of whom had probably voted for Weinberg (who now vigorously supported Street), to Street. Street's electoral base was the African-American vote, but the next building blocks in the coalition were the party and union loyalists of the white ethnic neighborhoods. Among the unions, the building trades offered the most vigorous support—including widely reported intimidation of Katz supporters at polling places. The building trades, traditionally among the most conservative of unions, saw Street as a candidate committed to building two new sports stadiums, enforcement of rigid union work rules at the city's convention center (that have been the rue of many convention sponsors), and major redevelopment of housing in the neighborhoods (*Philadelphia Inquirer* 2001). Halfway through the first term of the Street administration it is hard to imagine a mayor with a closer relationship to white ethnic union leaders. In fact, the building trades have already held re-election fund-raisers for Street at which the leadership publicly warned a highly popular white ethnic city councilman not to consider an electoral challenge to the mayor (Infield 2001).

Unions have emerged from behind the scenes and once again stand as a major actor in Philadelphia politics.

The party organization knows that John Street—in sharp contrast to Wilson Goode—believes in the patronage system and in the distribution of both lucrative city contracts and decent-paying city jobs to his friends. The electoral effort of Democratic party chairman and Congressman Robert Brady has ensured that the organization, not just Street's friends, will be the beneficiary of lucrative largesse in a city with a $206 million budget surplus. In the final weeks of the campaign, Street repeatedly offered the view that patronage was a time-honored norm in Philadelphia. When asked about his promises to distribute political jobs to his allies, he offered the classic machine response, "Who am I supposed to give them to, my enemies?" (*Philadelphia Weekly* 1999, 6). Though no hegemonic political machine exists in Philadelphia, machine politics remain; moreover, spoils are providing the lubrication for a smooth relationship between white ethnics and a sizable black faction.

An additional noteworthy factor in explaining Street's victory is a visit to Philadelphia in the final days of the campaign by President Bill Clinton. Clinton's visit further energized the local party and drove home to the black audiences that this was a close election in which every vote would count.

Finally, Latino voters gave about 75 percent of their votes to John Street in the general election. There are about 50,000 Latino voters (about 95 percent Puerto Rican) in the city, and about 10,000 voted, according to estimates of knowledgeable observers. Turnout of Latino voters was almost one-half the rate of registered voters across the city, which is typical for Philadelphia's transient and poor Latino voters. Because of the very narrow margin of Street's victory, Latino political leaders even made the claim that their votes were decisive in the outcome—and that John Street owed them much. They will be at the end of a long line of such claimants, however. In the primary, Latino votes had been divided among the Democrats, with Weinberg winning about 44 percent. Street won about 30 percent of the Latino vote in the primary, and the three black candidates together won about 46 percent. In addition, some Latino leaders have recently been caught up in scandals, and this has left the community further weakened.

THE STREET RECORD

By the summer of 2001, the Street administration had earned quite good evaluations from all observers. Before reviewing some of the achievements of the administration, we should recall how ephemeral a positive press can be—before the MOVE bombing, the Goode administration was nearly universally lauded.

Before Street's election, he was typically described with words such as *imperious* and *arrogant*. Street came to the mayor's office facing some hostility from the city council, which he had dominated as president during the Rendell years. At least four members, and perhaps others, promised to be watchdogs if not downright opponents of the Street administration. Three liberals—Michael Nutter (an African American with mayoral ambitions), Marian Tasco, and Angel Ortiz—chafed under Street's leadership of the council. Councilman James Kenney, a very popular white ethnic with mayoral ambitions, also promised to be a burr in the mayor's saddle. However, as mayor, Street has surprised most observers by demonstrating a willingness to compromise and, occasionally, accept defeat. He has also defused a number of potential crises in ways that have suggested leadership skills. Finally, the mayor has a few feel-good, bread-and-circuses initiatives that have won him widespread (if tenuous) admiration.

The mayor was a major advocate of a downtown baseball stadium for the Philadelphia Phillies. After months of working toward this goal, the mayor accepted that this option had too many negatives. He quickly accepted an alternative location and stated, "Mayors don't always get what they want" (Benson and Burton 2000, A1).

Mayor Street also settled a weekend-long strike by the Philadelphia Federation of Teachers with no school days missed. Street sought to take steps that would show that he was serious about improving both the quality of education and the financial mismanagement of the widely criticized Philadelphia school system. Street did not seek the full control over and responsibility for the schools that other mayors, like Daley of Chicago and Menino of Boston, have accepted. He sought a money-saving change in the health benefits package of the teachers, and when they refused, the mayor backed off. He did, however, seek and win acceptance from the unions for the creation of a new position of chief executive officer of the school district, a merit-based form of compensation for teachers, and an expansion of the workday by half an hour. Teachers also won a modest increase in salary as well as a $500 bonus. Most important, the concessions from the union in the direction of reform led Republican Governor Tom Ridge to agree to advocate an increase in state spending for the city's schools—something that the state had long resisted.

Street first big initiative was to remove 40,000 abandoned cars from the city streets. This was done quickly and efficiently, and it demonstrated the mayor's interest in the neighborhoods. The problems of these neighborhoods after 30 years of disinvestment, however, remain unchanged. Neighborhood revitalization is a linchpin of his mayoral agenda, and the test will be whether the administration moves from cosmetic initiatives to a major redevelopment program that makes the city more attractive to capital. Mayor Street's plan is to issue $250 million in bonds to pay for demolition of 14,000 houses; to renovate another 2,500 houses; to provide home-improvement loans, and to purchase tracts of land. Other funds have been allocated for the cleanup of 31,000 vacant lots and removal of 4,300 trees that began in the summer of 2001. The mayor hopes to hire a project-management firm to oversee the demolition and repair project over the next five years. Many of the mayor's advisers and political friends have lined up to bid on this job. At the time of this writing, the city council was mildly voicing concern about the propriety of this relationship (Burton 2001, B1).

Political connections appear to be highly correlated with acquisition of contracts for a major new construction effort at the Philadelphia International Airport as well. The mayor's new airport boss fired the firm that had won a competitive bidding process in the Rendell administration and handed the contracts to a general subcontractor who promised to meet the city's voluntary goals of giving 18 to

20 percent of subcontract work to minority firms. Through some clever machina-
tions, this new arrangement circumvented the requirements for competitive bidding
(Gelbart 2001). If Mayor Street continues to use his power to advance minority business interests, then black political incorporation will indeed yield black economic
advancement.

One conclusion here is that machine politics and reform politics remain useful
distinctions. Mayor Street's patronage contracting practices were steadfastly resisted
by Mayor Goode, and both the black and white communities of Philadelphia contain large groups of voters who identify with the tenets of both of these classical
political perspectives. But another, more tentative, conclusion is that both machine
and reform government may create significant gains for black working class people: city and private employment with good health and pension benefits that would
not otherwise be available.

In a crisis that involved a confrontation with the city's police department and
its widely respected police chief, Mayor Street took a firm stand for integrity. In
February 1998, a police captain got drunk at a bar. When he left the bar, he "crashed
into another vehicle, left the scene, and drove his unmarked car into North
Philadelphia with its front end crumpled, the air bag inflated, and steam rising from
the engine." A lieutenant then orchestrated a cover-up for the captain that included
directing a patrol officer to move the captain's car "onto the sidewalk, against a pillar, to make it appear that he had swerved to avoid another car" and filing a false
accident report. When the cover-up unraveled publicly in March 2001, Police
Commissioner John F. Timoney handed down 20-day suspensions for minor infractions to the captain and the lieutenant, who had been subsequently promoted to
captain. One day after defending this light punishment to the press—and after a
meeting with Mayor Street—the Police Commissioner accompanied the mayor to a
press conference and changed his mind. The captain who was intoxicated was
transferred to night duty and stripped of his command of the Homicide Division of
the department. Other than the Fraternal Order of Police, the public reaction to
Street's response to the crisis was highly laudatory (Fazlollah 2001, A1).

In his 2001 State of the Union address, President George W. Bush, Jr., singled
out the mayor as one leader of a city who has used faith-based organizations to
deliver social services, particularly in low-income neighborhoods. Philadelphia has
drawn attention specifically for community-based truancy programs and for efforts
in which religious congregations adopt convicts on their release from prison. The
significance and success of these programs remain open questions, but they
undoubtedly advance a number of agendas and produce a major public relations
coup for the mayor.

The mayor has also drawn national attention for putting the city on a diet. After
Philadelphia was named the most overweight city in America by a health magazine,
the trim mayor—who practices a spartan diet after once being on the paunchy
side—called on the city to lose 76 tons of weight in 76 days. The numerical reference was meant to capitalize on the popularity of the Philadelphia 76ers professional basketball team (and, of course, 1776 and the nation's Independence,
declared in Philadelphia). Citizens lost weight, joined health clubs which offered

discounts, and perhaps felt some greater sense of community, however fleeting. The mayor also got to display a cheerleading side of himself that reminded voters of the ever-popular Ed Rendell.

CONCLUSION

What is the future of Philadelphia politics? The mayor seems reasonably popular, and based on his support in the African-American community, the party organization, and labor leadership, he looks electorally impregnable. That his administration has moved back toward patronage and the distribution of major city contracts to friends of the mayor and the party leadership probably will not harm Street unless a major scandal reaches the mayor's office. Perhaps the only other threat to a second term for Mayor Street is Ed Rendell. Even with all the mutual praise that has been exchanged between Street and Rendell, seemingly small events have sown anger and division between the two. Rendell is likely to run for governor in 2002. If he does not win, he may turn back to Philadelphia and run for mayor again.

With respect to African-American incorporation, the Street administration raises important questions. However, after less than two years into the administration, it is still early for in-depth assessments. Can an electoral alliance of African Americans with the regular organization and conservative labor unions work? Middle-class blacks had been the least supportive of such an alliance in the Tate years, when blacks were only dealt the least desirable benefits of this coalition. Now that African Americans are full-fledged partners in the coalition and Mayor Street is funneling financially lucrative opportunities to pinstriped African Americans, can this coalition work? The answer appears to be yes. Party leader Brady has delivered votes for Goode and Street, and Street seems to thrive in a deal-making environment.

Will this coalition be able to increase the proportion of white voters who support a black mayor beyond the 20 percent threshold? I would say yes and point to the proportion of votes that all three black candidates received in the Democratic primary against Weinberg.

Will a sizable segment of the black community take a stand for a good-government candidate against a black mayor? Unless there is a huge scandal, I believe dissent will be minimal. It would not be surprising, however, if the GOP turned to a black good-government candidate in the future in an attempt to divide the black vote and portray the Democrats as corrupt.

Finally, will the Street administration, which has inherited a sizable city surplus, be able to deliver a greater share of the benefits of incorporation to African Americans below the middle class? Much depends on the health of the regional and national economies, particularly in light of what appears to be a trickle-down, development-led strategy by the Street administration. If the Street administration can increase its share of white electoral support and improve on distribution of the benefits of incorporation to all segments of the black community, then it will exemplify a biracial, machine politics path to minority political incorporation, governmental responsiveness, and economic benefit: a city government that is redistributive, but in a different way than the reformed city governments where biracial coalitions took control in California cities (see Chapter 1).

Does Philadelphia demonstrate a viable machine path to political incorporation, one that is closer to the governmental traditions of the large cities of the East and Midwest? The next few years should hold the answer.

REFERENCES

Adams, Carolyn Teich. 1991. Philadelphia: The Slide Toward Municipal Bankruptcy. In H. V. Savitch and John Clayton Thomas, eds., *Big City Politics in Transition*. Urban Affairs Annual Reviews, Vol. 38. Newbury Park, Calif.: Sage.

Balchunis, Mary Ellen. 1992. A Study of the Old and New Campaign Politics Models: A Comparative Analysis of Wilson Goode's 1983 and 1987 Philadelphia Mayoral Campaigns. Unpublished PhD dissertation, Temple University.

Beauregard, Robert A. 1989. Local Politics and the Employment Relation: Construction Jobs in Philadelphia. In Robert A. Beauregard, ed., *Economic Restructuring and Political Response*. Urban Affairs Annual Reviews, Vol. 34. Newbury Park, Calif.: Sage.

Benson, Clea, and Cynthia Burton. 2000. Ballpark Won't Be Downtown, Street Says. *Philadelphia Inquirer*, November 14, A1.

Burton, Cynthia. 2000. The Word on Street: How He Did in His First 100 Days. *Philadelphia Inquirer*, April 12, B1.

Burton, Cynthia. 2001. Verna Continues Fight over Blight. *Philadelphia Inquirer*, April 26, B1.

Christian Science Monitor. 1986. Goode's bright promise beset by MOVE, strike. July 22.

Edsall, Thomas, and Mary Edsall. 1991. *Chain Reaction: The Impact of Race, Rights, and Taxes on American Politics*. New York: Norton.

Ekstrom, Charles A. 1973. The Electoral Politics of Reform and Machine: The Political Behavior of Philadelphia's "Black" Wards, 1943–1969. In Miriam Ershkowitz and Joseph Zikmund II, eds., *Black Politics in Philadelphia*. New York: Basic Books.

Ershkowitz, Miriam, and Joseph Zikmund II. 1973. *Black Politics in Philadelphia*. New York: Basic Books.

Fazlollah, Mark. 2001. Timoney Does an About-Face. *Philadelphia Inquirer*, March 28, A1.

Featherman, Sandra, and William L. Rosenberg. 1979. *Jews, Blacks and Ethnics: The 1978 "Vote White" Charter Campaign in Philadelphia*. Philadelphia: American Jewish Committee.

Gelbart, Marcia. 2001. Airport Pact of Benefit to Street Donors. *Philadelphia Inquirer*, March 22.

Goode, W. Wilson, with Joann Stevens. 1992. *In Goode Faith*. Valley Forge, Penna.: Judson Press.

Infield, Tom. 2001. Trade Unions Rev Up for a Street Bid in 2003. *Philadelphia Inquirer*, December 6, B1.

Jennings, James. 1992. *The Politics of Black Empowerment*. Detroit: Wayne State University Press.

Keiser, Richard A. 1989. Black Political Incorporation or Subordination? Political Competitiveness and Leadership Formation prior to the Election of Black Mayors. Unpublished PhD dissertation, University of California, Berkeley.

Keiser, Richard A. 1990. The Rise of a Biracial Coalition in Philadelphia. In Rufus P. Browning, Dale Rogers Marshall, and David H. Tabb, eds., *Racial Politics in American Cities*. New York: Longman.

Keiser, Richard A. 1993. Explaining African-American Political Empowerment: Windy City Politics from 1900 to 1993. *Urban Affairs Quarterly* 29 (1): 84–116.

Keiser, Richard A. 1997. *Subordination or Empowerment? African-American Leadership and the Struggle for Urban Political Power.* New York: Oxford University Press.

Keiser, Richard A. 2000. Analyzing Urban Regime Change: Black Power, White Backlash, and Shades of Gray. In Richard A. Keiser and Katherine Underwood, eds., *Minority Politics at the Millennium.* New York: Garland.

Lowe, Jeanne. 1967. *Cities in a Race with Time.* New York: Random House.

New York Times. 1968. Philadelphia Poor Pledged $1 million by Business Group. May 12.

New York Times. 1983. Race is a Muted Issue in Philadelphia. April 12.

New York Times. 1989. 50% Cutback in Funds for Homeless is Fiercely Protested. September 15.

Paolantonio, S. A. 1993. *Frank Rizzo: The Last Big Man in Big City America.* Philadelphia: Camino Books.

Peterson, Paul E. 1967. City Politics and Community Action: The Implementation of the Community Action Program in Three American Cities, ch. 4. Unpublished PhD dissertation, University of Chicago.

Philadelphia Bulletin. 1965. Parties Court Negroes, Who Hold Key to Power. January 24, A3.

Philadelphia Bulletin. 1974. Tate Felt a Rizzo Win Would Save Democratic Control. January 23.

Philadelphia Daily News. 1982. Wilson Goode: He Transformed the Job. November 30, 6.

Philadelphia Inquirer. 1978. City's Religious Leaders Censure Racial Rhetoric. September 30.

Philadelphia Inquirer. 1983a. Business Leaders Give Less to Goode for this Campaign. October 31, B1.

Philadelphia Inquirer. 1983b. Philadelphia Was Also a Winner in the Primary. May 22.

Philadelphia Inquirer. 1984. Strong Start, Few Fumbles for the Mayor. April 22.

Philadelphia Inquirer. 1986. Goode's Re-election Is a Dilemma for Blacks, Also. November 27.

Philadelphia Inquirer. 1987a. Goode Pulled Black Vote for a Range of Reasons. May 24.

Philadelphia Inquirer. 1987b. Many on Green's Team Help Rendell. April 25.

Philadelphia Inquirer. 1987c. For Goode, a Year of Recovery. January 4.

Philadelphia Inquirer. 1993. Marching Side by Side Along a Divide. September 27.

Philadelphia Inquirer. 1994a. Police Accused of Beating Up Latinos. January 15.

Philadelphia Inquirer. 1994b. After Years of Losses, Area Jobs Up. April 7.

Philadelphia Inquirer. 1999a. Numbers Lie: Philadelphia's Turnout Not What It Seemed. November 6, B1.

Philadelphia Inquirer. 2001. Featherbedding: It May Jeopardize Convention Center. April 24, A20.

Philadelphia Inquirer Magazine. 1994a. Response Time. February 6.

Philadelphia Inquirer Magazine. 1994b. The Soul of an Old Machine. April 17.

Philadelphia Magazine. 1984. The No-Frills Mayor. December.

Philadelphia Weekly. 1999. Mayor Elect John F. Street. November 3, 6.

Portz, John. 1990. *The Politics of Plant Closings.* Lawrence: University Press of Kansas.

Reichley, James. 1959. *The Art of Government: Reform and Organization Politics in Philadelphia.* New York: The Fund for the Republic.

Rogers, David. 1971. *The Management of Big Cities.* Beverly Hills: Sage.

Sleeper, Jim. 1993. The End of the Rainbow. *The New Republic* 209 (18): 20–25.

Strange, John Hadley. 1966. The Negro in Philadelphia Politics: 1963–1965. Unpublished PhD dissertation, Princeton University.

Strange, John Hadley. 1969. The Negro and Philadelphia Politics. In Edward Banfield, ed., *Urban Government.* New York: Free Press.

Strange, John Hadley. 1973. Blacks and Philadelphia Politics. In Miriam Ershkowitz and Joseph Zikmund II, eds., *Black Politics in Philadelphia.* New York: Basic Books.

Summers, Anita, and Thomas Luce. 1987. *Economic Development Within the Philadelphia Metropolitan Area*. Philadelphia: University of Pennsylvania Press.

U.S. Conference of Mayors. May 1987. *A Status Report on Homeless Families in America's Cities*. Washington, DC: U.S. Conference of Mayors.

Weiler, Conrad. 1974. *Philadelphia: Neighborhood, Authority, and the Urban Crisis*. New York: Praeger.

Wolfinger, Raymond. 1977. Why Political Machines Have Not Withered Away and Other Revisionist Thoughts. In Harlan Hahn, ed., *Readings in Urban Politics*. Englewood Cliffs, NJ: Prentice Hall.

Part III

Barriers to Coalitions

Chapter 4

New York: Still the Great Anomaly

John Mollenkopf

EDITORS' NOTE

New York is still the largest city in the United States. Two-thirds of its residents are black, Latino, or Asian. Blacks and Latinos have a long history of sophisticated political participation and at times have formed an alliance with a sizable, politically active, white liberal population. Knowing these facts makes it easy to predict that blacks, Latinos, and white liberals have formed a strong and durable governing coalition in New York.

Easy, but wrong. As John Mollenkopf shows, blacks and Latinos have been politically much weaker in New York than we would expect. The contrast to other cities with nonwhite majorities is striking. It did not elect a black mayor until 1989, long after Los Angeles, Chicago, and Philadelphia had done so, and that mayor served only one term. Before and after, white mayors held sway, gaining support from white middle-class voters with relatively conservative programs that stressed fiscal prudence, fighting crime, and promoting development. Moreover, until redistricting in 1991, both blacks and Latinos were substantially underrepresented on the city council. Neither group can be considered part of the current governing coalition. Term limits forced out the popular Republican incumbent in 2001, but another Republican, a billionaire political newcomer, succeeded him by narrowly defeating a Democratic nominee supported by most minority voters.

Why have blacks and Latinos been so weak in New York? Read Mollenkopf's explanations as a sourcebook of barriers to minority incorporation: the reluctance of white voters to yield power to minority leaders; the persistence of regular Democratic party organizational influence; divisions among and competition between white liberals, blacks, and Latinos; and the absence of independent means for these groups to form a durable coalition. These barriers are not unique to New York City, but they come together with special intensity to deter minority political empowerment in that city.

Since 1977, the victor in every mayoral election in New York City, except for David Dinkins in 1989, has won office primarily on the basis of votes cast by relatively conservative white voters in a racially polarized contest. Indeed, for the first time since Greater New York was formed in 1898, a two-term Republican mayor, Rudolph W. Giuliani, was succeeded by another Republican, Michael Bloomberg, in 2001. Bloomberg was endorsed not only by Rudy Giuliani but also by former Mayor Ed Koch, both of whom governed largely without consulting the black and Puerto Rican political establishment. (Indeed, it took substantial protest over a police shooting of a black man to convince Mayor Giuliani even to meet with high-ranking African-American elected officials in his second term.) Both Koch and Giuliani were perceived as governing on behalf of their core white electoral constituencies.

Though it remains to be seen how the Bloomberg administration will govern, the 2001 mayoral election clearly continues this pattern of minority subordination. Fernando Ferrer, the Bronx Borough President, almost became the first Puerto Rican nominated by the Democrats. He was narrowly defeated in a bitter runoff primary, and the victor, Public Advocate Mark Green, then lost narrowly to Mike Bloomberg by 37,000 votes out of 1.5 million, leaving an angrily divided Democratic party. Support for Bloomberg in the 2001 general election closely paralleled that for Rudy Giuliani in 1993 (a precinct-level correlation of .903) and for Ed Koch in the 1989 Democratic primary (a correlation of .836). New York thus remains a challenging anomaly. Though non-Hispanic whites make up only 35 percent of its population, the mayor, two of the three citywide offices, the city council speaker (perhaps the second most powerful job in city government), and just over half the city council members are white. Unlike Los Angeles and Chicago, where white mayors preside over populations with even fewer whites, Bloomberg won without including a large minority vote in his electoral base.

Rufus Browning, Dale Marshall, and David Tabb's theory of minority political empowerment attributes its pace to the interplay between minority protest and the formation of an insurgent political coalition that can win mayoral elections (Browning, Marshall, and Tabb 1984, 1990, 1994). Only when white liberals joined with blacks and Latinos to displace a prior white coalition did some of the 10 California cities they studied become more responsive to minority interests, especially when blacks or Latinos led this coalition. Where such a coalition did not form or was not successful, leaving a coalition elected by relatively conservative white voters in power, city government continued to resist policy changes even in the face of minority protest. The prospects for forming a successful biracial insurgent coalition depend, in their view, on the extent of past minority political mobilization and the likelihood that white voters would support minority political advancement. Raphe Sonenshein extended this framework by arguing that whites would support minority political advancement not only when whites tended to be more liberal, but also when minority empowerment would advance the political interests of those white liberals. He added that the white-black collaboration would be fostered by a history of close personal ties between white and black leaders that enabled them to trust each other (Sonenshein 1993). In short, we should expect biracial coalitions to succeed where strong leaders emerged from the mobilization of large black and Latino populations for protest as well as electoral politics, and especially where these leaders had worked closely with and achieved power alongside white liberal elites.

From this perspective, New York City should have been an early—and leading—case of biracial insurgency and minority political incorporation. It was not. New York did not elect an African-American mayor until David Dinkins's victory in 1989, and he was defeated after only one term. In many respects, the key dynamic in New York City's political culture since the mid-1960s has been a series of reactions by white politicians and voters against failed or stalled bids for minority political power and persisting divisions among potential challengers.

This is not to say, of course, that minority elected officials did not make considerable headway at the lower levels of New York City's political system. The city council, for example, evolved from a relatively inconsequential body with only five minority members (out of 43) in 1978 to a far more powerful body with 14 black, 10 Latino, and one Asian member (out of 51) in 2002. In November 2001, New York also elected its first African-American comptroller and Queens Borough president, while Manhattan's borough president is a black woman and the Bronx's is a Puerto Rican man. Minority representation has also gradually increased in the city's Albany and Washington delegations.

At the same time, the New York City Charter invests a great deal of power in its chief executive. These executives (apart from Dinkins) won office mainly with white votes against candidates favored by blacks and Latinos, and they have not included members of black and Latino political establishments in their inner circle. Indeed, Mayors Koch and Giuliani arguably governed against the interests of their minority constituents, at least as conceptualized by the ranking black and Puerto Rican elected officials. They did not ignore or completely fail to respond to the needs, wants, and interests of the city's black and Latino residents, but they often crafted their responses to circumvent or subordinate minority leadership, not to empower it.

Why New York, the most liberal of America's big cities and certainly one that conservatives love to pillory as a sink of social democratic pathology (e.g., Siegel 1997), constitutes such a case study in the failure of minority empowerment is the central question addressed by this chapter.

NEW YORK AS AN ANOMALOUS CASE

New York City has long had the raw materials that Browning, Marshall, and Tabb suggested on the basis of their research on California cities would enable a liberal, biracial coalition to win office and bring about minority political incorporation. New York's non-Hispanic black, Hispanic, and Asian populations grew from 37 percent of the total in 1970 to 65 percent in 2000.[1] Each of these racial and ethnic groups has a long history of mobilization for electoral politics and protest. Moreover, the city's white voters are clearly far more liberal, Democratic-leaning, and favorable toward government programs than those of other cities or the nation as a whole (Goldberg and Arian 1990, Gifford 1978). Finally, white liberal, black, and Puerto Rican political elites have a long record of working together through electoral politics, trade unions, social service agencies, and civic organizations.

Black and Latino political mobilization dates to the Great Depression and World War II. Adam Powell, a Democrat, and Benjamin Davis, a Communist, became the city's first black elected officials when they won city council seats in the 1941 and 1943 elections, which were conducted under proportional representation. The first Puerto Rican state assemblyman was elected on the Republican and American Labor Party lines in 1938. After World War II, black and Puerto Rican political representation grew steadily, though not without setbacks. It reached one peak in 1969, when minority voters helped to elect Herman Badillo to be the first Puerto Rican borough president of the Bronx and Percy Sutton, an African American, as Manhattan Borough president, while providing pivotal votes for the re-election of Mayor John V. Lindsay (Kimball 1972, 170). Elsewhere in the city, blacks and Latinos also began to be elected in significant numbers to the state assembly and senate.

The fiscal crisis of the mid-1970s punctuated this trend, and poor results in the 1973 and 1977 mayoral elections caused Badillo and Sutton to seek other pursuits. Yet the steady growth of the city's black and Latino populations and the influence of the Voting Rights Act on redistricting enabled a growing cadre of minority politicians to win legislative offices during the 1970s and 1980s. After the 1990 round of redistricting, blacks and Latinos held 21 of the 51 city council seats, six of the city's 14 congressional seats, six of the 25 state senate seats, and 24 of the 60 state assembly seats. (Republicans control the redistricting of senate seats and Democrats control assembly seats. They jointly determine congressional districts. Separately, Democrats appointed by the council and mayor drew new city council district boundaries in 1991.) Ten years later, after the 2000 and 2001 general elections, the minority city council delegation increased to 25, including the first Asian American, but the other shares remained about the same. (At this writing, the 2001–2002 round of redistricting is still under way.) The slow turn of the demographic wheel has left the black share of local legislators about equal to their population proportion, while whites remain tremendously overrepresented and Latinos underrepresented. (Asians are just beginning to break into political representation.)

---

[1] The 2000 U.S. Census reports that New York's population of 8 million was 24.5 percent non-Hispanic black, 27.0 percent Hispanic, 9.7 percent non-Hispanic Asian, and 35 percent non-Hispanic white. References throughout this paper to black, Asian, and white populations exclude those of Hispanic origin, who are grouped together as Latino. (Some 7.8 percent of Hispanics are also black, however.) For an overview of demographic change in the 1980s, see Mollenkopf 1993.

Black and Latino protest also has a long and turbulent history in New York City. Highlights include the black boycott of white merchants along 125th Street in Harlem of the 1950s, the civil disturbances and school decentralization protests of the 1960s, marches led by the Reverend Al Sharpton and others during the late 1980s and early 1990s, and the protests against police brutality toward Abner Louima and the shooting of Amadou Diallo that culminated in many arrests in front of police headquarters in 1999. In short, many efforts have been made over the years to mobilize New York's large and growing black and Latino populations both for protest and for voting.

Equally important, a third of New York City's white voters call themselves liberals, and many cast ballots for white candidates heavily favored by and responsive to minority voters. In general election contests, about two-thirds of the city's white voters will back a white candidate who gets even more support from minority voters—typically the Democratic nominee. White Democratic elected officials and party leaders regularly work closely with black and Latino political elites to elect such candidates. White voters have even strongly supported black candidates in lower-profile general elections, such as Carl McCall's races for state controller in 1994 and 1998 or William Thompson's race for city comptroller in 2001. While far fewer whites were willing to support Puerto Rican and black candidates in the 1974, 1977, and 1985 mayoral primaries, roughly a third favored David Dinkins in the 1989 Democratic primary and general elections. Indeed, more white voters backed Dinkins in the 1989 general election than they did any other first-time black nominee in any other big city election beside Tom Bradley in his first run in Los Angeles (Arian, Goldberg, Mollenkopf, and Rogowsky 1991).

Given these antecedent conditions, Browning, Marshall, and Tabb's theoretical framework would lead us to expect that a liberal, insurgent, biracial coalition would have won the mayoralty in New York City by the early 1970s, and that this victory would have embedded minority political empowerment deeply into the New York City political system. Indeed, the early victories of African Americans and Puerto Ricans for legislative office and the election of John V. Lindsay as mayor in 1965 and 1969 suggested this might happen. However, it did not.

Lindsay's second mayoral term gave way to the fiscal crisis of 1975 to 1976 (blamed by many on Lindsay's expansion of programs serving or employing minority groups substantially beyond the local ability to pay for them) and a period of severe political as well as fiscal retrenchment. Black and Latino leaders were neither key participants in fiscal crisis decision making nor members of the dominant electoral and governing coalition erected in the wake of the fiscal crisis. While David Dinkins's victory in 1989 reawakened the struggle for minority empowerment, he and his allies failed to institutionalize their position, for the reasons discussed below. His defeat in 1993, Ruth Messinger's loss in 1997, Fernando Ferrer's defeat in the 2001 Democratic primary, and Mark Green's inability to win the 2001 mayoral election demonstrate the tenacity of this pattern.

The Lindsay administration offered the nation a model for liberal, biracial coalition politics between 1965 and 1973. It sought not only to incorporate minorities through such traditional means as extending welfare benefits and employing more blacks and Puerto Ricans on in public jobs but also through innovations like the Office of Neighborhood Government and community development corporations (Pecorella 1994; Katznelson 1981; Yates 1973). Yet the Lindsay experiment failed politically, engendering political turmoil over such issues as establishing a civilian police complaint review board, community control of the school system, and financing a widening fiscal gap caused in part by expansion of the public payroll (Morris 1980; Shefter 1985). Lindsay was succeeded by the white, ethnic, clubhouse politics of Mayor Abraham Beame (1973–1977), the fiscal crisis (1975–1977), and the conservative administrations of Mayor Edward I. Koch (1977–1989) and Rudolph W. Giuliani (1993–2001). Mayors Beame, Koch, and Giuliani all reduced the share of city spending flowing toward social programs and the poor, shifted priorities toward enhancing and protecting property, and used programs originally designed to promote minority interests to keep minority politicians in line (Katznelson 1981; Mollenkopf 1985, 1994; Shefter 1985; Brecher and Horton with Cropf and Mead 1993).

Although Dinkins's narrow victory as New York City's first African-American mayor in 1989 was undoubtedly a political breakthrough, he was soon defeated by Rudy Giuliani, an Italian-American, Republican, former prosecutor (Mollenkopf 1994). Using a severe budget crisis as the context, Giuliani began his mayoralty by terminating affirmative action programs, cutting social spending, and continuing the increase in the police department staffing and the crackdown on "quality of life" problems begun under Dinkins. Slashing the crime rate and welfare caseloads became the hallmarks of his administration. In the 1997 election, he rolled over Manhattan Borough President Ruth Messinger, a white, liberal, former social worker and reformer who had strongly supported David Dinkins. In 2001, Giuliani's endorsement helped Republican businessman Mike Bloomberg narrowly defeat Democrat Mark Green—spending a record $99 per vote in the process. Today, the city lacks either a liberal biracial governing coalition or broad political support for the spending and policy priorities such a regime would seek to put into place. Recently, a white city council member became that party's leader, holding the second most powerful job in city government. Of the eleven members originally appointed to the board of the Lower Manhattan Development Corporation, created by the Governor to direct the rebuilding process after September 11, only one member was an African American and none was Hispanic or Asian.

According to Browning, Marshall, and Tabb's classification system, minorities remain weakly incorporated in New York City politics, though doubtless in a stronger position than in 1994, because they now hold one citywide office and three of the five (relatively weak) borough presidencies. On the crucial question of participation in the mayor's electoral and governing coalition, however, they remain on the outside. In contrast to Mayor Giuliani, who seemed to go out of his way to snub minority officeholders, Mayor Bloomberg has met with most minority elected officials, particularly Freddy Ferrer, whose backers' tacit support for Bloomberg contributed to Mark Green's defeat. Bloomberg has, however, included relatively few blacks and Latinos among his deputy mayors and commissioners. With a severe budget crisis looming, the budget cuts he makes will define his administration.

Just as minority political leaders remain outside the mayoral circle of power, minority legislators exercise relatively little influence over the city's legislative bodies. Historically, the Board of Estimate was the city's key legislative body. The three citywide elected officials, the mayor, comptroller, and city council president, each cast two votes on this body, while the five borough presidents each cast one. Only two minority members served on the board between 1977 and 1991, when it was abolished: David Dinkins as Manhattan Borough President between 1985 and 1989 and mayor between 1989 and 1991, and Bronx Borough President Fernando Ferrer between 1987 and 1991. At their strongest, minorities thus cast only three of the board's 11 votes. Dinkins and Ferrer were wary of each other as well. Thus, neither constrained Mayor Koch, though each influenced decisions affecting his borough. Most of the time, the board had no minority members.

Minorities were also substantially underrepresented on the city council between 1977 and 1991. Overshadowed by the Board of Estimate, one former member called it "worse than a rubber stamp because it does not even leave an impression." At the beginning of this period, only five minority members served on a 43-member body. By 1989, when the board was abolished, only seven blacks and three Latinos held seats on a 35-member council (28.6 percent of the total), though blacks and Latinos then made up 42 percent of the voting-age citizen population and 46 percent of the 1989 Democratic mayoral primary electorate. Seven of the 10 were on the losing side of the 1986 factional fight in which Peter Vallone became the council speaker.

In 1989, in the wake of court rulings that declared the board's voting scheme unconstitutional, voters adopted a new city charter abolishing the board, enlarging the city council to 51 members, and giving it new powers. In 1991, the redistricting commission crafted substantially more majority-minority districts than in 1981. As a result, the 1991 election dramatically increased minority membership on the council to 41.2 percent (Macchiarola and Diaz 1993; Gartner 1993). Council Speaker Vallone nevertheless continued to direct the council's business through a centralized staff and punished council members who might challenge his policies. Black and Latino members did not constitute an independent voting bloc but, rather, shored up the speaker's leadership.

In naming a replacement for Speaker Vallone in early 2002, the Queens and Bronx county party leaders threw the support of the organization-backed council members from their boroughs behind a white council member from the Upper East Side, Gifford Miller, even though Miller's main competitor was a Latino incumbent from Brooklyn. The council members Miller appointed to head the most important committees, including finance, housing, land use, and oversight were white.

With the exception of Congressman Charles Rangel, the ranking Democrat on the House Ways and Means Committee, none of the city's minority legislators in Albany or Washington wields great influence within their legislative bodies. While minority members of the state assembly have an active caucus, a strong speaker also runs that body's affairs, and the black and Puerto Rican caucus does not often sway him. The city's minority legislators can and do extract rewards from the white leaders of their bodies, but they do not exert a strong and independent influence on the overall allocation of public benefits. Former Council Speaker Peter Vallone and Assembly Leader Sheldon Silver secured their co-operation with relatively low levels of patronage, contracts, and similar benefits. Neither had to rely on black and Latino votes to win election in their own districts, and neither had to worry that minority legislators would defect to a successful challenger for their position (in part because minority legislators are so deeply embedded in the machine political culture that produces these legislative leaders). As a result, minority elected officials still play subordinate roles in these bodies, generating a surprisingly low score on Browning, Marshall, and Tabb's index of political incorporation.

The quick roll-back of David Dinkins's initial victory also departs from Browning, Marshall, and Tabb's predicted path for New York. While Browning, Marshall, and Tabb conceded that the Reagan and Bush administrations threatened minority gains in their case study cities during the 1980s, none of the biracial coalitions that governed them experienced defeat. In New York, however, minority political breakthroughs have been defeated three times. In the latter 1970s, recession, fiscal crisis, and reductions of federal aid from the Reagan and Bush administrations prompted the Koch administration to undo the spending patterns of the Lindsay years (Brecher and Horton 1991). Similarly, the Giuliani administration, acting in response to the severe local recession of 1989 to 1991 and the Republican victory in the 1994 gubernatorial election, also reduced funding for programs serving minority communities. Though it is not yet clear what the Bloomberg administration will do, large city and state budget deficits for the 2002–2003 fiscal year make major budget reductions for social service programs almost inevitable.

New York is also anomalous in a third sense, because it does distribute public benefits to minority constituencies even though they have failed to forge a durable electoral majority. Browning, Marshall, and Tabb measure policy responsiveness through minority public employment, existence of a police complaint review board, minority appointments to commissions, and community development block grant funding for minority areas and contractors. On these indicators, minority beneficiaries do relatively well in New York City. Minority employees make up well over half the civil service, and even Mayors Giuliani and Bloomberg felt compelled to appoint significant numbers of blacks and Latinos to managerial positions. For example, 28 percent of Giuliani's first 32 appointments as commissioners were minority (though that number dropped over time), as were 32 percent of Bloomberg's first 43 senior appointments (Janison 2002). Almost all of these were in social services. Though aid to the individual poor drifted downward as a share of the city budget under Mayor Giuliani, mirroring the rest of the country, spending on social services and the education system, where many blacks and Latinos are employed, increased (Citizens Budget Commission 2001, 8–20).

When Mayor Giuliani opposed an independent civilian police complaint review board for the police department, the city council moved to establish one over his veto. The Koch and Giuliani administrations both opposed racial quotas and set-asides, but the Koch administration used community development funds, city capital funds, and other sources of creative financing to launch an ambitious $5.2 billion program to rehabilitate abandoned properties for use as subsidized housing.

Though the Giuliani administration reduced funding for this program, it continued to support it, as had the Dinkins administration.

Though it is hard to derive exactly analogous measurements to those used by Browning, Marshall, and Tabb, New York City would seem to compare favorably with the 10 California cities they studied. New York's minority public employment probably exceeds that of the median California city in that study (Browning, Marshall, and Tabb 1984, 172). Certainly, the Koch and Dinkins administrations appointed more minority managers than any California city, except for Oakland, though this figure fell under the Giuliani administration. The city has a vast array of social services aimed at minority communities, including use of the CDBG budget for housing development, and arguably spends more money on such functions than any other large city. Moreover, it adopted more public oversight regarding the police, despite Mayor Giuliani's opposition.

Browning, Marshall, and Tabb agree that external factors like federal regulations and demographic change may contribute to local policy responsiveness, and the Koch, Dinkins, and Giuliani administrations doubtless have had little choice but to hire minorities as welfare department case workers or traffic enforcement agents. (Many fewer succeeded in joining the uniformed services, especially the fire department, which remains 94 percent white.) Yet many city contracts continued to flow to community organizations run by and serving blacks and Latinos despite the weak, controlled, and divided nature of minority political incorporation in New York. These three anomalies prompt us to rethink the analysis presented in *Protest Is Not Enough*.

WHY NEW YORK IS AN ANOMALY: MACHINE POLITICS, THE DECAY OF WHITE REFORM, INTERETHNIC COMPETITION, AND CO-OPTATION

Three ways in which New York City differs from the 10 California cities that were studied suggest likely explanations for why its biracial impulse has been comparatively weak. First, New York City retains a strong "machine" political culture compared to the reformed political cultures of California cities (Shefter 1983). Machine politics has tended to slow the pace of minority empowerment across American cities. It certainly provides the main channel through which minority politicians have achieved upward mobility in New York City. A one-party system influenced by regular Democrats (black and Latino as well as white) deprives those who would construct an insurgent coalition of the organizational means by which to realize this end. Regular Democrats (black and Latino as well as white) also learned to use the programmatic tools invented in the Great Society to deter minority electoral challengers.

Second, the liberalism of the 1960s and 1970s has lost its political vitality and relevance in New York City. Its decay has multiple sources: white reformers and black insurgents were absorbed into New York's political establishment, demographic change undermined white leadership in the labor movement, and the Messinger and Green campaigns of 1997 and 2001 showed that white reformers were no longer acceptable to the minority political establishment as leaders of a biracial or multiethnic electoral coalition. (They nevertheless got the majority of the black and Hispanic vote.) As a result, minority political empowerment no longer clearly advances the political interests of white liberals in New York. To the contrary, minority advancement in the leadership of public employee and social service unions as well as many other civic and advocacy organizations has displaced white liberal leadership.

Finally, New York's African Americans and Latinos are more diverse and, therefore, potentially more politically divided and competitive than appears to be the case in the 10 California cities or, indeed, most other large American cities—save perhaps Los Angeles (Falcon 1988; Mollenkopf, Olson, and Ross 2001). Not only is each group divided between natives and immigrants (e.g., African Americans versus West Indians, Puerto Ricans versus Dominicans and South Americans), they all live in different neighborhoods across the five counties that make up New York City, and thus have different political centers of gravity. Uniting them is far more problematic than the rhetorical deployment of such terms of art as *people of color* might suggest. These groups all experience racial and ethnic disadvantage relative to whites, but they also experience substantial racial and ethnic differences among themselves.

Though political scientists usually classify New York as a reformed city, it still partakes deeply of an urban political culture characterized, to use Wolfinger's distinction, by machine politics if not by political machines (Wolfinger 1972). Regular county party organizations, which locals call "the machine" or "the regulars," exert a strong and persistent, if incomplete, hold on minority politics in New York's five boroughs. Though often reported to be in demise, these organizations remain quite vigorous compared to other parts of the country (Mayhew 1986).

These organizations are certainly not as strong as they once were. Fewer of the city's assembly districts have regular political clubs, these clubs have fewer members, and they are less active than in the 1950s (Ware 1985; Peel 1935; Adler and Blank 1975). Moreover, the county party organizations in Queens, the Bronx, and Brooklyn were rocked by political scandal during the mid-1980s, when the Queens county leader committed suicide, the Bronx leader went to jail, and the former Brooklyn leader was also convicted of a felony (Newfield and Barrett 1989).

At the same time, the county party organizations still hold important powers today and have rebounded from their low point in the late 1980s. For lesser offices, such as the city council and assembly seats, they continue to exercise a great deal of control over which candidates get on the ballot and are likely to be elected, and county party leaders also determine who will serve as judges in the New York Supreme Court and who gets hired as court personnel. Most members of the city council and state assembly are allied with the regular Democratic county party organizations. Legislative staff, funded by the state, often perform campaign and constituency service activities formerly done by political clubs (Gerson 1990). Some clubs, such as Thomas Jefferson Democratic Club in Canarsie, remain effective campaign organizations. In the 2001 city council primary, four of the five candidates endorsed by the Bronx County organization won, as did four of six backed by the Brooklyn organization and nine of 13 backed by the county leader in Queens. From their position on the city's periphery, the regular Democratic organizations thus exercise considerable influence over the city and state's decision-making centers and constrain Manhattan-based reformers.

The persistence of these regular county party organizations is particularly important. Many readers may not know that most New Yorkers, including its largest and fastest-growing minority communities, live outside Manhattan. The Brooklyn, Queens, and Bronx regular Democratic organizations have coped with racial and ethnic transition by promoting the careers of loyal minority politicians and absorbing minority insurgents. The former Bronx County leader was Roberto Ramirez, who was recently succeeded by state Assemblyman Jose Rivera, while Herman D. Farrell and Clarence Norman, both African-American assemblymen, lead the New York and Kings County party organizations. (Former congressman Tom Manton, an Irish American, heads the Queens organization.) In the 1985 and 1989 Democratic mayoral primaries, black and Latino machine politicians helped Mayor Koch to win more votes in their assembly districts against his black challengers than he got in similar districts represented by minority reformers. Minority regulars have also defeated—or at least made life extremely difficult for—insurgent minority opponents. Although Manhattan's county Democratic organization is considered to be "reformed," that borough's black elected officials continue to exhibit the "regular" traits skillfully deployed by J. Raymond Jones, the "Harlem Fox" (Walter 1989). Through these means, white mayors have often commanded substantial support in black and Latino districts.

These regular Democratic leaders (black and Latino as well as white) have learned to use tools initially developed to foster minority political incorporation instead to retard and absorb minority insurgents (Mollenkopf, 1985). They use appointments to community boards and city jobs as well as budget allocations to reward supporters and undermine challengers. While Mayor Koch reduced spending on public assistance, he appointed friendly blacks and Latinos to senior positions and initiated contracts with community organizations to consolidate his electoral base. This pattern continued under Mayor Giuliani, who deployed them even more effectively, because he was willing to cut off unco-operative groups. Even where community organizations win contracts "on the merits," they need political sponsors to protect them and know that mounting an overt challenge to a sitting mayor could cost them their funds.

It is worth noting that white regular Democrats in New York take a more "liberal" route to achieving influence over minority political mobilization than similar politicians in other eastern cities (e.g., Frank Rizzo of Philadelphia). While Jonathan Rieder's analysis of Canarsie in the 1970s accurately described Italian American and Jewish unease over racial change and school integration, he does not give sufficient weight to the ways in which the Thomas Jefferson Democratic Club, one of the city's premier regular Democratic clubs, worked against the school boycott, supported liberal Democrats for state and national office, and produced leaders like former Assembly Speaker Stanley Fink and the late Assemblyman Tony Genovese, who strongly supported social spending measures (Rieder 1985). Today, Canarsie is an increasingly West Indian neighborhood.

In some ways, New York resembles the South before the rise of the Republican party: it is a one-party Democratic system characterized by factionalism and a politics of personalism and invidious distinction (Key 1949, ch. 14). Browning,

Marshall, and Tabb's 10 California cities all had Republican mayors in the late 1950s, as did Los Angeles. White Democrats had an incentive to mobilize politically excluded minority groups so that they could challenge and defeat these mayors. In New York, the *ancien régime* was dominated by Democrats—albeit regular Democrats—not by Republicans. White liberals did not find the Democratic party a suitable vehicle with which to challenge the (regular Democratic) establishment. Instead, they formed reform Democratic clubs to contest for power in assembly districts where potential supporters lived, such as Greenwich Village, the Upper East Side, and brownstone Brooklyn. In the past, the Republican party provided the institutional basis for organizing a multiethnic challenge to entrenched white ethnic Democrats, as exemplified by the LaGuardia and Lindsay eras. By the 1980s, however, the Republicans had forsaken this role. As black and Latino regulars rose to prominence in the Democratic county party organizations, these bodies became even less suitable launching pads for white reformers. The tension between Freddy Ferrer, a product of the Bronx machine, and Mark Green, a former Naderite, consumer advocate, and Manhattan-based reformer, provides just one case in point.

The extrapartisan bases of organization for New York's white reformers and progressives have also atrophied. In the past, white reformers could occasionally exceed the influence of white regulars in citywide election campaigns. Even today, white reform candidates regularly win elections in Manhattan's Upper West Side and brownstone Brooklyn. The fervor of the civil rights movement and opposition to the Vietnam war, which prompted well-educated white baby-boomers to embrace a "the movement" has faded however. The resolution of old causes, the rise of racial identity politics, and the national and local cycles of fiscal retrenchment and political conservatism have rendered movement liberalism far less fashionable among whites.

As movement liberalism waned among whites, the incumbent establishment absorbed many of its proponents. White reformers elected to assembly and city council seats slowly melded into the regular hierarchy, while the young innovators of the Lindsay era aged and became cynical—though often still influential—during the Koch and Dinkins years. Challenging and seeking to overturn the political establishment no longer serves the career advancement goals of white baby-boomers, the youngest of whom are now in their late 30s. Periodically, a candidacy such as that of David Dinkins in 1989 and 1993, Ruth Messinger in 1997, or Mark Green in 2001, has reinvigorated parts of this constituency, but their electoral and political failures have been demoralizing. Nothing could be more emblematic of the decay of white liberalism than the lack of enthusiasm for Mark Green in the Upper West Side, Greenwich Village, and Park Slope, Brooklyn, in the 2001 election, where Republican Mike Bloomberg got 38 to 41 percent of the vote—in contrast to the 11 to 12 percent George W. Bush, Jr., got in the 2000 presidential election. These areas should have been Green's natural base.

Racial succession and competition, economic restructuring, and a conservative shift also squeezed the "old left" liberalism of unionized, blue-collar, and lower-middle-class Jewish constituencies that once so strongly characterized New York City's political culture. As Shefter has shown, this process began in the 1950s with the destruction of the American Labor Party as the price the Jewish left had to pay to join the Democratic establishment (Shefter 1986). In the 1960s, neighborhood change and competition over public jobs pushed the Jewish and Italian lower-middle-class further right (Rieder 1985). By the 1980s, generational aging and racial and ethnic succession had largely pushed whites out of the leadership of the trade unions and other organizations that had nurtured the old left. (Indeed, the current leaders of municipal and social service unions, many of whom belong to an aging generation of African Americans from the civil rights era, are themselves being challenged by their increasingly first- and second-generation immigrant membership.)

It vastly oversimplifies matters to say that New York City politics became conservative when the black and Puerto Rican bid for political power led Jews to abandon their alliance with minorities and find common cause with white Catholics, but this dictum contains an important element of truth. This shift was tempered by the commitment of regular Democrats to favor public service providers (e.g., public employee unions) and public service recipients. A substantial cadre of white, often Jewish social service professionals continue to bond with their minority leaders and coworkers. (Thus, the Jewish president of a teamsters local representing public employees supported Jesse Jackson's 1988 campaign in New York, while the Jewish former head of the local teachers union is married to a black man.) Most white ethnic voters, including Jewish voters, however, have defected in recent elections from the Democratic nominees (black in 1989 and 1991, white in 1997 and 2001) to support white Republicans. (In Forest Hills, Queens, for example, Mike Bloomberg got 58 percent of the vote in 2001, while George Bush got only 21 percent in 2000. Similarly, Bloomberg got 75 percent in Bensonhurst, compared to Bush's 37 percent.)

It also cannot be taken for granted that blacks and Latinos will find common political cause as "people of color." When they are after the same turf, as sometimes happens, black and Latino political leaders compete directly with each other. Moreover, the political cultures, racial identities, and class positions of their electoral constituencies differ significantly (Falcon 1988). The post-1965 wave of immigration has made interethnic relations among New York City's minority populations even more complex. West Indians and Dominicans are asserting political interests distinct from—and in some instances directly against—native-born African Americans and Puerto Ricans, such as when Jamaican-born Councilwoman Una Clarke challenged incumbent Democratic House member Major Owens in the 2000 Democratic primary, or when newly elected Queens Councilman Hiram Monserrate, a Puerto Rican, was tapped by the Queens County Democratic organization to run in a largely South American district. While Browning, Marshall, and Tabb note that tensions existed between blacks and Chicanos in the 10 California cities, they concluded that black incorporation strengthened Latino incorporation. Such a generalization would be far harder to sustain in New York, although the Bronx County Democratic organization has succeeded in balancing tickets of Puerto Ricans and blacks.

Generally, when voters in mixed-minority districts are faced with a contest between black and Latino candidates, each group favors its own candidate. Blacks and Latinos have had great difficulty coalescing around common mayoral candidates. In 1985, black elected officials belonging to the Coalition for a Just New York refused to support Herman Badillo in a challenge to Mayor Koch, because Badillo had not withdrawn from the 1977 primary in favor of Percy Sutton's mayoral candidacy. Instead, they ran a weak black candidate. In 1989, Latinos strongly supported David Dinkins's candidacy, but Puerto Rican leaders did not always feel that they got their "fair share" from the Dinkins administration. In 2001, many black leaders rallied to Fernando Ferrer, but many others, including former Mayor Dinkins, did not.

Political fragmentation among Latinos exacerbates this problem. Most Puerto Rican New Yorkers feel that blacks and Latinos are equally discriminated against, and should work together. However, many also feel that Puerto Rican elected officials are "more interested in their own careers than in serving the community" (Velazquez 1988, 11). Nine out of ten Latinos identified racially as white or "other" in the 2000 U.S. Census, not as black. Because most Latinos are Catholic and more describe themselves as conservatives than in any other ethnic group, Latinos are potentially open to appeals from white Catholic politicians, making the road to an effective black-Latino alliance something of a minefield.

Blacks and Latinos are heterogeneous categories, divided by ancestry and nativity. Native-stock African Americans and Puerto Ricans are now migrating out of New York City, and their populations are declining. Overall growth in the black and Latino population is driven by immigration from the West Indies, Haiti, the Dominican Republic, Mexico, and Central America and by the coming of age of the children of these immigrants. The native stock black population has dropped, and the immigrant black population has grown. Meanwhile, the non–Puerto Rican Latino population surged, and the Latino population has outdistanced the non-Latino black population.

As New York has become less white, it has not become more black in the manner of Detroit or Atlanta. Instead, it has become more diverse. For all these reasons, minority interethnic tensions have become more complex. Native-born African Americans and Puerto Rican political elites have generally not sought to mobilize and incorporate the new groups, leaving them to generate their own leadership—often in competition with sitting black and Puerto Rican officials. Two Jamaican-born and one Dominican-born member joined the city council after 1991, and in 2001, the first Chinese American was elected. While immigrant leaders largely supported David Dinkins in 1989 and 1991, their latent competition with native minority political elites provide fertile territory for those who would split immigrant minority voters from African-American or Puerto Rican candidates.

The persistence of machine politics, the decline of movement liberalism and of the labor left among whites, the division among minorities, and the absence of mechanisms promoting dialogue and co-operation among potential members of a biracial insurgent coalition all reinforce each other. Many of the other large "gateway" cities, like Los Angeles, have similar tensions (Mollenkopf, Olson, and Ross 2001). In the 10 California cities, these groups were all political outsiders, as was the Democratic party, at the beginning of the period examined by Browning, Marshall, and Tabb. They shared a political incentive to coalesce, and the Democratic Party had an organizational interest in helping them to do so. Neither the Democratic Party nor any other institutional mechanism serves this purpose in New York. Instead, New York City's political system plays on division. In this setting, it is less surprising that minority empowerment is weak than that it happened at all.

HOW NEW YORK ELECTED A BLACK MAYOR, AND WHY HE WAS DEFEATED

Mayor Harold Washington's victory in Chicago in 1983 prefigured and inspired the 1989 campaign to elect David Dinkins as mayor of New York. The Washington victory was preceded by racial polarization, the alienation of black leadership from the Cook County Democratic organization, a consensus-based candidate recruitment process, an upsurge in minority turnout (in which Latinos joined black voters), and a division among regular Democrats. Many of these same conditions also developed in New York City during the latter part of the 1980s.

According to Barker (1983), Chicago's black leaders undertook a survey that unearthed the names of 90 people as possible mayoral candidates. Twenty of these were submitted to a meeting attended by a thousand grass roots leaders, and these leaders overwhelmingly endorsed Harold Washington, producing a wave of grass roots mobilization. Registration increased by 29.5 percent in black wards, which then turned out at 73 percent or higher, giving Washington 73 percent of the black vote in the primary and 97 percent in the general election (Preston 1983; Kleppner 1985, 149). Washington also won half the Latino votes in the general election, even though he received only 20 percent in the primary. According to Peterson (1983), blacks used political resources gradually accumulated within the Cook County regular Democratic party organization to capitalize on a division among white regulars.

For most of the 1970s and 1980s, New York City offered a sharp contrast to these conditions. In 1985, the closed-door deliberations of the Coalition for a Just New York yielded a weak black candidate in preference to a liberal white woman and a potential Puerto Rican candidate. This black candidate got just 41 percent of a low black primary vote, even though the 1984 Jesse Jackson presidential race had produced a surge in black voter registration. He also received only 12 percent of the Latino vote, while Mayor Koch got 70 percent. Many black and Latino regular Democrats continued to support Koch. New York's black leaders did not coalesce around a mayoral candidate who could even mobilize black voters, much less build the necessary ethnic alliances.

This started to change in 1988, when Jesse Jackson won a plurality of New York City's votes in the Democratic presidential primary and showed that a black candidate might be able to win a Democratic mayoral primary in 1989. His 1984 campaign had mobilized blacks, but not Latinos. His 1988 campaign maintained a high level of black mobilization and also won 61 percent of the Latino vote and 15 percent of the white vote, producing a 43.5 percent plurality in the city. This included 9 percent of the Jewish vote—despite Mayor Koch's assertion that Jews would have to be crazy to vote for Jackson (*New York Times* 1988).

While Washington's 1983 and 1985 victories in Chicago and Jackson's 1988 victory in New York inspired Mayor Koch's black, white, and Latino opponents, other circumstances also facilitated Dinkins's victory. A corruption scandal in 1986 and 1987 led to the suicide of one borough president, the conviction of another, and the resignation of three of Mayor Koch's commissioners as well as numerous other senior appointees, all of whom were closely tied to the mayor. As a result, his approval rating plummeted, opening the way for three well-known, well-financed candidates to challenge him in the 1989 primary.

Dinkins had played a leading role in the 1988 Jackson campaign, uniting the previously divided black leadership and winning over many Latinos and white liberals. Public and social service trade unions, which had an increasingly black membership and leadership, provided a strong base both for the Jackson and the Dinkins campaigns, and white reform political clubs joined in. Having gotten his political start in Harlem clubhouse politics, Dinkins had drawn broad support from whites in his 1985 race for the Manhattan borough presidency and had used this office to criticize the policies of the Koch administration. The scandal-bred weakening of the county party organizations freed regular Democratic black leaders from Brooklyn, the Bronx, and Queens to back Dinkins in 1989. Jackson's ability to gain greater support among Latino voters in 1988 set the stage for greater black-Latino cooperation.

Finally, a series of polarizing events reawakened concern over race relations in 1988 and 1989. A fatal mob attack on three blacks in Howard Beach, a "wilding" assault by black teenagers on a white woman who was jogging in Central Park, and the murder of a black in the conservative Italian neighborhood of Bensonhurst sharply worsened racial tensions in the months leading up to the 1989 mayoral primary. Combined with frequent pronouncements from Mayor Koch that many observers thought were insensitive and racially polarizing, these events increased black and Latino dissatisfaction with the mayor, and they convinced many white voters to consider other options.

In the 1989 primary, Dinkins received virtually unanimous support from black voters, about half the liberal whites, and a substantial minority of Latinos, thus winning a majority of the primary votes and defeating Mayor Koch and two other white candidates. By maintaining his position with blacks and white liberals, increasing his Latino support, and retaining a quarter of the white Catholic and Jewish Democratic vote, he then narrowly beat Rudolph W. Giuliani, a Republican former prosecutor, in the general election (Arian, Goldberg, Mollenkopf, and Rogowsky 1991).

Crucial to these victories was the unity and mobilization of the black electorate, mirrored in virtually unanimous support from black elected officials. The promise of electing the city's first African-American mayor yielded major black turnout gains in the primary and general elections, enabling blacks to cast 34 percent of the Democratic vote, its largest ethnic component. It was crucial to the final victory that half the white liberals and a quarter of the white ethnic Democrats reported voting for a black nominee (Arian, Goldberg, Mollenkopf, and Rogowsky 1991; Mollenkopf 1994).

Dinkins did not convert his electoral triumph into a durable governing coalition, however. New York City experienced a severe recession between 1989 and 1992 that put great stress on the city's budget, leading Dinkins to reduce the growth rate of spending, increase taxes, and hold the line on rewarding various supportive constituencies. While Dinkins managed his fiscal difficulties without the Financial Control Board taking over—itself an accomplishment—he could not reward the public employee unions and social service providers at the level they had wanted. An upward spike in violent crime associated with the crack epidemic of the late 1980s also raised the salience of that issue. Dinkins responded by using much of his political capital to fund an increase in the number of police officers and to begin a crack down on street hustlers. In effect, the budget increases he did manage were flowing to communities that had not supported him.

Dinkins also faced the continuation of racially polarizing events that had worked in his favor in the 1989 mayoral election, but that led to subsequent disappointment among whites when they perceived him to have failed to bring them under control. In 1991, the largely black Crown Heights community erupted in a riot when an auto in the entourage of the Lubavitcher Hassidic Rebbe struck and killed a black child. A black person in the crowd stabbed a rabbinical student, who later died in Kings County Hospital when his wound was not properly diagnosed. In 1992, Hispanic Washington Heights nearly erupted in violence over the death of a Dominican man at the hands of the police. Police officers were dismayed when Dinkins showed concern for the man's family; police believed him to be a drug dealer. Dinkins also failed to halt a long-running boycott of a Korean merchant in Flatbush by black nationalists working on behalf of a Haitian woman who was treated roughly by its owner. Dinkins's expansion of the city's police force did not quell doubts among white ethnic voters about his ability to maintain racial harmony in the city.

On November 2, 1993, David Dinkins narrowly lost his rematch with Rudolph Giuliani and became the nation's first breakthrough black mayor to lose office after only one term. More than half of the margin of change since 1989 came from middle-class white Catholic and Jewish election districts (Mollenkopf 1994). They not only gave Dinkins less support, they turned out in increased numbers, particularly in Staten Island, where many voters went to the polls to support a referendum on secession from New York City.

Though increased mobilization by white ethnic voters was enough to put Giuliani over the top, black voters also turned out in lower numbers, though their level of support for Dinkins remained high. Latinos turned out in lower numbers and were somewhat less likely to support Dinkins, while white liberals continued to turn out in high numbers but also drifted away from Dinkins. Electoral demobilization was more pronounced among Latinos than among any other group; exit poll data suggest they were disappointed that Mayor Dinkins did not do more to foster Latino advancement and address the extreme problems facing their community.

In short, the factors that enabled a biracial coalition to elect an African-American mayor in New York City proved to be short-lived. Underlying conditions began to reassert themselves. Regular Democrats showed a surprising ability to restore their organizations in the wake of earlier scandals, and a number of white ethnic Democratic political clubs endorsed and campaigned for Giuliani in 1993 and 1997. Most white regular Democratic officials did endorse Dinkins, but they could not, or at any rate did not, deliver their constituencies for him. Dinkins's management of the Crown Heights riot and the Korean store boycott did not improve his support among white liberals. Finally, despite Dinkins's strong record on Latino appointments, black-Latino political relations also frayed, especially with regard to the City Council redistricting, where some Latinos charged that the mayor's appointees on the districting commission had favored blacks over Latinos in constructing minority districts.

THE FAILURE OF LIBERAL BIRACIAL POLITICS IN 2001

At the beginning of the 2001 election cycle in New York City, conditions appeared highly favorable for the renewal of a liberal, biracial political coalition in mayoral politics. A term-limits referendum first enacted in 1993 came into force in 2001, creating 38 open seats on the 51-member city council and four open seats among the five borough presidencies as well as requiring the three citywide office holders—Mayor Rudolph Giuliani, Comptroller Alan Hevesi, and Public Advocate Mark Green—to depart from their offices. Though Mayor Giuliani's popularity had obviously grown between his first and second mayoral race, his standing had fallen as a result of police community relations controversies, his autocratic style, and his shoddy treatment of his wife, from whom he separated. Giuliani also left no obvious heir apparent in the Republican party. Early in 2001, therefore, it seemed inevitable that a Democrat would return to the west wing of city hall.

Four well-known candidates entered the race on the Democratic side: Bronx Borough President Fernando Ferrer, Public Advocate Mark Green, Comptroller Alan Hevesi, and City Council Speaker Peter Vallone. Having switched his party registration in 2000 after determining that he could not win a Democratic primary, financial news service billionaire Michael Bloomberg spent the first 6 months of 2001 developing a campaign for the Republican nomination, formally announcing his candidacy in June. Another former Democrat, Herman Badillo, who was the first Puerto Rican elected to Congress but who had become a close advisor to the Giuliani administration, also mounted a contest for the Republican nomination. For much of 2001, most observers gave Bloomberg little chance to win, because of his complete lack of political experience and various stumbles on the campaign trail, and Badillo no chance at all, given Bloomberg's overwhelming financial resources and the party's largely white ethnic base.

The main political question thus seemed to be which Democrat would win the primary. Each candidate represented an important constituency within the party. Borough President Ferrer had become the city's leading Puerto Rican politician, and the Latino vote was a slowly but steadily growing factor in the Democratic electorate as the Latino population grew to exceed the city's black population. (Because of their relative youth, lack of citizenship, and low socioeconomic status, the ratio of actual voters to total population has consistently been lower for Latinos than for whites or blacks in New York City.) Ferrer had played a significant role in rebuilding the Bronx after its devastation in the 1960s and 1970s, but he was also a central cog in the Bronx machine. The Bronx also generally casts far fewer votes than Brooklyn, Queens, or Manhattan.

Mark Green had formerly worked as a public interest lawyer for Ralph Nader, was the consumer affairs commissioner in the Dinkins administration, and had twice been elected public advocate, a citywide office designated in the 1989 charter as a kind of in-house critic and ombudsman. Charismatic, smart, and articulate, Green also had a reputation as an egotist, outsider, and in the words of one *Daily News* columnist, a "liberal bomb-thrower" and persistent critic of the police (Kramer 2001). Though he lived on the Upper East Side and was an exemplar of the white professional reform political thrust in New York City, he also had substantial support in black neighborhoods, where he campaigned relentlessly (especially in black churches).

Controller Hevesi and Speaker Vallone represented the Democrats' white ethnic vote, with their respective bases in its outer borough Jewish and white Catholic populations. Both were considered to be somewhat less liberal than Ferrer or Green, and both arguably had deeper and stronger credentials in running the city. Hevesi had a doctorate in political science, had taught at Queens College, and had been a long-time member of the state assembly before becoming comptroller. He had extensive support from the city's business leaders, the teacher's union, and the Liberal Party. Vallone, on the other hand, had become a partner in governance with Mayor Giuliani, mainly supporting him but also departing from Giuliani's agenda at a few critical junctures, including establishment of a civilian complaint review board for the police and a living-wage bill for city contractors. Vallone stressed a neo–New Deal, lunch-bucket style of liberalism at the same time he attended mass every day and expressed personal reservations about abortion. Vallone was supported by the city employees union, District Council 37.

Between June and September 10, the day before the Democratic primary was scheduled to take place, Mark Green consistently ran ahead of the other candidates in polls of likely Democratic voters owing to strong support from white liberals (many of whom come from Jewish backgrounds) and blacks. Neither Hevesi, despite substantial spending on television commercials and support from Queens County Democratic leader Tom Manton, nor Vallone seemed able to coalesce sufficient support to block Green from the nomination. As Hevesi's campaign failed to catch on, some of his supporters apparently drifted toward Vallone.

Freddy Ferrer and his advisors made a strong effort to forge a black-Latino coalition on behalf of "the other New Yorkers," who had not shared in the city's prosperity during the 1990s. Ferrer's initial base was predicated on solid support from Latino (largely Puerto Rican) and black voters in the Bronx. His cause received an initial boost during the summer, when most of Harlem's political establishment, including Congressman Charles Rangel, State Controller Carl McCall, and former Borough President Percy Sutton, but excluding former mayor Dinkins, endorsed Ferrer. (Ferrer's campaign manager, Bill Lynch, had managed Dinkins's two campaigns, served as his deputy mayor, and was a vice-president of the Democratic National Committee. Dinkins, however, endorsed Green.) Ferrer also received the support of the two leading Dominican politicians from northern Manhattan, Councillor Guillermo Lineres and Assemblyman Adriano Espaillat. After receiving bad publicity in May, when he said he would endorse Ferrer only if Ferrer supported black candidates for Bronx borough president and comptroller, Reverend Al Sharpton ultimately endorsed Ferrer in late August, after having served jail time for a protest on the island of Vieques, Puerto Rico, with three Ferrer intimates—Bronx County Leader Roberto Ramirez, Bronx Borough President candidate Adolpho Carrion, Jr., and Assemblyman Jose Rivera—and after having been courted by Rangel and other Harlem elected officials. As the ranks of black leaders closed around Ferrer, his standing in the opinion polls steadily rose—and Green's dipped—as a significant share of black voters shifted to Ferrer while a smaller number of whites, fearing that their favored candidates would not win, shifted to Green. As it became clear that Ferrer had a good chance to win the nomination, Local 1199—the politically potent hospital workers union led by Dennis Rivera—also threw its support and political operation behind Ferrer. The *New York Times* endorsed Green. Polls taken on the eve of the election showed Green and Ferrer in a statistical tie, with Green slightly ahead.

Tuesday, September 11th, will be a day remembered by all New Yorkers and much of the rest of the world—but not for the outcome of the Democratic primary, which was suspended in the morning after the devastating attacks on the World Trade Center brought down the buildings, killed 2,800 people, caused downtown inhabitants to flee on foot, covered lower Manhattan and Brooklyn in ash, and sent the city into shock. The primary was postponed to September 25th, with a runoff on October 11th. If the devastation and shock of the attack were not enough to divert attention from politics during this period, the Yankees were also in the World Series.

The two weeks after September 11th, Ferrer continued to be robust in the polls, and on September 25th, a surprisingly large number of Democrats (some 780,000) turned out, giving 35.8 percent of their votes to Ferrer, 31.1 percent to Green, 19.9 percent to Vallone, and 12.2 percent to Hevesi. Voting turnout relative to past experience was particularly high in Latino areas of the city, which approached the city-wide average instead of being at the bottom.

The next two weeks also proved politically tumultuous. Because Ferrer had eroded Green's support among blacks, Green sought support among the largely white, relatively conservative voters who had favored Hevesi (who endorsed Green) and Vallone (who endorsed Ferrer). He strongly criticized Ferrer as lacking a sensible plan to rebuild lower Manhattan and to help the city recover—as well as for making racial appeals. However, he was also perceived as caving in to Mayor Giuliani's demand that he be allowed to remain in office for an additional three months. Ferrer would not agree to this and persisted with building a black-Latino alliance. Some 790,000 people voted in the runoff, giving Green a bare 51 percent of the vote.

In the wake of the runoff, Ferrer supporters were bitter that Green had thwarted the city from electing its first Puerto Rican and Latino mayor. Compounding this feeling were actions by some Green supporters in Brooklyn, who had distributed an unflattering cartoon from the New York *Post* showing Ferrer kissing the behind of a bloated Al Sharpton and who had made automated telephone calls to Jewish voters shrilly stating that voting for Ferrer would put Al Sharpton in city hall. The Green campaign also ran a highly negative television spot about Ferrer on the evening before the election. Some Ferrer supporters, particularly Bronx County party leader Roberto Ramirez and campaign manager Bill Lynch, felt these appeals were racist and insisted that the Green campaign apologize and fire any staff members involved—demands which the Green campaign did not feel inclined to meet.

Between the runoff election on October 11th and the general election three weeks later, as the Yankees played their way into a seventh game of the World Series, the Green campaign was plagued with difficulty in developing a united front with Ferrer supporters, while the Bloomberg campaign inundated virtually every possible channel of communication to voters with extremely well-crafted campaign messages. Mayor Giuliani, now a national hero, endorsed Bloomberg on the eve of the general election, and campaign strategist David Garth and his associates flooded the airwaves with an excellent commercial featuring Mayor Giuliani. The Bloomberg campaign's polling budget in the month before the election alone was half the amount spent by Green on his entire campaign. Increasingly desperate, the Green campaign mounted a shrill, negative attack on Bloomberg.

In the end, 1,511,986 voters cast ballots on November 7th, giving Bloomberg 744,757 votes to Green's 709,268. Just as in 1989 and 1993, the mayoral election was extremely close and racially polarized, though a few more whites voted for the candidate favored by blacks (Green), and a few more blacks supported the candidate favored by whites (Bloomberg) than those races. Overall, the Latino vote split roughly in half, though Puerto Ricans (including those living in the Bronx) favored Green while the South Americans living in Queens favored Bloomberg. If just 18,000 voters had shifted, Green would have won the election. Green ended up with only half the vote in the districts he had won in the primary—and only a quarter of the votes in districts won by Vallone. The correlation between his vote in the runoff against Ferrer and the general election vote for Bloomberg was .617. While low turnout in the Bronx hurt Green's chances and he did not win as many votes as white Democrats normally get in black neighborhoods, it was clearly the defection of the white middle-class Democrats to Bloomberg that cost Green the election. Once again, the coalition between white liberals, blacks, and Latinos failed to win a critical election. Indeed, that coalition lay in ruins. Mike Bloomberg's judgment that the best way for a moderate white Democrat to win the mayoralty was to run as a Republican while the Democrats threw themselves on the swords of racial and ethnic differences proved to be shrewd indeed.

LESSONS FOR THE THEORY AND PRACTICE OF BIRACIAL COALITION FORMATION

The New York City experience differs sharply from those of the relatively small California cities studied by Browning, Marshall, and Tabb as well as those of other cities where a permanent shift from white to minority empowerment has taken place, such as Atlanta or Detroit. It is more akin to that of Chicago or Los Angeles, which also elected African-American mayors only to see whites succeed them and new kinds of racial and ethnic cross-currents complicate the task of constructing a multiethnic liberal coalition. The New York experience suggests the need to revise and extend Browning, Marshall, and Tabb's theoretical approach (1984, 1990, 1994) in two basic directions.

First, we need to understand that the process of racial and ethnic succession in urban politics is often far more complex than the white-to-black trajectory that was the most common change in the California cities between 1960 and 1980. In the California cities, except for San Francisco, native-born blacks or native-born Latinos, typically Mexican Americans, were gaining ground, and in some cities one or both, in alliance with liberal whites, formed a new majority of the electorate. That experience and the continued growth of black and Latino populations seemed to signal a unidirectional shift from white control and minority exclusion to minority empowerment and inclusion and a more or less permanent rise to power of a liberal, biracial coalition in which one or another minority group held the leading position.

The case of New York City shows that while a city can become less white, it does not necessarily become more black, and that while a biracial coalition may come to power, it may not be able to consolidate its position. Urban politics, at least outside the older cities of the South and the Midwest, is no longer a simple matter of black political leaders consolidating minority empowerment based on appeals to black solidarity. This type of racial succession has already taken place in most of the large central cities where it will ever happen. Even in these cities, white minorities can now influence competition between black factions, as has happened in Detroit, Cleveland, Philadelphia, Washington, D.C., and elsewhere.

Many other large cities, including New York, Los Angeles, San Francisco, Boston, San Diego, Houston, and Miami, will never develop black majorities in their electorates. Indeed, immigration is making the populations of these cities more diverse. Whites may remain the single largest (though declining) group within an increasingly complex constellation of constituencies, most of whom will not defer to black leadership of "people of color." If racial division continues to mark these cities and the racial divide comes to be defined as "black/non-black" instead of "white/non-white," the prospects for black-led biracial or multiethnic coalitions may actually worsen. In the future, therefore, forming a dominant political coalition will depend on who can construct broader and more complex coalitions than the relatively simple biracial ones found in the northern California cities.

The New York experience also shows real differences of interest among potential components of multiracial insurgent coalitions. Prominent elements of this coalition in New York, including white liberals, native-born blacks, and Puerto Ricans, are on the wane. Given present economic and demographic trends, the white, professional stratum of New York and other large central cities is not likely to grow dramatically, and it will remain well ensconced and typically without great incentive to risk challenging the political establishment. It shares a group interest with more conservative white ethnic voters in controlling crime and holding the line on taxes. Its preferences for city spending probably lean more toward cultural institutions and environmental protection than welfare programs. As long as the "new breed" of relatively conservative mayors like Giuliani and his counterparts, Daley of Chicago, Rendell of Philadelphia, and Riordan of Los Angeles, avoided being trapped into socially conservative positions on abortion or gay rights, they could appeal to white liberals and not push them toward a multiracial insurgent coalition.

Similarly, the native stock black population of New York has been declining relative to other groups. More than Latinos or Asians, blacks rely on public sector and publicly supported, non-profit sector jobs. They have achieved proportionate legislative representation and are overrepresented within the Democratic party electorate. As a result, newer minority ethnic groups often see blacks as occupying—and blocking—rungs on the ladder that they would like to climb. Caribbean immigrants and their children provide most of the growth in the black population. African Americans in safe seats have little incentive to bring these new voters into the electorate.

Puerto Ricans are in an even more disadvantaged position. Their numbers are also declining, and while Puerto Rican elected officials like to talk of representing Latino interests, the rapidly growing Dominican population is a potential threat to them. The breakthrough candidacy of Fernando Ferrer elicited widespread and vigorous support in Dominican and South American neighborhoods, but ethnic competition also emerged in a number of multiethnic Latino council districts where Puerto Ricans ultimately won office in 2001. In this context, white mayors in predominantly minority cities, such as Daley in Chicago, Rendell in Philadelphia, Riordan in Los Angeles, and likely Bloomberg in New York City, can find enough support among the political elites of waning minority groups, as well as among rising immigrant groups, to keep them from uniting in a multiracial challenge.

These factors make it difficult for a biracial, multiethnic coalition to win office, institutionalize its position, and prevent a subsequent rollback of its policies. New York joins Los Angeles, Chicago, and Philadelphia as predominantly non-white cities where the strong mobilization of white voters, often in conjunction with the demobilization or lack of cohesion among minority voters, has enabled relatively conservative white mayors to defeat minority candidates—or even white candidates favored by minorities. These victories were characterized by the ability of the white candidate to exploit differences among the potential members of a liberal, multiracial coalition. In this respect, Mike Bloomberg's full court press to win a substantial share of the Latino vote was a harbinger of things to come. On this score, he can take lessons from how Mayor Daley has played off latent tensions between blacks and Latinos in Chicago, or how Mayor Hahn played off tensions between blacks, whites, and Latinos to win in Los Angeles.

Second, New York's experience suggests that we must give more theoretical attention to ways in which the institutions of a city's political system shape the expression of group interests and allocate access and influence across groups. In particular, the persistence of machine politics in New York City has had a crucial impact on hindering the construction of a durable multiracial insurgent coalition. The elements of a would-be insurgent coalition need an organizational framework through which to build the trust and cooperation necessary to overcome their differences. Suffice it to say, white Manhattan and Brooklyn reformers are going to be reluctant to forge common cause with former Bronx County party leader Roberto Ramirez—and vice versa. Browning, Marshall, and Tabb's California cities had reformed, nonpartisan political systems in which the Democratic party, or extraparty organizations, could unite out-groups. The entrenched nature of the Democratic party makes this problematic in New York and other large, old, eastern cities.

Other organizations that might help to forge such coalitions, like public employee or social service unions, have also failed to perform this function. Though District Council 37 of the municipal employees or Local 1199 of the hospital workers represent all the different components of the potential liberal multiracial coalition, they have been thrown on the defensive by city and state fiscal problems, have been distracted by internal conflicts, and have been unwilling or unable to reach outside their ranks to give equal partnership to community organizations in forming a new liberal coalition (Mantsios 2001; Thompson 2001). They also have their own material interests. Despite its radical history, Local 1199 will support Republican Governor George Pataki against African-American Democratic challenger Carl McCall, because Pataki has pushed their legislative agenda in Albany. This aspect of New York City's political system explains much of the weakness of biracial coalition politics in New York and elsewhere. The failure of Villaraigosa's campaign in Los Angeles, despite heavy backing from the county labor council, also bears examination.

The news for urban liberalism is not all bad, however. Just as proponents of minority empowerment have not solved the problem of constructing a durable political majority, the white mayors who have won office in New York, Los Angeles, Chicago, Philadelphia, and other majority-minority cities have also been unable to fashion a coherent, majoritarian governing coalition. Jim Sleeper has suggested that these "Rainbow II" mayors could build such majorities by opposing racial preferences and liberal social policies and by favoring lower taxes, tougher union contracts, fighting crime, and reinventing local government (Sleeper 1993). In his view, this platform would attract votes from entrepreneurial Latinos, Asians, and other immigrants as well as from white ethnics, giving these mayors claim to an ethnically diverse base of support. In practice, however, electoral victories for white mayors in majority-minority cities remains predicated on united white support, divided minority opponents, and pliant municipal unions.

Just how the Koch-Giuliani-Bloomberg electoral coalition will fare over the next eight years in New York City is uncertain. Many of Mayor Bloomberg's policies will generate opposition, such as when budget cutbacks have a disproportionately negative impact on services to black and Latino communities. While Mayor Bloomberg shows every indication of understanding that it will be pivotal for him to retain a good relationship with municipal unions and Democrats left unhappy by the 2001 Democratic primary and runoff, he must also satisfy his white, ethnic, and Republican electoral base. His efforts to do so are likely to give minority elected officials, community groups, and at least some union activists good cause to search for a political alternative.

To prevent this from happening, Mayor Bloomberg and his kindred leaders in other cities must broaden their appeal, keep their opponents divided, and develop their own organizational base. Mayor Daley of Chicago can rely on the traditions of regular Democratic organizational rule to keep minority politicians in his orbit. Mayor Bloomberg lacks an equivalent base in the Republican party, but he may be able to forge relations with regular Democrats from the Bronx, Brooklyn, and Queens, just as his predecessor Mayor Koch did.

In sum, New York City presents a less optimistic picture about the future of biracial coalition politics, minority incorporation, and urban liberalism than Browning, Marshall, and Tabb offered us two decades ago, but if the goal of a more democratic, inclusive, and responsive city government has proven elusive in New York City, it is not impossible. As Theodore Lowi (1964) observed, the reform impulse has been a long-standing, creative force in the political development of New York and, by example, many other cities. New York teaches us that progress toward this goal will depend on whether highly diverse racial, ethnic, and geographic locations can find new ways to engage in political dialogue, define common purposes that enable them to transcend group differences, and co-operate in practical politics. The 2001 mayoral primary and general elections provided a negative lesson in how to do so. If key participants learn this lesson, they may be more successful in the future.

REFERENCES

Adler, Norman and Blanche Blank. 1975. *Political Clubs in New York.* New York: Praeger.

Arian, Asher, Arthur Goldberg, John Mollenkopf, and Edward Rogowsky. 1991. *Changing New York City Politics.* New York: Routledge.

Barker, Twiley. 1983. Political Mobilization of Black Chicago: Drafting a Candidate. *PS* XVI (Summer): 482–485.

Brecher, Charles, and Raymond Horton. 1991. The Public Sector. In John Mollenkopf and Manuel Castells, eds., *Dual City: Restructuring New York.* New York: The Russell Sage Foundation, pp. 103–128.

Brecher, Charles and Raymond Horton with Robert A. Cropf and Dean Michael Mead. 1993. *Power Failure: New York City Politics and Policy Since 1960.* New York: Oxford University Press.

Browning, Rufus P., Dale Rogers Marshall, and David H. Tabb. 1984. *Protest Is Not Enough.* Berkeley: University of California Press.

Browning, Rufus P., Dale Rogers Marshall, and David H. Tabb, eds. 1990. *Racial Politics in American Cities.* New York: Longman.

Browning, Rufus P., Dale Rogers Marshall, and David H. Tabb. 1994. Political Incorporation and Changing Perspectives on Urban Politics. Paper presented to the 1994 annual meeting of the American Political Science Association, New York City, September 1–4.

Citizens Budget Commission. 2000. Managing the Budget in the Bloomberg Administration. Background paper for the Citizens Budget Commission Conference on New York City's Changing Fiscal Outlook.

Falcon, Angelo. 1988. Black and Latino Politics in New York City: Race and Ethnicity in a Changing Urban Context. In F. Chris Garcia, ed., *Latinos in the Political System*, 171–194. North Bend, IN: Notre Dame University Press.

Gartner, Alan. 1993. Public Involvement in the Work of the New York City Districting Commission: An Insider's View. Paper presented to the annual meeting of the Western Political Science Association, San Francisco, April 10–12.

Gerson, Jeffrey. 1990. Building the Brooklyn Machine: Irish, Jewish, and Black Succession in Central Brooklyn, 1919–1964. PhD dissertation, Political Science Program, City University Graduate Center.

Gifford, Bernard R. 1978. New York City and Cosmopolitan Liberalism. *Political Science Quarterly* 93 (Winter): 559–584.

Goldberg, Arthur and Asher Arian. 1989. The American Urban Electorate in the 1988 Presidential Election. Paper presented to the annual meeting of the American Political Science Association, Atlanta, August 31–September 3.

Janison, Dan. 2002. On Diversity, Room to Grow: Bloomberg's Picks Mirror Giuliani's Earlier Cabinet. *Newsday*, January 13.

Katznelson, Ira. 1981. *City Trenches*. New York: Pantheon.

Key, V.O., Jr. 1949. *Southern Politics in State and Nation*. New York: Vintage.

Kimball, Penn. 1972. *The Disconnected*. New York: Columbia University Press.

Kleppner, Paul. 1985. *Chicago Divided: The Making of a Black Mayor*. DeKalb, Ill.: Northern Illinois University Press.

Kramer, Michael. 2001. Mayors Race Edges Toward the Big Two. *New York Daily News*, May 17.

Lowi, Theodore. 1964. *At the Pleasure of the Mayor: Patronage and Politics in New York City, 1896–1956*. New York: The Free Press.

Macchiarola, Frank J. and Joseph G. Diaz. 1993. Minority Political Empowerment in New York City: Beyond the Voting Rights Act. *Political Science Quarterly* 108(1): 37–57.

Mantsios, Gregory. 2001. Labor and Community: Ambiguous Legacy, Promising Future? In John Mollenkopf and Ken Emerson, eds., *Rethinking the Urban Agenda: Reinvigorating the Liberal Tradition in New York City and Urban America*. New York: The Century Foundation, pp. 75–92.

Mayhew, David. 1986. *Placing Parties in American Politics*. Princeton: Princeton University Press.

Mollenkopf, John. 1985. The Politics of Racial Advancement and the Failure of Urban Reform: The Case of New York City. Paper commissioned for a colloquium at the Center for the Study of Industrial Societies, University of Chicago, April 25.

Mollenkopf, John. 1993. *New York in the 1980s: A Social, Economic, and Political Atlas*. New York: Simon and Schuster Academic Reference Books.

Mollenkopf, John. 1994. *A Phoenix in the Ashes: The Rise and Fall of the Koch Coalition in New York City Politics*. Princeton, NJ: Princeton University Press.

Mollenkopf, John, David Olson, and Timothy Ross. 2001. Immigrant Political Participation in New York and Los Angeles. In Michael Jones Correa, ed., *Governing Urban America: Immigrants, Natives, and Urban Politics*. New York: Russell Sage Foundation, pp. 17–70.

Morris, Charles. 1980. *The Cost of Good Intentions*. New York: W. W. Norton.

New York Times. 1988. New York Times/CBS Exit Poll, Thursday, April 21, D25.

Newfield, Jack and Wayne Barrett. 1989. *City for Sale: Ed Koch and the Betrayal of New York*. New York: Harper and Row.

Pecorella, Robert F. 1994. *Community Power in a Postreform City: Politics in New York City.* Armonk, NY: M. E. Sharpe.

Peel, Roy V. 1935. *Political Clubs of New York City.* New York: Putnam.

Peterson, Paul. 1983. Washington's Election in Chicago: The Other Half of the Story. *PS* XVI (Fall): 712–716.

Preston, Michael. 1983. The Election of Harold Washington: Black Voting Patterns in the 1983 Chicago Mayoral Race. *PS* XVI (Summer): 486–488.

Rieder, Jonathan. 1985. *Canarsie: The Jews and Italians of Brooklyn Against Liberalism.* Cambridge: Harvard University Press.

Shefter, Martin. 1983. Regional Receptivity to Reform. *Political Science Quarterly* 98 (Fall): 459–483.

Shefter, Martin. 1985. *Political Crisis/Fiscal Crisis: The Collapse and Revival of New York City.* New York: Basic Books.

Shefter, Martin. 1986. Political Incorporation and the Extrusion of the Left: Party Politics and Social Forces in New York City. *Studies in American Political Development.* 1: 50–90.

Fred Siegel. 1997. *The Future Once Happened Here: New York, DC, LA and the Fate of America's Big Cities.* New York: Free Press.

Sleeper, Jim. 1993. The End of the Rainbow. *The New Republic,* November 1: 20–25.

Sonenshein, Raphael. 1993. *Politics in Black and White: Race and Power in Los Angeles.* Princeton: Princeton University Press.

Thompson, J. Phillip. 2001. One Step Forward, Two Steps Back: Liberalism, Race, and Local Democracy. In John Mollenkopf and Ken Emerson, eds., *Rethinking the Urban Agenda: Reinvigorating the Liberal Tradition in New York City and Urban America.* New York: The Century Foundation, pp. 187–206.

Velazquez, Nydia. 1988. Puerto Rican Voter Registration in New York City: A Comparison of Attitudes Between Registered and Non-registered Puerto Ricans. Migration Division, Department of Labor and Human Resources, Commonwealth of Puerto Rico.

Walter, John C. 1989. *The Harlem Fox: J. Raymond Jones and Tammany, 1920–1970.* Albany, NY: State University of New York Press.

Ware, Alan. 1985. *The Breakdown of Democratic Party Organization, 1940–1980.* New York: Oxford University Press.

Wolfinger, Raymond. 1972. Why Political Machines Have Not Withered Away and Other Revisionist Thoughts. *Journal of Politics* 34 (May): 365–398.

Yates, Douglas. 1973. *Neighborhood Democracy: The Politics and Impacts of Decentralization.* Lexington, Mass.: Lexington Books.

Chapter 5

Chicago Politics: Political Incorporation and Restoration

Dianne M. Pinderhughes

EDITORS' NOTE

Chicago was well known for many years as a traditional machine city led by Mayor Richard J. Daley. The two decades after his death in 1975 were marked by challenges to the machine and by racial polarization and conflict. Even though blacks constituted more than one-third of the population, they did not gain substantial political power. In 1983, Harold Washington became the first black mayor of Chicago and fought rather successfully to reform the machine and move the city toward progressive politics and policy.

Dianne Pinderhughes puts that story in a larger context, emphasizing Chicago's adaptation to constant changes in ethnic politics over the years. She shows that Chicago's black activists used demand-protest to increase electoral mobilization and formed coalitions of organizations to unify black groups and to cross racial lines with support from Latino voters in building a winning coalition. It was difficult to translate the electoral coalition into a governing coalition, however, and after Washington's untimely death, the conflicts within the coalition could no longer be resolved. Ironically, increases in the black population and black electoral success were followed by intragroup conflict and by less attention to the growing Latino population. However, whites, when they were defeated, unified their efforts in ways they had not been able to do when they were a larger proportion of the population. Unity among whites and competition among blacks led to the success in 1991 of a new, increasingly multiracial, stable electoral coalition led by Richard M. Daley—the first Mayor Daley's son. Pinderhughes suggests, however, that Harold Washington's administration has had a lasting impact on black politics in Chicago and on the new electoral coalition.

INTRODUCTION

For nearly two decades, Chicago politics was synonymous with volatile racial and ethnic conflict expressed in the political system. Richard J. Daley's last mayoral election in 1975 marked the beginning of that era, and the re-elections of his son, Richard M. Daley, from 1991 through 1999 suggest the re-establishment of a stable electoral coalition. In between, Harold Washington's mayoral elections in 1983 and 1987 marked the creation of a distinctive political alternative, which proved unstable and short-lived after his death. That dynamic era has clearly been succeeded by a new Daley era. Therefore, several questions arise that serve as the focus for this review of racial and ethnic politics in Chicago in the context of Browning, Marshall, and Tabb's conception of the role of racial and ethnic groups in politics. What lasting impact has the Washington coalition had on Chicago politics? Has Mayor Richard M. Daley created a stable electoral and bargaining structure so as to constitute a new Chicago political regime? Stone (1989, 61) describes regimes as "the informal arrangements by which public bodies and private interests function together in order to be able to make and carry out governing decisions." What roles do racial and ethnic groups play in contemporary Chicago politics now that all post-Washington insurgent candidacies have failed? Does the Daley administration incorporate blacks and Hispanics in decision-making and policy-making structures and processes and, if so, on what terms?

Browning, Marshall, and Tabb (1984, 1990, 1997) framed racial and ethnic group politics in terms of group mobilization, coalition formation, political incorporation, and responsiveness. The era opened with the black challenge for citywide control of the Democratic political organization. As Richard M. Daley's terms in office have lengthened, however, that conception of single-group leadership has been replaced by a more complex framework of governance. As the city's racial and ethnic composition has become more diverse, Daley and other elected leaders have been forced to share office and to concede ground. Whether this reflects substantive incorporation will be answered over the coming years; this chapter examines the current evidence.

Specifically, this chapter provides a demographic portrait of Chicago in light of early data from the 2000 U.S. Census, briefly summarizes the dramatic changes in electoral representation the city has undergone in the last three decades, and illustrates the political constraints and opportunities these changes have provided politicians and groups. The complex array of leadership coalitions offered and rejected by the voters as well as the fusion of demand protest and electoral mobilization and governing activities developed by black activists are reviewed. Harold Washington's administration and the incorporation of blacks and Hispanics into the city council and other governmental bodies during his years in office and after are also considered. Finally, the role of blacks and Latinos, in terms of positions and policy, in this new Daley era is examined.

CHICAGO'S RACIAL AND ETHNIC CONTENDERS[1]

I use the broader conceptual framework of the political participation model to discuss changes that occurred in Chicago during this era. The political participation model predicts a group's likelihood of winning political leadership in terms of external variables that arise from outside the group's behavior, such as the structure and organization of the electoral system, demographic factors, and internal variables that have developed from the group's own specific history (Pinderhughes 1987). Political structures in Chicago reflect that city's long-term racial and ethnic heterogeneity. Since the late nineteenth century, Chicago has had densely complex ethnic populations that increased until the immigration reforms of the 1920s closed the nation's borders. Immigration reform in 1965 reopened the borders and ended preferences for European immigrants, and Asians, South and Central Americans, and Africans as well as African-descent populations from the Caribbean began to settle in the city. Others, such as Puerto Ricans and Mexican Americans, also increased their numbers through long-term migratory patterns.

Demographic changes significantly shape Chicago's political environment, but in citywide politics, the largest groups are not necessarily the electoral victors. Poles were the largest white ethnic bloc, but Polish candidates were unsuccessful in mayoral primary contests against Mayor Richard J. Daley in 1963 and against Daley's successor, Michael Bilandic, in 1977. Another large group, African Americans, offered challengers in the primary elections of 1975 and 1977, also unsuccessfully. The Irish, one of the smaller white groups, dominated the mayor's office and the machine for much of the twentieth century. Mayor Richard M. Daley is setting the city's agenda for the twenty-first century.

At the ward level, the nature of Chicago's political life rapidly translates demography into politics. The city council, with a large number of small wards, is organized around group-based representation and is especially sensitive to new groups. The building blocks of political life tend to rest on the geographic and political organization of these groups within wards. When a group settles within a single ward, as little as 2 percent of the voting-age population can elect an alderman.

By 1980, the city's total population had contracted by 10 percent, and by 1990, it had declined again. Long dominated by European ethnics and African Americans, the city's population became dramatically more diverse between 1970 and 2000 as new groups arrived and older groups left the city (Table 5.1). In 1970, two-thirds of the population identified themselves as white, and in 1980, this figure had fallen to 50.3 percent. By 1990, whites accounted for 45.5 percent; and by 2000, 42.0 percent of the city's total population. However, non-Hispanic whites constituted less than one-third of Chicago's population in 2000. (See Table 5.1 notes.)

---

[1] This section and part of the next are based on Pinderhughes 1994; see especially pp. 39–43 and 48–54.

TABLE 5.1   Chicago population by race, ethnicity and hispanic origin, 1970–2000

Race	1970	%	1980	%	1990	%	2000	%
African American	1,102,620	32.7	1,197,174	39.8	1,086,389	39.0	1,065,009	36.8
Asian/Pacific Islander	36,262	1.1	73,745	2.5	104,141	3.7	127,762	4.4
White	2,207,767	65.5	1,512,411	50.3	1,265,953	45.5	1,215,315	42.0
Other race[a]	20,308	0.6	221,748	7.4	327,243	11.8	403,493	13.9
Two or more races[b]							84,437	2.9
City total	3,366,957	100.0	3,005,078	100.0	2,783,726	100.0	2,896,016	100.0
Hispanic ethnicity[c]								
Hispanic	247,343	7.3	423,357	14.1	535,315	19.2	753,644	26.0
Non-Hispanic	3,119,614	92.7	2,581,721	85.9	2,248,411	80.8	2,142,372	74.0

[a]"Other race" includes 10,290 Native Americans as well as persons who self-identified as other races.

[b]The 2000 census introduced a new racial categorization system. For the first time, people were allowed to self-identify as two or more races. Single-race identifiers were tallied separately, as above, but there is no way of knowing how the multiple-race identifiers would have answered if they had identified one of the single-race categories; therefore, we can not calculate percentages that are strictly comparable with earlier censuses.

[c]In 2000, 41 percent of Chicago Hispanics identified themselves as "White"; 52 percent, as "Other race"; 5 percent, as "Multi-racial." Thirty-four percent of whites also identified themselves as Hispanic. Non-Hispanic whites constituted only 31.3 percent of Chicago's population in 2000.

Sources: 1970—U.S. Bureau of the Census, Illinois, Vol. 1, Part 15, Section 1, Chapter B, Table 23: 15–105; 1980—U.S. Bureau of the Census, Illinois, Vol 2, Part 15, Chapter 1, Table 59: 15–52; 1990—U.S. Bureau of the Census of Population and Housing, Summary Tape File 3A; 2000—U.S. Census Bureau, Census 2000 Redistricting Data (P.L. 94-171) Summary File, Matrices PL1 and PL2. GCT-PL. Race and Hispanic or Latino: 2000, Illinois—Place.

By 1990, the total populations of the city and the metropolitan region had declined again, as had the white and black populations. In 1970, blacks comprised about one-third of the city; their proportion peaked at 39.8 percent in 1980, dropping to 39 percent by 1990 and to 36.8 percent in 2000. Although blacks were still a significant group, they had also increased their outmigration to the suburbs from 1980 to 1990, with the result that the number of blacks declined by 9.3 percent.

Only Asian Pacific Islanders and Latinos grew during the 1980s and the 1990s. The largest change, however, involved the growth of the Latino population—from 7.3 percent of the total in 1970 to 14.1 percent in 1980, 19.2 percent in 1990, and 26 percent in 2000. Asians increased their numbers by nearly one-third, to 3.7 percent in 1990 and 4.4 percent in 2000. Their distribution was even greater in suburban Cook County, the "Collar" Counties (outside of Cook County, in which Chicago is located), and the larger metropolitan area (Chicago Urban League 1994, 6).

These broad identities are much simpler than the actual racial and ethnic categories. Whites, for example, include European nationality groups who are third- or fourth-generation citizens of the United States; the largest groups in 1990, in order of decreasing size, were Poles, Germans, and Irish, followed by Italians, Lithuanians, Russians, and Czechs. Asian Pacific groups include, also in order of size, Filipinos, Chinese, Asian Indians, Koreans, Japanese, and others. Most studies of Latinos in Chicago emphasize the city's atypical pan-ethnic diversity, including Mexican Americans, Puerto Ricans, and Cubans as the largest and most significant groups (Casuo and Camacho 1985; de la Garza et al. 1992; Padilla 1987). The 1990 U.S. Census showed that Guatemalans had replaced Cubans in number rank, followed by smaller groups from Central and South America (U.S. Bureau of the Census 1990).[2] The African-American population has declined but also grown more diverse in recent decades, with sub-Saharan Africans, blacks of Hispanic origin, and West Indians and Haitians in residence.

These shifts in the demographic character of the city directly affected political life in the last third of the twentieth century. In the 1970s and 1980s, whites competed among themselves, but as their proportion in the city fell, they were able to reduce conflict and form a coalition of loosely affiliated white ethnic groups in order to sustain citywide political leadership. Blacks forged a coalition of black leaders and organizations in the early 1980s that served as a basis for the broad, multiracial coalition that elected Harold Washington, but that disintegrated after his death, riven by class and ideological divisions. Blacks and whites competed for political leadership in the city partly as a result of the changes in the city's demographics and partly as a result of the differing character of the relationship of blacks to the city's political frame of reference. Although blacks and whites approximate each other in population size, Latinos now command significant political representation, because they serve as the balance of power between the older groups. Asian Pacifics are organizing for representation in the political arena, although they have not yet elected a representative to the city council or to state legislative public office. Redistricting efforts at the end of the twentieth century focused on limiting rather than enhancing their opportunities for elected office (Bush 1984; Padilla 1987; Torres 1991).

The size of racial and ethnic populations is not the same as their voting-age populations, their voter registration, or their actual voter turnout. Table 5.2 presents the composition of Chicago's voting-age population from 1950 to 1996. Whites fell from their dominant position in the electorate in 1950 to less than half the total in 1990; in 1996, they were just 40 percent of the voting age population. Blacks rose from less than one-tenth of the total in 1940 to 35.7 percent in 1990. In 1996, they constituted 34 percent of the total. The Hispanic voting-age population has been reported only since 1970, but by 1990, Latinos were 16.8 percent (Chicago Urban League 1994). In 1996, they were 20.6 percent. More than three-quarters of the city's total voting-age population was registered to vote at the beginning of the 1980s, and that proportion actually increased until the mayoral and presidential election years

---

[2] The census designations follow varying—and often changing—preferences of the populations in question. The long-term emphasis on race in the American group pantheon has arbitrarily required groups to be categorized by their relationship to whites. In censuses of the early 1900s, for example, Mexican Americans were moved into and out of the Caucasian category. In recent years, the census first used *Spanish speaking* as a category, then in 1980 shifted to *Hispanic,* in which the group in question might be of any race.

TABLE 5.2   Racial and ethnic composition of Chicago's voting-age population, 1950–1996

Year	White	African American	Latino	Other
1950	86.5%	13.4%[a]	NA[b]	NA
1960	79.7%	20.2%[a]	NA	NA
1970	67.2%	27.1%	5.6%	NA
1980	53.5%	37.5%	7.5%	1.3%
1990	43.5%	35.7%	16.8%	4.0%
1995[c]	40.9%	34.8%	20.0%	4.3%
1996[d]	40.3%	34.6%	20.6%	4.4%

[a]Before the 1970 U.S. Census, there were only two categories, "white" and "non-white." Most Latinos were counted only as "white."

[b] NA = not available.

[c]1995 data were projections in Chicago Urban League, Metro Chicago Information Center, and Northern Illinois University, 1994. *Metro Chicago Political Atlas—1994*, 9. Springfield, Ill.: Institute for Public Affairs, Sangamon State University.

[d]Estimates developed from data and analysis provided by the Metro Chicago Information Center.

Source: Lewis, James H., Garth D. Taylor, and Paul Kleppner. 1997. *Metro Chicago Political Atlas '97–'98*, 10. Springfield, Ill.: The Institute for Public Affairs, University of Illinois at Springfield.

of 1983 and 1984, with 79.9 percent and 78.9 percent, respectively (Chicago Urban League 1990, 61). In the 1988 and 1989 general elections, 74.4 percent and 73.6 percent, respectively, of the total voting-age population was registered (Chicago Urban League 1997, 12). After a decline in the late 1980s, registration had risen to 84.2 percent in 1992 and had fallen again in 1996 to 78.9 percent (Chicago Urban League 1994, 10). Of the 1.56 million registered voters in the city, 52.2 percent were white, 41.4 percent were black, and 5.7 percent were Latino.

Several factors explain the differences between a group's voting-age population and its voter registration. The somewhat older age of the white population relative to the black and Hispanic populations means both that more whites are eligible to vote and that they are also more likely to turn out and vote. Citizenship, language, and literacy are other factors. Puerto Ricans are citizens of the United States; many Mexican Americans and others from South America are neither citizens nor legal residents. The 1975 extension of the 1965 Voting Rights Act outlawed English literacy tests for voting, so illiteracy is not a formal barrier to political participation. It may, however, be an informal one, especially for non-English-speaking groups.

Electoral Representation

The city's racial and ethnic groups reside in distinct locations, so neighborhoods and wards are easily identifiable for political purposes. Chicago is also often noted as one of the country's most segregated cities (Massey and Denton 1988). Zikmund (1982), Kleppner (1985), and the atlas of the Chicago Urban League/Northern Illinois University (Chicago Urban League 1990) divides the neighborhoods into racial and ethnic political enclaves. These have shifted over the years as the black population has grown, the white population has shrunk, and the Puerto Rican and Mexican groups have established distinct residential locations on the northwest and south sides, respectively, and also grown in size. The city's politicians use detailed knowledge of racial and ethnic group location in the decennial redistrictings of local, state, and national office boundaries to acknowledge growth in some groups; more often, however, they use it to maintain the power of those designing the districts.

Chicago politics has traditionally been based on small unit politics. Whereas early twentieth century reform movements attacked ward politics and supported enlarged districts or at-large elections, Chicago embraced this pattern and moved from a 35-seat city council to a 50-seat council. New York City reorganized its council in this fashion in the 1990s (Mollenkopf 1992, 1995). Wards are a small enough prize to attract the interest of small and large groups and to enable these groups to win access to the city council. The wards also become the electoral building blocks used to campaign for the mayor's office and for the mayor's electoral coalition. The ability to control these wards in significant numbers, to turn out the vote, or to turn out voters in the numbers and for the candidates the party leaders have selected is of continuing concern to the party. The demographic changes in the city in recent decades and the policy issues that arose from them challenged the Democratic leadership at the most fundamental level.

THE SEARCH FOR AN ELECTORAL AND GOVERNING COALITION
The Balance of Power: Demographics and Partisan Politics

The size of racial and ethnic group populations is a critical factor shaping the opportunities for each to win election to office and to maintain control over the political process (Karnig and Welch 1980, 64). In the case of African Americans, cities with majority black populations, especially those over 65 percent, are especially likely to have elected black mayors on a sustained basis. Examples are Detroit; Washington, DC; Atlanta; and Gary, Indiana. When the black population is under 65 percent, the coalition is much less secure and more likely to be subject to the vagaries of partisan politics and/or intragroup fission. Black electorates in Cleveland after Carl Stokes, Los Angeles after Tom Bradley, and Chicago after Harold Washington's death were unable to maintain control of the mayor's office. Cities with black populations above 40 percent and below 65 percent find it possible to win control of city hall if they can minimize conflict within the group. Where the black electorate is a minority or only a narrow majority, possibilities of internal conflict *may* be more easily controlled, because the stakes are clearer. Even cities with minorities of 38 percent or less may elect a black mayor, as Charlotte, Hartford, Los Angeles, Kansas City, and New York have done. That individual, however, must rely on a significantly broader multiracial coalition to win election than would be needed with a larger black proportion of the population.

Chicago's African-American and European-American populations are each too small to dominate the mayor's office unilaterally and must seek broader support from each other and from Latino voters. In multiracial, multiethnic settings, one group may also be able to mediate among competing interests, whether they are divided along socioeconomic, religious, racial, ethnic, or language dimensions. For much of this century, Irish politicians have led or managed complex coalitions of groups. The first Mayor Daley—Richard J. Daley—was elected in 1955 with strong support from the black population, but black voters began to break away from the machine during the 1960s (Pinderhughes 1987, 240; Grimshaw 1982, 62; 1992). Middle-class black voters became more independent, and Daley began to rely more strongly on support from white ethnic wards that had not supported him in his earlier administrations. In the 1970s, poor black areas also shifted toward independent status as community organizations arranged voter registration drives and get-out-the-vote campaigns.

Though there were shifts from one group to another, the machine always had support from both black and white wards. Zikmund (1982) shows that despite these electoral shifts, the machine cultivated the loyalty of a continuing core of voters across all racial and ethnic groups: machine core, reform/northshore wards, black wards, southside white ethnics, Polish northwest, and northside ethnics. Richard Newhouse, Edward Hanrahan, and Dick Singer challenged Daley in the 1975 primary, and Harold Washington and Roman Pucinski challenged Michael Bilandic in 1977. Yet the black wards still produced a mean of 47.2 percent of their votes for Daley in 1975 and 46.2 percent for Bilandic in 1977 (Zikmund 1982, 49). Table 5.3 ranks mayoral winners' total votes by volume. Mayor Daley won the largest vote in the 1971 general election, with 70 percent of the total. His share dropped significantly in the 1975 primary, but even with three opponents, he still took 57.8 percent of the primary vote and 79.5 percent of the general election vote, winning majorities of the vote of the machine core, southside white ethnics, northside white ethnics, and Polish northwest. He won less than a majority only in the black wards and the reform/lakefront areas (Zikmund 1982, 49).

Mayor Bilandic was first elected by the Chicago city council after Daley's death in 1975. He won the mayoral primary in 1977 with only a plurality of the vote and the *lowest* voter turnout of all but two primaries and general elections between 1971 and 1995. In the general election, he improved his total turnout and won with 77.3 percent of the vote, but this election showed the first evidence of white ethnic conflict. In comparison to Daley's experience in 1975, Bilandic's mean proportion of support was stable in the machine core, the reform/northshore wards, and the black wards, but he lost support among southside and northside white ethnics and in the Polish northwest wards (Zikmund 1982, 49).

In 1979, Jane Byrne won 11 of the 12 black wards, all the reform/northshore wards, split the Polish areas, and took less than a third of the vote in the remaining white ethnic and racially mixed machine areas. In that year, Byrne won 83.6 percent, the second highest number of votes in this era in a general election, as shown in Table 5.3. She then proceeded to alienate her strongest base in an effort to lure white voters, at a point when demographic changes suggested this would probably not have been worth the investment. Byrne competed with the late Mayor's son, Richard M. Daley, for the white ethnic and machine vote in the 1983

TABLE 5.3   **Mayoral votes ranked by winner's total votes**

Winner's Total Votes	Year	Winner	Election[a]	Percentage of Total Votes Cast
740,137	1971	Daley	G	70.0
671,189	1979	Byrne	G	83.6
666,911	1983	Washington	G	51.6
600,252	1987	Washington	G	53.7
586,941	1987	Washington	P	53.5
576,620	1989	Daley II	G	55.4
542,817	1975	Daley	G	79.5
485,182	1989	Daley II	P	55.3
475,169	1977	Bilandic	G	77.3
463,623	1975	Daley	P	57.8
450,155	1991	Daley II	G	71.1
424,122	1983	Washington	P	38.1
418,211	1999	Daley	G	72.1
412,909	1979	Byrne	P	51.0
407,730	1991	Daley II	P	32.2
364,912	1995	Daley II	G	60.1
348,189	1995	Daley II	P	65.8
342,301	1977	Bilandic	P	49.3

[a] G = general election; P = primary election.

Sources: Pinderhughes, 1997, 124; Lewis, James H., Garth D. Taylor, and Paul Kleppner. 1997. *Metro Chicago Political Atlas '97–'98*, 10. Springfield, Ill.: The Institute for Public Affairs, University of Illinois at Springfield.; *Chicago Tribune*. 1999. Chicago Elections. February 25, Section 2, 8.

primary, abandoning the black vote to Washington; Bernard Epton, a previous unknown, became the Republican candidate in the general election. In the 1987 primary, Byrne challenged Washington for the Democratic nomination, while Edward Vrdolyak ran for the Solidarity party nomination and Donald Haider for the Republican nomination.

Alderman Eugene Sawyer was nominated by the city council to succeed Washington after his death in November 1987. Blacks saw Sawyer as the candidate of white northside and machine forces, and this produced internal conflict over succession. Black activists limited their focus to the black ward groups; as white groups had competed in 1983 and 1987, so blacks competed in 1989, 1991, and 1995 rather than offering a single candidate in the primary and general elections. Latino voters allied with Washington in 1983 and 1987, but when black alderman Tim Evans challenged Mayor Sawyer in 1989, they shifted their support to Daley, giving him 52.4 percent of their votes. In 1991, Latino wards gave Daley 90.8 percent of the vote in the general elections, but voters in black wards offered only 22 percent of their support. Daley has maintained the Latino vote while gradually increasing his support from black voters (Table 5.4). Metropolitan Water Reclamation District Commissioner Joseph Gardner challenged Daley in the 1995 primary, and former

TABLE 5.4 Mayor Richard M. Daley's percentage of the total, black, and Latino vote, 1989–1999

Year	Total Vote	Election[a]	Winner's %	% of Black Vote	% Latino
1989	485,182	P	55.3		
1989	576,620	G	55.4	3.6	52.4
1991	407,730	P	32.2		
1991	450,155	G	71.1	22.0	90.8
1995	348,189	P	65.8	23.1	90.5
1995	364,912	G	60.1	15.2	90.4
1999	418,211	G	72.1	44.4[b]	85.5[c]

[a] G = general election; P = primary election.

[b] Based on black wards (2–9, 15–17, 20, 21, 24, 27–29, and 37) and mixed ward 18.

[c] Based on Latino wards (1, 12, 22, 25, 26, 31, and 35).

Sources: Lewis, James H., Garth D. Taylor, and Paul Kleppner. 1997. *Metro Chicago Political Atlas '97–'98*, 10. Springfield, Ill.: The Institute for Public Affairs, University of Illinois at Springfield. Election results from *Chicago Tribune*. 1990. Chicago Elections. February 25, Section 2, 8.

Illinois Attorney General Roland Burris ran against Daley in the 1995 general election. Turnout remained below the 1980s mobilization, and both lost.

In 1999, former Black Panther and First District Congressman Bobby Rush challenged Daley in the city's first nonpartisan mayoral election. In black wards, Rush won 56 percent of the vote to Daley's 44 percent, which was a sharp turn from the 1980s, when black voter loyalty stayed well above 90 percent. Daley won 85 percent to Rush's 14 percent of support from Latino voters (Table 5.5).

The challengers from 1975 through 1995 represented stronger or weaker component units within the racial and ethnic elements of the machine. (Daley, already challenged by the reform and black sectors of the machine by 1975, was nevertheless able to hold a substantial portion of the vote in these areas.) Bilandic retained the same level of support as Daley in black and machine areas but lost support in the white ethnic areas to Pucinski. In 1977, Washington improved his showing over Newhouse in the 1975 mayoral primary but performed poorly in all other areas. Pucinski won more than half the vote in the Polish northwest and 41.6 percent in the reform/northshore areas, but no more than 30.5 percent in the rest (Zikmund 1982, 44–50).

TABLE 5.5 Support for 1999 mayoral candidates in black and Latino wards

	Total Votes	%
Daley	107,393	44.4
Rush	134,442	55.6

Source: Chicago Tribune. 1999. Chicago Elections. February 25, section 2, 8. Based on black and Latino wards (see Table 5.4).

The representatives of the major groups—Bilandic, Epton, Byrne, Daley, Washington, Sawyer, and Evans—and their challengers—Haider and Vrdolyak—in the years between 1977 and 1989 typically mobilized votes by race in only one or, at most, two of these ward groups. Put more simply, they were able to generate interest among some of the white ethnic groups or some sectors of the black population, but rarely were they able to cross racial lines or generate interest across a number of sectors—which by the end of this era also included the Hispanic population. Those who mobilized across racial lines and limited competition in the primaries were successful: Bilandic in 1977, Byrne in 1979, Washington in 1983, and Daley in 1989: Those who moved away from a multiracial coalition to concentrate on their own group were defeated after one term: Bilandic in 1979, Byrne in 1983, and Sawyer in 1989. Those who sustained interest across racial lines were reelected: Washington in 1987, and Daley in 1991, 1995, and 1999. Only a few of the challengers seemed able to understand the heterogeneous and competitive composition of the electorate and to plan an electoral strategy based on that new demographic reality.

THE WASHINGTON ERA
Mobilization and Government

In the 10 northern California cities studied by Browning, Marshall, and Tabb, electoral political incorporation followed an era of demand-protest. Chicago's activists fused demand-protest with electoral mobilization rather than engaging in periods of protest separated from and/or followed by electoral mobilization. Chicago's earliest black city council representation occurred in the second decade of the twentieth century; representation on the county commission had occurred even earlier. Membership in a dominant, racially liberal coalition, it can be argued, occurred on a number of occasions, as when William Hale Thompson was elected mayor in 1915, 1919, and 1927 in an alliance comparable to the relationship that Latinos had with Mayor Harold Washington in 1983 and 1987 as a small but loyal and decisive group.

Chicago's black grass roots community organizations had to create the energy, the strategy, and the network of political relationships to mobilize themselves to place substantive policy concerns on the city council's and the mayor's agenda. African Americans were represented inside the machine, but they had no real influence over the substantial racial discrimination in the city, which effectively demobilized them from the 1930s through the 1970s. They remobilized in the 1980s as a form of demand-protest. Black organizations used conflicts over Mayor Byrne's appointments to the school and public housing boards as well as over ChicagoFest as a basis for protest—but protest that was specifically framed within and used as an engine to respond electorally. They emphasized these issues in the October 1982 voter registration drive, which laid the foundation for a strong Washington challenge in the 1983 primary.

Starks and Preston (1990) described how the creation of coalitions of black organizations, combined with identification of a single enormously popular black candidate in the person of Harold Washington, framed the mayoral campaign. When the leaders of coalitions of organizations, the Task Force for Black Political Empowerment and Chicago Black United Communities, asked Harold Washington to run for mayor, he required them to increase voter registration by at least 50,000 and to raise $250,000 (Starks and Preston 1990, 95). Washington had legislative experience at the state and national levels, characterized himself as an "independent machine politician," and had deep roots in the labor movement (Travis 1987). His 1983 mayoral primary campaign, which was supported by a unified and mobilized black electorate, was balanced and enhanced by the competition between Byrne and Daley. Washington won nearly 80 percent and 73 percent of the vote in the southside and westside black wards, respectively, which with a majority of the Latino vote and small support from whites produced a 38.1 percent plurality in the primary and a 51.6 percent result in the general election.

Ironically, the successful fusion of demand-protest with electoral goals and the conventional structure of interest organizations left the black community with a serious political problem after Washington's election. An electoral coalition and a governing coalition, as Mayor Washington and his supporters discovered very quickly, are two different things. Most black leaders had little citywide leadership experience; there was neither a Chicago tradition of deliberative policy making by a broad popular coalition nor any integrative, citywide public structures to manage such a process (Squires, Bennett, McCourt, and Nyden 1987; Suttles, 1990).

It is important to consider what structures were available for participation in that process, what types of organizations existed, what types of tasks had been engaged in previously, and with what tasks the organizations were most familiar. Several associations of organizations had grown into structures that mobilized and unified the black community for the mayoral campaign: the Task Force for Black Political Empowerment, Chicago Black United Communities, VOTE, and a complex array of neighborhood groups, professional organizations, social groups, religious bodies, and even some ward organizations. Basically, most existing organizations that were not already linked to the Chicago Democratic party were transformed into electoral mobilizing committees in support of Washington's candidacy (Alkalimat and Gills 1984).

Traditionally, black organizations combine the sacred and the secular, with churches often serving as umbrellas for secular activities. Black religious, social, and professional organizations also integrate activities that might be treated separately by white interest groups at the national level. Chicago's black political groups reflected similar patterns. Harold Washington played the role of a secular substitute for religious leaders such as Congressman Adam Clayton Powell or the late Elijah Muhammad, founder of the Nation of Islam. He was also a sharp contrast to the late Chicago Congressman William Dawson, who by the 1970s was generally unwilling to raise substantive issues of black representation. Washington—elevated above the mass united by organizations of organizations in singular, hierarchical fashion—articulated the political and the material as well as the moral goals and the interests of the black community to the larger white city (Morris 1984; Hamilton 1991; Wilson 1960).

Mass mobilization worked for blacks in pressing forward the civil rights movement and in winning control of the Chicago mayor's office. It also works especially well for confronting crises, meeting political challenges, mounting protests, and mobilizing voters. This structure has not, however, developed or maintained grass roots interest in governing and policy making, in contacting and communicating with public officials, or in negotiating with or choosing among political leaders within the community.

During the election and for most of Washington's first term, the coalition protested, mobilized, and challenged the machine, which was controlled by white ethnic groups. Washington's election to office had not secured a voting majority in the city council or over city agencies, and his support of the Shakman decree, recognizing civil service protection over city jobs, weakened his control. In 1986, Washington's supporters defeated enough machine representatives in black or mixed wards to control the city council, and he was re-elected in 1987.

Black Chicagoans differed by class, education, income, occupation, and their choices of leaders and policy, and mediating among the complex range of interests that were part of the Washington coalition was a major task—even for Harold Washington. Differences appeared among African Americans and among the organizations over how to identify economic policy, to organize and manage the schools in light of poor student scores and rising deficits, and to judge environmental safety and other issues. At the time of Harold Washington's death, the African-American community and, therefore, the city was immediately confronted with many conflicts over leadership succession without a process or organizational network for resolving their disagreements. Consequently, they were not resolved successfully within the black population any more than they had been among white ethnics in the previous decade.

The black political structure that elected Harold Washington was not organized for the governance process, for contacting public officials, for concentrating on specialized policy areas, or for developing sustained accountability. This problem was neither new nor unique to Chicago black and white groups.

In the fusion of protest and electoral mobilization leading to the Washington era, race and representation were increasingly linked by grass roots organizations, as much by the nature of the organizational structure and process as by the policies they articulated. Washington's own preferences and understanding of the city's demographics meant that while he aimed at full mobilization of the black community, he also sustained ties with labor unions and reached out to other racial and ethnic groups that were willing to accept his leadership.

Liberal Tendencies and African-American Political Incorporation

Political incorporation, group mobilization, coalition formation, and responsiveness are the core variables in Browning, Marshall, and Tabb's study. Chicago has a political tradition that has demonstrated wide flexibility and creativity in its responsiveness to a series of racial and ethnic groups over the span of the twentieth century. Browning, Marshall, and Tabb also compare the demand-protest cycles they found in 10 northern California cities with the era of electoral participation in which blacks and Hispanics began to elect representatives to city councils and, in some cases, to the mayor's office.

New York City is the great anomaly, Mollenkopf has argued (see Chapter 4), because it produced relatively liberal policies even though blacks and Latinos remained outside its structure of power. Atlanta's regime politics links the large economic interests and the city's political leaders. San Franciscans' electoral politics involves competition among three sources of left politics. Chicago presents another type of anomaly. Its political structure produces routine, even swift descriptive political representation, especially at the ward level. Representatives of the masses of blacks and Latinos remain outside the substantive policy-making arenas, however, and there is little competition over or production of liberal policy. The city council, city government, and school system are domains in which racial representation can be found, but citywide arenas in which powerful economic interests dominate are not easily penetrated by ward-level racial and ethnic representatives.

The city's most significant economic interests tend to interact directly with the mayor outside of the electoral system. Racial and ethnic groups have limited access to the interactions between the mayor and large economic interests; therefore, liberal reform rarely occurs (DeLeon 1992; Mollenkopf 1995; Stone 1989). Before Washington, Chicago's politics during the twentieth century moved between unregulated, highly competitive group politics and highly centralized, regulated political monopoly. In neither case was policy making an expertise-based, deliberative policy process in which the various racial and ethnic groups might participate. The Washington administration moved the city away from the limited confines of the machine dimension onto another, more deliberative continuum that combined liberal policy, racial and ethnic interests, and ward politics.[3]

On the ethnic dimension–machine dimension, Washington's administration strengthened cross-group political alliances, continued detachment of the civil service from the machine, created policy-based entitlements in the form of civil rights ordinances for relatively weak groups, and promoted greater recognition of the political rights of several groups, including African Americans, gays and lesbians, women, and Latinos (Clavel and Wiewel 1991). On the policy-making dimension, Washington had to create policy-making infrastructures where none had existed, and bend those already in existence in directions where they had not yet gone. In effect, he had to create constituency, institutional, and policy-making connections simultaneously—a gargantuan task.

Starks and Preston (1990) noted that African Americans had already achieved participation, substantial representation, and "modest" incorporation in Chicago government and within the Democratic party for some time prior to Harold Washington's election to the mayoralty. Nevertheless, Starks and Preston felt this

---

[3] See Pinderhughes 1987, 39–48, for a more detailed discussion and conceptualizations of the evolution of competition and monopoly in Chicago politics.

gain was "sharply limited in its impact on policy" (1990, 92). They argued that "much more could be achieved if the reins of political power could be grasped by blacks as leaders of a multiracial coalition. Only in this way could government and party agendas be restructured so that black interests were protected and realized" (Starks and Preston 1990, 91).

Evaluations of political incorporation thus require examination of both these areas: the public electoral arena, in which fierce racial and ethnic competition occurs; and the more cloistered policy-making arena, in which large economic interests press their concerns. Before Washington, Chicago's white ethnic leaders had not been highly resistant to the demands and interests of the black community. Chicago's political regime differed from those found in most of the 10 northern California cities discussed in *Protest Is Not Enough*, except for Oakland in the 1960s and 1970s. Oakland was an industrial city with an industrial labor force and a strong, concentrated white power structure capable of considerable political and economic resistance to minority challenges against the racial status quo. Oakland and Chicago were similar in that minority incorporation at the highest levels outlined by Browning, Marshall, and Tabb—representation on the city council, representation within coalitions that controlled liberal reformist policy making on minority issues, and minority control of the mayor's office—was considerably delayed.[4] Despite considerable challenges, the Washington administration made some headway in the ward-level electoral arena and in the citywide policy arena.

In Chicago, only Hyde Park and north Lakeshore harbored a genuine white liberal constituency; there was only limited base for a white liberal professional group taking control of city hall from the immigrant, industrially employed population groups who controlled city hall after 1931. Race was such a powerful divide in the city that African Americans and white ethnics coexisted within the Democratic party but fought each other for political control of the city. In fact, the black challenge to segments of the traditional white ethnic machine's leadership was beneficial to white liberals and reformers. In a black administration elected with the support of Latino voters, white liberals had more space to influence policy than they had previously enjoyed.

Solving leadership succession crises and sustaining interest in policy making, even when the mayor in office represents black interests, was problematic. The literature on the Washington administration suggests that policy reform of at least a modest sort occurred. Pelissero and Holian examined six cities during the 1970s and 1980s that elected minority mayors, including Chicago, and a control group of six cities that elected white mayors. They found that "all minority mayor cities had an

---

[4] There were even similar reactions to their respective grass roots young male political activists. The Black Panthers in Oakland and Chicago and the Black Stone Rangers in Chicago were met with challenge, violence, and political repression by public officials. I think it can be argued that the response in Chicago was even more intense and decisive than that in Oakland, where some segments of the Panthers ran for political office.

increase in long-term expenditures" in comparison to the control cities, none of which had significant changes. They also found that "the election of a black mayor produced either a short-term decrease (Baltimore) or long-term increase (Chicago, New Orleans) in total debt per capita" (1994, 14).

Bennett (1993) shows that Washington distributed benefits to black wards, but to avoid being accused of favoritism, "he was careful to budget, if anything, a surplus of spending in anti-Washington wards" (432). Washington was not always able to balance the interests of his core black supporters and his Latino allies, according to Bennett's examination of hiring proportions, to the latter's satisfaction:

> For Washington, effectively delivered city services were perfectly consistent with minority empowerment. . . . Although Washington shied away from welfare-state-style redistribution of resources, his administration's collaboration with community-based organizations helped stretch city resources and offered neighborhoods across the city—not just on Chicago's black south and west sides—enhanced access to city government (Bennett 1993, 438).

MAYOR RICHARD M. DALEY: RESTORATION OF THE OLD REGIME OR INCORPORATION OF A NEW ONE?

Citywide Politics

By the mid-1990s, Mayor Daley had clearly increased his control of Chicago city politics, but the 1999 mayoral election clarified his control over the electorate, the city council, and increasingly, over the last and most resistant constituency—black voters. In recent years, he has moved aggressively to work in the citywide arena with its economic interests by reconstructing the city's lakefront and facilitating the gentrification of its neighborhoods. Finally, he has remade relationships with black ministers, voters, and economic interests. Racial and ethnic political incorporation has occurred in terms of descriptive representation. Whether full substantive incorporation has occurred is a matter of some debate, yet the Chicago of 2002 is considerably more integrated in terms of governmental and educational employment than it was before 1983. On the other hand, Reverend Albert Sampson, pastor of Fernwood United Methodist Church and an associate of Martin Luther King, Jr., during his 1966 Chicago campaign, commented that King "would be disappointed to see it's highly segregated. Gentrification is pitting people against each other" (Taylor 2002).

What has the second Mayor Daley done to merit this conclusion of mixed incorporation? First, Daley encouraged the black religious leadership to interact with his administration by naming a special envoy to the black ministers in the city. The mayor and Rainbow Push Director, Reverend Jesse Jackson, also communicate with each other regularly (Pinderhughes 2000; Starks 2000a).

The years of black electoral success have also generated an ironic—but unavoidable—pattern. Carol Moseley-Braun, who was elected to the U.S. Senate in 1992, and John Stroger, who was elected president of the Cook County board of commissioners in 1994, endorsed Mayor Daley, and the mayor offered his support when they were up for re-election. Braun was defeated by Republican Peter Fitzgerald, but it would have been very difficult for these statewide, countywide, and citywide leaders to ignore each other. Had Daley been more vulnerable, had he controlled fewer seats in the city council, or had the African-American middle class been less represented in city government, Braun and Stroger might have considered endorsing one of the black candidates for mayor in 1995 or 1999. The failure of the black political community to mobilize behind a single candidate, however, has meant that Daley has maintained the strategic advantage throughout the decade. The increasing presence of black elected officials in statewide and metropolitan positions has made it easier rather than more difficult for blacks to support Daley—and easier for others not to turn out to oppose him. These also reflect stronger class-based divisions within Chicago's black population. The black middle and upper classes that are close to and personally allied with the candidates who challenged Daley in the 1990s—Burris, Gardner, Judge Pincham, and others—have economic and institutional resources that make the defeat of black candidates unpleasant, but not necessarily devastating (*Chicago Tribune*, 1995a, 1995b; *Washington Post*, 1995a, 1995b).

How did the Chicago political environment deteriorate from Washington's strong electoral base and 40-vote governing coalition within just a few years? The 1987 mayoral election, held within the city council immediately after Mayor Washington's death, suggests that the black and white communities simultaneously polarized during the campaign (Hawking 1991). Whites and blacks each preferred one candidate and came to see the other as the nominee of their enemies. Their polarization identified black aldermen Eugene Sawyer and Timothy Evans as the nominees of whites and blacks, respectively. That split—and the African-American community's unwillingness to compromise—led it to offer two competing black candidates in the 1989 special election. This guaranteed internal competition among blacks, a minority of the city's voting-age population. The 1989 campaign established a pattern that was repeated in the 1991 and 1995 mayoral elections. A succession of black candidates competed against each other in the primary and in the general election, thereby strengthening rather than weakening the party's nominee. White voters had only one candidate, Richard M. Daley, in the primary and general election.

After his election in 1989, Mayor Daley could easily reinvigorate the traditional political alliances within the varying sectors of the white community, ensure strong support from Latino voters, and begin incrementally to increase his support in the black sector. The strategy that failed with Sawyer and Evans was used again—to Daley's increasing electoral advantage—in 1991. The black candidate in the mayoral primary from the West Side, former alderman Danny Davis, won only 198,000 votes. Washington's lowest vote total in the 1983 primary had produced 424,122 votes. Eugene Pincham ran as an independent in the general elections in April and lost with 159,608 votes. In 1995, Mayor Daley was re-elected when the black primary candidate, Joseph Gardner, the Metropolitan Water Reclamation District commissioner, lost with 164,969 votes, or 29 percent of the vote (to Daley's 70 percent in the primary). Turnout was only 40 percent of the city's registered voters. In the general election in 1995, black Democratic gubernatorial nominee Roland Burris, former Illinois comptroller and attorney general, challenged the mayor as an independent and won 207,464 votes, or 35.8 percent of the total turnout of about 41 percent of registered voters. Miriam Santos, a Latina, was elected treasurer on the Democratic ticket, running well ahead of the mayor by about 80,000 votes. Daley increased his support among black voters and won the Latino wards decisively. On the other hand, turnout dropped to about 40 percent in the primary and general elections; a significant proportion of the black population has withdrawn from participation. Daley defeated Congressman Bobby Rush with a substantial portion of the black vote in 1999.

The consolidation of a new Chicago electoral coalition took the following form: large turnout and high loyalty among white voters, combined with a small percentage of black voters, and strong majorities from the small but electorally significant Latino population. Several factors explain this change. African Americans lost the focus they created in the 1980s and competed over goals and leadership at the polls. Where they had supported only Harold Washington in the primaries and general elections of 1983 and 1987, they offered multiple candidates in both contests in 1989, 1991, and 1995. In the process, the black electorate gradually demobilized and generated lower turnout. By 1999, Daley won office with 44 percent of the vote in black wards. Robert Starks (2000b) of the Task Force for Black Political Empowerment explains:

> *We Have No Leaders*, we have followers. There are sporadic spokespersons, but . . . no consistent leadership that is constantly fighting for the Black community. Mayor Daley is only reacting to a void in the African American leadership . . . that is they cave in and go for their own individual interests.

European ethnic groups competed with Mayor Richard J. Daley in the 1970s and with each other with abandon in the early 1980s. After 1989, however, they constrained their disagreements and concentrated support on a single mayoral candidate in the primaries and in the general elections. Finally, Latino voters gave majority support for Mayor Washington in the 1987 primary and general elections but split their vote in the 1989 special elections. As African Americans competed with each other for office, Latinos moved increasingly toward support for Daley. By the end of the 1990s, more than 80 percent of Latinos supported Mayor Daley.

Daley consolidated his hold on the mayor's office with large white turnouts and high loyalty, reduced turnout but increasing proportions of black voters, and small turnouts but increasing support from Latino voters. The 1995 and 1999 elections confirmed this pattern. Mayor Daley was re-elected again (and again), making him the mayor with the greatest longevity "after Daley" (Gove and Masotti 1982).

Daley's mixed record of support and conciliation for the black community is reflected in recent divergent actions. Councilwoman Dorothy Tillman sponsored a resolution asking Congress to examine the possibility of reparations. The mayor supported the resolution: "We must apologize when there is apologizing to do . . . It's about time that America does this." The City Council passed the resolution 46-1 (*CBS News* 2000).

On the other side of the ledger, Daley's increasing mastery of the city's many political domains has led to efforts to dismantle constraints on patronage politics instituted during the Washington administration. The 1983 Shakman decree, a federal ruling, had made it illegal for the city to hire employees for political purposes. In September 2001, a federal district court ruling extended the Shakman requirements to temporary employees. In response, in January 2002 Mayor Daley incorporated the Shakman provisions into Chicago's own personnel rules, where they could be altered by executive order—but then also asked that the Shakman ruling be rescinded. Daley, seeking to preserve some control over the number of city employees who serve at the mayor's pleasure, argued that the incorporation of the policies within Chicago's own personnel rules would eliminate the need for federal controls. Original plaintiff Michael Shakman and others disagreed. This is an extremely important policy issue to watch (Ford and Martin 2002; Pearson and Kovac 2002).

Ward-Level Politics

At the ward level, Chicago's African-American and Latino electoral representation, although significant, was subject to competition, bargaining, and lawsuits in the 1990s. The first decade of the twenty-first century, however, promises to be considerably less contentious. As of this writing, only a few months after the U.S. Census Bureau released redistricting data, the 2000 redistricting process has moved remarkably quickly toward resolution in the Chicago city council. The council voted 48-1 in support of a ward map with 20 African-American wards, 13 majority-white wards, 11 Latino wards, and six majority-minority wards (Table 5.6). While the possibility of lawsuits still remains, the near-unanimous city council vote suggests that none will originate from the city's aldermen, as was the case during the 1990s. MALDEF (the Mexican-American Legal Defense and Education Fund, a public interest legal organization) has left open the possibility that it may file suit when more detailed census data are available; the organization feels Latinos may be underrepresented by the city council's plan (*Chicago Tribune* 2001; Washburn 2001b).

The 1990s were marked by intense competition over racial and ethnic control of wards. At the beginning of the decade, blacks held 18 seats, Latinos four, and whites the rest. Black representation increased when Fifth Ward alderman Larry Bloom entered the 1995 race for city treasurer, opening his seat to a win by Barbara

TABLE 5.6   Chicago city council wards

	Voting Majorities			Majority-Minority
	White	*Black*	*Latino*	
1990	23	20	7	
2000	13	20	11	6

Source: Chicago Tribune. 2001. Mapping Hispanic Clout. December 20, 12.

Holt; the ward, which includes Hyde Park and the University of Chicago, had been majority-black for some decades. Latinos gained three new wards in the redistricting necessitated by the 1990 U.S. Census. There were 20 majority-black wards and 19 black aldermen (in the Eighteenth, blacks hold a narrow majority and a white alderman represents it) and seven majority-Latino wards with Latino aldermen. Representation of blacks on the council (38 percent) approximated their proportion of the population (37 percent), whereas Latinos were somewhat underrepresented on the council (14 percent) in comparison with their 26 percent of the population.

After the 1990 U.S. Census, the city and racial and ethnic group leaders engaged in a long, painful process that took up the entire decade. City council redistricting culminated in a 1992 citywide referendum on alternative redistricting proposals offered by administration versus independent aldermen. The mayor and administration aldermen proposed an "Equity Map" that preserved greater representation for whites, although there were 200,000 fewer whites in the city in 1990 than there had been in 1980, with 23 white wards and 20 black wards. Black and white independent aldermen proposed the "Fair Map," which increased the number of black wards to 22, gave the Eighteenth a large majority, and reduced the number of white wards to 21. Both groups proposed seven Latino wards, but white wards were preserved in the administration's proposal by stabilizing black and staunching Latino expansion. The alternative proposal split southeast side Hispanics into two wards.

The administration's map won 61 percent of the vote and reflected an electoral pattern that began with the 1989 mayoral election. Richard M. Daley and his allies turned out overwhelming proportions of white voters, about one-fifth of black voters, and at least three-quarters of Latino voters. Black aldermen turned out lower proportions of their supporters and won only about three-quarters to four-fifths of their votes. Latino turnout was low but directed primarily toward Mayor Daley's position.

Three lawsuits were filed in federal court charging discrimination in the equity redistricting plan. Independents and Latinos sued the city for greater black (22 wards) and Latino (eight or nine wards) city council representation. After a decade of legal conflict, which cost the city $20 million, the court made little change in the city's ward balance.

CONCLUSION

First, what impact has the Washington coalition had on Chicago politics? Has Mayor Richard M. Daley created a stable electoral and bargaining structure and restored a new Chicago political regime that resembles the post–World War II Democratic regime? What role do race and ethnicity play in contemporary Chicago politics now that black mayoral candidacies are clearly not viable? Does the post-Washington city government incorporate blacks and Hispanics in decision-making and policy-making structures and processes?

Harold Washington's campaigns and administration had a dramatic impact on African-American participation, mobilization, and incorporation. Although Chicago no longer has a black mayor, for the first time blacks now hold countywide and they have held statewide positions; elections are not always polarized if voters can be mobilized by simultaneous appeals to race and to some other factors, such as gender, their status as independent voters, or class. Carol Moseley-Braun served in the U.S. Senate from 1994 through 2000, while John Stroger was elected chairman of the Cook County board in 1994 and re-elected in 2002. Inside the city, elections remain highly polarized, although portions of the black population, including opinion leaders like former Senator Moseley-Braun and Dempsey Travis, have begun to support Mayor Daley. In the wards, competition for office remains intense and highly group oriented. Daley has placed some blacks in office to sustain his support in black areas. In policy-making areas, Daley has begun to move away from the reforms initiated during the Washington era.

In the last 20 years, Chicago's voters have sampled different political leaders, substantive policies, and policy approaches. Mayor Richard J. Daley's death offered the city an opportunity to consider racial and ethnic candidates from an array of political coalitions, different substantive policy emphases (e.g., economic development, physical infrastructure, school reform, and housing), and different strategies of resource distribution and fiscal policy. This chapter has examined the differing political resolutions that successive mayoral elections offered and why they did— or did not—result in stable coalitions.

Some coalitions, such as the Bilandic and Evans solutions, were not tenable. Others could not survive the death of their leader, Harold Washington. Still others were tenable but could not survive, subject to coalition drift or instability—namely, the Byrne and Sawyer coalitions. Mayor Richard M. Daley took office with a predominantly white coalition and has gradually won support from Latino voters and added increasing numbers of black voters. The city council, reflecting the city's increasing racial and ethnic heterogeneity, has shifted from majority-to minority-white. While Asians are not yet represented, some of the minority-white wards may be the source of representation for well-mobilized, newer groups with high turnout. Balancing the competing interests in the political leadership of diverse groups that also relate to economic status makes management of the city's political and economic life a complex challenge. While some argue that blacks remain unincorporated, the era of demand-protest and political mobilization elected African Americans to metropolitan and statewide office. Latinos, a small proportion of the population in the 1980s, nevertheless served as the electoral balance of power, both in Washington's campaigns and again in Daley's elections in the 1990s. Neither Richard M. Daley nor any other mayor who wants to remain in office can afford to ignore the electoral influence or the substantive and economic concerns of the city's racial and ethnic interest groups. While substantive policy interests are still subject to conflict and competition, African Americans and Latinos are increasingly integrated into the electoral and administrative structures of the city.

REFERENCES

Alkalimat, Abdul (Gerald McWorter), and Doug Gills. 1984. Black Power vs. Racism: Harold Washington Becomes Mayor. In Rod Bush, ed., *The New Black Vote: Politics and Power in Four American Cities*, 53–180. San Francisco: Synthesis.

Bennett, Larry. 1993. Harold Washington and the Black Urban Regime. *Urban Affairs Quarterly* 28 (March): 423–440.

Browning, Rufus P., Dale Rogers Marshall, and David H. Tabb. 1984. *Protest Is Not Enough: The Struggle of Blacks and Hispanics for Equality in Urban Politics.* Berkeley: University of California Press.

Browning, Rufus P., Dale Rogers Marshall, David H. Tabb. 1990. *Racial Politics in American Cities.* New York: Longman.

Browning, Rufus P., Dale Rogers Marshall, David H. Tabb. 1997. *Racial Politics in American Cities.* 2nd ed. New York: Longman.

Bush, Rod, ed. 1984. *The New Black Vote: Politics and Power in Four American Cities.* San Francisco: Synthesis.

Casuo, Jorge, and Eduardo Camacho. 1985. Hispanics in Chicago, Conclusion. *The Chicago Reporter* 14 (April): 1–4.

CBS News. 2000. Chicago Urges Reparations Hearings. May 17. cbsnews.com.

Chicago Tribune. 1999. Citywide Races. February 25, 8.

Chicago Tribune. 2001. Mapping Hispanic Clout. December 20, 26.

Chicago Urban League and Northern Illinois University. 1990. *CUL/NIU Atlas: Chicago Politics 1990.* Chicago and DeKalb: Social Science Research Institute, Northern Illinois University, and the Chicago Urban League.

Chicago Urban League, Metro Chicago Information Center, and Northern Illinois University. 1994. *Metro Chicago Political Atlas—1994.* Springfield, Ill.: Institute for Public Affairs, Sangamon State University.

Clavel, Pierre, and Wim Wiewel, eds. 1991. *Harold Washington and the Neighborhoods: Progressive City Government in Chicago, 1983–1987.* New Brunswick, NJ: Rutgers University Press.

De La Garza, Rudolfo O., Louis DeSipio, F. Chris Garcia, John Garcia, and Angelo Falcon. 1992. *Latino Voices: Mexican, Puerto Rican, and Cuban Perspectives on American Politics.* Boulder, Colo.: Westview Press.

DeLeon, Richard Edward. 1992. *Left Coast City Progressive Politics in San Francisco, 1975–1991.* Lawrence: University Press of Kansas.

Ford, Liam and Andrew Martin. 2002. Daley Seeking to Void Decree on Patronage. *Chicago Tribune,* January 11, 1.

Gove, Samuel K., and Louis H. Masotti, eds. 1982. *After Daley: Chicago Politics in Transition.* Urbana: University of Illinois Press.

Grimshaw, William. 1982. The Daley Legacy and Declining Politics of Party, Race and Public Unions. In Samuel K. Gove and Louis H. Masotti, eds., *After Daley: Chicago Politics in Transition,* 57–87. Urbana: University of Illinois Press.

Grimshaw, William. 1992. *Bitter Fruit: Black Politics and the Chicago Machine, 1931–1991.* Chicago: University of Chicago Press.

Hamilton, Charles V. 1991. *Adam Clayton Powell, Jr.: The Political Biography of an American Dilemma.* New York: Macmillan.

Hardy, Thomas. 1995. Daley Now Has to Win Over State GOP. *Chicago Tribune,* April 6, 1.

Hawking, Jim. 1991. We Have a Mayor. *Chicago Reporter* 20 (December): 3–5, 10.

Karnig, Albert, and Susan Welch. 1980. *Black Representation and Urban Policy.* Chicago: University of Chicago Press.

Kleppner, Paul. 1985. *Chicago Divided, the Making of a Black Mayor.* DeKalb: Northern Illinois University Press.

Massey, Douglas S., and Nancy A. Denton. 1988. Suburbanization and Segregation in U.S. Metropolitan Areas. *American Journal of Sociology* 94 (November): 592–626.

Mollenkopf, John Hull. 1992. *A Phoenix in the Ashes: The Rise and Fall of the Koch Coalition in New York City Politics.* Princeton, NJ: Princeton University Press.

Mollenkopf, John. 1995. New York, The Great Anomaly. Paper prepared for presentation at the American Political Science Association, August 31-September 3.

Morris, Aldon M. 1984. *The Origins of the Civil Rights Movement: Black Communities Organizing for Change.* New York: Free Press.

Padilla, Felix. 1987. *Puerto Rican Chicago.* Notre Dame, Ind.: University of Notre Dame Press.

Pearson, Rick and Adam Kovac. 2002. Keep Shakman Rule, Candidates Say. *Chicago Tribune.* January 13, Section 4, 3.

Pearson, Rick, and Gary Washburn. 2001. High Court's Democrats Keep Party Remap Lines; Mell Rushes to File New City Ward Map. *Chicago Tribune*, November 29, 1.

Pelissero, John P., and David B. Holian, II. 1994. Electing a Minority Mayor: The Impact on City Finances and Employment. Paper presented at the American Political Science Association, New York, September 1–4.

Pinderhughes, Dianne M. 1987. *Race and Ethnicity in Chicago Politics: A Re-examination of Pluralist Theory.* Urbana: University of Illinois Press.

Pinderhughes, Dianne M. 1994. Racial and Ethnic Politics in Chicago Mayoral Elections. In George E. Peterson, ed., *Big City Politics: Governance and Fiscal Constraints*, 37–62. Washington, DC: Urban Institute Press.

Pinderhughes, Dianne M. 1997. An Examination of Chicago Politics for Evidence of Political Incorporation and Representation. In Browning, Rufus P., Dale Rogers Marshall, and David H. Tabb, eds., *Racial Politics in American Cities*, 2nd ed., 117–135. New York: Longman.

Pinderhughes, Dianne M. 2000. Twenty-First Century Chicago Politics: Ten Years Later. In *Commissioned Research Reports Handbook 1999–2000, Social and Public Policy Series*, 1–23. Chicago; Human Relations Foundation of Chicago.

Squires, Gregory D., Larry Bennett, Kathleen McCourt, and Philip Nyden. 1987. *Race, Class and the Response to Urban Decline.* Philadelphia: Temple University Press.

Starks, Robert T. 2000a. Speech, Annual Black Studies Conference, Olive Harvey College, Chicago, Illinois, April 15.

Starks, Robert T. 2000b. Telephone interview, August 25.

Starks, Robert T., and Michael B. Preston. 1990. Harold Washington and the Politics of Reform in Chicago 1983–1987. In Rufus P. Browning, Dale Rogers Marshall, and David H. Tabb, eds., *Racial Politics in American Cities*, 88–107. White Plains, NY: Longman.

Stone, Clarence N. 1989. *Regime Politics Governing Atlanta 1946–1988.* Lawrence: University Press of Kansas.

Suttles, Gerald D. 1990. *The Man-Made City: The Land Use Confidence Game in Chicago.* Chicago: University of Chicago Press.

Taylor, Elizabeth. 2002. Attachments. *Chicago Tribune Magazine*, January 13, 31.

Torres, Maria de los Angeles. 1991. The Commission on Latino Affairs: A Case Study of Community Empowerment. In Pierre Clavel and Wim Wiewel, eds., *Harold Washington and the Neighborhoods. Progressive City Government in Chicago*, 165–187. New Brunswick, NJ: Rutgers University Press.

Travis, Dempsey J. 1987. *An Autobiography of Black Politics.* Chicago: Urban Research Press.

U.S. Bureau of the Census. 1990. Census of Population, Summary Tape File 3A, Illinois, Ancestry, Hispanic Origin. CD-ROM.

Walsh, Edward. 1995. In Chicago, the Politics of Race Appear to Be Set Aside for Daley. *The Washington Post*, February 26, A3.

Warren, Ellen, and Mark Caro. 1995. Happy or Mad, Voters Stay Away in Historic Totals. *Chicago Tribune*, March 2, 1.

Washburn, Gary. 2001. City Ward Remap OKd by 48-1 Vote. *Chicago Tribune*, December 20, 3.

Washington Post. 1995. Daley Wins by Knockout in Chicago Primary Vote. March 1, A3.

Wilson, James Q. 1960. Two Negro Politicians. *Midwest Journal of Political Science* 4 November: 346–369.

Zikmund, Joseph, II. 1982. Mayoral Voting and Ethnic Politics in the Daley-Bilandic-Byrne Era. In Samuel K. Gove and Louis H. Masotti, eds., *After Daley: Chicago Politics in Transition*, 27–56. Urbana: University of Illinois Press.

Chapter 6

San Francisco: The Politics of Race, Land Use, and Ideology

Richard E. DeLeon

EDITORS' NOTE

Many observers view San Francisco as the last outpost of urban liberalism among large U.S. cities. Richard E. DeLeon agrees and offers recent comparative survey data to support that claim. He also shows that as San Francisco enters its second decade as a majority-minority city, its major racial and ethnic minority groups still have not converted the full potential of their growing numbers into political power. The expanding Asian and Latino populations, which include many recently arrived and non-citizen immigrants, continue their struggle to mobilize electorally toward greater political incorporation. At the same time, the city's African Americans are fighting to protect their hard-won political gains from new competition even as their population base continues to shrink and their economic hardships worsen.

DeLeon's analysis of the "political chemistry" of multiracial coalition building shows how different combinations of group interest and ideology can attract or repel potential allies. He argues that African Americans in particular confront difficult obstacles in forging stable electoral alliances with any of the other major racial/ethnic groups. Liberal on economic issues but conservative on social and environmental issues, many African Americans have come to feel isolated and estranged from mainstream city politics.

DeLeon also gives an account of Mayor Willie Brown's first six years as mayor. Elected in 1995 as the city's first African-American mayor, Brown promised to make his administration the most racially and ethnically inclusive in the city's history as well as more responsive to the needs of the city's low-income families and long-neglected neighborhood communities. As DeLeon shows, however, Mayor Brown's pro-growth approach to that agenda had the paradoxical effect of encouraging the invasion of dot-com firms and investment capital that threatened to displace the very families and neighborhood communities he had hoped to serve. Combined with the return of district elections and the mobilization of a new slow-growth movement, the resulting anti-Brown backlash created the "perfect political storm" in the November 2000 election that broke his vaunted political machine and ushered in a new, progressive supermajority on the Board of Supervisors, which has opposed him since at every turn.

DeLeon concludes with the argument that leaders of the city's major racial/ethnic groups must expand their agendas to include land-use issues as a priority. He also argues they must master the practice of what Robert Bailey calls "identity multiplexing" to be able to build the kinds of stable and inclusive multiracial coalitions that are required as the foundation for a new urban progressivism.

In January 1996, following his election as San Francisco's first African-American mayor, Willie L. Brown, Jr., took charge of his office with high expectations. Demographic changes over the previous decade had made San Francisco a majority-minority city, and Brown was prepared to act on his promise to take immediate steps to make his administration the most racially and ethnically inclusive in the city's history. The local economy, which had sputtered for years, was springing to life with new growth and investment in leading high-tech industries. The budget crises that had plagued his predecessors, Mayor Art Agnos (1988–1991) and Mayor Frank Jordan (1992–1995), were behind him as new business-generated revenues flowed into the city's coffers. With the powers of his office enhanced by recent charter reforms, Brown enjoyed unprecedented mayoral control of the city's bureaucracy, expanded budget authority, and greater influence over the city's many policy-making boards and commissions. Planned departures of incumbents from the 11-member Board of Supervisors, the legislative body for the consolidated city and county of San Francisco, opened vacancies that he could fill early on to build a loyal working majority to pass his legislative initiatives—or at least not oppose them. As a nationally known liberal and leading figure in the Democratic Party, he had moved into city hall as the most formidable politician ever to have served as Speaker of the California State Assembly. He had connections with supporters and bankrollers in high places and reputational power to burn. Under these favorable conditions, if he had become mayor of some other big U.S. city, the voters might have made him king.

That was not to happen in San Francisco, however. In 1999, running for re-election, Brown was forced into a runoff against the city's leading progressive, Tom Ammiano, a nationally known gay activist and current president of the Board of Supervisors. Mayor Brown defeated Ammiano and won a second term, but only at the price of courting the city's Republicans and conservatives and by pulling out all stops in raising funds for his campaign. Earlier, in 1996, the city's voters had dumped the at-large system and restored district elections for supervisor—over Brown's objections. In November 2000, those same voters, voting in districts for the first time since 1979, rejected his plans for land use and development, defeated virtually all of his anointed and lavishly funded candidates, and elected a new, progressive supermajority to the board, which has opposed him since at every turn. In November 2001, to be sure the little red light went out on the ruined Willie Brown machine, leaders of the new board majority introduced ballot measures to dilute the mayor's appointment powers, restrict his control over the redistricting process, and mandate campaign spending limits and public financing of board elections. The voters passed them all. By the end of 2001, the local economy had also tanked in the midst of a general nationwide recession, which only added to the mayor's reversals of political fortune. As revenue shortfalls loomed, Mayor Brown began to withdraw from public view to plan a campaign for a State Senate seat in 2004.

Why did this happen? And how could it have happened to one of the nation's leading liberal politicians in what is arguably the nation's most liberal city?

In this chapter, after sketching a larger picture and presenting some background data on the city's racial and ethnic diversity, I explore possible answers to these questions through a more focused analysis of important moments in San Francisco's recent political history. The first was Willie Brown's election in 1995 as the city's first African-American mayor. The second was the successful campaign by community activists in 1996 to restore district elections for supervisors after 16 years under an at-large system. The third was Mayor Brown's campaign for re-election in 1999, particularly his runoff victory over challenger Tom Ammiano. And the fourth was the November 7, 2000, election, which I view as a watershed event and transformational turning point in San Francisco's political development. This history is deliberately selective and elliptical, and a great many things happened that are politically significant before, between, and after these highlighted moments. However, the evidence drawn from those cases is sufficient, I believe, to explain the rise and fall of Willie Brown as mayor of San Francisco. At the end, I state my conclusions and conjectures on that matter. I also advance a few propositions inspired by this study about the changing meaning of *liberalism* and *conservatism* in the urban context and about the future place of race and identity politics in what, I believe, is an emerging, new urban progressivism.

SAN FRANCISCO AS A LIBERAL OASIS AND CITY OF REFUGE

San Francisco has evolved politically over the last quarter-century into the nation's most liberal city and the urban capital of progressivism. Although that claim has been challenged (for reasons to be discussed), the city has reached certain milestones that most observers from the left would judge to be liberal or progressive achievements. One such milestone was the election of George Moscone as mayor in 1975, marking the historical point of origin of San Francisco's progressive movement. The tragic assassinations of Mayor Moscone and of gay supervisor Harvey Milk in 1978 set the movement back for years. In 1986, however, after a decade of grass roots revolts against a business-dominated, pro-growth coalition, slow-growth activists fulfilled part of Moscone's vision by persuading the voters to approve stringent caps on high-rise office development, linkage fees, neighborhood preservation policies, and expanded citizen participation requirements in land-use planning.

These new policies loosened the grip of business and capital on the city's physical and economic development (Wirt 1974; Mollenkopf 1983; Hartman 1984; DeLeon 1992). The city's voters followed this by electing liberal Art Agnos as mayor in 1987, passing residential rent controls that same year, and electing the first liberal-progressive majority on the Board of Supervisors in 1988. The movement came to a halt once again in 1991, however, when popular disenchantment with Mayor Agnos's abrasive personality and pro-growth initiatives fractured the progressive coalition, sabotaged his re-election campaign, and ushered an even less friendly and more conservative leader into office, ex–police chief Frank Jordan.

As the nation began to turn to the right with the Republican onslaught that toppled Democrats from power in the 1994 elections, the liberal-progressive majority on the Board of Supervisors held Mayor Jordan at bay, and the voters re-elected all local Democrats holding seats in the state legislature and in the U.S. House of Representatives. "Some people think of us as the United States of San Francisco," joked Mayor Jordan after the election. Supervisor Terence Hallinan, then the most liberal of liberals on the board, commented: "We're conservative about being liberal. Our traditions are well entrenched. They're not subject to swings the way the rest of the state and country are" (*San Francisco Chronicle* 1994: A6).

Since Willie Brown's election as mayor in 1995, San Francisco has solidified its reputation as the nation's "left coast city" in a number of policy areas. The city adopted landmark domestic partners legislation in advancing gay rights (DeLeon 1999), asserted its local autonomy by resisting the state government's repressive anti-immigrant and anti–affirmative action policies, and defied attempts by state and federal authorities to crack down on the city's needle exchange and medicinal marijuana programs. More generally, over the last quarter century, San Franciscans have pioneered a new vision of urban progressivism that encourages an expanded role for local government in achieving distributive justice, limits on growth, neighborhood preservation, and ethnic-cultural diversity under conditions of public accountability and direct citizen participation (DeLeon 1992, 33).

The Roper Social Capital Benchmark 2000 Survey (see Appendix) provides evidence to support the claim that San Francisco is the nation's capital of progressivism—not only at the level of local government policies and programs, but also at the level of public values and political culture. Conducted during the period July through November 2000, the Roper Project administered the same battery of questions to a national sample of 3,003 adults and to independent samples of adults in 40 participating communities (cities, counties, regions, and states), including San Francisco.

Figure 6.1 plots the percentage of non-whites who identified themselves as moderately or very liberal in each of these community samples against the percentage of whites who did so. The graph dramatically reveals that San Francisco, ideologically speaking, stands alone and far apart from all other communities surveyed as well as from the national norm. None even comes close to matching the estimated 71.9 percent of San Francisco white respondents who identified themselves as liberals, and only Seattle can rival San Francisco's estimated 46.2 percent of non-whites who claimed the same label. The multiple and changing meanings of

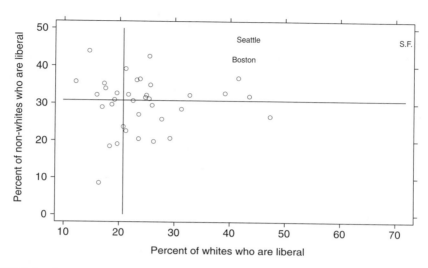

FIGURE 6.1 **Scatterplot of the percentage of non-white adults in each sample who identified themselves as liberals versus the percentage of white adults who did the same**

Plotted data points are based on weighted point estimates of percentages in each of the 40 communities sampled by the Roper Social Capital Benchmark Survey 2000 project. The cross-hatch locates the co-ordinates of the national norm (30.9, 20.9) based on the Roper national sample survey results.

Source: Roper Social Capital Benchmark Survey, 2000 (see Appendix).

the term *liberal* will be explored later in this chapter, but for now, these results may speak for themselves: San Francisco is, indeed, an exceedingly liberal city, and its white population is the most liberal of all.

Renowned for its culture of tolerance and celebration of diversity, San Francisco in 1985 officially declared itself to be a "city of refuge" and has since enacted a series of "sanctuary city" policies to protect immigrants and refugees. One would expect, therefore, that the Roper Survey would show San Franciscans to be especially welcoming and sympathetic toward immigrants. Figure 6.2 offers evidence to support that claim. It plots the percentage of white citizens in each sample who *disagreed* strongly with the statement that "immigrants are getting too demanding in their push for equal rights" against the percentage of white citizens who *agreed* strongly with it. Once again, San Francisco stands alone and far apart from all other communities surveyed as well as from the national norm. An estimated 56.2 percent of the city's white citizen respondents disagreed strongly with the statement, and only 2.4 percent agreed strongly with it. Nationally and in some other cities, public opinion is sharply polarized on immigration issues. That is not the case in San Francisco, where the popular consensus supporting immigrants is very firm and unified.

It is important to locate San Francisco within the larger picture of national politics and public opinion, because the city's fame—or notoriety—as a bastion of liberalism is a source of pride for many leaders and activists. San Franciscans

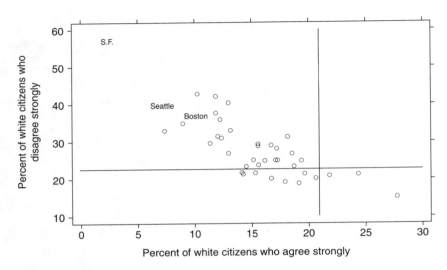

FIGURE 6.2 **Scatterplot of the percentage of white citizens in each sample who disagreed strongly with the statement that "immigrants are getting too demanding in their push for equal rights" versus the percentage of white citizens who strongly agreed with the statement**

Plotted data points are based on weighted point estimates of percentages in each of the 40 communities sampled by the Roper Social Capital Benchmark Survey 2000 project. The cross-hatch locates the co-ordinates of the national norm (22.6, 21.0) based on the Roper national sample survey results.

Source: Roper Social Capital Benchmark Survey, 2000 (see Appendix).

enjoy being in the national spotlight, leading the way toward reform and social change, and stirring things up. It is true that other cities have led the way in certain policy domains (Baltimore, for example, in the case of the living wage movement), but there will always be San Franciscans who will push city hall to compete for that honor. The general point is that San Francisco's progressive agenda is rarely strictly local; many local activists see themselves as performing on a larger stage before a national audience. Such ambition motivates behavior, and it explains much about San Francisco politics that cannot be explained in simply local terms.

SAN FRANCISCO AS A MAJORITY-MINORITY CITY

San Francisco officially became a majority-minority city in 1990, when the U.S. Census reported that the Anglo population had dropped to under 47 percent of the total. Since 1990, the city's racial and ethnic composition has continued to change, immigration has continued significantly affecting city life, important socioeconomic differences and disparities among racial/ethnic groups have persisted, and the intergroup struggle for political representation and power has not stopped.

Shifts and Trends in the City's Racial and Ethnic Diversity

The racial and ethnic composition of San Francisco's population has changed significantly since 1990, but the overall direction of that change has stayed the same since the 1970s: Anglos and African Americans down, and Asians and Latinos up.

Anglos   As shown in Table 6.1, the city's Anglo population has continued to decline both in absolute numbers and in share of the total population, further reinforcing San Francisco's recently acquired status as a majority-minority city. The Anglo population still constitutes 47.1 percent of the city's total voter-age population (VAP), however, and its relatively high voter turnout rates consistently produce large white majorities, especially in low-turnout, non–presidential year elections.

Blacks   Also following an established trend, African Americans have continued to lose numbers and relative size at a faster rate than in any other U.S. city (McCormick 2001). Always a small minority (13.9 percent at their height in 1970), the black population has now fallen to 7.6 percent of the total—and a tiny 6.9 percent of the VAP. Chipped away by rising housing costs, loss of blue-collar jobs, migration to the suburbs, and actuarial attrition, the black population base has lost ground, figuratively

TABLE 6.1   Racial/ethnic composition of San Francisco population, 1990 and 2000

Racial/Ethnic Groups	1990 Total Population[a]		2000 Total Population[b]		2000 VAP[b]		Estimated Voter Turnout Rate (% of VAP) in November 7, 2000, Election
	Number	*%*	*Number*	*%*	*Number*	*%*	
Hispanic or Latino	96,258	13.3	109,504	14.1	84,719	12.8	15.8
Non-Hispanic or Latino							
White	339,452	46.9	338,909	43.6	312,942	47.1	71.2
Black or African American	77,518	10.7	58,791	7.6	45,998	6.9	31.8
Asian	206,003	28.5	238,173	30.7	197,158	29.7	24.6
Other race	6,000	0.6	31,356	4.0	23,114	3.5	—
Totals:	723,626	100.0	776,733	100.0	663,931	100.0	—

[a]Asian category includes Pacific Islanders.

[b]Other race category includes American Indian, Native Alaskan, Native Hawaiian, Pacific Islander, some other race, and mixed race.

Sources: 1990 Total Population—U.S. Census 5% Public Use Microdata Sample (PUMS) for 1990; 2000 Total Population and VAP—U.S. Census Table QT-PL, Race, Hispanic or Latino, and Age: 2000, for San Francisco County. Data set: Census 2000 Redistricting Data (Public Law 94-171) Summary File, Matrices PL1, PL2, PL3, and PL4; Estimated Voter Turnout—see Appendix.

and literally, to the ascendant Asians and Latinos and has eroded to the point of endangering its hard-won place in the city's political power structures (Nieves 2001; Ness 2001a). Nieves writes:

> The result, in one of the few major cities with a black mayor and a liberal political sensibility in sync with a majority of African-Americans, is a San Francisco with whole neighborhoods where it is rare to see a black person. It is a city where blacks have little clout, few cultural institutions and only one remaining neighborhood, the homely, lonely Bayview-Hunters Point, best known for a sewage treatment plant and a radioactive Superfund site. For many blacks here, San Francisco is the sweetheart who loved 'em and left 'em, who promised the moon and stars only to forget them when new blood came to town. (Nieves 2001, Y21).

Asians   The city's diverse Asian population has continued to grow in both absolute and relative terms, and it has spread both west and south into new areas of the city. Although three of every 10 residents are now Asians (about half of them Chinese), many are recently arrived immigrants and non-citizens (Table 6.2), and the political conversion of residents into citizens and voters has only recently picked up steam (Chao 1998; Ong and Lee 2001).

Latinos   The city's Latinos (most with origins in Mexico and Central America) have achieved a modest net growth since 1990 in both numbers and relative share. Based on official U.S. Census counts, Latinos now comprise 14.1 percent of the total population and 12.8 percent of the VAP, moving past African Americans on the charts. The same forces that have whittled down the black population, however, have also kept the Latino population smaller than it might otherwise be. Rising housing costs and limited blue-collar jobs in particular have driven many Latino families across the Bay or down the peninsula in search of employment opportunities and affordable housing (DelVecchio 2001). Those who have remained in the city continue to concentrate mainly in the Mission district, with expanding enclaves in the southern parts of the city. Until very recently, Latinos have been the least politically mobilized and most poorly represented of all the city's major racial/ethnic groups (DeLeon 1997).

San Francisco's Immigrants

Compiled in Table 6.2 are recent statistics that demonstrate the contribution immigrants have made to the city's overall population growth and remarkable diversity. Fully 37 percent of the city's current residents are foreign-born, and at least 16 percent are non-citizens. Nearly 40 percent of the foreign-born have arrived in San Francisco since 1990, and nearly three out of four in that cohort are not citizens. Most of the foreign-born and nearly half of the non-citizens came from Asian countries, mainly China. Nearly 20 percent of the foreign-born came from Mexico and other parts of Central America; Latino immigrants constitute more than 27 percent

TABLE 6.2 **Percentage estimates of foreign-born, non-citizens, immigrant cohorts, language spoken at home, and linguistic isolation**

1. Estimated number and % foreign-born of total population, 2000: 279,967; 37.0%
2. Estimated number and % non-citizens of total population, 2000: 121,774; 16.1%
3. Breakdown of foreign-born and non-citizen populations, 2000, by place of birth:

Place of Birth	% of Foreign-Born	% Non-Citizens
Europe	14.2	17.5
Asia	61.1	47.7
Mexico	7.7	13.1
Other Central America	10.8	14.1
Other	6.2	7.6
Total:	100.0	100.0

4. Breakdown of total foreign-born population, 2000, by year of arrival:

Year of Arrival	% of Foreign-Born	% Non-Citizens in Cohort
Before 1980	31.7	15.5
1980–1989	29.2	34.1
1990–2000	39.1	73.2
Total:	100.0	

5. Language spoken at home and linguistic isolation, 1999 (households):

	Language Spoken at Home[a] (% of all households)	Linguistically Isolated[b] (% of language group)
English	56.3	—
Spanish	11.5	30.6
Other Indo-European	7.7	26.8
Asian or Pacific-Islander language	23.6	37.3
Other language	0.9	15.3
Total:	100.0	

[a]Language spoken at home is indicated by household respondent reporting speaking a language other than English sometimes or always at home.

[b]Linguistically isolated households are those in which all adults have some limitation in communicating in English. Website URL for data, definitions, and other documentation: http://factfinder.census.gov/home/en/acsdata.html

Source: Computations based on sample estimates from U.S. Census, American Community Survey, 1999 and 2000, for San Francisco City, CA. Summary Tables 2000: P038, P039, and P040; Summary Tables 1999: P107, P109.

of the city's officially counted non-citizen population. At least one resident in more than 40 percent of the city's households speaks a language other than English at home either sometimes or always. Within these major non–English language groups, particularly among Asians and Latinos, the rates of linguistic isolation are high, ranging from 27 to 37 percent.

Guided by San Francisco's city of refuge policies, the mayor and other local officials, including the police, have consistently refused to co-operate with the Immigration and Naturalization Service in facilitating raids and detentions, particularly in the city's predominately Latino Mission district (Chao 1999). Following the September 11th terrorist attack, on grounds that it would constitute racial profiling, city officials refused to co-operate with federal agents seeking to detain and interview foreign persons who were not actual suspects in the crime (Herel and Hendricks 2001). San Francisco also became the first city or county in the nation to require all city agencies to officially honor "matricula consulare" ID cards as legal identification. In the wake of September 11th, the cards became hot items as immigrants were required to prove their identities more often and federal authorities cracked down on even minor visa infractions. When the new policy was challenged by anti-immigration groups, the city's police chief, Fred Lau, replied that enforcing immigration law "really isn't our job. That's the INS's. . . . This is a sanctuary city, and we have city policies we have to abide by" (Ness 2001b).

Racial/Ethnic Group Differences and Disparities in Needs and Resources

Table 6.3 reveals significant socioeconomic differences and disparities among San Francisco's major racial/ethnic groups. By nearly all indicators, the city's Anglos are better off, on average, than are members of other racial/ethnic groups. Based on 1999 U.S. Census estimates, more Anglo households (25.6 percent) earn at least $100,000 a year compared to those that earn less than $25,000 (20.5 percent). At the other extreme, an estimated 45 percent of African-American households earn less than $25,000, and only 3.9 percent earn $100,000 or more. Nearly one in four African Americans lives below the official 100 percent poverty line, which tops the poverty rates of other or mixed-race categories (15.6 percent) and Latinos (14 percent) and is much worse than Asians (10.9 percent) and Anglos (6.7 percent). Nearly 20 percent of African-American families have a single female head of household who cares for children under the age of 18 living at home. No other major racial/ethnic group comes close to that statistic. Furthermore, the city's Asians, Latinos, and those of other or mixed race are much more likely than Anglos or African Americans to live in overcrowded housing units.

Table 6.3 also shows that blacks in the labor force in 1999 had the highest unemployment rate of all major racial/ethnic groups—more than four times the unemployment rate of Anglos, more than twice that of Asians, and nearly twice that of Latinos. These intergroup differences are even more dramatic among younger job seekers. An estimated 29.9 percent of black males between the ages of 16 and 29 were unemployed in 1999, compared to 3.8 percent for Anglos, 5.3 percent for Asians, 7.4 percent for those of other or mixed race, and 9.4 percent for Latinos.

TABLE 6.3   Breakdown of household income, poverty rates, education, unemployment, and overcrowding by race and ethnicity: San Francisco residents, 1999

Item	Anglos	Blacks	Asians	Other/ Mixed[a]	Hispanic	All
% of households earning less than $25,000	20.5	45.0	27.8	27.0	28.9	26.3
% of households earning at least $100,000	25.6	3.9	18.1	11.1	11.3	18.1
% of persons below 100% poverty line	6.7	24.1	10.9	15.6	14.0	11.5
% of families with single female head of household and children under 18 years	1.2	18.1	2.4	6.5	4.8	4.1
% of persons 25 years or older with at least a bachelor's degree	58.9	20.5	32.9	25.7	26.1	41.5
% unemployed of persons 16 years or older in the labor force	2.9	12.1	4.8	5.9	7.0	4.9
% unemployed of males 16–29	3.8	29.9	5.3	7.4	9.4	7.5
% of occupied housing units with 1.01+ persons per room	1.9	4.0	18.0	21.8	18.9	—

[a]Other/mixed race excludes Hawaiians, Pacific Islanders, American Indians, and Alaskans. Website URL for data, definitions, and other documentation: http://factfinder.census.gov/home/en/acsdata.html

Source: Computations based on sample estimates from U.S. Census, American Community Survey, 1999, for San Francisco City, CA. Summary Tables P42, P42A-I, PCT24, PCT24A-I, P76, P76A-I, P123, P123A-I, P31, P31A-I, HCT161A-I.

These statistics do not bode well for the city's already declining African-American community, which has been beset in recent years by a sharp rise in gang violence and related crimes, especially in Bayview-Hunters Point (Sward 2001).

Table 6.3 shows striking disparities in education among the city's major racial/ethnic groups as well. An estimated 59 percent of Anglos 25 years or older have at least a bachelor's degree, a level of educational attainment nearly three times that of the African-American population and more than twice that of Latinos. About one-third of Asians in that age group have at least a bachelor's degree. San Francisco's touted "new economy" continues to move away from manufacturing and distribution to leading-edge, high-tech sectors, such as the digital media, biotechnology, and advanced corporate services (Sims 2000). These statistics, therefore, indicate that African Americans and Latinos will be particularly disadvantaged in competing for jobs that will allow them to remain in the city. As documented by urban labor economist Michael Potepan (1998), only about 28 percent of the total of 535,000 jobs in San Francisco in 1996 were held by workers with a high school education or less. Of the 35,068 new city jobs created between 1994 and 1997, an estimated 7,924 (27 percent) were filled by workers with a high school education or less. Many of these less educated workers, Potepan concluded, "are employed around the margins in San Francisco's economy in industries and occupations that tend to pay relatively low wages, do not offer benefits, and provide few opportunities for advancement. These included jobs in restaurants, garment factories, as private security guards, and as custodians and janitors" (1998, 18).

Political Mobilization and Incorporation of Racial and Ethnic Minorities

A leading theory of urban politics (Browning, Marshall, and Tabb 1984) asserts that protest in the form of demonstrations, boycotts, rallies, and so on is not enough for disadvantaged racial and ethnic minority groups to succeed in their struggle for equality. Given sufficient population numbers, they must also mobilize electorally and form alliances with other disadvantaged groups and supportive white liberals to achieve political incorporation within the city's dominant governing coalition. Only then will they gain sustained political access to—and responsive policies from—local government on issues of most concern to them.

Political incorporation is key, and it involves a combination of formal representation and informal inclusion in the power centers that make policy. A group has achieved substantial political incorporation, argue Browning, Marshall and Tabb, when it "is in a position to articulate its interests, its demands will be heard, and through the dominant coalition it can ensure that certain interests will be protected, even though it may not win on every issue" (1984, 27).

It can be questioned whether San Francisco has either a dominant coalition or the governing capacity needed to respond effectively to minority-group interests. There have also been recent and complicating changes afoot in the definition of issues that most concern various racial/ethnic groups and in the range of interests they pursue and seek to protect. However, we can at least provide some rough indicators for the level of electoral mobilization and political incorporation achieved by each of the city's major racial/ethnic groups.

Anglos   Anglos typically register and turn out to vote at a much higher rate than do the VAPs of the city's other major racial/ethnic groups. For example, an estimated 71 percent of the Anglo VAP turned out to vote for the November 2000 election (see Table 6.1). As of January 2002, seven Anglos (64 percent of the total) serve on the 11-member Board of Supervisors. All are men; two are gay (Tom Ammiano and Mark Leno). Based on 1990 U.S. Census statistics, 1994 Equal Employment Opportunity reports, and other data for 1993 to 1995 (see DeLeon 1997, 146), Anglos in the early 1990s constituted 58 percent of the membership on the city's 32 boards and commissions and 56 percent of the presidents of boards and commissions. Finally, Anglos in 1990 held 39 percent of all local government jobs and 55 percent of the official/administrator and professional positions. All these percentages come close to or exceed the Anglo group's current 43.6 percent share of the total population.

Blacks   As an indicator of electoral mobilization, an estimated 32 percent of the black VAP turned out to vote for the November 2000 election—a higher turnout rate than that of Asians and Latinos, but much lower than that of Anglos. As of January 2002, an African American, Willie Brown, holds the mayor's office (100 percent of the total). One African American (9 percent of the total) serves on the Board of Supervisors, and it happens that this supervisor, Sophie Maxwell, is also the only woman on the board. Blacks in the early 1990s constituted 14 percent of the membership on the city's boards and commissions and 6 percent of the presidents of boards and commissions. Finally, blacks in 1990 held 19 percent of all local government jobs and 12 percent of the official/administrator and professional positions. All these percentages come close to or exceed the African-American group's current 7.6 percent share of the total population.

Asians   An estimated 25 percent of the Asian VAP turned out to vote for the November 2000 election—a higher turnout rate than that of Latinos, but lower than that of African Americans and much lower than that of Anglos. As shown in Table 6.2 for both Asians and Latinos, however, many of the city's Asians are non-citizen immigrants or have achieved citizenship only recently. Despite apparently successful voter registration drives in recent years (McLeod 1997; Ong and Lee 2001), only one Asian American, Leland Yee, currently serves on the Board of Supervisors (9 percent of the total). Significantly, in late 2000, before the shift to district elections, three Asian Americans held seats on the board (27 percent). Asian Americans in the early 1990s constituted 20 percent of the membership on the city's boards and commissions and 31 percent of the presidents of boards and commissions. Finally, Asians in 1990 held 29 percent of all local government jobs and 23 percent of the official/administrator and professional positions. Most of these percentages are below but close to the Asian group's current 31 percent share of the total population.

Latinos   An estimated 16 percent of the Latino VAP turned out to vote for the November 2000 election—the lowest turnout rate of all major racial/ethnic groups. As with Asians, however, many of the city's Latinos are non-citizen immigrants or have achieved citizenship only recently, suggesting a long road ahead before this group's full political mobilization. Anecdotal evidence suggests that the state's anti-immigrant policies in the 1990s (particularly Proposition 187) have mobilized growing numbers of Latinos into the local electorate. Furthermore, the gentrification/displacement impacts of recent economic change in the Mission district (discussed later) as well as the federal government's crackdown on immigrants following the September 11th terrorist attacks have added to the motivation driving Latinos to naturalize, register, and vote. Two Latino men, Matt Gonzalez and Gerado Sandoval, both elected in November 2000, currently serve on the Board of Supervisors (18 percent of the total). Latinos in the early 1990s constituted 7 percent of the membership on the city's boards and commissions—and zero percent of the presidents of boards and commissions. Finally, Latinos in 1990 held 13 percent of all local government jobs and 9 percent of the official/administrator and professional positions. Latino representation on boards and commissions and in higher administrative positions falls below the 14 percent Latino share of the total population.

Summary   These admittedly rough statistics accord with impressions gained from personal observations and interviews with local political experts. In general, Anglos achieve high levels of electoral mobilization and political incorporation out of proportion to their declining share of the population base. Blacks have a level of political incorporation close to parity with their population base, but demographic trends point toward reduced presence and influence in the city's political power structures. Asians continue to expand their population base but have had difficulty achieving full political mobilization. It remains to be seen whether they can hold a representative share of governing offices. Latinos, like Asians, continue to expand their population base, but at a slower rate. Also like Asians, and for many of the same reasons, Latinos have had only limited success in achieving full political mobilization and incorporation. The recent election of two Latinos to the Board of Supervisors, however, might foretell a more promising political future.

POLITICAL CHEMISTRY OF MULTIRACIAL COALITION BUILDING IN SAN FRANCISCO

Demographic realities in San Francisco dictate the necessity of building multiracial electoral coalitions for any racial/ethnic group to achieve power and influence in San Francisco politics. Leaders of the city's racial/ethnic minority groups in particular face difficult strategic and tactical choices in selecting political allies, negotiating agendas, and organizing campaigns. Electoral majorities tend to disintegrate rather quickly in the city's highly fissionable political culture. Many electoral coalitions are theoretically possible, but only a few have realistic prospects of stability and success. What kinds of coalitions are feasible, and what kinds are not? What holds them together or tears them apart? What price must be paid to participate in such coalitions—and is that price worth it?

According to Raphael Sonenshein (1997), the "glue" that holds coalitions together is a mixture of group self-interest and shared ideology: "The optimists focus on the role of *ideology* and emphasize the enduring and solid character of biracial coalitions based on common beliefs. The pessimists tend to see *interest* as the glue of coalitions and to view biracial coalitions as at best short-lived compromises between self-centered groups" (262). Regarding progressive multiracial coalition building, Sonenshein writes that as an organizing principle, "color is an unreliable glue. Using ethnicity as a bond for coalitions—rather than addressing the serious economic and social issues of community life—will have the paradoxical effect of exacerbating coalition tensions" (274).

Sonenshein's analysis of the roles played by interest and ideology in building successful coalitions illuminates important aspects of multiracial coalition building in San Francisco. (One might add "identity" politics to this recipe, as will be done later in this chapter, though it is admittedly difficult at times to differentiate interests from ideology and both of those from identity. Robert Bailey [1999] draws some usefully clear distinctions between identity and interests in particular that have guided my own thinking on this issue.) What follows is a summary (visually aided by graphs) of the "rules" of political chemistry that appear to govern the mutual attraction and repulsion of potential coalition partners in San Francisco's multiracial political universe.

1. Definitions of *postmaterialism* and *materialism* in the urban political context: Postmaterialism is a term advanced by Ronald Inglehart (1990) to describe a new political polarization found increasingly in advanced industrial societies. It is a value-based political cleavage that cuts across traditional class and racial divisions. It is focused on social and environmental issues that relate more to the meaning and quality of life than to its materialist basis in property and economic growth. At the city level, postmaterialist values and interests motivate political conflict on matters such as environmental protection, neighborhood preservation, urban aesthetics, individual liberties, and citizen empowerment (DeLeon 1991). Materialist values and interests motivate political conflict on matters such as jobs, housing, education, and local government services.

2. Two distinct Left-Right axes structure San Francisco's ideological space. There is a "materialist" Left and Right and a "postmaterialist" Left and Right. San Francisco voters can be classified as Left on both, Right on both, Left on one and Right on the other, or in some kind of centrist position on one or the other.

3. The city's white voters in particular tend to be ideologically polarized between those who are Left on both axes ("white progressives") and those who are Right on both ("white conservatives").

4. Latino voters tend to align with white progressives on most issues and with black voters on materialist issues involving jobs, housing, schools, and local government services.

5. Asian voters tend to align with white conservatives on most issues, but as a group, they occupy an overall middle position in the city's two-dimensional ideological space. The major exception to this rule is voting on certain cultural policy issues, such as gay rights, in which case Asian voters as a group tend to vote even more conservatively than white conservatives. Overall, however, Asians voters appear to be strategically located to play an important mediating and brokering role in building future multiracial coalitions.

6. Black voters tend to align with white progressives and Latinos on materialist issues and with white conservatives and Asians on postmaterialist issues, especially those that relate to social and cultural policies. Ideologically, as a group they are both Left and Right, and which it will be at any given time depends on the type of issue in question. In this sense, blacks are an anomaly in San Francisco politics. To apply Sonenshein's glue metaphor, they

don't "stick" very well or for very long with coalition partners that are consistently Left-Left (white progressives and Latinos) or Right-Right (white conservatives) in their voting patterns and political agendas. This apparent mismatch undermines the prospects of blacks forming stable alliances or coalitions with such groups.

7. San Francisco's two-dimensional ideological space is somewhat warped and wrinkled by the forces of group self-interest, especially in candidate races for elective office. Even in this more competitive and zero-sum arena of politics, however, a substantial amount of coalition building takes place consistent with each group's ideological position.

These "rules" of coalitional political chemistry are empirical generalizations based on observation and study that apply mainly to San Francisco. The graphical analyses that follow are intended merely to illustrate how these rules work with respect to selected political issues, not to provide convincing evidence of their validity and scope. Viewed as a model of political reality, they are a work in progress.

Two graphs are presented and briefly interpreted. Each is a scatterplot of the city's precinct-level vote on a pair of ballot measures. The plotting symbols used in each graph identify precinct electorates classified as white progressive (P), white conservative (C), Asian majority (A), black plurality (B), or Hispanic/Latino plurality (H). (For more details, see the definitions in the graph legends and the Appendix.) The overall pattern revealed by these graphs gives insight into the degree of coalignment or opposition that exists between various racial/ethnic groups in voting on different types of issues. Somewhat whimsically, these patterns might be called "graphical molecules," because they resemble textbook pictures of chemical molecules.

Case 1: Racial/Ethnic Group Voting on Materialist Issues

Figure 6.3 plots the precinct yes vote on a local community college bonds measure (Proposition A, November 2001) against the precinct yes vote on a local charter amendment (Proposition D, November 2000) extending the city's Children's Fund to the year 2016. Proposition A asked voters to approve or reject $195 million in bonds for City College campuses. Proposition D asked voters to approve or reject an extension of the city's annual set-aside of property tax revenues for children's services programs. For purposes of this analysis, both are classified as materialist issues.

As shown in Figure 6.3, there is an overall, strong, positive, and linear relationship between the precinct vote on Proposition A and the precinct vote on Proposition D. Black, Latino, and white progressive precinct electorates are all clustered together at the upper-right (high percentage yes vote on both propositions), and white conservative and Asian precinct electorates are clustered at the lower-left (low percentage yes vote on both), with considerable scattering of the Asian precinct electorates into the middle range of voting yes on these measures. If local government policy making focused strictly on issues like these, there would be only

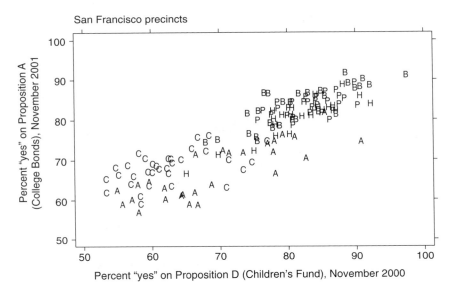

FIGURE 6.3   **Scatterplot of precinct percentage yes vote for Proposition A (College Bonds) in November 2001 versus precinct percentage vote for Proposition D (Children's Fund) in November 2000**

"P" identifies precinct electorates in which Anglos are at least 70 percent of the 2000 VAP and that score in the top 20 percent on the Progressive Voting Index. "C" identifies precinct electorates in which Anglos are at least 70 percent of the 2000 VAP and that score in the bottom 20 percent on the Progressive Voting Index. "B" identifies precinct electorates in which blacks are at least 40 percent of the 2000 VAP. "H" identifies precinct electorates in which Hispanics are at least 40 percent of the 2000 VAP, and "A" identifies precinct electorates in which Asians are at least 60 percent of the 2000 VAP. Precincts that do not meet these criteria are not plotted in the graph.

Sources: San Francisco Department of Elections, Statements of Vote, December 14, 1999, and November 7, 2000. Precinct 2000 VAP by DOJ-defined race/ethnicity (U.S. Census PL94-171 2000 precinct dataset downloaded from the UC Berkeley/IGS Statewide Database website http://swdb.berkeley.edu.)

one Left-Right (liberal-conservative) ideological axis structuring racial and ethnic group politics in San Francisco.

Case 2: Racial/Ethnic Group Voting on a Postmaterialist Issue and a Materialist Issue

Figure 6.4 plots the precinct yes vote on a statewide proposition to constitutionalize a ban on gay marriages (Proposition 22, March 2000) against the precinct yes vote on a local community college bonds measure (Proposition A, November 2001; see above). For this analysis, the first is classified as a postmaterialist issue and the second as a materialist issue.

As shown in Figure 6.4, there is an overall weak, slightly negative, and distinctly nonlinear relationship between the precinct vote on Proposition 22 (with a yes vote

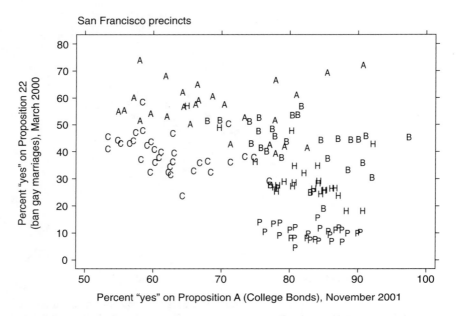

FIGURE 6.4   Scatterplot of precinct percentage yes vote for Proposition 22 (Ban on Gay Marriages) in March 2000 versus precinct percentage vote for Proposition A (College Bonds) in November 2001

"P" identifies precinct electorates in which Anglos are at least 70 percent of the 2000 VAP and that score in the top 20 percent on the Progressive Voting Index. "C" identifies precinct electorates in which Anglos are at least 70 percent of the 2000 VAP and that score in the bottom 20% on the Progressive Voting Index. "B" identifies precinct electorates in which blacks are at least 40 percent of the 2000 VAP. "H" identifies precinct electorates in which Hispanics are at least 40 percent of the 2000 VAP, and "A" identifies precinct electorates in which Asians are at least 60 percent of the 2000 VAP. Precincts that do not meet these criteria are not plotted in the graph.

Sources: San Francisco Department of Elections, Statements of Vote, March 7, 2002, and November 7, 2000. Precinct 2000 VAP by Department of Justice–defined race/ethnicity (U.S. Census PL94-171 2000 precinct dataset downloaded from the UC Berkeley/IGS Statewide Database website http://swdb.berkeley.edu.)

interpreted as conservative and a no vote as liberal) and the precinct vote on Proposition A. We can see immediately that collapsing the two axes into a single Left-Right spectrum, as was possible in the case of Figure 6.3, will not work here. Looking up at the distribution from the bottom axis, we can see the group ordering of C-A-B-H-P moving from left to right on the graph and from Right to Left ideologically. Looking across the distribution from the left axis, we can see the group ordering of A-B-C-H-P. Interpreted in two-dimensional ideological terms, black precinct electorates that voted liberally with Latino and white progressive precincts on college bonds voted much more conservatively on Proposition 22, in alignment with white conservative and Asian precincts. Asian precinct electorates jumped from voting somewhat conservatively on college bonds to voting very conservatively on Proposition 22. Latino precinct electorates—and especially white progressive precincts—remained close together and consistently Left-Left in voting on both propositions.

In sum, this particular "graphical molecule" reveals much that is interesting about the political chemistry involved in building multiracial coalitions with sufficient scope to cover more than one type of issue agenda. Indeed, these graphical insights agree with observations that the two most stable electoral coalitions in San Francisco politics are the essentially biracial alignments of Asians–white conservatives versus Latinos–white progressives. This analysis also illustrates why African Americans in San Francisco have had a difficult time over the years building durable and broad-based coalitional partnerships with any of the other major racial/ethnic groups. (On this last point, see Baca 1992 and Ness 2001a.) This is especially unfortunate, because the city's small and shrinking African-American community needs all the political help it can get to address the severe hardships and inequalities documented earlier in Table 6.3. Space does not allow a deeper exploration of the causes of this phenomenon, except to suggest that a generational divide is growing within San Francisco's African-American community between older, more culturally conservative black liberals with political roots in the civil rights era and younger, more culturally liberal progressives (such as newly elected Supervisor Sophie Maxwell) who are more informed about, and sympathetic to, a broader Left agenda.

SAN FRANCISCO'S FIRST BLACK MAYOR: THE WILLIE BROWN YEARS

In this chapter, it is impossible to provide more than a sketch of the most politically significant events and developments that occurred during Willie Brown's first 6 years as mayor. At least several books will be required to tell the whole tale of Mayor Willie Brown. In this section, I provide a highly selective and roughly chronological account of the most important political moments. In the next section, I focus on the November 7, 2000, election as a case study that illustrates many of the themes and theses advanced thus far and that helps to justify my assessment of the November 7 election as a transformational turning point in San Francisco's recent political history.

Running for Mayor: The 1995 Election

Facing term limits on his long career as a state assemblyman representing San Francisco, Willie L. Brown, Jr., retired early from his powerful role as speaker in 1995 to run for mayor of his city. The move surprised some observers, who knew of Brown's disdain for local government officials and recalled his comment in 1994 that "street lights, dog-doo and parking meters are not my cup of tea" (Richardson 1996, 385). Flamboyant and charismatic, Brown was a major player in state and national Democratic party politics. Despite his long track record as a paid lobbyist for virtually every large corporation and developer in the Bay Area (Richardson 1996)—and despite his freely acknowledged eagerness as speaker to accept huge campaign donations from anybody and everybody willing to pay to keep

Democrats in power (Clucas 1995)—Brown commanded impressive support from the city's liberal-progressive community. Even his detractors conceded that Brown had used his power in the state assembly to channel millions of state and federal dollars into the city, defend civil rights and individual liberties, expand educational and economic opportunities for blacks and other disadvantaged minorities, and protect the "left coast city" from wrathful and intolerant right-wing attacks.

Christened by many local observers as the front-runner in the race for mayor, Brown organized a formidable campaign against the incumbent, Frank Jordan, a pro-growth conservative Democrat, and against rival challenger Roberta Achtenberg, a nationally known lesbian activist and civil rights advocate. After the ballots were counted on November 7, Willie Brown came out on top with 33.6 percent of the votes, followed by Frank Jordan with 32.1 percent and Roberta Achtenberg with 26.8 percent. Brown and Jordan then faced each other in the December 12 runoff election, which Brown won by a vote of 54 percent to 46 percent.

Following his inauguration on January 8, 1996, Mayor Brown took charge of city hall with electrifying zeal. On day one, he appointed African-American Robert Demmons as fire chief and Chinese-American Fred Lau as police chief, thus acting on his promise to take immediate steps to make his administration the most racially and ethnically inclusive in the city's history. He also signaled that a very high priority would be given to economic development, business growth, and job creation, particularly in the working-class neighborhoods of the long-neglected southern and eastern parts of the city. Thus, San Francisco's working-class liberals and racial minorities had good reasons for expecting that Mayor Brown would be responsive to their needs, interests, and aspirations in the years ahead. For those very same reasons, however, the city's white progressives and slow-growth activists braced themselves for the latest mayoral assault on their hard-won growth limits and neighborhood preservation policies.

Charter Reforms Increase Mayoral Authority

In 1995, in addition to electing Willie Brown as mayor, the voters also approved major amendments to the city charter that enhanced the mayor's office by giving it greater budget authority, more power vis-à-vis boards and commissions in choosing department heads, and (by replacing the city's independent chief administrative officer with a city administrator under the mayor's control) consolidated authority over the city's previously bifurcated bureaucracy (Cain, Mullin, and Peele 2001).

Return of District Elections

In 1996, after many earlier failed attempts, neighborhood leaders and community activists mounted a successful campaign to replace the city's at-large system for Board of Supervisors elections with district elections. At the same time, voters rejected a more radical electoral reform—preference (or choice) voting—that would have installed the single transferable vote system of proportional representation. There was strong support for electoral reform of some kind in virtually every major sociodemographic and racial/ethnic category of voter, particularly African Americans, and even the local GOP endorsed district elections in the desperate hope of achieving at least token representation on the board (DeLeon, Hill, and Blash 1998). Proposition G (district elections) won overwhelmingly with 57 percent of the vote. Starting 4 years later, on November 7, 2000, voters in each of the 11 new districts (Figure 6.5) would elect one supervisor to represent them on the board. District elections for supervisor had been used twice before, in 1977 and 1979, but they were repealed by the voters in 1980 following the assassinations of Mayor George Moscone and Supervisor Harvey Milk in 1978.

"What Mayors Are Known For": Mayor Brown's Land Use and Development Projects

In Mayor Brown's first term, the local economy turned from cold to hot, the commercial real estate market revived after 10 years of doldrums, and investment capital began to flow once again into the city. Willie Brown, the most brazenly pro-business and pro-growth mayor in recent memory, was in his element. "Mayors are known for what they build and not anything else," Mayor Brown declared in June 1997, "and I intend to cover every inch of ground that isn't open space" (J. King 1997, A21).

Mayor Brown's allies on the Board of Supervisors and his appointees on the Redevelopment Agency Commission and Planning Commission read his marching orders and did his bidding. Major land use and development projects that had been on hold for years took off (Finnie 1998, A1). These included the long-dormant, 313-acre Mission Bay development project; completion of the new San Francisco Giants Pacific Bell ballpark; repair and restoration of the earthquake-damaged city hall; new and long-delayed high-rise office buildings and condominium housing complexes; razing of dilapidated public housing projects, and building of replacement

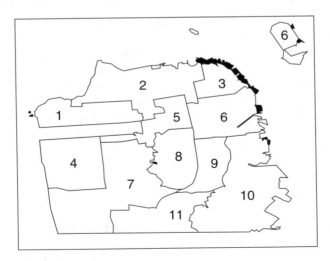

FIGURE 6.5   **Map of districts, San Francisco Board of Supervisors**

units; improved transit and beautification projects along the city's northern water-front; serious planning to extend light-rail transit from the central business district to the long-neglected Bayview-Hunters Point neighborhood; and launching of a successful campaign to persuade voters to contribute $100 million toward replacing the aging Candlestick Park (now named 3-Com Park), home of the 49ers football team, with a new stadium–shopping mall complex near that site.

Invasion of the Dot-Coms, Displacement Impacts, and Growth Control Wars, Round 2

Starting around 1997, shortly after Mayor Brown took office, a rogue wave of cap-ital investment hit the city. The economic and political forces unleashed were dif-ferent from those that had Manhattan-ized the city's skyline during the late 1970s and early 1980s. That earlier investment surge had been driven by high-rise office developers funded mainly by banks and tax syndicates. The negative impacts of unregulated growth on transportation and housing gave rise to a grass roots slow-growth movement led by white middle-class professionals and neighborhood activists. In 1986, the city's voters approved Proposition M, which imposed strin-gent caps and controls on future high-rise office development. This latest surge of investment, however, was driven by droves of Internet dot-com entrepreneurs funded mainly by Silicon Valley venture capitalists. All were eager to locate their start-up firms in or near the famous Multimedia Gulch in the city's South of Market neighborhood. (For a lively and informative account of these developments, see Borsook 1999.)

Mayor Brown, his allies on the Board of Supervisors, and his downtown busi-ness friends all welcomed this latest chaos of capitalism with open arms. Under Mayor Brown's supervision, the Planning Commission and Board of Permit Appeals approved dozens of building projects and live-work developments that violated the spirit, if not the letter, of Proposition M; ignored the city's neighborhood preserva-tion priorities; and made mush of other planning codes. The sudden gentrification and displacement impacts of this high-tech gold rush on low-income residents, merchants, artists, and non-profit workers living in the South of Market, Mission, and Portrero Hill neighborhoods provoked another grass roots slow-growth move-ment. Mobilized by new umbrella organizations, principally the Mission Anti-Displacement Coalition (MAC) and the South of Market Anti-Displacement Coalition (SOMAD), this new round of growth control politics more directly engaged work-ing-class renters and people of color in leadership roles. Leaders of these new groups and organizations, with help from the original architects of Proposition M, said bad things about Mayor Brown, fought his planners and bureaucrats, and worked hard to crush his pro-growth governing coalition.

Willie Brown Versus Tom Ammiano: The Voter Revolt of 1999

In 1999, Mayor Brown launched his re-election campaign into the first winds of a brewing political storm. Initially, his chances looked good, despite his plummeting popularity, to win an outright majority in the November 2 mayoral election. His main rivals were former mayor Frank Jordan, whose political stock was low, and Clinton Reilly, a locally well-known political consultant who invested $4 million of his own money for media promos to accent the positives in his combative career. These individuals posed no real threat to Willie Brown.

The one potential contender who did threaten Willie Brown a bit was Tom Ammiano, president of the Board of Supervisors. Ammiano's outspoken opposition to Mayor Brown's pro-growth policies and his own legislative initiatives, including the city's new landmark domestic partners law, had earned him the reputation of being a tough political fighter and a champion of progressive causes. In San Francisco, he could compete with Willie Brown, but he had announced early on that he would not run for election and was all but counted out. Then, 6 weeks before the election, sensing the spread of the anti-Brown backlash and the surge of a new slow-growth movement in the making, Ammiano changed his mind. Having missed the deadline for declaring his candidacy on the formal ballot, he and his supporters mobilized an unprecedented and intensive grass roots write-in campaign that, astonishingly, worked to win him enough votes on November 2 (25 percent of the total cast) to place him in the December 14 runoff against Mayor Brown.

Although many outside observers and reporters framed the runoff election campaign as a contest between a black liberal incumbent and a gay progressive challenger, the discourse of racial and sexual identity politics was rarely heard from the local media, from the voters, or from the candidates themselves. The essential content of the candidate debates focused on issues like affordable housing, public transit, schools, and most prominently, the destructive impact of the dot-com invasion and what do about it.

Apart from the debates, however, the campaigns were very unequally matched. Mayor Brown had the support of the state and local Democratic Party establishment, the downtown business elites, most labor union chiefs (despite grumbles from some rank and file), a large share of the gay and lesbian vote (including an endorsement from the increasingly conservative Alice B. Toklas Lesbian and Gay Democratic Club), most Asian political organizations, and rock solidarity from African Americans. He also summoned and unleashed an avalanche of corporate soft money through his affiliated political action committees. Ammiano's main support came from the Haight-Ashbury and Portrero Hill white progressives, gays and lesbians affiliated with the progressive Harvey Milk Lesbian and Gay Democratic Club, some sectors of organized labor (especially in the public employee and teachers unions), and the growing cadres of militant slow-growth organizers in the Mission and South of Market. In addition, the campaign funds he raised were paltry compared to Mayor Brown's.

The electoral weights of these two constituencies alone might have balanced out, but Mayor Brown, insuring his odds, tipped the scales strongly in his favor by appealing to a largely silent third constituency (and not his) made up of politically conservative white homeowners in the Sunset, West of Twin Peaks, and other neighborhoods. These were voters who were not amused to be forced to witness a runoff battle between a liberal and a progressive. Mayor Brown got their votes, however, helped by an official endorsement of his candidacy by the San Francisco Republican Party. (That endorsement, the final insult inflicted by Willie Brown on state GOP warlords, caused a scandal at the California Republican Convention in early 2000. The San Francisco chapter was vigorously and formally rebuked for it [Salladay and Coile 2000].)

At the end, on December 14, Mayor Brown soundly defeated Supervisor Tom Ammiano by a 60-40 vote to win a new term as mayor. (See Gallagher 2000 for a more detailed account of the 1999 campaigns and election.) The winds, however, were blowing.

"A PERFECT POLITICAL STORM": THE NOVEMBER 7, 2000, ELECTION

In August 2000, weeks before the November 7 general election, Richard Marquez, a leader of the recently formed MAC, spoke to a crowd at a MAC-sponsored rally in the Mission: "We have the potential in November to build the perfect political storm," he said. "We've got no choice, because our backs are up against the wall. We've got to come out swinging" (Kim 2000, B1). The "perfect political storm" that he envisioned combined four powerful forces that were converging to cause political ruin for Mayor Brown.

The Dot-Com Invasion, Proposition L, Anti–Willie Brown, and District Elections

Dot-Com Invasion   The first force entering the storm was the cresting of the dot-com tidal wave (discussed earlier) at the peak of its sharpest impacts on commercial real estate, housing prices, and low-income neighborhood communities, especially in the Mission and South of Market (Districts 9 and 6 in Figure 6.5).

Proposition L   The second force was a grass roots mobilization of voters to support a citizen-initiated ballot measure, Proposition L, that would (1) impose a ban on new development in parts of the Mission and South of Market districts, (2) apply an indefinite moratorium on new development in two other neighborhoods and other parts of South of Market, (3) significantly raise the per-square-foot development exaction fees to pay for growth-induced demands on housing and public transit, (4) halt further live-work loft construction, (5) redefine the zoning codes to place more dot-com firms in a business class requiring higher exaction fees, and (6) allow only a few of the exemptions from the growth caps imposed by Proposition M in 1986 being demanded by high-rise developers and dot-com entrepreneurs (Nieves 2000). Widely called the "daughter of Proposition M," Proposition L would close all the loopholes and bar all the gates that had allowed the dot-commers to enter the city so suddenly and displace its most vulnerable populations.

Anti-Willie Brown   The third force was the continuing and unabated fury of the anti–Willie Brown backlash that had fueled Tom Ammiano's write-in campaign for mayor in November 1999. This backlash intensified in late June 2000, when Mayor Brown summarily rejected a compromise plan for growth controls that had been thrashed out by an informal task force of corporate CEOs, civic leaders, and community activists (Robson 2000). It intensified further in August, when he placed his own watered-down growth control measure, Proposition K, on the ballot, delighting the developers, entrepreneurs, and speculators who chaffed at any restrictions but infuriating others, including some of his own business friends, who had hoped to work out something reasonable behind the scenes. Abrupt and impatient with his critics, Mayor Brown tried to justify his actions. "The same people jumping up and down and yelling about the growth are the same people who were yelling about unemployment in disadvantaged neighborhoods five year ago," he said. "You can't have it both ways" (Matier and Ross 2000, A15). That kind of pro-growth logic might have been compelling in another city or at an earlier stage of San Francisco's physical development, but at this point, it seemed vestigial. It did not placate or persuade—it only made things worse.

District Elections   The fourth force at work that converged with and magnified the other three was the scheduled change from at-large to district elections of supervisors. All 11 seats were up for grabs, meaning that all the mayor's loyal allies on the board who sought re-election would have to stand trial before neighborhood electorates. The timing of this shift to district representation coincided perfectly with the peaking of the grass roots neighborhood revolt against Mayor Brown and his pro-growth agenda.

The Outcome: A New Progressive Supermajority and the Collapse of the Willie Brown Machine

By August 2000, a total of 87 candidates had filed for candidacy in the 11 new districts. The number of candidates ranged from only one, incumbent Gavin Newsom, running unopposed in District 2 to the 17 running in District 6. Eight of the 87 candidates were board incumbents seeking re-election in different districts, guaranteeing that at least three new supervisors would serve on the board. Of those eight, four (Michael Yaki, Mabel Teng, Alicia Becerril, and the Reverend Amos Brown) were loyal supporters of Mayor Brown and formed the core of his working majority on the board. Two (Mark Leno and Gavin Newsom) supported the mayor's agenda on many issues, and another two (Tom Ammiano and Leland Yee) were the core of Mayor Brown's disloyal opposition.

To retain his working majority on the board, Mayor Brown and his political and business allies pulled out all the stops to re-elect his favored incumbents or challengers in nine of the 11 districts, writing off District 2 (the unopposed Gavin Newsom) as a sure thing and District 9 (the unbeatable Tom Ammiano) as a lost cause. One of the things Willie Brown is most famous for is his ability to raise and spend money in political campaigns and to use those funds to secure his own power and support his allies. As the assembly speaker, that special talent in the cloakrooms and boardrooms of Sacramento made him king (Clucas 1995; Richardson 1996). In the fishbowl of San Francisco politics circa November 2000, however, that kind of top-down, money-driven approach to winning elections backfired on him—and in a big way.

On October 30, a week before the election, the *San Francisco Examiner* published two front-page investigative reports on Mayor Brown's behind-the-scenes orchestration of district campaigns (Lelchuk 2000; Finnie 2000). Most damaging was a detailed analysis, complete with flowcharts, of the organized network of political action committees, political clubs, and highly paid consultants that he had put in place to raise, distribute, and spend an unprecedented amount of money in support of his loyal candidates in the field. This was a flowchart that ran from the top to the bottom. At the top was Mayor Brown and the corporate executives, and at the bottom, below all the froth of money, were the voters, many of whom saw their suspicions confirmed that Willie Brown really did own and operate a political machine here in the midst of a city renowned for its neighborhood activism and grass roots democracy. For many voters, especially the progressives, the picture did not fit the frame.

The issues of land use, displacement, and growth controls defined the main agenda for debate in most of the district campaigns. Where these issues did not arise naturally on the local turf, they were made into issues by the MAC, SOMAD, and Yes-on-L campaign operations that sent organizers and volunteers out from Mission, South of Market, and other growth-impacted neighborhoods into the city to educate the residents and do battle. All candidates in every district were put on the hook to state their positions on these issues, especially their positions on Propositions K and L.

Meanwhile, the city's long tradition of racial and identity politics was suspended, at least for this election. The paradoxical title of an election eve column by gay political writer Bruce Mirken conveys the Alice-in-Wonderland quality of what happened: *Save Queer S.F.: Vote Straight* (Mirken 2000; also see Blackwell 2000). Mirken was writing about the split in the city's gay community between the Alice B. Toklas Lesbian and Gay Democratic Club (pro–Willie Brown) and the Harvey Milk Lesbian and Gay Democratic Club (pro–Tom Ammiano). He wanted to expose what he and many others saw as a cynical attempt by Alice's leaders to exploit gay solidarity by promoting a "Lavender Slate" of gay and lesbian candidates in district races against straight challengers. It was not merely coincidental, Mirken pointed out, that all of those slate candidates, with the exception of Tom Ammiano, just happened to be Willie Brown allies and strong opponents of restrictions on growth.

Many other examples of this ideological reframing of the politics of identity as usual could be given, such as the Chinese-American Democratic Club's endorsement of white progressive Jake McGoldrick in his race against incumbent Chinese-American Michael Yaki in the heavily Asian-populated District 1. The general conclusion, however, is that this election was not fundamentally about race or identity but about land use, ideology, and Willie Brown.

The complete story of the Proposition K and L campaigns and of the various district election campaigns would take too long to tell here. Skipping to the end, there were three main outcomes. First, Propositions K and L both lost, though Proposition L just barely, meaning that Proposition M's tight restrictions on growth would continue to apply by default. Second, nearly all the progressive, slow-growth, anti–Willie Brown candidates for supervisor won in their districts, creating an unprecedented 8-3 progressive supermajority on the Board of Supervisors. And

TABLE 6.4   Breakdown of winners and runoff losers (December 12, 2000), key political statistics, and racial/ethnic composition of 2000 VAP by Board of Supervisors' election districts

District	Winner	Runoff Loser	Mean % W. Brown (Dec, 1999)	Mean % Yes Prop. L (Nov, 2000)	Mean Score Progressive Voting Index	White	Black	Asian	Hispanic
						Mean % of 2000 VAP			
1	McGoldrick	Yaki[a]	62	49	47	48	2	44	4
2	Newsom[a]	(won Nov.)	67	38	37	80	1	13	4
3	Peskin	Wong	59	48	52	50	2	43	4
4	Yee[a]	Shanley	70	44	30	40	1	52	5
5	Gonzalez	Owens	44	57	77	63	15	13	7
6	Daly	Dittenhafer	44	57	74	46	10	25	15
7	Hall	Teng[a]	67	43	33	57	4	31	7
8	Leno[a]	Hansen	41	55	66	74	3	9	11
9	Ammiano[a]	(won Nov.)	41	64	81	37	4	14	41
10	Maxwell	Richardson	78	45	51	20	31	29	15
11	Sandoval	A. Brown[a]	76	45	41	18	11	46	22

[a]Board incumbent who ran for re-election on November 7, 2000.

Sources: Reported statistics are means of precinct data (Ns vary from 631 to 646). Precinct voting statistics are from San Francisco Department of Elections, Statements of Vote, December 14, 1999, November 7, 2000, and December 12, 2000. See text and Appendix for details on construction of the Progressive Voting Index. Precinct data on 2000 VAP by Department of Justice–defined race/ethnicity (U.S. Census PL94-171 2000 are from precinct dataset downloaded from the UC Berkeley/IGS Statewide Database website (http://swdb.berkeley.edu/).

third, Mayor Brown's slate of well-funded, loyal incumbents and challengers was blown to smithereens.

Table 6.4 compactly summarizes the outcomes of each of the 11 district races and of nine runoffs, provides information on three key indicators of each district electorate's political character and voting behavior, and gives statistics describing each district's current racial/ethnic composition.

At the end, Mayor Brown's political machine was in ruins. Its moving parts worked well enough under the at-large system and during tranquil economic times. Under district elections and in turbulent times, however, its parts and pieces no longer meshed. The result was a ghastly political nightmare for Willie Brown, who now could look forward to a progressive supermajority voting against him on the Board of Supervisors and to demands from the downtown corporate CEOs for an accounting of how their huge financial investment in local political control could have been so wildly misspent.

BEYOND RACIAL AND IDENTITY POLITICS: A NEW URBAN PROGRESSIVISM?

Robert Bailey, in his seminal book on gay politics and urban regimes, proposed the term *identity multiplexing* to describe the "layering and ranking by individuals of their different identities in different arenas" (Bailey 1999, 31). For example, a person might express the identity of "African American" when pursuing goals of racial equality, of "feminist" when joining other women to combat sex discrimination in hiring, and of "lesbian" when writing to a legislator in support of same-sex marriages.

The very concept of identity multiplexing is corrosive to the political mindset of an older generation of urban liberals, especially those who became politically active during the civil rights movement and are inclined to think of liberalism and conservatism strictly in terms of race. That mindset is perfectly captured in the words of former Supervisor Willie Kennedy, who reportedly exclaimed, "I want someone who is black all the way!" while objecting to the nomination of a black lesbian activist for a seat on an important city commission (Zachary 1995, A1). Kennedy was convinced that the nominee, if selected, would be more likely to give a higher priority to her sexual identity than to her racial identity as a guide to making public policy.

The crucial point that Bailey makes and the San Francisco case illustrates is that identity politics in any form—gay politics, black politics, and so on—has the potential to restrict an individual's freedom of political self-expression under the punishing norms of coerced solidarity. Even worse, it can lock in an inflexible, exclusionary, and ultimately counterproductive strategy of collective action that views identity multiplexing by insiders as a form of betrayal and by outsiders as the basis for suspicion and mistrust. Under these conditions, coalitions with out-groups are, at best, merely tactical and temporary, at worst, impossible.

In some U.S. cities—San Francisco is exemplary—the visible presence of multiple and highly organized identity groups mobilizing followers and interacting in a fragmented political environment creates a problem for political theory and collective action. There is no problem of this sort in cities where the political order has institutionalized only one kind of identity in the structures of urban governance while suppressing the rest. In some cities, for example, identity politics is only about race and, under that category, only about black and white. All the rest is mainly about business, interests, and who gets what. In such settings, individual citizens lack the means and opportunity to practice identity multiplexing as a form of political art, or even to recognize that they are, in fact, engaging in a kind of sanctioned identity politics reduced to one dimension. In cities like San Francisco, however, identity multiplexing is essential not only for individual political survival but also as the foundation for effective collective action.

Broad and stable progressive coalitions can be built that are able to contain and harness the political energy of the fissions and fusions of identity that occur within them. Land-use issues are key, especially in dense and impacted cities like San Francisco. Sidney Plotkin (1987) writes that "the stakes of modern-day battles for power to control land use should be seen in the widest social context, for they involve nothing less than the meanings of community itself amid larger corporate tendencies to convert work and residence into mutually reinforcing production sites within more efficient business networks" (59). As witnessed in the recent San Francisco elections, the deep conflicts between community and capital over land-use issues provide the broader framework required for building these kinds of coalitions as the foundation of a new urban progressivism.

APPENDIX

Notes on the Roper Social Capital Benchmark Survey, 2000

Source: Roper Center. 2000. U.S. Social Capital Benchmark Survey.

Description: A national sample of 3,003 adults and of 40 independent community samples with sample sizes ranging from 388 (rural southeast South Dakota) to 1505 (Peninsula–Silicon Valley). The sample *n* for San Francisco was 500.

Method: Telephone surveys.

Survey organization: Saguaro Seminar at John F. Kennedy School of Government, Harvard University. TNS Intersearch conducted the interviewing.

Field Survey dates: July–November, 2000.

Dataset: USMISC2000-SOCCAP.

Download data and codebook from: http://www.ropercenter.uconn.edu/scc_bench.html. The Stata 7.0 "svyprop" command was used with weights on each sample to produce the percentage estimates plotted in Figures 6.1 and 6.2. Sampling errors, which are larger for smaller samples, are not shown on the graphs.

Notes on Estimates of Voter Turnout Rate (% of the VAP) in the November 7, 2000, Election

Citywide estimates of voter turnout rates were obtained using Gary King's EZI ecological inference software (http://GKing.Harvard.edu) on precinct voting turnout data (San Francisco Department of Elections, Statement of Vote, November 7, 2000) and precinct VAP for 2000 by Department of Justice–defined race/ethnicity (U.S. Census PL94-171 2000 precinct dataset downloaded from the UC Berkeley/IGS Statewide Database website [http://swdb.berkeley.edu/]). Also see King 1997.

Notes on Construction of the San Francisco Progressive Voting Index

The Index was constructed from a principal factor analysis of voting data for the city's 646 precincts on 12 local and state ballot measures presented to the voters in the November 7, 2000, and November 6, 2001, elections. The twelve items (see list below) were selected to tap the several key facets of my own conceptual definition of urban progressivism as "a system of values, beliefs, and ideas that encourages an expanded role for local government in achieving distributive justice, limits on growth, neighborhood preservation, and ethnic-cultural diversity under conditions of public accountability and direct citizen participation" (DeLeon 1992, 33). The analysis extracted one factor with an eigenvalue of greater than 1.0. Precinct factor scores were computed and then rescaled to a minimum of 0 and a maximum of 100 to create the Index. The Cronbach's Alpha scale reliability coefficient for the Index is .97.

The 12 Index items were as follows:

1. % Yes Prop. D (Nov 2000) Extend Children's Fund to 2016.
2. % Yes Prop. F (Nov 2000) JFK/GG Park Saturday Closure.

3. % Yes Prop. H (Nov 2000) Limit Tenant Pass-Through Costs.
4. % Yes Prop. L (Nov 2000) Office Development Live Work Controls.
5. % Yes Prop. N (Nov 2000) Limit on TIC Condo Conversions.
6. % Yes Prop. O (Nov 2000) Public Financing Board of Supervisors Elections.
7. % Yes Prop. 36 (Nov 2000) Drugs, Probation Treatment.
8. % Yes Prop. 39 (Nov 2000) 55% Local Vote on School Bonds.
9. % Yes Prop. B (Nov 2001) Revenue Bonds Local Renewable Energy.
10. % Yes Prop. D (Nov 2001) Require Voter Approval of SF Bay Land Fill.
11. % Yes Prop. E (Nov 2001) Ethics, Elections, Outside Counsel.
12. % Yes Prop. F (Nov 2001) Municipal Water Power Agency.

Data sources: San Francisco Department of Elections, Official Statements of Vote for November 7, 2000, and November 6, 2001, general elections. Numbered ballot measures were statewide propositions; lettered ballot measures were local propositions.

REFERENCES

Baca, Kathleen. 1992. Clash on the Left: The Broad-Based Coalition Behind the Success of Progressives in San Francisco Is on the Verge of Blowing Up Along Racial Lines. *SF Weekly*, November 25, pp. 16–19.

Bailey, Robert W. 1999. *Gay Politics, Urban Politics: Identity and Economics in the Urban Setting*. New York: Columbia University Press.

Blackwell, Savannah. 2000. Gay-Vote Games: The Machine's "Lavender Sweep" Plan to Divide Gay and Progressive Voters. *San Francisco Bay Guardian*, September 20.

Borsook, Paulina. 1999. How the Internet Ruined San Francisco. *Salon.com*, October 28.

Browning, Rufus P., Dale Rogers Marshall, and David H. Tabb. 1984. *Protest Is Not Enough*. Berkeley: University of California Press.

Cain, Bruce E., Megan Mullin, and Gillian Peele. 2001. City Caesars? An Examination of Mayoral Power in California. Paper presented at the 2001 Annual Meeting of the American Political Science Association, San Francisco, August 29–September 2.

Chao, Julie. 1998. Poll Finds Asians Lag Politically: Despite Gains, City's Asian Americans Care Less About Politics than Other Groups. *San Francisco Examiner*, December 6, C1.

Chao, Julie. 1999. Mission Seethes with Fear of INS: S.F. Mayor Brown Promises at Latino Meeting to Fight Any Incidents of Injustice. *San Francisco Examiner*, September 26, C1.

Clucas, Richard A. 1995. *The Speaker's Electoral Connection: Willie Brown and the California Assembly*. Berkeley: Institute of Governmental Studies.

DeLeon, Richard E. 1991. San Francisco: Postmaterialist Populism in a Global City. In H. V. Savitch and John Clayton Thomas, eds., *Big City Politics in Transition*. Beverly Hills: Sage, pp. 202–215.

DeLeon, Richard E. 1992. *Left Coast City: Progressive Politics in San Francisco, 1975–1991*. Lawrence: University Press of Kansas.

DeLeon, Richard E. 1997. Progressive Politics in the Left Coast City: San Francisco. In Rufus P. Browning, Dale Rogers Marshall, and David H. Tabb, eds., *Racial Politics in American Cities*, 2nd ed. White Plains, NY: Longman, pp. 137–159.

DeLeon, Richard E. 1999. San Francisco and Domestic Partners: New Fields of Battle in the Culture War. In Elaine B. Sharp, ed., *Culture Wars and Local Politics*. Lawrence: University Press of Kansas, pp. 117–136.

DeLeon, Richard E., Steven Hill, and Lisel Blash. 1998. The Campaign for Proposition H and Preference Voting in San Francisco, 1996. *Representation* 35 (4): 265–274.

DelVecchio, Rick. 2001. Hispanics Move from S.F., San Jose into Suburbs. *San Francisco Chronicle*, May 24, A19.

Finnie, Chuck. 1998. Brown Leaving His Stamp on City: Building Projects Define Mayor's Term. *San Francisco Examiner*, January 6, A1.

Finnie, Chuck. 2000. 800-Pound Gorilla of Political Spending: S.F. Consultants Channel Corporate Soft Money to Favored Campaigns. *San Francisco Examiner*, October 30, A1.

Gallagher, Tom. 2000. The San Francisco Voter Revolt of 1999. *Social Policy* 31 (2); 24–34.

Hartman, Chester. 1984. *The Transformation of San Francisco*. Totowa, NJ: Rowman and Allanheld.

Herel, Suzanne, and Tyche Hendricks. 2001. Fremont Police Turn Down ACLU, Will Help FBI with Questioning. *San Francisco Chronicle*, December 5, A9.

Inglehart, Ronald. 1990. *Culture Shift in Advanced Industrial Society*. Princeton, NJ: Princeton University Press.

Kim, Ryan. 2000. Mission Marchers Show Pride of Place. *San Francisco Examiner*, August 13, B1.

King, Gary. 1997. *A Solution to the Ecological Inference Problem: Reconstructing Individual Behavior from Aggregate Data*. Princeton, NJ: Princeton University Press.

King, John. 1997. The Boom Is Back: Economy Prompts Growth Without Controversy of '80s. *San Francisco Chronicle*, June 27, A21.

Lelchuk, Ilene. 2000. Mayor Pulls Campaign Strings: With Power Base at Risk, He Fights for S.F. Propositions, Supe Candidates. *San Francisco Examiner*, October 30, A1.

Matier, Phillip, and Andrew Ross. 2000. Pledge Cards and Bagels. *San Francisco Chronicle*, September 18, A15.

McCormick, Erin. 2001. Black Population Plummeting in S.F. *San Francisco Chronicle*, June 17, A1.

McLeod, Ramon G. 1997. More Asians Turning Out: Voting in S.F. Record Levels Contrast with Past Uninvolvement. *San Francisco Chronicle*, July 11, A19.

Mirken, Bruce. 2000. Save Queer S.F.: Vote Straight. *San Francisco Bay Guardian*, October 11.

Mollenkopf, John H. 1983. *The Contested City*. Princeton, NJ: Princeton University Press.

Ness, Carol. 2001a. Blacks Fear Losing Their Political Clout in State. *San Francisco Chronicle*, June 17, A17.

Ness, Carol. 2001b. Hundreds Line Up to Get Consular ID Cards: Mexican Immigrants Brave Rain to Take Advantage of S.F. Policy. *San Francisco Chronicle*, December 6, A21.

Nieves, Evelyn. 2000. Mission District Fights Case of Dot-Com Fever. *New York Times*, November 5, Y21.

Nieves, Evelyn. 2001. Blacks Hit by Housing Costs Leave San Francisco Behind. *New York Times*, August 2, A12.

Ong, Paul M., and David E. Lee. 2001. Changing of the Guard? The Emerging Immigrant Majority in Asian American Politics. In Gordon H. Chang, ed., *Asian Americans and Politics: Perspectives, Experiences, Prospects*. Stanford, Calif.: Stanford University Press, pp. 153–172.

Plotkin, Sidney. 1987. *Keep Out. The Struggle for Land Use Control*. Berkeley and Los Angeles: University of California Press.

Potepan, Michael J. 1998. *Jobs and Recent Job Growth for Low Educated Workers in San Francisco*. San Francisco; San Francisco Urban Institute.

Richardson, James. 1996. *Willie Brown: A Biography*. Berkeley and Los Angeles: University of California Press.

Robson, Douglas. 2000. Willie Brown Slaps Growth Proposal. *San Francisco Business Times*, June 30–July 6, 1.

Salladay, Robert, and Zachary Coile. 2000. S.F. Republicans Rebuked for Endorsing Democrat. *San Francisco Examiner*, February 6, A17.

San Francisco Chronicle. 1994. City's Liberal Reputation Intact in Elections. November 12, A6.

Sims, Kent. 2000. San Francisco Economy—Implications for Public Policy: A Report to the San Francisco Planning and Urban Research Association. San Francisco: SPUR, July 10.

Sonenshein, Raphael J. 1997. The Prospects for Multiracial Coalitions: Lessons from America's Three Largest Cities. In Rufus P. Browning, Dale Rogers Marshall, and David H. Tabb, eds., *Racial Politics in American Cities*, 2nd ed. White Plains, NY: Longman, pp. 261–276.

Sward, Susan. 2001. The Killing Streets: A Cycle of Vengeance Blood Feud in Bayview-Hunters Point. *San Francisco Chronicle*, December 16, A1.

Wirt, Frederick. 1974. *Power in the City: Decision Making in San Francisco*. Berkeley and Los Angeles: University of California Press.

Zachary, G. Pascal. 1995. Who Needs Oprah? San Francisco Has Board of Supervisors. *Wall Street Journal*, February 2, A1.

Part IV

Class and Leadership in the South

Chapter 7

Is Strong Incorporation Enough? Black Empowerment and the Fate of Atlanta's Low-Income Blacks

Michael Leo Owens and Michael J. Rich

EDITORS' NOTE

African Americans constitute about two-thirds of the population in Atlanta, and they have held a substantial majority of the elected positions in the city—including the office of mayor—for nearly 30 years. Incorporation would seem to be strong and well established. What more is there?

Plenty, according to Michael Leo Owens and Michael Rich. They demonstrate that despite nearly three decades of black control of the city's major political institutions and the economic opportunities provided by one of the nation's fastest-growing regional economies, the gap between black and white in Atlanta is greater now than it was 30 years ago. Owens and Rich attribute the lack of tangible progress for Atlanta's poorest blacks to a number of factors, including squandered opportunities with major federal urban initiatives, an extensive spatial mismatch between the job opportunities provided by the region's growing economy and the residential locations of the city's low-income black neighborhoods, a growing mismatch between the skills of the city's low-income blacks and available jobs, political alienation and demobilization in the city's low-income black neighborhoods, and the increased importance of money in municipal elections, which has further muted the needs and concerns of low-income blacks.

Owens and Rich note that while low-income blacks have little to show for nearly 30 years of black rule, current demographic trends (reverse white flight in some black neighborhoods, population growth in many white neighborhoods, and increased suburbanization of the city's black middle class) may yield a new biracial coalition capable of electing a white mayor. They conclude that under such a scenario, low-income blacks may emerge as the pivotal voting block and, ultimately, may attain the policy responsiveness they have sought for so long.

Atlanta is novel politically. It is one of four major cities where blacks have governed continuously for nearly three decades (the others being Detroit, Newark, and Washington, DC). Since the early 1970s, black mayors have consistently governed the city. Since the 1980s, Atlanta has had a majority-black city council and a majority-black school board, and the city's superintendent of the public school system, chief of police, and a majority of its mayoral administrative appointees have been black. The majority of Atlanta's municipal workforce has also been black.

Tony Affigne (1997, 78) notes "Atlanta can appear to be the 'promised land' to Black Americans in other, less empowered communities." On its surface, the city displays the strongest form of black political incorporation. Blacks are a core constituency in the electoral politics of Atlanta, comprising a majority (58 percent) of registered voters in the city. Black representatives are incorporated in both the government and the regime that governs Atlanta (Stone 1989), which in turn allows them to influence governmental responsiveness to black interests, such as jobs, contracts, and oversight of the police department. Consequently, blacks hold a majority of municipal jobs, city agencies award high proportions of contracts to black businesses, affirmative action is a hallmark of city policy making, despite continued legal opposition, and a civilian police review board exists.

The dawn of the twenty-first century—and the elections that inaugurated it—brought few changes to the racial composition of the city government. In 2001, Atlanta voters elected Shirley Franklin as the city's fourth black mayor and also elected a majority-black city council, though in the process they replaced the outgoing black city council president with a white gay councilperson. As for the school board, it remains majority-black. Within the city bureaucracy, blacks continue to hold a majority of the key appointed positions of administrative authority, including superintendent of public schools, as well as a majority among the ranks of the civil service.

In many ways, however, Atlanta is a critical test case for the benefits of strong political incorporation, because nearly 30 years of black rule has not translated into tangible benefits for all of Atlanta's African Americans. Cleavages matter. In Atlanta, as Clarence Stone and Carol Pierannunzi (1997, 167) contend, "there is a fault line within the African-American community between the haves and the have-nots" as well as those who have some but want more. The black regime recognizes these cleavages—and stands on the side of the advantaged. The city government privileges the interests and values of the black middle class over the black working class. In the end, low-income blacks receive few rewards for their political mobilization and alliance with middle-class blacks. That the city government can routinely advantage the values of the black elite and black middle class over those of the black masses is a testament to the power of symbolic politics, the political demobilization of the working class and the poor, and the complexities of reducing poverty.

This chapter explores the limits of strong racial incorporation, especially as it pertains to the interests of low-income blacks. It contends that the black-led city government has been and continues to be unresponsive to the needs of low-income blacks and their neighborhoods. This is not to say that Atlanta's political elite does not provide the black masses with symbolic benefits. It has not, however, provided them with substantive benefits or the design of effective policy initiatives to improve the quality of life in those black neighborhoods with the least resources, which comprise about half the city's neighborhood areas.

THE LAND OF MILK AND HONEY: POPULATION AND EMPLOYMENT GROWTH IN THE ATLANTA REGION

Within the real estate development community, the Atlanta region is known as the "land of milk and honey" because of the abundant development opportunities that it provides (Valley 2000). Over the past 20 years, the Atlanta metropolitan area has ranked either at or near the top among all major metropolitan areas in terms of population growth and job creation. Using the 10-county Atlanta Regional Commission as a reference base for the Atlanta metropolitan area, the region's population nearly doubled—and the number of jobs more than tripled—between 1980 and 2000 (Table 7.1). Even the official U.S. Census Bureau designation for the metropolitan region has expanded dramatically, increasing from five counties in 1970 to 20 in 2000—an increase in land area from about 1,700 to more than 6,100 square miles (or 259 percent). This growth prompted a March 1999 *Time* magazine cover story entitled "The Brawl Over Sprawl" that proclaimed Atlanta "the fastest spreading human settlement in history" (Lacayo 1999).

According to the Atlanta Regional Commission (1999), the defining characteristic of metropolitan Atlanta's economy has been its diversity, with no single sector or industry providing a preponderant share of employment. The largest industry sector is services, which accounted for about 30 percent of the region's employment in 1998. The primary factors driving growth in the regional economy—today as well as throughout its history—are Atlanta's location at the crossroads of the southeastern United States and its transportation infrastructure (e.g., railroads, interstate highways, and Hartsfield International Airport, which has become the nation's busiest).

Despite the abundance of economic opportunities in the region, the city's share of those opportunities has declined sharply during the post–World War II era. Whereas once the city of Atlanta accounted for about half of the metropolitan region's population (1960) and more than three-fourths of its jobs (1950), today Atlanta is home to slightly more than 10 percent of the region's population and only about one-fifth of its employment (Table 7.1). The Atlanta region has become a multinodal metropolitan area with several suburban downtowns or Edge Cities, each with their own skylines and employment mix.

Unlike many northeastern and midwestern U.S. cities, however, the region's growth has not necessarily come at the expense of the central city's decline. Employment in the city of Atlanta has increased in every decade but one (the 1970s), and city employment in 1997 was 72 percent higher than in 1977. According to one study, the two most important factors contributing to the decentralization of employment in the Atlanta metropolitan region over the past two decades were decentralization of the population (jobs following people) and expansion of firms already located in the suburbs as opposed to outmigration of jobs from the central city or new businesses locating in the region (Hartshorn and Ihlanfeldt 1993).

TABLE 7.1   Selected characteristics of Atlanta, city and metropolitan area, 1950–2000

	1950	1960	1970	1980	1990	2000
Atlanta Metropolitan Area—U.S. Census						
Number of counties	3	5	5	15	18	20
Square miles	1,137	1,713	1,713	4,319	5,122	6,126
Total population	672	1,017	1,388	2,030	2,833	4,112
% Change over previous decade	29.7	51.3	36.5	46.3	39.6	45.1
% Black	24.7	22.7	22.4	24.6	25.8	29.2
Atlanta Metropolitan Area						
Total population (in thousands)[a]	794	1,095	1,503	1,898	2,516	3,431
% Change over previous decade	27.7	37.9	37.3	26.3	32.6	36.4
% Black	23.6	22.6	21.8	25.1	27.1	32.1
Total employment (in thousands)[a]	139	202	295	392	783	1,216
% Change over previous decade	—	45.3	46.0	32.9	99.7	55.3
City of Atlanta						
Total population (in thousands)	331	487	497	425	394	416
% Change over previous decade	9.6	47.1	2.1	-14.5	-7.3	5.6
% Of metro area population	41.7	44.5	33.1	22.4	15.7	12.1
% Black	36.6	38.3	51.6	65.9	66.7	61.6
Total employment (in thousands)	107	142	170	153	203	263
% Change over previous decade	—	32.7	19.7	-10.0	32.7	29.6
% Of metro area	77.0	70.3	57.6	39.0	25.9	21.6
Citywide Demographic Characteristics						
Median family income	2,664	5,029	8,399	13,591	25,173	37,231
% Of metro median family income	90.7	87.3	78.5	63.7	60.5	62.8
% Of persons below the poverty line	—	—	20.4	27.5	27.3	24.4
% High school graduates	34.1	40.5	47.1	62.1	69.9	76.9
% College graduates	8.9	9.3	16.2	25	26.6	34.6
% Unemployed	3.7	3.6	4.0	8.1	9.2	9.0
% Owner-occupied housing	39.9	45.6	41.2	46.3	43.1	43.7
Median housing value	8,204	12,000	17,000	31,800	70,800	130,600
% Of metro median housing value	102.1	96.8	85.9	66.7	80.2	96.5
Median rent	28	54	80	148	341	606
% Of metro median rent	93.3	100.0	81.6	70.8	77.3	81.2
Atlanta Neighborhood Characteristics						
Number of census tracts	75	100	119	116	118	124
Number of tracts majority-black	21	34	54	73	78	83
% Of tracts majority-black	28.0	34.0	45.4	62.9	66.1	66.9
Number of high-poverty tracts	—	—	33	54	55	—
% Of high-poverty tracts	—	—	27.7	46.6	46.6	—
Index of Dissimilarity[b]						
City of Atlanta	82.7	83.2	83.3	79.5	81.3	81.6
Atlanta metropolitan area	—	—	—	77.0	68.6	65.6

[a]Population and employment figures for all years were calculated based on the 10-county Atlanta Regional Commission boundaries (Cherokee, Clayton, Cobb, DeKalb, Douglas, Fayette, Fulton, Gwinnett, Henry, and Rockdale counties). Employment data based on economic census years 1948, 1958, 1967, 1977, 1987, and 1997 and include total employment for the following sectors: manufacturing, wholesale trade, retail trade, and services.

[b]Based on the distribution of non-Hispanic black and white populations residing in Atlanta census tracts. Index values range from 0 to 100, with higher scores indicating a greater degree of residential segregation.

Sources: U.S. Bureau of the Census, Atlanta Regional Commission.

Demographically, Atlanta (the region and the city) is largely a metropolis in black and white, and the spatial distribution of the population has had important implications for the extent to which African Americans have shared in the economic opportunities generated by the region's robust economy. According to the 2000 U.S. Census, about six out of every 10 residents in the Atlanta metropolitan area were white, and about three of every 10 were black. The proportions in the city, however, were nearly the reverse (61 percent black, 31 percent white).

Residential patterns in both the city and the suburbs are highly segregated, though they appear to be moving in different directions. As Table 7.1 reports, the index of dissimilarity for the Atlanta metropolitan area has declined from 77 in 1980 to 66 in 2000, reflecting in part the substantial increase of Atlanta's suburban black population—especially the black middle class—during the past two decades. The in-migration of half a million African Americans to the region over the last decade, which is the largest increase in African Americans recorded by any metropolitan area, propelled the increase in black suburbanization (Tamman and Suggs 2001). In the city, however, racial segregation as measured by the index of dissimilarity has actually increased slightly during this same time period. As Figure 7.1 illustrates, neighborhoods in Atlanta tend to be either predominantly black or predominantly white, and there is a definite demarcation line between the two areas.

Atlanta is also a city with sharp class divisions. The city's overall poverty rate in 1990 was 27.3 percent, the fifth-highest among major cities and exceeded only by Detroit, New Orleans, Miami, and Cleveland. Nearly half the city's census tracts were high tracts (30 percent or more in poverty) in 1990 and in 20 tracts (17 percent), a majority of persons were living below the poverty line. As Figure 7.2 illustrates, there is fairly high correlation between the neighborhood areas with high concentrations of African Americans and those with large proportions of poor persons ($r = .61$).

In the introduction to a recent edited volume on Atlanta, David Sjoquist (2000, 2) describes Atlanta

> as a paradox of extreme racial and economic inequality—of abject poverty in a region of tremendous wealth, of a poor and economically declining city population in the face of dramatic economic growth, and of a black Mecca in a "city too busy to hate" . . . confronting a highly racially segregated population and the substantial problems associated with racism and poverty that pervade the city.

Thus, Atlanta presents a critical test case for the importance of strong black political incorporation. Is control over the reins of the city's political institutions enough to improve the quality of life for black Atlantans? The remainder of this chapter attempts to answer that question, first by summarizing the evolution of black incorporation in Atlanta and then by reviewing the subsequent policy impacts of that incorporation.

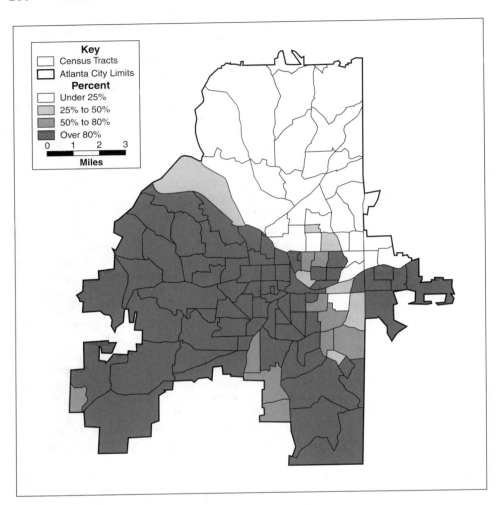

FIGURE 7.1 **Percentage black population, 1990**

BLACK MOBILIZATION AND WEAK INCORPORATION, 1949–1969

The 1946 abolition of the whites-only Democratic primary, along with the eventual end of other vote suppression devices (e.g., poll taxes, literacy tests, and property ownership requirements), gave blacks in Atlanta the legal right to participate regularly in all city elections. The courts, Mayor William B. Hartsfield remarked at the time, gave a black man "a front ticket for any-damn-wheres he wants to sit, if he knows how to use it. And Atlanta Negroes know how to use it" (Bayor 1996, 21). At the time, blacks accounted for 8 percent of the Atlanta electorate.

In the Democratic primary of 1949, Atlanta's blacks, whose share of the city's electorate had increased to 27 percent, proved that they knew how to use the ballot strategically to advance their collective interests (Stone 1989, 28). In the four-way race for mayor, Hartsfield won 50.1 percent of the votes cast, assuring his return to

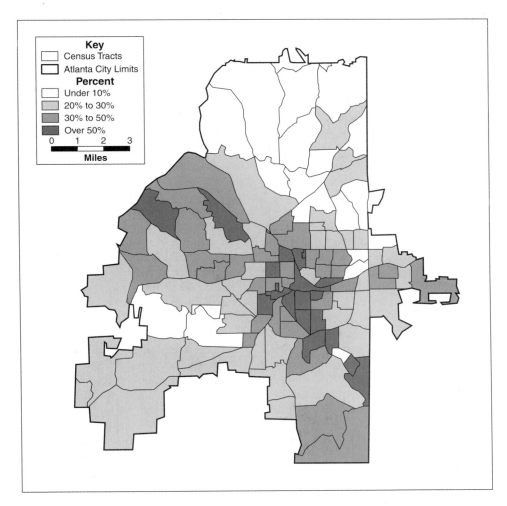

FIGURE 7.2 **Percentage in poverty, 1990**

city hall by a margin of approximately 100 votes (Stone 1989, 30). Black voters made the difference, casting most of their ballots for the mayor, who they perceived as being less oppositional than other candidates to their political interests.

The 1949 election signified the ascendance of black power and the formation of a biracial governing coalition uniting whites (mainly business elites with economic power) from the northside and blacks (chiefly civil rights leaders with influence over black votes) from south Atlanta (Stone 1989). Over the next 20 years, Atlanta's three white mayors—Hartsfield (1937–1961), Ivan Allen, Jr. (1961–1969), and Sam Massell (1969–1973)—would need the support of this biracial coalition, especially the votes of its black members, to govern, for the white vote in the city, beginning in 1949 and extending through the 1960s, would split between incumbents and white challengers or multiple candidates in open races. Accordingly, to win an election, a mayor needed the endorsements and voter mobilization efforts of black institutions, especially churches. Blacks never disappointed them, voting as a bloc for the incumbents in every election until 1973.

Mayoral candidates, along with white members of the biracial coalition, used selective and group incentives to curry support for a development agenda favoring growth tilted toward the northern, solidly white neighborhoods and the central business district as opposed to the predominantly black neighborhoods of the city's south and west (Stone 1989). Inducements to attract the black vote included endorsements and financial support for black candidates, such as the 1953 election of the first black to the Atlanta School Board, as well new low-income housing units, token city contracts, bank deposits, board and commission appointments, and city jobs (Stone 1989). The incentives often muted black opposition and prevented dramatic socioeconomic change or significant physical improvements in the black neighborhoods. Consequently, Atlanta remained "a tightly segregated city with little power-sharing and significant race-related problems in regards to schools, city services, housing, and jobs" (Bayor 1996, 32). Blacks earned slightly more than half the income of whites, were more likely to have families living below the poverty line, were less likely to graduate from high school, and were more likely to be unemployed than whites (Jones 1978, 95–96; U.S. Department of Commerce 1977, 639).

By the 1969 election, the black population of the city had swelled beyond 250,000 but remained mainly in majority-black neighborhoods south and west of the central business district (White 1982). Blacks comprised more than half the city's population and 49 percent of its registered voters. They translated their numbers in the population and on the voter rolls into a formidable political presence, winning five at-large seats on the powerful 18-member Board of Aldermen, three of nine seats on the Atlanta School Board, and the office of vice-mayor, which gave blacks an ex-officio membership on all city council committees (Jones 1978, 98).

Despite the electoral success and influence of blacks in the 1969 municipal elections, Atlanta was still not a city of strong black political incorporation; it was, however, a city with increased black representation in city government. Blacks held one-fourth of the seats on the city council and one-third of the seats on the school board. However, they still lacked membership in the dominant governing coalitions that affected black interests within each institution. Moreover, white elites continued to exercise majority influence over the political character of the biracial coalition and its governance of the city, despite the white population decreasing dramatically due to a massive middle-class migration to the Atlanta suburbs. Black electoral success did not achieve black political power, but it did permit blacks to associate more with those who wielded it (Jones 1978).

BLACK POWER AND STRONG INCORPORATION, 1974–PRESENT

Blacks were pivotal in the 1969 election of Sam Massell as mayor. Massell, a Jew, received 26 percent of the votes cast by northside whites but 92 percent of the votes cast by blacks (Bayor 1996, 43). This upset the white business community, which did not support Massell. An internal Atlanta Chamber of Commerce correspondence assessed the outcome of the 1969 elections, observing that "the 'junior partner' role of the black leadership [and electorate] in the last decade has been rejected by black leaders" (Bayor 1996, 44). Nevertheless, blacks did not support Massell's re-election bid in 1973, choosing instead to support a candidate of their own, Maynard Jackson, the vice-mayor and grandson of an esteemed black civil rights leader.

During the campaign, Massell alienated blacks by appealing to the fears of white voters. For example, Massell proclaimed that "Atlanta is too young to die," which suggested a black mayor would destroy the city's finances and threaten its continued economic growth. Massell also attempted to increase white electoral strength by calling for the annexation of affluent white communities north of Atlanta's city limits, preferably before election day.

Despite incumbency and past black support, Massell received only 5 percent of the black vote in the general election. Jackson captured the remainder to become the city's first black mayor, and he took office with formal political powers unknown to his predecessors due to an extensive charter reform that was adopted by voters in the 1973 election. The new charter called for a strong mayor–weak council system of government, providing the city with a clearer separation of executive from legislative powers than the old system of shared powers between the mayor and the board of aldermen. The new system gave the mayor the power to veto council legislation, appoint the heads of municipal agencies, prepare the city budget, formulate comprehensive city planning policies to guide growth and development, negotiate city contracts, and reorganize the city government (Atlanta City Charter Commission 1973). The amended charter also changed the at-large board of aldermen to a city council composed of 12 ward-based representatives and six at-large representatives. It also replaced the vice-mayor position with a president having appointment and tie-breaking powers in the legislature.

The city politics of the early 1970s demonstrated that black power in the electoral arena and in city government was not only possible in Atlanta; it was achieved. In 1974, blacks gained control of city hall and its powers over patronage and the city's budget. They also were victorious in city council and board of education elections, achieving parity with whites (50-50) in the city council and a majority (five of nine seats) on the school board. With black control of city hall and enough black members to manage the dominant coalitions in the city council and board of education, Atlanta had become a city of strong black political incorporation.

The Jackson Regime, 1973–1981

During his first term, Maynard Jackson pursued a progressive political agenda. For example, his administration attempted to improve police–community relations by appointing a public safety commissioner to oversee the police department as well as hiring more black officers. At the conclusion of the Massell administration, blacks comprised only 19 percent of the police force in a city that was now majority-black (Jones 1978, 101). Reports of excessive force by the police against black suspects were common. Four years later, blacks had increased their presence in the department to 35 percent (Jones 1978, 116). Between 1974 and 1976, blacks accounted for

74 percent of those hired by the department—and whites accounted for 87 percent of those who left it (Bayor 1996, 185). Claims of police brutality declined as the complexion of the police force changed (Eisinger 1980, 155).

Another progressive act of the Jackson administration, aided by a coalition in the city council, was its efforts to use a newly formed neighborhood planning system to increase citizen participation in neighborhood land-use decisions. The Neighborhood Planning Unit (NPU) system, which resulted from the 1973 charter revisions, required the mayor's office to devise multiyear and annual comprehensive plans for the city and its neighborhoods. The city council created 24 formal neighborhood councils composed of community representatives. Though the NPU councils lacked veto power, they could comment on planning and zoning proposals and recommend alternative policies and projects to influence planning decisions, the capital budget, and the allocation of millions of dollars in federal aid through programs such as general revenue sharing and community development block grants (CDBG) (Rohe and Gates 1985, 97–98; Stone 1989, 86–87). They also had professional staff at their disposal in the form of designated city planners assigned to work with the NPUs and based in a new Division of Neighborhood Planning that Jackson established.

Central Atlanta Progress (CAP), the downtown business community's advocacy group, took issue with much of Jackson's agenda. In a 1974 letter to the mayor, CAP President Harold Brockey informed Jackson of his constituents' concerns. Jones (1978, 112) reports that the contents of the letter stated CAP's "fears of the increasing crime rate, the growing racial imbalance in the city's workforce, and the perceived attitude of the mayor as anti-white." Through the local newspaper, the business community publicly criticized Jackson as a maverick and a reverse racist. The media campaign of the business community characterized Atlanta as a crisis city. Responding to the criticism and a need to govern more effectively (i.e., work in tandem with the private sector), the second term of the Jackson administration focused less on neighborhood groups and more on the land-based economic interests of the city's growth machine. Parity issues and democratic reform became less important than the development interests of the private sector (Reed 1999; Stone 1989).

In line with the interests of the white business community—as well as with those of middle-class black entrepreneurs, Jackson advanced an agenda of publicly aided redevelopment and growth. He also decreased his commitment to the NPU system, reducing the access of neighborhood groups to the resources of the planning department, especially its planners. In addition, Jackson broke a municipal strike called by low-income city workers, especially sewer and sanitation workers, lobbying for an hourly raise of 50 cents. His administration consistently socialized the costs of white-led development while privatizing its benefits to the disadvantage of most blacks, especially the poor (Reed 1999). For example, funding for the public–private development initiatives of the city came from a host of sources, including federal programs like CDBG, which was intended to be targeted to aid low- and moderate-income persons and neighborhoods. Increasingly, the Jackson regime relied on CDBG funds to subsidize the financial components and infrastructure of private development projects, resulting in fewer funds for social services initiatives and neighborhood improvement projects (Reed 1999, 170).

The Young Regime, 1981–1989

Andrew Young, who previously had served three terms in Congress and as ambassador to the United Nations under President Carter, succeeded Jackson as mayor in 1981. Early in his tenure, the city council became majority-black. By the halfway point of Young's first term, blacks had secured 32 elected local government positions: the mayoralty, 13 city council seats, six board of education seats, nine city judgeships, and three county commissioner seats (Bullard and Thomas 1989, 95). The potential was present for the administration to promote more equitable and progressive public policies, and many voters had high hopes of it, which they based on Young's roots in the church and the civil rights movement (Young had served as a top aide to Martin Luther King, Jr.). Yet the Young administration produced no noticeable policy outputs that improved the general condition of nonelites (Keating 2001; Reed 1999; Stone 1989).

Although Young had campaigned in defense of neighborhoods, as mayor he reduced the efficacy of the NPU system by downsizing its staff to a single planner, and he reneged on promises to neighborhood groups to oppose construction of new intracity expressways (Stone 1989). In terms of taxes, Young was regressive, favoring increased sales taxes over increased property taxes. In partnership with CAP, the downtown business community's advocacy group, the Young administration revived old development projects and pursued new ones that benefited private investors more than the general public. Young also used public money (primarily federal) to finance the redevelopment of Underground Atlanta, a subterranean shopping and entertainment complex billed as a festival marketplace in the hope of attracting tourists and conventioneers in the central business district. Yet when city council members tried to link funding for Underground Atlanta to employment quotas for unemployed Atlanta residents, the Young administration opposed them (Stone 1989, 139).

The Young regime could have acted on behalf of marginal groups in other instances as well. When presented with an opportunity to invest public funds in the Auburn Avenue district, a historic commercial strip in a black neighborhood immediately east of the central business district, the administration balked. The Young regime also showed little interest in redeveloping the majority-black neighborhoods in south Atlanta. In addition, rather than channel city resources to reduce housing costs and homelessness through non-profit, community-based affordable housing production like New York City and other cities were doing in the 1980s, city hall focused instead on creating tax incentives to encourage the development of upper- and middle-income high-rise apartments and condominiums north of the central business district.

Like Jackson, Young did not receive the support of the white business community during his first election campaign. Nevertheless, the Young administration sought to reconstitute the biracial coalition of yore. For example, shortly after his election, Young met with Atlanta's business leaders and told them "I didn't get elected with your help, . . . I can't govern without you" (Stone 1989, 110). Young strengthened ties with the business community by becoming Atlanta's chief booster, ultimately gaining private sector support by convincing the International Olympic Committee to hold the 1996 Summer Games in Atlanta. His success at winning the Olympic bid, and spurring private development in the central business district and foreign investment in other parts of the city, albeit not on the majority-black southern side of the city, were his hallmarks.

The Campbell Regime, 1993–2001

Maynard Jackson returned to city hall as mayor in 1989 to complete a single term. Black City Councilman Bill Campbell, Jackson's protégé and floor leader in the council, succeeded him. Campbell had a good political reputation, earned primarily through his representation of a diverse district of affluent majority-white and poor majority-black neighborhoods (Holmes 1994, 6). He was a strong advocate for black enterprise and neighborhood preservation. He had promise. However, he ended his 8 years as mayor dogged by allegations of graft and corruption, and despite his claims to the contrary ("Ultimately, you leave the city in better shape than you found it"; Tofig 2002, 1H), he left Atlanta with a number of staggering problems (Bennett 2001).

When Campbell took office, the crime and poverty rates in Atlanta were among the highest in the nation. The city's infrastructure was in disrepair, especially its water mains and sewer system, requiring a projected $1 billion in repairs. The city also faced a multiple-million dollar budget shortfall. In response, Campbell stressed the need for increased private and intergovernmental investment in the city and fiscal responsibility. For example, the administration used $913.5 million in capital improvements and an estimated $140 million in administrative costs to encourage the private sector to invest in the city before the 1996 Atlanta Olympic Games (Keating 2001, 148–155). The city investments leveraged approximately $70 million for revitalization projects in the neighborhoods proximate to the Olympic venues (Keating 2001, 159). Furthermore, the city won a coveted federal award— Empowerment Zone designation. This award provided the city with a $100 million grant and approximately $150 million in federal tax incentives to be used over a 10-year period to help revitalize some of Atlanta's poorest neighborhoods.

In response to budget shortfalls, the Campbell administration routinely reduced the municipal workforce. Between 1993 and 2000, the city reduced its workforce by 300 jobs, mainly through early retirements and attrition (City of Atlanta 1993, 2000). It imposed budget cuts among administrative agencies (Holmes 1999) and had some success using bond referendums to raise revenues for capital projects. Overall, however, the administration was no more valuable materially to low-income blacks than its predecessors had been and, given the difficulties the city's Empowerment Zone initiative encountered, may have been even less responsive to their needs.

The last years of the Campbell regime were shrouded by rumors of corruption, which led one local newspaper article to compare it to a kleptocracy (Woods 2001) and another to suggest that "Campbell may have presided over the most corrupt administration in city history" (*Atlanta Journal-Constitution* 2001, 13A). Business leaders, community groups, and politicians criticized the administration for ethical lapses, fiscal and administrative incompetence, greed, and cronyism. In 2000, the U.S. Department of Justice opened an extensive corruption investigation of city hall that focused specifically on the mayor and issues pertaining to city contracts, favoritism, and campaign finance irregularities. Critics pilloried the mayor for decisions such as accepting trips financed by local businesses with city contracts or contracts pending. Associates of the mayor both in and outside city hall faced federal indictments on corruption charges. His former deputy chief operating officer pleaded guilty to accepting bribes from a company seeking to do business with the city. Key financial contributors to Campbell's re-election campaign pleaded guilty to raising campaign funds in exchange for city contracts. By the end of his term, Campbell was a discredited leader who handed over a city with a $90 million deficit (equivalent to about 20 percent of the city's operating budget) to a fourth black mayor.

The Franklin Regime, 2001–Present

In November 2001, Shirley Franklin became the first black woman to become mayor of a major southeastern U.S. city. She won the election with 50.1 percent of the vote, defeating two African-American challengers and avoiding a runoff by a mere 189 votes, equivalent to about a vote per precinct (Figure 7.3). Franklin had never held elected office. Still, she is considered by many to be the consummate insider based on several important, previously held policy-making positions in the private and public sectors. For example, she was a senior policy advisor and managing director of the quasigovernmental Atlanta Committee on the Olympic Games (ACOG), which according to Larry Keating (2001, 147) was a "new, formal version of the old downtown business elite. Like downtown business interests, it had so much power and influence that it actually functioned to a great extent as an unelected government." The ACOG also gave Franklin high visibility among the city's economic elites, as did her brief stint as a board member of the Georgia Regional Transportation Authority, to which she was appointed by Governor Roy Barnes. In addition, Franklin had served as chief administrative officer in the Young administration and, according to some informed observers, was actually mayor during that period given Young's extensive foreign travel schedule. She also had served as commissioner of cultural affairs in the Jackson administration.

Franklin's background in public administration gave her the credibility to run for mayor. Her ties to Jackson and Young gave her legitimacy with black voters. Her access to the business community gave her a fund-raising advantage of more than $1 million over her closest competition in the mayor's race, the outgoing president of the city council (with 24 years of legislative experience). Her campaign stressed themes relating to ethical, efficient, and effective government. As the *Atlanta*

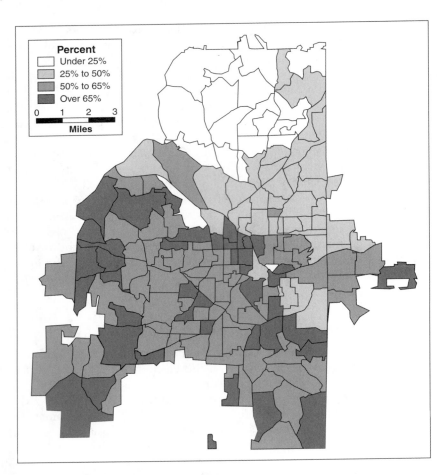

FIGURE 7.3   General vote for Shirley Franklin, 2001

Business Chronicle reported (Williams 2001, 11), "she talked of restoring faith in City Hall without naming names. It was as if she were succeeding Jackson and Andy Young, her mentors, and the years from 1992 to 2001 were just some vague unpleasantness." Franklin never worked for Campbell, but she needed to distinguish herself from him because like Campbell, she too had been a protégé of the earlier black mayors and had benefited from her affiliations with them.

If history repeats itself, Franklin will govern for 8 years, extending the legacy of black power in city hall to beyond 30 years. Franklin's campaign rhetoric gave voters—especially the 30 percent of whites who voted for her—hope that her governance of the city would be better than what occurred during the Campbell era. To govern well, however, she will need the assistance of the city council, especially the president, who appoints committee chairs and breaks tie votes. Yet Franklin will have to govern with a white city council president, who could be an important factor in forging consensus in a city council where a majority of its members are new.

Councilwoman Cathy Woolard won the council presidency in 2001, defeating Councilman Michael Bond, who had served as Campbell's floor leader in the city council and was also the son of civil rights leader Julian Bond, by almost 4,000 votes in a close runoff election (Figure 7.4). Woolard's election marks the return of whites to a position of leadership in city politics, which may also signal the emergence of a new biracial electoral coalition as well as a renewed interest among whites seeking to ensure that city government is responsive to their interests. Depending on the extent of racial population changes over the next decade (during the 1990s, the white population in the city increased by 9 percent, whereas the black population declined by 2 percent), it may also foreshadow the end of black control of city hall and, perhaps, of the city council as well.

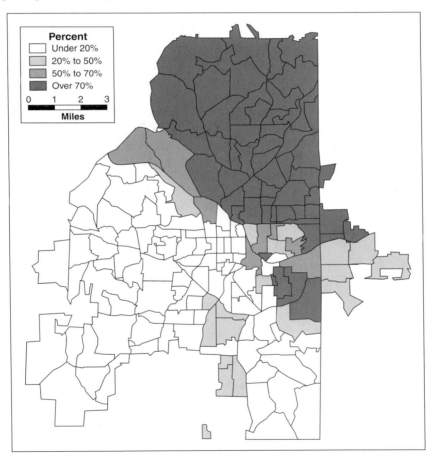

FIGURE 7.4   **Runoff vote for Cathy Woolard, 2001**

GOVERNMENT RESPONSIVENESS

The prize of strong political incorporation is what put blacks in a position where they could assume major influence over municipal policies and the distribution of public benefits. This section examines the impacts of black incorporation in Atlanta, particularly regarding city government employment, public contracts, use of federal grants-in-aid, and public education.

City Government Employment

During the 1960s, blacks held mainly low-tier jobs in the city government, mostly as laborers (Brimmer and Marshall 1990). Blacks were absent from the city's administrative and managerial positions in the Allen administration, and professionals accounted for only 1 percent of black city workers. By the early 1970s, under the Massell administration, whites still held the majority of jobs in city government. However, while Massell had tried to increase the proportion of blacks in city government, aiming for 50 percent, by 1972—a year before Massell's re-election campaign—38 percent of city government jobs belonged to blacks (Jones 1978, 101). The proportion of professional and managerial positions in city government that blacks held increased to 19 percent and 14 percent, respectively (Bayor 1996, 121). In summary, black power, as defined by increased political incorporation in the city council and city hall, ultimately changed the racial composition of the city government to advantage blacks (Table 7.2).

The place of whites among the ranks of city employees began to diminish during the Jackson administration, partially due to enactment of a residency requirement for appointed city employees and reductions in the importance of

TABLE 7.2   Black employment, Atlanta city government, 1970–2000

Job Category	1970	1978	2000
Administrative	7.1	32.6	65.9
Professional	15.2	42.2	71.4
Police	15.9	—[a]	64.2
Fire	16.0	—[a]	58.7
Office/clerical	17.2	—[a]	90.1
Service/maintenance	90.6	—[a]	94.5
Total % black	38.1	55.6	80.1

[a]Data unavailable.

Sources: Jones, Mack. 1978. Black Political Empowerment in Atlanta. *Annals of the American Academy of Political and Social Science*, 439 (September): 90–117; Eisinger, Peter K. 1982. Black Employment in Municipal Jobs: The Impact of Black Political Power. *American Political Science Review* 76 (June): 380–392; and City of Atlanta, Bureau of Labor, Department of Personnel, EEO-4 Report, 2000.

standardized examinations (Bayor 1996, 122; Stone 1989, 87). By the end of Jackson's first term in 1978, blacks accounted for 56 percent of city employees (Eisinger 1982b, 385). Among civil service professionals, the proportion of jobs that blacks held increased to 42 percent, while the proportion of blacks in administrative positions grew to 33 percent (Jones 1978, 101; Eisinger 1982a, 756).

As of 2000, blacks had a disproportionate share of city jobs. According to unpublished personnel data from the city government, blacks held 80 percent of all positions (full- and part-time) in city government. Whites hold most of the remainder (18 percent). Across the 10 functional categories of government under authority of the mayor, blacks hold majorities in all. In three categories, blacks hold nine of every 10 positions—Community Development (97 percent), Natural Resources (94 percent), and Corrections (92 percent). Their presence is dominant even in the functional areas where they have their lowest proportions, such as Fire (59 percent), Housing (64 percent), and Police (64 percent), which are the areas that continue to employ the most whites.

Blacks dominate all classes and ranks of employment in the city government, especially positions of authority and bureaucratic discretion. Among policy-making positions, blacks are 70 percent of the city's officials and administrators. As well, blacks hold seven of every 10 professional positions in the workforce. This pattern also exists in agencies that are independent of city hall. For example, unpublished personnel data from the Atlanta public school system for 2000 show that blacks account for 78 percent of the system's central office administrators and 95 percent of its school principals. The effect of black administrators and principals on black teacher hiring and retention seems positive. From 1989 to 1993, the proportion of black teachers in the public schools was 82 percent (Henig, Hula, Orr, and Pedescleaux 1999, 121). This is striking when one considers that blacks were only 47 percent of the city's teachers in 1963 (Bayor 1996, 230).

As in the past, blacks are unevenly distributed throughout city government. In the 1970s, most black city workers in Atlanta were in laborer, clerical, and service positions (Jones 1978, 101). These positions, which imposed few requirements for employment, benefited many low-skilled and low-income blacks, providing them with hundreds of well-paying jobs. At the end of the 1990s, however, service positions provided fewer jobs than in the past. Instead, protective services positions and paraprofessional positions accounted for approximately one-half of the jobs held by blacks in city government. In most instances, these positions required postsecondary education, meaning that mainly middle- or even working-class blacks, not poorer blacks, probably acquired these positions.

Generally, access to government jobs and advancement within the public sector has furthered the overall progress of blacks. Not only does public employment improve household income, advance educational attainment, and move people out of poverty, it also provides blacks with greater opportunities for descriptive representation as well as participation in and influence over the direction of public policy (Collins 1983; Eisinger 1980).

Unfortunately, city government employment, at least during the 1980s, did little to affect the overall employment situation of Atlanta's blacks. From 1980 to 1990, the black unemployment rate increased from 10.6 percent to 13.3 percent (Keating 2001, 34). At the conclusion of the 1990s, city government was no longer a growth sector for blacks in Atlanta. There had been idiosyncratic increases in the municipal workforce, such as growth in the police force during the years preceding the 1996 Atlanta Olympic Games, but the overall trend of the black regimes was to downsize the municipal workforce. Between 1980 and 2000, black mayors and the city council reduced the municipal workforce by 28 percent, from 10,500 to 7,607 (City of Atlanta 1979, 2000). Likewise, the Atlanta public school system cut its teacher rolls by 20 percent, from a high of 4,788 in the 1980s to 3,800 at the end of the 1990s (City of Atlanta 1979, 2000).

City Contracts

In 1973, black firms received .13 percent of the city's expenditures through contracts (Brimmer and Marshall 1990, Boston 1999). The proportion would change over the next 4 years under the first Jackson administration, increasing from 2 percent to 39 percent (Research Atlanta 1986, 41). The Jackson administration deliberately used race as a criterion for awarding city contracts to increase the share going to black firms. Jackson acknowledged it: "Let me be clear, MBE's [minority business enterprises] in the City of Atlanta did not improve their status until the first term of my administration. Without concerted governmental action there would have been no improvement" (Boston 1999, 13). Black entrepreneurs agreed. A 1995 survey of black firms found that 88 percent of entrepreneurs responded that the city's affirmative action policies had significantly assisted black business development in Atlanta (Boston 1999). Few, however, identified the "political correctness" of the city as being influential in their decision to locate their business in Atlanta.

The prevalence of black governmental leadership and policies aimed at their core racial constituency, the middle-class, made a difference to the growth and financial viability of black firms. From 1982 to 1997, the number of black-owned firms grew from 3,496 to 7,853, an increase of 125 percent (Boston 1999). The number of black businesses per 1,000 blacks in Atlanta also increased by 125 percent (Boston 1999, 19). Increased black access to municipal contracts for services and procurement may have spurred the growth in black enterprise within the city limits of Atlanta, as economist Thomas Boston (1995a, 87) contends. By 1995, public sector contracts accounted for 40 percent of the revenue of black-owned firms located in the city of Atlanta, with black construction firms receiving more than half (55 per cent) of their revenue from public contracts (Boston 1999, 58).

Black influence over public contracting also may have improved the employment prospects of some blacks in the city. A survey of black-owned firms in Atlanta suggests the degree to which their presence and growth matters to blacks (Boston 1999). A majority (83 per cent) of black entrepreneurs assert that they have a responsibility to assist in the improvement of black neighborhoods, and they manifest it by hiring local blacks. Overall, blacks held 82 percent of the positions at black firms, with 59 percent of the employees of black firms residing within the city of Atlanta. Moreover, one-third of their employees reside in neighborhoods proximate to Atlanta's downtown central business district. Generally, the average proportion of blacks in the neighborhoods of black-owned firms is 57 percent. For black-owned construction firms, which rely mainly on government contracts for their revenue, the proportion of black employees is 64 percent.

There is a caveat, however, to the story of contracting and employment under the black regimes of Atlanta. Black firms with the highest revenues recruit heavily from low-income black neighborhoods but tend to locate themselves elsewhere in the city. Boston (1995b) reports that the majority of "successful" black-owned firms in Atlanta are located in black communities other than poor and working-class neighborhoods. Specifically, whereas 3 percent of black firms are located in low-income neighborhoods and another 24 percent in moderate-income neighborhoods, middle-income black neighborhoods account for the greatest proportion of black firms (64 percent), and upper-income black neighborhoods account for nearly 10 percent of black businesses.

As Boston (1995b) has shown, black firms in low-income neighborhoods are more likely to employ more black workers than firms in higher-income neighborhoods, and they count a higher percentage (82 percent) of blacks among their employees. The publicly assisted growth of black firms in the city, however, occurred mainly in affluent and middle-income black neighborhoods, which did little to improve the conditions of the city's poor black neighborhoods. Historian Ronald Bayor (1996, 123) concludes:

> In the lower income levels, employment conditions remained dismal. Jackson's affirmative action, MBE, and other economic uplift efforts did not benefit all. This was partly the result of the focus of the [mayor's] programs, which stressed economic development for the city as a way to help the poor. This approach was based on the concept that as the city's economy expanded, all Atlantans benefit. But it did not happen this way.

Low-income blacks likely fared even worse under the Campbell administration's affirmative action/minority business program. Near the end of Campbell's second term, the Southeastern Legal Foundation, a conservative public interest group, sued the city in federal court on the grounds that its minority business program was unconstitutional. Campbell's initial response was a vow "to fight to the death" to defend the city's program, and he indicated that the city's defense would resemble the "shootout at the O.K. Corral" (Cook 1999, 2c). As in the past, Atlanta's business and civic leaders quickly moved to defuse a potentially ugly—and public—racial conflict by encouraging both parties to reach a settlement. Other developments also weakened the city's prospects for a successful defense. A federal court judge threw out Fulton County's affirmative action program, which was very similar to Atlanta's, and one of the mayor's close associates and campaign contributors, who was charged with tax evasion, acknowledged that his business was nothing more than a front for white-owned companies that needed to certify they worked with black businesses as a prerequisite for getting city contracts. In December 2000, after spending nearly $2 million in legal fees, the city decided not to go forward with its defense and, instead, sought a settlement with the Southeastern Legal Foundation. A few months later, the city council adopted a revised program, which did not differ dramatically from the program it replaced.

Federal Programs

Historically, Atlanta has fared well in the competition for federal funding under major urban initiatives. It participated in the urban renewal, community action, and model cities programs of the 1950s and 1960s as well as the urban development action grant program of the 1980s. Most recently, Atlanta was one of six cities designated as a federal Empowerment Zone in 1994. Each of these programs brought millions of dollars in federal aid for Atlanta's distressed areas—and the potential to leverage millions of additional dollars in private investment.

The record, however, as former Atlanta Congressman Charles Weltner (1977), whose district included Atlanta's model cities neighborhoods, observed, is "a sobering scorecard."

As Stone (1976) has extensively documented, the city's urban renewal efforts, and the federal dollars underwriting much of them, did not benefit most black Atlantans. Black entrepreneurs and churches struck financial deals with the city's white elite to relocate African-Americans from the central business district and move them to outlying neighborhoods to the south and west of downtown. This protected the elite's substantial investment in the central business district and established a buffer zone between the downtown area and the encroaching blight of nearby black neighborhoods.

Under the model cities program, more than $173 million in public funds (federal, state, and local) were invested in some of Atlanta's poorest neighborhoods during the 6-year initiative to address a variety of physical, social, and economic problems. According to Weltner, "it is inescapable that we made very little difference and in some cases we clearly had a negative impact on the lives of people we were sincerely trying to help." Atlanta had intended to construct 6,000 units of new housing in its model cities target areas, but by the end of the program, only 42 units had been completed, another 307 were under construction, and 69 had been rehabilitated (Blackmon and Harris 1994).

Urban renewal and model cities, however, were programs run under the old regime of white mayors, a white business elite, and neighborhood "advisory" panels. Yet in many respects, the city's current Empowerment Zone initiative, run under conditions of full black political incorporation and in many of the same target neighborhoods as the model cities program, has yielded no better result. According to Atlanta's strategic plan, the majority of Empowerment Zone funds ($36 million) were to be invested in activities focused on "lifting youth and families out of poverty," including the creation of several comprehensive, family-based service centers; expanded child care; expanded prekindergarten education; and a number of programs to improve the quality of education. This investment, in conjunction with $10 million to promote "safe and livable communities" and $21 million to provide "adequate housing for all," was to enhance the community context for the investment of $32 million to "expand employment and investment opportunities," primarily through promotion of neighborhood-based businesses, microenterprise, and creation of home-based businesses (City of Atlanta 1994).

Seven years into the 10-year Empowerment Zone initiative—one that has been plagued by controversy, power struggles between the mayor and zone residents serving on the corporate board overseeing it, and an inability to execute projects—the actual uses of Empowerment Zone funds have turned out to be quite different than those originally anticipated by participants in the strategic planning process. The preponderance of funding ($50 million) has been directed toward economic development activities, including a $5 million grant to support development of an office park abutting the western boundary of the central business district that was promoted by a development spin-off of the CAP. Moreover, the style of economic development that has been funded to date has been either large-scale redevelopment projects or business loans to entice companies to relocate to the zone, not the creation of small, resident-owned and -operated businesses as originally envisioned. On the other hand, allocations for activities to "lift youth and families out of poverty" have totaled slightly more than $1 million, and of this amount, only about $50,000 had been spent at the halfway mark of the 10-year initiative.

Schools

In response to white flight, inequality among public schools in the city, and decades of protracted disagreement over school desegregation and especially the issue of busing, the Atlanta Compromise of 1973 radically changed the Atlanta public school system, especially its administration (Bayor 1996, 243–251; Stone 1989, 103–106). The majority-white school board agreed to hire a black superintendent, create new administrative positions for blacks, and recruit blacks to replace retiring white administrators. Its goal was to achieve black-white parity among its administrative ranks. In return for black administrative control, black leaders shelved a large-scale busing plan.

Black "bureaucratic enfranchisement" (i.e., the ability to formally affect the policies of an administrative agency through positions of governmental authority) was expected to make a difference regarding segregation (Fainstein, Fainstein, and Armistead 1983). Yet educational segregation continued. In 1970, public schools in Atlanta were 64 percent black, but by 1985, they were 90 percent black (Bullard and Thomas 1989, 93). As of October 2000, enrollment was 89 percent black. Moreover, as Table 7.3 shows, there are sharp disparities in the composition and performance of Atlanta's public schools. For example, test scores in elementary schools in majority-white census tracts are twice as high as those reported for elementary schools in majority-black neighborhoods. In the white elementary schools, test scores average around the 65th percentile, a level comparable to the average for public elementary schools in suburban Cobb and Gwinnett counties. On the other hand, in the city's majority-black census tracts, test scores average around the 30th percentile—with some individual schools showing averages as low as the 10th percentile (or lower).

TABLE 7.3   Selected characteristics of Atlanta public schools

	Census Tracts	
	Majority-White	*Majority-Black*
Number of elementary schools	8	57
Enrollment, 2000–2001	472	456
% Black	31.2	96.4
% Eligibile for school lunch program	35.5	86.8
Mobility index[a]	33.1	46.9
Test Scores (Stanford 9, national percentiles)		
Reading, grade 3	67	26
Math, grade 3	65	30
Reading, grade 5	65	32
Math, grade 5	64	35

[a]The mobility index is defined as the number of students who enter and leave the school during the school year in proportion to the average active enrollment at the beginning and end of the school year. The lower the mobility index, the more stable the student population is throughout the school year.

Sources: Atlanta Public Schools, *2000–01 School Reports* and *Statistical Reports*, various years.

WHY THE BLACK POOR HAVE NOT BENEFITED FROM BLACK POWER

Despite nearly three decades of black control of city political institutions and the opportunities provided by one of the nation's fastest-growing regional economies, the socioeconomic gap between black and white Atlantans is greater now than it was 30 years ago (Sjoquist 2000). Why have poor African Americans in Atlanta not fared better under black rule? We think that several factors account for this.

During the 1960s and 1970s, as the black mayor became a more prominent part of the urban landscape, some observers speculated that blacks had achieved a "hollow prize" (Friesma 1969). That is, some argued that blacks came to power during a time when cities were reeling in an urban crisis brought about by disinvestment in housing and economic activities as population and jobs moved to the suburbs. Similarly, the heady days of the War on Poverty had ended, and Washington was showing less interest in urban problems than it had during the 1960s. However, though Nixon's New Federalism extended federal aid to many suburban communities, such aid continued to pour into central cities during most of the 1970s. Mayors were often the big winners as programs such as general revenue sharing, community development block grants, and comprehensive employment and training grants annually brought millions of dollars in assistance that were extremely flexible in their use. Thus, mayors (and city councils) had control over relatively large sums of discretionary funds. Federal grants to cities declined sharply during the Reagan years. New initiatives were launched during the Clinton years, however, and funding for many ongoing programs was increased.

As noted above, Atlanta participated in several major federal urban initiatives, but those resources were not always effectively invested in the city's most distressed neighborhoods. In many instances, the major beneficiaries of these programs were more likely to be the administrators and consultants running the programs as opposed to low-income African Americans.

A second factor that has impeded poor black Atlantans from sharing in the region's prosperity has been the spatial mismatch between the location of economic opportunities and the city's low-income neighborhoods. As noted earlier, much of the region's growth has occurred in the northern portions of the city and in the northern suburbs. The suburban areas in particular have experienced substantial employment growth, but much of this area is beyond the reach of public transit, largely due to voters in Cobb and Gwinnett counties repeatedly rejecting referendums that would have increased the sales tax rate to raise revenue needed for those counties to become part of the MARTA system. Each county now has its own separate bus system. One recent study (Rich and Coughlin 1998) examined the geographic distribution of jobs listed in the city's major newspaper and found that only three of every 100 jobs listed were entry-level positions (high school education or less and 6 months experience or less), accessible by public transportation, and paid more than $15,000 per year.

Third, even if Atlanta's low-income African Americans could utilize a regional transportation system to access job opportunities in the northern suburbs, would they have the requisite skills and experience needed to secure those jobs? Generally, the skill deficit of low-income blacks is deep compared to whites in the region (Ihlanfeldt and Sjoquist 2000). Although most graduates of the majority-black Atlanta public school system are employed or in postsecondary programs, system data suggest they may be poorly educated. As noted earlier, black students from low-income neighborhoods consistently score poorly on standardized tests and perform below grade-level in reading and math, which ultimately retard their prospects for well-paying jobs, either in the city or outside of it.

A fourth factor that may explain why black incorporation in Atlanta has failed to improve the conditions of low-income blacks is political alienation and demobilization. The poor participate less. From 1973 through 1989, black voter turnout surpassed white voter turnout (Gilliam and Kaufmann 1998). By 1993, however, whites were more likely to mobilize than blacks (Gilliam and Kaufman 1998; Affigne 1997). The declines in black voter registration and turnout observed in Atlanta from the 1970s to the 1990s occurred mainly among the residents of low-income black neighborhoods (Affigne 1997; Banks 2000). Turnout in the most recent municipal election was lowest in the city's poorest neighborhoods. Perhaps disappointed by the inability of black regimes to convert campaign rhetoric into policy responsiveness, low-income blacks in the city are "standing down" politically, retreating with their resources (i.e., votes) from the electoral sphere. The result is that the foundation for cross-class collective action to pressure the city government to enact and implement policies that improve low-income black neighborhoods is weak. Consequently, black policy makers may disregard the political interests of the black poor, so these neighborhoods remain impoverished or worsen.

Fifth, due to the increased importance of money in municipal elections, the needs and concerns of Atlanta's lowest-income residents have likely been muted by more affluent residents and special interests who provide the campaign contributions to those seeking office. Atlanta's most recent mayoral election was also its costliest. The two major candidates together spent more than $5 million on the campaign and the $3.18 million raised by Shirley Franklin in the 2001 race nearly matched what former Mayor Bill Campbell spent on both the general election and the runoff in 1997 (Miller and Judd 2001).

CONCLUSION

The Atlanta experience demonstrates that sustained, strong black political incorporation has not been enough to attain policy responsiveness to the needs and concerns of the city's low-income blacks. Despite nearly 30 years of black control over the major city institutions, black poverty is pervasive, and city government appears to be no more—and perhaps even less—responsive to low-income blacks than when whites ruled.

That low-income blacks in Atlanta have few tangible benefits to show for black political gains may simply reflect a black elite that was more interested in improving its material standing than that of all blacks. It also may reflect a set of unrealistic expectations regarding the ability of city government to improve conditions in poor black neighborhoods given the complexity of urban poverty and the spatial distribution of economic opportunities in the Atlanta region, patterns that were shaped largely by white flight and disengagement from a majority-black city where blacks controlled the governing institutions.

Yet current demographic trends—manifest in the form of reverse white flight in some black neighborhoods, significant population growth in many white neighborhoods, and increased suburbanization of many middle-class blacks—suggest that the political dynamics in Atlanta are likely to be volatile over the next decade and may yield a new biracial coalition capable of electing a white mayor. Regardless of whether the city continues to elect a black mayor or the pattern breaks and a white candidate is elected, low-income blacks could play the pivotal role in determining that outcome and, ultimately, may achieve the policy responsiveness they have sought for so long.

REFERENCES

Affigne, Tony. 1997. Black Voters and Urban Regime: The Case of Atlanta. In James Jennings, ed., *Race and Politics in the United States.* London: Verso Books, pp. 67–81.

Atlanta City Charter Commission. 1973. *The New City Charter.* Atlanta: Atlanta City Charter Commission.

Atlanta Journal Constitution. 2001. Our Opinions: Campbell Fostered Climate of Rampant Corruption. December 17, 13A.

Atlanta Regional Commission. 1999. *Atlanta Region Outlook.* December.

Banks, Manley Elliot, Jr. 2000. A Changing Electorate in a Majority Black City: The Emergence of a Neo-Conservative Black Urban Regime in Contemporary Atlanta. *Journal of Urban Affairs* 22 (3): 265–279.

Bayor, Ronald H. 1996. *Race and the Shaping of Twentieth-Century Atlanta.* Chapel Hill: University of North Carolina Press.

Bennett, D. L. 2001. Atlanta's Woes Await Franklin. *Atlanta Journal-Constitution*, November 18, 1C.

Blackmon, Douglas A. and Lyle V. Harris. 1994. Cash Infusion Welcome, But Will It Work? *Atlanta Journal-Constitution*, 26 December, D2.

Boston, Thomas D. 1995a. Characteristics of Black-Owned Corporations in Atlanta: With Comments on the SMOBE Undercount. *Review of Black Political Economy* 24 (Winter): 85–100.

Boston, Thomas D. 1995b. Location Preferences of Successful African American–Owned Businesses in Atlanta. *Review of Black Political Economy* 24 (Summer–Fall): 337–358.

Boston, Thomas D. 1999. *Affirmative Action and Black Entrepreneurship*. London: Routledge.

Brimmer, Andrew and Ray Marshall. 1990. *Public Policy and Promotion of Minority Economic Development: City of Atlanta and Fulton County, Georgia—Part II. Discrimination in the Atlanta Marketplace*. Washington, DC: Brimmer and Marshall Consulting.

Bullard, Robert D. and E. Kiki Thomas. 1989. Atlanta: Mecca of the Southeast. In Robert D. Bullard, ed., *In Search of the New South*. Tuscaloosa; University of Alabama Press, pp. 75–97.

City of Atlanta. 1994. *Creating an Urban Village: Atlanta's Community-Driven Vision for the Empowerment Zone*. Atlanta

City of Atlanta. Various years. *Comprehensive Annual Financial Report*. Atlanta: Department of Finance, City of Atlanta.

Collins, Sharon. 1983. The Making of the Black Middle Class. *Social Problems* 30 (April): 369–382.

Cook, Rhonda. 1999. Affirmative Action Lawsuit: Mayor Gets Political at MLK Stamp Event. *Atlanta Journal-Constitution*, August 29, 2C.

Eisinger, Peter K. 1980. *The Politics of Displacement: Racial and Ethnic Transition in Three American Cities*. New York: Academic Press.

Eisinger, Peter K. 1982a. The Economic Conditions of Black Employment in Municipal Bureaucracies. *American Journal of Political Science* 26 (November): 754–771.

Eisinger, Peter K. 1982b. Black Employment in Municipal Jobs: The Impact of Black Political Power. *American Political Science Review* 76 (June): 380–392.

Fainstein, Susan S., Norman I. Fainstein, and P. Jefferson Armistead. 1983. Bureaucratic Enfranchisement under the Community Development Block Grant Program. *Journal of Urban Affairs* 5 (Summer): 123–139.

Friesma, H. Paul 1969. Black Control of Central Cities: The Hollow Prize. *Journal of the American Institute of Planners* 55: 75–79.

Gilliam, Jr., Franklin D. and Karen M. Kaufman. 1998. Is There an Empowerment Life Cycle? Long-Term Black Empowerment and Its Influence on Voter Participation. *Urban Affairs Review* 33: 741–766.

Hartshorn, Truman and Keith Ihlanfeldt. 1993. *The Dynamics of Change: An Analysis of Growth in Metropolitan Atlanta Over the Past Two Decades*. Atlanta: Research Atlanta, Inc., Georgia State University.

Henig, Jeffrey R., Richard C. Hula, Marion Orr, and Desiree S. Pedescleaux. 1999. *The Color of School Reform: Race, Politics, and the Challenge of Urban Education*. Princeton, NJ: Princeton University Press.

Holmes, Bob. 1994. The 1993 Elections and Politics in Atlanta. In Bob Holmes, ed., *The Status of Black Atlanta, 1994*. Atlanta: Southern Center for Studies in Public Policy, Clark Atlanta University, pp. 1–22.

Holmes, Bob. 1999. Atlanta Politics on the Eve of the Millennium. In Bob Holmes, ed., *The Status of Black Atlanta, 1999*. Atlanta: Southern Center for Studies in Public Policy, Clark Atlanta University, pp. 1–39.

Ihlanfeldt, Keith R. and David L. Sjoquist. 2000. Earnings Inequality. In David L. Sjoquist, ed. *The Atlanta Paradox.* New York: Russell Sage Foundation, 116–127.

Jones, Mack H. 1978. Black Political Empowerment in Atlanta: Myth and Reality. *Annals of the American Academy of Political Science* 439 (September): 90–117.

Keating, Larry. 2001. *Atlanta: Race, Class, and Urban Expansion.* Philadelphia: Temple University Press.

Lacayo, Richard. 1999. The Brawl Over Sprawl. *Time*, March 22, 45–48.

Miller, Jill Young and Alan Judd. 2001. Franklin Clinches Money-Making Reign. *Atlanta Journal-Constitution*, November 3, 1H +.

Reed, Jr., Adolph. 1999. *Stirrings in the Jug: Black Politics in the Post-Segregation Era.* Minneapolis: University of Minnesota Press.

Research Atlanta. 1986. *The Impact of Local Government Programs to Encourage Minority Business Development.* Atlanta: Research Atlanta.

Rich, Michael J. and Joseph Coughlin. 1998. The Spatial Distribution of Economic Opportunities: Access and Accessibility Issues for Welfare Households in Metropolitan Atlanta. Paper presented at the annual meeting of the American Association of Geographers, Boston, MA.

Rohe, William M. and Lauren B. Gates. 1985. *Planning with Neighborhoods.* Chapel Hill, NC: University of North Carolina Press.

Sjoquist, David L., ed. 2000. *The Atlanta Paradox.* New York. Russell Sage Foundation.

Stone, Clarence and Carol Pierannunzi. 1997. Atlanta and the Limited Reach of Electoral Control. In Rufus P. Browning, Dale Rogers Marshall, and David H. Tabb, eds. *Racial Politics in American Cities*, 2nd ed. New York: Longman, pp. 163–178.

Stone, Clarence N. 1989. *Regime Politics: Governing Atlanta, 1946–1988.* Lawrence: University Press of Kansas.

Stone, Clarence N. 1976. *Economic Growth and Neighborhood Discontent: System Bias in the Urban Renewal Program in Atlanta.* Chapel Hill: University of North Carolina Press, 1976.

Tamman, Maurice and Ernie Suggs. 2001. Atlanta Is Top Magnet for Blacks. *Atlanta Journal-Constitution*, July 8, 1A.

Tofig, Dana. 2002. As He Predicted, Campbell Still Standing at Term's End. *Atlanta Journal-Constitution*, January 5, 1H.

U.S. Department of Commerce. 1977. *County and City Data Book: A Statistical Supplement.* Washington, DC: Bureau of the Census, U.S. Department of Commerce.

Valley, Matt. 2000. Can the No. 1 Growth City Keep on Growing? *National Real Estate Investor*, May 1, 90–96.

Weltner, Charles Longstreet. 1977. The Model Cities Program: A Sobering Scorecard. *Policy Review* 2 (Fall): 73–87.

White, Dana F. 1982. The Black Sides of Atlanta: A Geography of Expansion and Containment, 1970–1870. *Atlanta History Journal* 26 (Summer/Fall): 199–225.

Williams, Dick. 2001. Shirley Franklin's Victory Isn't a Mandate for More of the Same. *Atlanta Business Chronicle*, November 9, 11.

Woods, Walter. 2001. City Hall Is a Kleptocracy. *Atlanta Business Chronicle*, October 26, 1–2.

Chapter 8

The Evolution and Impact of Biracial Coalitions and Black Mayors in Birmingham and New Orleans

Huey L. Perry

EDITORS' NOTE

How much difference do leaders make? How do their styles and strategies shape black–white politics? This chapter documents the astonishing change from white—and more or less racist—regimes in two cities of the Deep South to regimes in which blacks play leading roles. The chapter demonstrates also that black leadership may unfold in quite different ways despite regional and developmental similarities. As Huey Perry shows, Richard Arrington, mayor of Birmingham, Alabama, from 1979 to 1999, was a consensus builder who established co-operative relations with business and gained control over city council elections. In contrast, Ernest Morial, mayor of New Orleans from 1977 to 1985, was unsuccessful in controlling council elections and had a more confrontational style.

Perry credits both Arrington and Morial with progressive actions and policies for blacks in executive appointments, municipal employment, and minority business programs. Have their different styles led to significantly different governmental outcomes? When two black candidates for mayor run against each other, as in New Orleans, what difference does it make for the structure and policy commitments of their competing coalitions? Finally, how do these cities compare with other southern U.S. cities having large black populations and black mayors? The reader might ask whether black successes have been greater in these two cities than in Atlanta (Ch. 7), or whether the marked difference in the assessment of black regimes in Chapters 7 and 8 reflects different evaluative criteria of the authors.

[1] I wish to express my appreciation to the National Science Foundation (NSF) for supporting my research on the impact of African-American political participation in urban polities. Some of the research in this chapter was conducted as part of a 14-city study funded by NSF. I also want to thank my undergraduate research assistant Marcus Augustine for making a substantive contribution to my work on this chapter. Marcus is the recipient of a 2002 National Science Foundation Graduate Fellowship.

Birmingham, Alabama, and New Orleans, Louisiana, have both had black mayors long enough to assess their impact—Birmingham since 1979 (Richard Arrington, Jr., for 20 years until 1999, followed by Bernard Kincaid in 1999), and New Orleans since 1977 (Ernest Morial followed by Sidney Barthelemy in 1985, Marc Morial in 1993, and Ray Nagin in 2002). In both cities, developing biracial coalitions exerted significant political influence during the late 1960s and early 1970s. By the mid-1970s, these were the governing coalitions in the two cities. They were responsible for the election of Arrington in Birmingham and of both Morials in New Orleans. The biracial coalitions that elected these mayors evolved in different ways, however, with different consequences for the programs and policies of the two city governments and for their black populations.

This chapter analyzes the development of black politics and biracial coalitions in Birmingham and New Orleans. The overall trend in this regard has been the rapid strengthening of black political organizations and the steady rise of black politicians since the 1960s. Within that common trend, this chapter focuses on the impact of different mayoral styles and strategies on the evolution of coalition politics and the actions and policies of city governments, especially regarding the allocation of municipal resources to African Americans. The impact of mayoral governance on governmental outputs is assessed with respect to police treatment of citizens, municipal employment, executive appointments, and minority business assistance. Finally, this chapter addresses new developments in the racial dynamics of politics in these two cities that provide powerful new insights for understanding the future of politics in U.S. cities.

Significant black political participation in both Birmingham and New Orleans, as with most localities in the South, is a post–World War II development. In both cities, the push for black inclusion in the political process was orchestrated by black political organizations. In Birmingham, the organization principally involved was the Jefferson County Progressive Democratic Council (JCPDC), which was formed in 1936 to work for the end of white supremacy in Alabama. The leaders of the JCPDC filed a lawsuit in federal court that successfully contested the exclusion of blacks from participation in the Democratic Party in Alabama. The lawsuit, the formation of a state black political party (the National Democratic Party of Alabama), and pressure from the national Democratic party resulted in blacks winning the right to participate in politics in Birmingham and in the rest of Alabama within the structure of the state Democratic Party.

During the 1950s and early 1960s, blacks in Birmingham encountered substantial resistance from whites to their desire for participation in the political process. White resistance to black demands for political rights was more severe in Birmingham than in any southern city of comparable size (Strong 1972, 443; Perry 1983, 206–207; Perry 2000). The number of black voters began to increase appreciably during the early 1960s, however, and as their numbers increased, blacks, in coalition with middle-class whites, began to exert a greater impact on electoral outcomes. The growing black vote in Birmingham played an increasingly important role within the structure of the biracial coalition in electing seriatim the city's first racially moderate white mayor, first racially liberal white mayor, and first black mayor (Table 8.1).

TABLE 8.1 Election of black mayors and percent black of registered voters in Birmingham and New Orleans

Key Elections	Birmingham		New Orleans	
	Year	*% Black Voters*	*Year*	*% Black Voters*
	1960	10	1960	17
	1967	36	1967	25
	1970	40		
Racially liberal mayor	1975	41	1969	30
Black mayor (first time)	1979	45	1977	43
Black mayor (second time)	1983	51	1981	46
Black mayor (second generation)			1986	51
Black mayor (third generation)			1994	59
Black mayor (third term)	1987	55		
Black mayor (fourth term)	1991	60		
Black mayor (fifth term)	1995	63		
Black mayor (third generation—second term)			1998	68
Black mayor (second generation—first term)	1999	69		
Black mayor (fourth generation—first term)			2002	72

Source: Registration data for this table were provided by the Registrar of Voters, Parish of Orleans, State of Louisiana, and the Registrar of Voters, County of Jefferson, State of Alabama.

The growing black vote in Birmingham also played an important role in electing, over several city elections, a more racially progressive city council, which eventually resulted in a black majority on the council. Black voters in Birmingham over the last two decades have also played a significant role in passing bond measures that allowed the city to dramatically improve its physical infrastructure and educational system and to increase other public amenities important to the quality of life, such as libraries, museums, and the arts. African Americans have benefited as recipients of these resources through the governmental allocation process. These developments constitute what Browning, Marshall, and Tabb refer to as *political incorporation*, which is "the extent to which" minorities "have achieved not only representation but positions of influence in local policy making" (1984, 12), and what Bobo and Gilliam refer to as African-American *political empowerment*, which is the extent to which "African Americans have achieved significant influence in the decision-making process" (1990, 378).

The biracial coalition has played a critical role in shaping political life and policy outcomes in Birmingham. The coalition first emerged in the election of 1962 with a successful effort to change the type of government from the commission form to the mayor–council form. The basis of the coalition was the development of a consensus among blacks, a small number of liberal whites, and members of the business community that Police Commissioner Eugene "Bull" Connor had become a liability to the city. The leaders of these groups decided that because Connor had approximately two years remaining in office, the best way to remove him was to change the form of city government. The strategy was successful. The government was changed from a commission to a mayor–council form, and because of this change, Connor and the two other commissioners were removed from office (Perry 1983, 207; Perry 2000, 108–110). This was a coalition of necessity; without the black vote, even small as it was at that time, the effort to remove Connor would not have been successful. The coalition was not one of equals, however, as business interests and middle-class white reformers clearly dominated its decision making. Even so, it was black demonstrations over the rigidity of racial segregation in all aspects of life in Birmingham—and the city being embarrassed by national television coverage of how the Birmingham police, under Connor's orders, abused the demonstrators, including women and children—that caused the coalition to be formed in the first place.

The next major point in the development of the coalition was the mayoral election of 1967, in which the biracial coalition was responsible for the election of George Seibels, the city's first moderate mayor. The coalition consisted of a large number of blacks, a somewhat smaller number of liberal and moderate whites, and a small number of people from the business community.

The third major point in the coalition's development involved the mayoral election of 1975, when blacks and liberal whites helped to elect David Vann, the city's first liberal mayor. At this point, the coalition consisted of a significant black minority and a white majority. The 1975 election represented the greatest racial integration of the coalition. The fourth major point in the development of the coalition was the election of Richard Arrington as the first black mayor in 1979. The composition of the biracial coalition that elected Arrington in 1979—and that re-elected him in 1983, 1987, 1991, and 1995—differed from the composition of the coalition that elected Vann. The composition of the Arrington coalition was a large black majority with a small but significant proportion of liberal whites and businesspersons.

After several years of increased black voter registration and officeholding in Jefferson County and Birmingham in particular, a split emerged in the JCPDC, the organization most responsible for the increased black political participation, and another organization, the biracial Citizens Action Coalition, was formed. The split was basically generational. Younger, emerging black leaders grew uncomfortable with the conservative leadership style of the older black leaders. Tensions between the younger black leaders and the old-guard leadership of the JCPDC likely were more ideological as well. It was also a contest for power, because the younger, emerging leaders and the older JCPDC leadership saw each other as being in competition for the leadership of black politics in Birmingham. Arrington provided the central leadership in the formation of the Citizens Action Coalition in 1983, which later became the Alabama Citizens Coalition as Arrington's influence grew beyond the city of Birmingham and reached statewide. The Coalition soon became the ascendant political organization in the city. It was the single most important organizational forum in Birmingham for debating black political issues, developing the black political agenda, recruiting blacks to public office, and electing both blacks and whites to public office.

In New Orleans, the organization most prominently associated with the emergence of black political participation was the Orleans Parish Progressive Voters

League (OPPVL), which was formed in 1949 to push for increased black political participation in the city. OPPVL and JCPDC were formed for the same reason—to call attention to the exclusion of blacks from public life in their city, and to pave the way for blacks to be integrated into the mainstream of public life in their city, with their organization serving as the negotiator and bargaining agent for the ascendancy of blacks in public life. As with JCPDC in Birmingham, and for the same reason, the influence of OPPVL eventually began to wane, and its role as the organizational leader of black politics in the city was successfully challenged by another black political organization consisting also of younger, emerging black leaders. As with JCPDC in Birmingham, the tensions between the younger black leaders and OPPVL leadership was in part ideological and in part a contest for the leadership of black politics in New Orleans.

The evolution of black political empowerment in New Orleans and Birmingham can be attributed in part to changes in the total population and the percentage of black registered voters since 1960. Currently, the population of New Orleans is 484,674 and blacks constitute 72 percent of the voters. New Orleans's demographic trends for the last 40 years resemble those of declining industrial cities of the Northeast and the Midwest in a number of respects. The city's population pattern for the years under review has been one of decline and stagnation. In the 1970s the population change was essentially white flight to the suburbs, especially Jefferson Parish, located west of New Orleans. From 1986 through 1988, the New Orleans Metropolitan Statistical Area (MSA) suffered an average annual net outmigration of about 8,000 people seeking jobs elsewhere.

New Orleans became a black-majority city in the 1970s, changing from 45 percent black and 54 percent white in 1970 to 55 percent black and 43 percent white in 1980. Registered voters have reflected the same trends. New Orleans has had a tradition of black voter registration since the 1940s. In 1960, blacks comprised 17 percent of the city registered voters. By the 1986 mayoral election, blacks were a majority 51 percent of the electorate (Vanderleeuw 1990).

New Orleans's place in the hierarchy of American cities has changed considerably in 30 years. It is hard to believe today that New Orleans was the third-largest city in the country in the 1840 Census. New Orleans retained its status as the largest Southern city until the 1950 Census, when it was surpassed by Houston. New Orleans's southern competitors are now cities such as Orlando (Fogelsong 1989), Nashville, Memphis, and Birmingham (Perry 1990a).

Currently, the population of Birmingham is 242,820 and blacks constitute 71 percent of the voters. By the time of its fifteenth birthday in 1921, Birmingham had grown to become the leading industrial city of the American South. Birmingham, much like New Orleans, experienced the same problems as other cities—annexation, sizable ethnic population, zoning problems, and demands for new and improved municipal services. Also, like New Orleans, Birmingham's population pattern has been one of decline and stagnation and one that has been affected by white flight to the surrounding suburban areas. Birmingham became a black-majority city in the 1970–1980 decade.

As in Birmingham, the growing number of black voters in New Orleans in coalition with middle-class white voters played an increasingly important role in electing the city's first racially moderate white mayor, first racially liberal white mayor, and first black mayor (Table 8.1). Also, as in Birmingham, the growing black vote in New Orleans was central to the election of a more racially progressive city council and, eventually, a majority-black council.

A key dissimilarity in the strength of the governing biracial coalitions in Birmingham and New Orleans was their record in bond issue and other revenue-enhancing elections and referenda. In Birmingham, blacks as part of the biracial coalition have played a consistently pivotal role in passing bond issues that have improved municipal services; in New Orleans, the voters have generally rejected revenue-enhancing proposals. In New Orleans, the biracial coalition that made Morial the first black mayor in the city's history in 1977 and that re-elected him in 1982 repeatedly broke down on revenue-enhancing proposals. Both Mayor Ernest Morial and Mayor Barthelemy failed in their efforts to convince voters to pass revenue-enhancing proposals. This difference has had important implications for the quality of life enjoyed by residents of the two cities, as discussed later.

Another difference in the politics of the two cities concerns city council elections. In Birmingham, Mayor Arrington, working through the Citizens Action Coalition and, later, the Alabama Citizens Coalition, controlled city council elections. Arrington's control over these elections resulted in the election of a majority-black council in 1987 and the selection of a black president by the council—both for the first time in the city's history. The New Orleans experience has been the opposite of Birmingham's, despite the fact that in 1987, New Orleans also elected its first majority-black city council and the first black was chosen president of the council by council members. Mayor Ernest Morial was unsuccessful in his efforts to control elections to the city council.

DIFFERENCE IN MAYORAL STYLE AND MANAGING CONFLICT

The difference between the accomplishments of the mayors in the two cities is of such magnitude that a close examination is warranted. One possible explanation is the difference in personal style between Morial and Arrington. Morial's style during his eight-year mayoral tenure was confrontational—a style developed during his tenure as a civil rights activist in New Orleans during the 1960s. Arrington was a more consensus-oriented leader. Another factor that may have contributed to Morial's governance problems was the poor state of the New Orleans economy. At the time of Morial's first election as mayor, New Orleans was overwhelmed with economic problems. These ranged from "low income and poverty, maldistribution of income, unemployment and subemployment to low educational attainment" (Schexnider 1982, 223). According to James R. Bobo, the crux of New Orleans's economic problem was not growth but inadequate economic development:

The local economy has experienced economic stagnation tendencies since the mid and late 1950s, with chronic and severe stagnation since 1966, not because there was an absence of economic growth, but because economic development did not provide adequate employment opportunities for an expanding labor force. . . . Employment opportunities have been inadequate since 1966 . . . consequently, unemployment has increased both absolutely and as a percentage of the labor force since 1966, reaching 9.0 percent in 1975 (Bobo 1975, 1–2).

Many believe that the main reason for Morial's limited success in his mayoral leadership was his problematic relationship with the business community. Morial asserted that he was pro-economic development and that he had no problem with the business community in its entirety—only with certain business leaders. Morial by and large thought he had a fairly good relationship with the business community. According to Morial, his problem with certain business leaders involved whether the city should play a substantive role in economic development or should the city let the private sector handle economic development. Additionally, Morial blamed the press for creating the friction between himself and the business community. Morial indicated that he only wanted to ensure that the city received some of the benefits from economic development activities, and that certain business leaders did not want the city to benefit in that way.[2]

In Birmingham, Arrington's style was that of a consensus builder. Arrington had cooperative relationships with the business community, whereas Morial's relationship with the business community was tenuous at best. As a consensus builder, Arrington made whites feel comfortable with a black political leadership majority in Birmingham, whereas Morial made whites feel uncomfortable with majority black political leadership in New Orleans.

Throughout his mayoral tenure, Arrington demonstrated a genuine willingness to cooperate with the business community and to make it a part of the governing coalition. An important symbolic manifestation of this approach was the monthly breakfast meetings that Arrington held with business leaders. Moreover, he made economic development the key policy objective of his second term, and this emphasis continued during his third and fourth terms. The principal beneficiary of this policy initiative has been business interests. Even when the city's leading banks failed to give Arrington his highest-priority request, a Minority Enterprise Sector and Business Initiative Cooperation Program, Arrington refused to terminate accounts the city had with some of those banks.

This difference in personal style influences the ability of a black mayor to establish a political power base. To the extent that a consensus builder like Arrington can win the trust of whites in general, and of the business community in particular, and still influence blacks, he can exert tremendous influence over city council elections and, thus, over the success or failure of his policies and programmatic initiatives. Arrington controlled not only the routes to office, particularly to the city

---

[2] Personal interview with Ernest "Dutch" Morial, former mayor of New Orleans, Louisiana.

council, but also the substantive agenda of city government—and perhaps more than any other contemporary big city mayor did. In this respect, Arrington, during the zenith of his political power, was probably the most powerful urban mayor since Mayor Richard J. Daley of Chicago during the zenith of his political power in the 1960s.

The difference in mayoral leadership between Arrington and Morial was primarily one of style rather than of issues. The overriding concern facing both administrations was basically the same: how to maintain city services in the face of dramatically reduced support from the federal government and a declining tax base. Morial, however, had an additional problem that Arrington did not have: Morial's policy and programmatic initiatives were continually opposed by the second most powerful black in city government, City Council President Sidney Barthelemy, who later became mayor. Barthelemy's opposition to Morial's initiatives weakened the support of the black community for them and made it easier for other interests to oppose them.

Not only did Morial have a problem with Barthelemy, he had a problem with the entire city council. Morial was not on the council when he was elected mayor. He was something of an outsider in New Orleans black politics, but he tried to build rapport with the city council. As a symbolic gesture, he had private brunches for the council members and their wives. According to Morial, some council members expected his support for traditional patronage politics in exchange for their support of his policy initiatives, but he was opposed to conducting the city's business that way. As a result, Morial believed the council killed many of his proposals in retribution. The relationship between Morial and the city council was not what he had wanted it to be in either term, and that was his biggest disappointment.[3]

City council opposition explains the difficulty that Morial had in translating proposals into public policies. A majority of the council generally opposed Morial's proposals. The New Orleans city council is composed of seven members, of whom five were black and two were white during Morial's mayoral tenure. The city council in Birmingham has nine members; six were black and three were white during Arrington's third and fourth terms. Morial was not nearly as successful as Arrington in shaping the council to support his proposals. Arrington achieved this objective by his influence over city council elections. He was successful in helping to elect a council majority that felt some political allegiance to him. By contrast, Morial was able to rely on only two of the seven council members for consistent support. Black politics in Birmingham under Arrington was unicentered in the mayor's office; black politics in New Orleans under Morial was dual-centered—in the mayor's office and in the city council. These competing forces in black politics in New Orleans have severely limited the ability of black political participation to produce public resources for African Americans.

---

[3] Personal interview with Ernest "Dutch" Morial, former mayor of New Orleans, Louisiana.

THE IMPACT OF BLACK POLITICAL INCORPORATION ON GOVERNMENTAL ACTIONS AND POLICIES

Black political incorporation has generally meant that blacks in both cities have favorably influenced governmental actions and policies. This section assesses the impact of black political incorporation on governmental actions and policies in four categories of public-sector activity: police treatment of citizens, municipal employment, executive appointments, and minority business assistance.

Police Treatment of Citizens

It is important to establish the intellectual parameters of this analysis based on insight from previous research findings as well as careful reflection on the dynamics of African-American penetration of police enforcement and management of racio-structural hierarchicalism. Two principal components of police-community relations are examined here: the increased hiring of African-American police officers and the reduced police abuse of African Americans, and the relationship of both of these components to a reduction of racio-structural hierarchicalism. Regarding the former, it is expected that the increased representation of African Americans in police departments will reduce police abuse of African Americans but that the reductions will occur over time rather than in the short run. The powerful influence of police culture and norms probably predisposes new African-American police officers to accept and support the prevailing norms and practices of the police force as an institution. Indeed, these acculturation forces may be so powerful as to lead new African-American recruits in the department to be especially zealous in their display of police behavior in order to demonstrate their complete commitment to the culture and norms of the department. It is expected that these forces will hold sway only in the short run and that over time increased African-American political participation will produce a climate and a demand to end police abuse of African Americans that will overcome these short term forces.

It is further expected that the reduced police abuse of African Americans will be reflected in a reduced number of excessive force complaints being filed by African Americans against police officers. Here previous research helps us to understand the impact of increased African-American political participation on the filing of excessive force complaints against the police by African Americans. Elsewhere I have argued that full scale African-American political participation, including the election of an African-American mayor committed to ending police abuse of African Americans, is likely to result initially in an increase in excessive force complaints against the police filed by African Americans rather than initial decrease as popular wisdom might suggest. These initial results occur because African Americans who are abused by the police will be motivated to file complaints under these changed circumstances because they feel that something will be done to penalize abusive police officers, whereas previously they would not bother to file complaints because they felt that nothing would be done to penalize abusive police officers.

As police officers get the message that police abuse of African Americans will no longer be tolerated, the number of excessive force complaints against the police filed by African Americans is likely to decrease. Therefore, full scale African-American political participation is likely to produce an initial increase in excessive force complaints filed against the police by African Americans followed by a decrease in excessive force complaints filed against the police by African Americans (Perry 2000). The relationship of hiring more African-American police officers and a reduction in police abuse of African Americans to racio-structural hierarchicalism appears to be fairly straightforward. It seems reasonable that these two factors would reduce racio-structural hierarchicalism. One study of police abuse of citizens in selected major cities by the U.S. Department of Justice found that police brutality in New Orleans was a major problem (1991). New Orleans was rated number one out of more than 100 cities in that study in complaints of police brutality made to the Department of Justice. A study for the New Orleans Human Relations Commission examined data on brutality complaints filed against the New Orleans Police Department in 1990, 1991, and 1992 (Perry and Delmas 1992). According to the study, 140 complaints were filed against black officers by black complainants, and 16 complaints were filed against black officers by white complainants. Also, 86 complaints were filed against white officers by black complainants and 19 against white officers by white complainants (Perry and Delmas 1992, 23). These findings lead to two major conclusions: blacks are significantly more likely than whites to file police brutality complaints, and white officers are much less likely than black officers to be the subject of black complaints (Perry and Delmas 1992, 22; Perry 2003, 111–113). The latter conclusion stands out in stark contrast to the popular perception that blacks are frequently subjected to abuse by white police officers. More systematic research on police abuse of citizens by race of complainants and race of alleged abusive officers is needed for us to know whether the Perry and Delmas findings are anomalous or representative.

The situation regarding police treatment of citizens in Birmingham is entirely different from that of New Orleans. In fact, Birmingham could be a model for New Orleans and other cities in this regard. Mayor Arrington's efforts to eliminate police brutality in Birmingham is an excellent example of how mayors can substantially improve the relations between black citizens and the police. During the 1950s, 1960s, and 1970s, Birmingham had a widespread problem of white police officers abusing black citizens. Professionalization of the police department was a high priority for Arrington during his first term, and his efforts were very successful: Police officers used less force in making arrests, and charges for resisting officers and assaults against police officers decreased. In fact, police brutality complaints dropped by 75 percent during Arrington's first term (Franklin 1989).

Police brutality continued to decline in Birmingham after Arrington's first term. Table 8.2 presents data on excessive force by race of complainants for the city of Birmingham between 1973 and 2000, including annual data on excessive force complaints in addition to two-year averages. The importance of the two-year averages is that they produce a better determination of trend lines given wide fluctuations in

TABLE 8.2 **Excessive force complaints by race of complainants for the city of Birmingham, 1973–2000**

Year	Total Number of Complaints	Total Two-Year Avg.	Black			White		
			No.	%	Two–Year Avg.	No.	%	Two–Year Avg.
1973	27		—	—	—	—	—	—
1974	39	33	—	—	—	—	—	—
1975	54		34	63	—	20	37	—
1976	19	36.5	13	68	23.5	6	22	13
1977	33		15	45	—	18	55	—
1978	—		—	—	—	—	—	—
1979	26		17	65	—	9	35	—
1980	35	30.5	21	60	19	14	40	11.5
1981	18		11	61	—	7	39	—
1982	18	18	11	61	11	7	39	7
1983	39		26	67	—	13	39	—
1984	15	27	10	67	18	5	33	9
1985	21		15	71	—	6	29	—
1986	39	30	—	—	—	—	—	—
1987	37		—	—	—	—	—	—
1988	43	40	—	—	—	—	—	—
1989	34		—	—	—	—	—	—
1990	39	36.5	—	—	—	—	—	—
1991	45		—	—	—	—	—	—
1992	52	48.5	37	71	15	15	29	—
1993	43		19	44	28	24	56	19.5
1994	41	45	28	68	—	13	32	—
1995	46		30	65	29	16	35	14.5
1996	44	45	25	57	—	19	43	—
1997	40		19	48	22	21	52	20
1998	45	43.5	20	44	—	25	56	—
1999	42		21	50	20.5	21	50	23
2000	48	45	42	88	—	26	12	—

Source: Data on the number of complaints provided by the Birmingham, Alabama, Police Department.

the annual data. In terms of the total number of excessive force complaints, the annual data generally reveal that the number of complaints decreased between 1973 and 1982 and increased between 1982 and 1991. The two-year averages reflect this general trend but place it in starker relief. Between 1973 and 1982, the two-year averages show that the total number of excessive force complaints declined by 45 percent, although an 11 percent increase occurred between 1974 and 1976. The two-year averages also show that between 1982 and 1988, the number of excessive force complaints increased by 122 percent, with a 9 percent decrease by 1990. In

2000 there were 48 complaints of excessive force. This is the second highest number in the entire series of available data since 1973. Clearly, police brutality in Birmingham has not been eliminated.

Table 8.2 also presents annual data on black and white excessive force complaints and two-year averages of the annual data for the years between 1975 and 1985. The annual data show that between 1975 and 1985, black excessive force complaints declined substantially over the period to less than half the beginning number. White excessive force complaints declined more than black excessive force complaints between 1975 and 1985. Extraordinarily, Mayor Arrington reported in 1990 that police brutality simply did not exist in Birmingham (Perry 1992). This optimistic assessment belies the data presented in Table 8.2.

The key lessons to be learned from an analysis of the police brutality issue in Birmingham and New Orleans are that African Americans can use political participation to change policies and actions of city government and that outstanding political leadership matters greatly in this process. Over the course of less than two decades African Americans in Birmingham—led first by city Councilman Arrington and subsequently by Mayor Arrington—helped to transform a situation that for them was emotionally and physically abusive and intolerable. In the early 1960s, African Americans in Birmingham were on the margins of political power in the city and were subjected to police abuse orchestrated by a racist police commissioner. By 1979, African Americans in Birmingham had played a key role in eliminating the form of government that supported the racism of Bull Connor, removing Bull Connor from power and electing Richard Arrington as the first black mayor. A similar situation occurred in New Orleans, but the police brutality issue in New Orleans historically was not as well-known across the country as Birmingham's police brutality situation was.

Once in office, Mayor Arrington adopted reforms of the police department that over time succeeded in reducing police abuse in Birmingham. In New Orleans, Mayor Ernest Morial was not successful in introducing substantive police reform to reduce abuse of citizens. Police reform in New Orleans did not occur until the administration of Mayor Marc Morial.

Municipal Employment

The capacity of increased black political participation to produce an increased share of municipal employment has received much attention in the scholarly literature on black politics (Eisinger 1980, 1982; Perry 1983, 1990a, 1990b, 1992; Browning, Marshall, and Tabb 1984; Stein 1986; Perry and Stokes 1987, 1993; Stein and Condrey 1987; Mladenka 1989a, 1989b; McClain 1993). Earlier research has confirmed the strength of that relationship in Birmingham and New Orleans (Perry 1983; Perry and Stokes 1987; Perry 1990a, 1990b, 1992).

In Birmingham by 1985, blacks had succeeded in integrating the city's workforce at all occupational levels, but they were disproportionately employed in the lower-paying and less prestigious service/maintenance and office/clerical cate-

TABLE 8.3 Full-time employees for the city of Birmingham by race, 2000

Occupation Classification	Black			White			Other		
	No.	*%*	*IOR*[a]	*No.*	*%*	*IOR*[a]	*No.*	*%*	*IOR*[a]
Officials/Administrators	33	54.1	0.74	28	45.8	1.9	0	0	0
Professionals	337	48.7	0.67	344	49.7	2.1	11	1.6	0.26
Technicians	86	44.3	0.6	108	55.7	2.3	0	0	0
Protective Services	675	52.9	0.72	597	46.8	1.95	4	3	0.05
Para-Professionals	88	76.5	1.36	27	22.6	0.94	1	0.9	0.015
Office/Clericals	322	76.5	1.36	99	23.5	0.98	0	0	0
Skilled Craft Workers	185	54.4	0.74	113	45.6	1.9	0	0	0
Service/Maintenance Workers	724	84.2	1.15	132	15.3	0.63	4	5	0.8
Totals	2450	61.51	0.92	1448	38.12	1.59	20	1.31	0.05

[a]Index of representation

Source: Data on the number of full-time employees provided by the City of Birmingham, Alabama.

gories. Table 8.3 presents municipal employment data for Birmingham in 2000 by race using an index of representation[4] to indicate the extent to which blacks and whites were under- or overrepresented in the standard Equal Opportunity Office occupational classifications. The table confirms the pattern of the 1985 and 1995 data. Blacks remained fully integrated into the city's workforce, but they were still overrepresented in low-skill, low-wage classifications (service/maintenance and paraprofessionals).

Table 8.3 also shows that blacks were underrepresented in the higher-skill, higher-paying occupational classifications (professionals, technicians, skilled craft workers, and officials/administrators). For whites, Table 8.3 shows the exact opposite pattern—except for the paraprofessional classification, in which blacks and whites are virtually equally represented.

The tendency for blacks to be employed in low-skill, low-wage occupational classifications reflects a limitation on black political participation, but this pattern can also be interpreted to reflect quasipositively on black political participation. The employment of blacks in low-skill, low-wage classifications is important, because the jobs in these classifications are significant sources of employment for low-income blacks who, were it not for these jobs, would perhaps not be employed at

---

[4] The index of representation is a standard statistical technique for determining the extent to which target groups are under- or overrepresented in certain classifications using their percentage in the general population or the labor force as a baseline. The index of representation is computed by dividing a group's percentage in a target classification by its percentage in the baseline category. A quotient of 1 indicates perfect representation. A quotient of less than 1 indicates underrepresentation. A quotient of greater than 1 indicates overrepresentation.

all. This is an important consideration, because an enduring criticism of black politics is that the benefits produced by increased black political incorporation have only gone to members of the black middle class who possessed the education, occupational, and social skills necessary to take advantage of these new opportunities. There is considerable validity to this criticism. The irony is that the increased black political participation and influence in cities during the 1970s and 1980s is, in large part, a result of the entry of a significantly larger proportion of the black lower class into electoral politics, and their political awakening was often stimulated by the prospect of electing a viable black candidate to a high-level political office. By increasing employment opportunities for blacks in the office/clerical and, especially, the service/maintenance classifications, black politics in Birmingham has produced significant benefits for members of the black working class.

Although blacks in Birmingham have clearly not achieved an equitable proportion of municipal employment commensurate with their approximately 69 percent of the city's population, they have significantly increased their representation in municipal employment. In addition to strong representation of blacks in the service/maintenance and office/clerical categories, blacks, as Table 8.3 shows, were also well represented in the mid-level occupational classifications, which generally consist of jobs that require more skills and pay better than the service/maintenance and office/clerical classifications. These classifications include skilled craft workers, paraprofessionals, protective services, and technicians. Blacks made up 54.4 percent of skilled craft workers, 76.5 percent of paraprofessionals, 52.9 percent of protective services workers, and 44.3 percent of technicians. Blacks were also well represented in the two high-skill, high-wage categories: professionals (48.7 percent), and officials/administrators (54.1 percent). As a result of black political empowerment in Birmingham, the representation of blacks in municipal employment has increased. One of the strongest relationships in the literature on black politics is that between increased black political participation and increased black municipal employment (Eisinger 1980; Stein 1986).

Increases in black political employment in New Orleans have been similar to those in Birmingham. Between 1960 and 1985, the last year of the first Morial administration, the black proportion of the New Orleans municipal workforce increased from a neglibile amount to 53 percent. The bulk of that increase occurred during the eight-year mayoralty of Moon Landrieu, the city's first white liberal mayor. Table 8.4 provides data on municipal employment for the city of New Orleans by race for 1993, also using the index of representation as the critical measure of black representation in city employment. The index of representation in this table indicates the same general pattern as Birmingham: Blacks were overrepresented in the low-skill, low-paying occupational classifications and underrepresented in the high-skill, high-paying occupational classifications.

Executive Appointments

Executive appointments include appointments by the mayor of his top personal executive staff and heads of city departments. Previous research has shown that increased black political participation and influence in both Birmingham and New

TABLE 8.4 Full-time employees of the city of New Orleans by race, 1993

	Black			White			Other			Unknown	
Occupation Classification	*No.*	*%*	*IOR*[a]	*No.*	*%*	*IOR*[a]	*No.*	*%*	*IOR*[a]	*No.*	*%*
Officials/Administrators	167	38.83	0.65	248	57.67	1.43	12	2.79	0.44	3	0.70
Professionals	451	42.31	0.7	561	52.67	1.3	53	4.98	0.79	1	0.09
Technicians	300	42.44	0.71	373	52.76	1.3	31	4.38	0.67	3	0.42
Protective Services Workers	763	41.81	0.7	1021	55.94	1.38	39	2.14	0.34	2	0.11
Paraprofessionals	281	77.83	1.30	70	19.39	0.48	10	2.77	0.44	0	0.00
Clerical Workers	956	84.08	1.4	155	13.64	0.33	22	1.94	0.31	4	0.35
Skilled Craft Workers	248	68.51	1.14	86	23.75	0.58	25	6.91	1.11	3	0.83
Maintenance Workers	736	89.10	1.49	61	07.38	0.18	28	3.39	0.53	1	0.12
Totals	3902	58.12	0.97	2575	38.35	0.95	220	3.28	0.58	17	0.25

[a]Index of representation.

Source: Work Force Demographics, City of New Orleans, Louisiana, 1993.

Orleans has resulted in significantly increased black representation in these key executive positions. In Birmingham, black representation in key executive positions increased from zero percent in 1975—before the election of David Vann, the city's first racially liberal white mayor—to 44 percent of the mayor's top personal executive staff positions (four of nine positions) and one department head during Vann's administration (Perry 1983, 212). Throughout his mayoral tenure, at least 50 percent of Arrington's top personal executive staff was black.

In New Orleans, the percentage of black department heads increased from zero percent in 1969—before the election of Moon Landrieu, the city's first racially liberal white mayor—to 42 percent (five of 12) during Landrieu's mayoralty. Landrieu appointed the city's first black chief administrative officer, Terrence Duvernay, in addition to "a significant number of blacks to important administrative positions just below the department head level" (Perry and Stokes 1987, 244). During Ernest Morial's mayoralty, the number of black department heads increased to seven of 12 (or 58 percent) which included a black chief administrative officer; the city's first black police chief, Warren Woodfork; and a black sanitation department head (Perry and Stokes 1987, 245). Succeeding Morial, Barthelemy appointed a white chief administrative officer and eight of 12 (67 percent) black department heads. In the administration of Mayor Marc Morial, half the mayor's executive staff was black.

The appointment of blacks to executive positions in city government is important for several reasons. First, though these positions are few, they provide additional financially rewarding and prestigious employment opportunities for blacks. Second, executive positions are generally policy-making positions; therefore, blacks who hold these positions can make or influence policies that advance black interests. Third, because these appointments have historically gone to whites, the appointment of blacks to these positions represents an important symbolic benefit. Finally, service in these key positions provides a small number of blacks with valuable experience, which should make them especially attractive for service in future mayoral administrations—or as candidates should they seek elective office. The experience that black urban government executives are currently gaining in running city government should have positive significance for future urban governance.

Minority Business Assistance

Black municipal officials can use the authority of city government's control over contracts for services and products to award city contracts to black businesses and to provide technical assistance to those businesses. Until recently, this important possibility had been ignored in the literature on black politics (Perry and Stokes 1987, 245–246). Because ethnic politics earlier in the twentieth century widely used this practice, and because its applicability to blacks has been frequently questioned, this omission in the scholarly literature is conspicuous.

Increased black political participation in both Birmingham and New Orleans has not significantly increased the dollar amount of municipal contracts awarded to black businesses. In Birmingham, the minority business assistance program was begun by a city ordinance in 1977. Arrington acknowledged that his major disappointment during his mayoral tenure was his failure to advance black businesses in the city. Edward LaMonte, Arrington's chief of staff, shared this sentiment during his first term: "The city's minority assistance program has not helped black businesses much. Blacks have not moved into the mainstream of the business sector. In every other way, blacks in Birmingham have been successful."[5]

Mayor Arrington, however, persisted in his efforts to increase minority participation in the business sector. In 1989, he proposed the Birmingham Plan to civic and community leaders. The Birmingham Plan involved partnerships between public and private entities designed to increase the participation of minority and disadvantaged business enterprises in Birmingham's economic development over a sustained period of time (City of Birmingham 1992).

Several societal and legal issues explain why the city's leaders made a concerted effort to ensure the participation of minority and disadvantaged citizens in Birmingham's economy by use of the Birmingham Plan. Since 1989, blacks in Birmingham have made up more than 60 percent of the city's population. The black majority expected benefits in return for its political support of Arrington and the predominantly black city council. In effect, blacks expected a quid pro quo for their political support of the black political leadership class, and they expected tangible resources rather than just symbolic racial, group-pride benefits. In the legal arena, the construction industry opposed the city's minority business assistance programs. In addition, the decisions handed down by the U.S. Supreme Court in *City of*

---

5 Personal interview with Dr. Edward LaMonte, former executive secretary to Dr. Richard Arrington, mayor of Birmingham, Alabama. Arrington had hoped that his minority business assistance program would create a strong black business sector to complement outstanding success of blacks in the public sector. This had not occurred by 1989.

Richmond v. J. S. Croson and *Martin v. Wilkes* struck down minority set-aside programs in areas where patterns of discrimination could not be documented.

Three initiatives of the Birmingham Plan are most pertinent to understanding Arrington's efforts to create opportunities for minority businesses: the Birmingham Community Development Corporation, Inc.; the Birmingham Residential Mortgage Program; and the Birmingham Construction Industry Authority (BCIA). The Birmingham Community Development Corporation, Inc., was created by nine local financial institutions to provide loans for business startup and equipment costs and as a credit enhancement for new bank financing. As of 1992, the financial institutions and the city had pledged $8 million. The Birmingham Residential Mortgage Program was started in cooperation with the city and the same lending institutions. The program makes available $25 million in FHA and VA residential mortgage loans to low- and moderate-income buyers in the metropolitan Birmingham area. Some closing costs are waived, and the city provides up to $1,500 for closing costs and down payment assistance. The BCIA resulted as a settlement of a 12-year legal dispute involving the City of Birmingham and the Alabama Chapter of the Associated General Contractors over the city's practice of setting goals for minority participation in public construction projects. The BCIA set voluntary goals for minority and disadvantaged business enterprise participation in public and private sector construction projects, and assisted minority and disadvantaged businesses with certification, marketing assistance, and project reporting and tracking (City of Birmingham 1992).

Implementation of the Birmingham Plan has resulted in markedly increased minority participation in the public and private sectors. In 1991, according to a report prepared by the mayor's office (Office of Mayor Richard Arrington, Jr. 1992), the city of Birmingham awarded 31 percent of its contracts to minority and disadvantaged business enterprises. By contrast, the University of Alabama at Birmingham, which is the largest employer in the city, awarded 5 percent of its contracts to minority and disadvantaged business enterprises. The BCIA has provided training and development seminars to minority contractors and sponsors scholarships for minority high-school and college students pursuing careers in construction. General contractors in the city reported that the minority and disadvantaged business enterprise participation rate in BCIA-sponsored programs was 13 percent of 136 monitored projects. The Birmingham Residential Mortgage Program, as of December 1991, had approved 83 loans in the amount of $2.5 million. As of March 1992, the Birmingham Community Development Corporation, Inc., had approved 80 loans in the amount of more than $2.8 million.

The New Orleans business assistance program has not been as successful as the Birmingham business assistance program. Ernest Morial authorized a minority business assistance program in late 1983 by issuing Executive Order No. 83-02, which required 25 percent minority labor force participation; however, implementation of the program did not begin until 1985. By the end of Morial's second and final term in 1986, the city's minority business assistance program was widely regarded as a failure (Perry and Stokes 1987). The failure of black political leadership in New Orleans to increase significantly the number of municipal contracts awarded to black businesses and the slow success of comparable efforts in Birmingham demonstrate a limitation of black political participation as a vehicle for producing private-sector benefits for blacks. Finally, in 1989, minority business assistance programs were discontinued nationwide because of the landmark decision by the U.S. Supreme Court in *City of Richmond v. J. S. Croson,* (1989), which ruled that " 'minority set-aside' programs must be based on documented evidence of discrimination." The Court ruled that arbitrary goals were unconstitutional. The *Croson* decision, in effect, mandated that political jurisdictions that wanted to reinstate minority set-aside programs had to conduct disparity studies that found evidence of willful discrimination to reinstate these programs.

A 1993 disparity study conducted for the city of New Orleans indicated that minority businesses were discriminated against in the allocation of city contracts (Metro Consultants, 1992). The study, conducted by the Massachusetts-based National Economic Research Associates, found that minority business enterprises (MBEs) and women's business enterprises (WBEs) have been discriminated against in the allocation of city contracts. WBEs received 3 percent of all construction contracts, whereas MBEs received 2 percent of construction contracts, 10 percent of service contracts, and 3 percent of commodity purchasing contracts.

The city of New Orleans sought to improve its record of allocating contracts to minority and women's businesses by setting utilization goals of 17.23 percent for black businesses and 14.78 percent for women's businesses. The city did not set a higher utilization goal for black businesses because of the disproportionately small number of black businesses and the fact that many of them did not own—and could not obtain—the equipment required to perform certain contract jobs.

THE SOCIAL AND ECONOMIC IMPACT OF INCREASED ALLOCATION OF GOVERNMENTAL RESOURCES TO AFRICAN AMERICANS

The public resources that African Americans have received from their increased political power and influence in Birmingham and New Orleans have been both symbolic and substantive. Some observers feel that symbolic benefits are not important. To the contrary, symbolic benefits are very important in American politics (Edelman 1964, 1971, 1975; Elder and Cobb 1983), and blacks, like all other groups in American society, are affected by symbolic politics. Symbolic benefits that confer an aura of legitimacy, respect, and equal standing to previously disadvantaged, discriminated against, and subordinate groups are very important (Barker 1987). Increased black political participation and especially increased black officeholding have moved blacks toward enhanced group social standing, which concomitantly has elevated their self-esteem.

A derivative of the symbolic resources that accrue to African Americans from holding important governmental positions is that it becomes easier for other African Americans to move into important positions of public responsibility. Mayor Arrington's former chief of staff Edward LaMonte describes the symbolic importance of Arrington's serving successfully as the black mayor of Birmingham:

> Arrington provides a personal example for blacks to move into leadership positions. Arrington serving as the mayor has made it easy for other blacks

to move into other visible positions. Having Dick Arrington as mayor made it easier for Walter Harris to be appointed superintendent of public schools.[6]

In other words, blacks who serve successfully in high positions of public responsibility not only benefit blacks generally by improving their individual and group self-esteem but also make it easier for whites to accept blacks in other high positions of public responsibility. Thus, the benefits that blacks achieve in the symbolic realm from their political success substantially improve their social status.

The substantive benefits that blacks in Birmingham and New Orleans have received from their increased participation in the political process have significantly improved their social and economic conditions. Improvements in this regard have clearly been more in the social than in the economic realm. Minority business assistance and efforts to improve police treatment of citizens have not been as successful as municipal employment and executive appointments in both cities in terms of areas of governmental activity that have been influenced by black political participation. Increased executive appointments and municipal employment are examples of the substantive public resources now available to blacks in the two cities. These resources, in addition to the symbolic benefits, have collectively enhanced the social and economic conditions of blacks.

It is more difficult to show that improvements in the economic status of blacks follow directly from the benefits they have obtained from city government, because so many other factors may be involved in the economic elevation that African Americans have experienced in both cities. In New Orleans, the percentage of black middle-class families increased from 10 percent in 1970 to 31 percent in 1985. Gains in municipal employment likely have contributed to improved economic conditions for blacks by providing significant, stable employment for them that would not have existed otherwise.

BIRACIAL COALITIONS IN THE 1990s

In both Birmingham and New Orleans, the major politically relevant groups are blacks, liberal whites, the white business community, and the remainder of the white populace. In New Orleans, organized labor is another center of power. In both cities, no one center of power is ascendant over all major policy issues. The strong biracial coalition of blacks and upper-income liberal whites in Birmingham, which controlled elections in the city from 1967 to 1997, and the less strong biracial coalition in New Orleans, which controlled city elections from 1969 to 1986, have not won all—or even most—policy battles. The same is true for the white business community, which is generally acknowledged to be the most influential group once elections are decided. These observations support the central tenets of pluralist theory that the decision-making process in the United States is influenced

---

[6] Personal interview with Dr. Edward LaMonte, former executive secretary to Dr. Richard Arrington, mayor of Birmingham, Alabama.

by many different groups and that no single group can dominate the process across all issue areas.

The least identifiable group in Birmingham city politics—the amorphous remainder of the white populace, which principally consists of low-income, conservative whites—has not fared poorly in either city. Arrington averred that he gave more services to the conservative white areas of the city than any other mayor in Birmingham's history, despite the fact that whites in these areas did not vote for him. The wisdom of Arrington's actions in this regard is supported by political developments in New Orleans.

In the New Orleans mayoral election of 1986, in which the two principal candidates were black, whites divided their vote by voting overwhelmingly for the candidate perceived to be less threatening to their interests. In other words, whites are now in the exact same position that blacks were in before they became the majority population. The election result had the potential to stimulate low-income conservative whites to become more politically active and, perhaps, even more organized for political action. This would clearly be a significant development, given that low-income whites generally are less politically active than other groups and they demonstrate little interest in political organizations.

Low-income whites are the least identifiable group in both cities because they are not nearly as organized as other groups in the two cities. In fact, it is more of a latent group than a group in the traditional sense of interest group pluralism. That low-income whites are not as politically active and organized as other groups, including low-income blacks, is consistent with prior research on black and white participation rates (Verba and Nie 1972; Shingles 1981). Low-income whites in both cities continue to be only periodically politically active, and they continue to demonstrate little interest in becoming politically organized.

The 1986 New Orleans election results also mean that the biracial coalition that controlled election outcomes in New Orleans between 1969 and 1986 was moribund. Mayoral elections in New Orleans since 1986 have been and will likely continue to be contested by two viable African-American candidates, and as long as that condition holds, the once-powerful coalition will not be able to function. Thus, the character of biracial politics in New Orleans has changed. It has evolved into two biracial coalitions split along ideological lines—a liberal coalition, and a conservative coalition. The liberal biracial coalition is made up of a large black majority and a small white minority. The conservative biracial coalition is composed of a white majority and a significant black minority. Two points are relevant here. First, having the population of a city align in two contending biracial coalitions based on ideology is better than having an alignment based on race alone because of the divisive impact that race as a social cleavage can have on the fabric of a political community in the United States (Carmines and Stimson 1989). Compared to race, ideology is a much milder social cleavage in American politics; thus, it is much easier to bridge ideological breeches than racial breeches for the betterment of the body politic. Second, blacks are strongly incorporated in both coalitions and, therefore, stand to gain from whichever coalition wins.

The results of the 1990 mayoral election in New Orleans confirm the observation that the city is evolving into two biracial coalitions. The liberal biracial coalition succeeded in influencing Mayor Barthelemy's victory over his opponent Donald Mintz, a white liberal. Barthelemy had the support of a large black majority and small white minority. (The incumbency-ideological-racial character of this election was comparable to the 1981 contest between then-incumbent Ernest Morial and Ronald Faucheaux, a white liberal candidate.) Barthelemy won re-election, capturing 86 percent of the black vote and 23 percent of the white vote, whereas Mintz received 75 percent of the white vote and 14 percent of the black vote (Perry 1990c, 157). The keys to Barthelemy's victory were support from black voters and the significant cross-over support from white voters. Surprisingly, high black voter turnout, a feature usually associated with black mayoral victories, was not a factor in Barthelemy's victory. The low turnout among black voters may suggest their lack of enthusiasm for Barthelemy, a phenomenon that makes the 1990 re-election of Barthelemy both significant and unique. Most black candidates require strong black voter support and a strong black turnout to win an election (Perry 1990c, 157).

In Birmingham, the influence of the liberal biracial coalition over electoral outcomes was not threatened as long as Arrington remained the ascendant person in the city's politics. For 20 years, Arrington was so firmly entrenched in his informal role as the leader of politics—black and white—in the city that he did not face significant black *or* white opposition after his second re-election race. In each of his elections, Arrington combined solid black support with limited white support to win. In the 1991 mayoral election, Arrington received solid support from the city's black voters and, as in the past three elections, did not receive much support in the city's predominantly white areas—particularly in the city's eastern section. Because Arrington had no significant black opposition, the biracial coalition had enough political influence to overcome his lack of substantial white support.

NEW DEVELOPMENTS IN BIRMINGHAM AND NEW ORLEANS POLITICS

In his 1998 re-election campaign, Mayor Marc Morial received very strong support from New Orleans voters and increased support from white voters. Morial received about 43 percent of the white vote, which represented nearly a fivefold increase over the estimated 9 percent of the white vote he received in 1994. Morial increased his support among black voters from 90 percent in 1994 to about 93 percent in 1998. Morial's popularity was so strong after a very successful first term in office that he won the 1998 general election by a majority vote over two challengers, thus obviating a runoff election. Overall, Morial received 79 percent of the vote—the widest margin in a New Orleans mayoral race since 1962, when Victor Schiro won with 81 percent against a token Republican opponent. In this election, Morial defeated two white challengers, lawyer Kathleen Cresson and arts store manager Paul Borrello. Morial defeated his two rivals in 83 percent of the city's 455 voting precincts. He won in all but one of the city's 17 wards, losing only in the Fourth Ward, which includes much of the predominately white Lakeview area.

Marc Morial was the most popular mayor of New Orleans since Moon Landrieu and the most popular of the city's three African-American mayors. Yet despite his popularity, he failed to persuade voters in a referendum election in 2001 to change the city's charter to allow him to run for a third term. The city charter of New Orleans limits a mayor's tenure in office to a maximum of two full, consecutive terms, or eight years. The vote on the initiative to amend the city's charter was 61 percent opposed and 39 percent in favor. The turnout in the referendum election was 40 percent. The margin of defeat for Morial was resounding given his immense popularity. The failure of the referendum left in place the city charter's limit of two consecutive terms for mayors. In not supporting Morial's proposal, voters rejected his argument that they should keep an experienced mayor in office to reform the city's troubled public schools and to guide New Orleans through the dangerous economic and public safety problems created by the September 11 terrorist attacks on the World Trade Center and the Pentagon. Following the lead of the city's voters in 1961, 1983, and 1985 when faced with a similar challenge, the voters of New Orleans upheld the two-term limit provision placed in the city's charter in 1954 to keep any New Orleans mayor from becoming too powerful.

Marc Morial's father, Ernest, had also unsuccessfully tried to persuade the voters to change the city's charter to allow him to run for a third term. Actually, Ernest Morial tried twice to persuade the voters to change the city's charter to allow him to run for a third term. There are nuanced differences between the three attempts of the Morial mayors to change the city charter to allow a third-term campaign. In 1983, voters rejected Ernest Morial's proposal to let mayors run for unlimited terms by a margin of 62 percent to 38 percent. Two years later, in 1985, voters also rejected Morial's proposal to extend the two-term limit to three terms by a margin of 61 percent to 39 percent. The first effort by the senior Morial was to totally eliminate term limits in mayoral service; the second effort attempted to assuage concerns about extended mayoral tenure by a powerful mayor by limiting mayoral tenure to three terms. Marc Morial's proposal for a third-term campaign represented an additional refinement of the third-term concept to make it more appealing to voters. Without eliminating the two-term limit, Marc Morial's proposed amendment would have allowed Morial to seek a third term and would have allowed any future second-term mayor who wanted to run for a third term to also seek voter approval to do so.

Ironically, despite his greater popularity with voters and the fact that his proposal to seek a third term was a much gentler version than his father's proposals, Marc Morial did no better than his father in persuading the voters to change the city charter to remove the two-term limit on mayoral service. The irony is that the senior Morial was not as popular with voters and enjoyed much less voter support and less favorable approval ratings by white voters compared to the younger Morial. This suggests that New Orleans voters have a deep-seated fear that extending the tenure of mayoral service would lead to an abuse of power by a politically popular and powerful mayor. Their fear in this regard is held whether the mayor is relatively unpopular, as the senior Morial was when he twice attempted to change the city charter, or is enormously popular, as Marc Morial was. Part of this fear undoubtedly has to do with the pervasive culture of political corruption and scandal that historically has characterized New Orleans politics in particular and Louisiana politics in general.

Because Marc Morial could not run for re-election, his popular reform police chief, Richard Pennington, ran for mayor in the 2002 election, and in this regard, Pennington was popularly viewed as a surrogate candidate for Morial. The expectation was that Pennington would be well received by the voters, because he is widely regarded for doing an outstanding job in cleaning up one of the most corrupt and scandal-ridden police departments in the nation. On a leave of absence from his duties as superintendent of police, Pennington finished second in the general election, trailing the front-runner, Ray Nagin, by 6 percentage points, which placed the two candidates in a runoff election. Both Pennington and Nagin are African American. Nagin, who like Pennington is a Democrat, is a wealthy former cable television executive. Nagin, who had never run for elective office previously, won the runoff election by a substantial margin over Pennington.

It is interesting that Nagin, a political unknown, defeated a popular reform police chief who was widely perceived to be the person that Morial most preferred to succeed him, and that Morial himself remained enormously popular with the voters during the last six months of his mayoralty. Two interrelated reasons explain this seeming paradox. First, the people of New Orleans, both African American and white, after eight years of one mayor were ready for new mayoral leadership. This is clearly suggested by the vote on the third-term charter change referendum. Second, the people of New Orleans apparently did not want a mayor who was widely perceived to be a surrogate for Morial. In the eyes of the voters, allowing this to happen would have been a disingenuous end run around their rejection of Mayor Marc Morial's third-term charter change proposal. So, New Orleans has two competing strains in the city's contemporary politics. The distrust of mayors staying in office for more than two terms is so powerful in the city's contemporary political culture that no future effort to change the city's charter to allow a third mayoral term is likely to be successful. A huge part of the reason for this is the political disjointedness of the African-American political leadership in the city and the unwillingness of emerging African-American mayoral prospects positioning themselves for a mayoral candidacy to wait for their chance to run for office beyond a maximum of two terms.

New Orleans is not the only city in which a popular mayor has tried to select his successor. Recent mayoral election dynamics in Birmingham provide additional useful insight regarding this phenomenon. In 1995, Richard Arrington, Jr., was elected to a fifth term as mayor of Birmingham after having served as mayor for 16 years since 1979. For a substantial portion of his career, Arrington was political godfather to council member and, later, council president William Bell. In 1999, Arrington resigned from office two years short of completing his fifth term. He did this so that Bell could serve as mayor for the remainder of his term,[7] thereby gaining experience in the office and, hopefully, a competitive edge over the other candidates for the next mayoral election. The hope was that Bell would acquire greater

---

[7] Under Birmingham law, the city council president automatically becomes interim mayor when a vacancy occurs in the mayor's office with less than two years remaining in the mayoral term.

name recognition and incumbent-like status over the other candidates during his service as interim mayor. Similar to New Orleans in the 2002 mayoral general election, Bell finished second to little-known Republican city council member Bernard Kincaid in Birmingham's 1999 mayoral and city council elections. In the runoff election, Bell lost to Kincaid, handing Arrington a bitter repudiation of his leadership and stewardship of city politics in Birmingham for almost 20 years.

Arrington's political humiliation in the 1999 elections extended beyond Bell's loss to Kincaid. In addition to Bell's defeat, seven of the eight city council incumbents seeking re-election to the city council, all of whom were endorsed by Arrington's political organization, the Alabama Citizens Coalition, were defeated, and none received more than 40 percent of the vote. Although the Alabama Citizens Coalition was not given its name until much later, this was in effect the same coalition that helped Arrington to become Birmingham's first African-American mayor in 1979 and that dominated city council elections in African-American and, later, white city council districts for years. Interestingly, Birmingham voters, even long-time Arrington supporters, eventually grew tired of Arrington's historic fight to eliminate police brutality against African Americans by the Birmingham police.

The first signs of substantial resistance to Arrington's leadership appeared two years earlier, in 1997, when four incumbent city council members lost and Kincaid, a former University of Alabama Birmingham administrator, became the first non–Alabama Citizens Coalition candidate to win a race in a majority African-American district in at least 10 years. After Bell lost the mayoral election to Kincaid, he returned to his position as city council president—and led the council in opposing many of Kincaid's initiatives. Bell was defeated in the city council elections of 2001.

SUMMARY AND CONCLUSION

Black organizations in both Birmingham and New Orleans had enough political resources to successfully energize blacks to increase their participation in politics despite opposition from some white individuals, groups, and political leaders who possessed greater political resources. The principal resource that black organizations used to increase their voting strength was protest activity. Specifically, the protests of the civil rights movement in the South resulted in actions and policies by the national government that fully extended the franchise to southern blacks. After southern blacks obtained the full franchise in the mid-1960s, black organizations and political leaders used increased black voting as the principal resource to extract favorable actions and policies from city governments in Birmingham and New Orleans.

Overall, increased black political participation is positively associated with African Americans receiving an increased proportion of resources allocated by city governments in both Birmingham and New Orleans. Consistent with prior research, black political participation in the two cities is strongly associated with African Americans receiving increased municipal employment. Black political participation in the two cities is also strongly associated with increased executive appointments of African Americans. The benefits of increased municipal employment and executive appointments that accrued to African Americans were significant in both cities.

In contrast, the public resources that accrued to African Americans in minority business assistance were not as significant as those in municipal employment and executive appointments in both cities. Increased black political participation has exerted its weakest influence in both Birmingham and New Orleans in this category. That black political participation has not been able to increase significantly the number of city contracts awarded to African-American businesses in New Orleans and was slow in doing so in Birmingham indicates a limitation of black political participation in producing publicly generated, private-sector benefits for African Americans. William Keech (1968) first observed this limitation. The findings of this chapter confirm the continued saliency of Keech's observation in this regard, and they provide a mixed assessment regarding the ability of black political participation to substantially reduce police brutality against blacks in the two cities. In Birmingham, the results were uniformly strong in that direction. In New Orleans, however, black political participation has not substantially reduced police brutality against blacks.

The benefits that African Americans have received from increased participation in the political process in both cities have contributed significantly to improving their social and economic conditions. The gains in this regard have clearly been more substantial in the social than in the economic realm. To those who would criticize the impact of increased black political participation because it has not revolutionized the social and economic conditions of blacks, an appropriate response is that such an expectation was unrealistic in the first place. There is no precedent for expecting political participation to produce revolutionary outcomes for any group in American urban politics specifically or American politics in general. Given the inherent limitations of political participation as a medium for social and economic exchange, blacks in Birmingham and New Orleans have gained significant public resources from their incorporation in the political process.

Finally, in New Orleans, survey data suggest preliminarily that the economic gap between middle- and upper-income African Americans may be in the process of overpowering the racial divide in that city (Howell 2002). In light of this observation, in the 2002 mayoral runoff between Ray Nagin, a wealthy African-American businessman, and Richard Pennington, the very successful reform police chief of New Orleans and the handpicked choice of the very popular outgoing mayor Marc Morial, it is not surprising that Nagin easily defeated Pennington. The powerful implication of Nagin's victory is that not only are white voters returning to the business model as the premier desirable leadership attribute for the chief public executive of the city, but that African-American voters in New Orleans appear to be buying into that orientation for the first time. For African-American voters, the premier leadership attribute in their preferred choice of African-American mayoral candidates has historically been a strong civil rights background.

Another powerful implication of current developments in New Orleans that is clearly related to the rise of the business model in mayoral leadership preference and the growing importance of economic performance is that police brutality, long the premier issue among African-American voters in that city, is no longer the issue of primary saliency. Police Chief Pennington's defeat by Nagin in the 2002 mayoral election dramatically supports this conclusion. The decline in the saliency of police brutality as an issue of primary concern to African Americans is also occurring in Birmingham. Police brutality was the premier issue that helped to elect Richard Arrington, Jr., as mayor of Birmingham in 1979 and that provided the basis for his re-election four additional times. Arrington's handpicked candidate to replace him, Birmingham City Council President William Bell, lost to Bernard Kincaid, who promoted a platform of economic development, in the 1999 mayoral race.

These developments in Birmingham and New Orleans clearly suggest that African-American voters are becoming more concerned with economic development issues, and that they want a mayor who can promote a successful economic development agenda for the city. This new preference of African Americans for economic development in terms of local public policy suggests that Arrington and Morial, as more traditional civil rights–oriented leaders, were, in fact, successful in reforming their police departments and reducing the historic level of police abuse of African Americans in their cities, thereby eliminating police abuse as the issue of primary saliency to African-American voters. The key shortcoming of both Arrington and Morial in their leadership was their inability to realize they had successfully addressed their primary policy concern, police brutality, and that they should have switched their attention to establishing a successful economic development agenda. Doing so may not have allowed them to remain in office, but it may have allowed them to anoint their successor. This is clearly a failure of leadership on their part.

REFERENCES

Barker, Lucius J. 1987. Ronald Reagan, Jesse Jackson, and the 1984 Presidential Election: The Continuing American Dilemma of Race. In Michael B. Preston, Lenneal J. Henderson, and Paul Puryear, eds., *The New Black Politics: The Search for Political Power*, 2nd ed. White Plains, N.Y.: Longman, pp. 29–44.

Bobo, James R. 1975. *The New Orleans Economy: Pro Bono Publico?* New Orleans: College of Business Administration, University of New Orleans.

Bobo, Lawrence, and Franklin Gilliam, Jr. 1990. Race, Sociopolitical Participation, and Black Empowerment. *American Political Science Review* 84 (June 1990–1993): 377–393.

Browning, Rufus P., Dale Rogers Marshall, and David H. Tabb. 1984. *Protest Is Not Enough: The Struggle of Blacks and Hispanics for Equality in Urban Politics*. Berkeley: University of California Press.

Carmines, Edward G., and James A. Stimson. 1989. *Issue Evolution: Race and the Transformation of American Politics*. Princeton, N.J.: Princeton University Press.

City of Birmingham. 1992. *Birmingham Plan at a Glance*. Office of Economic Development.

City of Richmond v. J. S. Croson, 488 U.S. 469 (1989).

Edelman, Murray. 1964. *The Symbolic Uses of Politics*. Urbana: University of Illinois Press.

Edelman, Murray. 1971. *Politics as Symbolic Action*. Chicago: Markham.

Edelman, Murray. 1975. *Political Language*. New York: Academic Press.

Elder, Charles D., and Roger W. Cobb. 1983. *The Political Uses of Symbols*. White Plains, N.Y.: Longman.

Eisinger, Peter K. 1980. *Politics of Displacement: Racial and Ethnic Transition in Three American Cities*. New York: Academic Press.

Eisinger, Peter K. 1982. Black Employment in Municipal Jobs: The Impact of Black Political Power. *American Political Science Review* 76 (June): 380–392.

Franklin, Jimmy Lewis. 1989. *Back to Birmingham: Richard Arrington, Jr., and His Times.* Tuscaloosa: University of Alabama Press.

Howell, Susan. 2002. 2002 Mayoral Runoff Survey. UNO Survey Research Center. www.uno.edu poli.

Keech, William. 1968. *The Impact of Negro Voting: The Role of the Vote in the Quest for Equality.* Chicago: Rand McNally.

Martin v. Wilkes, 490 U.S. 84 (1989).

McClain, Paula D. 1993. The Changing Dynamics of Urban Politics: Black and Hispanic Municipal Employment—Is There Competition? *Journal of Politics* 55 (May): 399–414.

Metro Consultants Research Firm. 1992. Disparity in the City of New Orleans, Louisianna.

Mladenka, Kenneth R. 1989a. Blacks and Hispanics in Urban Politics. *American Political Science Review* 83 (March): 165–191.

Mladenka, Kenneth R. 1989b. The Distribution of an Urban Public Service: The Changing Role of Race and Politics. *Urban Affairs Quarterly* 24 (June): 556–583.

Office of Mayor Richard Arrington, Jr. 1992. 1991 Birmingham Plan Year-End Status Report. Birmingham, Ala., February 15.

Perry, Huey L. 1983. The Impact of Black Political Participation on Public Sector Employment and Representation on Municipal Boards and Commissions. *Review of Black Political Economy* 12 (Winter): 203–217.

Perry, Huey L. 1990a. Black Politics and Mayoral Leadership in Birmingham and New Orleans. *National Political Science Review* 2: 154–160.

Perry, Huey L. 1990b. The Evolution and Impact of Biracial Coalitions and Black Mayors in Birmingham and New Orleans. In Rufus P. Browning, Dale Rogers Marshall, and David H. Tabb, eds., *Racial Politics in American Cities.* White Plains, N.Y.: Longman, pp. 140–152.

Perry, Huey L. 1990c. The Re-election of Sidney Barthelemy as Mayor of New Orleans. In Huey L. Perry, ed., Recent Advances in Black Electoral Politics (Symposium). *PS: Political Science & Politics* XXIII: 156–157.

Perry, Huey L. 1992. The Political Reincorporation of Southern Blacks: The Case of Birmingham. *National Political Science Review* 3: 230–237.

Perry, Huey. 2002. Richard Arrington, Jr. and Police-Community Relations in Birmingham, Alabama, in James R. Bowers and Wilbar C. Rich, eds., *Governing Middle-Sized Cities: Studies in Mayoral Leadership.* pp. 103–118.

Perry, Huey L., and Judith C. Delmas. 1992. A Report on Police Abuse in New Orleans, Louisiana. Prepared for the New Orleans Human Relations Commission.

Perry, Huey L., and Alfred Stokes. 1987. Politics and Power in the Sunbelt: Mayor Morial of New Orleans. In Michael B. Preston, Lenneal J. Henderson, Jr., and Paul Puryear, eds., *The New Black Politics: The Search for Political Power,* 2nd ed. White Plains, N.Y.: Longman, pp. 222–255.

Perry, Huey L., and Alfred Stokes. 1993. Politics and Power in the Sunbelt: Mayor Morial of New Orleans. Reprinted in Harry A. Bailey, Jr., and Jay M. Shafritz, eds., *State and Local Government and Politics: Essential Reading.* Itasca, Ill.: F. E. Peacock, pp. 129–166.

Schexnider, Alvin J. 1982. Political Mobilization in the South: The Election of a Black Mayor in New Orleans. In Michael B. Preston, Lenneal J. Henderson, Jr. and Paul Puryear, eds., *The New Black Politics: The Search For Political Power.* White Plains, N.Y.: Longman, pp. 221–237.

Shingles, Richard D. 1981. Black Consciousness and Political Participation: The Missing Link. *American Political Science Review* 75: 76–90.

Stein, Lana. 1986. Representative Local Government: Minorities in the Municipal Workforce. *Journal of Politics* 48 (August): 694–713.

Stein, Lana, and Stephen E. Condrey. 1987. Integrating Municipal Workforces: A Comparative Study of Six Southern Cities. *Publius: The Journal of Federalism* 17 (Spring): 93–103.

Strong, Donald S. 1972. Alabama: Transition and Alienation. In William C. Harvard, ed., *The Changing Politics of the South.* Baton Rouge: Louisiana State University Press.

U.S. Department of Justice, Civil Rights Division, Criminal Section. 1991. *Police Brutality Study.* Washington DC.

Verba, Sidney, and Norman H. Nie. 1972. *Participation in America.* Chicago: University of Chicago Press.

Chapter 9

The Struggle for Black Empowerment in Baltimore

Marion Orr

EDITORS' NOTE

From the mid-1970s through the mid-1980s, when other big cities with large black populations were electing their first African-American mayors, Baltimore, despite its huge black population, was unable to elect a black chief executive. The powerful and popular Mayor William Donald Schaefer was able to retain the mayor's office for several years after Baltimore reached a black majority. In addition, whites maintained a majority of the city council seats until 1995—more than 15 years after blacks reached a numerical majority of the population.

In many ways, the struggle for black political empowerment in Baltimore confirms many of Browning, Marshall, and Tabb's findings. The election of Mayor Kurt L. Schmoke and increased black representation on the city council brought about significant changes in city government. In 1999, Martin O'Malley, a white city councilman, was elected mayor. During the first two years of his administration, O'Malley focused on lowering the city's violent crime rate and worked to maintain the support of the city's African-American residents. It remains to be seen what long-term impact O'Malley's election will have on black incorporation. This chapter also raises the issue of how effective electoral incorporation is in addressing public education, a critical challenge facing many major cities.

In 1935, long before the national civil rights movement, a little-known but excellent study commissioned by the Baltimore Urban League urged the city's black citizens to make more use of their right to vote. The report referred to the underutilized black vote as a "sleeping giant" (Reid 1935, 43) and stated:

> If ever the Negro population of Baltimore became aware of its political power, the changes in the governmental, economic and racial set-up of the community would under-go a profound change. . . . Despite the curtailment of the vote through registration laws, there is sufficient strength to bring about many reforms which hitherto have been sought through pleading. We refer, particularly, to such matters of librarians, policemen, firemen, et al. The power of organized political strength has never been effectively tested in Baltimore. (Reid 1935, 46)

Black politics in Baltimore has changed greatly since the Urban League released its report more than 60 years ago. African Americans have consistently used their political power to achieve access to city government. During the decades leading up to the 1970s and 1980s, the proportion of blacks on the Baltimore city council never reached parity with the percentage of blacks in the city. Today, African Americans hold a majority of the 19 seats on the council, including the seat of council president, who is elected citywide. The position of comptroller, a citywide post, is also held by a black woman. In 1987, Kurt Schmoke won the Democratic mayoral primary and became the first African American to be elected mayor of Baltimore. Schmoke held the post for 12 years, further showing that blacks had achieved a high level of incorporation and access to government. In 1999, Martin O'Malley, a white city councilman, became mayor of the majority-black city. Two years after his election, African Americans remain highly incorporated in city government, occupying many of the top executive positions.

This chapter examines the struggle of African Americans in Baltimore for political access and responsive policies at the local level. It provides an account of the political challenges that black Baltimoreans overcame to gain incorporation in Baltimore city government. It also shows how Browning, Marshall, and Tabb's theory of "political incorporation" applies to African-American politics in Baltimore.

The first section provides some important background information on Baltimore's economic, social, and political history. I examine the impact of Baltimore's tradition of machines and patronage on black political empowerment, assess the level of black incorporation on the Baltimore city council, and analyze the effort by blacks to gain control of the mayor's office. Next, I assess the impact of Kurt Schmoke's election on black incorporation, focusing specifically on minority municipal employment and education policy. This is followed by a discussion of the election of Martin O'Malley. I describe how a white candidate became mayor of a city in which blacks constitute a significant majority, and I speculate about the long-term impact of O'Malley's election on African-American incorporation. In a concluding section, I reflect on the lessons that can be drawn from the Baltimore experience.

BACKGROUND AND HISTORY

With its economy built on heavy industry, Baltimore has many features of an old frostbelt city (Browne 1980, 177–195). For most of its history, Baltimore had a diversified industrial base, with clothing factories, chemical plants, steel mills, and auto assembly plants dotting its boundaries. Such employment opportunities attracted people to the city. During the nineteenth century, European immigrants arrived from Ireland, Germany, and later Italy and Poland, along with smaller numbers from Russia and Lithuania, making Baltimore a city of ethnic neighborhoods (Fee, Shopes, and Zeidman 1991). Blacks and whites from rural Maryland and other southern states also came in search of jobs.

Baltimore's location makes it unique among other large industrial cities. Situated just below the Mason-Dixon line, Baltimore has many traditions that are characteristic of the Deep South. Historian Joseph Arnold described Baltimore as a city with a "southern culture and a northern economy" (1990, 25). The majority of whites in the city traced their roots to rural Maryland or other southern states, and they kept black residents firmly "in place" through a southern system of legal and social segregation. African Americans were never disenfranchised, but they were relegated to second-class citizenship. Racial segregation was enforced by custom and law in schools, public facilities, neighborhoods, churches, and employment (Reid 1935; Hollander Foundation 1960; Callcott 1988). Baltimore was the first city to enact an ordinance prohibiting blacks and whites from living in the same neighborhood (Power 1983). Supreme Court Justice Thurgood Marshall often described his native city as "up-South Baltimore" (Watson 1990, 81).

In the 1950s and 1960s, the city underwent a profound transformation. First, suburbanization of the white population triggered the numerical dominance of the city's black residents. By the mid-1970s, black residents became the majority; by 2000, as Table 9.1 shows, blacks made up 64 percent of the total population. The total population of Baltimore is composed primarily of whites and blacks. The "new immigrant" groups from Asia and Latin America are about 5 percent of the residents. Second, the civil rights movement and the rise to power of African-American elected officials changed the social and political life of the city; by the 1980s, in fact, it had shed most of its southern orientation. Third, the economic structure of the city changed profoundly: Baltimore is no longer a manufacturing center (Garland 1980). Since 1950, the number of manufacturing jobs has declined by nearly 70 percent. Growth in the economy has taken place primarily in the service sector, and much of this growth has been centered in the Inner Harbor redevelopment area

TABLE 9.1   Population of Baltimore, 1950–2000 (in thousands)

Year	Total	% Change	White	% of Total	Black	% of Total
1950	950		724	76	225	24
1960	939	−1	611	65	326	35
1970	906	−4	480	53	420	46
1980	787	−31	347	44	431	55
1990	736	−6	288	39	436	59
2000	651	−13	202	31	417	64

Source: U.S. Bureau of the Census.

and downtown. Some view the redevelopment of downtown as the most successful redevelopment project in urban America, yet Baltimore is "a city declining"
(Szanton 1986, 45). The suburbanization of middle-class whites (and increasingly of
middle-class blacks as well) has left behind many residents who are poor (Rusk
1996). The out-movement of retail and wholesale trade and manufacturing jobs has
contributed to high unemployment and a weakened tax base. Finally, the continued decline in the city's population has diluted the city's political standing in state
politics and government.

Machine Politics and the Black Community

Like many large eastern U.S. cities with sizable racial and ethnic communities,
Baltimore developed a machine tradition. In most big cities with strong machine traditions, black political leadership and the black vote were often tightly controlled
by machine leaders (Banfield and Wilson 1961; Gosnell 1968; Walton 1973, 56–69;
Pinderhughes 1987; Wright, 2000). For example, Banfield and Wilson observed that
blacks in Chicago were organized as a "submachine" (1961, 259). Black voters were
expected to support the machine's white candidates in return for specific induce-
ment or patronage—city jobs, zoning and housing code decisions, and police matters. In those wards or districts dominated by black voters, a black "boss" led the
submachine. Congressman William Dawson was Chicago's leading black machine-
style politician (Grimshaw 1993; Pinderhughes 1987; Walton 1973). In the end, however, machine politics in Chicago delayed black political empowerment.

Minority mobilization in Baltimore seems to have followed the pattern in
Chicago and other cities where partisan, ward-based machines were prevalent.
From the late nineteenth century until the 1960s, the formal machinery of government in Baltimore was controlled by a multitude of district-level Democratic party
organizations or "clubs" (Arnold 1976; Bain 1970; Wong 1990). Between 1930 and
the early 1960s, the Fourth District in west Baltimore, where the majority of the
black residents lived, was controlled by James "Jack" Pollack, the political boss and
leader of the Trenton Democratic Club (Wheeler 1955; Fleming 1964). Although
African Americans were a majority of the Fourth District's population, Pollack
refused to support black candidates for Fourth District seats on the city council or
in the state legislature (Fleming 1964).[1]

In 1954, three black candidates—foremost among them Harry Cole, who later
became a justice on Maryland's highest court—defeated Pollack-backed incumbents
for seats in the state legislature from the Fourth District (Callcott 1988, 151; Fleming
1964; McDougall 1993, 92). One year later, Pollack responded by running Walter
Dixon, a black, on his Fourth District city council slate. Dixon won election and

---

[1] Baltimore's six state legislative seats were coterminous to the six council seats. During this
    time, the Fourth District elected six members to the House of Delegates and one member
    to the state senate.

became the first black in 25 years to hold a seat on the city council.[2] In 1958, a biracial Pollack slate recaptured the three legislative seats he had lost four years earlier. Even with partially black tickets, however, Pollack was not able to control black voters who were moving into his district in the 1950s. Pollack was eventually overthrown by population change.

A smaller but significant number of black residents lived in east Baltimore. The black precincts there were the bailiwick of a black submachine boss, Clarence "Du" Burns (O'Keeffe 1986). Burns was one of only two African Americans working for the Bohemian Club, a party organization led by conservative white ethnics. Burns worked his way up the Bohemian Club "through precinct work" (Russo 1986, 1). Burns carried his precinct for the white bosses and became, in his own words, "one of the boys" (quoted in Russo 1986, 1). Burns acknowledged that he was being used by white bosses, but this did not bother him. He considered it a part of the game of politics. Burns later formed his own political club, the East Side Democratic Club, and in 1970 was elected to a seat on the city council.

Machine politics tend to create a considerable amount of distrust and jealousy between black voters and black politicians—and among the political leaders themselves (Nelson and Meranto 1977, 58). Within Baltimore's black leadership, the most important ideological division was between machine-style black politicians and those black leaders with roots in the civil rights movement. Members of the influential Mitchell family were leaders in Baltimore's civil rights community (Watson 1990; Callcott 1988; Hollander Foundation 1960). The Mitchells often challenged black machine-style politicians as pawns of white political operatives, criticizing them for forsaking the goals of equality and equal representation for personal and economic gain. Clarence "Du" Burns "received a great deal of criticism . . . because of his willingness to cut deals with white political operatives" (O'Keeffe 1986, 15). Black club leaders and their white patrons were in constant battle with civil rights leaders for political hegemony in the black community.

Baltimore City Council, 1955–2000

Baltimore's governmental structure is different from that of the 10 cities discussed in *Protest Is Not Enough* (Browning, Marshall, and Tabb 1984). Constitutionally, those 10 cities have council-manager forms of government. Under a council-manager system, all city policy is established by the city council and carried out by the city manager. The Baltimore city charter, however, allows for a strong mayor–weak

---

[2] In 1890, Republican Harry S. Cummings, an attorney, became the city council's first black member. Six different black Republicans served on the council between 1890 and 1931. The defeat of the last of two of them, Warner T. McGuinn and Walter S. Emerson, meant the exclusion of African Americans from the council until 1955. For more on Cummings and other black Republican city councilors, see Greene 1979 and Smith 1993, 145–146.

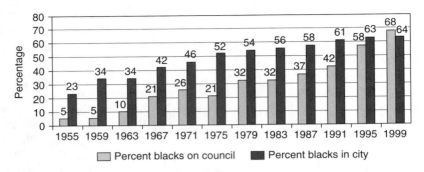

FIGURE 9.1 **Black representation on the Baltimore City Council, 1955–1999**

council form of government (Krefetz 1976). The city council is divided into six districts, each of which elects three councilors. The council is presided over by its president, who is elected at large. Although the council is relatively weak compared to the mayor, several successful politicians have used their tenure on the city council to win election to higher offices.

Weak incorporation best characterizes the position of blacks on Baltimore's city council during much of the post–World War II era. Figure 9.1 shows the relationship between Baltimore's black population and the number and percentage of black council members for selected years from 1955 through 1999. The data show that African-American representation on the city council did not approach its share of the population until the 1995 elections. For example, in 1955, blacks made up 23 percent of the population but held only one city council seat—just 5 percent of the council.[3] Four years later, the African-American population rose to 34 percent, but the number of blacks on the council remained at one. In 1987, when 60 percent of the city's population was black, 11 of the 18 council members were white, as was the council president. As late as 1991, African Americans made up 61 percent of the city's population but held only 42 percent of the city council seats.

What explains the history of black underrepresentation on the Baltimore city council? After the U.S. Supreme Court's decision in *Baker v. Carr*, the city charter was amended to require a redistricting following the results of each census. In 1971, and again in 1980, incumbents in four of Baltimore's six council districts gerrymandered the district lines to dilute the voting power of the city's growing black population (Bachrach and Baratz 1970). With blacks consolidated into a 90-percent black Fourth District, white majorities were preserved in the First, Third, and Sixth

---

[3] In 1946, the city charter was amended to allow for a fourth council member in any district with more than 75,000 registered voters. Because two of the six districts satisfied this criterion, the membership of the council stood at 20 from 1955 to 1963. A charter revision adopted in 1966 capped the total number of councilors at 19—three for each of the six districts and a council president.

Districts. Slim black majorities in the Second and Fifth Districts were overcome by highly organized white political clubs, which often handpicked a "token" black to integrate an otherwise all-white ticket.

Whites have been reluctant to form biracial coalitions at the district level. To win election to the city council, blacks have had to run in the three majority-black districts. As of 1980, only the Second, Fourth, and Fifth Districts fell into this category. Yet unlike white-majority districts, black-majority districts have shown a willingness to cross racial lines in elections. For instance, though blacks make up more than two-thirds of the Second District's population, they have regularly elected a white to one of its three city council positions. And in the Fifth District, where African Americans account for slightly more than half the population, a white candidate has won one of the three seats (Wickham 1987, 14–15). In the First, Third, and Sixth Districts, however, where the African-American populations range between 20 percent and 40 percent, white voters have rejected black candidates at the polls. A commentator for the *Baltimore Evening Sun* observed in 1991, "Black candidates for City Council lose by huge margins in white, working class precincts controlled by old-line political clubs fielding all-white tickets. No black city council member has been elected from a district with a white majority" (Fletcher 1991, BI).

The frustration of black leaders with their minority status on the city council came to the fore in 1991 during the decennial redistricting. A coalition of councilors, led by the seven blacks and supported by the white councilors from the majority-black Second and Fifth Districts and the white council president, pushed through a redistricting plan that established five majority-black districts. Several white council members objected to the plan, describing it as the "rape of our communities" (Thompson 1991, A1). At one dramatic moment, Sheila Dixon, a black councilor, took off her shoe and waved it in the faces of her white colleagues, saying, "You've been running things for the last 20 years. Now the shoe is on the other foot. See how you like it" (Olesker 1991, 131). In the ensuing municipal election, a black was elected for the first time to a Sixth District council seat. A black activist, Melvin Stukes, was elected without the endorsement of the district's Stonewall Democratic Club (Banisky 1991). Stukes's election was viewed by many as the beginning of the empowerment of the city's black majority on the city council.

Black incorporation on the council was strengthened after the 1995 municipal elections (Daemmrich 1995). Lawrence Bell became the second black to win election as council president. He was joined by 10 other blacks on the council, including the first black to win a Third District seat and the second black representative chosen in the Sixth District. Hence, the 1995 city council election produced a city council milestone: 105 years after the first black was elected to that legislative body, African Americans—for the first time—formed the council's majority. After the 1999 elections, the percentage of African Americans on the city council finally reached parity with the total percentage of black residents. Blacks controlled 14 (68 percent) of the 19 council positions. Sheila Dixon held the council presidency. Continued white out-migration helped African Americans to capture another of the Third District's council seats. At the dawn of the new century, black political incorporation on the city council was at it strongest.

Baltimore's Failure to Elect a Black Mayor

In Baltimore's strong-mayor form of government, gaining control of the mayor's office is the culminating step in the process of electoral incorporation. The mayor appoints all the department heads, has considerable budgetary authority, and controls the important Board of Estimates. The Baltimore City Public Schools (BCPS), for example, is a department of city government operated by a nine-member school board appointed by the mayor. Because city council members are, for the most part, concerned with providing constituent services, the mayor's domination over city affairs is unchallenged.

The groundwork for electing the city's first black mayor was laid in 1967, when Joseph C. Howard won a seat on the Supreme Bench (a city judicial post), becoming the first African American to win a citywide election (Welcome 1991, 193). Three years later, Milton Allen was elected to a prominent citywide post, Baltimore State's Attorney (or district attorney). Also in 1970, Parren Mitchell became the first black from Maryland elected to Congress. These early black citywide victories showed that African Americans could successfully compete in citywide elections.

In early 1971, after Mayor Thomas D'Alesandro, III, announced that he would not run for re-election, there was considerable speculation that Baltimore would follow Gary, Indiana, and Cleveland, Ohio, and elect its first black mayor. With no incumbent, the September 1971 Democratic primary was viewed by observers as a competition to determine which group—the black club leaders or the black civil rights establishment—would dominate as the city became majority African American.[4]

City Solicitor George Russell, a black, was the first to announce for mayor and was a leading candidate. Russell had broad support among white and black political leaders (Fleming 1972, 4), but he surrounded himself with many whom the civil rights establishment had opposed and was the choice of many of Baltimore's black club leaders, including Clarence "Du" Burns.

The desire of civil rights leaders to direct the political future of Baltimore was a major factor in the decision by State Senator Clarence Mitchell, III, to enter the mayor's race. His candidacy was viewed by many as an effort to siphon black votes away from Russell. Mitchell's candidacy also boosted that of the principal white aspirant, then–city council president William Donald Schaefer. Schaefer had citywide backing and developed tremendous popularity with city voters—both black and white (Fleming 1972). In the end, Schaefer won the primary with 57 percent of the vote.

Baltimore's failure to elect a black mayor in 1971 was the result of division in the black community. Many blacks who were active in the civil rights movement

---

[4] With Democrats outnumbering Republicans in Baltimore by a 9-1 ratio, a win in the Democratic primary is tantamount to victory. The last Republican member of the city council left office in 1942. A Republican has been elected mayor of Baltimore only twice in the last 50 years: Theodore Roosevelt McKeldin in 1943 and again in 1963.

and who helped to elect Judge Howard, Parren Mitchell, and Milton Allen did not work for Russell, did not raise money for him, and refused to endorse any black candidate. Perhaps the best indication of black division is reflected in the statement of Congressman Parren Mitchell, who despite his nephew's defeat, declared the election a victory. "This is a victory night for us," Mitchell said. "We have accomplished what we set out to accomplish" (Fleming 1972, 17).

The Schaefer Years: 1971–1987

Many observers agree that William Donald Schaefer became the most powerful mayor in Baltimore history (Levine 1987a; Arnold 1990; Smith 1999). He was not seriously challenged in his re-election bids, and in 1975, 1979, and 1983, he received 71 percent, 80 percent, and 73 percent, respectively, of the Democratic primary vote.

After Baltimore became majority-black in the mid-1970s, Schaefer was able to hold the mayor's office largely because he had developed a close association with black leaders (Arnold 1990, 30; Welcome 1991). When Schaefer became mayor, his black supporters were rewarded and given greater responsibilities in the city government (Wong 1990, 87). For example, he used his formal authority over the BCPS to maintain black support. The first majority-black school board was named during Schaefer's first term. Many of Schaefer's black supporters were appointed as school administrators as well, and many more received jobs throughout the school district (Wong 1990, 115; Crew et al. 1982). In 1965, 20 percent of the elementary and secondary assistant principals and principals were African American; by 1993, 70 percent were. The percentage of black teachers rose from 59 percent in 1972 to 71 percent by 1984. By 1995, African Americans held more than 70 percent of BCPS jobs, including lower-level positions such as janitors, secretaries, and teacher's aides (Orr 1998).

In general, downtown development became the hallmark of the Schaefer administration. The famous Inner Harbor redevelopment project, the World Trade Center, the National Aquarium, and luxury hotels all were constructed during his 15-year tenure (Levine 1987b). Under Schaefer's leadership, Baltimore rose to national prominence as a "renaissance" city. Black residents, however, were not included in Baltimore's transformation. In 1983, the U.S. Commission on Civil Rights held hearings in Baltimore and found that the city had not done enough to include African Americans in the city's downtown redevelopment projects (U.S. Commission on Civil Rights 1983, 1). Levine (1987b) presents census data showing that during the renaissance era, black neighborhoods continued to experience social and economic decay.

To finance downtown redevelopment projects and maintain a good bond rating, city agencies received reduced budgets. For example, local spending on the schools decreased (Vobejda and Ifill 1986). As a result, the BCPS operated with both a shortage of books and low staffing levels in libraries and counseling offices. Enrichment programs, such as art and music, were eliminated. The influential *Baltimore 2000* report (Szanton 1986), commissioned in 1986 to examine

Baltimore's future, was critical of Baltimore's schools: "The system is now widely condemned as ineffective, undisciplined and dangerous. The fact remains that, on leaving the school system, very few Baltimore students have been pressed to the limit of their intellectual potential, many are unprepared for any but menial employment and some are unready for jobs of any kind" (10). *Baltimore 2000* maintained that the city faced a bleak future, growing smaller, poorer, and more isolated by the year 2000, unless steps were taken to improve public education. Even in its diplomatic language, the fact that Schaefer did little to help improve the public schools is clear. Future mayors, the report argued, should play a more substantial role.

The black community, however, remained patient, waiting for Mayor Schaefer to retire or move on to higher office (O'Keeffe 1986). Their chance finally came in 1987 after Schaefer was elected governor.

The Election of Kurt Schmoke

In the 1987 mayoral election, one thing was certain: Baltimore would elect a black mayor. The Democratic primary was the first all-black mayoral primary in Baltimore history. The two candidates, however, represented radically different generations and backgrounds.

Clarence "Du" Burns, 68 years old, largely self-educated, and outgoing, had worked for 22 years as a janitor at a high school (a patronage appointment), formed his own political club, and was elected to the city council in 1971 (Arnold 1990, 31). In 1983, he ran citywide and became the first black to win election as president of the city council. As council president, Burns automatically became mayor when his friend, Schaefer, resigned to become governor in 1986.

Nearly 30 years younger than Burns, Kurt Schmoke grew up on Baltimore's west side as the son of college-educated parents. Schmoke was a high school and college sports star. A graduate of Yale University and Harvard Law School, he also was a Rhodes Scholar. In 1982, in his first bid for elected office, Schmoke was elected state's attorney (Noah 1990). Schmoke was able to unite the black community behind his candidacy, and he also received considerable support from liberal whites and many of the city's prominent civic leaders (O'Keeffe 1986, 63–90).

Among the several issues dominating the 1987 mayoral campaign, development and education were perhaps the most important. Schmoke expressed the view that Baltimore's economic goals had not balanced neighborhood improvement with downtown development. He concluded that Baltimore was prettier but poorer. Schmoke also emphasized his desire to improve the city's public schools (Orr 1996, 1999).

Burns was less critical of Baltimore's "renaissance." As Mayor Schaefer's floor leader, Burns had helped to guide many of the city's downtown projects through the city council. He argued that the Inner Harbor and other redevelopment projects were necessary to expand the city's tax base. Burns also indicated that he too was unhappy with the condition of the city's schools and would work to improve them.

During the campaign, a grass roots, church-based organization called Baltimoreans United in Leadership Development (BUILD) sought to shape the debate by launching a petition drive to show support for its antipoverty program, which included a school compact program, site-based school management, reduction in school class sizes, creation of more low-income housing, and improvement in municipal services (Orr 1992, 2000). BUILD collected more than 70,000 signatures of voters. BUILD is perhaps the most influential community-based organization in the city. As a non-profit organization, it could not endorse political candidates; instead, BUILD leaders asked each candidate to endorse its antipoverty agenda. Schmoke did so without reluctance. Burns initially rejected it as unrealistic, but he later changed his mind and confirmed his commitment and the city's commitment to the BUILD municipal agenda. Schmoke won the 1987 primary election with 51 percent of the total vote, and he was easily re-elected in 1991 and 1995.

During the Schmoke administrations, the number and percentage of African Americans as department heads and top city hall staffers increased, confirming earlier studies showing an increase in the number of black government executives after the election of an African-American mayor (Eisinger 1984; Rich 1989). When Mayor Schaefer left office in 1986, African Americans headed 40 percent of the 15 major departments. By 1994, Mayor Schmoke had increased the percentage of blacks heading major departments to 73 percent. These appointments included a number of departments that were never previously headed by a black. For example, Schmoke appointed the first black to head the Department of Planning, the agency charged with preparing and updating the city's physical redevelopment plan. In 1992, Schmoke named Herman Williams the city's first black fire chief.

The data for Baltimore during the Schmoke administration also confirm Browning, Marshall, and Tabb's findings that black municipal employment is a function of electoral incorporation and size of the black population (Browning, Marshall, and Tabb 1984, 171–204; Mladenka 1989; Perry 1990). As the black population of Baltimore increased and blacks gained controlled of city hall, black Baltimoreans gained a fairer share of municipal jobs. Table 9.2 shows that in 1986, the last year of the Schaefer administration, the black percentage of the municipal workforce leveled off at 45 percent; by 1999, the proportion of black employees rose to 55 percent. Although the percentage of blacks in the municipal workforce had increased across nearly all occupational levels, blacks remained heavily represented in the service maintenance and office/clerical categories (78 percent and 72 percent, respectively), jobs characterized by low skill levels and low wages.

Table 9.2 shows that blacks are well represented in the middle-level categories, which generally require more skills and training than the service maintenance and office/clerical positions. These categories include paraprofessionals, protective services workers, and technicians. In fact, the largest percentage of African Americans is not found at the low skill level; the largest proportion of blacks (79 percent) is paraprofessionals. The proportion of blacks in protective services rose from 30 percent in 1986 to 44 percent in 1999; these data confirm earlier research that showed black mayors have had a special interest in police and community relations (Saltzstein 1989).

The Schmoke administration attempted to address a number of vexing urban problems, including drug abuse, literacy, teenage pregnancy, and housing. These

TABLE 9.2   Black employment, Baltimore city government, 1986–1999

| | 1986 | | | | |
Category	White	Black	Other	Total	% Black
Administrative	266	81	4	351	23
Professional	1,586	785	81	2,452	32
Technical	1,447	795	17	2,259	35
Protective services	2,860	1,229	24	4,113	30
Paraprofessional	106	420	1	527	80
Office/clerical	969	1,214	18	2,201	55
Skill crafts	206	136	1	343	40
Service maintenance	1,109	2,368	13	3,491	68
Total	8,549	7,028	159	15,737	45
	1999				
Category	White	Black	Other	Total	% Black
Administrative	215	137	9	361	38
Professional	1,123	817	86	2,026	40
Technical	1,294	1,034	32	2,360	44
Protective services	2,198	1,805	69	4,072	44
Paraprofessional	90	353	4	447	79
Office/clerical	489	1,311	10	1,810	72
Skill crafts	265	245	10	520	47
Service maintenance	573	2,079	9	2,661	78
Total	6,247	7,781	229	14,257	55

Source: City of Baltimore, Office of Equal Opportunity, State and Local Government Information, EEO-4 Report, 1986 and 1999.

are tough policy matters, and Schmoke brought a "policy wonk" perspective to dealing with many of them. For example, he approved implementation of a controversial program making the Norplant contraceptive implant available to public school teenagers. Early in his first term, he received a barrage of criticism for advocating drug decriminalization. Schmoke argued that the illegal drug problem facing Baltimore and other major cities should be addressed as a public health problem, and Baltimore became one of the first major U.S. cities to institute a needle-exchange program for intravenous drug users. With help from the federal government, the city also replaced antiquated public housing high rises with new townhouse communities.

Improving public education, however, was Schmoke's chief policy concern. In his first inaugural speech, he vowed to make Baltimore "the city that reads" (Schmoke 1987). Schmoke used his formal authority over the city's budget to increase the city's financial support to the BCPS. In the first year that the Schmoke administration presented a budget, the share of local revenues dedicated to education increased 11 percent (Orr 1992, 183). Indeed, in a reversal from the Schaefer administration, the city's contribution to the BCPS budget increased each fiscal year during Schmoke's first eight years in office. With a limited tax base, however, per-pupil spending in Baltimore remained considerably less than the state average.

Because he appointed the nine-member school board, Schmoke successfully encouraged the board to appoint superintendents who embraced policies that he believed would improve the management of the school system and student achievement. Schmoke supported site-based management (SBM)—giving principals, teachers, and community members more authority to make management decisions concerning the operation of their individual schools. Richard Hunter, Schmoke's first handpicked superintendent, had pledged to move the BCPS toward SBM. Schmoke discovered after his appointment, however, that Hunter was not a strong supporter of SBM. Eventually, the school board, under orders from the mayor, voted not to renew Hunter's three-year contract.

As Schmoke began this second four-year term as mayor, the BCPS had reformed very little, and Baltimore's students continued to perform poorly. Between 1994 and 1997, all but two of the 52 schools the state designated as being eligible for state intervention were in Baltimore. Management of the BCPS was increasingly scrutinized. One report, released in 1992, found that many of the system's school-based and central-office administrators were incompetent, and that a "culture of complacency" existed in the school system that did not support "effective management" (Associated Black Charities 1992, 1–4 and 3–24). The school system's bureaucracy, as Schmoke concluded, "was finding a way to slow it [reform] down to choke it" (Orr 1999, 90).

Schmoke's decision in 1992 to hire a private firm, Education Alternatives, Inc. (EAI), to manage nine of the city's public schools was an attempt to maneuver around the system's bureaucracy. It was a bold, risky, and controversial move, making Baltimore one of the first major U.S. cities to turn over management of its schools to a private, for-profit corporation. The experiment ended in early 1996, however, after the teachers union, school activists, and religious leaders mobilized to kill it. Political opposition to EAI was strong, but the experiment's demise became apparent after an independent evaluator found that the EAI schools showed little difference from comparable city-run schools on test results, attendance, and parental involvement.

Meanwhile, Maryland joined a number of other states by adopting an intervention policy for schools with poor performance and lack of progress on statewide assessments. Baltimore officials and school leaders opposed the new school accountability and intervention program, fearing that BCPS schools would be singled out as underperforming. Parents, clergy, teachers union officials, and community activists maintained that Maryland was requiring school improvement without providing the city with adequate financial support.

In March 1995, a few months after being sworn in for his third four-year term, Schmoke reluctantly filed a lawsuit aimed at forcing the state to provide tens of millions of dollars more each year in funding for the BCPS. The lawsuit argued that the BCPS could not be expected to meet state educational standards while being given insufficient resources. The state, however, filed a countersuit, noting that

Baltimore received $400 million annually from the state for education, representing more than 65 percent of the BCPS budget and more than any of Maryland's other school districts.

After lengthy and heated negotiations, the lawsuits were eventually settled out of court. Mayor Schmoke and top state education officials agreed to a "partnership" that significantly increased the state's role in management of the BCPS in exchange for additional education aid to the city ($254 million over five years). The partnership legislation abolished the city school board and the superintendency, replacing them with a board appointed jointly by the governor and the mayor and with a chief executive officer (CEO) appointed by the new school board. The city also agreed to a series of management reforms.

At a news conference in November 1996, reportedly near tears, his voice cracking with emotion, and over the opposition of many African-American clergy and community activists who considered the partnership an "outrageous" state "takeover" that threatened the long tradition of African-American control of the BCPS, Schmoke announced that Baltimore had entered into this historic partnership with the state: "When I came into office, I said it was my goal to make this the city that reads. It became clearer and clearer to me that our community could not achieve that goal without a partnership with the state" (Thompson and Siegel 1996, A1).

In December 1998, Schmoke announced that he would not run for re-election. As he noted, "There are some who will be disappointed. Others will say, 'Hallelujah.' " Although polls showed him having a nearly 60 percent approval rating from city residents, Schmoke declared that "right now, my gut tells me it's the right time" to depart (Penn and Shields 1998, A1).

The 1999 Election of Martin O'Malley

After Schmoke's announcement, a number of city politicians expressed interest in succeeding him. School board member Carl Stokes was the first major candidate to announce. An African American, Stokes had also served eight years on the city council. Stokes eventually gained the endorsement of the editors of the *Baltimore Sun* and the Interdenominational Ministerial Alliance (IMA), an influential coalition of African-American ministers.

Lawrence Bell, leader of the anti-Schmoke faction on the city council, also announced. In 1987, at the age of 25, Bell stunned the political establishment when he won a seat on the council from the city's Fourth District. In 1995, he became the second African-American to be elected city council president. Bell and Stokes quickly became the front-runners in the pivotal Democratic mayoral primary.

Shortly after Stokes and Bell declared their candidacies, however, a number of powerful civic and political leaders began to publicly question if either man could effectively lead Baltimore. Howard "Pete" Rawlings was the most vocal skeptic. A Baltimore state legislator, Rawlings was chairman of the House of Delegates Appropriations Committee and considered the most politically powerful African American in the state. Rawlings declined to enter the mayor's race, saying that he could do more for the city by remaining in the legislature, but his mission, he announced, was to find a strong candidate to succeed Schmoke. Those already in the race, Rawlings declared, were "frightening to people" (Penn 1999, B3). According to Rawlings, neither Stokes nor Bell possessed the leadership or vision to move the city forward.

Rawlings and other city and state politicians believed that Kweisi Mfume, the president and CEO of the National Association for the Advancement of Colored People (NAACP) and a former congressman and Baltimore city council member, would make a strong mayor and give the guidance the city needed. A full-fledged campaign to draft Mfume was launched with a diverse set of players, including the pastors of the city's largest churches, business executives, and three former mayors—including William Donald Schaefer. The group took out newspaper advertisements, held a public rally, and circulated lawn signs urging Mfume to run. That Mfume never made a public commitment to run did not discourage the efforts of Rawlings and others to put him on the ballot.

The draft-Mfume coalition had to overcome several obstacles. First, Mfume was not a resident of the city; he lived in neighboring Baltimore County. Candidates were required to live in the city for a year before the September 1999 Democratic primary. To overcome that hurdle, Rawlings successfully pushed through the legislature a law changing the residency requirement from a year to six months. There also was concern that the $95,000 annual mayoral salary wasn't enough to entice Mfume, who earned $220,000 as NAACP president (not including substantial speaking fees and other outside income). In response, some members of the city council moved to raise the mayor's salary to $150,000. Several Baltimore business leaders floated the idea of allowing Mfume, if elected, to serve on corporate boards and receive honoraria to augment his income (Mishra and Fletcher 1999).

The draft-Mfume committee, however, could not overcome the most significant hurdle—convincing Mfume to leave a well-paying, high-profile position to take on the job of mayor of his hometown. In late May 1999, Mfume announced that he would not run. He decided, as he put it, to stay where he could "do the greatest good for the greatest number of people" (Fletcher and Pierre 1999, B1).

On June 22 (two weeks before the filing deadline), the race took an unexpected turn. Martin O'Malley, a 36-year-old white city councilman representing a majority-black district, entered the Democratic primary for mayor. At a street corner widely known for illegal drug sales, O'Malley stated that city leaders must address Baltimore's high murder rate, much of it linked to illegal drugs. He announced that he would make fighting crime his top priority and that, if elected, he would implement a zero tolerance crime-fighting strategy (O'Malley 1999). O'Malley added:

> When we make fighting crime and closing down open-air drug markets the top priority of Baltimore City government, then, and only then, will we be able to build a stable and growing City tax base. Then, and only then, will we dramatically improve schools. Then, and only then, will the new jobs created by increased private investment be things of City's present and future. We will create jobs and improve schools by first improving public safety. (O'Malley 1999)

O'Malley's emphasis on public safety resonated with Baltimore's voters. While the crime rate had declined in New York, Boston, and other major U.S. cities, the number of murders in Baltimore had soared, reaching more than 300 each year during the 1990s.

O'Malley's candidacy was aided by the fact that Stokes and Bell ran ineffective campaigns and received a barrage of unflattering media coverage. For example, the media reported that Bell had managed to spend more than $4,000 from his campaign donations for new clothes. While making a campaign appearance, his personal automobile was repossessed. In addition, two of Bell's campaign supporters were forced to acknowledge making thousands of copies of white supremacist literature endorsing O'Malley and distributing them in Baltimore's black neighborhoods. Stokes, while picking up critical endorsements, was also forced to address miscues, including driving with a suspended license, being served with a four-year federal tax lien during his council tenure, and falsely claiming a college degree on his campaign literature. Stokes's troubles cost him support among the city's white liberal community.

The campaign predictably took on racial overtones. A number of prominent black leaders labeled O'Malley as a political opportunist who was trying to capitalize on the expected split in the African-American vote. At one campaign appearance, Bell urged the black crowd to vote for "a man who looks like you do." Reverend Doug Miles, a black Stokes supporter, announced, "An O'Malley victory is the worst thing that could happen to the city, it would tear the city apart" (Texeira 1999).

O'Malley, by most accounts, ran a nearly flawless campaign, which he took across the city, including the city's black neighborhoods. O'Malley also won the endorsement of a number of black elected officials and civic leaders. State Senator Joan Carter Conway was the first African-American official to publicly support O'Malley. Pete Rawlings, who after failing to entice Mfume into the race tried unsuccessfully to encourage other blacks to become candidates, was poised to support Stokes. The revelation that Stokes had misrepresented his educational background on his resume, however, led Rawlings to endorse O'Malley. "We as a people should not seek the best black candidate or the best white candidate. We ought to seek the best candidate," Rawlings declared (Olesker 1999). Local observers noted that Rawlings's "stature brought increasing legitimacy" to O'Malley's candidacy (Penn 1999, B3). Rawlings reportedly helped O'Malley to win the support of the Reverend Frank M. Reid, pastor of the largest African-American congregation, who broke with the IMA and endorsed O'Malley. Reid's endorsement signaled to many African-American voters that it was "okay" to support the white candidate.

O'Malley outpolled a field of 17 candidates, winning 53 percent of the vote—including 30 percent of the black vote. Carl Stokes won 27 percent of the vote; Bell won 17 percent. In the November 1999 general election, O'Malley trounced the Republican mayoral candidate.

It is too early to assess definitively the impact of O'Malley's election on African-American political incorporation. Once in office, he formed a biracial administration, appointing two African Americans among three deputy mayors. In addition, 10

(67 percent) of the city's 15 major departments are headed by an African American. This is a slight drop from the 73 percent during the Schmoke administration. O'Malley elevated a high-ranking, veteran black police commander, Ronald Daniel, to police chief. Daniel, however, was asked to resign after two months, reportedly because he and O'Malley differed on crime-fighting strategies. O'Malley then hired Edward T. Norris, who had played a critical part in New York's efforts to lower that city's crime rate, as the new police chief.

From a policy perspective, reducing violent crime has been the focus of O'Malley's administration. "You can't have a healthy city for very long if you can't protect the lives of your people, including the children," he said in an interview (O'Malley 2001). Law enforcement officers have focused on the city's most violent neighborhoods, especially open-air drug corners. Overall, black and white residents appear to approve of his public safety focus. O'Malley pledged to bring down the annual number of murders to 175 by the end of 2002.

Public education has long been a policy area of special significance to African Americans. As of early 2002, O'Malley's involvement in schools has been limited. While Kurt Schmoke talked daily with the two superintendents who served during his tenure, O'Malley admits that his contact with the school system's new CEO is much more limited. "I talk daily to my police commissioner," O'Malley says (O'Malley 2001). Mayor O'Malley has left school affairs to the schools system's CEO and the new school board. O'Malley's limited involvement in school affairs is partly a result of his focus on public safety but more a consequence of the city-state partnership that reduced the mayor's influence in the BCPS.

CONCLUSION

What lessons do we draw from the Baltimore experience? First, the experience of blacks and machine politics in Baltimore confirms earlier research showing that the tradition of patronage and machines can delay black political empowerment. The Baltimore case shows that machines can hamper the development of strong, independent black political leadership and foster internal division within the African-American community. White machine bosses worked to prevent blacks from challenging the dominant power structure and even designated "token" blacks to keep progressive coalitions from challenging the dominant mobilization of bias. Machine-style politics was virtually absent in the 10 northern California cities originally examined by Browning, Marshall, and Tabb (1984). The Baltimore experience suggests a need to reformulate the incorporation model to account for existing arrangements and traditions that tend to divide minority communities.

An essential lesson to be drawn from the Baltimore case is that ideology varies from city to city. V. O. Key's (1949) seminal work on southern culture and politics found racial ideology to be a significant contextual variable that determined the political behavior and success of African Americans. Baltimore, a city with a southern culture, has been characterized by the absence of an organized liberal white leadership willing to forge a biracial electoral coalition. For much of the post–World War II era, a majority of the 18 seats on the city council were controlled by whites who represented districts that voted strongly for George Wallace in 1968 and Ronald Reagan in 1980 and 1984.[5] Conservative whites successfully resisted black political incorporation.

A central component of the theory of minority political incorporation is the necessity to form coalitions with racially liberal voters in cities where a nonwhite group actually comprises a minority of the electorate. Strong political incorporation in the 10 California cities studied by Browning, Marshall, and Tabb was associated with the presence in sufficient numbers of non-black liberals—mostly whites—who were willing to form coalitions with black minorities (1984, 18–45). Liberal whites were probably easier to find in Berkeley and San Francisco, or even in Oakland, than they were in Baltimore, where white leadership willing to form a biracial electoral alliance did not step forward. As a result, black incorporation was delayed until Baltimore's black population became a near-majority in the city.

In Baltimore, the election of a black mayor brought about important changes in city policy. The author of the 1935 Urban League report quoted in the opening of this chapter would be pleased. Sixty years later, blacks are well represented as firefighters, librarians, and other municipal workers. In fact, the head of the city's public library system is a black woman.

Although these findings are heartening, they should be viewed in the context of an aging city with an extremely needy population, shrinking revenues, and erosion of federal aid (Walton and Orr 1997). Throughout the Schmoke years, there were long-standing hiring freezes in most city agencies, allowing many jobs to be phased out as workers retired. O'Malley instituted a similar hiring freeze. Between 1986 and 1999, the number of municipal jobs fell from 15,737 to 14,257. This means that fewer African Americans benefited from black electoral incorporation (Fletcher 1992; Terry 1991).

The election of Martin O'Malley put Baltimore in the category of cities where white mayoral candidates have emerged to replace African-American mayors. Running against a field of weak candidates gave O'Malley a favorable position during the 1999 election. He also embraced an issue—public safety—that connected with citizens across the city. In many of its communities, Baltimore never became "the city that reads." For these residents, Baltimore could best be characterized as "the city that bleeds." O'Malley's strongest support in the African-American community came from voters in precincts most affected by crime. O'Malley built his victory in Baltimore's white neighborhoods (90 percent of white voters supported him). As we have seen, African-American voters in Baltimore have not been reluctant to vote for white candidates. The thousands of African Americans who crossed over and voted for him sealed O'Malley's victory.

---

[5] The leaders of the political clubs that controlled these districts were typically conservative. Some of them, like Dominic Mimi DiPietro, a councilman from the First District and founding member of the United Democratic Club, occasionally used racial epithets when referring to blacks.

It is too early to predict the impact of O'Malley's election on black incorporation. At this stage, however, it does not appear that blacks have lost significant ground in terms of appointments to high-level positions within city government. In November 2000, O'Malley signed a new "minority contracting" ordinance, allowing the Board of Estimates to annually set the percentage of city contracts awarded to minority businesses. The city had stopped enforcing a previous minority-contracting ordinance after a federal judge ruled the city had failed to collect data showing that racial disparities continued to exist. The new ordinance, O'Malley declared, "says to all, we are not retreating from the goals, we're advancing" (Shields 2000). He also issued an executive order to all city departments, setting a goal of 35 percent of city contracts to be awarded to minority-owned businesses. Two years into his administration, O'Malley has not given any sign that he plans to lead an effort to roll back black incorporation in city government.

The argument is often made that the benefits of minority electoral incorporation—access to city jobs, contracts, appointments to city boards—go disproportionately to minority middle-class communities (Barnes 1994; Jones 1978; Reed 1988; Stone 1989). During the Schaefer and Schmoke years, the learning opportunities for poor children were limited, while opportunities for the middle-class expanded.

The population and economic trends discussed in the opening of this chapter strongly affected public education in Baltimore. In 1955, the year after the U.S. Supreme Court's *Brown* decision, 60 percent of the students in the BCPS were white. By September 1960, 51 percent of the students were African American. The percentage of black students rose to 87 percent in 1999. By the late 1990s, nearly 70 percent of the BCPS students were eligible for free or reduced meals, an indication of their poverty status. In fact, in Maryland, Baltimore serves the largest concentration of students in poverty and with special needs. In part, the demographic shift in the BCPS reflected changes in the overall city population, but it also reflected the reluctance of financially secure families to send their children to the city's public schools, opting instead to send them to private schools or, as many did, move to the surrounding suburbs. The out-migration of whites opened employment and other opportunities for African Americans, but it also meant that matters of race and poverty were disproportionately felt in the city's school system.

Baltimore leaders also became increasingly reliant on the state to help support its schools. Growing suburban strength in state politics and the legislature, however, has meant that as the level of black political incorporation increased, the city became more answerable to state officials. This suggests that in education and other challenging policy areas, black political incorporation may have to include the development of coalitions with suburban whites, who increasingly dominate state politics and control the state's purse strings. These coalitions, however, are difficult to forge and sustain. Reflecting on the state partnership that forced Baltimore to relinquish considerable authority over its schools, former Mayor Schmoke summed up the matter succinctly:

What the partnership recognizes, and what I didn't realize until I got very involved in the issue, is that local government only controls about one-third of the budget in public school systems, and in public education, like so many other areas of life, the "golden rule" applies, that is, "he who has the gold rules." To me the partnership simply was a positive recognition that the education of our children is a shared responsibility of the city and the state. (Schmoke 2001)

Perhaps, when it comes to education policy in many big cities, political incorporation at the local level may not be enough. Baltimore's experience suggests that something more is needed.

REFERENCES

Arnold, Joseph. 1976. The Last of the Good Old Days: Politics in Baltimore, 1920–1950. *Maryland Historical Magazine* 7 (Spring): 443–448.

Arnold, Joseph. 1990. Baltimore: Southern Culture and a Northern Economy. In Richard M. Bernard, ed., *Snowbelt Cities: Metropolitan Politics in the Northeast and Midwest since World War II*, 25–39. Bloomington: Indiana University Press.

Associated Black Charities. 1992. *A Report of a Management Study of the Baltimore City Public Schools*. Baltimore: Author.

Bachrach, Peter, and Morton S. Baratz. 1970. *Power and Poverty. Theory and Practice*. New York: Oxford University Press.

Bain, Henry. 1970. Five Kinds of Politics: Politics in Five Maryland Communities. PhD dissertation, Harvard University.

Banfield, Edward, and James Q. Wilson. 1961. *City Politics*. New York: Vintage Press.

Banisky, Sandy. 1991. Increased Black Role Foreseen in Baltimore Politics. *Baltimore Sun*, March 24, B1.

Barnes, Claude W. 1994. Black Mecca Reconsidered: An Analysis of Atlanta's Post-Civil Rights Political Economy. In Marilyn Lashley and Melanie N. Jackson, eds., *African Americans and the New Policy Consensus: Retreat of the Liberal State?*, 179–199. Westport, Conn.: Greenwood Press.

Browne, Gary L. 1980. *Baltimore in the Nation, 1789–1861*. Chapel Hill: University of North Carolina Press.

Browning, Rufus P., Dale Rogers Marshall, and David H. Tabb. 1984. *Protest Is Not Enough*. Berkeley: University of California Press.

Callcott, George H. 1988. *Maryland and America, 1940–1980*. Baltimore: Johns Hopkins University Press.

City of Baltimore. 1993. *City Charter*.

Crew, John et al. 1982. *Effective Public Education: The Baltimore Story*. New York: New Dimensions.

Daemmrich, Joanna. 1995. Council Likely to Reach Race and Gender Balance. *Baltimore Sun*, February 26, C1.

Eisinger, Peter. 1984. Black Mayors and the Politics of Racial Advancement. In H. Hahn and C. Levine, eds., *Readings in Urban Politics*. White Plains, NY: Longman, pp. 25–37.

Fee, Elizabeth, Linda Shopes, and Linda Zeidman, eds. 1991. *The Baltimore Book*. Philadelphia: Temple University Press.

Fleming, G. James. 1964. *An All-Negro Ticket in Baltimore*. New York: McGraw-Hill.

Fleming, G. James. 1972. *Baltimore's Failure to Elect a Black Mayor in 1971*. Washington, DC: Joint Center for Political Studies.

Fletcher, Michael. 1991. Blacks May Need More than Numbers to Gain: Political Clubs' Voting Patterns Affect Black Groups. *Baltimore Evening Sun*, March 3, B1.

Fletcher, Michael. 1992. Job Cuts by City Especially Pain Its Black Workers. *Baltimore Sun*, January 26, B1.

Fletcher, Michael, and Robert Pierre. 1999. Mfume Nixes Draft for Baltimore Mayor. *Washington Post*, May 25, B1.

Garland, Robert. 1980. Baltimore Is No Longer a Blue-Collar Town. *Baltimore Magazine*, March, 5–21.

Gosnell, Harold. 1968. *Machine Politics: Chicago Model*, 2nd ed. Chicago: University of Chicago Press.

Greene, Suzanne E. 1979. Black Republicans on the Baltimore City Council, 1890–1931. *Maryland Historical Magazine* 74 (September): 203–222.

Grimshaw, William. 1993. *Bitter Fruit: Black Politics in Chicago*. Chicago: University of Chicago Press.

Hollander Foundation. 1960. *Toward Equality: Baltimore's Progress Report*. Baltimore: Sidney Hollander Foundation.

Jones, Mack H. 1978. Black Political Empowerment in Atlanta: Myth and Reality. *Annals of the American Academy of Political and Social Science* 439 (September): 90–117.

Key, V. O. 1949. *Southern Politics in State and Nation*. New York: Knopf.

Krefetz, Sharon. 1976. *Welfare: Policy Making and City Politics*. New York: Praeger.

Levine, Marc. 1987a. Response to Berkowitz Economic Development in Baltimore: Some Additional Perspectives. *Journal of Urban Affairs* 9 (Spring): 133–138.

Levine Marc. 1987b. Downtown Redevelopment as an Urban Growth Strategy: A Critical Appraisal of the Baltimore Renaissance. *Journal of Urban Affairs* 9 (Fall): 103–123.

McDougall, Harold. 1993. *Black Baltimore: A Theory of Community*. Philadelphia: Temple University Press.

Mishra, Raja, and Michael Fletcher. 1999. Baltimore's Movers and Shakers Push Mfume for Top Job. *Washington Post*, May 1, B1.

Mladenka, Kenneth. 1989. Blacks and Hispanics in Urban Politics. *American Political Science Review* 83 (March): 165–191.

Nelson, William, and Philip Meranto. 1977. *Electing Black Mayors*. Columbus: Ohio State University Press.

Noah, Timothy. 1990. The Testing of Kurt Schmoke. *Washington Post Magazine*, May 27, 13–17, 27–31.

O'Keeffe, Kevin. 1986. *Baltimore Politics in 1971–1986: The Schaefer Years and the Struggle for Succession*. Washington, DC: Georgetown University Press.

Olesker, Michael. 1991. Recalling the Night that Sheila Dixon Let the Shoe Drop. *Baltimore Sun*, March 21, B1.

Olesker, Michael. 1999. Baltimore Deserves Better than Antics of Bell's Bullies. *Baltimore Sun*, August 8, B1.

O'Malley, Martin. 1999. Martin O'Malley announcement speech, Baltimore, City Hall, June 22.

O'Malley, Martin. 2001. Interview with author, Baltimore, July 1.

Orr, Marion. 1992. Urban Regimes and Human Capital Policies: A Study of Baltimore. *Journal of Urban Affairs* 14 (Summer): 173–187.

Orr, Marion. 1996. Urban Politics and School Reform: The Case of Baltimore. *Urban Affairs Review* 31 (January): 314–345.

Orr, Marion. 1998. The Challenge of School Reform in Baltimore: Race, Jobs, and Politics. In Clarence N. Stone, ed., *Changing Urban Education*. Lawrence: University Press of Kansas, pp. 93–117.

Orr, Marion. 1999. *Black Social Capital: The Politics of School Reform in Baltimore, 1986–1998*. Lawrence: University Press of Kansas.

Orr, Marion. 2000. Baltimoreans United in Leadership Development: Exploring the Role of Governing Nonprofits. In Richard Hula and Cynthia Jackson–Elmoore, eds., *Nonprofits in Urban America*. Westport, Conn.: Quorum Books, pp. 151–167.

Penn, Ivan. 1999. Rawlings Declines to Run for Mayor. *Baltimore Sun*, January 14, B3.

Penn, Ivan, and Gerald Shields. 1998. Schmoke Calls This "the Right Time," Mayor Says Officially He Won't Seek 4th Term. *Baltimore Sun*, December 4, A1.

Perry, Huey L. 1990. The Evolution and Impact of Biracial Coalitions and Black Mayors in Birmingham and New Orleans. In Rufus P. Browning, Dale Rogers Marshall, and David H. Tabb, eds., *Racial Politics in American Cities*, 140–152. White Plains, N.Y.: Longman.

Pinderhughes, Diane. 1987. *Race and Ethnicity in Chicago Politics*. Urbana: University of Illinois Press.

Power, Garrett. 1983. Apartheid Baltimore Style: The Residential Segregation Ordinances of 1910–1913. *Maryland Law Review* 42 (Fall): 289–328.

Reed, Adolph. 1988. The Black Urban Regime: Structural Origins and Constraints. In Michael Peter Smith, ed., *Power, Community and the City. Comparative Urban and Community Research*, Vol. 1. New Brunswick, N.J.: Transaction Books, pp. 138–189.

Reid, Ira. 1935. *The Negro Community of Baltimore*. Report of a study conducted for the Baltimore Urban League.

Rich, Wilbur. 1989. *Coleman Young and Detroit Politics*. Detroit: Wayne State University Press.

Rusk, David. 1996. *Baltimore Unbound: A Strategy for Regional Renewal*. Baltimore: Abell Foundation.

Russo, Bud. 1986. The Rise of Clarence "Du" Burns: From Collecting Cardboard to City Council President. *The Baltimore Chronicle*, March 5, A1.

Saltzstein, Grace. 1989. Black Mayors and Police Policies. *Journal of Politics* 51 (3): 525–544.

Schmoke, Kurt L. 1987. Inaugural Address of Mayor Kurt L. Schmoke. Baltimore: Office of the Mayor.

Schmoke, Kurt. 2001. Correspondence to author. July 25.

Shields, Gerald. 2000. Mayor Signs Minority Contracting Ordinance. *Baltimore Sun*, November 29, B1.

Smith, C. Fraser. 1999. *William Donald Schaefer: A Political Biography*. Baltimore: The Johns Hopkins University Press.

Smith, J. Clay. 1993. *Emancipation: The Making of the Black Lawyer, 1844–1944*. Philadelphia: University of Pennsylvania Press.

Stone, Clarence. 1989. *Regime Politics: Governing Atlanta, 1946–1988*. Lawrence: University Press of Kansas.

Szanton, Peter. 1986. *Baltimore 2000: A Choice of Futures*. Baltimore: Morris Goldseker Foundation.

Terry, Don. 1991. Cuts in Public Jobs May Hurt Blacks Most. *New York Times*, December 10, A1.

Texeira, Erin. Color Fades from Race for Mayor. *Baltimore Sun*, September 3, A1.

Thompson, Ginger. 1991. City Council OKs Plan for 5 Majority Black Districts. *Baltimore Sun*, March 24, A1.

Thompson, Jean, and Eric Siegel. 1996. City, State Sign Deal for Schools. *Baltimore Sun*, November 7, A1.

U.S. Bureau of the Census. 1950, 1960, 1970, 1980, 1990, and 2000.

U.S. Commission on Civil Rights. 1983. *Greater Baltimore Commitment: A Study of Urban Minority Economic Development*. Washington, DC: U.S. Government Printing Office.

Vobejda, B., and Gwen Ifill. 1986. Education Issue May Spell Trouble for Schaefer. *Washington Post,* July 28, C1.

Walton, Jr., Hanes. 1973. *Black Politics.* Philadelphia: Lippincott Press.

Walton, Jr., Hanes, and Marion Orr. 1997. African American Mayors and National Urban Policy: The Fiscal Politics of Urban Federalism. In Hanes Walton, Jr., *African American Power and Politics.* New York: Columbia University Press, pp. 341–351.

Watson, Denton L. 1990. *Lion in the Lobby: Clarence Mitchell, Jr.'s Struggle for the Passage of Civil Rights Laws.* New York: William Morrow.

Welcome, Verda, with James Abraham. 1991. *My Life and Times.* Englewood Cliffs, NJ: Henry House.

Wheeler, Harvey. 1955. Yesterday's Robin Hood: The Rise and Fall of Baltimore's Trenton Democratic Club. *American Quarterly* 7 No. 4 (Winter): 332–344.

Wickman, Dwayne. 1987. *Destiny 2000: The State of Black Baltimore.* A report from the Baltimore Urban League.

Wong, Kenneth. 1990. *City Choices.* Albany: State University of New York Press.

Wright, Sharon D. 2000. *Race, Power, and Political Emergence in Memphis.* New York: Garland Publishing.

Part V

Latinos

Chapter 10

Power Without a Program: Hispanic Incorporation in Miami

Christopher L. Warren and Dario V. Moreno

EDITORS' NOTE

Miami is a medium-size city constituting the geographic, political, and economic center of Miami–Dade County. Although it remains the hub of urban life in south Florida, it is only one segment of a more complex metropolitan form of government (Metropolitan Miami–Dade County) that encompasses more than 30 municipalities as well as a sprawling unincorporated area. Because of the enormous influx of refugees over the last 42 years from Cuba, Haiti, and other Latin American and Caribbean countries, Miami has undergone the single most dramatic ethnic transformation of any major city in the past 100 years. As of the 2000 Census, the city of Miami also ranked as the poorest large city in the United States, as measured by the percentage of its population living below the poverty line. Although the complex intersection of a unique governmental structure with multi-ethnic political and economic adjustments makes its politics unique, metropolitan Miami may also stand as a portent for other cities with rapidly changing international populations.

Warren and Moreno show that in Miami, Hispanics—especially Cuban Americans—unlike blacks and unlike Latinos in many other cities, have achieved rapid economic and political incorporation. They have been successful in Miami's internationalized economy and in various attempts to overturn at-large elections in favor of district representation at both the county and municipal levels—resulting in dramatic increases in the number of Hispanic elected officials. These achievements, combined with other factors, have made Hispanics the core electoral constituency as well as an integral part of local political-economic elite leadership.

Although Hispanic political incorporation arises in significant ways from growing numerical superiority, economic success, and the structural reform of local government, the dominant coalition that institutionalizes their incorporation is neither likely to include blacks nor be especially liberal. In such a context, the emergence of new minority groups as major players in local politics does not necessarily result in shifts in substantive policy or the redistribution of locally controlled resources in ways that enhance the political position or policy interests of blacks and low-income Hispanics.

Miami has always been a place that forces people to reclaim their past and identity—or even to discover them for the first time. As it was for playwright William Inge, when he observed, "It wasn't until I got to New York that I became Kansan" (Clapp 1984, 123), so it is for most of Miami's population. In this city of emigrés, migrants, and immigrants, attributes such as national and state origin, race, and ethnicity usually eclipse other possible bases of identity. For that reason, political participation usually cuts along these same lines. Coalitions between different ethnic, racial, and national groups—when they exist at all—are usually strategic and issue- or candidate-specific and, thus, not broadly conducive to the general shaping or redirection of local public policy over time. Out of this diverse mix of peoples, however, Hispanics,[1] and especially Cuban Americans, have emerged as a catalytic and increasingly dominant group. This chapter probes the manifestations of that political ascendancy and its implications for other groups and political agendas in metropolitan Miami.

The dramatic demographic changes accompanying the internationalization of Miami's population have combined with historical, structural, and systemic factors to produce several dramatic statistics. Based on the 2000 U.S. Census, the City of Miami now ranks as the poorest major city (250,000 or more residents) in the country, with 32 percent of its population living below the poverty line. Forty percent of all households have an income of $15,000 or less. Sixty-one percent of the population are foreign born, surpassing every other major city in the country, and fully two-thirds of the population speak Spanish at home, placing Miami third in the nation in this category. Examined countywide, throughout the Miami-Dade[2] metropolitan area, the figures are only slightly less dramatic, even though proportionally fewer immigrants reside in metropolitan Miami-Dade and the area also encom-

---

[1] Although for many the term *Latino* is preferred when referring to Spanish-speaking people from the Americas, in Miami the term is rarely encountered and infrequently used by Cuban Americans in self-identification. Therefore, the terms *Hispanic* or *Latin,* which are more common in local usage, are used throughout this chapter.

[2] Even the term *Miami* can be a source of confusion. In common usage, it often refers to the entire metropolitan area, which encompasses all of Miami-Dade County and its 30 municipalities. It also refers to the City of Miami, which is the core municipality in the Miami Metropolitan Statistical Area (MSA). In this chapter, the term *Miami* refers to the Miami-Dade County metropolitan area. The City of Miami will be referred to as such. Also note that the name of Dade County was changed to Miami-Dade County in 1997.

passes a number of very affluent suburban towns and neighborhoods (U.S. Census Bureau 2000; Elliott and Grotto 2001; Grotto and Yardley 2001; Viglucci 2001).

In the 1980s and 1990s, Cuban Americans, the area's largest immigrant group, increasingly became the key players at all levels of Miami electoral politics and in many of its most important economic and civic affairs. Four decades of extensive Hispanic population growth, structural reforms in local government resulting in the election of more Hispanic officials, an impressive level of economic incorporation, establishment of durable cultural institutions, and unifying political experiences and issues combined to facilitate the growing importance and clout of Miami's Cuban population in municipal, county, state, and even national affairs. This rapid and multifaceted incorporation even gave rise to new metaphors to describe the phenomenon. Portes and Stepick (1993, 8) view Miami as an area that has experienced "acculturation in reverse"—a process by which foreign customs, institutions, and language are diffused within the native population to the extent that opponents of biculturalism are compelled to "either withdraw into their own diminished circles or exit the community." Consistent with this observation, many non-Hispanic whites have either migrated out of Miami-Dade County or have sought to incorporate new, suburban municipalities within it to retain more political control over their own neighborhoods. For many African Americans, who also witnessed the internationalization of the black population due to Caribbean immigration, such changes have also meant that long-deferred political goals and agendas are now further complicated and frequently superseded by the needs, size, and political assertiveness of a newly arrived, multinational immigrant population.

In the face of such transformations, the question for Miami still lingers: In terms of substantive local policy, what difference has Hispanic incorporation made? Hispanic political and economic incorporation has certainly injected a number of volatile issues into local political campaigns and made for a more representative, albeit complex, policy-making environment. Frequently, however, these new agenda items have been mostly symbolic in terms of the intents and purposes of local policy, are often rooted in the respective homelands of the different immigrant groups, and typically have little to do with matters most directly affecting the day-to-day lives of residents. The degree of controversy and local political activity that surrounded the Elián González case from November 1999 through June 2000, and the extent to which the issue dominated and continues to affect Miami politics, stands as only one of the most recent and dramatic of examples of this tendency.

In that regard, Hispanic political incorporation has been extremely important as a symbol of growing success and clout and a boon to the emergence of a Latin business class, but as yet, it has not had significant implications for long-standing patterns in the distribution or redistribution of resources controlled by local government. In Miami, minority incorporation, including significantly greater representation for blacks on policy-making bodies, has thus far resulted in a high level of continuity with historic patterns and practices evident in local policy-making. In effect, the ethnic makeup of the political and business leadership of the community has changed dramatically, but the broader socioeconomic and political tone of local public policy has not. Thus, the proposition that minority empowerment might lead to a redirection in the flow of resources through local public policy programs, or that issues rooted in the conditions of poorer or working-class neighborhoods might achieve greater attention, has not yet received any significant validation in the Miami experience.

Of great utility in studying cities like Miami has been the recent emergence of several theoretical frameworks. These frameworks have encouraged research to characterize local politics broadly, in ways that transcend both the descriptive case study and an exclusive focus on only one or a few important variables. Individuals such as Browning, Marshall, and Tabb (1984, 1994, 1997) as well as Mollenkopf (1992) and Stone (1989), whether they speak in terms of *political incorporation, dominant coalitions,* or *regimes,* have sought to focus on variables that, while broadly heuristic, nonetheless provide common reference points in the study and comparison of divergent urban areas.

The framework used by Browning, Marshall, and Tabb is particularly apt in the analysis of this most group conscious of cities, given its specific focus on minority group mobilization, dominant coalition formation, political incorporation, and resultant policy responsiveness to minority interests. Insights derived from the study of Miami might then be harbingers for other large metropolitan areas affected by the "internationalization" of their populations, economies, and politics through the incorporation of new immigrant populations.

While claims of uniqueness can be made with regard to any city's politics, aspects of Miami's political environment place minority mobilization and incorporation, as well as the resultant questions of coalition building and local government responsiveness to minority policy agendas, in a context quite different from those of most other cities analyzed in this book. Four features of the Miami setting are especially noteworthy for how they combine to shape the area's minority politics:

1. Miami's distinctive political geography, particularly the ethnic diversity of its population, its neighborhood settlement patterns, and the structure of its two-tiered metropolitan form of government.
2. Heightened group consciousness and conflict resulting from the respective roles played by each of the area's three major ethnic groups (Hispanics, non-Hispanic whites, and blacks) in determining election outcomes and influencing local government policy making.
3. Growing system complexity, as evidenced by the continued intrusion of international affairs into local politics and the need to manage conflict over both symbolic and substantive policy issues as diverse as the ongoing influx of refugees, neighborhood redevelopment, police violence, non-Hispanic white flight, and local anti-Communism.
4. Ongoing efforts to reform local government structure, including a shift from at-large to district representation in elections for city and county commissions, increased advocacy of strong-mayor models of government, and attempts to incorporate new municipalities within Miami-Dade County.

This chapter analyzes Miami politics in light of these features, with the objective of explaining (1) the basic contours of Hispanic (especially Cuban) and black (especially African American) political mobilization and incorporation, (2) the area's well-publicized political and social upheaval (e.g., massive influxes of political and economic refugees, race riots, and clashes over largely symbolic issues rooted in the experiences and sensitivities of each group), and (3) possible scenarios for the future of minority politics.

THE POLITICAL GEOGRAPHY OF METROPOLITAN MIAMI

Three aspects of metropolitan Miami's political geography are of particular relevance to minority politics. First, considerable intragroup diversity along lines of national origin makes analyses of minority group politics problematic. Second, the area's unique metropolitan form of government creates a complex system of overlapping governments with varying authorities that are difficult to analyze. The Miami-Dade Metropolitan Government system (Metro) combines mechanisms of a strong county government with those of the area's 30 municipalities and a very large unincorporated area. These municipalities range in size from the City of Miami, with a population of 362,470, to Islandia, with a population of six. Third, this political structure is superimposed on paradoxical neighborhood settlement patterns that variously concentrate and disperse minority populations, dramatically affecting the relative influence of blacks, Hispanics, and non-Hispanic whites in the different municipal and county jurisdictions.

Ethnic Diversity and Neighborhood Settlement Patterns

During the past 40 years in Miami, the combined forces of immigration and non-Hispanic white flight have brought about the most dramatic ethnic transformation of any major American metropolitan area in the twentieth century (Metro-Dade Planning Department 1986). With the internationalization of Miami's population, the once overwhelmingly dominant non-Hispanic white population has not only seen its numbers shrink, both in relative and real terms, but also lost external recognition of their own varied ethnic and regional backgrounds. The tendency is for native or transplanted southerners, northerners, Jews, Irish, and even expatriate white Canadians and Europeans to be grouped together as "Anglos." The 2000 census placed the number of non-Hispanic whites in Miami-Dade at 466,000, or just slightly more than 20 percent of the total. This is approximately the same size as the county's black population. In 1960, non-Hispanic whites constituted 80 percent of the county's total population, at 744,000 (Table 10.1).

As Table 10.1 shows, the rapid demographic change in Miami-Dade County is a post-1960 phenomenon, largely precipitated by the Cuban Revolution and the resultant influx of refugees and exiles. The emergence of a Cuban cultural and economic enclave, combined with the rapid penetration of international capital into the local economy, had a multiplier effect on the influx of additional refugees and immigrants from throughout the hemisphere (Portes and Stepick, 1993). Today, the

TABLE 10.1   Population for Miami-Dade County, 1960–2000

Year	Non-Hispanic White	%	Non-Hispanic Black	%	Hispanic	%	Non-Hispanic Other	%	Total	%
1960	744,000	79.6	139,000	14.9	50,000	5.3	2,000	0.2	935,000	100.0
1970	776,000	61.2	189,000	14.9	298,000	23.5	5,000	0.4	1,268,000	100.0
1980	763,000	46.9	276,000	17.0	574,000	35.3	13,000	0.8	1,626,000	100.0
1990	586,000	30.3	370,000	19.1	953,000	49.2	28,000	1.4	1,937,000	100.0
2000	466,000	20.6	427,000	19.0	1,291,000	57.3	69,000	3.1	2,253,000	100.0

Sources: 1960–1980: total populations according to the census are combined with estimates of group populations in Boswell (1994a). 1990: Census SFT 1, Table P10. 2000: Census SF 1, Table P8. Totals rounded to nearest thousand.

county's Hispanic population exceeds 1.25 million people (about 57 percent of the total), making Miami-Dade the first county in the nation with a population greater than 1 million to have a Hispanic majority. Cubans, the Hispanic group almost singularly associated with Miami in the popular consciousness, now constitute barely 50 percent of Miami's Latin population—a decline of more than 40 percentage points since 1970, when they constituted about 90 percent of the total (Castro 2001; Boswell 1994a, 1994b). By remaining the largest and most established Hispanic national group by far, however, Cubans continue to assert largely uncontested political and economic leadership within the Hispanic community.

Adding to the area's diversity, Miami's black population has had a significant Caribbean component, even going back to before the city's incorporation in 1896, when Bahamian laborers were brought to the area. Since then, Haitian and other Caribbean immigrants and refugees have added tremendously to the black population's diversity, as has the arrival of more black Hispanics from Cuba and elsewhere (Dunn 1997; Dunn and Stepick 1992; Stepick 1992). However, despite significant increases in the black population the increase as a proportion of the total, has been slow and gradual, from 15 percent in 1950 to 19 percent in more recent years.

Even given the difficulty inherent in defining broad categories of minority groups in Miami, political analysis within the general context of the tri-ethnic framework remains useful. The hundreds of thousands of non-Cuban immigrants and refugees from throughout the hemisphere represent a rapidly expanding portion of the overall population and contribute significantly to intragroup diversity, but these other national groups mostly remain politically, economically, and socially insulated and isolated. Questions of immigration status, citizenship, group size, and economic subsistence loom large for many of them, making questions of political mobilization, incorporation, and shaping local public policy distant considerations. An important exception—and a likely forerunner of things to come—is that Haitian Americans have established an important political base in the city of North Miami (the county's fourth most populous municipality), where they now hold the mayor's office and a majority of city council seats. The increasingly assertive Haitian Americans and native African Americans often divide over scarce political and economic resources, local agendas, and issues of self-definition. It remains to be seen whether other black and Hispanic national groups that reach "critical mass" follow a similar pattern of political mobilization.

Another factor shaping minority politics in Miami is the extent to which this diverse population has been superimposed on complex political boundaries, resulting in several of the area's 30 municipalities being predominantly Hispanic (12 in all, including the three largest: Miami, Hialeah, and Miami Beach), black (the moderate to very small towns of North Miami, Opa Locka, Florida City, and El Portal), or non-Hispanic white (several of the smallest and most affluent incorporated residential areas). At the same time, rapid growth of the unincorporated-area population, which exceeds that of all the municipalities combined, has marginalized the influence of the municipal governments on the area at large. City of Miami residents, for example, made up almost 65 percent of the total county population in 1940, but that proportion had dropped to 16 percent by 2000.

Black settlement patterns have had an especially negative effect on political mobilization. Historically, due to both the legacy of southern racism and the conscious placement of some black settlements in unincorporated areas (Mohl 1987, 1992), blacks played an almost insignificant role in the politics of most municipalities. Sixty-two percent of the black population still resides in unincorporated Miami-Dade County, making blacks particularly dependent on decisions of the county government, where historically their electoral clout has been most diffused.

Overall, about a dozen identifiable black neighborhoods are spread throughout the metropolitan area. In the northern reaches of the county are the densely populated public housing developments of Liberty City, which is not a city at all but a mostly unincorporated area bordering the City of Miami in northwest Dade. Closest to the City of Miami's central business district is Overtown, which historically has served as the black downtown section. In the agricultural south end of the county lie several less densely settled black neighborhoods. This settlement pattern—and the extent to which it undermines black influence in both the county and the individual municipalities and complicates grass roots organizing—has been a formidable barrier to political mobilization. Even in the majority-black towns of Florida City and Opa Locka, black electoral success has always been tempered by the marginal roles played by these municipalities in the area's affairs. Use of these two cities as a base for articulating black political interests is even more profoundly limited by the severe economic problems they face. As of the mid-1980s, both were among the 10 poorest of all suburban incorporated areas in the nation (Johnson 1987).

In contrast to Miami's black population, a majority of Hispanics reside in various municipalities. Also, rather than their numbers being geographically dispersed throughout the county, Cubans in particular originally settled in a largely uninterrupted corridor of residential areas, extending from the City of Miami's Little Havana section to the western limits of Miami-Dade County and north into Hialeah. This contiguous neighborhood base in Dade's two largest municipalities, combined with the more recent institution of district elections for county, municipal, and state legislative offices, has facilitated the emergence of Cuban Americans as the often dominant participants in both municipal and county politics. Moreover, rather than isolating them, political success at the municipal level has been an effective spring-board to higher local and state office for many Cubans.

Meanwhile, the declining non-Hispanic white population is now in the minor-ity in all but a number of modest to extremely small municipalities, and its clout in county elections has been increasingly diminished. As recently as the early 1990s, when the non-Hispanic white population had already shrunk to less than one-third of the total, the two major bases of "Anglo" power remained the Miami-Dade County Commission and the major downtown business, civic, and media institu-tions involved in community affairs. As explained in detail later, however, these sig-nificant bases of political power have also recently experienced dramatic changes, and non-Hispanic white influence has waned in these sectors too.

In short, in the complex political geography of Miami, the three major ethnic groups are not spread uniformly across the metropolitan area. Instead, they reside in a mixed pattern of enclaves and neighborhoods, the locations of which deter-mine their respective bases of power and possible arenas for effective political participation.

Metro's Structure and Minority Group Representation

Unlike metropolitan areas such as Boston, Chicago, or Atlanta, where core cities with a clear sense of identity are the dominant governmental structures, Miami's metro-politan government is fragmented both structurally and in the public consciousness, blurring jurisdictional lines as well as local governmental responsibility and account-ability. In 1957, Miami-Dade County established the first metropolitan form of gov-ernment in the United States. Popularly referred to as "Metro," the new system provided for a two-tiered government that left the municipalities intact while grant-ing the county certain powers over them. The large unincorporated area was to be solely governed by Metro. A Metro county commission, an executive mayor, and a county manager hold most policy-making and administrative authority and are the dominant forces in area-wide concerns (e.g., land use and zoning, mass transit and infrastructure, social services, and parks and recreation). The county also sets mini-mum performance standards for many of those services still provided by the munic-ipalities. For their part, municipalities retain the authority to maintain their own police departments, set municipal taxes, and exceed county standards in zoning and serv-ice delivery, among other narrower powers (Sofen 1961, 1966; Lotz 1984).

From 1963 until 1993, the Metro commission was composed of nine members who were elected at-large, on nonpartisan ballots, with provisions for runoffs in the event that no candidate for a seat received a majority. A Metro mayor with no exec-utive or administrative authority served as one of the nine commissioners, as first among equals, and the county manager exercised most executive and administra-tive authority (Mohl 1984).

The Metro system was created at a time when political power was overwhelm-ingly in the hands of Miami's non-Hispanic white population. Blacks, who as of 1960 were still seriously disenfranchised, made up only 15 percent of the popula-tion. Hispanics, who were mostly noncitizens, constituted a meager 5 percent of the total population, and by one estimate, "probably fewer than 5,000" actually voted (Banfield 1965, 104). Thus, concern for minority representation was not part of the political calculus that created or initially reformed the Metro system, nor was it a significant factor in its subsequent policies (Sofen 1961, 1966).

Characterized by a council-manager form of government, nonpartisan/at-large elections, and recognition of an "at-large community interest" in local government policy making, Metro stood as a model of reformed local government. A concomitant de-emphasis of party, neighborhood, and minority racial or ethnic interests meant that Metro's structure buffered subsequent attempts to use minority- and neighborhood-based political power to influence public policy (Stack and Warren 1992).

Over time, at-large elections and the runoff provision proved to be particularly effective deterrents to minority candidates. By the early 1990s, when Hispanics and blacks made up about 70 percent of the population, there had never been more than one black and one Hispanic commissioner serving on the nine-member Metro Commission at any given time (Table 10.2). From Metro's inception in 1957 through 1992, a total of five black and two Hispanic officials served on the commission, and of those, only two blacks and one Hispanic had been elected outright, without first having been appointed to fill a vacancy. Ironically, in those instances when a minority candidate was elected outright, it usually proved to be the case that the candidate would win without carrying the votes of his or her own group. Indeed, generalized social and political antagonism between blacks and Hispanics combined with a tendency for bloc voting in all three ethnic groups, essentially assuring that non-Hispanic whites would remain the decisive swing vote in most at-large county elections even as their numbers had declined from 80 percent of the total population in 1960 to barely more than 30 percent in 1990 (Warren 1991).

The high costs of running countywide campaigns also meant that successful candidates usually received significant financial support from major private-sector interests—especially those tied to development and tourism. In competitive races, private interests commonly contributed to each of the major candidates running for the same seat—a practice known in local campaign parlance as CYA (Cover Your

TABLE 10.2   Ethnic representation on the Metro Commission: Pre- and post-court intervention[a]

	Non-Hispanic White			Black			Hispanic			Total		
	1992	*1993*	*2001*	*1992*	*1993*	*2001*	*1992*	*1993*	*2001*	*1992*	*1993*	*2001*
No. of seats	7	3	2	1	4	4	1	6	7	9	13	13
% of seats	78	23	15	11	31	31	11	46	54	100	100	100
% of population	30	30	21	19	19	19	49	49	57	100	100	100

[a]The 1992 Metro Commission had nine members elected at-large, including a mayor with no executive authority. The 1992 U.S. District Court order expanded the commission to 13 members elected by district and eliminated the mayoral seat. A separate charter change established an executive mayor in 1996.

Assets) (Soto 1988). Unless minority candidates could attract similar financial backing and combine it with policy stands that cultivated non-Hispanic white support, they had little chance of winning office.

Court Intervention   Over the years, one of the few issues that provided common political ground for Miami's black and Hispanic political leadership was reforming at-large election structures in favor of district representation for local and state legislative offices (Moreno and Warren 1992). Within Metro, however, a steadfast majority of incumbent commissioners resisted all recommendations and attempts to create district elections. As a result, black and Hispanic plaintiffs filed a class action suit in federal court against Metro under Section Two of the amended 1965 Voting Rights Act (*Meek v. Metropolitan Dade County* 1992).

Before this case, the federal courts had ruled that plaintiffs in voting-rights cases no longer had to demonstrate "intent" to discriminate in the creation of at-large electoral systems for those systems to be overturned on constitutional grounds. Instead, plaintiffs needed only to demonstrate that "under the totality of circumstances," the electoral system had the effect of diminishing minority access to the electoral process and hindered the election of representatives of their choice (*Thornburg v. Gingles* 1986). In an elaborate 62-page order handed down in August 1992, the judge in the Metro case ruled that Miami-Dade County's system of elections discriminated against both blacks and Hispanics. Ironically, central to the judge's reasoning was his recognition of "the severe degree of racially polarized voting and the keen hostility that exists between blacks and Hispanics" (*Meek v. Metropolitan Dade County* 1992). The judge concluded that such polarization led each group to forge separate strategic voting coalitions with non-Hispanic whites to defeat those candidates most strongly supported by either minority group. Pursuant to its ruling, the court approved a plan that replaced the nine-member, at-large system with a 13-member commission elected from districts—with as many districts as practicable having either Hispanic or black voting majorities. Under the court's orders, not even the position of mayor was retained. Separate action taken under provisions for reforming the county's home-rule charter, however, established a separate, executive mayor with substantial executive and administrative authority who works in conjunction with a county manager appointed by the mayor and approved by the commission.

With the first election under the new system in April 1993, the county commission went from a nine-member body with never more than one black and one Hispanic commissioner at a time to a 13-member body with six Hispanics, four blacks, and three non-Hispanic whites. Overnight, non-Hispanic white representation dropped from 78 percent to 23 percent of the seats (Table 10.2). After the success of the suit against Metro, many of the same plaintiffs immediately proceeded to bring suit against the Miami-Dade County School Board and the City of Miami. Seeing the trajectory of court decision making, both bodies settled the suits and shifted to district elections.

The newly created mayor's seat was not imbued with all the powers associated with the classic "strong mayor" model of local governance. Nonetheless, it offered an unprecedented opportunity for visibility and leadership in the Metro system. Ironically, the first election for the office in 1996 came down to a runoff between a black and a Hispanic. Moreover, although technically a nonpartisan race, the runoff "witnessed tens of thousands of Cuban American Republicans crossing party lines to vote for a well known Cuban Democrat (Alex Penelas), at the same time that tens of thousands of African American Democrats crossed party lines to vote for a prominent black Republican (Arthur Teele)" (Hill, Moreno, and Cue 1997, 1). Penelas— who would later gain national visibility as the local official who most visibly opposed Janet Reno and the U.S. Department of Justice's efforts to return Elián González to his father's custody in Cuba—won on the strength of solid Cuban-American support combined with a greater share of the non-Hispanic white vote. Among other things, the race demonstrated that as of the mid-1990s, not only did race and ethnicity "trump" partisanship in Miami politics, non-Hispanic white candidates and voters no longer held center stage even in county-wide races.

CHANGING POLITICAL FORTUNES

With such profound changes in both the structure and the substance of Miami government and politics, Miami-Dade County has become a significant testing ground for the extent to which local electoral reform can be a significant force in promoting minority group political power. Certainly, at the level of Hispanic and black representation on locally elected boards and commissions, it is difficult to envision more rapid or fundamental changes.

These are not insignificant gains. In the case of black Miamians, to move in 30 years from virtual political exclusion, frequently reinforced by both racist law and practice, to proportional representation on key policy-making bodies has deep symbolic significance and inherent value in the representation of people and agendas long denied. Cuban Americans have experienced one of the most rapid political incorporations of any immigrant group in American history. Such achievements provide legitimacy, forums for the articulation of policy agendas, the potential to forge new governing coalitions, and an opportunity to steer resources in new directions. As Browning, Marshall, and Tabb (1994) point out, however, in the drive by minority groups to attain political power and equality, "it is the nature of issues to change over time from what is urgently demanded to what is taken for granted." There are always the lingering questions of "What difference does it make?" and "What's next?" Thus, the electoral successes of minority group leadership must ultimately be gauged in terms of "the production of policies responsive to the concerns of the group" (Browning, Marshall, and Tabb 1994, 18, 12).

An analysis of policy responsiveness, however, must go beyond representation of group and constituency interests on policy-making bodies. One must also examine the influence of economic structures and power on local government decision making and the ways in which such influence can either nurture or hinder certain policy outcomes. As Mollenkopf has argued (1992, 38), the two "primary interactions" between the leaders of local government and the numerous other players and forces in urban political systems are, "first, between the leaders of city government and their political/electoral base; and second, between the leaders of city government and their economic environment." It is the broader analysis of these interactions, and the extent to which they provide further insight regarding the political fortunes of Miami's three major ethnic groups, to which we now turn.

An End to Non-Hispanic White Dominance in a Pervasive Political–Economic Context

Court-imposed reform meant that non-Hispanic whites were supplanted in terms of electoral dominance, but this group has remained powerful in the major non-governmental civic, media, and business institutions. Recently, however, these bases of elite power have also been transformed. They are no longer the bastions of Anglo control they once were, but as with electoral systems and policy-making bodies, there is more to altering the business community's role in local affairs than simply enhancing ethnic diversity in civic organizations and boardrooms. Absent strong political leadership and pressures on the private sector, the status quo is sustained by continuing to limit the range of issues and policy alternatives that make it onto the public and private sectors's agendas. To a very substantial degree, those elements of the business community that monitor and involve themselves in local public affairs have always played—and continue to play—a significant role in setting the broad parameters of what is "possible" or in the "public interest" in Miami-Dade County. In doing so, policy initiatives that generally support business development have almost always taken precedence over policies that rechannel a larger share of the community's resources into neighborhood development.

Historically, private-sector influence in Miami has been especially linked to the establishment and growth of the city's central business district as well as to the development and tourism interests long essential to the health and well-being of the local economy. With rapid growth in the 1940s and 1950s came new demands for physical and social infrastructure and expanded local initiatives to promote and stabilize business activity. Such objectives facilitated business leadership in community affairs. As Mohl documented (1987), even early social programs such as slum clearance were shaped by the "hidden agenda of the downtown civic elite," which sought to expand the business section into the black downtown area known as Overtown.

With population growth, the proliferation of dozens of local governments, and the resultant fragmentation in local policy making, local elites in the 1950s became active in the effort to establish a metropolitan government. Endorsement of the proposition was also forthcoming from a variety of "good government" groups, prominent law firms, professional administrators, the *Miami Herald*, and others who saw inherent advantage in being able to work with a more centralized government. This pro-Metro coalition became—and long remained—the dominant force in shaping the community's basic political-economic agenda (Sofen 1966; Mohl 1984). Many of Sofen's (1961) early observations regarding Miami's power structure remain essentially valid:

> In the case of Miami, the lack of countervailing organizations in the form of either cohesive labor or minority groups has meant that the business com-

munity had no real competitors in the political arena. Moreover, since the cause of "good government" groups coincided with the desires of the more powerful Miami business organizations, the latter were quite content to allow the newspapers, professional groups, the university professors, and the League of Women Voters to assume the positions of catalytic leadership in civic affairs. (p. 30)

The one significant caveat to Sofen's statement is, of course, that Miami has seen the emergence of cohesive minority groups and significantly increased Hispanic and black involvement in some of the top echelons of the civic and business establishment. However, this increased involvement has not produced significant change in the interactions or agendas that have characterized relations between local government and business.

During the 1970s and 1980s, the role played by the business sector became even more formalized and institutionalized through the establishment of organizations such as the ironically self-described "Non-Group" (an association of Miami's top business and civic leaders), the Beacon Council (a publicly and privately funded agency chartered to encourage business development), and various appendages of the traditionally Anglo Greater Miami Chamber of Commerce. Each organization has served as an important vehicle in the formation and articulation of the policy preferences of major private economic interests—constituting what one former Miami mayor and Metro commissioner called "the shadow government" (Slevin 1994, 1B).

At the same time, because of the social upheaval experienced in Miami during the 1980s and 1990s, the leadership of the business community could no longer define the public interest in a social and political vacuum. Profound demographic change, increasingly brittle relations among the major ethnic groups, and a series of highly publicized events, such as the Liberty City riots, the Mariel boatlift, and the arrival of tens of thousands of Haitian "boatpeople," all underscored Miami's growing reputation as a "paradise lost." Given the negative impact of these events on the image and economy of the area, civic and business leaders led the call for increased government action to deal with the community's problems. They also began to acknowledge the need to incorporate more representatives from the Hispanic and black communities into their own ranks. In other instances, Hispanic-owned firms, such as the telecommunications company MasTec and beverage giant Bacardi, have emerged as important players in the local political economy, even as "Anglo"-dominated companies like Knight-Ridder, which owns the *Miami Herald*, have left.

The nongovernmental sector has also seen the emergence of parallel business and civic institutions controlled by Hispanics and blacks, such as *Mesa Redondo*, the Cuban American National Foundation, the Latin Builders Association, and the Black Lawyers Association. None of these significant changes in the ranks of civic and business leadership, however, can alter the fact that the overall prosperity of the business community invariably remains the top priority not only within this sector but with local governing authorities as well (Freedberg and Soto 1989). The prominence of an affluent Cuban-American business class has also meant that while faces, names, and accents have changed, the essential ways in which the business community defines the public interest has not.

Although the business community has often been at the forefront of pointing to some of Miami's many social, political, and economic problems and often encouraged government action, there usually has not been a concomitant pledge of significant private-sector resources. Nor has there been a willingness to see resources shifted from the promotion of business development to dealing with the problems of low-income and working-class neighborhoods. In actual practice, the pattern of action from most important nongovernmental civic and business institutions has been sporadic and almost entirely reactive even as Hispanic and, to a lesser extent, black leadership has expanded in this sector.

Throughout most of its history, Miami's business interests and reformist governmental structures and values converged to create an environment in which issues of primary concern to poorer or working class minority neighborhoods were frequently dismissed as not being in the best interest of the community as a whole. The idea that advancement for minorities might require policies inconsistent with the interests of influential economic institutions has not—and still is not—generally countenanced. Greater ethnic diversity within the leadership ranks of nongovernmental institutions has been an important development in its own right, but it has not resulted in a demonstrably more progressive stance regarding local public policy priorities.

At the citizen level, as indicated earlier, many non-Hispanic whites have "voted with their feet" and left Miami-Dade county, cutting the non-Hispanic white population to approximately half of what it was at its peak in the early 1970s. Many of those who remain have either adapted to the "Latinization" of Miami or have continued to confront a diminished sense of place and a growing sense of powerlessness, often vented through letters to the editor and calls to English-language radio talk shows. During the controversy over whether Elián González should be returned to Cuba, there were also street demonstrations by non-Hispanic whites that went beyond the issue at hand and usually became forums for decrying the "Cuban takeover."

Beyond such cathartic expressions of accumulated resentments, Miami has also seen several affluent areas with significant non-Hispanic white populations seek to become newly incorporated municipalities. Thus far, four such efforts have been successful: Key Biscayne, Pinecrest, Aventura, and Miami Lakes. At least two more are pending. In Miami's Metro system, municipal status provides more direct control over zoning, law enforcement, and other quality-of-life services while also assuring that a larger share of tax revenues are retained by the local municipality. Substantively, this means that lower levels of revenue from more affluent areas can be funneled into services for other parts of Miami-Dade. Symbolically, the move to incorporate more affluent neighborhoods suggests a "circling of the wagons" mentality, driven by considerations of both ethnicity and class.

Black Incorporation and the Limits of Structural Reform

As in most areas of the country, the 1950s and 1960s promised a positive political future for Miami's black population. The civil rights movement, federal court decisions, and national legislation encouraged local mobilization efforts. Although lacking the high level of organization and larger population found in some southern U.S. cities, substantive gains for blacks through community organizing and protest activity were realized in the desegregation of public and private facilities and in voter registration.

Once black voter registration increased, election to a limited number of local political offices followed. Blacks also gradually made significant gains in the area of appointed office, holding at various times the positions of Miami city manager, superintendent of schools, and several other high- and mid-level positions. Ultimately, local government jobs also became an essential source of employment for black Miamians, with blacks holding approximately one-third of the tens of thousands of Dade County and City of Miami jobs.

Apart from overcoming *de jure* segregation and lack of access to government offices and jobs, the most significant milestone in black political incorporation has been restructuring of the Metro commission and institution of district elections, resulting in the election of four black commissioners. As a result, the proportion of commission seats held by blacks rose from 11 percent to 30 percent in 1993. Yet despite greatly enhanced representation, what has generally been lacking in efforts to promote a coherent agenda that speaks to the needs of Miami's black community has been the absence of strong leadership from black officials. To date, the four African Americans who presently serve on the Metro commission have been among the least visible and vocal of all the commissioners.

Although black Miamians have no formal policy agenda as such, most of the concerns repeatedly voiced by civic leaders fall into a few major categories. First, concerns that cut across the breadth of law enforcement have been ongoing, including high incidence of crime, poor police–community relations, and repeated instances of police violence against black citizens. Second, public housing and neighborhood revitalization have been consistent areas of complaint. Finally, and most significantly, general issues of expanded economic opportunity, especially in the private sector, are not only critically important but, because of the need for sustained response from the business community, particularly resistant to improvement. The perceptions and the realities of limited progress on these issues indicate the limitations of political incorporation for black Miamians.

In the area of law enforcement, under the Metro charter incorporated areas maintain their own police departments, while unincorporated areas, including some of the most densely populated black neighborhoods, are policed by the county force. A long history of friction between blacks and police has been a particular problem in the unincorporated neighborhoods and in the City of Miami, and it was a catalyst in each of the four riots that occurred in the 1980s (Porter and Dunn 1984). At the same time, crime rates in these areas run high, and the obvious need for safety and stability in black neighborhoods clashes with a generalized mistrust and resentment toward law-enforcement officials, making the multidimensional problem particularly recalcitrant.

In the 1980s, Liberty City (which experienced one of the most violent riots of the twentieth century in May 1980) and Overtown (which experienced several nights of disorder in December 1982, the spring of 1984, and January 1989) replaced Watts and Detroit as the contemporary symbols of racial upheaval in America. For some, the pattern of rioting symbolized a host of fundamental problems faced by the black community, leading them to describe the riots as "rebellions" (Marable 1980). Yet in this community, still dependent on tourist dollars and hypersensitive to bad publicity, efforts were often made to downplay recurrent outbreaks of violence. Furthermore, just as the 1980 riots coincided with the influx of more than 150,000 Mariel and Haitian refugees, the racial violence of 1989 accompanied the arrival of tens of thousands of Nicaraguan and other Central American refugees. The coincidence of such events seems to reinforce the contention that in Miami, the problems evident in the black community are frequently undercut or upstaged by the pressing needs of the most recently arrived refugees, who are often viewed as receiving more immediate, concentrated, and dedicated assistance from local, state, and federal officials as well as from the private sector.

In the area of housing and neighborhood revitalization, there have been chronic complaints about the administration and maintenance of public housing through the county's "Little HUD" office, but the housing problem is in turn linked to a broader problem—that black Miamians frequently lack the power to shape those policies most directly affecting their own residential neighborhoods. Over the years, a greatly disproportionate number of development projects have negatively affected black neighborhoods. A football stadium to house the Miami Dolphins was built in northwest Dade, disrupting one of the county's few middle-class black neighborhoods. Since the 1930s, Overtown itself has been repeatedly disrupted by redevelopment plans and massive highway construction, virtually none of which have focused directly on improving conditions for the residents. The last major effort, in the 1980s, called for the area of Overtown bordering the central business district to be the site of a publicly funded arena to house the Miami Heat basketball franchise and the development of hundreds of units of middle-class housing and shops. Only the arena and the first housing units were ever completed, and after six years of operation, the Miami Heat franchise declared the facility inadequate. They then lobbied the county and city into subsidizing the completion and operation of a new arena less than a mile away, but removed from Overtown and squarely in the heart of the business district.

In the meantime, mere blocks from the Overtown neighborhood, two major government-subsidized retail projects have been completed on the bayfront, tens of millions of dollars were spent on a downtown auto-racing facility used a few times and then abandoned, the main downtown park (which lies mostly unutilized) and the adjoining Biscayne Boulevard have received more than $35 million in improvements, $120 million have been pledged for construction of an opera-and-symphony facility, and hundreds of millions more in public funds have been spent within about a three-square-mile area adjoining Overtown. Frequently, even monies initially dedicated for neighborhood development are subsequently funneled into the business district. One $40 million City of Miami bond issue, known as "Parks for People," was approved with support from black voters on promises that most of the funds would be used to create and improve neighborhood parks throughout the city. More than two-thirds of the money ultimately went to expanding the downtown Port of Miami and improving the main downtown park (Goldfarb 1992).

While it is impossible to calculate the direct and indirect returns generated by such projects for local government or business, such anecdotal evidence at least suggests the general direction of resource allocation. At each juncture, policy makers have justified redevelopment projects in the business district in terms of the broader economic interest of the community and the spin-off benefits for blacks and other residents through expanded job opportunities and better overall living conditions. Many blacks have remained skeptical of such justifications, because they are either (1) premised on the seemingly contradictory logic that improved circumstances for blacks are often linked to disruption of their neighborhoods and dislocation of residents or (2) linked to expensive projects and programs that provide little or no direct benefit to black residents and neighborhoods but, rather, are intended to bring macroeconomic benefits. Policies aimed at improving black neighborhoods outright have been few in number, have had low visibility, and have experienced weak followthrough.

The final category of policy concerns especially relevant to Miami's black community is directly linked to the need for greater economic opportunity. As a group, blacks have the worst living conditions, the lowest median income, the largest percentage of families in poverty, the worst housing conditions, and usually double the rate of non-Hispanic white and Hispanic unemployment. In sharp contrast to many Hispanics, blacks are not in a position to use economic clout as a means of enhancing their political status. There are comparatively few black-owned businesses (approximately 16,918 as of 1997), and of those, only 1,806 (less than 11 percent) provide employment for anyone other than the owners (U.S. Economic Census 1997).

Even the pledges of public and private support for efforts to promote black economic opportunity that were forthcoming after the 1980 and 1982 riots were short-lived. The Metro-Miami Action Plan (MMAP), which was to be the centerpiece of a co-ordinated public/private revitalization effort, all but folded after five years of operation. As one Hispanic former MMAP board member stated, "MMAP has been abandoned by almost everyone. There is not a sense of urgency about black problems. . . . A lot of prominent corporate leaders began to disappear after the second year. In Miami, you only get the corporate world to react in times of crisis. There's not a conscience that endures" (Dugger 1987, 1C).

Thus far, expanded and more secure black representation on the Metro commission and other policy-making bodies has not provided the necessary pressures to assure better followthrough on those programs that are established, much less provided an effective base for actual policy initiation. To that extent, protest, though rarely seen in an organized or sustained way, is still viewed as a necessary tool for the black community. One particularly illustrative example was provoked by local government and business leaders' snubbing of Nelson Mandela when he visited Miami in 1990. Mandela was slated to receive a grand welcome to the city until, soon after his arrival in the United States, he was asked about ties between the African National Congress, Fidel Castro, and Yasser Arafat. Refusing to renounce those who had lent support to him and his organization, Mandela's comments angered anti-Castro activist groups as well as many leaders in the Jewish community.

In response, local officials (Cuban and Anglo alike) refused to greet Mandela and withdrew the honors to be presented. Little organized response was forthcoming from the black community until a prominent local black attorney, H. T. Smith, worked on organizing a convention boycott of Miami. Gradually, the initial call to apologize for the snubbing of Mandela evolved into a more substantive list of demands aimed at expanding opportunities for blacks in the private sector. After three years of the boycott, during which Miami is estimated to have lost tens of millions of dollars in convention business (Croucher 1997, 151), a 20-point negotiated settlement was announced in May of 1993. At the time of the agreement, Smith reminded community leaders of their poor followthrough in past efforts to focus on issues of greatest concern to the black community: "Failure to keep the promises we have made will have serious consequences, because we believe in the future we will not have the credibility to harness the rage, the frustration, and the indignation of the black community" (Smith 1993). The boycott strategy, while effective in this instance, may also conceal a tragic flaw over the longer term. By relying heavily on outside players as opposed to local organizing, the boycott may have more effectively pressured the private sector in this one instance, but it contributed little to long-term mobilization and incorporation efforts that could bring Miami's black citizens and political leaders together in common cause. Since the announcement of the settlement, there has been neither government and private-sector action—nor further protest mobilization.

While advances for blacks in voter registration, elections, appointment politics, and public-sector employment have provided important opportunities, their incorporation to date has not provided the occasion to forge a competitive governing coalition able to move policy in ways that directly benefit black neighborhoods and their residents or to capture the attention and commitment of the major business and civic institutions. Group size, holding a minority of seats without consistent allies on fragmented boards and commissions, holding a majority of seats in some of the poorest municipalities, and having generally diffuse and weak political leadership either unable or unwilling to consistently promote an agenda to benefit the black community are all factors in limiting the achievements associated with black political incorporation. Black Miamians have discovered that even when the electoral structure has "delivered" all that it reasonably can, numerous obstacles to real influence over policy remain.

The Political and Economic Dimensions of Hispanic Incorporation

Standing in a city once called the "capital of Latin America" (Levine 1985), it is difficult to appreciate that 40 years ago, Hispanic influence in Miami was practically nonexistent. After the Cuban Revolution of 1959, the first waves of Cuban immigrants were not the dispossessed poor of that country; they included numerous accomplished professionals who combined personal initiative with an open-armed immigration policy and U.S. economic assistance for establishing themselves in Miami. Subsequent waves of immigrants throughout the 1960s brought a large portion of the Cuban middle class as well as an upwardly mobile working class to the area. In collective terms, notions of Cuban wealth are often more valid as allegory than as fact, but Cuban immigration has been accompanied by rapid economic incorporation and a number of dramatic success stories. As of the late 1980s, the median income for Cubans nationally was $26,770, as opposed to $14,584 for Puerto Ricans and $19,326 for Mexicans (Marquis 1989). More dramatically, by 1997 Hispanics in Miami had founded close to 121,000 businesses, including banks, television and radio stations, development companies, restaurants, and a variety of service and industrial enterprises. These businesses provide employment to hundreds of thousands and have a combined annual payroll of close to $3 billion (U.S. Economic Census 1997).

The 1980 Mariel refugees and many of the Cuban entrants since then have included far larger numbers of refugees who are poor, nonwhite, unskilled, and without family ties in the United States. Thus, in more recent years, class and racial differences have sometimes tested the durability of nationalistic ties; however, such divisions have yet to manifest themselves in politically significant ways. Ultimately, the numerical, economic, and political force of the middle- and upper-class Cuban community has the greatest impact on Miami politics. Invoking issues and symbols in campaigns that are meaningful to now-older, first-generation exiles is also a potent tactic in running for office and has served as the political bridge between a more successful and acculturated leadership and working-class, rank-and-file voters.

For many years, Cuban-American political incorporation lagged behind their economic accomplishments. As of the late 1970s, few Miami precincts had a majority of Hispanic registrants, and only a handful of Hispanics held local political office. Fortunes began to change dramatically in the 1980s, as Cuban Americans became more pervasive in municipal and county government as well as in the state legislature and Miami-Dade's U.S. House of Representatives delegation. Bloc voting for Cuban candidates, higher-than-average voter turnout, and fuller use of the once-weak local Republican Party apparatus were all important factors in early Cuban political mobilization.

In the area of appointive politics, Hispanic incorporation progressed just as rapidly. In what may be the capstone of their ascendancy in this area, at different junctures Cuban Americans have held the positions of county manager, Miami city manager, and superintendent of the county school system. County and municipal employment for Hispanics has progressed apace with these other developments—sometimes leading to charges of political patronage, cronyism, and machine politics. Such charges have been especially common in several Hispanic majority cities, such as Hialeah and Sweetwater.

While the immigrant experience, antipathy toward Fidel Castro, and other more local factors have channeled Miami Cuban-American politics in particular directions, it is a mistake to view their political activity as monolithic. Some political rivalries were transplanted from Cuba, and there are no leaders behind whom Cubans are truly united. Cubans running against Cubans is a growing phenomenon in elections at all levels. Even the Cuban American National Foundation, the most visible and influential of Cuban civic and lobbying organizations, has been disrupted and weakened by internal strife.

Thus, the long-term impact of Cuban-American incorporation on local policy making has been uneven and inconsistent at best, especially considering the unusual nature of their accompanying policy agenda. In addition to routine issues of service delivery and small business development, Cubans in Miami have frequently emphasized issues that, in a local context, are more symbolic than substantive—especially those related to their homeland and ongoing opposition to the Castro government:

> On the local level, symbolic politics have . . . frequently been at the core of local political mobilization, candidate selection, and issue articulation. . . . Certain largely symbolic political issues became particularly significant, not only because of the controversy surrounding them, but also because of the role they played in galvanizing Cuban ethnic group consciousness and converting it into local political activism. (Stack and Warren 1990, 12)

Although there are many examples of this phenomenon, the controversy surrounding the return of Elián González stands as the best recent illustration of largely symbolic issues taking priority over substantive local policy concerns. No other figure, issue, or symbol—beyond Fidel Castro himself—has ever so thoroughly galvanized such a large proportion of the Cuban community in common cause. Found alone at sea on Thanksgiving Day 1999, clinging to an inner tube off the coast of Miami, 5-year-old Elián was one of only three survivors from a small boat holding 14 Cuban refugees that capsized while escaping from Cuba to Miami. The attendant publicity surrounding the boy's dramatic story of survival, the death of his mother in the Straits of Florida, the desire of the child's Miami relatives to keep him in the United States, and his father's adamant demands for Elián's return to his custody in Cuba seemed to evoke every issue, image, symbol, and experience that has served to unify the otherwise diverse Cuban-American population. In many respects, the Elián González case evolved into the ultimate litmus test of Cuban-American political clout and the continued viability of the Cuban exile political agenda in the post–Cold War era.

For most non-Cubans, including many other Hispanics in Miami, the Elián affair underscored much of what was "wrong" with Miami. Not only did most seem to view the core issue as a simple one of returning a boy to his father, many came to increasingly resent the extent to which the entire community, including most of its local political leadership, became so singularly preoccupied with the case when clearly so many other matters required attention. There was also resentment over the feeling that political orthodoxy on issues involving Cuba and Cubans was now being imposed on those who were not part of the exile community. Disagreement with the mainstream Cuban-American view over the Elián case was often condemned, ridiculed, or dismissed. Ultimately, the controversy over the boy's fate—and his forced return after a raid by armed federal agents—further fueled lingering resentments over what was sometimes perceived as the arrogance of Cuban-American power.

What the return of Elián González to Cuba may ultimately come to symbolize more than anything else is the diminished potency of the traditional Cuban exile political agenda. Notwithstanding the emotions surrounding this one case, some Cuban leaders have been trying to gradually distance themselves from such issues and devote more attention to the substantive concerns of local government. The broadening of some Cuban officials' participation in an array of policy areas suggests a newfound confidence in the power and influence they have gained at the local level, even if their influence regarding policies affecting their homeland is on the wane. It also signals a gradual shift from more militant and internationally oriented exile politics to more mainstream, domestic ethnic politics.

Of more critical significance is the extent to which Hispanic economic and political incorporation in Miami has not raised policy issues that challenge the power of traditionally influential downtown business elites. Cuban-American political successes have displaced a number of non-Hispanic white officials, but the Latinization of the economy has proven to be functional for the major Anglo business interests, providing international linkages and increased stability. The overlap of Hispanic and Anglo economic interests reduces the non-Hispanic white elite's anxieties over the growing political strength of the Latin population, diminishing any motivation to enlist black support in a non-Hispanic political coalition. This process differs from the political and economic co-optation of minorities that has been described in other cities, and it represents a genuine convergence of economic and class-based interests between Miami's private sector establishment and upper- and middle-class Hispanics.

Overall, Hispanic incorporation in Miami contradicts in six important ways most generalizations made about other cities with large Hispanic populations. First, the makeup of Miami's Hispanic population differs from that of most other cities, being predominantly Cuban and generally more affluent. Second, Hispanic political incorporation has proceeded so rapidly and to such an extent that they now are the dominant electoral group in local politics, demonstrating significant levels of cohesion and bloc voting. Third, the economic incorporation of middle- and upper-class Hispanics in Miami has facilitated their political incorporation. Fourth, Hispanic incorporation in Miami has preceded, rather than followed, the incorporation of blacks. Fifth, whereas black and Hispanic mobilization and incorporation may be complementary processes in some cities, in Miami the political and—just as important—economic incorporation of Hispanics is widely perceived as not benefiting blacks. Finally, Hispanic incorporation in Miami has not been associated with the building of more liberal coalitions but has generally complemented rather than challenged the traditional leadership and agenda of downtown business elites. At the same time, a frequent preoccupation with symbolic issues rooted in the exile experience and mutual antipathy toward Fidel Castro galvanize the Cuban-American electorate while shrouding other potentially more divisive political and economic divisions.

INCREASING SYSTEM COMPLEXITY

As detailed in the foregoing analysis, great variation is found in the respective struggles of blacks and Hispanics in Miami, resulting in neither common patterns of mobilization nor a convergence of political-economic and policy interests. Unlike the gradual, incremental working out of different stands on policy issues as discussed by Peter Eisinger (1980), minority politics in Miami has often shown signs of intransigence in an atmosphere of group polarization. Black and Hispanic political mobilization often has been at cross-purposes, as in the New York scenario described by Mollenkopf (see Chapter 4), but unlike New York and most other cities, Hispanic incorporation in Miami has superseded that of blacks in every respect. Given the coincidence of ethnic and class divisions in Miami, however, juxtaposing middle- and upper-class Hispanics and non-Hispanic whites with poorer blacks and more recently arrived immigrants and refugees, the substantive policy implications of Hispanic incorporation are very different for non-Hispanic whites and for blacks. In short, while Hispanic incorporation has injected new, sometimes contentious issues into the community, it has not presented a fundamental challenge to the community's essential conservatism in matters of local government policy.

As the complexities of Miami's politics and the turbulence and unpredictability of its recent history suggest, a thorough assessment of possible scenarios for the future is a risky endeavor. However, based on recent events, it is possible to highlight certain political possibilities relevant to the ongoing efforts by Miami's diverse minority populations to have their disparate interests effectively represented in local policy making.

Political Prospects

Browning, Marshall, and Tabb (1984, 1994, 1997) have discussed the respective roles of both *electoral politics* and *demand-protest* in effective minority group mobilization. They have also underscored the importance of *coalition building* between minorities and supportive whites in challenging more conservative groups in the making of policy. The emphasis placed on these foci is appropriate in assessing the future of Miami politics. By distinguishing what seems to be feasible in the context of these factors, as opposed to what might otherwise be viewed by some as ideal, one can focus on those political prospects that are most likely to emerge in the near future.

Electoral Politics   The most important determinant in Miami's electoral politics has long been—and will continue to be—the area's governmental structure. Until the advent of district elections in the mid-1990s, the Metro system did not lend itself to increased levels of minority incorporation, and it was found by the federal court to comprise an unconstitutional hindrance. For black citizens, the restructuring of Metro and the City of Miami commissions has, for the first time, provided secure representation at a level proportionate to their population on the metropolitan area's most important policy-making bodies. For Hispanics, long underrepresented as well, district elections have assisted in consolidating their status as the dominant electoral force in both the city and the county. In the process, non-Hispanic white representation has declined precipitously from the days of at-large elections. Despite predictions from mostly non-Hispanic white critics of the court ruling that district elections would usher in an era of ethnically based "ward politics" and the "Balkanization" of Miami's ethnic groups, district elections have also provided the best opportunity for non-Hispanic whites to secure their own future representation on elected bodies and to provide at least the potential for the more effective representation of the diversity of group interests evident throughout the community. If it has provided nothing more than parity in representation and the potential for representatives of each group to broker competing demands and forge new coalitions, then on that basis alone, district representation has had some beneficial impact.

Protest   Given the often spontaneous and opportunistic nature of political protest, it is difficult to estimate its future role in Miami politics. Of the three major ethnic groups, blacks have used protest as a tool to pressure local government most frequently. As seen with the boycott over the snubbing of Nelson Mandela, however, when such actions do not involve local, grass-roots citizen mobilization, they do not necessarily lead to enhanced mobilization or incorporation. Instead, Miami has had more experience in the last 23 years with occasional outbreaks of racial violence, but the lack of substantive results in the wake of numerous promises for post-riot relief has amply demonstrated the limitations of protest as a policy lever. In the end, protest and outbreaks of violence have drawn attention to grievances but, to date, have been ineffective in assuring a sustained response from either government or the private sector.

Protest has been used less frequently by Hispanics and non-Hispanic whites to pressure local government. On occasion, groups of angry residents from a particular neighborhood will turn out at a commission meeting to oppose changes in neighborhood zoning, and there have been numerous demonstrations by Hispanics and Haitians over immigration policy as well as displays of anti-Communist sentiment. During the Elián González affair, street demonstrations by Cubans and non-Hispanic whites were common, but they often seemed to take on the tone of competing, "in-your-face" pep rallies. All such examples fall short of protest that is used as a tool to shape the policies of local government in any sustained way. Notwithstanding its recurrence in various forms and its being directed at different targets, it seems unlikely at present that protest will play a substantively different role in the future of Miami politics.

Coalition Building   The entry of new groups and issues into Miami's political process over the past several years and its reinforcement through structural reform might be thought to provide numerous opportunities for the emergence of new political coalitions. For years, however, the City of Miami and Metro systems made policy according to a fixed, if not always gladly accepted, set of rules. Anglo and private-sector elite dominance in the political arena seemed to be unchallengeable. In the 1960s, efforts at black mobilization and the earlier phases of Latin immigration suggested emergent divisions in the community, transforming Miami's black–white racial setting into a much more complex, multiethnic political environment. That diversity is now better represented in the electoral and policy-making processes. Yet while such changes have increased the number of groups and actors participating in community politics, there has not been a subsequent emergence of new coalitions able to bring about a major shift in the content of local public policies. The divisions between blacks and Cubans especially are so steeped in economic and group differences, as well as in cultural and ideological sensitivities, that finding acceptable compromises is difficult under the best of circumstances. Nor have white liberals played a determinant role in the formation of new coalitions. Liberal political organizations in Miami are few, and local government has lacked the mechanisms that could bring liberals from various groups together in support of particular candidates or policy initiatives.

Occasional instances of increased voting across ethnic lines does present some opportunity for the creation of new coalitions within the electorate. The nature of Miami elections, however, given the absence of a role for political parties, the highly individualistic nature of campaigning, and the ever-changing ad hoc coalitions that are a constant in local policy making, severely limit the opportunity for building lasting coalitions between officials on policy-making bodies.

The shift to executive/strong mayors from pure council–manager systems in both Metro and the City of Miami, and the ongoing proposals to further empower those positions through charter reforms, has also afforded some opportunity for the emergence of stronger political leadership with broader bases in Miami. Although only in place for one election cycle as of this writing, Metro and City of Miami mayors have come under pressure to broker group differences and to craft policy agendas that cut across the respective concerns of the area's increasingly multiethnic and multinational constituencies. In particular, the outcome of the 2001 City of Miami mayoral election may presage a positive future in terms of the emergence of new leadership adept at political brokerage and more attuned to building coalitions than to playing one group off another.

In the 2001 City of Miami mayor's race, the original field of candidates included four serious contenders, all of whom were Hispanic (three Cuban Americans and one of Puerto Rican descent). The then-incumbent mayor, Joe Carollo, and a former mayor, Xavier Suarez, both of whom are Cuban American and extremely controversial figures, split the largest share of that constituency in the initial vote; thus, neither made the runoff election. Another former mayor, Maurice Ferre, the only non-Cuban in the race, was the first Hispanic to be elected to significant office in Miami-Dade and was a proven vote-getter among non-Hispanic whites and blacks. Ferre faced the ultimate winner, Manny Diaz, a Cuban American and a newcomer to elected office, in the runoff election. Diaz entered the race having never sought elected office, but he had established himself prominently as an attorney and local political and civic activist.[3] Diaz represented what has been rare in Miami politics— he had credibility, especially at elite levels, in each of the ethnic communities as well as in the business sector. Given his past work as a Democratic Party activist on behalf of various African-American and non-Hispanic white candidates and as an attorney with important clients in the business community, he generated endorsements from several prominent black and non-Hispanic whites. Moreover, while not

---

[3] The authors acknowledge both a professional and personal relationship with Mayor Manny Diaz, who is an alumnus of the political science program at Florida International University. One author was also involved in polling work for his mayoral campaign.

as well known among rank-and-file voters, Diaz had capital among Cuban exiles given his work both as an attorney on behalf of the family members who sought to keep Elián González in the United States and as former director of the Spanish American League Against Discrimination.

In the runoff against Ferre, voters divided quite strictly along ethnic lines. Diaz won on the strength of strong Hispanic support; non-Hispanic whites and blacks voted disproportionately for Ferre. Diaz, however, was not seen as a polarizing figure, and his campaign consciously set a conciliatory tone. Even many who endorsed other candidates were quick to state that Diaz also represented a good choice. In his November 2001 inauguration speech, Diaz delivered his initial greeting in English, Spanish, and Haitian Creole, saying, "Good morning and welcome to a new Miami—one city, one future" (Corral 2001, 1B). Entering office with "low negatives" among otherwise divided constituencies, however, is only one small part of translating an electoral victory driven by Cuban-American voters into a much broader governing coalition that, of necessity, involves brokering very complex ethnic, racial, and socioeconomic class interests. Even so, the Diaz campaign and election speak to a significant shift in tone and rhetoric that, if at all successful, could emerge as a new model for others to emulate.

CONCLUSIONS

In the attempts of social scientists to understand black and Hispanic struggles for power and equality in urban politics, Miami is particularly important in suggesting a scenario of increased division between the nation's two largest minority groups. Regarding both substantive and symbolic issues, zero-sum perceptions may widen the gulf between blacks and Hispanics as well as between both groups and non-Hispanic whites.

Those who remain most optimistic about the future of ethnic group relations in Miami have at times been blinded by civic boosterism. On many occasions, it has been proclaimed that Miami was to at long last address the intractable problems of its poor and politically disenfranchised, who are disproportionately of minority populations. At some junctures, one or more ingredients in fact did seem to be in place for just such action. However, bringing the right elements together at the same time, over a sustained period of time, has been a particularly elusive goal. There is the potential for key policy-making institutions to represent Miami's divergent group interests and provide an arena for working out differences between them and political-economic notables on issues of resource allocation. With less than 10 years passing since the institution of district elections and executive mayors in both Metro and the City of Miami, however, it is still too short a period for definitive assessments. To date, little evidence suggests significant shifts in agendas or the flow of resources. On occasion, usually in the face of crisis, major private-sector players have been jostled to independent action. Here again, however, what has not been observed is the political system's ability to be the source of a sustained effort to harness the energies of both sectors, public and private, in common purpose to deal with long-neglected problems.

The political and social problems faced by blacks in Miami require particular attention. Reforms have boosted representation and provided more direct electoral linkages between black officeholders and the problems of black neighborhoods. Yet without strong leadership promoting a coherent agenda, such changes do little to bring about substantive shifts in local policy. This may especially be the case if there is an increased trend for affluent areas to distance themselves from the Metro system through their own incorporation—a move that is usually viewed as a means for neighborhoods to keep more of their resources to themselves. In such an environment, poor and working-class blacks and Hispanics could find themselves becoming more influential over a rapidly shrinking resource pool.

Miami's experiences may also point to the possibility of Hispanics emerging as a dominant political force in more cities. With continued rapid population growth, Hispanics may increasingly achieve political power on their own, without support from white or black coalitions. Such a pattern may prove especially evident in cities like Miami, where Hispanic economic and political incorporation are complementary.

Finally, although it is a new twist in urban politics, the alienation—and even underrepresentation—of white residents in majority-minority cities and the phenomenon of non-Hispanic white flight will likely demand increased attention from policy makers and students of urban politics alike. Such problems are in many ways different in both character and degree from those of groups that historically have been disenfranchised; nonetheless, they relate to the continued viability of our cities and the representative nature of their governments. The often related issues of private economic power, the deference that should—or should not—be accorded it by local government, and the role of business in shaping important public policies are even more complex when placed against the backdrop of minority group power and agenda articulation. Ultimately, each urban area faces its own unique circumstances relating to minority political mobilization and incorporation, but Miami may represent a microcosm of change, conflict, and adaptation that could alter previous explanations of minority politics in America's cities.

REFERENCES

Banfield, Edward C. 1965. *Big City Politics*. New York: Random House.

Boswell, Thomas D. 1994a. *The Cubanization and Hispanicization of Metropolitan Miami*. Miami: Cuban American Policy Center of the Cuban American National Council.

Boswell, Thomas D. 1994b. *A Demographic Profile of Cuban Americans*. Miami: Cuban American Policy Center of the Cuban American National Council.

Browning, Rufus P., Dale Rogers Marshall, and David H. Tabb. 1984. *Protest Is Not Enough: The Struggle of Blacks and Hispanics for Equality in Urban Politics*. Berkeley: University of California Press.

Browning, Rufus P., Dale Rogers Marshall, and David H. Tabb. 1994. Political Incorporation and Competing Perspectives on Urban Politics. Paper Presented at the Annual Meeting of the American Political Science Association, New York, September 1–4.

Browning, Rufus P., Dale Rogers Marshall, and David H. Tabb. 1997. *Racial Politics in American Cities*, 2nd ed. New York: Longman.

Castro, Max. 2001. Hispanic Equation Shifting. *Miami Herald*, July 31, 7B.

Clapp, James A. 1984. *The City: A Dictionary of Quotable Thoughts on Cities and Urban Life*. New Brunswick, N.J.: Center for Urban Policy Research, Rutgers University, 123.

Corral, Oscar. 2001. Diaz Honors Diversity at Swearing-In. *Miami Herald*. November 18, 1B.

Croucher, Sheila L. 1997. *Imagining Miami: Ethnic Politics in a Postmodern World*. Charlottesville: University Press of Virginia.

Dugger, Celia W. 1987. MMAP Losing Punch. *Miami Herald*, July 17, 1C.

Dunn, Marvin. 1997. *Black Miami in the Twentieth Century*. Gainesville: University Presses of Florida.

Dunn, Marvin, and Alex Stepick. 1992. Blacks in Miami. In Guillermo J. Grenier and Alex Stepick, eds., *Miami Now!: Immigration, Ethnicity and Social Change*. Gainesville: University Presses of Florida, 41–56.

Eisinger, Peter K. 1980. *The Politics of Displacement*. New York: Academic Press.

Elliott, Andrea, and Jason Grotto. 2001. Fifty-One Percent in Miami-Dade Born in Other Nations. *Miami Herald*, November 20, 1A.

Freedberg, Sydney P., and Luis Feldstein Soto. 1989. Miami Splinters in Three Parts. *Miami Herald*, February 13, 1B.

Goldfarb, Carl. 1992. Time's Right to Help Inner City, Non-Group, Other Leaders Say. *Miami Herald*, May 16, 1B.

Grotto, Jason, and William Yardley. 2001. Poverty Rate a Distinctive Challenge for Miami. *Miami Herald*, November 20, 17A.

Hill, Kevin A., Dario V. Moreno, and Lourdes C. Cue. 1997. Racial and Partisan Voting in a Tri-Ethnic City: The 1996 Dade County, Florida Mayoral Election. Paper presented at the Midwest Political Science Association, Chicago, April 10–12.

Johnson, Dirk. 1987. The View from the Poorest U.S. Suburbs. *New York Times*, April 30, 10.

Levine, Barry B. 1985. The Capital of Latin America. *The Wilson Quarterly* 9 (Winter): 46–69.

Lotz, Aileen. 1984. *Metropolitan Dade County: Two-Tier Government in Action*. Boston: Allyn and Bacon.

Marable, Manning. 1980. The Fire This Time: The Miami Rebellion, May 1980. *The Black Scholar* 11 (July): 2–18.

Marquis, Christopher. 1989. Cubans Still Better Off than Other Latins. *Miami Herald*, February 6, 1B.

Metro-Dade Planning Department: Research Division. 1986. *Hispanic Profile: Dade County's Hispanic Origin Population*. Miami.

Meek v. Metropolitan Dade County. 1992. 805 F. Supp. 967.

Mohl, Raymond A. 1984. Miami's Metropolitan Government: Retrospect and Prospect. *Florida Historical Quarterly* 63 (July): 24–50.

Mohl, Raymond A. 1987. Trouble in Paradise: Race and Housing in Miami During the New Deal Era. *Prologue* 19: 7–21.

Mohl, Ramond A. 1992. Race Relations and the Second Ghetto in Miami: 1940–1960. Paper presented at the annual meeting of the American Historical Association, Washington, DC, December 28.

Mollenkopf, John H. 1992. *A Phoenix in the Ashes: The Rise and Fall of the Koch Coalition in New York City Politics*. Princeton: Princeton University Press.

Moreno, Dario, and Christopher L. Warren. 1992. The Conservative Enclave: Cubans in Florida. In Rodolfo O. de la Garza and Louis DeSipio, eds., *From Rhetoric to Reality: Latino Politics in the 1988 Elections*. Boulder; Colo. Westview Press, 127–145.

Porter, Bruce, and Marvin Dunn. 1984. *The Miami Riot of 1980: Crossing the Bounds*. Lanham, MD: Lexington Books.

Portes, Alejandro, and Alex Stepick. 1993. *City on the Edge: The Transformation of Miami.* Berkeley: University of California Press.

Pugh, Tony. 1993. A Biracial Blueprint for Change: Boycott Ends with Pact, Promises. *Miami Herald,* May 13, 1A.

Slevin, Peter. 1994. The Non-Group Seeks to Answer, "What Are We?" *Miami Herald,* November 21, 1B.

Sofen, Edward. 1961. Problems of Metropolitan Leadership: The Miami Experience. *Midwest Journal of Political Science,* 5 (1): 18–38.

Sofen, Edward. 1966. *The Metropolitan Experiment,* 2nd ed. New York: Doubleday Anchor.

Soto, Luis Feldstein. 1988. Donors Hedged Their Bets. *Miami Herald,* October 10, 1B.

Stack, John F., Jr., and Christopher L. Warren. 1990. Ethnicity and the Politics of Symbolism in Miami's Cuban Community. *Cuban Studies* 20: 11–28.

Stack, John F., Jr., and Christopher L. Warren. 1992. The Reform Tradition and Ethnic Politics: Metropolitan Miami Confronts the 1990s. In Guillermo J. Grenier and Alex Stepick, eds., *Miami Now!: Immigration, Ethnicity and Social Change.* Gainesville: University Press of Florida, 160–185.

Stepick, Alex. 1992. The Refugees Nobody Wants: Haitians in Miami. In Guillermo J. Grenier and Alex Stepick, eds., *Miami Now!: Immigration, Ethnicity and Social Change.* Gainesville: University Press of Florida, 57–82.

Stone, Clarence N. 1989. *Regime Politics: Governing Atlanta, 1946–1988.* Lawrence: University Press of Kansas.

Thornburg v. Gingles. 1986. 106 S.Ct. 2752.

U.S. Census Bureau. 2000. P.L. 94–171, Miami-Dade County.

U.S. Economic Census. 1997. Minority and Women Owned Businesses, Dade County, Florida.

Viglucci, Andres. 2001. Cultural Mix Is Rapidly Diversifying. *Miami Herald,* May 23, 21A.

Warren, Christopher L. 1991. Affidavit in Support of Plaintiffs' Motion for Summary Judgment and in Response to the Court's 2/13/91 Order. *Meek vs. Metropolitan Dade County.*

Chapter 11

Latinos, Blacks, and Multiethnic Politics in Denver: Realigning Power and Influence in the Struggle for Equality

Rodney E. Hero and Susan E. Clarke[1]

EDITORS' NOTE

As Rodney E. Hero and Susan E. Clarke note, "During the 1990s, the political advances of Latinos in Denver were, by commonly used measures, quite impressive and surpassed by Latinos in but a few cities; African-American political influence similarly was quite high." This "steady-state" previously characterizing Latino and black struggles to achieve equality in Denver (Hero 1997) is challenged by recent developments, however. The dramatic growth of Latinos in Denver evident in the 2000 U.S. Census modifies previous perceptions of the status of Latinos and blacks in the cities. Though this surge in population might seem to signal a takeoff for Latino political influence in the city, a number of constraints caution against an unqualified assessment.

Despite some evidence that would suggest growing Latino political influence, other factors complicate predictions. There is little consensus on a Latino political agenda, much less on one that would reflect the shared concerns of blacks and Latinos about poverty, affordable housing, safety, health care, and neighborhood well-being. And many especially salient issues, including education, are beyond the control of city government officials.

Whether whites, Latinos, African Americans, and Asians in Denver collaborate, compete, or "go their own way" on these issues remains to be seen. Our analysis suggests that the political and cultural dimensions of African-American and Latino identities will make the development of common, converging patterns difficult. Contested political identities, complicated by class, cultural, and generational splits, make further political mobilization and incorporation a complex matter in Denver.

---

[1] The authors acknowledge the expert and good-natured research assistance of Meg McCroskey in helping to update recent developments in Denver.

The "steady-state" previously characterizing Latino and black struggles to achieve equality in Denver (Hero 1997) is challenged by evidence from the 2000 U.S. Census. The stunning growth of Latinos in Denver—and throughout the state of Colorado—upsets previous calculations regarding the status of Latinos and blacks in the city. As one local observer put it, these new data "turn politics on its head" in Denver. While the political implications have yet to unfold, the demographic tilt toward Latinos in this multiethnic, multiracial city will have profound effects. Despite some evidence that would suggest growing Latino political influence in Denver, other factors complicate this prediction. Against this backdrop of dramatic demographic change and constrained political influence, this chapter examines and compares the political status of Latinos (Mexican Americans) and blacks in Denver, Colorado.

UPSETTING THE "STEADY-STATE" IN MULTIETHNIC POLITICS IN DENVER

As in the past, the extent and nature of Latino and black political influence in Denver does not lend itself to easy explanations. Nonetheless, the theoretical model put forth by Browning, Marshall, and Tabb (1984, 1990; 9–18 ; also see Chapter 1) provides a useful and systematic approach for assessing minority politics (cf. Hero 1992, ch. 10). The analysis below follows that framework to a large degree. Latino and black political influence in Denver appears to be shaped by forces, factors, and processes delineated in the mobilization/representation/incorporation model, including growing minority populations, the potential and reality for coalitions, and city size. Additionally, governmental structure and individual leadership or political entrepreneurialism appear to be significant factors.

During the 1990s, the political gains of Latinos in Denver were, by commonly used measures, quite impressive and surpassed by Latinos in but a few cities; African American political influence similarly was quite high. On the whole, the political influence of Latinos and blacks in Denver over this period was as great—or greater than—that found in a number of cities, including those in northern California and elsewhere, such as New York City, Los Angeles, and Chicago (Browning, Marshall, and Tabb 1984, 1990, 1997; Hero 1992). Yet these successes sometimes seem to be more apparent than real, and restricted to only some arenas of city governance. Even though the recent surge in population would seem to signal the takeoff stage for Latino political influence in the city, a number of constraints caution against an unqualified assessment. The grounds for these observations and the conditions that produced these outcomes are discussed below.

Background

Mexican Americans continue to be the largest "minority" group in Denver and in the state of Colorado (now 735,601 statewide). The Latino population in Colorado and Denver remains largely Mexican in origin, though there are signs of greater diversity. Nearly two-thirds of the Hispanic population is Mexican American, but there has been a slight decline statewide (from 66.6 percent in 1990 to 61.3 percent in 2000) as the Latino/Hispanic population slowly became more diverse, with growth in Central and South American, Puerto Rican, and Cuban groups. Until recently, the Latino population in Colorado has been notable for its low rates of non-citizens. By most estimates, well over 90 percent of Colorado Latinos are U.S. citizens, and the vast majority are native-born, with many tracing U.S citizenship back over several generations. These characteristics distinguished Denver Latinos from those in a number of U.S. cities with diverse and/or very large non-citizen or recent immigrant Latino populations (cf. Meier and Stewart 1991).

Analyses of the 2000 U.S. Census, however, classify Colorado as one of 19 "new growth" states whose foreign-born population is growing faster than in the rest of the nation (Aguilar 2001). The 80 percent growth rate in the foreign-born population in Colorado over the last 10 years—from 142,000 to 255,000—is driven by Hispanic and Asian immigration to the state (Aguilar 2001). Not all of this immigration fits the traditional urban pattern, however. With labor shortages in the mountain tourism sectors as well as in meat-packing and agricultural sectors, many new immigrants head to rural resort and agribusiness communities in Colorado. So, even with the statewide growth in foreign-born population, Denver remains distinctive relative to other cities with high non-citizen populations; this increasing diversity among Latinos, however, further complicates the prospects for mobilization and incorporation.

PRECONDITIONS TO MINORITY MOBILIZATION

According to the Browning, Marshall, and Tabb model, certain contextual variables or preconditions to mobilization need to be considered to understand political representation and incorporation of Latinos and blacks in Denver.

Growth Rates

The differential growth rates of the Latino and black populations and their disparate socioeconomic features shape the political dynamics of the city. Overall, there has been considerable growth of the minority (especially Latino) populations in the last decade: In 2000, 51.9 percent of the city were non-Hispanic/white, and 42.9 percent were Latino and black. As noted, the stunning growth in Latino population (64 percent growth from 1990 to 2000) accounts for a large share of this minority population. By 2000, the Latino population grew to 31.7 percent of Denver's population, a dramatic gain since 1990, when Latinos comprised about 23 percent of the population, and relative to their 18 percent share in the 1980s, when Latinos achieved notable political gains in Denver politics. Denver's African-American population has grown modestly from 7 percent in 1960, peaking in the mid-1990s at 14.3 percent and, by 2000, reaching only 11 percent of the population. Although the black population in Denver is substantial, its recent growth rates (4 percent growth from 1990 to 2000) are modest relative to those of Latinos, and it is losing ground to Latino groups in terms of rate of growth and share of the population.

The location of this growth is especially significant. Over the last decade, historically black neighborhoods such as Five Points and Cole witnessed an influx of Hispanic families; both neighborhoods now have Hispanic majorities, with school populations even more predominately Latino. Similarly, the primarily white neighborhood of Ruby Hill is now majority-Hispanic. As a result of these trends, several city council members now represent districts with dramatically different ethnic and racial characteristics than when they were first elected.

Denver's biggest suburban growth occurred in the 1970s and 1980s, but over the past 20 years, suburbanization of Latino and black families is slowly altering the makeup of the metropolitan region. In 1980, 57.5 percent of the region's minority population lived in Denver; by 1995, that number had decreased to 45.3 percent as minority populations in suburban counties grew rapidly. Denver's city-suburb poverty gap is one of the widest in the American west (Piton 1994), but the metropolitan suburbs are decidedly "less white" in 2000 than they were in the 1980s: 88.7 percent white in 1980, 77 percent white in 2000 (U.S. Department of Housing and Urban Development 2001). Though Latino groups are primarily clustered within Denver, there is some modest suburbanization beyond the city limits into the northern and western suburbs. In contrast, blacks remain more concentrated in Denver and neighboring Adams County in the northeast, but their growth rates in the surrounding counties are higher than in the city.

Demand-Protest Activities

"Demand-protest" activities have been extensive in Denver for both Latinos (Hero 1992) and blacks. Denver's substantial black presence mobilized locally during the national (black) civil rights movement, which served as a model and a catalyst for Latino political efforts. Denver was also the home of the "Crusade for Justice," which was headed by one of the most prominent leaders of the "Chicano Movement" of the 1960s and 1970s, Rodolfo "Corky" Gonzalez. Throughout this period, and continuing to the present, white liberal support for minorities in Denver has been substantial. One example is the electoral support for a Latino mayoral candidate, Federico Peña (first elected in 1983 and re-elected in 1987) from white liberals and from blacks. Yet Peña's electoral coalition was always somewhat fragile and had its origins in white middle-class support as much as in the Latino neighborhoods (see Hero 1987; Hero and Beatty 1989). The broad-based white middle-class electoral support for Denver's first African-American mayor, Wellington Webb, also proved to be critical during his time in office, from 1991 to the present (Hero 1989).

Population Size and Relative Inequalities

The city's population size and levels of socioeconomic inequality—population related to sheer numbers, and inequality as a spur to more activism—also would suggest substantial mobilization in Denver. During the 1990s, Denver rebounded from the slump of the 1980s. After losing population during the 1980s (467,610 population in 1990, down from 492,000 in 1980), the city grew to 554,636 by 2000—a more than 18 percent population change. Local officials refer to the 1990s as "the Denver Decade." Denver now is consistently rated one of the best places for business in the United States, with unemployment rates lower than the national average. The economic base diversified in the 1990s, bringing in more telecommunication, biomedical, and computer enterprises and making the city more resilient to future economic downturns. More than 41 percent of the jobs in the city are in the service sector; in contrast to many other cities, many entry-level jobs with tracks to livable wages remain available to low-skill workers in Denver (Piton 1999). A significant share of these jobs, however, continues to migrate to the suburbs.

This growth climate brought benefits to many in the city, but it sharpened inequalities as well, especially for people of color. As one reporter put it, "the Vail (Colorado) syndrome" began to emerge in Denver in the mid-1990s as workers' wages proved to be insufficient for securing affordable housing (Booth 1997). The consequences of economic growth for those lacking the skills and education in demand became a matter of concern for local officials. By 1999, Mayor Webb was articulating the need for more regional and integrated strategies and drawing parallels between city incentives available to businesses with those that should be provided for supporting the working poor.

Overall, the black population in Denver continues to fare somewhat better than Latinos by some measures of socioeconomic well-being. However, blacks and Latinos historically do much less well than Anglos on these indicators. In 1989, the per-capita income for whites in Denver was $18,191, for blacks $10,442, and for Hispanics $7,778. With the booming economy of the 1990s, Denver County reported a per-capita income of $31,533 in 1999. Although the average household income in 1995 was $42,426, the disparities across neighborhoods ranged from $13,879 in the Latino neighborhood of Sun Valley to $25,384 in the primarily black neighborhood of Clayton to $95,821 in the Country Club neighborhood. In Denver, home ownership is now at 52.5 percent, but black and Latino homeownership rates are lower than those for whites: 71 percent of whites and Asians own their own home, compared to 53 percent of Hispanics and only 45 percent of blacks (*Denver Post* 2001).

By 1990, Latinos were more visible in executive, administrative, and managerial positions than blacks, comprising 6.2 percent, compared to 3.4 percent for blacks and 88.6 percent for whites, but they were more visible in service occupations as well (18 percent, compared to 8.2 percent for blacks and 70 percent whites) (Colorado Department of Labor and Employment 1999). Every year, however, Latinos in Denver public schools trail graduation rates of both blacks and whites, and poverty rates remain high: In 1989, the African-American poverty rate was 26.7 percent (up from 23.3 percent in 1979), while Latinos had a 30.6 percent poverty rate (up from 23.9 percent in 1979, nearly double the rate of increase for blacks) (Piton 1994).

In short, there is clearly continued socioeconomic *in*equality of both blacks and Mexican Americans relative to Anglos and/or the general population in Denver. Despite recent economic growth, 53.8 percent of children in the Denver public school system were eligible for free lunches; in the public school system, Latinos and African American children are now 70 percent of the school population. In the face of these persistent inequalities, poverty in Denver is increasingly concentrated in Latino neighborhoods and has a "Latino face." According to the respected Piton Foundation, poor neighborhoods are becoming increasingly Latino, while historically black neighborhoods are transforming through gentrification as well as by in-migration of whites and Latinos (Piton 1999; see also Hero 1992).

Governmental Structure and Political Constituencies

Governmental structure is often perceived to be related to minority political activity and influence (e.g., Browning, Marshall and Tabb 1984, 84–85). "Unreformed" structures are commonly assumed to provide more outlets for minority political influence. Denver's governmental structure is relatively unreformed, with a strong mayor–council system and a heavily district-based, relatively large council (11 of the 13 council members are elected by district). The salience of city council size to the minority communities is reflected in the recent (unsuccessful) effort by a Latina council member to add two more council seats to reflect the growing city population. Moreover, the Denver mayor is a formally "strong" mayor, with extensive budgetary, appointment, and veto powers. Finally, Denver is a consolidated city and county; given Colorado's history of devolving programs to county governments, this has become more salient as federal programs are shifted to state control.

New Democratic majorities among voters and on the council are another precondition for minority political mobilization in the Browning, Marshall, and Tabb model. This occurs despite the formally non-partisan electoral nature of many cities in the western United States, including Denver. Since at least 1963, Denver has had a majority of Democrats on its city council, and since the mid-1970s, that majority has exceeded 60 percent. Democrats appear to have been overrepresented on city council relative to registered Democratic voters. At the same time, however, Republican membership on the council exceeded Republican voter registration for every year until about 1987 (Hero 1992). This ostensible overrepresentation of both Democrats and Republicans on the council is partly the result of high levels of "unaffiliated" or "independent" registration in Denver (and, indeed, in Colorado as a whole). In 2001, 47 percent of the 235,012 registered voters in Denver were Democrat, 24 percent Republican, and 29 percent Independent.

MINORITY REPRESENTATION AND INCORPORATION

Representation

"Descriptive" or "sociological" representation—having city council/mayoral positions held by members of the minority population—is another major dimension of minority politics in cities. Representational "parity" means having representation in approximate proportion to population numbers in the city as a whole.

City Council   From the 1960s to late 1970s, Latinos in Denver were generally underrepresented (or below parity) on the council relative to their numbers in the general population (Hero 1992). From 1955 to 1975, there were no Latinos on the Denver city council, despite the all-district (nine-member) council before 1971 and the expansion of that council (to 13 members, with 11 district and 2 at-large seats) in a way that was intended to enhance the likelihood of Mexican-American representation (Lovrich and Marenin 1976). (A Latino member on the Denver city council, a Republican, was elected in 1943, however, and served until the mid-1950s [Leonard and Noel 1990, 393]). In 1975, two Latinos were elected to district-based seats on the Denver city council and held those seats until 1987, when both decided not to seek re-election. Both were succeeded by two Latinas who had been their former aides. Both Latinas were re-elected to their council seats in 1991, and each has subsequently held the position of "President" of the council. It thus appears that Latino/a representation on the city council is well established—indeed, even "institutionalized."

Latinos in Denver had substantially higher scores on representational parity—more than double—during the mid- to late 1970s than the average for Hispanics in the northern California cities (during the same period) studied by Browning, Marshall, and Tabb (1984). Indeed, the average parity ratio for Denver from the mid-1960s to the mid-1980s, which includes several years in which there was no Latino representation, is somewhat greater than the average for the northern California cities in 1975 to 1978.

There have been two or three Latino/as holding city council positions along with a Latino mayor for most of the 1980s, producing something at or close to parity between the size of the Latino population and the proportion of elected officials. In 1997, there were 2 Latino/as on the city council; assuming roughly 26 percent Latinos in the city population at that time, the Latino parity score was .59. By 2000, there were still two Latino/as on the council, but the Latino population growth was significant—assuming 30 percent Latinos in the city population, the parity score was .50 (Table 11.1).

Similar stability exists in parity scores for African-American council representation. The first black was elected to the Denver city council in 1956. From the early

TABLE 11.1   Representation on Denver city council, 1990–2001

Year	Whites	Blacks	Hispanics
1990–1991	9	2	2
1991–1992	8	2	3
1992–1993	8	2	3
1993–1994	8	2	3
1994–1995	8	2	3
1995–1996	9	2	2
1996–1997	9	2	2
1997–1998	9	2	2
1998–1999	9	2	2
1999–2000	9	2	2
2000–2001	9	2	2

1960s to the present, black representation on the Denver city council has actually been above parity, averaging 2.9 (where 1.0 equals parity). In 1994, two of the 13 city council members were black. In 1997, the two blacks on the city council garnered a 1.28 parity score, assuming blacks were about 12 percent of the population. As the black population share declined in 2000, however, the same two members generated a parity score of 1.36. This stability in Latino and African-American council representation may shift, because many current council members will be term-limited out of office in 2002.

Mayor's Office   In 1983, Federico Peña, who had previously served in the Colorado House of Representatives and been quite visible and active in several Chicano/Latino policy concerns—but who had no previous city government background—became Denver's first Mexican-American mayor. He was re-elected in 1987, but he did not seek re-election in 1991. It was the first time that a Latino mayor was elected in a major U.S. city without a Latino majority. Indeed, Peña's initial election surprised many observers, because few minority mayors have been elected in cities with such relatively small minority populations (at the time, 18 percent Latino and 12 percent black). In fact, Latinos and blacks comprised only about 12 and 10 percent of eligible voters, respectively.

This pattern continued with Peña's successor. Denver's first African-American mayor, Wellington Webb, also served in the Colorado House of Representatives in the early 1970s, ran for city auditor (a traditional stepping-stone to the mayor's office), and successfully ran for mayor in 1991 after defeating a black challenger in a runoff election. He won his re-election bid, but term-limit legislation prevents him from seeking a third term in 2003.

Political Incorporation

As these figures suggest, the "face" of Denver politics reflects the multiethnic composition of the city's population. Political "incorporation" refers not only to representation, however, but also to the position of minority representatives vis-à-vis the dominant coalition on the city council. That is, incorporation measures the extent to which minorities are represented in coalitions that dominate city policy-making on minority-related issues (Browning, Marshall, and Tabb 1984, 25, 18). Our previous estimates of incorporation (based on interviews and other evidence) suggested that Denver's overall minority incorporation scores in 1984 and 1987 were quite high—and well above that for any of the northern California cities studied by Browning, Marshall, and Tabb (the highest of which was 3, in 1978)—and its 1976 to 1980 score of 2 is well above the average (.5) for the 10 northern California cities in 1978. In 2000, that level of incorporation remains high: a black mayor and four minority council members, who have held important positions within the council and appear to be quite active on issues central to minority communities. Thus, the basic patterns found in Denver for the late 1980s continue to hold into the present.

Underlying these scores, however, is a dramatic process of political incorporation unfolding from the 1980s to the present in ways that suggest, to many observers, a "regime change" in which new configurations of interests—including African Americans and Latinos—displaced the dominant governing coalition. Peña's upset election in 1983 signaled the end of the Old Guard political elite dominating city politics since the 1950s and 1960s and the movement toward a political order more reflective of the city's changing demographic and economic character (see Clarke and Saiz 2002). Peña's electoral coalition included blacks, Latinos, labor, gays, feminists, environmentalists, neighborhood groups, and organizations of people with disabilities; most critically, Peña also drew a core group of business leaders, especially developers, to his campaign. Peña's campaigns were notable in emphasizing distributive or developmental concerns and in bringing attention to "minority" or "redistributive" concerns only indirectly (Hero 1992). Once elected, the projects unveiled by the Peña administration pulled together a governing coalition of business, media, public economic development professionals, historic preservationists, neighborhood activists, and land developers.

To many, the Peña administration is distinguished as a more liberal and ethnically/racially "aware" political regime, despite its tenuous electoral base. Peña's mayoral agenda sought to achieve both economic development, linked to minority opportunities and neighborhood development, and governmental "openness." While Peña stressed issues such as building a new convention center and a new airport, and bringing a major league baseball team to the city, he linked these projects to minority employment and business opportunities. He also expanded the city's minority contracting program and appointed many minorities to administrative positions and to city boards and commissions. The full or "real" benefits for minorities of the Peña administration have been debated (cf. Saiz 1988; Judd and Ready 1986; Hero 1992, chs. 8 and 10), but the administration clearly was dramatically more "progressive" or liberal than its conservative Democratic predecessors.

Webb's election in 1991 is another watershed in Denver's political history. Wellington Webb ran as someone seeking to carry on and, essentially, to complete the progressive agenda of his predecessor. Webb's administration (his third and last term expires in 2003) has also emphasized economic development, neighborhood development, and completion of the tourist infrastructure advocated by Peña. Webb also explicitly set out to outdo former Mayor Speer, a progressive mayor of the 1920s, in public infrastructure development and doubling of the city's parks and public areas. He emphasized development of housing downtown and, later, in inner ring neighborhoods by spearheading private activity bonds and creating a revolving loan fund for housing. In addition, Webb articulates a growing concern with the working poor in Denver, which includes primarily Hispanic and black families, as it becomes clear that "the Denver Decade" is not benefiting every family in the city. With a large influx of federal funds for workforce development and youth opportunity programs and state funds devolved to counties for workfare programs, the Webb administration is creating Individual Development Accounts to facilitate homeownership, new business startups, and further education and training for working families. Drawing on General Funds and unexpended TANF (Temporary Assistance to Needy Family) funds, Denver is the first city in the nation to establish a local Earned Income Tax Credit program to benefit working poor families.

The early 1990s thus have witnessed a maintenance and consolidation of the black and Latino political incorporation in Denver that emerged in the 1980s. In the coming decade, Latino political incorporation and influence relative to that of African Americans is likely to be the key issue. Denver is consistently named by *Hispanic Magazine* as one of the "top ten cities in the nation for Hispanics," thanks to the economy, cultural activities, and political opportunities for Hispanics. However, Latino incorporation or "presence" seems not yet to have increased relative to their growth surge: Little evidence suggests it has had an impact beyond a fairly narrow set of concerns in the governmental arena, nor has it altered minority socioeconomic conditions. That is, minority and/or equality concerns do not routinely receive equal footing in general policy processes. The socioeconomic status of minorities also has declined relative to whites (Latino immigration has not been a major issue in Denver until recently). While Denver is willing to extend distributive policies and there has been some redistribution within public sector programs, broader "economic imperatives" limit much activity beyond this. The renewed interest in affordable housing and federal funds now available for workforce development and youth opportunity programs may open the door to new social initiatives in Denver, as in other cities. Whether Latinos and blacks are in a position to shape these policies, however, remains to be seen.

Accounting for Relatively High Latino and Black Political Incorporation

Latino incorporation is relatively high in Denver compared to the 10 northern California cities. At least two variables that were not considered in the Browning, Marshall, and Tabb study seem to be particularly significant regarding the higher representation and incorporation in Denver.

First is the link between residential segregation and minority representation on city council (Vedlitz and Johnson 1982). Denver Latinos have been more residentially segregated than in the northern California cities. Mexican–Anglo segregation in 1970 in Denver was 52.8, but it averaged 37.3 in the five northern California cities for which data were available (see Lopez 1981; Hero 1992).

Residential segregation by ethnicity and race is a persistent pattern in Denver; in the 1990s, dissimilarity indices reported very high rates of segregation for nearly all groups (Table 11.2). Trends toward more diverse neighborhoods are evident, however, especially as whites and blacks lose population share; the overlap of black and Latino communities is especially notable. According to the Lewis Mumford Center (2001), the dissimilarity index for white with black in 2000 dropped to 62.96 from 66.75 in 1990 (60 or higher is ranked as very high segregation). Similar declines occurred for white with Asian (30.75 in 2000, 35.04 in 1990), black with Hispanic (62.27 in 2000, 72.18 in 1990), and black with Asian (58.29 in 2000, 60.6 in 1990). Scores for white with Hispanic increased (57.05 in 2000, 54.95 in 1990), and scores for Hispanic with Asian changed little (46.75 in 2000, 46.31 in 1990). The Isolation Index for Denver shows some greater diversity in primarily white neighborhoods (67.08 per cent white with white in 2000, 73.72 per cent in 1990) and primarily black neighborhoods (35.46 percent black with black in 2000,

TABLE 11.2 **Residential segregation patterns in Denver**

Groups	1990	2000
Dissimilarity Index[a]		
White with black	66.75	62.96
White with Hispanic	54.95	57.05
White with Asian	35.04	30.75
Black with Hispanic	72.18	62.27
Black with Asian	60.60	58.29
Hispanic with Asian	46.31	46.75
Isolation Index[b]		
White with white	73.72	67.08
Black with black	48.21	35.46
Hispanic with Hispanic	44.50	51.86
Asian with Asian	3.72	4.84
Exposure to Other Groups[c]		
White with black	6.98	7.37
White with Hispanic	16.26	20.52
White with Asian	2.25	3.52
Black with Hispanic	14.64	27.43
Black with Asian	2.02	2.83
Hispanic with Asian	2.45	2.86

[a]A score of 60 or higher is ranked as very high segregation. If the score is 40, that means 40 percent of the population would have to move to reach neighborhood parity. A very high score indicates that groups tend to live in different tracts.

[b]Racial/ethnic composition of the tract where the average member of a given group lives. Indicates percentage of the same-group population in the census tract where the average member of a racial/ethnic group lives.

[c]A large value means that the average group member lives in a tract with a higher percentage of persons from another group.

Source: Lewis Mumford Center, 2001.

48.21 percent in 1990). Hispanics were more likely to be clustered together in 2000 (51.86 per cent Hispanic with Hispanic in 2000, 44.5 percent in 1990), as were Asians (4.84 percent Asian with Asian in 2000, 3.72 percent in 1990).

Second, Denver's largely "unreformed" governmental structure also seems to be important. Its strong mayor system, with extensive budgetary and appointment power, permits executive leadership. Its district-based and "professionalized" city council are also distinctive from the cities studied by Browning, Marshall, and Tabb. Minorities seem to be more willing to contact city council members about governmental concerns when those members are elected from districts and are themselves minorities (Heilig and Mundt 1984). Legislative professionalism has impacts on policy outputs (Carmines 1974). It also may have a significant role in institutionalizing influence, including minority influence, at the urban level, in that it provides resources for councilors to give more time and attention to their legislative and related activities, such as "constituency service" or "casework." Historically, Denver's city council members are substantially better paid ($18,675 in 1982, $36,000 in 1994) than those in the California cities studied (*Municipal Yearbook* 1982): by 2001, council member salaries averaged $60,120, with the president of the council earning $67,344. Denver councilors also have staff support, and the council appears to have a more formalized committee structure than in many other cities. These factors would, in turn, be expected to have implications for questions of policy responsiveness.

Given these advantages, we might expect significant minority influence in Denver politics. While the incorporation of blacks and Latinos is beyond question, there are a number of constraints on their ability to fully develop their potential influence in the future. Despite their growing numbers, nearly one-third of the Hispanic population is too young to vote, and many of voting age are not registered (Griego 2001). Latinos also remain constrained by the growing diversity of the Latino population and the divisions of Latinos into citizens and undocumented migrants. These are familiar features in any city with a strong Latino presence, but Latinos in Denver continue to be saddled with historical divisions within their community. These cleavages can be traced back for generations; their current expression seems to be in terms of embracing Latino identity or taking a more pragmatic, meritocratic stance on political issues.

POLICY RESPONSIVENESS

Representation and incorporation are important in themselves, but they must also be considered relative to policy responsiveness. The expectation—and finding—of earlier research was that greater incorporation is related to greater policy responsiveness. Several measures of policy responsiveness have typically been used; the major indicators are replicated here for Denver.

City Government Employment

One measure of policy responsiveness is the proportion of minority employment in city government. When all occupations are considered, Denver is, and has been since at least 1973, above parity for both Latinos and blacks. This employment parity resulted from the demand-protest activities of the mid-1960s in both the black and Chicano communities. The relatively conservative Democratic mayors during this period addressed the demands in part with limited political appointments and through civil service employment. The Peña administration, along with a majority of the council, was supportive of minority public employment, including some at the upper levels and viewed this as something to be addressed because it was the right thing to do, and not only because of political expediency.

Overall, the Peña administration made significant progress in the incorporation of minorities, particularly in key positions of government. Equally notable is the incorporation of minorities into the city's top administrative positions, including the mayor's cabinet and most of the department directors and deputy directors: These appointments—53 positions—are solely under the mayor's discretion, because they are exempt from the city's Career Service Board. In Peña's administration, minorities occupied the most prominent positions in the administration, including the manager of safety, fire chief, manager of general services, director of health and hospitals, and director of parks and recreation.

In the past, however, Denver Latinos also tended to be heavily concentrated in low-level positions and occupations (Hero 1992), with concomitant low employment among officials and administrators in classified positions. In the late 1980s, Denver's parity score for Latino officials and administrators was .62; the black parity score in Denver for this category of employment was about the same as that for Latinos. The data for the 10 northern California cities in 1978 indicates an average of .45; Denver, at about the same time, was somewhat higher (estimate of .57).

The 2000 parity scores for the higher level official and administrator positions demonstrate uneven gains for minority groups in Denver. Based on EEOC reports, the parity score for Latino officials and administrators is now .48. This lower score can be attributed in part to the larger size of the Latino population, but it indicates, at a minimum, a lag in Latino access to upper level employment. In contrast, the parity score for black officials and administrators is 1.23. With one exception, the parity scores for blacks are higher than for Latinos in every job status category; Latinos are overrepresented (1.57) relative to blacks (1.26, also overrepresented) in service/maintenance jobs. Blacks are below parity only in the professional classification (.89); Latinos also are below parity on this job status (.46) and slightly below on technicians and protective services.

There is a gender dimension to this occupational segregation as well: Hispanic women are more likely to be found in higher management, professional, and technical positions than Hispanic men, but they are also more likely to be in paraprofessional, clerical, and skilled craft positions. Black women are less prevalent in higher management positions than black men but are more likely than black men to be in professional and technician as well as paraprofessional, clerical, and skilled craft positions. In contrast, Hispanics (especially women) are hired as contract workers at a much higher rate (57.7 percent vs. 29.7 percent) than blacks.

Contracts and Loans

Another indicator of responsiveness focuses on minority contracting policies. Several measures were used to evaluate city policies regarding special efforts to enhance the opportunities of minority businesses to receive city contracts. First, an assessment was made as to whether the cities had adopted various contracting practices (cf. Browning, Marshall, and Tabb 1984, 161, 284–285), such as specifically targeting minority contractors even if they are not the lowest bidders. Interview responses revealed that, of the six such practices identified, Denver has adopted essentially *all* of them, and the actual *implementation* in Denver of those policies has been seen as moderately aggressive, according to interviewee responses.

Several points are noteworthy here. First, Denver established its policy under the conservative administration of (Democrat) William McNichols at the behest of minority and liberal white council members. Prior to Peña taking office, there were no explicit goals for awarding contracts to minorities and women; consequently, the city only awarded 10 percent of its contracts to minorities—and only 1 percent to women. In 1984, the Peña administration set affirmative action goals for design and construction contracts: to award 20 percent of the city's public works contracts to minority-owned business enterprises and 5 percent to women-owned business enterprises. In 1986, the Peña administration increased its affirmative action goals to 30 percent for minority firms and 6 percent for women. Construction contracts for minorities and women quadrupled after 1984; and all affirmative action goals were met for all years during the Peña administration except 1986. In 1987, the administration announced that a record 35 percent of public works contracts went to minority or women firms (*Rocky Mountain News* 1988).

In the aftermath of the 1989 U.S. Supreme Court decision in *Richmond v. Croson*, which significantly narrowed the grounds on which such minority set-aside programs could withstand judicial scrutiny, Denver undertook studies to justify the continuance of such programs. In 1998, Mayor Webb lowered the goals for minority- and women-owned contracting from 16 percent and 12 percent, respectively, to 10 percent for both.

Another measure of city minority contracting policies has to do with the Community Development Block Grant (CDBG) program, created by the federal government in the mid-1970s, which allocates monies to cities. The legislation called for cities to identify the ethnic/racial background of the owners of firms that receive contracts to carry out work under the program. For the period 1983 to 1987, estimates indicated that, relative to the overall Latino population, Latino businesses in Denver received 64 percent of the contract dollars that parity would imply (based on the authors' calculations and estimates from CDBG data obtained from the U.S. Department of Housing and Urban Development Regional Office, Denver). That for blacks was somewhat higher, over 80 percent. While below parity, these percentages appear comparable to the average for the northern California cities (at an earlier period, 1978; see Browning, Marshall, and Tabb 1984, 162).

In Denver, the CDBG funds are important sources of economic development support, targeted primarily at neighborhoods and businesses. The targeted neighborhoods remain the same as in previous generations of federal programs, but the rapidly shifting ethnic and racial composition of these neighborhoods blurs the identification of beneficiary groups. Through loan programs in these neighborhoods, typically around one-third (in 2000) of the small businesses assisted are owned by minorities (CAPER 2000).

Membership on City Boards and Commissions

"Appointments to [city boards and] commissions enable elected officials to reward supporters, to give at least symbolic representation to groups, and to give ambitious activists the opportunity to gain visibility for future political candidacies" (Browning,

Marshall, and Tabb 1984, 156–157). In Denver, both Peña and Webb have been acutely attuned to this opportunity. As a mayoral candidate, Peña strongly emphasized the importance of such "descriptive" representation in his appointments to boards and commissions. Peña's appointments to boards and commissions during his first administration reflected the city's population, with 16 percent (60) African Americans and 17 percent (64) Latinos in the 373 appointed positions (as reported in Clarke and Saiz 2002). By 1987, Latinos in Denver had a parity score approaching 1.0, while blacks already were above parity (1.34). With the surge in Latino population in the 1990s, the parity score for Latinos on many boards and commissions has declined even though the numbers of representatives may have remained the same. On the Workforce Development Board, the key forum for considering allocations of Workforce Investment Act funds, for example, six of the 30 members are Latino, giving a parity score of .66, whereas black parity is 1.25.

Civilian Police Review Board

Civilian police review boards have been seen as a way of dealing with concerns surrounding police treatment of minorities. Therefore, the presence (or absence) of such a board is another measure of policy responsiveness (Browning, Marshall, and Tabb 1984, 152–155).

The Denver was slow to establish a civilian police review board, though such a board was discussed with some frequency during the late 1970s and 1980s. Interestingly, the election of Peña in 1983 seemed to dampen rather than increase discussions on this matter (cf. Browning, Marshall, and Tabb 1984, 155–156). Peña's election—and his position as chief executive of the city's bureaucracy, with the power to appoint the head of the Department of Public Safety and the police chief—seemingly allayed minority concerns about police treatment (author interviews). In 1992, however, with the leadership of a black city council member and over the opposition of the police department and the black mayor, a civilian review board was established. For the last five years, black representation on the Public Safety Review Commission has been above parity; Latino representation has been near parity (.97) (Table 11.3). Though a Latino headed the public safety department, a series of controversies appeared to weaken public support. The board is now headed by a Latina, with another Latina serving on the Commission.

TABLE 11.3   Representation on Denver Public Safety Review Commission, 1996–2000

Year	Whites	Latinos	Blacks	Asians
1996	2	2	2	1
1997	3	2	1	1
1998	3	2	1	1
1999	2	1	1	0
2000	2	2	2	0

School Reform

While the remarkable Latino growth reflected in the 2000 U.S. Census figures surprised many observers, the signs were evident in the public school system throughout the 1990s. By the end of the 1990s, the Denver public school system was 51 percent Hispanic, 23.4 percent white, and 26 percent African American. With the end of the desegregation orders in 1996, various constraints on local control of the schools were removed; however, like many cities, Denver has an independently elected school board and superintendent rather than any direct, formal authority granted to city officials. As a result, many of the issues most salient and significant to parents of color are settled in an arena separate from the influence of the mayor and city council.

Political incorporation and representation in citywide offices can pale in significance to the influence wielded by the officials who control local schools. Thus, we consider the Denver public school system an arena of great significance to Latinos and blacks as the new public school constituencies. Applying measures of representational parity on the school board (as we did for the city council and other city government bodies), we find that blacks were near or above parity for 4 of the 6 years (1993–1996) when comparing their board representation to their share of the public school population as well as of city population (Table 11.4). During the past five years, an African-American male served as president of the school board; no Latino/as have ever been in this position.

In contrast to black scores, Latinos were substantially below parity all six years on both measures. Somewhat similar patterns exist for school administrators: Blacks were significantly above parity for all six years on both measures, and Latinos were

TABLE 11.4   Representation in Denver public school governance, 1992–2001

Year	Whites	Latinos	Blacks
Board of Education			
1992	5	1	1
1993	6	1	2
1994	4	0	2
1995	7	1	2
1996	6	1	2
2001	4	2	1
Denver School Administrators			
1992	4	3	2
1993	4	3	2
1994	4	3	2
1995	4	2	3
1996	5	2	2
2001	5	1	3

above parity from 1992 to 1994 relative to their share of the city population but well below parity every year compared to their share of the school population. A black woman served as school superintendent for several years in the early 1990s, while no Latino/as have held this position.

As in other public school systems (Stone, Henig, and Jones 2001; Henig, Hula, Orr, and Pedescleaux 1999; Hess 1999), the lifting of the desegregation orders in Denver opened the door to myriad reform options and advocates. While Colorado voters consistently reject school vouchers at the polls, the state and the city of Denver are home to numerous charter and magnet schools. Denver also relies on open enrollment, school-based, collaborative decision-making units, neighborhood schools, and other school reform options. The state recently embarked on a statewide "report card" initiative aimed at increasing school-based accountability, though it does not take into account the differing contexts in which schools operate or the resources available to them.

Despite this flurry of school reform, the performance of Latino and black children in the Denver public schools remains low. The introduction of the Colorado State Assessment Program (CSAP) in 1997 allowed comparisons of students and schools on a yearly basis. While Denver schools consistently score below state averages, there is no strict correlation between student ethnicity or racial identity and CSAP scores. The most heartening description of CSAP scores is "a mixed bag". Some Denver schools with high enrollments of students of color and from disadvantaged backgrounds report gains in proficiency, but most struggle with scores significantly lower than those of more diverse schools in more affluent neighborhoods.

In 2000, for the first time, more than 50 percent of third-graders in each major ethnic group, including black, Hispanic, and American Indian, were proficient or advanced in reading. The percentage of white students passing the test exceeded 80 percent for the first time. In addition, more than 50 percent of students in federally funded Title I programs, which target schools with high numbers of low-income students, were proficient or advanced in reading, up from 33 percent only three years before. Nevertheless, the Colorado Civil Rights Commission is investigating a petition filed on behalf of black children regarding failure of the public high schools to educate them.

Literacy and school achievement are not the only concerns for parents of color. Representation issues arise in teacher patterns: more than three-fourths of the teachers in Denver public schools are white, while less than one-fourth of the students are. In the 1998–1999 school year, 36 percent of suspended or expelled students were black (with blacks accounting for only 20 percent of the school population). Racial tracking is also a concern: although only 24 percent of students are white, 46 percent of the gifted and talented students are. Students 4 Justice, a student group linked to the Colorado Progressive Coalition, surveyed students at East High School and reported that minority students were three times less likely to be placed in advanced placement or accelerated classes than white students.

One of the most salient concerns—bilingual education—splits the Latino community. There is little agreement among Latinos on the best language acquisition strategies—and little interest among blacks in this debate. Several high schools now teach predominantly Spanish-speaking math and science classes, and many elementary and middle schools feature such classes. The school district adopted a compromise English Acquisition Program in 1999, but a Latina activist formerly on the school board joined forces with the English Only advocate from California, Ron Unz, to promote a initiative for the 2001 ballot that would dismantle bilingual education programs throughout the state. This issue is now before the state court.

With these continuing issues of school reform and disparities in school achievement, the salient representation and incorporation issues in Denver often extend beyond the formal structures of city government. Latinos lag seriously in representation and incorporation in the education arena. Blacks are better represented and incorporated in school administration, but black students remain ill-served by the public school system as well. The lifting of the desegregation order and the end of busing, along with the annual publication of student and school proficiency scores, generated renewed local and neighborhood interest in schools. Latinos and blacks bring different experiences and preferences to school reform issues (Clarke et al. 2001), however, so the prospects for multiethnic coalitions are tenuous. As the dominant groups in Denver public schools, blacks and especially Latinos are the new public school constituencies, but their voices are often competing and have yet to shape the educational agenda in Denver in the post-desegregation era.

CONCLUSION

This analysis affirms that the variables previously specified by Browning, Marshall, and Tabb continue to be significant in understanding racial politics in U.S. cities. These variables, particularly those concerning city population size, minority growth rates, and governmental structure, seem to be significant in explaining the different levels of political mobilization of Denver's minority communities relative to the northern California cities. At minimum, these findings indicate that the low levels of Latino and African-American representation and incorporation—and the resultant low policy responsiveness—found in a number of other cities are *not* universal.

A complete understanding of why this is the case escapes easy explanation, but we highlight the importance of governmental structure and professionalism, residential segregation, city position, and ethnic and racial balance. The Browning, Marshall, and Tabb study was quite cognizant regarding the potential impact of governmental structure but was unable to systematically or extensively examine its impact. The 10 cities they studied were all basically "reformed"; thus, there simply was not sufficient variation for analysis. It is therefore notable that in Denver, with its unreformed structure, including a strong mayor system and minority mayors since 1983, political representation, incorporation, and responsiveness are substantially greater than in the northern California cities. Denver's well-paid, well-staffed city council underscores the importance of legislative professionalism; the mix of at-large and district seats means that local representatives have both the motivation and the resources to respond to their neighborhood constituencies. Given the continuing patterns of residential segregation in Denver, these neighborhood constituencies are often distinguished by their ethnic or racial character. In the wake of the 2000 U.S. Census and in the context of term limits, the changing ethnic and racial mix in many neighborhoods could result in greater descriptive representation on the city council if Latinos can overcome their historical divisions.

Denver is the largest and most visible city in the state, the state capital, and the most prominent city in the Rocky Mountain region. These factors—alone and in combination—magnify the importance of such variables as city population size, governmental structure, and the like. Moreover, Denver's minority population, while substantial, is not as large or, perhaps, as "threatening" as those in other cities. Whether the remarkable increase in Latino population upsets this delicate balance remains to be seen. The minority politicians who have emerged have, for the most part, been moderate to liberal, but they also have pursued agendas that are compatible with larger city concerns. Indeed, despite the signal successes of Peña as the city's first Mexican-American Mayor and of Webb as its first African-American mayor, their policy agendas are not informed by ethnic and racial concerns. Given the structural constraints on American mayors, every mayor of Denver will be oriented to the "big picture, big ticket" priorities, such as convention centers and other economic development concerns. Peña and Webb recognized the importance of "small opportunities" as well: both appointed significant numbers of Latino, African American, and some Asians to top exempt positions in their administrations as well as to the many boards and commissions involved in local governance. Both also changed the "rules of the game" during their administrations to give greater voice to neighborhood interests in planning, transportation, housing, and workforce development issues. This not only contributed to the sense of political representation and incorporation of African Americans and Latinos, it also created an intricate web of personal ties, shared language, and common experiences among the multiethnic, multiracial community leadership.

Although some outcomes for racial/ethnic minority groups in Denver seem "better" than in other cities, the struggle of Latinos and blacks for equality clearly continues. In the past, emerging trends, both locally and nationally, suggested a "steady-state" for minority influence in Denver (Hero 1997); indeed, the concern was for the decline of that influence as prominent national, state, and local officials openly and aggressively challenged policies that contributed to the level of minority incorporation and policy responsiveness found in Denver and elsewhere. Now, the demographic shift in Denver indicates that the "sleeping giant" of Latino political influence may be rising, with the prospects for a very different political future. There is little consensus on a Latino political agenda, however, much less one that would reflect the shared concerns of blacks and Latinos over poverty, affordable housing, safety, health care, and neighborhood well-being. Many salient issues also seem to be beyond the control of local officials: affirmative action is circumscribed by the courts, health care and welfare reform have devolved to state levels, local schools are independent of city officials, and old age and pension programs are threatened at the national level.

Whether whites, Latinos, African Americans, and Asians in Denver collaborate, compete, or go their own way on these issues remains to be seen. In a sense, anticipating a policy consensus among Latinos and/or blacks implies their political incorporation patterns will parallel those of white ethnics. That is a possible outcome, but our analysis suggests that the political and cultural dimensions of African-American and Latino identities, at least in the American west, preclude such common, converging patterns. These contested political identities—complicated by class, cultural, and generational splits—make political mobilization and incorporation a complex matter in western U.S. cities.

In many ways, the "successes" of Peña and Webb in Denver are similar to those of Tom Bradley in Los Angeles and of Norman Rice in Seattle, suggesting that large, multiethnic, multiracial cities in the western United States offer a distinctive version of political incorporation. Although the seeming successes of mayors of color and their relatively progressive, multiracial regimes in these cities are compelling, they also are vulnerable to the frailties that undermined the equally visible biracial coalition in Atlanta. As Stone (2001) notes, Atlanta's biracial coalition functioned effectively on physical redevelopment and school desegregation issues, but it faltered in the face of changing economic and social conditions demanding different capacities and new forms of collaboration. Now, as city agendas evolve to include the working poor, low-performing schools, workforce development and livable wages, and lack of health care, the coalitions mobilized by Peña and Webb around making Denver a world-class city will be open to similar challenges. As Denver and other cities grapple with increasingly multiethnic and multiracial populations and the politics of democratic inclusion that this entails, the factors identified in the mobilization/representation/incorporation framework (Browning, Marshall, and Tabb, 1984) may prove to be necessary, if not sufficient, elements for understanding these new political alignments and agendas.

REFERENCES

Aguilar, Louis. 2001. "New Growth" of Immigrants Adds to State's Boom. *Denver Post*, May 3, C1.

Bingham, Janet. 2001. CSAP's a Mixed Bag. *Denver Post*, July 21.

Booth, Michael. 1997. "Reclaiming the Rockies: Where's a Worker to Live?" *The Denver Post*, October 27, A–01.

Browning, Rufus P., Dale Rogers Marshall, and David H. Tabb. 1984. *Protest Is Not Enough: The Struggle of Blacks and Hispanics for Equality in Urban Politics*. Berkeley: University of California Press.

Browning, Rufus P., Dale Rogers Marshall, and David H. Tabb. 1990. *Racial Politics in American Cities*. New York: Longman.

Browning, Rufus P., Dale Rogers Marshall, and David H. Tabb. 1997. *Racial Politics in American Cities*, 2nd ed. New York: Longman.

CAPER (Consolidated Annual Performance and Evaluation Report). 2000. Strengthening Denver's Community. Denver: Housing and Neighborhood Development Services.

Carmines, Edward. 1974. The Mediating Influence of State Legislatures on the Linkage Between Interparty Competition and Welfare Policies. *American Political Science Review* 68 (September): 1118–1124.

Clarke, Susan E., and Martin Saiz. 2002. From Waterhole to World City: Place-Luck and Public Agendas in Denver. In Dennis Judd and Alan Artibise, eds., *The Infrastructure of Urban Tourism*. New York: M. E. Sharpe.

Clarke, Susan E., and Rodney E. Hero, with Mara Sidney, Luis Fraga, and Bari Anhalt Erlichson. 2001. *The New Populism: The Multiethnic Politics of Education Reform*. Manuscript in preparation.

Colorado Department of Labor and Employment. 1990. Census EEO Special File: Detailed Occupations by Sex and Race, Ethnicity.

Denver Post. 2001. Editorial: Equity Missing in Housing. July 6, Section A.

Griego, Tina. 2001. Hispanics a Multicultural Nation of Our Own. *Denver Post*, March 21, B1.

Heilig, Peggy, and Robert J. Mundt. 1984. *Your Voice at City Hall*. Albany: State University of New York Press.

Henig, Jeffrey R., Richard C. Hula, Marion Orr, and Desiree S. Pedescleaux. 1999. *The Color of School Reform*. Princeton, NJ: Princeton University Press.

Hero, Rodney E. 1987. The Election of Hispanics in City Government: An Analysis of the Election of Federico Pena as Mayor of Denver. *Western Political Quarterly* 40 (March): 93–105.

Hero, Rodney E. 1992. *Latinos and the U.S. Political System: Two-tiered Pluralism*. Philadelphia: Temple University Press.

Hero, Rodney E. 1997. Latinos and Politics in Denver and Pueblo, Colorado: Differences, Explanations, and the "Steady-State" of the Struggle for Equality. In Rufus P. Browning, Dale Rogers Marshall, and David H. Tabb, eds., *Racial Politics in American Cities*, 247–258. New York: Longman.

Hero, Rodney E., and Kathleen M. Beatty. 1989. The Elections of Federico Peña as Mayor of Denver: Analysis and Implications. *Social Science Quarterly* 70 (June): 300–310.

Hess, Frederick M. 1999 *Spinning Wheels: The Politics of Urban School Reform*. Washington, DC: Brookings.

Judd, Dennis, and Randy Ready. 1986. Entrepreneurial Cities and the New Economic Development. In George Peterson and Carol Lewis, eds., *Reagan and the Cities*, 209–247. Washington, DC: Urban Institute Press.

Leonard, Stephen J., and Thomas J. Noel. 1990. *Denver: Mining Camp to Metropolis*. Niwot: University Press of Colorado.

Lewis Mumford Center for Comparative Urban and Regional Research, State University of Albany. 2001. Metropolitan Racial and Ethnic Change—Census 2000 (http://mumford1 .dyndns.org/cen2000/WholePop/WPsegdata.htm)

Lopez, Manuel M. 1981. Pattern of Interethnic Residential Segregation in the Urban Southwest. *Social Science Quarterly* 62 1 (March): 50–63.

Lovrich, Nicholas, and Otwin Marenin. 1976. A Comparison of Black and Mexican-American Voters in Denver: Assertive Versus Acquiescent Political Orientations and Voting Behavior in an Urban Electorate. *Western Political Quarterly* 29 (June): 284–294.

Meier, Kenneth, and Joseph Stewart, Jr. 1991. *The Politics of Hispanic Education*. Albany, NY: State University of New York Press.

Municipal Yearbook. 1982. International City Managers' Association.

Piton Foundation. 1994. *Poverty in Denver: Facing the Facts*. Denver: The Piton Foundation.

Piton Foundation. 1999. *Neighborhood Facts 1999*. Denver: The Piton Foundation.

Rocky Mountain News. 1988. February 18.

Saiz, Martin. 1988. Progressive Politics and Fiscal Austerity: The Experience of the Peña Administration. Paper presented at the annual meeting of the Western Political Science Association, San Francisco.

Stone, Clarence. 2001. The Atlanta Experience Re-examined: The Link Between Agenda and Regime Change. *International Journal of Urban and Regional Research* 25: 20–34.

Stone, Clarence, Jeff Henig, and Bryan Jones. 2001. *Building Civic Capacity*. Lawrence: University Press of Kansas.

Stone, Clarence N. 1990. Race and Regime in Atlanta. In Rufus P. Browning, Dale Rogers Marshall, and David H. Tabb, eds., *Racial Politics in American Cities*, 125–139. New York: Longman.

U.S. Department of Housing and Urban Development. 2001. *State of the Cities Data System* (http://socds.huduser.org/Census).

Vedlitz, Arnold, and Charles A. Johnson. 1982. Community Racial Segregation, Electoral Structure, and Minority Representation. *Social Science Quarterly* 63 (December): 729–736.

Part VI

Strategies and Prospects

Chapter 12

The Prospects for Multiracial Coalitions: Lessons from America's Three Largest Cities

Raphael J. Sonenshein

EDITORS' NOTE

Politically excluded groups often debate the best strategies to improve their position. Should they go it alone or form coalitions? If they enter into coalitions, will an appeal to shared ideology be sufficient to hold the coalition together, or will it be necessary to make major concessions to the material interests of other members? And can the experience gained through the minority incorporation model be helpful in the more diverse and multipolar world of today's big city arena? What does the rise of white-led regimes in most large cities mean for the study of minority incorporation? What are the implications of the sudden rise of Latino politics in major cities?

In this chapter, Raphael J. Sonenshein explores in the multiracial setting a model of coalition politics he developed in the study of biracial coalitions. His approach begins with a critique of the idea that only self-interest can animate coalitions; ideology is crucial to coalition success. Good will alone is not enough, but neither is cold self-interest. But even ideology is not enough without creative and determined leadership to navigate the shoals of interest conflict. He finds that in America's largest cities, the linkages of ideology and interest among potential minority allies have weakened, and that progressive leadership for such coalitions is in severe disrepair.

Sonenshein finds that white-led regimes have capitalized on interest and ideology conflicts within the minority-progressive alliance and have been able to capture the community's ideological center. Progressive leaders have become bogged down in the politics of diversity rather than developing agendas for solving community-wide problems. The rise of Latinos creates a new setting for minority politics in which the old paradigms of ideology and race have been dramatically altered and in which a two-headed minority struggle for equality by both African Americans and Latinos animates and complicates coalition politics. In addition to new options for minority

333

coalitions and the possibility of mix-and-match coalition politics, there is increased danger of minority isolation. To bring about a resurgence of minority-progressive influence, leaders of potential coalitions must both relearn the lessons of earlier coalitions and stake out new and creative territory in issues that concern both minority and non-minority communities.

T he debate over the viability of interracial coalition politics has been an enduring and intensely argued one. Should racial minorities go it alone, join forces
with other minorities against the majority, or form alliances with elements of the
majority group?

I have previously developed a theory of interracial coalition within the context
of black–white relations. Only a mixture of interest and ideology, shaped by leadership, can overcome the numerous barriers to the success of coalitions crossing
racial and ethnic lines (Sonenshein 1993). In this chapter, I apply the same three-
part model to the complex task of evaluating the prospects for multiracial coalitions.
Are multiracial coalitions viable in political settings of increasing diversity and
weakening liberal strength? What are the implications of the defeat of black-led
electoral coalitions by white-led alliances in the three largest U.S. cities in the closing years of the twentieth century? How does the rising level of participation by
Latinos affect the prospects for multiracial coalitions? What roles do institutional differences in the three cities play in the prospects for multiracial coalitions?

A THEORY OF COALITION

Since the mid-1960s, urban politics have been profoundly influenced by race and
the ideological divisions that grow from racial division. Indeed, throughout
American politics, the racial barrier redefined opinions, attitudes, and alignments.
The meanings of conservative and liberal ideologies have been deeply influenced
by their relationship to race (Edsall and Edsall 1991; Carmines and Stimson 1989).

As racial matters came to a boil in the mid-1960s, African Americans had to
choose among several paths. This practical decision in turn depended on a more
theoretical question: What is the most solid basis on which to build coalitions?

The debate over interracial coalitions is highly political and pragmatic, but it is
also an argument over a *theory* of biracial coalitions. The optimists focus on the
role of *ideology* and emphasize the enduring and solid character of biracial coalitions based on common beliefs. The pessimists see *interest* as the glue of coalitions
and view biracial coalitions as, at best, short-lived compromises between self-centered groups.

An active scholarly debate on racial issues divides along roughly the same lines.
One school of thought suggests that pre-existing racial attitudes deeply influence
perception of racial issues; in this sense, racial politics is at root ideological (Kinder
and Sears 1981). Regardless of the political situation, some whites are more racially
liberal than others, and this attitude shapes their political actions. A contrasting view

holds that racial conflict can be understood as a realistic power struggle between groups. Because whites identify with other whites in the face of a black challenge, they protect their group interests through racial hostility (Giles and Gatlin 1980; Bobo 1983; Giles and Evans 1986). In this view, political actions are affected by the political situation of individuals and groups.

Thus, the study of biracial electoral coalitions can be seen as a test case in a more general debate regarding the roots of racial conflict and co-operation. What is more important in racial coalitions: good will, or practical calculation?

In their classic *Black Power* (1967), Carmichael and Hamilton argued that the good will that underlay the civil rights movement was no longer adequate for the new era of racial polarization. Rather, they favored self-interest as the glue of coalitions and believed that communities of color and class had the best chance of forming such pragmatic alliances. This view coincided with a widespread move to exclude white liberals from minority political organizations. As African-American communities moved toward citywide power in many cities, the evidence both supported and contradicted Carmichael and Hamilton's view.

Minority power arose from a combination of minority unity and mobilization, as suggested by Carmichael and Hamilton, and the support of liberal whites, as suggested by those who favored a role for liberal ideology. Starting in 1967, cities with large African-American populations began to generate black mayoral candidacies. The first black mayors were elected in 1967 in Cleveland and Gary. Newark elected a black mayor in 1970, and Los Angeles and Detroit followed suit in 1973.

Despite enormous differences among cities, the coalitions of the African-American candidates, and the alliances that opposed them, were similar across cities. Black mayoral candidates drew overwhelming black support; the youngest, most liberal, and best-educated whites, particularly Jews; and mixed support from Latinos. Less educated, less liberal whites provided the hard core of opposition (Pettigrew 1971; Halley, Acock, and Greene 1976; Hahn, Klingman, and Pachon 1976).

Win or lose, African-American candidates could rely on black voters to provide virtually unanimous and enthusiastic support. The margin of victory would come from inroads into white constituencies and increasing support among Latinos. Instead of a class alliance of the economically disadvantaged, the biracial coalitions that carried black candidates into power were a mixture of racial identification among blacks, ideological affinity with some whites, and some racial and class solidarity with Latinos.

Browning, Marshall, and Tabb's study of the political incorporation of minorities in 10 northern California cities (1984) found that whether or not African Americans were mayoral candidates, the coalitions for minority "incorporation" involved the same mixture of groups. Mobilization and unity among blacks were combined with the support of liberal whites (and often Latinos) into a winning liberal coalition. Their research strongly supported the roles of race and ideology in the development of minority power. Their work also pointed to the importance of coalitions between African Americans and liberal whites, with additional support from Latinos.

My application of the Browning, Marshall, and Tabb model found that the same pattern defined modern Los Angeles politics (Sonenshein 1993). Whether the issue was taxes, board of education races, voting for partisan offices, or ballot measures to ensure police accountability, the pattern was the same: Blacks were the most liberal, joined in coalition to liberal whites and Latinos in opposition to the most conservative whites. Tom Bradley's six mayoral campaigns between 1969 and 1989 (all but one of which was successful) confirmed the pattern: he carried the African-American community; did extremely well with liberal whites, particularly Jews; and drew increasingly strong support from Latinos (Sonenshein 1993).

The ideological underpinnings of minority political incorporation have been so consistent that ideology must be considered the central factor in the success of such coalitions. Ideological differences among whites, as demonstrated by Browning, Marshall, and Tabb, are indeed crucial to minority political success. The case of limited and precarious minority incorporation in New York City, however, where historically white liberalism has been very strong, creates what John Mollenkopf, in this volume, has called "the great anomaly." Los Angeles has been a less liberal city than New York City, but its level of minority incorporation has been far greater and more durable.

Just as Carmichael and Hamilton predicted, conflict of interest between minorities and white liberals greatly weakened the possibilities for interracial coalitions in New York City. White liberals were highly represented in the civic institutions, particularly the schools, that came under attack by minority activists during the 1960s. By contrast, the minority surge in Los Angeles was tied to the struggle of white liberals, particularly Jews, for representation in Los Angeles civic life; the coalition of outsiders represented a fundamental alliance of interest.

Neither ideology nor interest fully explains coalition outcomes, however. Group relations are not simply the outcome of objective interests or poll-measured attitudes. Political actions are taken by human beings and are therefore affected by the actions of leaders who themselves seek out trusting relationships with other political actors.

Drawing on Hinckley's (1981) critique of coalition theory, I argue that the outcome of interracial coalitions is profoundly shaped and influenced by leadership. Leaders and organizers have an impact on how group interests are perceived. The prospects for biracial coalitions depend heavily on the willingness and ability of leaders to create and sustain such coalitions. In matters of race, leaders may find it easier to overcome interest conflicts among ideological allies than to create an interest alliance among ideological foes.

The presence of outstanding interracial leadership in Los Angeles made a great contribution to the black community's extraordinary success in winning political incorporation. The trust among the long-time Bradley forces made them coherent, cohesive, and united in the face of political challenges. The effective leadership of Harold Washington was critical to the Chicago success story, as demonstrated by that coalition's collapse after his sudden death in 1987. In New York City, interracial leadership networks were weak, internally divided, and vulnerable to demagoguery from the outside.

In the last decade of the twentieth century, the prospects for interracial coalitions were clouded by changes in political context and demographics. First, the rise of white Republican mayors in Los Angeles and New York City and of moderate white Democratic mayors in Philadelphia and Chicago during the late 1980s and early 1990s showed that the electoral base for minority incorporation had dramatically declined. Second, immigration changed the demographics of American cities, creating a greater degree of multiethnicity. Coalition politics became more than a matter of crossing the white–black divide. New forms of minority assertion appeared, exemplified by strong Latino mayoral candidacies in both New York City and Los Angeles in 2001.

Has electoral defeat for African Americans by whites and the increasing prominence of Latinos meant the rollback of minority political gains? Has there been a long-term change in the structure of urban politics? Has the period marked by racial and ideological divisions ended, or were these divisions merely a shift of victors in a political structure that had not fundamentally altered? How durable was the realignment of urban politics that began in the mid-1960s, when the racial struggle moved from the South into the big cities of the nation? What are the prospects for multiracial coalitions as a replacement for the liberal biracial coalitions of the recent past?

The historical approach to coalition presented by Hinckley (1981) suggests caution in declaring the old world dead. Coalition patterns evolve slowly; old patterns die hard and can even be regenerated. The challenge is to separate the enduring from the new as cities move from a biracial to a multiracial focus.

To some conservatives and moderates, the earlier pattern of racial and ethnic division has become obsolete. In this view, African-American politicians and their white liberal allies were keeping alive a set of racial divisions against the wishes of the voters. Jim Sleeper (1993, 20), a perceptive New York City journalist, referred to "the rainbow ideology's tendency to deepen racial and other differences in the name of respecting them; in the zero-sum game of urban governance, politics implodes." Sleeper (1993, 20) attributed the victories of new mayors, most of them white, to new coalitions:

> It's a familiar pattern. Beyond New York, the Rainbow habit of crying racism has found itself discounted by voters of all colors who want better governance and less rhetoric. Politically centrist mayoral candidates, many of them, ironically, white men, have drawn substantial numbers of nonwhite voters into new coalitions—call them Rainbow II—by touting a can-do pragmatism and a common civic identity that is more than the sum of skin tones, genders, sexual orientations, and resentments.

The implication of Sleeper's argument is that some change has occurred in the structure of city politics—one that black leaders and their supporters have failed to grasp—in which race and ideology play less central roles than before. Others argue there has been no real decline in the election of African-American mayors (Alozie 2000), and that the "new" mayors are more anomalies than indicators of a broad turn away from urban liberalism (Keiser 1997).

To assess these views of the future of minority politics, we turn to the experience of the nation's three largest cities, in which the defeat of minority-led coalitions and the rise of diverse populations have challenged the nature of coalition politics.

NEW YORK, LOS ANGELES, AND CHICAGO

The three largest American cities represent alternative urban models. New York City and Chicago are both older cities with traditional party structures deriving from their industrialization in the nineteenth century. In that sense, they share many qualities with a large number of eastern and midwestern U.S. cities. Liberalism and the norms of the welfare state have dominated New York City, while pragmatic governance by a political machine has been the leading force in Chicago.

The institutional structure of cities has been increasingly recognized as a profound influence on how groups compete for power and how policy is made. Barbara Ferman's (1996) influential analysis of citizen participation contrasted the success of neighborhood organizations in Pittsburgh with the pattern of resistance they experienced in Chicago, and she traced these differences to the contrasting political structures of the cities.

Institutional structure and the political culture that shapes it should also affect how interest, ideology, and leadership develop in *racial* politics. Michael Jones-Correa (2001) has built on Ferman's model to contrast the "horizontal" structure of Los Angeles, with its reform institutions and decentralized politics, to the "vertical" structure of New York City. His analysis helps to explain why Los Angeles responded to the 1992 civil disorder with a private-sector response while New York City responded more successfully to such challenges with a greater focus on government. Mollenkopf, Olson, and Ross (2001) have presented a similar analysis comparing the incorporation of immigrants in New York City and Los Angeles. They argued that New York City has more political institutions that can play an integrating role for immigrants than Los Angeles.

A three-way comparison among the three largest cities is useful, because with Chicago in the mix, New York City appears more vertical than Los Angeles but less vertical than Chicago. With its dominant Democratic party organization, Chicago offers the possibility of truly centralized control. Under Mayor Richard M. Daley, the city government exercises great sway. The Chicago city council is virtually a rubber stamp for the mayor (McCann 2001). By contrast, the long-derided New York city council is at least potentially troublesome for the mayor since 1989 Charter reforms increased its authority (Schwartz and Lane 1998). The Los Angeles city council is by far the strongest of the three, even after 1999 Charter reforms shaved back some of its administrative authority.

Los Angeles has the greater affinity to the model presented by Browning, Marshall, and Tabb. Like the 10 northern California cities they studied, Los Angeles has been deeply imbued with the reform philosophy and nonpartisan local structure that found its greatest expression in the West (Shefter 1983). With the Democratic party organization weak or absent, biracial coalition politics became the vehicle by which excluded minorities and their white liberal allies went from the outside to the inside, winning strong incorporation into the city government (Sonenshein 1993).

Los Angeles is a model of the newer western U.S. cities developed in the late nineteenth and early twentieth centuries and shaped by midwestern Protestant migrants who hoped to devise an urban alternative to the "old, corrupt" cities of the east and midwest (Fogelson 1967; Singleton 1979). The antiparty norms of the Progressive movement found their greatest expression in the West (Shefter 1983) and were central to development of the Los Angeles political community. Party organization has been virtually nonexistent in Los Angeles (Adrian 1959; Carney 1964), representing the polar opposite of Chicago.

In demographic terms, the three cities represent different points on a spectrum (Table 12.1). Chicago has the largest black population, nearly 40 percent. Los Angeles is the smallest at 11 percent (a decline from 14 percent in 1990). New York City is in the middle at 25 percent. Both New York City and Chicago have large populations of Eastern European Catholic immigrant groups, but New York is by far the larger center of Jewish population. Together, metropolitan New York and Los Angeles hold 60 percent of America's Jews (Fisher 1979).

Los Angeles has by far the largest Latino population (47 percent) of the three cities, and it lacks the working-class white Catholic group so prominent in New York City and Chicago. Its black population is the smallest of the three cities. Of the three, New York has the largest Jewish population and Chicago the smallest (3 percent). Los Angeles has the second-largest Jewish community in the nation (an estimated 6 percent). Chicago's Latino population has dramatically increased from the 1990 U.S. Census, to a quarter of the city.

In my earlier work (1993), I proposed to explain why coalition politics developed so differently in the nation's three largest cities. Why had Los Angeles, the city with the smallest black population, managed to develop by far the strongest biracial coalition? Why had New York City, with its long tradition of liberalism, been most notable for the failure of its interracial politics? Why had Chicago reached a higher degree of biracial politics around Harold Washington than occurred in the more liberal climate of New York City?

In the 1990s, these cities continued to differ among themselves, but there was also one striking commonality. All three were marked by the succession of white mayors not supported by the vast majority of African Americans to posts previously held by black mayors. In Los Angeles and New York City, voters elected Republican mayors. In Chicago, Richard M. Daley replaced the powerful minority-led regime of Harold Washington with a highly stable and politically successful restoration of the Democratic party machine built around white and Latino voters.

TABLE 12.1   Population by group, 2000

		Percent			
	Population	*White*	*Black*	*Latino*	*Asian*
New York City	8,008,278	35.0	24.5	27.0	9.7
Los Angeles	3,694,820	29.7	10.9	46.5	9.9
Chicago	2,896,016	31.3	36.4	26.0	4.3

Source: U.S. Bureau of the Census, 2000.

In all three cities, progressive forces have been stymied in mounting a challenge to the new white-led regimes. Although African-American mayors continue to be elected in American cities (Alozie 2000), the disproportionate impact of the largest cities on the formation of political coalitions requires special attention.

Why did minority liberalism falter in America's three largest cities? What does that failure mean for the future of minority politics? Los Angeles had by far the longest run of biracial coalition rule. In Chicago, Harold Washington's death in 1987 was followed almost immediately by the defeat of the liberal coalition he had built to win the mayor's office in 1983 and 1987. In New York City, David Dinkins's mayoralty lasted only one term, ending with his defeat in 1993. By contrast, Tom Bradley held office in Los Angeles for 20 years, finally stepping down in 1993. His predicted successor, Michael Woo, was solidly defeated by white Republican Richard Riordan. Liberal coalitions have been unable to create citywide winning majorities in all three of the largest American cities.

As the twentieth century ended, however, the cities diverged once again. Chicago maintained its white-dominated Democratic party regime behind Richard M. Daley, Jr., and New York City voters elected another white Republican, Michael Bloomberg, as mayor after Rudolph Giuliani. According to Mollenkopf (this volume), Bloomberg's coalition strongly resembled the white-dominated alliance behind Giuliani. Bloomberg's election overcame term limits to continue the Giuliani alliance, marked by the outgoing mayor's strong endorsement. Chicago and New York City continued with their white-led moderate coalitions; in each city, African-American and Hispanic political forces were muted.

Los Angeles went in a different direction, however, and ventured into uncharted territory. Los Angeles voters chose a new mayor, James K. Hahn, whose victory was built on the unlikely foundation of African Americans and conservative and moderate whites. A liberal Latino candidate also came close to winning the mayoralty. Once again, Los Angeles had diverged from the path of the other two largest cities. Oddly, the city with the decentralized, horizontal structure had fostered the creation of not one but two minority movements that were strong enough to compete for citywide leadership. This result casts some doubt on both Mollenkopf's and Jones-Correa's conclusions that Los Angeles' reform structure made interracial coalition building and minority empowerment more difficult than in New York City and Chicago in a multiethic era.

Ironically, the new condition in Los Angeles has made white liberals politically vulnerable even as new forms of minority assertion have arisen. The mayor's election was supported by blacks (although dismay at his refusal to call for the reappointment of black police chief Bernard Parks soon devastated that support), but also by the conservative police union. The council president, Alex Padilla, is Latino and allied with Hahn.

Even in the absence of a ruling liberal coalition, African Americans have managed to pull partially out of their political isolation under Riordan to join the winning mayoral coalition and to hold their 20 percent share of city council seats. There is no denying the rising power of Latinos compared to African Americans, but the black community has not gone away or lost all its sway.

In the 2002 redistricting of Los Angeles city council seats, the citizens's commission appointed by the city council to advise it on a plan for the 15 seats adopted as its main principles maintenance of the three African-American seats, an increase in Latino seats from four to five, and five seats in the San Fernando Valley. In other words, the political representation of minorities has been institutionalized. In fact, the one community that was likely to lose a seat in the Los Angeles Council redistricting was the white liberal Westside (McGreevy 2002).

Thus, only in Los Angeles has minority empowerment adapted itself in a new way to the two sets of pressures on the old system: the difficulty of liberal coalitions in defeating white moderate alliances, and the rise of Latinos. Yet this has not increased the odds of liberal interracial coalitions. What, then, are the roles of ideology, interest, and leadership in interracial coalitions during the early part of the twenty-first century?

IDEOLOGY

A central pillar of biracial coalition politics has been ideological affinity between minority groups and whites. Racial liberalism among whites was the principal predictor of white support for minority political interests (Browning, Marshall, and Tabb 1984). A second pillar has been the ideological affinity among minority groups, specifically African Americans and Latinos. Where that affinity has not appeared— for example, in Miami—blacks have experienced severe political isolation.

In the early 1990s, it still made sense to treat African Americans as the measure of urban liberalism. Distance from black voting could stand for distance from liberalism. Racial liberalism defined urban liberalism.

With the rise of Latinos, and the election of white moderate and conservative mayors, blacks have begun to develop a more complicated stance, sometimes progressive, and at other times protective of a status quo threatened by the rise of a new group or against reforms proposed by mayors considered unsympathetic to blacks. Thus, Riordan's mayoralty brought him into constant conflict with city employee unions, which had strong black representation. To many blacks, "reinventing government" in the hands of a white Republican businessman meant getting rid of black employees.

The conflict between African Americans and white mayors with their own reform agendas further cracked the ideological framework of urban politics. Part of the link between minority assertion and white liberalism was a shared commitment to government reform, often in opposition to party regulars (Sonenshein 1993). With Riordan, Daley, and Giuliani successfully offering themselves as non-liberal reformers, the tie between African Americans and urban reform weakened.

Many white moderates and even some liberals were drawn to these mayors because of their tough stances on crime and community order. The new mayors made strong—and often successful—appeals to Latinos, placing blacks in a position of further defensiveness. As blacks became more politically isolated, they became less rather than more inclined to reach out to white liberals, in turn pushing these whites even further from the interracial realm.

In New York City, Mollenkopf found that Rudolph Giuliani's 1993 mayoral victor was due to several factors. "More than half of the margin of change since 1989 came from middle-class white Catholic and Jewish election districts. They not only gave Dinkins less support, but they turned out in increased numbers. . . . Black voters turned out in lower numbers, though their level of support for Dinkins remained high." Latinos turned out in lower numbers and defected from Dinkins, and white liberals also defected from Dinkins. "Electoral demobilization was more pronounced among Latinos than any other group" (Chapter 4, 129).

In Chicago's 1989 mayoral election, Richard M. Daley reversed Harold Washington's success by taking the lion's share of white votes and a high percentage of Latino votes. He made strong inroads in the small but key areas of white liberal reform strength on the Lakefront. Pinderhughes found that, in subsequent elections, "Daley consolidated his hold on the mayor's office with large white turnouts and high loyalty, reduced turnout but increasing proportions of black voters, and small turnouts but increasing support from Latino voters" (Chapter 5, 160). He had created a white-led multiracial coalition of surprising stability.

In Los Angeles, Richard Riordan did much better among Jews and Latinos than any conservative opponent had ever done against Tom Bradley. Shockingly, he even won the most powerful white liberal council district in the city, the Fifth, with 57 percent of the vote. In modern times, the Fifth District had never supported a conservative over a liberal candidate for any citywide office (Sonenshein, ch. 2). Riordan received nearly half of Jewish votes. Woo desperately needed this generally liberal constituency, which Bradley had regularly tapped for two-thirds or more of their ballots. Among Latinos, Riordan also exceeded 40 percent, a significantly higher level than previous conservative candidates had achieved. As in the other cities, turnout was higher in areas of Riordan's strength than in areas of Woo's strength.

White liberals remain distinctive from white conservatives, however. In each city, white liberals were pulled to the right, but other whites were farther down that road. Exit polls in both New York City and Los Angeles reveal the persistence of this ideological split among whites. At the same time, the shift of other groups rightward left the black community more isolated than at any time in decades. Now more distant from white liberals and Latinos, the black community found itself alone on the left.

Thus, in all three cities, mayoral elections revealed a shift in the support and enthusiasm of key groups. Those on the minority-progressive side were less enthusiastic and less supportive of their candidate. Those on the white conservative side were more enthusiastic about their candidate and made significant inroads into the liberal constituency. The citywide momentum of racial politics shifted rightward.

The ideological prospects for multiracial coalitions from the progressive side are therefore mixed. Ideological differences among whites remain potent, but as a whole, whites seem to be moving farther away from minority concerns. Among minorities, blacks must compete against conservative and moderate appeals to class and ethnic interests. This could be seen in the support given to white mayoral candidates in all three cities by leading Latino politicians. The main pillar that remains intact is Democratic identification and voting among white liberals, blacks, and Latinos.

Broad support for racial liberalism remains among most blacks, many whites, and many Latinos. There has not yet been a fundamental and irreversible restructuring of political support against black interests and in favor of racial conservatism. Obviously, something else is taking place in these cities that holds great implications for the future prospects of minority incorporation.

The rise of Latinos, however, created a new ideological dynamic, at least in Los Angeles. The Latino candidate for mayor, Antonio Villaraigosa, ran as a liberal against a moderate Democrat backed by African Americans. While Riordan's defeat of Woo marked a shift from a liberal to a conservative winning coalition, the 2001 Los Angeles mayoral race also revealed a new structure of coalitions. White liberals were on the left, with Latinos and African Americans competing for the mayoralty. A two-headed minority movement created new opportunities for conservative and moderate whites to act as the balance of power. Hahn won in 2001 by gathering the votes of this white group to supplement his solid support from African Americans. In New York City, the Latino candidate, Fernando Ferrer, ran a close second in the Democratic primary to liberal Mark Green. In the runoff election, the Republican candidate, Michael Bloomberg, defeated Green. By contrast to both New York City and Los Angeles, Chicago offered no such expression of the independent Latino political surge, except for Daley's ability to hold the strong support of Latino voters.

There has been a significant decline in both white and Latino support for the expressed position of the African-American community. In Los Angeles, New York City, and Chicago, white liberal voters were less likely than in the past to support the mayoral candidate backed by the African-American community, and white conservative voters mobilized at a higher level than minority voters. The more remarkable fact, however, is that in the face of surging Latino participation, African-American liberalism has itself been transformed—often into a defense of the status quo. In the 2001 Los Angeles city elections, blacks voted for the moderate white candidate for mayor and the moderate Latino candidate for city attorney against a Latino liberal and a Jewish liberal, respectively.

Urban liberalism has become increasingly ill-defined. Conservatism also has little coherence. Can cities become less liberal *and* less conservative at the same time? The shift in ideological lines caused by the surge of reformist white moderates and conservatives and the rise of Latinos has raised new issues concerning the roles of ideology and interest in urban politics.

INTEREST

Carmichael and Hamilton suggested that the ideological support white liberals give to blacks is contingent on self-interest:

> We do not seek to condemn these groups for being what they are so much as we seek to emphasize a fact of life: they are unreliable allies when a conflict of interest arises. Morality and sentiment cannot weather such conflicts, and black people must realize this. (1967, 76)

Interests helped mightily to explain why biracial coalition politics succeeded in Los Angeles to a far greater degree than in the more liberal New York City. A fundamental conflict of interest arose between blacks and many white liberals in New York City, due in part to the very liberalism of New York. That city developed a huge public sector in which thousands of white liberals held a central stake at the very moment minority assertion collided with city government in the 1960s.

By contrast, blacks and Jews (and other white liberals) in Los Angeles were largely excluded from the city's civic culture. The public sector was poorly developed in Los Angeles, setting up far fewer stakes for intergroup conflict. As the two groups began to cohere, they were able to simultaneously erase their outsider status by taking over city hall together.

In Chicago, the interests of blacks were in sync with those of the small, white liberal reform community that had been excluded by the powerful Democratic machine and with elements of the similarly excluded Latino community. Thus, prospects for a biracial alliance were, oddly, greater in Chicago than in the more liberal New York City.

In the contemporary era of each city, however, the balance of interests has shifted in a way that is less amenable to liberal multiracial coalitions. White-led coalitions have managed to appear as guarantors of the interests of many whites and Latinos who would otherwise be open to supporting a citywide minority movement. Unlike the earlier white-led coalitions of raging populists with a strong racist flavor, such as those of Frank Rizzo in Philadelphia and Sam Yorty in Los Angeles, the new mayors are pragmatists who are just as open to the ideas of white reformers as black mayors had been. And they are more likely than minority opponents to speak directly to the interests of these communities.

Thus, when Daley campaigned on the Chicago lakefront, he presented himself much as a black mayoral candidate might: a pragmatic centrist who would protect the interests of the people in the area and provide good government. One politician noted, "What Richard Daley offered to the lakefront was a combination of what the lakefront, in my opinion, always wanted. It was an efficient, honest operation that works well and is reasonably progressive on social issues" (quoted in Hinz 1991, 77).

Riordan campaigned on the liberal westside of Los Angeles as a centrist, non-ideological candidate who understood that even liberal communities are deeply afraid of crime. His slogan, "Tough enough to turn L.A. around," implied a measured strength—no more toughness than absolutely necessary—rather than the alienating bombast of a Sam Yorty.

By appealing directly to the interests of key centrist constituencies, the new white-led coalitions overcame the ideological leaning toward racial equality. Unlike Bradley and Washington, liberal candidates relied heavily on ideological arguments to win over these communities. Cross-pressured voters in white and Latino communities had a sense of moral obligation to vote for the liberal but a powerful urge toward self-preservation to vote for the conservative. While whites might vote for Woo or for Dinkins out of a sense of guilt or hope, there was less of the potent combination of self-interest and ideology that guided earlier votes for liberal candidates.

Pivotal to the decline of white and Latino support for black political interests is the changing perception these groups hold about the city and their place within it. In Los Angeles, for example, white liberal voting for Richard Riordan was related to voters' attitudes about immigration. The principal issue that whites mention is crime and the government's response to it (Kauffman 1998). The growing divide between economic classes further separates white and minority interests.

For other minorities, tensions with blacks are built around day-to-day economic and political competition. The rainbow assumption that color will play a special role was under severe challenge between black and Korean Americans in Los Angeles and New York City. Color is not necessarily an interest. Economic interests are probably far more important than broad appeals to color as a unifying force.

The dilemma for multiracial coalitions is this: They have not made a successful argument that they can protect the interests of the key groups they hope to represent. Conservative and moderate coalitions have more successfully addressed this interest question.

The framework of the ideological debate over racial equality in America's three largest cities has shifted so that good will is the main pillar of the liberal argument. Goodwill alone is not enough, however, especially when the conservative side effectively avoids the more blatant opposite of good will—racial polarization—in its message. The liberal side says the city will work better if we all get along better. The conservative side says we will all get along better if the city works better. The second argument is both more realistic and more appealing to an electoral majority.

As Latinos emerge in big city politics, they bring their own definition of interest to the table. Though often friendly to the black-led regimes in the three cities, Latinos rarely felt that they were at the political head table. As their long-predicted political rise flowers, Latinos seem to be charting their own course around ethnic identification. This stance places them in potential conflict and alliance with both African Americans and whites. Thus, in Houston, a conservative Republican Latino backed by conservative whites nearly unseated the African-American Democratic mayor, Lee Brown. In Los Angeles, a liberal Latino backed by liberal whites nearly defeated a white candidate backed by African Americans and conservative whites. Yet both Latino voting communities provided huge support for their candidate, regardless of ideology.

One reason that Latinos bring a new angle to city politics is that unlike African Americans, they are the subject of competition between the political parties. The Republican party in the 1960s largely reshaped itself into a party opposed to black interests, and the Democrats became the sole party interested in helping blacks (Edsall and Edsall 1991). Latinos have a different card to play than African Americans did, because Republicans consider them both necessary and winnable voters. In fact, the Republican search for Latino votes is the next stage in their racially based coalition that excludes blacks. There are not, as President Bush's political advisor warned him, enough whites to keep electing Republicans to national office.

The tremendous importance of ideology in the black search for urban equality grew out of the limited options that African Americans possessed. Race was so powerful that only a strong, ideological liberalism could overcome the racial barrier. For Latinos, the possibility of short-term, interest-based alliances is greater, and that suggests a greater role for interest in urban politics. Certainly, interest is emerging as central to racial politics in Los Angeles (Wright and Middleton 2001).

Here, political structure plays a role. In the partisan structures of New York City and Chicago, it still seems to be more difficult for new forms of minority incorporation to emerge. Mayors are structurally much stronger in those traditional cities than in Los Angeles, and other bodies (such as city councils) are weaker. A strong, unified party organization like that in Chicago becomes the sole source of political innovation. In New York City, the partisan primaries strengthen the hand of a Republican candidate (even if he is a recent Democrat) who stands out from the field. In nonpartisan Los Angeles, minority council membership is highly significant because of the sway of the council. There may be more elective posts in New York City and Chicago, but most of them are not worth much compared to being a Los Angeles city council member.

The redistricting battles of 2001–2002 in the three cities illustrate the extent to which a system in which ideological lines are no longer clear will degenerate into a battle of interests. Rather than dividing along ideological lines, the redistricting battles are shaping up (at the time of this writing) as numbers games among whites, blacks, Latinos, and other groups. The politics of recognition and representation are emerging as central. In Los Angeles, the political imperative in council redistricting is keeping African-American seats even as their population declines, and increasing the representation of Latinos and alienated suburban whites in the San Fernando Valley. In Chicago, the key factors are also the maintenance of African-American seats, as well as the protection of white Democrats without frustrating Latinos too visibly (Speilman 2001).

In this new climate of shifting minority interests, the African-American community has been both cut adrift and offered a wider range of political choices. This change has major implications for interracial coalitions and the role of African Americans within them. As a group with a stake in the system, resulting from years of minority incorporation, blacks have assets with which to bargain. They often vote as a single community, and the interests of the group are widely communicated internally. If they are not predictably in one camp politically, they will be sought after by various political factions. Latinos also have a wider range of options than before, as they represent potential swing voters in numerous coalitions. No longer are they limited to the supporting role in black-led coalitions.

A problem that emerged from the era of biracial coalition politics was the *dependence* of African Americans on white liberal support. Because of the ideological nature of racial politics in America, the only available allies for blacks were the most liberal whites. While the support of such whites was gratefully accepted, there was limited choice in alliance partners. Some of the tension between blacks and white liberals, particularly Jews, can be traced to this dynamic (Sonenshein 1993, ch. 16).

If in Los Angeles blacks and white liberals are on different sides of the mayoral race and even on the question of reappointing the police chief, that actually opens up the possibility of a more balanced relationship based on mutual choice—essentially a restatement of Carmichael and Hamilton's criteria for healthy coalitions. In New York City, blacks may find themselves more comfortable with the Republican mayor Michael Bloomberg than they were with either Giuliani or Democratic nominee Mark Green (Wyatt 2002; Caldwell 2002). While there are more options, however, there is also a loss of shared experience and trust among groups. Coalitions built on leadership trust are based on the repetition of successful patterns of interaction. *Ad hoc* alliances rarely have that enduring quality.

In short, neither color nor liberalism are by themselves sufficient to create multiracial progressive coalitions. The ability to reach groups who have a choice to go elsewhere, by linking ideologies to self-interest, is the path to coalition success. Understanding these dynamics is the task of leaders.

LEADERSHIP

In the face of urban stresses and fading ideological affinities, the burden on liberal multiracial leadership has become heavy. In these three cities, one fact stands out: On the leadership front, conservatives and moderates have come to overshadow liberals. Just as black mayors of the 1960s, 1970s, and 1980s contrasted themselves with the often corrupt—and even racist—mayors they fought, white mayors have positively contrasted themselves to the leaders generated by the left in urban politics. As cities become more diverse, liberals have had a more difficult time projecting themselves into the leadership roles than might be expected with a diverse population.

In 1993, Los Angeles voters were asked in a private poll to evaluate the two candidates for mayor on the dimension of leadership. Even though voters narrowly preferred Riordan in the horse race, they overwhelmingly rated him ahead of the liberal Woo on the dimension of leadership (Sonenshein, ch. 2). In a comparable manner, New York City voters in that same year, even though closely divided in the horse race, clearly saw Giuliani as a stronger leader than Dinkins. Mollenkopf's analysis reveals that even some of Dinkins's strongest supporters had questions about his leadership ability:

> Registered voters were evenly divided on the . . . question of whether Dinkins was a strong leader. Three-quarters of blacks felt so, but all other groups had a much more negative evaluation of Dinkins's leadership. By contrast, a clear majority of the voters thought Giuliani was a strong leader, including 44 percent of the black voters. (1994, 214)

The death of Harold Washington in 1987 showed in the most dramatic possible terms that the dynamics of coalition building are not abstract or mathematical but painfully human. Between his first election in 1983 and his reelection in 1987, Washington revealed outstanding skills of political leadership in the face of highly entrenched opposition. He held—and expanded—his political base and became the dominant figure in Chicago politics. When Washington suddenly died, the entire framework of minority incorporation in that city literally collapsed.

In both Chicago and New York City, mayors acted in key instances to jeopardize their credibility. During the Chicago mayoralty of Eugene Sawyer, a top mayoral deputy, Steve Cokely, was quoted as charging Jewish doctors with inventing the AIDS virus to kill blacks. This set off a storm in the city, with special intensity among Jews and other whites. Mayor Sawyer delayed firing Cokely until the political pressures became too intense to resist. Thus, the firing came far too late to dispel the impression that the mayor could not bring himself to totally disown Cokely without being forced to do so.

Even more damaging were two events during Mayor Dinkins's tenure. A black-led boycott of a Korean-owned grocery store in Brooklyn strained tempers in that city to the boiling point. Dinkins maintained an extremely low profile, only later taking the symbolic action of visiting the store. This delay allowed the perception to grow that he would not oppose black interests in conflict with those of another minority group. Then, when several days of rioting by blacks in the Crown Heights section of Brooklyn terrorized the orthodox Jewish community, Dinkins again seemed to delay the deployment of sufficient police forces to stem the violence. The Crown Heights events left an indelible impression that Jews could not count on Dinkins to protect their most basic interests in life and property.

Interests are not simply objective. People come to understand their interests, at least in part, by the actions of leaders either to protect or to jeopardize them. With interests seen as being unprotected, the white vote for Dinkins depended far too heavily on ideologically based good will.

The apparent ability of white-led coalitions to consolidate their support indicates something else about the leadership competition: The edge favoring these coalitions depends partly on their greater responsiveness to the concrete problems of their cities. These are not new Sam Yortys; these are generally pragmatists with serious policies. Much like the African-American mayors of an earlier time, they are charting a path down the city's center and holding the high ground on the core issues of public safety and economics. It is very difficult to challenge these new mayors from the left as long as the left struggles for a counter-philosophy of governing.

When Antonio Villaraigosa campaigned against James K. Hahn in Los Angeles in 2001, he built an appealing coalition of Latinos, white liberals, and young African Americans. Hahn skewered him on the issue of crime, however, contrasting his tough-on-crime record as city attorney with Villaraigosa's "root causes" approach. Near the end of the campaign, polling showed that Hahn led Villaraigosa on the crime issue by a massive margin.

With the top leadership of the progressive side of urban politics having difficulty with the voters, there have been many attempts from others to generate a dialogue that can advance liberal multiracial ideals. These attempts, while successful to a degree, have been hampered by the inherent difficulty of making *diversity* into an effective political concept.

Part of the problem is that leadership from the left in urban politics has had difficulty making the transition from the biracial to the multiracial. Basically, progressives need to reach significant numbers of whites *and* to unify and mobilize minorities. This task is substantially more formidable than the challenge that faced black mayors. To a great degree, many progressives have treated the multiracial challenge as a reason to build rainbow coalitions around color. This strategy is doomed to failure.

Under a biracial approach, as pioneered by black mayoral candidates, minority leaders make genuine and extensive efforts to recruit whites to their cause and to make clear that their leadership will make the city safer and better run. Under the rainbow approach, the bond of color and nonwhite status is the vehicle for inclusion, but the rainbow and biracial approaches conflict with each other. Leaders have been forced to split the difference, which makes no one happy. A revealing example was Woo's admission in 1993 that he referred to the violence of 1992 as a *rebellion* among blacks and as a *riot* among whites. Dinkins, trying to bridge a harsh black–Korean battle in Brooklyn in 1991, ended up seeming rudderless and ineffective.

In the search for rainbow coalitions, the appealing concept of diversity has fragmented progressive politics. As a symbol of harmony, diversity is a useful and relatively benign concept. As a political coalition strategy, it is problematic. Diversity appears to be a "soft" way to avoid the hard edges of coalition politics—namely, which groups are potential allies with a serious stake in the system—and also the hard edge of racial polarization.

Diversity evades the tough decisions among deserving interests that are the essence of urban leadership. Unlike the successful biracial coalitions of the 1970s and 1980s, the diversity coalition begins with appeals to member groups rather than with an overall rationale for leadership that will appeal to a number of groups.

In effect, many of the new progressives have confused the inner leadership role (building networks of key leaders) and the outer leadership role (crafting and presenting a rationale for governing). They have misunderstood the experience of biracial coalitions and have begun with the coalition question rather than subordinating the coalition to the development of broad political messages and evidence of governing credibility. The diversity discourse about rainbow coalitions has transformed a coalition from a means to an end and, in so doing, has forfeited the high ground essential to citywide political victory.

Diversity promises an easy answer to racial issues: talk less about race and slide past hard choices among the few truly available partners. And diversity is hardly benign to many voters in American cities, for whom it symbolizes not the "gorgeous mosaic" of David Dinkins or the cosmopolitan walkways of Michael Woo but the very breakdown of the social order.

The white-led mayoralties in large cities are not the only challenge to the biracial model of urban politics. The rise of Latino voting and Latino candidates in major cities has the potential to create a new model for minority incorporation. In fact, the white-led mayoralties may have served as a means to weaken the old order, thus opening doors for a new political system with multiple minority movements, kaleidescopic interests, and diverse ideologies. Rather than being the long-term shift to the right that conservatives dream about or the short-term aberration that many liberals perceive, it has instead been a very important transitional, catalytic phenomenon.

The long-awaited rise of the sleeping giant of Latino communities was spurred in California by the 1994 controversy over Proposition 187. The impact was felt immediately in higher voting participation. In 1993, Latinos cast 10 percent of all votes in the mayoral runoff election; in 2001, they cast 22 percent. Major Latino mayoral candidates arose in New York City (Fernando Ferrer) and in Los Angeles (Antonio Villaraigosa). In Houston, a conservative Latino nearly unseated the incumbent African-American mayor.

The "diversity model" suggests that the rise of these Latino candidacies would be an extension of the liberal minority politics of the African-American community. This has not been the case, however. First, the Latino candidates were not predicably liberal. Villaraigosa was a liberal, but other Latino candidates in Los Angeles have been moderates. Second, Latino candidates, as insurgents and challengers, found themselves on the opposite side of African Americans. In Los Angeles, the winning mayoral candidate built a coalition that little resembled the model of Browning, Marshall, and Tabb: African Americans and white moderates and conservatives against white liberals and Latinos. Hahn's coalition had nothing in common ideologically but shared a fear of the change represented by rising Latinos.

The implications of the Latino rise are that a new form of urban politics is emerging. Unlike the relatively simple black versus white, liberal versus conservative model that underlay urban politics for decades, urban politics is becoming more multilateral and competitive. Because Latinos are not as locked into a single point of view as African Americans have been, they are seen as "in play," which brings Republicans back into city politics. No single policy agenda is attached to the Latino rise, unlike the black rise, which opens the possibility of numerous deals and bargains. The politics of recognition seems to be high on the agenda.

The outcomes in the three cities in the post-post-incorporation era show an element of dizzying changes. African Americans, threatened politically by whites and Latinos, made a big comeback in the election of Los Angeles mayor James K. Hahn. Oddly, they came back not as liberals but as moderates, not as avatars of police reform but as staunch backers of a black police chief opposed to reform. Latinos came up and lost as liberals in the mayoral race but won as moderates in the city attorney race. The Riordan phenemenon was not carried over by his endorsements, but Riordan voters provided the edge for the black-supported Hahn's victory.

A four-cornered relationship is evolving among blacks, Latinos, liberal whites, and moderate and conservative whites. There is a mix-and-match quality to urban coalitions, now that ideology has become somewhat muddled.

One reason that ideology was so central to the black struggle for equality is that race seems to trump everything else in American politics. Latinos, however, start from a different standpoint. Certainly, they are subject to racial stereotyping, and anti-Latino sentiment is a dangerous force. Yet Latinos are not yet seen as locked into one party or ideology. Thus, national Republicans fought hard for the Latino Republican candidate for mayor of Houston, who lost narrowly to a black Democrat, Mayor Lee Brown. Latinos have certain options that blacks do not; blacks have considerable political power that Latinos do not.

The Latino rise has expressed itself differently in the three largest cities. These various outcomes are influenced by the institutional structure of each city and how that structure shapes interests, ideology, and leadership. In Chicago, it has been difficult for Latinos to develop an independent political challenge in the face of the effective, vertically organized regime of Mayor Daley. In New York City, Latinos have become a bigger force, reflected in Ferrer's campaign and its attempts to forge a black-Latino alliance. However, as Mollenkopf notes in Chapter 4 (see pages 118–120), Latinos were unable to wield much power at city hall or in the state house. By contrast, Latinos in Los Angeles have moved from little incorporation before 1994 to major influence, with a nearly victorious mayoral candidate, important posts in the city council, and widespread influence in the State Capitol. Democrats rule California in no small part due to the political outpouring of Latinos behind the Democratic party.

In Los Angeles, once again, the lack of strong partisan institutions, and the presence of weak political institutions, created opportunities for new groups to go from low power to major influence in unexpected ways. The lack of vertically organized institutions creates, in Los Angeles, the simultaneous possibility of minority exclusion and sudden minority incorporation, and the contrast between a spectactularly successful black-white coalition and the real possibility of a white-led secession movement that would carve the city in half.

What did we learn about the white-led regimes in the three largest cities? They were not brief anomalies. Their political success continues in Chicago and New York City. But in Los Angeles they have become something different, neither the coalition of the past nor the white-led regimes. In all cases, though, these political phenomena functioned to stall and block the transition from a biracial to a multiracial liberalism in big cities. They succeeded because the storehouse of liberal ideas had lost influence, because its leaders were in decline, and because the problems of the day were not addressed by liberalism. The replacement was not, however, urban conservatism. The old-fashioned right-wing ideas of urban governance were also in decline. In the broadest sense, these regimes helped reduce the role of both liberalism and conservatism in city politics. They also helped open the gates to new forms of political participation by Latinos.

MINORITY INCORPORATION AND MULTIRACIAL COALITIONS

Looking at the present era in historical perspective, we see that we are entering uncharted waters. We have reached the end of a great wave of American minority politics: the experiment in minority incorporation. Its achievements were historic, and many of its gains have been institutionalized within city government. Like all waves, it will continue to flow unevenly—and perhaps permanently, like the civil rights movement before it. We should ask, however, as

Martin Luther King, Jr., did in 1967: Where do we go from here? In the answer to this question, the meaning and potential of multiracial coalitions will emerge. After all, creating electoral coalitions for minority incorporation is not an end in itself but, like the civil rights movement, an inspiring tool toward the more profound prize: equality.

The movement for racial equality traversed a similar bridge more than 30 years ago in the transition from the civil rights movement to the battle for minority incorporation. Few saw the significance of the changes at the time, because many were demoralized by how badly the civil rights relationship had deteriorated. Actually, the relationship had evolved, opening up a greater range of choices of coalition partners.

To an even greater degree than in the movement for minority incorporation, the civil rights movement was built around good will. There was an overpowering moral dimension to it, so much so that many whites could feel themselves cleansed of the evils of racism by participating. Blacks, who had the most at stake, were dependent on such morally based support and, without it, could not have succeeded.

When blacks turned to the levers of powers in American cities, however, they found their choice of allies blocked both by ideological racial resistance and by conflict of interest over highly valued resources in urban communities. Thus, the strategy of minority incorporation required a different set of choices and strategies than the civil rights movement. Once again, blacks found it easier to ally with liberal whites, but balancing the political and social interests of these allies required sophisticated politics and nuanced responsiveness. Thus, theories of minority incorporation built only around ideology are insufficient to explain why successes occurred in some cities but not in others.

With institutionalization of the movement for minority incorporation in such policies as city hiring and political representation during redistricting, the coalition struggle is evolving again. Once more, progressives are blocked, frustrated, and at times, demoralized. Interest conflicts, which may take the form of increased ethnic voting, lie like geological strata atop the continuing ideological and racial divisions that mark urban politics.

The challenge for leaders is to accept this change as an opportunity to reforge the relationships among minorities and between minorities and whites, with a recognition that minority politics has matured in its resources and available choices even as the needs of minority communities remain extremely pressing and the necessity for progressive urban politics as great as ever. It will also be a challenge for minority leaders to recast and refocus the grounds for their appeals to whites who are uncertain where their beliefs and interests will find a home.

If the civil rights movement was about applying moral force against unjust laws and the movement for minority incorporation was about the development of political power to change unjust practices, what is next? The most fundamental battleground in American society is about neither rights nor political power but rather about gaining majority consent through the art of political communication. Both the civil rights movement and the movement for minority incorporation represented expressions of that broader strategic necessity.

The literature on minority incorporation tends to assume the importance of electoral coalitions and voting alliances as central features of minority success. And indeed participation in a winning coalition did make a significant difference in policy outcomes. But in contemporary American cities, there are good reasons to go beyond the electoral in searching for vehicles for equality.

In the preincorporation era, minority groups and their liberal allies could see the value of gaining electoral power. But there is also the downside: Power can be lost. A minority strategy that depends only on winning successful incorporation will be subject to the partisan and ideological winds. If incorporation increases positive change, how can unincorporation be hedged against?

The battle over public opinion and governmental power cannot solely depend on turning demographics into political power. Far more than even a decade ago, American political life is now dominated by competing agendas advanced in highly sophisticated ways through the mass media. These agendas are advanced by interest groups, political parties, candidates, bureaucracies, and even foreign nations. In the place of an Establishment that could be appealed to, we have instead a political marketplace. If it gets caught up in a limited dialogue on color and diversity, *the movement for minority equality runs the serious risk of not contending on that awesome battleground of public opinion.* The shaping of public opinion rules budgets and determines national, state, and local priorities. It is the ability to compete and succeed in that competitive arena that will underlie the success of multiracial coalitions.

CONCLUSIONS

The prospects for building multiracial coalitions are bleak unless progressives fully understand the wrong turns that can derail the minority search for equality. Coalition politics are means to an end. The ability to link ideologies of fairness and equity and to respond to the legitimate interests of groups and masses, as well as the intangible quality of leadership, give them life.

Regardless of the appeal of strategies of color in the search for racial equality, cross-racial appeals remain fundamentally important. As Mollenkopf noted on New York City: "Proponents of such a [multiracial liberal coalition] must also address the issues that deeply concern all voters, but especially middle-class white voters. Foremost among them is the perception that crime is rampant, the streets unsafe, intergroup relations uncivil, and the quality of life decaying" (1994, 226). Although it is tempting to turn sympathetic whites into "flak-catchers" for the long-unexpressed anger of minority activists, they are actually potential members of a progressive coalition whose interests must be respected and whose values should be appealed to.

A progressive movement cannot, in its desire to move "beyond black and white," make two fundamental errors. One is to treat multiracial coalition politics as simply a numerical extension of the same black–white dynamics that underlie biracial coalitions. Latinos and Asian Americans have their own ideologies, interests, and internal divisions, and in responding to appeals from conservative forces, these groups may not have the same goals and objectives as blacks and whites. The actual rise of Latinos has had all sorts of surprises that a more theoretical model did not predict.

The other error is to underestimate the continuing power of race in American politics. As Sears, Citrin, and van Laar (1995) have demonstrated, race continues to shape a wide range of issues, including American attitudes toward the very diversity that leads many of us to downplay the significance of black–white divisions.

As an organizing principle for new progressive multiracial coalitions, color is an unreliable glue. As a bond for coalitions, using ethnicity rather than addressing the serious economic and social issues of community life will have the paradoxical effect of exacerbating coalition tensions. The evidence is that there must be goals beyond race relations to make coalitions succeed. Coalitions must be able to make a difference, to cut deeper, and to provide leadership.

We continue to learn that good will is not enough, but neither is cold self-interest. While the idea of color-blindness distorts the reality of American life, color alone is an insufficient basis for enduring coalitions for equality. We can be neither color-blind nor color-coded. The struggle for equality still requires leaders who can create—and sustain—enduring systems of belief, manage conflicts of interest, promote interest alliances, and cross society's racial and ethnic barriers in the interest of a humane vision for the whole society.

Minorities must continue to try to be part of the leadership coalitions in government, and to engage in the battle to frame public issues. These struggles inevitably call for communication and coalitions across racial and ethnic lines, and for connecting the aspirations of minorities to such broad symbols of good governance as reform, efficiency, and responsiveness.

REFERENCES

Adrian, Charles R. 1959. A Typology for Nonpartisan Elections. *Western Political Quarterly* 12: 449–458.

Alozie, Nicholas O. 2000. The Promise of Urban Democracy: Big-City Black Mayoral Service in the Early 1990's. 35 *Urban Affairs Review* 3 (January): 422–434.

Bobo, Lawrence. 1983. Whites' Opposition to School Busing: Symbolic Racism or Realistic Group Conflict. *Journal of Personality and Social Psychology* 45: 1196–1210.

Browning, Rufus P., Dale Rogers Marshall, and David H. Tabb. 1984. *Protest Is Not Enough: The Struggle of Blacks and Hispanics for Equality in Urban Politics.* Berkeley: University of California Press.

Caldwell, Diane. 2002. Mayor to Mark King's Birthday with Sharpton. *New York Times*, January 19.

Carmichael, Stokely, and Charles V. Hamilton. 1967. *Black Power: The Politics of Liberation in America.* New York: Random House.

Carmines, E. G., and J. A. Stimson. 1989. *Issue Evolution: Race and the Transformation of American Politics.* Princeton, N.J.: Princeton University Press.

Carney, Francis. 1964. The Decentralized Politics of Los Angeles. *Annals of the American Academy of Political and Social Sciences* 353 (May): 107–121.

Edsall, Thomas B., and Mary D. Edsall. 1991. *Chain Reaction: The Impact of Race, Rights and Taxes on American Politics.* New York: Norton.

Ferman, Barbara. 1996. *Challenging the Growth Machine: Neighborhood Politics in Chicago and Pittsburgh.* Lawrence: University of Kansas Press.

Fisher, A. M. 1979. Realignment of the Jewish Vote? *Political Science Quarterly* 94: 97–116.

Fogelson, Robert. 1967. *The Fragmented Metropolis: Los Angeles, 1850–1930.* Cambridge, Mass.: Harvard University Press.

Giles, Micheal W., and Arthur Evans. 1986. The Power Approach to Intergroup Hostility. *Journal of Conflict Resolution* 30: 469–486.

Giles, Micheal W., and Douglas S. Gatlin. 1980. Mass-Level Compliance with Public Policy: The Case of School Desegregation. *Journal of Politics* 42: 722–746.

Hahn, Harlan, David Klingman, and Harry Pachon. 1976. Cleavages, Coalitions, and the Black Candidate: The Los Angeles Mayoralty Elections of 1969 and 1973. *Western Political Quarterly* 29 (December): 521–530.

Halley, Robert M., Alan C. Acock, and Thomas H. Greene. 1976. Ethnicity and Social Class: Voting in the 1973 Los Angeles Municipal Elections. *Western Political Quarterly* 29 (December): 521–530.

Hinckley, Barbara. 1981. *Coalitions and Politics.* New York: Harcourt Brace Jovanovich.

Hinz, Greg. 1991. Lakefronters. In Paul M. Green and Melvin G. Holli, eds., *Restoration 1989: Chicago Elects a New Daley*, 74–90. Chicago: Lyceum Books.

Jones-Correa, Michael. 2001. Structural Shifts and Institutional Capacity: Possibilities for Ethnic Co-operation and Conflict in Urban Settings. In Jones-Correa, ed., *Governing American Cities: Interethnic Coalitions, Competition, and Conflict*, 183–209. New York: Russell Sage Foundation.

Kauffman, Karen. 1998. Racial Conflict and Political Choice: A Study of Mayoral Voting Behavior in Los Angeles and New York. 32 *Urban Affairs Review* 3 (January): 291–318.

Keiser, Richard A. 1997. Analyzing Urban Regime Change: Black Power, White Backlash, and Shades of Gray. In Richard A. Keiser and Katherine Underwood, eds., *Minority Politics at the Millennium*, 157–178. New York: Garland Publishing.

Kinder, Donald R., and D. O. Sears. 1981. Prejudice and Politics: Symbolic Racism Versus Racial Threats to the Good Life. *Journal of Personality and Social Psychology* 40: 414–431.

McCann, Herbert G. 2001. Daley's Rubber Stamp? *Associated Press*, December 9.

McGreevy, Patrick. 2002. Latinos May Gain Majority in Another District. *Los Angeles Times*, January 27.

Mollenkopf, John, David Olson, and Timothy Ross. 2001. Immigrant Political Participation in New York and Los Angeles. In Michael Jones-Correa, ed. *Governing American Cities: Interethnic Coalitions, Competition, and Conflict*, 17–70. New York: Russell Sage Foundation.

Pettigrew, Thomas. 1971. When a Black Candidate Runs for Mayor: Race and Voting Behavior. In Harlan Hahn, ed., *People and Politics in Urban Society*, 99–105. Beverly Hills, Calif.: Sage Publications.

Schwartz, Frederick A. O., Jr., and Eric Lane. 1998. The Policy and Politics of Charter Making: The Story of New York City's 1989 Charter. 42 *New York Law School Law Review* 3 & 4, 723–1015.

Sears, David O., Jack Citrin, and Colette van Laar. 1995. Black Exceptionalism in a Multicultural Society. Paper presented at the annual meeting of the American Political Science Association, Chicago, August 31–September 3.

Shefter, Martin. 1983. Regional Receptivity to Reform. *Political Science Quarterly* 98: 459–484.

Singleton, Gregory H. 1979. *Religion in the City of the Angels: American Protestant Culture and Urbanization, Los Angeles, 1850–1930.* Ann Arbor: University of Michigan Research Press.

Sleeper, Jim. 1993. The End of the Rainbow? America's Changing Urban Politics. *The New Republic* (November): 20–25.

Spielman, Fran. 2001. Proposed Ward Map Angers Hispanics. *Chicago Sun-Times*, November 21.

Sonenshein, Raphael J. 1993. *Politics in Black and White: Race and Power in Los Angeles.* Princeton, N.J.: Princeton University Press.

Wright, Sharon, and Richard T. Middleton IV. 2001. The 2001 Los Angeles Mayoral Election: Implications for Deracialization and Biracial Coalition Theories. 29 *Politics and Policy* 4 (December): 692–707.

Wyatt, Edward. 2002. On King's Day, Warm Response by Blacks to Bloomberg Embrace. *New York Times*, January 22.

Chapter 13

Has Political Incorporation Been Achieved? Is It Enough?

Rufus P. Browning, Dale Rogers Marshall,
and David H. Tabb

The question, again: Can people of color achieve power—and equality—in city government? We answer this question with five others.

Have people of color achieved strong political incorporation in the 20 cities examined in this book? Sometimes. They did overcome exclusion in most cities. In the past 40 years, African Americans and, to a lesser extent, Latinos and Asians, have increased their political power in many of the 20 cities. However, minority incorporation is uneven and incomplete; its achievement, ongoing.

Have minorities held the power they built? Not always. They and their liberal allies suffered significant defeats in several cities, and fear arose that these reversals might result in renewed exclusion and subordinate status. They did not. Defeat does not necessarily mean renewed exclusion or the end of minority influence. However, minority political power has become more varied and complex, with crosscutting and shifting coalitions.

Where they did achieve incorporation, have minority-oriented city governments produced gains for minority people? Yes, in significant, but limited, areas, but the performance of too many minority-oriented regimes is disappointing.

Have these governments achieved the broader social and economic goals of the movement for political incorporation? No. Political incorporation in cities is not enough to achieve the broadest goals of minority mobilization: redistributive policies that would significantly reduce economic equality, disadvantage, and social decay. Can cities make a difference with respect to these goals? In some ways, yes. Will they? Only if leaders and activists find better ways to bring diverse groups together. The jury is always out, however; the trial continues, and there is no final decision. Racial politics is a struggle, not a promised land.

Is there a future for minority political incorporation? Yes, but the ground on which coalitions are built has been transformed by immigration. In many cities the future of incorporation will be very different from the enduring biracial coalitions that produced strong incorporation of African Americans in some cities in the last decades of the twentieth century. African Americans especially will have to adapt quickly to the new demographic reality if they are to sustain or improve their political position. Issues that reach across immigrant and racial groups will increasingly structure urban coalitions.

In this chapter, we will first summarize the findings of the preceding chapters on minority mobilization and incorporation and the conditions that promote or hinder it. Then we will take up the record of minority-oriented city governments, what we have learned about the coalitions that sustain them, the recent reversals they have met in several cities, the possible futures of racial politics, and the strategies that can advance the goals of the movement toward ethnoracial incorporation.

MOBILIZATION AND INCORPORATION: FUNDAMENTALS

Withholding, for the moment, judgment about the value of minority incorporation in city governments, we bring together here findings and interpretations about resources for—and barriers to—mobilization and incorporation, in the struggle to overcome racial exclusion.

Weak and Strong Forms of Minority Incorporation

Representation alone gained little influence for minorities. Minority participation in liberal dominant coalitions led to much stronger minority influence in city governments and greater policy responsiveness, and coalitions led by black mayors typically incorporated still stronger commitments to minority objectives.[1] As Stokely Carmichael and Charles Hamilton put it in 1967:

> When black people lack a majority, Black Power means proper representation and sharing of control. It means the creation of power bases, of strength, from which black people can press to change local or nation-wide patterns of oppression—instead of from weakness.
>
> It does not mean merely putting black faces into office. Black visibility is not Black Power. (1967, 46)

In our terms, Carmichael and Hamilton's "proper representation" was potentially achievable through participation in liberal dominant coalitions; "sharing of control" was the fundamental premise of the most successful of those coalitions.

---

[1] Mollenkopf suggests in Chapter 4 that New York may be an anomaly in this regard—that a regime in which blacks are weakly incorporated nevertheless produces substantial benefits for them. We deal with that possibility later in this chapter.

Interest Group and Electoral Strategies

Mobilization that produced sustained incorporation built on interest-group organization, demand, and protest as well as on electoral effort, including the formation of party or party-like coalitions. Electoral mobilization and coalition were the essential foundation of enduring incorporation. Group organization, demand, and protest were the foundation of successful electoral effort, despite instances when too-intense protest hindered and delayed the formation of coalitions.

Cities in which blacks or Latinos achieved the most powerful participation in electoral coalitions and, subsequently, in city governments were those in which the development of autonomous, solidary minority leadership and organization preceded it, confirming Carmichael and Hamilton's argument for the period in which the struggle to overcome racial exclusion was paramount:

> The concept of Black Power rests on a fundamental premise: Before a group can enter the open society, it must first close ranks. By this we mean that group solidarity is necessary before a group can operate effectively from a bargaining position of strength in a pluralistic society. (1967, 44)

The linkage between achievement of solidarity within the minority group and achievement of strong incorporation was very close in the cities studied. The early, strong incorporation of blacks in Berkeley depended on the unusually strong organization of black leadership in the Berkeley Black Caucus. Conversely, the long delay in the election of a black mayor in Oakland resulted in part from the split between the Black Panther Party and middle-class black leadership (Browning, Marshall, and Tabb 1984, 114–116). Failure to achieve solidarity both within and between minority populations in New York explains in part the failure of blacks and Latinos to obtain incorporation corresponding to their numbers in that city (see ch. 4). Failure to achieve black unity delayed black incorporation in Baltimore (see ch. 9). In Philadelphia, two black candidates split the black vote; as a result, a white man won (see ch. 3). Breaking away from the Democratic machine and organizing a grass roots process to pull black community organizations together—and the inclusion of Latinos in a coalition—were prerequisites for Harold Washington's victory in Chicago. After his death, competing black candidates split the black vote, and blacks lost their position of strong political incorporation (see ch. 5). All this is evidence for the critical role of group solidarity.

The Importance of Coalitions

Regardless of the election system (partisan or nonpartisan), the political incorporation of minorities—the extent of their role in dominant coalitions that controlled city government—depended on their ability to form and maintain cohesive electoral coalitions. In particular, where blacks and Latinos constituted a minority of the effective electorate, their incorporation depended on the formation of biracial or multiracial coalitions that selected candidates, controlled the number of minority candidacies to prevent splitting the vote, organized slates, co-ordinated campaigns, and controlled city councils and departments. Mayor Tom Bradley's success in forging a biracial coalition of blacks and white liberals was particularly noteworthy in Los Angeles, where blacks never exceeded 17 percent of the population (see chs. 2 and 12).

Fundamental resources of group size formed the basis of these coalitions. Depending on historical patterns of competition and conflict, on leadership, and on the sizes of black, Latino, and supportive white groups, coalitions were variously composed of blacks and whites, Latinos and whites, or all three groups. The black-white biracial coalition was the most common pattern during the period of the struggle to overcome exclusion, from the 1950s on.

The Importance of Leadership

Historically, competition and conflict between groups are typical, so the structure, size, and timing of new coalitions have depended on the ability of leaders to overcome divisions and to shape issues in a way that minimizes antagonism and sustains joint effort. The flow of issues, partly under the control of coalition leaders, and the willingness and ability of the available leadership to reach out across racial boundaries—a difficult task—shaped the structure of the coalitions that actually formed, that won control of city government, and that maintained their commitment and position (see ch. 12). The structure of local leadership and the dynamic of group conflict are shaped by historical experience—for example, innovative co-operation took hold and became accepted practice in Philadelphia (see ch. 3). The civil rights movement provided a mobilizing and coalition-defining agenda for liberals and blacks in the northern California cities, creating new opportunities and powerful incentives for coalition.

GROUP SIZE AND PATTERNS OF MOBILIZATION

In Chapter 1, we set forth expectations about mobilization based on sizes of ethnoracial groups in 10 northern California cities—namely, that a successful multiracial coalition will form and take control of city government where the minority population, plus support from liberal whites, approaches 50 percent of the electorate. Patterns of mobilization that emerged in the other cities analyzed in this book correspond in part to those expectations. Of the 20 cities presented, six—Atlanta, Baltimore, Birmingham, New Orleans, Oakland, and Richmond, California—had majority or near-majority black populations by 1980. In all these cities, black mayors who led biracial or multiracial coalitions were elected, though in cities where blacks constituted a majority of the electorate on their own—Birmingham and New Orleans—they were no longer dependent on support from other groups. In those cities, as Huey Perry carefully delineates in Chapter 8, biracial coalitions had formed earlier and first elected racially liberal white and then black mayors. Similarly, in Miami, Latinos constituted a majority by 1980 and elected a Latino mayor.

In a second group of cities, neither blacks nor Latinos constituted majorities in 1980, and neither group had an overwhelming share of the city's population of color. The two groups together, however, made up at least 40 percent of city population in Los Angeles, Philadelphia, Chicago, and New York City.[2] In all these cities, a biracial or multiracial electoral alliance with a strong commitment to minority (primarily black) interests had taken control of the mayor's office by 1987. In New York, this was a biracial coalition under Mayor John Lindsay, elected in 1967 and 1971. Thus, the experience in these cities was at first glance consistent with the simple model, derived from the northern California experience, that predicts coalition formation and takeover of city government.

New York, however, has oscillated between explicitly multiracial coalitions— Mayor Lindsay's and an uneasy coalition that elected David Dinkins mayor in 1990—and considerably less liberal coalitions led by mayors Ed Koch and Rudolph Giuliani. The inability of multiracial coalitions to sustain themselves in New York is anomalous in terms of the simple model, as Mollenkopf argues in Chapter 4. In Chicago, a successful black-Latino-liberal coalition led by Harold Washington also could not maintain itself after his death.

New York since 1975 and Chicago before and after Harold Washington all exemplify co-optation, in which segments of black and Latino leadership and electoral support are brought into a dominant coalition where whites play the primary roles and that does not make so strong a commitment to minority interests. We discuss these cities and those with similar group size and political characteristics in "Barriers to Incorporation."

Denver constitutes a modest anomaly on the other side, with a combined black and Latino population of only 30.8 percent in 1980 but a Latino mayor by mid-decade—the first major U.S. city without a Latino majority to elect a Latino mayor. Federico Peña had broad, multiracial support but also the backing of a core business elite. Peña was followed by Wellington Webb, Denver's first African-American mayor, in a city with only 10.8 percent black population in 2000 (see Table I.1). Both mayors publicly emphasized economic development; both also gave much more attention to minority concerns than previous regimes, especially Webb (see ch. 11).

BARRIERS TO INCORPORATION

The passage of time has seen the defeat of biracial and multiracial coalitions in several cities. This history enlarges our view of the barriers to incorporation. Now we see not only the problems that prevented or restricted incorporation in the first

---

[2] The 40 percent minority figure is a rule of thumb—an approximation for circumstances that vary from city to city. Evidence from many cities suggests that, typically, 10 percent to 20 percent of the white population will support a biracial coalition (Preston, Henderson, and Puryear 1987). This amounts to 6 percent to 12 percent of the total population. Combined with a 40 percent minority population, we have a potential coalition of 46 percent to 52 percent of the population—within striking distance of an electoral majority if the coalition's supporters can be mobilized.

place, but also the decline of once-successful minority-oriented coalitions, the threat of countermobilization, and the resurgence and success of conservative coalitions. Maintaining a coalition that supports minority interests during a period of governance is different from mobilizing to elect it in the first place. Restructuring such a coalition after its defeat is likely to be different still, requiring altered expectations, new visions, and different skills. We review first the barriers to incorporation that are apparent from the history of minority incorporation in cities since the 1950s, then turn to the threat of reversal and the fear of renewed exclusion that defeat brought to the fore.

Urban Machines

New York since 1975 and Chicago before and after Harold Washington present characteristics that were not found in the 10 northern California cities and that constitute additional barriers to minority mobilization and incorporation. In these cities, party organizations co-opted minorities—bringing in carefully selected minority activists and officeholders who are expected to remain loyal to the organization and its leadership rather than to an autonomous leadership that arises from the minority community itself.

The machines were well-institutionalized coalitions that predated the widespread minority mobilization of the 1960s. Not oriented toward reform and determined to protect the power of the organization and the economic interests of its ultimately white leadership and business support, machines attempted to prevent the formation of multiracial challenging coalitions through co-optation, building on and generating divisions among minority leaders and groups, and establishing minority officeholders against whom other minority candidates found it difficult to run. Machines created some minority incorporation and produced some minority-oriented policies, but also helped to prevent the mobilization of more liberal, unified, minority-based coalitions.

Thus, the machine stood as a barrier to the formation and success of reform-oriented coalitions in which more autonomous minority leadership could play central and dominant roles. Some benefits flow to minority populations from such machines—as they do from co-optive regimes in general—such as city government employment and city contracts—but the machines did not reorient city government across a broad range of policy areas.

In Chicago, unlike New York, a weakened machine was defeated by a multiracial coalition led by black insurgents. Harold Washington's election as mayor and, later, his success in gaining a council majority showed that even a long-entrenched machine and its structure of co-optation can be overthrown given appropriate leadership, fundamental resources of minority population, and some support from outside the minority community.

The Chicago case also demonstrates the difficulty of accomplishing such an overthrow. As Pinderhughes shows in Chapter 5, Washington's coalition and leadership were unusual (see also ch. 4 and 12). The coalition conducted an extraordinary grass roots mobilization and involvement in the decision to select Washington as its candidate for mayor in the first place. Washington himself was capable of reaching out across racial lines to Chicago's Latino population, including them as respected partners in his ultimately victorious coalition. Not every leader with the ability to win majority support in his own group also has the will, the credibility, and the skill to create a liberal biracial or multiracial coalition. (See ch. 12 on the importance of leadership.)

The fragile dependence of such coalitions on leadership was sadly illustrated when Washington died in office. The black candidates competing to succeed him split his coalition, leading to election of the white machine candidate, Mayor Richard M. Daley, in 1989.

The recent election of an African-American mayor, John Street, in Philadelphia, presents an interesting counter-example to the pattern of the machine as an obstruction. Unlike the first black mayor, Wilson Goode, who was a reform candidate, Street was supported by the traditional machine Democratic organization. This is the only example among our cities of a machine government with blacks as full-fledged partners in the coalition. Unlike other machine-based city governments, Street's administration may allocate resources that significantly benefit Philadelphia's large black working-class population (see ch. 3).

Fragmentation of Minority Groups

In addition to the party machine as a barrier to minority mobilization, New York City illustrates also the possibility—and the consequences—of extreme fragmentation of minority groups. The 1980 U.S. Census counted more than 45 percent of New York's population as black or "of Hispanic origin," and these groups probably made up more than half of New York's population by the late 1980s. By the standards of the other cities studied in this book, resources of such size should have been more than ample to found a liberal multiracial coalition that could control city government over a long period. A major reason this has not happened, as seen in Chapter 4, is the extent to which both blacks and Latinos in New York have been divided.

In contrast to the California cities, where most blacks and Latinos have arrived since World War II, New York's black and Latino populations have had a long history of competition, conflict, established leadership, and political division. This is not new clay that a skillful leader can readily mold into a unified force but a congeries of minority populations between which the divisions are deep and solid. Blacks and Latinos in New York are further split within each group by ancestry and nativity—blacks of West Indian birth or origin as well as blacks of southern origin; Latinos of Puerto Rican birth or ancestry but also Dominicans and other Latino immigrant groups—and by place of residence in the boroughs.

Fragmentation of minority populations in New York results not only from differences in ancestry and nationality but also from a long history of conflict, competition, and the habituation of organizations and leaders to that history, as Mollenkopf notes (see ch. 4). This is utterly unlike the experience of black communities in the California cities, where they arrived in large numbers mainly during and after World War II. Coming predominantly from the American South, they were not divided by different ancestry. Their organizational structure and leadership still emerging, they were mobilized by the civil rights and the Black Power movements and were presented with an opportunity to overthrow conservative regimes—if they could coalesce among themselves and with others. For California blacks, the civil rights movement was the formative historical context for political mobilization. In contrast, the political fragmentation of New York's black population was well established long before the civil rights movement. This population's ability to overcome fragmentation was tested again in the 1989 New York mayoral election that pitted Mayor Koch against David N. Dinkins, the black Manhattan borough president. Dinkins formed a biracial coalition and won, but he subsequently lost support and was defeated in his bid for re-election in 1993.

Intense fragmentation both between and within minority groups impedes the formation of multiracial coalitions. New York, Chicago, and San Francisco all illustrate the difficulty of combining the potential electoral strength of two or more groups. We should expect it to be more difficult to form the multiethnic coalitions necessary to take control of city government in such settings than it is to form biracial black–white or Latino–white coalitions in cities where one "minority" group dominates. It is not impossible—witness Sacramento and the sometimes-successful efforts of multiethnic coalitions in all these cities—but it is more difficult and, therefore, more dependent on circumstances, on special qualities of leadership, or on learning new ways of framing issues to reach across group lines.

Fragmentation of ethnoracial groups can obstruct stable coalition building in cities where no political machine is established—witness San Francisco. Fragmentation, however, makes co-optation a convenient tool for a well-organized machine—witness New York.

Issues, Interests, and the Loss of White Support

The formation and survival of biracial and multiracial coalitions depend in part on the ideological commitment of liberal whites to the minority cause. Mollenkopf's analysis of New York (see ch. 4) and Sonenshein's comparative study of New York, Chicago, and Los Angeles (see ch. 12) delineate the limits of this commitment. The New York case especially illustrates the potential for drastic loss of earlier support and the long-term eclipse of progressive multiracial coalitions.

In some cities, and certainly in New York and Los Angeles, Jews have accounted for a large share of white support for blacks, reflecting the experience of Jews with discrimination and their special moral determination to oppose it. Unfortunately for coalitions, blacks and whites in general but Jews in particular have a special potential for conflict of interests around anti-Semitism, city government fiscal problems, residential and labor market succession, and control over city government functions and employment.

Anti-Semitism   A few black leaders express openly anti-Semitic attitudes, and these expressions of anti-Semitism—and the failure of some black leaders to denounce them—reduced support for biracial coalitions among Jews in New York. As a result, two-thirds of the Jewish voters defected from the Democratic Party in 1989 and 1993 to support a Republican for mayor. The broader message: Expressions of racial or ethnic prejudice can destroy a multiethnic coalition.

Fiscal Problems   In New York, severe fiscal crisis has dominated the agenda of city government off and on for decades and has turned white supporters away from the problems of minority groups. "Recession, fiscal crisis, and reductions of federal aid from the Reagan and Bush administrations prompted the Koch administration to undo the spending patterns of the Lindsay years," and the Giuliani administration also "reduced funding for programs serving minority communities" (ch. 4, 120).

Residential and Labor Market Succession   In New York in particular, many Jews were affected by the transition of Jewish lower-middle and working-class neighborhoods to black or Latino neighborhoods. Such transitions are likely to kindle racial, class, and cultural antagonisms and, thus, to reduce support for coalitions.

Control over City Government Functions and Employment   In the 1968 school strikes in New York, black activists were:

> pitted . . . as "outs" against a school bureaucracy led and staffed disproportionately by liberal and moderate whites (including many Jews). Liberals were cast as "ins" in traditionally liberal New York City; it was a strike against [white] institutional liberalism. The high degree of black-Jewish conflict produced by the strikes shifted much of the city's liberal base into a moderate/conservative alliance with white Catholics; this link became the base for the Koch regime. The result left blacks without political incorporation. (Sonenshein 1993, 234–235)

Conflicts arising from these and other issues can destroy or prevent the formation of biracial and multiracial coalitions. Liberal coalitions have split and lost power in many cities:

- In Los Angeles, as Latinos and Jews moved to a conservative coalition.
- In Philadelphia, as a nonreform coalition of Democrats replaced a reform-oriented Democratic coalition.
- In New York, as conservatives exploited conflict within the liberal multiracial coalition.
- In Chicago, as blacks split among themselves and were unable to retain the allegiance of Latinos.
- In San Francisco, as progressive whites and blacks split over social and environmental issues.
- In New Orleans, as both conservatives and liberals formed biracial coalitions.

These issues involved conflict between whites and blacks, blacks and Latinos, whites and Latinos, blacks and Asians, and so on. The general problem is the management of issues in a way that allows an effective coalition to form and be maintained, even in the presence of actual or potential conflict with respect to interests.

THE INCREASING SIGNIFICANCE OF LATINOS AND ASIANS IN THE NEW URBAN LANDSCAPE

The Immigration Act of 1965 led to large-scale immigration and rapid growth in the Latino and Asian populations, which is driving major changes in racial politics. The tide of newcomers is running at an all-time high, with 9.1 million people immigrating legally to the United States in the 1990s—more than the 8.8 million who came in the earlier great wave of immigration (1900–1910). More than half of the 1990s immigrants came from Latin America, mainly Mexico, and they settled mainly in the big cities. The Asian immigrants are mainly of Chinese origin—China, Taiwan, and Hong Kong. Eleven percent of the U.S. population was foreign born in 2000 (U.S. Bureau of the Census 2000b; Borrus and Smith 2001). A diverse population is becoming ever more diverse.

The changing demographics mean that two-way competition for power between blacks and whites will characterize fewer cities than in the past, and black–white biracial coalitions are less likely to be a solution. Racial politics will be increasingly multiracial, multiethnic politics in many cities.

Latino and Asian Mobilization and Coalition Formation

As the numbers of Latinos and Asians rise, they organize to gain political office. Latinos were important in the mayoral races in Los Angeles and New York (see chs. 2 and 4), even though both Latino candidates lost to whites, and they were an essential component of Harold Washington's victories in Chicago mayoral elections in the 1980s (see ch. 5). The mayor of San Jose and four members of the city council are Latino. Mexican Americans have been mayors of other important cities (Denver and San Antonio, for example), speaker of the California Assembly, and lieutenant governor of California, and they are increasingly running for major offices in California and Texas as well as in Florida. The National Association of Latino Elected and Appointed Officials (NALEO) reports more than 5,400 such officeholders (Gonzalez 2002). NALEO has organized Latino leadership recruitment and training for many years.

Asians constitute a smaller and more concentrated fraction of the nation's population than Latinos and blacks—about 4 percent, compared with 12.9 percent for blacks and 12.5 percent for Latinos (who may be any race). In 2000, Asians were a majority in Hawaii and 12.3 percent of California's population, but they comprised less than 7 percent in New York state, New Jersey, and Washington state, the states with the next largest Asian populations (U.S. Bureau of the Census 2000a). The first-ever National Asian Pacific American Voter Registration Campaign gave a boost in 1996 to Asian political mobilization nationwide, producing 75,000 new registrations, and similar efforts were carried out in 2000. Twelve Asian Americans, primarily of Japanese origin, had served or were serving in the U.S. Congress by 2000, other than nonvoting delegates from Guam and American Samoa (Lien 2001, 73, 90).

This does not mean that Latino and Asian political mobilization has followed—or will follow—a trajectory like that of African Americans. Latinos and Asians are different. First, they do not suffer the stigma of blackness in American society, except among Latinos in relatively small numbers, and many Latinos consider themselves white. Second, both groups are more diverse than blacks, and the diversities count: Cuban Americans are not Puerto Ricans, who are not Dominicans, and Mexican Americans are not Central Americans, either culturally or in socioeconomic status. Similarly, Chinese are not Filipinos, who are not Japanese, who are not Korean. Working toward greater mobilization among both Latinos and Asians, on the other hand, are social interaction, intermarriage, and the need for political support following legislative attacks on immigrants in the 1990s, which created strong incentives to identify for political purposes with pan-ethnic organizations, movements, candidates, and campaigns (on Asians, see Lien 2001). Still, notwithstanding the intensity and determination of Asian and Latino mobilization by many leaders, activists, and organizations, these groups overall are still probably less likely than African Americans to see political action as a preferred or even necessary means of improvement.

Cubans are likely to be Republican in party affiliation and other Latinos Democratic, but both parties compete for their votes. Asians nationwide appear to be split between the two major parties and are more likely than the other large ethnoracial groups to be independent, to decline to state a party preference, or to say they are moderate in their views (Lien 2001, 154).

Latinos are more likely to be Roman Catholic, while blacks are predominantly Protestant. Asians are diverse in religion, including Catholic, Buddhist, and no religion. Finally, though poverty continues to be a major problem in many Latino and some Asian communities, Latinos on average appear to assimilate economically more rapidly than blacks, while Asians overall are doing relatively well educationally and economically.

Some of these differences come down to the simple and important fact that Latinos and Asians are less intensely and rigidly racialized in American society than African Americans are, despite the discrimination and racism that Latinos and Asians also have experienced—and that they continue to experience.[3] Taken together, these considerations reduce the urgency of political mobilization for Latinos and Asians compared to African Americans, interfere with coalition formation with blacks, and lessen political mobilization in general.

Latinos have supported multiracial coalitions led by whites (Philip Isenberg in Sacramento) and by blacks (Harold Washington in Chicago, Tom Bradley in Los Angeles). Significant political careers can develop from such affiliations. In Sacramento, Joe Serna led Chicano organizing efforts in the 1960s, was Isenberg's

---

[3] In publicity for its annual conference in June 2001, the NALEO Educational Fund listed as the first of many workshops "Campaign Training: Beyond Race, Ethnicity and Gender— Winning in Any District" (NALEO Educational Fund 2001). This is the emphasis of a group that is confident of the ability of its members to win deracialized campaigns in diverse settings.

political associate in the 1970s, won election to city council in 1981, and eventually served as mayor of Sacramento. "In spite of the belated entry of mainland Asians into electoral politics," they too have joined forces with other groups in a wide range of electoral and governing coalitions since the 1940s (Lien 2001, 123–124).

In the 1990s, continued immigration and high birth rates produced dramatic increases in the absolute and relative size of Latino and Asian populations in many cities and corresponding increases in electoral effort and officeholding. This trend is real. Overall, leaders and activists see the urgency of mobilization, but it is more a response to the opportunity created by steadily increasing population than the intensely organized, frequently enraged mass mobilization that characterized the Black Power movement. This reflects the less racialized position of Latinos and Asians. Like any distinct group, they are gratified to help members break through the barriers to political incorporation and will support candidates of their group— and all group mobilization now takes place in the context of the successful civil rights and Black Power movements and the breakthroughs in black electoral mobilization and incorporation.[4]

Latino and Asian Incorporation

Latino and Asian incorporation, as seen in the cities studied in this book, draws more narrowly from the comprehensive socioeconomic goals of the black power movement and has a more limited view regarding the proper role of government. The political leadership of these groups has responded to an electoral base that has been more diverse and, typically, somewhat more conservative in certain respects.

The conservatism of Latino and Asian mobilization and incorporation has, of course, implications for the responsiveness of city governments in which these groups are incorporated. The question is, responsiveness to whose demands and interests? To what ultimate goals? We should expect Latino-run city governments, for example, to end discrimination at least against Latinos in hiring, in the routine administration of city affairs, and in the award of government contracts to minority-owned businesses. Should we expect such governments to equalize the delivery of city services and improvements in general? Perhaps somewhat, alleviating the most glaring inequities, but not much, if it means significantly reallocating municipal resources toward low-income neighborhoods, their residents, and their businesses and raising taxes to pay for new programs. The programs of minority-governed cities depend on the nature of the coalitions that control city government. If these are multiethnic coalitions, they are likely to be based on a careful and equitable distribution of the benefits available from city government to all the groups involved.

---

[4] From an Asian-American perspective: "Monumental changes in the social, economic, and political orders on both the domestic and international fronts in the post-1965 era have significantly improved the opportunity structure for Asians to voice their concerns in electoral politics." (Lien 2001, 123)

If they are dominated by one group that constitutes a majority of the electorate, this group—whether Latino, Asian, black, or white—typically will grasp the lion's share of the benefits.

The studies in this book confirm the difficulty of forming multiracial coalitions including blacks and Latinos. The tensions between these groups are often high, because they compete both in labor markets and for political positions and governmental benefits. Of the cities discussed in this book, the obstacles seem greatest in New York and Miami. There, the two groups are in direct conflict. Political relationships are problematic in Los Angeles as well. The most successful black–Latino coalition seems to have been Harold Washington's in Chicago. The process of coalition formation in that city should be a model for similar efforts elsewhere. The collapse of Washington's coalition when he died, however, underscores again the special problem of maintaining multiracial coalitions and the special importance of leadership in such settings.

BLACK POLITICAL INCORPORATION: IS IT IN DECLINE?

The cities examined in this book reveal many patterns of change in black political incorporation. In some, strong black political incorporation has been achieved and sustained over time. In others, coalitions that strongly incorporated black leadership have been defeated. In still others, strong incorporation has not been achieved.

In 1988—with the important exceptions of New York and Miami, where black incorporation was weaker than we might expect based on population alone— blacks were well placed in dominant coalitions in all nine cities (of the 20 studied in this book) in which they constituted at least 20 percent of the city's population in 1980: Berkeley, Atlanta, Los Angeles, New Orleans, Oakland, Birmingham, Chicago, Philadelphia, and Baltimore. Where blacks were smaller proportions of the populations, they have fared less well. Nevertheless, the enormous gain from the virtual exclusion of blacks in 1950 to their achievement of governmental positions and leadership in 1988 cannot be denied.

In the early 1990s, the picture was more complex. Liberal coalitions in five cities experienced defeat after 1990: New York, Los Angeles, Chicago, Philadelphia, and San Francisco. In these cities, previously dominant liberal coalitions were turned out of office, the alliances that sustained them were significantly weakened, and their futures were highly uncertain.

In the second half of the 1990s, however, the picture changed again. San Francisco quickly reversed the earlier defeat: Willie Brown, the African-American former speaker of the California Assembly, won election to the mayor's office in December 1995—a gift of term limits to splintered liberal, progressive, and multiracial groups in San Francisco.

Developments in New York, Los Angeles, Chicago, and Philadelphia suggest that a collapse of black political power is not inevitable after the defeat of the first black mayor. Incorporation is a variable, not an either-or attribute. Being represented on a city council or important electorally to a new dominant coalition are also forms and levels of incorporation that are not without importance, especially once a group or groups have controlled city government for a time in a dominant coalition.

In 11 other cities, biracial and multiracial coalitions have not experienced defeat, or the local political system has evolved into competing coalitions, both of which are biracial or multiracial. In New Orleans, two blacks leading biracial coalitions ran against each other for mayor. One biracial coalition was liberal, the other conservative; the alignment was based on ideology, not on race (see ch. 8). Stable, party-like, biracial progressive and moderate coalitions have competed for decades in Berkeley, and less fixed multiethnic progressive and moderate coalitions are competing in San Francisco and Oakland.

The levels of incorporation that groups achieve are changeable. The aging of coalitions in office, demographic change that presents new interests and challenges, investment of coalition leadership in the successful commitments and statuses of the past, and the likelihood that their mistakes and programs will eventually stimulate opposition all work to undermine established coalitions in which African Americans are strongly incorporated.

The rapid growth of Latino and Asian populations in the 1990s, largely as a result of immigration, has been a major feature of the new era in minority politics. This growth shifts the ground beneath biracial coalitions that were founded on the premise that the fundamental alliance is a compact between blacks and whites.

The chapters of this book provide many examples of how competing coalitions exploit differences within liberal biracial coalitions, the potential for fragmentation of groups once they have achieved some success or lose a unifying leader (Chicago and Sacramento), and the difficulty of translating successful electoral coalitions into successful governing coalitions (Chicago, New York, and Philadelphia).

DEFEAT OR EVOLUTION IN A NEW ERA?

In the second edition, several authors wrote of "rollbacks" in black or Latino political incorporation. This term seemed to signify a return to an earlier stage of minority political incorporation. The possibilities are really more diverse than "rollback" implies, however, and it is important to be clear about the possibilities.

Defeat and Its Consequences

What happens when a governing coalition is defeated in an election and loses control over the legislative and executive functions of city government? Defeat certainly does not mean a return to the 1950s. Minority communities typically have far greater resources at their disposal now than they did then—money, leadership, experience, education, political awareness, organization, position, and relationships in private, public, and nonprofit organizations. Defeat is not the end of the road for the interests in a losing coalition, because these resources do not go away with defeat. Instead, they are likely to be organized to conduct vigorous advocacy on behalf of their communities. Later, they turn to building and rebuilding alliances.

Perhaps the most important resource of a defeated coalition is its potential to regroup and compete again. A coalition that maintains its structure even though it has lost an election—especially a close one—is likely to instill caution in the victorious coalition. The cautionary impact of a still-viable coalition is a form of influence over policy and programs. Coalitions can be influential even when not in office. While that is not as good as control, it is much better than nothing, as in Philadelphia during the Rendell years (see ch. 3).

Defeat may be more serious than that, however. It may signify the disintegration of a coalition—even perhaps its irretrievable demise. At one point, the end of the Bradley era in Los Angeles seemed to be such an instance, but even the complete disintegration of the Bradley coalition did not mean the end of the political road for people of color in Los Angeles. By opening up political space, the end of a coalition creates opportunities for new leaders and new alliances while the old patterns fall apart. New alliances in which people of color participate will eventually form to take advantage of their potentially mobilizable numbers.

Evolution and Complexity: Settings and Scenarios

The chapters in this third edition indicate that racial politics have evolved into new patterns characterized by much more fluidity and complexity. The new era is marked *not* by a return to a previous status quo of exclusion and subordination but by qualitative shifts in issues, mobilization, coalitions, leadership, incorporation, and responsiveness. New forces have intervened to generate more complex and varied patterns.

Black–white relations dominated the decades following the civil rights movement in most of the cities analyzed in this book. They are still the main interracial relationship in the four cities where blacks are a majority of the population: Atlanta, Baltimore, Birmingham, and New Orleans.

In the other cities, what is most striking is the complexity and fluidity of crosscutting and shifting coalitions as Latino and Asian populations grow and interests around particular issues play a larger role in coalition formation. The importance of leaders grows when politicized racial identities give way to interests that can no longer be counted on to preserve group unity.

Latinos are now a much more formidable force. Of the 16 cities where blacks are not a majority, Latinos are a majority in Miami but, strikingly, constitute 20 percent or more of the population in 10 more cities: Chicago, Denver, Los Angeles, and the northern California cities of Daly City, Hayward, Oakland, Richmond, Sacramento, San Jose, and Stockton. In only six cities where blacks are not in the majority do they constitute 20 percent or more of the population—Miami, New York, Chicago, Oakland, Richmond, and Vallejo.

The growth of Latino populations is changing dramatically the political ground on which urban racial politics is played out.[5] Black–white relations and biracial politics were the dominant mode; now biracial politics is becoming sometimes multiracial politics but more often a politics of candidates and issues in which voters or leaders of different groups join forces temporarily. Only a few years ago, the future of cities seemed to be in African-American majorities. Today, only two of these 20 cities are majority-white—Denver and Berkeley, where minorities make up 48 percent and 45 percent of the population, respectively—and the others are "minority-majority" cities. In 12 of the minority-majority cities, no single minority group constitutes a majority of the population.

Multiracial Coalitions   From these numbers alone, one might expect that formation of multiracial coalitions would be an increasingly popular and prevalent pattern. Indeed, many minority leaders over the last decades have advocated such coalitions, from Jesse Jackson's Rainbow Coalition to William Julius Wilson's (1999) and Lani Guinier's (2002) recent advocacy of progressive, multiracial coalitions.

Forming multiracial coalitions is difficult, as the chapters in this book have illustrated. The groups are different in many ways, and their entry into political participation inevitably carries a strong commitment to the defense and benefit of the group and an unformed sense of the possibilities of collaboration with other groups. A systematic analysis of competition between African Americans, Latinos, and Asians in American cities reports that across cities, socioeconomic levels of these groups are mostly positively correlated (McClain and Tauber 2001). At least at the aggregate level of the data, this finding does not support the proposition that these groups are locked in the sharpest sort of zero-sum economic competition. The number of mayoral and council positions is usually fixed, of course, so the levels of representation of each group tend to be negatively correlated with levels of other groups—the groups are in direct competition for these positions, and preventing such competition from turning into conflict is a primary task of the leaders of any interracial coalition.

The biracial coalition model paired racially liberal whites with racially mobilized blacks—to their mutual benefit. In multiracial cities and as issues arise that divide the allied groups, other pairings become more viable. The new pairings may not include African Americans, and they may be pro-entrepreneurial rather than "virtually by definition 'progressive' or 'liberal'," as we might have assumed in the past (see ch. 12 and Sonenshein 2001, 215).

Similarly, Edward and John Park (2001, 91–93) suggest that the liberal coalition model centered on African Americans was predicated on the "realities of another generation," in particular on the unifying force of the civil rights movement. As personal experience with *de jure* racism recedes, the ideological force of that coalition model also recedes, and a range of other options now opens.

---

[5] Asians are almost at or above 20 percent in five of the cities, all in California—Daly City, San Francisco, San Jose, Stockton, and Vallejo (see Table I.1).

The very phrase "multiracial coalition" implies that racial groups are the building blocks of coalitions and that multiracial coalitions might extend across many issues and play the same role in minority incorporation that biracial coalitions played in the 1960s. The experience of the 1990s described in this book suggests that this is increasingly unlikely. More likely is a pattern in which groups are sometimes split internally on issues, so that divisions are on other lines, often economic, or in which groups are united and are able to come together to pass legislative proposals but do not form a stable coalition across many issues. Shifting, issue-oriented coalitions are the order of the day. Policy entrepreneurs and candidates will get support wherever they can, from organizations and officeholders representing any group. In some cities, stable, competing coalitions both draw on members of most or all groups. Consider the competing black-led coalitions in Philadelphia and the competing progressive and moderate coalitions in Berkeley, Oakland, and San Francisco (see ch. 6).

Exclusion   Vigorous resistance to minority demands and exclusion from city government is another pattern that characterized many cities before biracial coalitions took control. Two (in)famous cases were Los Angeles under Sam Yorty and Philadelphia under Frank Rizzo. A more contemporary scenario has African Americans becoming increasingly isolated from other groups. In this scenario, cities become increasingly multiracial, but Latino and Asian-American populations grow more rapidly than black populations. The first two groups are increasingly assimilated—at least their relatively light-skinned and educated members—and co-opted into white-dominated coalitions from which African Americans are largely excluded. The latter find themselves increasingly unwanted as partners in urban political alliances. This scenario is given impetus both by legitimate apprehension about the pervasiveness and persistence of racism and by knowledge of the real differences in political orientations and social values and identities between these groups. Richard DeLeon's data on the political isolation of African Americans in San Francisco—and their shrinking population—lends support to this possibility in the future (see ch. 6).

Unfortunately, the record of city governments dominated by majorities or near-majorities of one minority group is not good with respect to exclusion of the other groups. Cuban Americans in Miami, a large majority, pay little heed to a substantial but much smaller black population (see ch. 10). African Americans, the first to gain political incorporation in Oakland and Richmond, California, defend their city hall turf as if the next new claimants, Latinos and Asians, who also want access to city government and positions in it, should not be allowed on it. Exclusion is attempted even where whites are not in power.

Politicoeconomic Co-optation   Atlanta illustrates this pattern (see ch. 7). In this scenario, black politicians control city government, but they have been co-opted by a white economic elite. An African-American economic and professional elite emerges that enriches itself but abandons low-income blacks, who are politically isolated and powerless. In this story, the great escape from black political exclusion engineered during the 1960s and 1970s ends in the assertion of class interests and power and the perpetuation of poverty and hopelessness, determined by both class and race.

IS INCORPORATION ENOUGH?

No one who favors political equality objects in principle to the formation of multiracial coalitions or to minority officeholding. The question is, what do minority officeholders and coalitions do with their positions? Do they make city government responsive to the interests and needs of minority communities? Especially, do they use the powers of city government to pursue the broader aims of the Black Power movement, including expansion of assistance and provision of employment to economically marginal populations of all races and redistribution of the resources of city government?

There is "an inherent value in officeholding. . . . A race of people who are excluded from public office will always be second class citizens" (McCain 1981). Officeholding *does* confer legitimacy on a hitherto-excluded group, as Perry argues (see ch. 8). These are symbolic but nonetheless terribly important considerations.

Still, some authors in this book criticize some largely black regimes and some black leaders. These criticisms lead toward the conclusion that these leaders are not as active as they should be in redistributive efforts; that they are less powerful than their political positions imply, because of the pervasive systemic power of white business interests and a pro-growth ideology that prefers to ignore the needs of ordinary citizens; and that they are too narrowly self-interested, too focused on their own interests and on those of the black (and white) middle and upper class.

The case of Atlanta reminds us that minority political leadership may ally itself more tightly to a white business elite than to the working-class and poor of their own race. In the memorable words of one observer, a meeting of black and white leaders in Atlanta "is nothing but a room full of people trying to cut a deal" (Painton 1987, A1). In such a setting, the dominance of the governing biracial coalition does not overthrow extreme inequalities in the socioeconomic realm, it replicates them— Atlanta is second only to Newark in poverty, and the mass of black constituents remains effectively excluded (see ch. 7).

In such a situation, we might hope eagerly for black political incorporation but, when it arrives, find it is an obstacle to achieving a broader set of goals. Even if we do not conclude that incorporation is *only* a sham, *only* the illusion of empowerment, we might still be profoundly ambivalent toward it.

The authors of this book do not conclude that black incorporation is only a sham. Biracial and multiracial regimes have accomplished substantial good overall. What has been accomplished varies from city to city, however, and it is clearly not enough to prevent the perpetuation of racial discrimination, disadvantage, poverty, and social decay.

HAVE MINORITY REGIMES BEEN RESPONSIVE?

By "minority regimes," we mean city governments dominated by biracial or multiracial coalitions in which blacks or Latinos play significant roles. Primarily, these are biracial regimes in which blacks play leading roles.

City Government Employment

All the minority regimes studied in this book have effectively reduced discrimination in city government employment. They have often created strongly affirmative recruitment and hiring practices that have resulted in minority workforces close to or above parity with the size of minority populations. Even governments like New York City's with limited minority incorporation, have pushed ahead rapidly with minority hiring (see ch. 4). All the minority regimes have greatly increased minority representation in professional, managerial, and executive positions, including department heads.

Some commentators deride city government employment as the weakest of weak rewards, "a few government jobs" with which elites buy off minority protest. We do not agree. One analysis concludes:

> About 55 percent of the increase in black professional, managerial, and technical employment between 1960 and 1976 occurred in the public sector, and employment in social welfare programs accounted for approximately half of that increase. (Murray 1984, citing Brown and Erie 1981, 308)

This suggests that gains in city government employment contributed significantly to gains in middle-class black employment during this period. Our own analysis of city workforces in the 10 California cities showed that minority employees of city governments ranged from 2 percent to 6 percent of total minority residents in the workforce, with more in the older, larger cities with the highest proportions of black residents—again, not an insignificant contribution to total minority (especially black) employment.

The argument is also sometimes made that the advantages of city government accrue almost entirely to middle-class minorities, but the pattern varies a great deal from city to city. Older cities with broader governmental functions also hire large numbers of blue-collar workers. From an antipoverty perspective, bolstering the employment opportunities of middle-class—or of potentially middle-class—minority persons is obviously not the same as enhancing employment opportunities for low-income persons. On the other hand, support for a nascent minority middle class is not to be scoffed at either.

Police–Community Relations

Establishment of civilian police review boards was one of the points for which minority incorporation in the 10 California cities did make a difference, and some authors in this volume report progress along these lines. Police review boards are, of course, only one of several strategies for reducing the use of lethal force against minority people. Minority hiring onto police forces and changing top leadership are common—and probably more effective—steps taken by minority regimes. Reviewing the literature on black regimes, Adolph Reed concludes:

> Black regimes generally have been successful in curbing police brutality, which often has been prominent among black constituents' concerns. . . .

Black regimes have made substantial gains in black police employment, which contributes to the reduction in police brutality. (1988, 156)

Development of Minority Businesses

Development of minority business is typically supposed to be accomplished by set-asides or other special efforts to channel city spending for supplies and services to such businesses, thus encouraging growth of the minority-owned private sector. The record of minority regimes in this area is murky. Perry reports little or no progress in New Orleans and Birmingham (see ch. 8). Atlanta, with its business-oriented black elite, dispenses more than $250 million a year to black vendors and contractors (Whitaker 2002, 158) and may have significantly increased the number and revenues of black-owned businesses (see ch. 7). The record in other cities is mixed. Minority contracting is sometimes distorted by favoritism for a few firms with special ties to the regime (see ch. 3), as governmental contracting frequently is. Some minority contractors have been paper corporations—fronts for white-owned businesses. There are success stories of city government support for minority businesses, but recent U.S. Supreme Court decisions now make set-asides more difficult to implement even when city governments are willing to develop strong programs.

Appointments to Boards and Commissions

All the minority regimes studied in this volume have made substantial minority appointments to city boards and commissions in terms of both numbers and proportions. No doubt the significance of these appointments varies enormously. In some cities, they may be entirely symbolic; in others, they may be key steps in the extension of control over city government and associated agencies. In Oakland, for example, minority control of commissions with real governmental authority was essential to establishing control over city departments and public authorities, such as the Port Authority, associated with the city. This in turn allowed the dominant coalition to change the policies of those agencies to emphasize direct minority hiring, employment-related development, increased provision of facilities and services to minority residents and neighborhoods, and co-ordination with other minority-oriented programs of city government.

In these respects, the minority regimes studied here have typically been responsive. We simply do not have sufficient evidence in this volume about other areas of need in which minorities may or may not have made substantial progress. Adolph Reed, reviewing the available evidence in the late 1980s, concluded that "the presence of a black mayor or regime has some, but less than dramatic, racially redistributive effect on allocation of public resources" (1988, 139). It may be too much to expect more than "some" racially redistributive effect. Yet worsening poverty and other signs of social breakdown among inner-city populations would seem to be critical conditions with which a city government—and certainly one that purports to be responsive to its minority population, as minority regimes do—must deal.

Several authors in this volume note that the regimes they studied had done little to meet the needs or even heed the objections of lower-income minority populations.

Unfortunately, it is extremely difficult for city governments to have much impact on poverty. The federal government can no longer be depended on to lead this effort, and city governments lack both the fiscal resources and the structural capability to do so even if they were willing to take up where the federal government left off.

STRUCTURAL LIMITS AND INSTITUTIONAL CAPACITY

The painful truth is that many of the forces shaping the conditions under which the mass of low-income minority people live are not under the control of city governments—even city governments run by minority regimes (Peterson 1981). Big cities with large minority populations are undergoing two radical transformations that have been under way for several decades and are continuing today (Kasarda 1985; Wilson 1985; Downs 1985; Jones-Correa 2001). One is economic—the shift from manufacturing and distribution activities to administration, information, and other services, many of which are highly technical in nature. The number of low-skill jobs in such cities is dropping. This trend accelerates during difficult economic times.

Big-city populations are being transformed as well. As Latinos, mainly poor and unskilled, increase in number, many poor and unskilled blacks remain. Other blacks and many whites are moving to the suburbs, the latter partly for racial reasons:

> This transformation is occurring in part because of the white majority's deliberate policy of segregating itself from both poor and nonpoor minority group members. Such segregation . . . operates by excluding nearly all poor households and most minority households from new suburban areas. Segregation is less evident in workplaces, although residential segregation also produces massive racial separation of jobs.
>
> As a result, many minority group members live in areas that provide a much lower quality of life in every respect than that enjoyed by most whites. Confronted by a triple handicap of shrinking job opportunities, poor education, and low-quality neighborhoods [and increasing competition for low-skill jobs from new immigration and from high birth rates in the inner city], these minority citizens are caught in a situation from which there appears to be no escape. (Downs 1985, 285)

If the twentieth century saw the construction of the great cities of the United States, the twenty-first may be "the Suburban Century" (Keiser and Underwood 2000, 8). Not only the white population but also its taxable wealth and the investments of corporations are being suburbanized. Migration to the suburbs has decreased the electoral power of central cities and increased the concentration of minority populations in them. At the same time, the minority populations of central cities face severe and intractable problems, and their cities are losing resources to cope with them.

The roots of this knot of problems and constraints are many, but again, they are essentially outside the control of city governments. In the 1970s and 1980s, increased competition from foreign manufacturers and national policies that fought inflation by keeping interest rates high—thus increasing demand for the dollar, raising the exchange value of the dollar, and raising the prices of U.S. goods—led to the permanent closure of many older manufacturing plants, typically in big cities where African Americans were and are concentrated.

Long-standing policies that had nothing to do with race in their origins have produced racially distributed outcomes. Construction of freeways beginning in the 1950s helped to accelerate suburban development relative to the central city. The income tax deduction for mortgage loan interest increased the demand for new homes, which were—and continue to be—built in the suburbs.

Trends and pressures as well as the shifting strength of coalitions at the state and national levels are also at work. Republicans made major gains in state legislatures in 1994 and took control of both houses of Congress. Even though public support is weak for Republican initiatives to overturn 40 years of social policy, Republicans control the presidency and the U.S. House of Representatives at this writing in spring 2002. Further cutbacks in federal aid to cities, together with state-imposed spending and taxing limits and other legislative barriers, make it that much more difficult for liberal-to-progressive coalitions to achieve their goals. The aid that is available is more likely to be funneled to the suburbs and to find its way to cities with Republican rather than with Democratic mayors. The prosperity of the mid-1990s helped to reduce poverty among minorities of color, but with the end of that boom, cities and states again face rising deficits and calls for cutbacks in spending in areas of critical need to minorities, especially education.

Thus, the tendency of whites to segregate themselves from people of color is compounded by global economic trends, long-standing national policies, the American tradition of local government that permits the wealth and incomes of suburban populations to be separated from the problems of the central city, and by Republican gains. The forces operating against big cities and their minority populations are powerful and manifold, and there is no immediate or direct way out of their dilemmas.

Nevertheless, cities vary in their economic fortunes and in the extent to which they can or wish to negotiate arrangements with investors and residents that foster economic growth and employment, support affordable housing, job training, and other services, and maintain city revenues at a level that permits expanding programs. Even majority-black cities and their mayors vary significantly in the extent to which they confront or ally themselves with business interests (see ch. 8).

Cities also vary in governmental structures, which shape the ways they institutionalize and respond to emerging group demands. Clarke and Hero attribute part of the minority incorporation and responsiveness of Denver city government to its largely "unreformed" governmental structure, with a strong mayor who wields substantial budgetary and appointment powers (see ch. 11). In many older cities where political parties were never excluded from local politics by the reform requirement of nonpartisan elections, such as New York City, Philadelphia, and Chicago, party organizations have long experience deflecting and absorbing emerging groups. They will coopt leaders and structure the policy response to meet their organizational needs, but they may also attend to emerging demands more consistently than "reform" cities that lack party organizations.

Cities restructured during the reform era usually lack party-like coalitions with organizational continuity and an institutional stake in the long-term future. Coalitions in these cities tend to be more fluid and candidate-centered, and community-based organizations, often with an ethnic basis, are likely to play more important roles. In the absence of party politics and the presence of district elections, and given that ethnoracial groups tend to be geographically concentrated, city council elections tend to be based on ethnicity rather than on "thinking about the longer-range benefits of ethnic cooperation or the importance of introducing new players into city politics" (Jones-Correa 2001, 203). A related finding is that in the presence of conflict between African Americans and Korean Americans, organized protest in the form of boycotts was more likely to occur in cities with strong traditional party organizations than in cities with reformed institutions (Joyce 2001; in press). It may be that cities with reformed institutions are more insulated from community activism, which discourages protest.

WHAT SHOULD BE DONE?

It is in the nature of partly successful movements that their accomplishments, once taken as great victories, are more or less quickly taken for granted. Leadership, a vision, and an agenda emerged from the early civil rights movement and mobilized millions of people against great odds. The movement's great accomplishments—including the establishment of voting rights and the election of many thousands of African Americans to public office—were not enough to end discrimination or to lead or assist sufficient numbers of other African Americans out of poverty. In the shadow of these persistent and painful problems, we should not be surprised if the widespread achievement of an end to discrimination in city government employment does not shine as brightly as it once did and cannot be accepted as enough.

The civil rights movement drew power from the great ideas of freedom, equality, justice, and brotherhood—from "the American dream that one day this nation will rise up and live out the true meaning of its creed—we hold these truths to be self-evident, that all men are created equal" (King 1992, 104). In this new century, when African Americans and, increasingly, Latinos and Asians are found in considerable numbers at high levels of achievement in the professions, government, universities and schools, and business, can renewed minority mobilization draw on those ideas and the hope that they offer?

If a renewed movement could emerge, what would it want? What concrete steps would it demand? It is one thing to demand an end to legal segregation of public accommodations and of public universities and schools and to get affirmative action in city hiring. It is quite another to get equal financing for inner-city and suburban schools or equal employment rates for people of color and for whites. If whites move to the suburbs in part to avoid racial integration, achievement of integrated housing such that people of color would have the same rate of access to suburban schools as whites lies at still another level of impossibility.

The U.S. Supreme Court's decision in *Brown v. Board of Education* (1954) was an attack on separate but unequal education, yet de facto segregation and grossly unequal education are still largely what we have. Perhaps a renewed movement would mount a renewed attack on de facto segregation, but perhaps not.[6] Even if integration is a dream still deferred, much better education must be high on the rational priorities of inner-city families of all races. More jobs and better neighborhood conditions are also common goals for people of color in many settings—not only African Americans but Latinos, Asians, and Native Americans as well—and for whites.

Jobs, education, a living wage, affordable housing, better neighborhoods, available and affordable health care, drug prevention and treatment programs, affordable day care—a plausible set of concrete goals for a progressive agenda is not much of a puzzle. The mobilization that would be necessary to achieve them, however, *is* a puzzle, though local efforts pursue them now in countless different settings, with limited success overall. What is noteworthy about these issues is that they are not defined by race.

WHAT CAN BE DONE?

City governments and the coalitions that control them are not entirely without resources. Anthony Downs has pointed out that "minority control over big-city government"—we would now say, control by coalitions with a progressive agenda and responsive to minority interests—"greatly increases the bargaining power of minorities in relation to major property owners who pay taxes, and increases their political power in Congress and the state legislatures" (1985, 291). This is true, but it is also true that suburbs are gaining population and political power more rapidly than the big cities.

Finding New Allies

Minorities need allies not only to win elections but also to mobilize, to the fullest extent possible, the resources of the community to improve education and job training. Whereas in earlier decades supporters of minority demands for improved edu-

---

6 Anthony Downs's conclusion written more than a decade ago (1985, 290) is still accurate: "There is no point in advocating racial integration as the central social strategy for coping with big-city problems. . . . The political leaders of all large metropolitan areas do not have the slightest interest in pursuing this strategy in any meaningful way. . . . So devoting scarce political energy and resources to integration must be considered a marginal activity."

cation and job training were powerful at the federal level, that is no longer true. Now, as Downs put it in 1985:

> The best natural allies are those who stand to lose most if the minority community cannot produce competent workers. That means businesses locked into the city itself, such as downtown property owners, nonbranching banks, or newspapers. They might support more ghetto enrichment as a quid pro quo for further integrated core development benefiting them. (1985, 292)

Of course, "ghetto enrichment," such as greatly increased financing for schools, is likely to involve raising property taxes, where a pro-minority coalition will face an electorate as well as business interests.

Many cities have progressive elements of significant size and vigor, people who are committed ideologically to living wage, affordable housing, improved child care, and similar programs. Denver targeted its working poor, primarily black and Hispanic, with several programs, and implemented a local Earned Income Tax Credit for working poor families (see ch. 11). The size of the supportive progressive population, regardless of race, continues, of course, to make a difference in the ability to move cities through a progressive agenda that can offer some advantages to low-income populations. Labor unions representing ethnically diverse workers in some of the cities studied have played active roles in campaigns for these issues.

Bargaining with Business

The governments of large cities that are economic and administrative centers with stable or growing economies are in a better position to bargain with—and to extract concessions from—business interests about the form, location, and mix of development and about the use of minority-owned firms and employment of minority workers. The record of minority-oriented and progressive regimes in actually extracting such concessions is mixed, and such concessions are not a solution to all the problems of education, jobs, and poverty. Such regimes clearly do more in this regard, however, than do nonminority regimes.

As Adolph Reed explains, this strategy means "neither a reflexive opposition to economic growth nor an adversarial relationship with concrete business interests." Rather, the goal is to use "public authority to articulate policy agendas that accommodate economic growth as much as possible to the needs of the municipality and its citizenry rather than vice versa" (Reed 1988, 167).

Expanding Advocacy

Downs and Reed both emphasize the leadership role of the minority community— and of minority mayors in particular. Reed suggests that regimes use the "cultural authority of office to draw attention to unpalatable conditions that affect constituents but are beyond the scope of municipal control." They can also engage in forms of official protest, such as:

passing unconstitutional tax ordinances, to dramatize existing inequities, thereby opening them to public awareness and debate and providing opportunities for political mobilization. Along each of these dimensions of advocacy for justice and equity, the record of black regimes is poor. (Reed 1988, 168)

Downs also stresses the possibilities for effective advocacy that go beyond the current political efforts of minority-oriented regimes. One tactic that might be effective "is constantly emphasizing that spending more on educating minority group children is investing in the city's future, not just aiding the poor." Another tactic "would be launching a series of nonviolent demonstrations in white areas and schools about the poor quality of minority schools," resembling civil rights protests of the 1960s (Downs 1985, 292). Such advocacy might eventually lead to metropolitan tax sharing or other measures to channel state or local funds to inner-city schools, investment, and employment programs. Minority-oriented regimes could do more to organize and publicize demands on suburban governments in metropolitan regions and on state and national governments for resources and programs to alleviate their problems.

Although these tactics could be undertaken, there are strong reasons why big-city mayors and other elected officials are not likely to pursue them with great vigor. These officeholders have typically won office without such tactics in the first instance; if they harbor ambitions for higher office, they will typically have to appeal to a less minority-oriented constituency than the one that initially elected them. This creates a disincentive to use dramatic or radical tactics.

Self-Help

Self-help in minority communities can be important to their development and success. Though not political in the narrow sense, self-help has important social and political implications. Even if the path of political mobilization is unpromising, self-help efforts can make an enormous difference in the lives of individuals and groups. Some Asian communities, for example, have successfully operated loan pools so that immigrants can acquire small businesses. Self-help efforts and the discipline they demonstrate also probably help minority communities appeal successfully to middle-class and business interests (Downs 1985, 292). African-American, Latino, and Native-American communities have also initiated forms of self-help that we simply do not know enough about.

Minority-oriented regimes can play an important leadership role in the development of self-help efforts and, with relatively modest governmental resources or private support, can help communities to organize such activities that involve recyclable financial resources. Leadership in self-help efforts would be an effective tactic politically, in addition to the direct help it generates, because it would assure nonminority people that minority communities are doing what they can to help themselves while giving those minority communities increased hope and confidence in the relevance of local government.

The fundamental point is that many minority-oriented and progressive regimes, even with the constraints they operate under, could undertake significant new efforts. For this to happen, however, may require new coalitions that are faced with "greatly increased and informed pressure from the black electoral constituency" (Reed 1988, 196) and from liberal whites, Latinos, and Asians, which in turn implies broad public debate on the issues—a debate that is not now heard.

New Agendas and New Tasks for Leaders

Clarence Stone has written about the possibility of an "opportunity-expansion" regime—a coalition of public and private interests in cities that would pursue "enriched education and job training, improved transportation access, and enlarged opportunities for business and home ownership" for the lower-class residents of big cities (1993, 20). No city is wholly of this kind, but several large cities (San Francisco, Cleveland, and Boston) have undertaken "significant moves to open benefits to the lower class. . . . Each of these cities has edged toward a more class-inclusionary regime" (Stone, Orr, and Imbroscio 1991, 236). The achievement of such a regime would require at least some mobilization of a lower-class constituency and "overcoming a cycle of disappointment and cynicism" (Stone 1993, 21).

By this vision, coalitions should form around the goals of much better education, more jobs, state and local subsidies for affordable housing, and enlarged opportunities for home ownership. These are key goals for many members of diverse groups, including liberal and progressive whites and labor, and they might be cast convincingly as goals for some business interests as well. With vigorous, persistent effort and skillful leadership, such coalitions might be able to mobilize and unite a broad range of groups and interests around issues of fairness, equal opportunity, and reduction of social conflict and crime through better education and access to employment.

Public education, a necessary cornerstone of an opportunity-expansion regime, is now one of the most hotly contested policy arenas in the United States. At the local level, school systems in some multiethnic cities are battlegrounds of racialized rage and frustration, with groups in bitter conflict both with each other and with school officials over resources, academic results, and standardized testing. The move toward more testing and higher standards sometimes conflicts with parental desires to keep their children from becoming discouraged and to make sure that they receive necessary remedial instruction.

Because groups are often locked in such conflict over public education, it may be very difficult to bring them together. On the other hand, they do have fundamental goals in common—improving the quality of education for lower- and middle-income children. The problem is actually improving education in any given school system, as well as fairly allocating resources among communities within a given system. People who can do these things appear to be in distinctly short supply and difficult to identify.

That many state governments now fund large shares of the revenues of schools poses a special problem. Baltimore mayor Kurt Schmoke summed it up: "Local government only controls about one-third of the budget in public school systems, and in public education, like so many other areas of life, the 'golden rule' applies, that is, 'he who has the gold rules' " (see ch. 9, 273–274).

Because of the new diversity in American cities from the rapid rise of Latino and Asian populations and the obvious differences and distances among the contending groups, leaders who want to advance a more progressive agenda should emphasize not simply racial interests and demands but proposals that tap the shared values of all these groups—values of opportunity expansion, helping people out of poverty, ensuring good education, and the like. Certainly, the biracial, black–white, racially liberal electoral coalition of the 1960s and 1970s, which was a solution to a problem then, is not a viable solution now in many cities. In others, however, it may still be appropriate and needed.

Given the cultural and socioeconomic distances between blacks, whites, Latinos, and Asians, the diversity of their views, and the absence of a great mobilizing movement, highly visible *electoral* coalitions may be less feasible now than they were in the 1960s through the 1980s, but electoral coalitions are not the only possibility. Another is that representatives of diverse groups gain office and form more fluid, issue-based coalitions with each other. It is not proving difficult, for example, for African-American and Latino council members and for white and Asian members with progressive or lower-income constituencies to band together to pass a living-wage ordinance, which 79 cities have done (CBS News 2002; Neumark 2002). If care is taken on the distribution of affordable housing, it should not be impossible for them to band together on that issue as well. The point is that there are issues on which these groups can come together, and stable electoral coalitions are not the only possibility. Issue-based coalitions that shift from issue to issue are also possible and may be more feasible in many situations.

Because American cities are becoming increasingly multiracial, there is no alternative but to continue exploring the possibilities of multigroup coalitions and learning what works to bring groups together, if not at the electoral stage then at the policy-making stage. Clearly, what does not work in a multiethnic setting is a single-minded focus on one's own race or ethnicity. Leaders and activists who hope to put together multiracial coalitions must formulate issues and ways of dealing with each other that both focus on common interests and respect the different histories of each group. These are not new skills in the history of coalition formation, but they will be new to many established leaders whose careers have been based on cultivation of their group alone or of biracial relationships. Forward-looking leaders of all these groups recognize this, and many efforts are going forward on this front.[7]

---

[7] For example, an initiative of the Joint Center for Political and Economic Studies is the Network of Alliances Bridging Race and Ethnicity (NABRE, pronounced "neighbor"). "Our mission is to cultivate and nurture local leaders as they build and sustain alliances that break down and transcend artificial barriers of race and ethnicity in all sectors of civil society and in communities across our country" (Joint Center 2000). Another initiative of the Center is the Minority Business Round Table, also a deliberately inclusive organization. On Asians, see Lien (2001, ch. 4).

Leaders trying to organize winning coalitions may pursue a race-blind approach, downplaying racial themes to stress common interests that cross racial groups, as William Julius Wilson has suggested (1999). Or, leaders may adopt a consciously multiracial approach that appeals to different groups by touching on themes that are important to them and that explicitly acknowledges the continuing importance of diverse minority interests in urban politics (McKeever 2001, 245–246). Raphael Sonenshein provides a nuanced and grounded guide to leadership choices that can make or break multiethnic coalitions (see ch. 12). Hochschild and Rogers, reviewing a great deal of survey data as well as big-city case studies, point out that the views of African Americans, nonwhite immigrants, and poor whites are quite similar in support of redistributive policies (2000, 74). But, they write, to bring groups together around such issues requires at least four conditions. These conditions are only part of her advice to leaders and activists, but they are worth quoting here in their entirety for their compelling clarity and logic and because they address barriers to interracial coalitions noted in this book:

- Where possible, racial issues should not be the center of discussion and action; the focus instead should be on shared substantive policy and political goals such as jobs in the primary sector, better schooling, nonbrutal crime control, neighborhood development, immigrant incorporation, and decent housing.
- When attention to race is deemed desirable or essential, everything possible should be done to avoid zero-sum conflicts over processes (such as redistricting and the selection of candidates) and outcomes (such as affirmative action or the funding of particular programs).
- African Americans need to pay more attention to civil rights issues of concern to immigrants such as welfare rights, deportation, and immigration restrictions. They also need to recognize that other groups have the same intense desire for descriptive representation that they themselves have evinced.
- Latinos, Asian Americans, and sympathetic whites, in return, need to accept that blacks' history of enslavement and their continued suffering from poverty and racial discrimination are qualitatively different from the history of all voluntary immigrant groups, and perhaps require distinctive treatment as a consequence. (Hochschild and Rogers 2000, 74)

Political incorporation must be the start, but it cannot be the limit of minority governmental effectiveness. Minority-oriented and progressive regimes that adopt a broader, opportunity-expansion program possess unique resources with which to pursue renewed mobilization and advocacy, so that issues of poverty, employment, housing, isolation, and terribly inadequate education—for disadvantaged people of any color—find their way onto local, state, and national agendas. Understanding the histories of leadership, mobilization, coalition formation, and incorporation described in this volume will, we hope, help people to fashion the vision and the coalitions that will carry to a new plane the historical struggle to build democracy and a greater equality out of the centuries-long practice of racial domination.

REFERENCES

Borrus, Amy, and Geri Smith. 2001. Spotlight on the Border: A Viable Plan on Immigration Tops the Bush-Fox Agenda. *Business Week* (September 10): 40.

Brown v. Board of Education. 1954. 347 U.S. 483, 494.

Brown, Michael K., and Stephen P. Erie. 1981. Blacks and the Legacy of the Great Society: The Economic and Political Impact of Federal Social Policy. *Public Policy* 12 (Summer): 299–330.

Browning, Rufus P., Dale Rogers Marshall, and David H. Tabb. 1984. *Protest Is Not Enough: The Struggle of Blacks and Hispanics for Equality in Urban Politics*. Berkeley: University of California Press.

Browning, Rufus P., Dale Rogers Marshall, and David H. Tabb. 2000. Taken In or Just Taken? Political Incorporation of African Americans in Cities. In Richard A. Keiser and Katherine Underwood, eds. *Minority Politics at the Millenium*, 131–156. New York: Garland Publishing.

Carmichael, Stokely, and Charles V. Hamilton. 1967. *Black Power*. New York: Random House.

CBS News. 2002. *CBS Evening News Sunday*. March 17.

Downs, Anthony. 1985. The Future of Industrial Cities. In Paul E. Peterson, ed., *The New Urban Reality*. Washington, DC: The Brookings Institution.

Gonzales, Lawrence, 2002. Testimony before the United States House of Representatives Subcommittee on Immigration & Claims. National Association of Latino Elected and Appointed Officials (http://www.naleo.org/special/NALEOTestimonyINS.pdf), April 9.

Guinier, Lani, and Gerald Torres. 2002. *The Miner's Canary: Enlisting Race, Resisting Power, Transforming Democracy*. Cambridge, Mass.: Harvard University Press.

Hochschild, Jennifer L., and Reuel R. Rogers. 2001. Race Relations in a Diversifying Nation. In James Jackson, ed., *New Directions: African Americans in a Diversifying Nation*, 45–85. Washington, D.C.: National Policy Association.

Joint Center for Political and Economic Studies. 2000. The Network of Alliances Bridging Race and Ethnicity (www.jointcenter.org/nabre/).

Jones-Correa, Michael. 2001. Structural Shifts and Institutional Capacity. In Michael Jones-Correa, ed., *Governing American Cities: Interethnic Coalitions, Competition, and Conflict*, 183–209. New York: Russell Sage Foundation.

Joyce, Patrick D. 2001. Protest or Violence: Political Process and Patterns of Black-Korean Conflict. In Michael Jones-Correa, ed., *Governing American Cities: Interethnic Coalitions, Competition, and Conflict*, 158–179. New York: Russell Sage Foundation.

Joyce, Patrick D. In press. *No Fire Next Time: Protest, Politics and Violence in Black-Korean Conflicts*. Ithaca: Cornell University Press.

Kasarda, John D. 1985. Urban Change and Minority Opportunities. In Paul E. Peterson, ed., *The New Urban Reality*. Washington, DC: The Brookings Institution.

Keiser, Richard A., and Katherine Underwood. 2000. *Minority Politics at the Millenium*. New York: Garland Publishing.

King, Martin Luther, Jr. 1992. I Have a Dream. Speech to the March on Washington, August 28, 1963. In James M. Washington, ed., *I Have a Dream: Writings and Speeches That Changed the World*. Glenview, Ill.: Scott, Foresman.

Lien, Pei-te. 2001. *The Making of Asian America Through Political Participation*. Philadelphia: Temple University Press.

McCain, Tom. 1981. Quoted in *American Civil Liberties Union News*.

McClain, Paula D., and Steven C. Tauber. 2001. Racial Minority Group Relations in a Multiracial Society. In Michael Jones-Correa, ed., *Governing American Cities: Interethnic Coalitions, Competition, and Conflict*, 158–179. New York: Russell Sage Foundation.

McKeever, Matthew. 2001. Interethnic Politics in the Consensus City. In Michael Jones-Correa, ed. *Governing American Cities: Interethnic Coalitions, Competition, and Conflict*, 230–248. New York: Russell Sage Foundation.

Mollenkopf, John M. 1997. New York: The Great Anomaly. In Rufus P. Browning, Dale Rogers Marshall, and David H. Tabb, eds. *Racial Politics in American Cities*, 2nd ed, 97–115. White Plains, NY: Longman.

Murray, Charles. 1984. *Losing Ground: American Social Policy 1950–1980*. New York: Basic Books.

NALEO Educational Fund. 2001. Latinos Are Changing the Political Map. Press Alert, June 17 (www.naleo.org/PressReleases/Press003.html).

Neumark, David. 2002. *How Living Wage Laws Affect Low-Wage Workers and Low-Income Families*. San Francisco: Public Policy Institute of California.

Painton, Priscilla. 1987. The Shaping of Atlanta, Part 3: Race and Politics. Black and White Detente Evolved from an Enlightened Self-Interest. *Atlanta Constitution*, August 11, A1.

Park, Edward J. W., and John S. W. Park. 2001. Korean Americans and the Crisis of the Liberal Coalition: Immigrants and Politics in Los Angeles. In Michael Jones-Correa, ed. *Governing American Cities: Interethnic Coalitions, Competition, and Conflict*, 91–108. New York: Russell Sage Foundation.

Peterson, Paul E. 1981. *City Limits*. Chicago: University of Chicago Press.

Preston, Michael B., Lenneal J. Henderson, and Paul Puryear, eds. 1987. *The New Black Politics*, 2nd ed. White Plains, N.Y.: Longman.

Reed, Adolph. 1988. The Black Urban Regime: Structural Origins and Constraints. In Michael Peter Smith, ed., *Power, Community and the City*. Vol. 1, *Comparative Urban and Community Research*. New Brunswick, N.J.: Transaction Books.

Sonenshein, Raphael J. 1993. *Politics in Black and White: Race and Power in Los Angeles*. Princeton, N.J.: Princeton University Press.

Sonenshein, Raphael J. 2001. When Ideologies Agree and Interests Collide, What's a Leader to Do? The Prospects for Latino-Jewish Coalition in Los Angeles. In Michael Jones-Correa, ed. *Governing American Cities: Interethnic Coalitions, Competition, and Conflict*, 210–229. New York: Russell Sage Foundation.

Stone, Clarence N. (1993). Urban Regimes and the Capacity to Govern: A Political Economy Approach. *Journal of Urban Affairs* 15 (1): 1–28.

Stone, Clarence N., Marion E. Orr, and David Imbroscio. 1991. The Reshaping of Urban Leadership in U.S. Cities: A Regime Analysis. In M. Gottdiener and Chris G. Pickvance, eds., *Urban Life in Transition*, Vol. 39, *Urban Affairs Annual Reviews*. Newbury Park, Calif.: Sage.

U.S. Bureau of the Census. 2000a. DP-1. Profile of General Demographic Characteristics: 2000. Census 2000 Summary File 1 (SF 1) 100-Percent Data (http://factfinder.census.gov/).

U.S. Bureau of the Census. 2000b. QT-02. Profile of Selected Social Characteristics: 2000. Census 2000 Supplementary Survey Summary Tables (http://factfinder.census.gov/).

Whitaker, Charles. 2002. Is Atlanta the New Black Mecca? *Ebony*, March, 148–162.

Wilson, William Julius. 1985. The Urban Underclass in Advanced Industrial Society. In Paul E. Peterson, ed., *The New Urban Reality*. Washington, DC: Brookings Institution.

Wilson, William Julius. 1999. *The Bridge Over the Racial Divide: Rising Inequality and Coalition Politics*. Berkeley: University of California Press.

Index